Playing and Learning in Early Childhood Education

SECOND EDITION

BEVERLIE DIETZE

Okanagan College

DIANE KASHIN

Ryerson University

Vice President, Editorial: Anne Williams
Executive Acquisition Editor: Kimberley Veevers
Marketing Manager: Michelle Bish
Content Manager: Madhu Ranadive
Project Manager: Susan Johnson/Christina Veeren
Content Developer: Christine Langone
Production Services: Cenveo® Publisher Services
Permissions Project Management: Integra Publishing Services
Photo Researcher: Integra Publishing Services
Text Permissions Research: Integra Publishing Services
Cover Designer: Anthony Leung
Interior Designer: Anthony Leung
Cover Image: Rawpixel.com/Shutterstock

Pearson Canada Inc., 26 Prince Andrew Place, North York, Ontario M3C 2H4.

Copyright © 2019, 2012 Pearson Canada Inc. All rights reserved.

Printed in the United States of America. This publication is protected by copyright, and permission should be obtained from the publisher prior to any prohibited reproduction, storage in a retrieval system, or transmission in any form or by any means, electronic, mechanical, photocopying, recording, or otherwise. For information regarding permissions, request forms, and the appropriate contacts, please contact Pearson Canada's Rights and Permissions Department by visiting www.pearsoncanada.ca/contact-information/permissions-requests.

Attributions of third-party content appear on the appropriate page within the text.

PEARSON is an exclusive trademark owned by Pearson Canada Inc. or its affiliates in Canada and/or other countries.

Unless otherwise indicated herein, any third party trademarks that may appear in this work are the property of their respective owners and any references to third party trademarks, logos, or other trade dress are for demonstrative or descriptive purposes only. Such references are not intended to imply any sponsorship, endorsement, authorization, or promotion of Pearson Canada products by the owners of such marks, or any relationship between the owner and Pearson Canada or its affiliates, authors, licensees, or distributors.

If you purchased this book outside the United States or Canada, you should be aware that it has been imported without the approval of the publisher or the author.

9780134639277

Library and Archives Canada Cataloguing in Publication

Dietze, Beverlie, 1957- author
    Playing and learning in early childhood education/Beverlie Dietze, Okanagan College, Diane Kashin, Ryerson University.—Second Canadian edition.

Includes bibliographical references and index.
ISBN 978-0-13-463927-7 (softcover)

    1. Play—Textbooks. 2. Learning—Textbooks. 3. Early childhood education—Textbooks. 4. Textbooks. I. Kashin, Diane, author II. Title.

LB1139.35.P55D53 2017   372.21   C2017-907141-6

5 2020

Dedication

I dedicate this book to my late mother, Eileen Lucy Arthurs, and my late father, William Christie Arthurs, who knew intuitively the importance of their eight children having the freedom to play outdoors—in the woods, at the brook, on the lawn, and in makeshift playhouses. And to my childhood playmates, my sister Myrna, and our late brother, Philip, who shared adventure, risk-taking, intrigue, and surprise in our play and learning. And to my sister Nancy, my brother Paul, and my loving husband, Peter, who inspire me to continue to play and learn.

—B.D.

I dedicate this book to my children, Jeremy, Ben, and Dory, whose early playful ways were a joy to behold and experience. To my mother, Reeva; I thank her for my artistic and creative side. To my late father, Gerald; I thank him for my passion for knowledge and love of research. I want to recognize my husband, Lorne, for his tireless support and encouragement. Finally, to my grandson, Griffen; I look forward to many playful days ahead.

—D.K.

Brief Contents

CHAPTER 1	Exploring the Foundations of Play	1
CHAPTER 2	The Process of Play	36
CHAPTER 3	Observing, Documenting, and Interpreting Children's Play	74
CHAPTER 4	Outdoor and Nature Play: Unscripted and Unstructured	109
CHAPTER 5	Planning Play Spaces	153
CHAPTER 6	Loose Parts and Children's Play	185
CHAPTER 7	Art and Play	217
CHAPTER 8	Blocks and Child's Play	251
CHAPTER 9	Dramatic Play	285
CHAPTER 10	Language, Emergent Literacy, and Play	319
CHAPTER 11	Math and Science and Play	354
CHAPTER 12	Music, Movement, and Play	390
CHAPTER 13	Bringing Technology into Child's Play: A New Perspective	416
CHAPTER 14	Taking Play to the Next Level	451

Detailed Contents

Preface xiii
Acknowledgments xviii

1 Exploring the Foundations of Play 1

Chapter Preview 2
The Origin of the Word *Play* 4
  Defining Play 4
The United Nations Convention on the Rights of the Child 9
The Importance of Examining Societal Concerns and Child's Play 10
  Childhood Obesity 11
  Outdoor Play 14
  Electronic Devices 17
  Culture 18
  Consumerism 22
  Poverty 23
Brain Development 25
An Overview of the Classical, Modern, and Contemporary Perspectives on Play 28
Terms That Influence Early Learning Play Environments 31
Position Statements on Children's Play 32

Summary 33
Review Questions 34
Making Connections 35

2 The Process of Play 36

Chapter Preview 37
Child's Play: From an Ecological Theory Perspective 39
Components of Play and Unique Features of Play 43
  Ecological Theory 43
  Play, Learning, and Intrinsic Motivation 44
  Play, Learning, and Active Engagement 49
  Play, Learning, and Play as Process Rather Than Product 50
Characteristics of Play 54
The Play Process 56
  Phase I: Body Play 56
  Phase II: Motoring Movement Play 57
  Phase III: Imaginative Play 57
  Phase IV: Intentional Imaginative Play 59
  Phase V: Peer Play with Rules 59
  Phase VI: Adult Play 60
Classifying Play Experiences 60
  Piaget's Stages of Play 60
  Smilansky's Contributions to the Stages of Play 63
  Parten's Classifications of Social Play 63
  Seagoe's Contributions to Play 64
Children and the Theories of Play 65
  Theories of Play 65
  Classical Theories 65
  Modern Theories 65
  Contemporary Theories 67
Putting the Play Processes into Perspective: Building on Children's Strengths 67
The Roles of Early Learning Teachers in Play 68
  Adults' Participation in Child's Play 69
Terms That Influence Early Learning Play Environments 70

Summary 71
Review Questions 72
Making Connections 73

3 Observing, Documenting, and Interpreting Children's Play 74

Chapter Preview 75
Children and Learning through Play 78
The Relationship of Observation to Play and Learning 80
Observation, Documentation, and Interpretation: A Twenty-First-Century Approach 84
  Observation 84
  Documentation 86
  Interpretation 89
  Reflective Practice 90

Examining the Difference between
Child Observation and Pedagogical
Documentation 91
Authentic Assessment 92
Ways of Acquiring Information to Support
Student Early Learning Teachers in
Understanding the Whole Child 94
Documentation Strategies 99
　Where Does Documentation Occur? 100
Discovering and Making Meaning of
Children's Play 101
The Types of Discoveries Made through
Watching, Listening, and Discussing Play with
Children 102
Terms That Influence Early Learning Play
Environments 105

Summary 105
Review Questions 107
Making Connections 107

4 Outdoor and Nature Play: Unscripted and Unstructured 109

Chapter Preview 110
The Complexities of Outdoor Play and Early
Learning Programs 112
Historical Perspective on Outdoor Play 113
Outdoor Play for Today and Tomorrow 117
The Importance of Outdoor Play to Child
Development 117
　Cognitive Development 119
　Social Development 120
　Emotional Development 120
　Physical Development and Movement 121
　Outdoor Play and Exposure to Natural Light 122
　Developing an Appreciation for Outdoor Play 123
　Children's Outdoor Play: Risky, Challenging, and
　Adventurous 125
　Planning Outdoor Play Spaces 129
Play Spaces for Infants, Toddlers,
Preschoolers, and School-aged Children 132
　Examining the Use of Play Space 134
　Analyzing Play Spaces 134
Choosing Materials for Outdoor Play:
Why Loose Parts 137
Active Outdoor and Constructive Play
Experience Areas 138

　Blocks 139
　Woodworking 139
　Art 139
　Discovery and Science 139
　Sociodramatic Play 140
　Games with Rules 141
The Roles of Early Learning Teachers in Outdoor
Play 141
　Early Learning Teachers' Attitudes and Abilities 141
　Program Schedules for Outdoor Play 142
　Early Learning Teacher's Facilitation Roles 142
Observing and Documenting Children's Play
Outdoors 145
　Examining the Environment for Health
　and Safety Issues 146
Terms That Influence Early Learning Play
Environments 149

Summary 149
Review Questions 151
Making Connections 152

5 Planning Play Spaces 153

Chapter Preview 154
Children's Play 155
　Sensorimotor Play 156
　Symbolic Play 156
　Construction Play 157
The Environment as the Third Teacher 157
Children's Places 158
Characteristics of Responsive Play Space
Environments 163
　Feeling Tone 164
　Listening to the Children 165
　A Caring Place to Play 166
　Inviting Engagement in Environments with
　Provocations 167
　Environmental Aesthetics 168
　Natural Light 171
　Stress-Free 171
Reflects Cultural and Community
Attributes 172
　Places for Exploration and Freedom to Play 173
Flexible Schedules and Order 174
Characteristics of Effective Play Space
Environments 176
　The Physical Environment 176

Space 176
Design Considerations for Effective Play Spaces 177
Traditional Physical Play Space Considerations 179

How Play Spaces Affect Children's Behaviour 181

Terms That Influence Early Learning Play Environments 182

Summary 183
Making Connections 184

6 Loose Parts and Children's Play 185

Chapter Preview 186

Understanding the Concept of Loose Parts 187

Classification of Loose Parts 190

Examining the Theory of Loose Parts 193

Intelligent Materials 194

Children's Play and Development with Loose Parts 195

Children's Play and Schemas with Loose Parts 197

Choosing Loose Parts for Early Learning Environments 198

Loose Parts Outdoors and Indoors 200

The Value of Loose Parts in Comparison to Fixed Equipment Outdoors 201

Loose Parts, Tinkering, and the Maker Movement 202

What Tinkering in Play Looks Like 202

Children's Play Types and Learning That Evolve with Loose Parts 205

Dramatic Play 205
Constructive Play 206
Social Play 206
Creative Play 207

Early Learning Teachers, Play, and Loose Parts 209

Strategies for Enhancing the Use of Loose Parts in Early Learning Environments 210

Terms That Influence Early Learning Play Environments 212

Summary 213
Review Questions 215
Making Connections 216

7 Art and Play 217

Chapter Preview 218

Defining Art 220

Educational Approaches Influencing the Visual Arts in Early Childhood Programs 221
Art and Child Development 225
Principles of Children Developing Their Visual Language through Art Experiences 231

Stages of Children's Artwork 232

Stages of Children's Drawing 233
Stages of Clay Development 234

The Process of Art and the Product 235

Strategies for Encouraging Creativity with Art Experiences 238

Types of Open-Ended Art Materials 239

The Role of Early Learning Teachers in Art Experiences 242

1. Children Require Early Learning Teachers Who View Themselves as Embracing Play, Creativity, and Art 243
2. Children Require Early Learning Teachers Who Have an Understanding of the Elements of the Materials 244
3. Children Require Early Learning Teachers Who Know When to Be Supportive and When to Allow Children to Be Free and to Problem Solve the Area of Challenge 245
4. Children Require a Learning Environment with a Variety of Materials and Places to Use the Materials 245
5. Children Benefit from Early Learning Teachers Who Encourage Children to Discuss Their Creations 245
6. Children Benefit from Early Learning Teachers Who Observe Children and Engage in Documentation 246
7. Children Require Early Learning Teachers to Have Rich Dialogue with Them about Their Art Creations 246
8. Children Benefit from Early Learning Teachers Who Know about the Relationship of Art to Child Development 246

Terms That Influence Early Learning Play Environments 247

Summary 248
Review Questions 249
Making Connections 249

8 Blocks and Child's Play 251

Chapter Preview 252
Defining Block Play 253
The Historical Perspective of Blocks 254
   Beginning in the 1700s 254
   Late-Nineteenth-Century Block Systems 255
   The Twentieth Century 255
   The Stages of Block Play 257
Types of Blocks 260
   Table Blocks 260
   Picture and Alphabet Blocks 261
   Parquetry Blocks 261
   Bristle Blocks 261
   Duplo® Blocks 261
   Foam Blocks 261
   Floor Blocks 261
   Unit Blocks 261
   Tree Blocks 261
   Hollow Blocks 262
   Cardboard Bricks 262
Loose Parts and Accessories 263
How Blocks Support Great Learning Opportunities for Children 263
   Blocks and Cognitive Development 267
   Blocks and the Affective Domain 267
   Blocks and Physical Skills 267
   Block Play and Language Development 268
   Block Building and Math 269
   Block Building, Science, and Engineering 270
   Block Play, Creativity, and the Arts 271
   Block Play and Gender 272
   Blocks and Inclusive Practice 272
The Role of Early Learning Teachers in Block Play 272
   Determining One's Philosophical Perspective 273
   The Early Learning Environment 274
   Organizing the Space 276
   Observing and Documenting Children's Block Play 277
   Role Modelling 280
   Starting Dialogue with Children about Block Play 281
   Reflection and Development 282
Terms That Influence Early Learning Play Environments 282

Summary 282
Review Questions 283
Making Connections 284

9 Dramatic Play 285

Chapter Preview 286
Theoretical Foundation 287
What Is Dramatic Play? 290
   Characteristics of Dramatic Play 291
   Stages of Dramatic Play Development 292
   Experiences for Children in Dramatic Play across Ages 295
   The Importance of Dramatic Play 295
   Variations in Sociodramatic Play 298
The Role of the Early Learning Teacher 299
Observation and Documentation 301
   Planning and Facilitating Dramatic Play 302
   Types of Dramatic Play 304
   Story Drama 306
   Provocations for Dramatic Play 309
   Setting Up for Dramatic Play 309
   Time to Play 310
Weaving Dramatic Play into the Early Learning Environment 311
   Guns, War Play, and Superheroes 312
Terms That Influence Early Learning Play Environments 314

Summary 314
Review Questions 317
Making Connections 318

10 Language, Emergent Literacy, and Play 319

Chapter Preview 320
Theoretical Frameworks 322
From Theory to Trends 323
Defining Language Development 325
Defining Literacy Development 325
   Play and Language 325
   Characteristics of Language Development 327
   Stages of Language Development 330
Children's Conversational Roles 331

Observing, Waiting, and Listening
(The Hanen Centre OWL Strategy) 331
  Language Skills and Play 332
  Characteristics of Literacy Development 333
  Stages of Literacy Development 334
  The Importance of Child Participation in Emerging Literacy 335
Literacy Skills and Play 336
Narratives or Storytelling 337
  Variations in Language and Literacy Development 338
The Roles of Early Learning Teachers 341
  Early Learning Teacher Interactions 341
The Early Learning Environment 343
  Creating a Community Culture for Language and Literacy 343
Setting Up a Literacy-Rich Environment 347
Terms That Influence Early Learning Play Environments 348

Summary 349
Review Questions 352
Making Connections 353

11 Math and Science and Play 354

Chapter Preview 355
Theoretical Foundation 357
Defining Science, Mathematics, and Scientific Inquiry 361
  The Importance of Math and Science 362
  Concept Development in Science and Mathematics 364
  Science, Mathematics, and Development 365
Learning Science and Math through Play 367
Playing with Science Is to Celebrate Wonder 369
The Scientific Method for Young Children 371
  The Role of Early Learning Teachers in Outdoor Math and Science 372
  Setting Up an Environment to Support Scientific Inquiry 373
  The Development of Mathematical Concepts 375
The Language of Mathematics 380
A Numbers-Rich Environment 381
  Mathematical Invitations and Provocations 381
Observation 382
  Science and Math Connections 383

Terms That Influence Early Learning Play Environments 385

Summary 385
Review Questions 388
Making Connections 388

12 Music, Movement, and Play 390

Chapter Preview 391
Historical Influences of Music and Movement 393
The Importance of Music and Movement 395
  Music, Movement, and Child Development 399
  Psychomotor Development 400
  Social and Emotional Development 402
  Cognitive Development 403
Aesthetic Appreciation 405
  Presenting Music and Movement to Children 406
  Presenting Songs to Children 407
The Role of the Early Learning Teacher in Promoting Music and Movement 408
Music and Movement Experience Centres 410
  Musical Instruments 411
  When Early Learning Teachers Have Limited Skills in Music and Movement 411
Observations and Documentation 412
Terms That Influence Early Learning Play Environments 413

Summary 413
Review Questions 415
Making Connections 415

13 Bringing Technology into Child's Play: A New Perspective 416

Chapter Preview 417
Defining Technology 419
Various Perspectives about the Use of Technology with Young Children 422
Technology and Children's Creativity 424
Technology and Early Learning 427
The Benefits of Using Technology with Young Children 428
The Role of Information and Communication Technologies 429
  Computers 431
  Tablets 431

    Interactive Whiteboards 434
    Digital Games 434
    Coding 434
    Robotics 435
Technology and Play 436
Technology and Children's Development 438
    Technology Supports Inclusivity 441
    Is There a Digital Divide? 441
The Role of the Early Learning Teacher 442
    Facilitating Children's Play with Technology 443
    Choosing Applications 444
    Observing Children 445
    Professional Learning and Development 446
Terms That Influence Early Learning Play Environments 447

Summary 447
Review Questions 449
Making Connections 450

14 Taking Play to the Next Level 451

Chapter Preview 453
Terminology Challenges and Debates 454
Programming and Curriculum 455
    Emergent Programming 456
    Communities of Practice 457
    Postmodernism 458
The Truth and Reconciliation Commission of Canada: A Call to Action 459

Intercultural Communication Competence 460
Voice and Empowerment 461
Critical Pedagogy 463
Reconceptualization in Early Learning 463
    Integrating Twenty-First-Century Skills in Early Learning 464
    Values and Beliefs 464
    The Image of the Child 465
    Critically Rethinking Practice 467
Professional Dispositions 467
    Reflective Practice 468
    Children's Rights 470
    Becoming an Advocate of Play 471
    Action Research 471
    Health Determinants 472
    Healthy Living and Sustainability 473
Family Rights and Family Engagement 474
Final Thoughts 475
Terms That Influence Early Learning Play Environments 476

Summary 477
Review Questions 480
Making Connections 480

References 482
Index 502

Preface

Children's play—it sounds so simple, yet it is a complex process, as you will discover as you read, examine, debate, and synthesize the information presented throughout this book. Play is as important to children as their nutrition, family nurturing, culture, and community engagement. Children reap so many benefits when early learning teachers and families invest in providing rich play environments, experiences, access, and opportunities to explore and discover through play. For example, play ultimately enhances children's sense of curiosity and wonderment, which in turn influences every aspect of their social, emotional, cognitive, and physical development.

Contemporary children are growing up in fast-paced societies in which many adults are replacing or reducing play opportunities and options with activities that focus on academic skills, technological gadgets, organized events such as sports, and passive activities indoors, including video games and television. This societal shift is eroding opportunities for children to play. Early learning teachers are encouraged to collectively work with children, families, neighbourhoods, policymakers, educational institutions, children's organizations, and governments to refocus our knowledge about play and, more importantly, to bring play back into the centre of a child's world. Why? Because children's play = learning for life.

The first edition of *Playing and Learning in Early Childhood Education* evolved from many factors. When Beverlie was working with early learning teachers, she was intrigued and distressed to discover that some did not have childhood experiences such as making mud cakes, creating snow angels or snow people, or having tea parties. Some had never built a fort out of wood pieces or blocks. A sizable percentage of early learning teachers felt that outdoor play was a time for children to run off energy rather than recognizing how outdoor play can be an incubator for incredible exploration and discovery. It was common for some early learning teachers to view outdoor play as a time for a "break." Still others believed that it was more important to offer children "academic-type" exercises than play opportunities. These perspectives led Beverlie to want to create a textbook that would provide up-and-coming early learning teachers with an examination of how children's play influences every part of a child's being and development—a book that would examine both indoor and outdoor play in terms of risk-taking skills, problem-solving abilities, interpersonal relationships with peers and others, and the use of natural and loose materials in play: "Plant the seeds, weave the ideas [and] nurture the growth" (Dietze, 2005) of children's being.

This edition brings together the wisdom and perspectives of both Beverlie and Diane. It is grounded in sharing new research, practices, and ways of knowing about play; the contribution that play makes to the lives of children; and how play sets the foundation for later academic and life dispositions. This new edition reinforces how play prepares children to develop critical thinking, problem solving, their desire to be curious, and creative expression that facilitates their communication skills and their ability to embrace place, community, culture, and diversity among peers. These skills form the foundation for the twenty-first-century skills that focus on STEAM—science, technology, engineering, arts, and math. This edition is intended to further support early learning teachers in engaging in discussions about their changing roles and responsibilities in working with children to create indoor and outdoor environments that challenge children to think, wonder, imagine, discuss, and discover through various play, tinkering, and research experiences.

We have been inspired by the knowledge and skills that we have gained from our early learning students, our graduates, the children, and our colleagues who work in or influence various types of early learning settings. This book represents a compilation of our learning acquired from our life journeys and from our work in the early learning field. We hope that by reading this text you, too, will gain knowledge, skills, and renewed passion that you can share with colleagues and the most precious resource in our communities—the children and their families.

OUR VISION FOR THIS BOOK

As we began to discuss our vision for this edition and examined new research that would influence our writing, we reaffirmed that our initial vision of developing a text that would support early learning student teachers by providing an in-depth examination of how play contributes to children's overall development was still valid. We wanted this new edition to:

- Support early learning student teachers in exploring the "who, what, when, how, and why" of children and play
- Spark readers to engage in discussion and debate about the concepts and ideas presented
- Highlight new research to advance thinking, dialogue, debate, and learning about the importance of children's curiosity to play and to learning
- Stimulate new and experienced early learning teachers to examine their roles and responsibilities in partnering with children to create stimulating, challenging, exciting, and unique play environments and experiences in both indoor and outdoor environments
- Offer our readers tools to support them in engaging in dialogue with families about how early play experiences provide children with the foundational knowledge, skills, and attributes needed for later academic learning and lifelong dispositions
- Support early learning student teachers in gaining the knowledge and skills needed to commit to ensuring that children in both urban and rural settings have access to quality play experiences
- Provide early learning student teachers with evidence-based information about the importance of play that can be incorporated into their working philosophy
- Contribute to early learning student teachers developing or deepening their passion for and commitment to children and their play

APPROACH TO THE TEXT

This text is intended to be user friendly and a valuable resource that early learning student teachers will use during their studies and refer to as they enter any number of exciting career options with young children. Each chapter begins with a message from an early learning teacher to students. These messages and the application examples in each chapter are intended to help readers understand how the theoretical framework is used by early learning teachers to inform their practice.

Learning and Playing in Early Childhood Education differs from other texts in several ways:

- First, many of the chapters discuss the concepts and programming perspectives from both an indoor- and an outdoor-play perspective. This book not only has a chapter devoted to outdoor play and loose parts but also clearly weaves in the importance of outdoor play to the development of the whole child throughout the text.

- A second important feature of this book is the emphasis on play and learning from infancy to school age. Many of the examples are relevant to all phases of childhood.
- Third, this book introduces you to Canadian content and Canadian and international researchers who are influencing the research and application of play around the world.
- Another key feature is the discussion of family and community culture, loose parts, technology, and environmental sustainability in relation to children's play.
- This book offers readers opportunities to see play from multiple perspectives. It introduces the concepts of reconceptualization and critical thinking and analysis about play.
- The final attribute of this book that differs from others like it is the approach taken in planning play space. The importance of creating a positive feeling tone within the early learning space and among the staff, children, parents, and community is emphasized.

This text has many unique features and would be ideal for use in both play- and curriculum-related courses. We envision it having many applications across curriculum in early childhood education diploma and degree programs. Observation courses, methods or curriculum courses, and content-specific courses (such as those focusing on art, planning, the environment, language and literacy, or math and science) will benefit from the content presented in this text. This textbook can be used from one semester to the next, as we recognize that it is unlikely that all of the chapter topics could be addressed in one course. We hope it will be a text that early learning student teachers will refer to during their studies and as they launch their careers as early learning teachers.

The Content and Features of the Text

We believe that learning occurs when students are engaged in exploring subjects and concepts with others in their learning community. The pedagogical layout of the text is designed to support learners in exploring the theoretical concepts through stories, examples, and discussions among faculty and other learners.

The text begins with the first three chapters introducing you to the foundational information on play. Chapter 1 examines the foundations of play. Chapter 2 discusses the process of play. Chapter 3 highlights the importance of conducting observations and documentation of children's play.

In Chapter 4 we highlight the importance and power of outdoor play. In Chapter 5 we examine the considerations to be made when planning for play. Chapters 6 through 13 highlight the relationship of play to programming areas, including dramatic play, outdoor play, blocks, language and literacy, math and science, art, technology, and music. Chapter 14, the final chapter, examines how we can take play to the next level in our practice.

The pedagogical features of this edition include the following:

- *Opening Quotes:* Each chapter begins with a quote that is intended to offer the reader "a place to begin" in thinking about one aspect of child's play.
- *Stories of Practice:* At the beginning of each chapter, early learning teachers share their perspective on the topic the chapter will address. These messages help set the stage for you to become familiar with how theory has informed practice, how new learning is essential in the profession, and how the combination of theory and practice guides early learning teachers in their daily work with children and families.

- *Learning Outcomes:* Each chapter begins with a series of learning outcomes that will be presented in the chapter. This helps the reader to become familiar with the core concepts of each chapter.
- *Stop . . . Think . . . Discuss . . . Reflect Boxes:* These boxes provide probing questions that prompt you and members of your learning community to explore and trigger ideas, passion, and research interests beyond the content presented in the chapter.
- *Invitations to Search the Internet:* The magnifying glass represents an invitation to students to further the learning in each chapter by accessing readings and resources online.
- *Key Terms with Definitions:* Throughout the text, key terms are shown in boldface, and definitions are presented in the margins.
- *Terms That Influence Early Learning Play Environments:* We conclude each chapter with three additional terms that support the theory of children's play
- *Chapter Summary:* At the end of each chapter, key points summarize the core concepts of the chapter and reflect the learning outcomes presented at the beginning of the chapter.
- *Review Questions:* Each chapter offers the learner questions to explore based on the content of the chapter.
- *Making Connections: Theory to Practice:* Each chapter provides scenarios based on the content of the chapter. This section is intended to help the reader make the connection between theory and practice.
- *Digital Portfolio Entries:* This end-of-chapter section includes suggestions for potential portfolio entries based on the content of each chapter.

New to This Edition

This edition of *Playing and Learning in Early Childhood Education* has new features and research resources, as follows:

- A new chapter that focuses on loose parts and their importance to children's play and learning
- An enhanced chapter on outdoor play
- Key terms that are bolded in the text and defined in the margin
- Colour photos, figures, and illustrations
- Action boxes that offer new research options or learning tasks to support theoretical highlights
- A Digital Portfolio section

The chapter order for this edition has been revised. The chapters have been repositioned to support the importance of examining environments and the curriculum planning process so that students gain knowledge and skills in a sequential process that will support them in transferring the theory to practice in both the indoor and the outdoor environments equally.

The content also reflects current research and practices. Discussion of risky and rough-and-tumble play, pedagogical documentation, sustainability, and outdoor play has been enhanced to reflect these areas' importance to early learning environments. This is particularly important as children's access to and opportunities for play and learning are being highlighted internationally as a right and need for children.

SUPPLEMENTS

Playing and Learning in Early Childhood Education is accompanied by the following supplements, which all instructors will find helpful.

An **Instructor's Manual**, which offers case studies, teaching and learning methods for consideration, and other resources to support active learning with students.

A **Test Item File** (in Microsoft Word format) consisting of multiple-choice, short-answer/short-essay, and essay questions.

PowerPoint Presentations for each chapter that help to highlight and illustrate key themes in the text.

Please note that all of these supplements are available online. They can be downloaded by instructors from a password-protected location on Pearson Canada's online catalogue (**vig.pearsoned.ca**). Simply search for the text, then click on "Instructor" under "Resources" in the left-hand menu. Contact your local sales representative for further information.

Acknowledgments

We would like to sincerely thank Pearson Canada for providing us with this opportunity. We are particularly grateful to Christine Langone, who has worked with us on three texts now. Christine has helped us make the text what it is. We also thank Kimberley Veevers, Madhu Ranadive, and Christina Veeren, whose guidance and support have allowed this project to evolve. We thank the reviewers, whose feedback helped us shape the content and the layout of the text, including the following:

- Kimberly Bezaire, George Brown College
- Deb Bumstead, Georgian College
- Tricia Dumais, Conestoga College
- Frances French, Canadian Business Skills College of Technology
- Alison Gaston, Sheridan College
- Lisa Lamarre, Algonquin College
- Terrah Lindsay, Grande Prairie Regional College
- Mary Lou Lummiss, Fleming College
- Heather McLeod, Memorial University

We would like to thank all of the children, families, and early learning centres that have allowed us to use their photos throughout the book. The photos help us emphasize key aspects of the content through the actions of the children.

We must also thank our families, extended families, and friends. A project such as this is made possible only when families and friends are encouraging, supportive, and positive. We appreciate your patience and your encouragement along the way. Thank you for listening to us, challenging our thoughts and perspectives, and helping us to engage in and focus on making this project the best it can be.

Diane Kashin

In particular, I wish to thank my husband, Lorne, and my children, Jeremy, Ben, and Dory, for the space, support, and inspiration to take on new challenges. Finally, thank you to my mother, whose joy for life reminds me that play is a lifelong endeavour.

Beverlie Dietze

I wish to thank my brother, Paul, and sisters, Nancy and Myrna, for accepting my need to be curious and embark on new challenges. Thank you for always believing in me. Your encouragement has led me to examine, explore, and discover so many new ideas, perspectives, and opportunities. Thank you, Peter, for continuing to support me in my quest to gain new knowledge and make a difference in teaching and learning. Without your support and encouragement, these learning adventures would not occur. You are a great husband and partner in learning!

Finally, we want to acknowledge that this project brought us together as new colleagues. We are grateful to Pearson Canada for allowing us to engage in such a stimulating, collaborative learning experience. We have challenged each other, mentored each other, learned significantly from each other, and shared a collective spirit, enthusiasm, and commitment that helped us bring this project to fruition.

—Beverlie Dietze
—Diane Kashin

CHAPTER 1
Exploring the Foundations of Play

Rawpixel.com/Shutterstock

> " Play is the highest expression of human development in childhood for it alone is the free expression of what is in a child's soul. "
>
> —Friedrich Froebel (1782–1852)

LEARNING OUTCOMES

After exploring this chapter you should be able to:

- Describe five perspectives on play, including the similarities and differences of each perspective.
- Explain the relationship of the United Nations Convention on the Rights of the Child to play.
- Outline how obesity, outdoor play, culture, consumerism, technology, and poverty influence children's play and their development.
- Discuss how various theorists such as Comenius, Locke, Rousseau, Pestalozzi, and Froebel influence early learning teachers' knowledge and practice about play and learning.
- Describe how position statements on play inform practice.

Sharing Stories of Practice

When I began my college education, I thought that taking an early childhood education course would be easy—after all, I had been a camp counsellor and a swimming instructor, and I was a babysitter in my neighbourhood during my teen years. I also grew up in a family with parents who believed in providing children with active learning experiences.

Prior to starting the compulsory play course, I thought, "Oh, this is going to be a bit boring—why do we need to study play? Play is play—that is what children do." When the professor started teaching the course, I soon realized that play is a comprehensive and complicated topic. Children make play look easy and natural, but it is not. Play is a process. Each aspect of children's play has a developmental purpose—play lays the foundation for academic, social, physical, and emotional life skills.

Now I work with children daily, and I often reflect on the content of my play course. Although I did not appreciate all the theory at the time, I now draw upon that theory of play in my daily practice. How the children play influences the types of observations I engage in with the children and the conversations I have with children and their families, and contributes to how I document their play experiences. Understanding the relationship between play and child development is, in essence, the foundation of early childhood education. This foundational knowledge has contributed to how I analyze the documentation and how I plan for children's play. It has helped my documentation become pedagogical.

I believe that understanding the various facets of play is an important investment in my practice. Every day I use my knowledge about play in my work with children. Understanding play becomes my guide, my touch point, my reference for programming, and my anchor for programming, interacting, and respecting the important work of children—that is, playing.

Melinda, early learning teacher, 2016

CHAPTER PREVIEW

We all have different play-life experiences. Some of us have fond memories of playing in mud during the spring or jumping in the leaves come fall. In the summer, you may have played at the beach, and in the winter, in the snow. You may have memories of going to the neighbourhood parks to swing, pumping as much as you could to give you the feeling of going higher and higher in the sky. Perhaps you remember your first street hockey game or when you arrived home so dirty from your play that you worried about what your mom or dad might say. These childhood memories will serve you well as you consider play as a topic of study. As you begin your journey in examining the theory related to children's play, you will note that it is complex and vital to children's lives and their development. Play today differs drastically from play during your childhood and ours. As you will soon discover, play is the foundation of childhood. This text has been written to support you in examining play from a variety of perspectives and to allow you to gain new knowledge and practice in looking at play with children in mind.

Play—what is it and how important is it to children? Does play have a defined "textbook" meaning? Is child's play the same across cultures, genders, and age groups? Are there different types of play? Does it differ from urban to rural environments? Do children go through stages of play? Have children always played throughout history? Do all children play? Does play affect us later in life? Can and should adults play?

As you can see, the word *play* brings forth many questions. It may also generate many images in your mind. Take a moment and visualize play—what do you see in your mind's eye? Do you see yourself in dress-up clothes, making mud cakes, or playing with a favourite toy? Or do your play memories take place outdoors with your siblings and friends rolling on the freshly cut grass? You might remember playing with others in an early learning program, building with blocks or making sand castles. Some of you may have vague or limited memories of play and childhood. There are many reasons for this, which may include stressful childhoods, lack of opportunity for quality play experiences, or limited exposure to other children and group play. Play is an important part of childhood. As you explore the concepts of play, we hope that it will trigger positive childhood memories. Ultimately, you will begin to connect the theory of play with the play experiences that you remember and the ones that you are now observing as an early learning student.

Children's play has long been important to early learning teachers, families, community advocates, and health and education professionals who have an interest in child development and human thought (Barnett & Owens, 2015; Christian, 2012). Throughout history, in every culture, children have played. Play is a vehicle in which cultural attributes are passed from one generation to another. Through play, children communicate their feelings and ideas to other children and adults (Smirnova & Riabkova, 2016). Children gain physical development and experimentation opportunities during play (Sandseter & Sando, 2016). In essence, the subject of children's play is complex, as it formulates the foundation for child development. Understanding children's play is pivotal to the role and responsibilities of early learning teachers.

Observing children's play is one of the most important roles and responsibilities of early learning teachers. That may seem strange to you at this point in your studies, but as you continue to learn, you will discover that the young child is at the centre of early

Photo 1.1 Children's play can be with simple materials.

Used with Permission of Family Space Quinte, Inc.

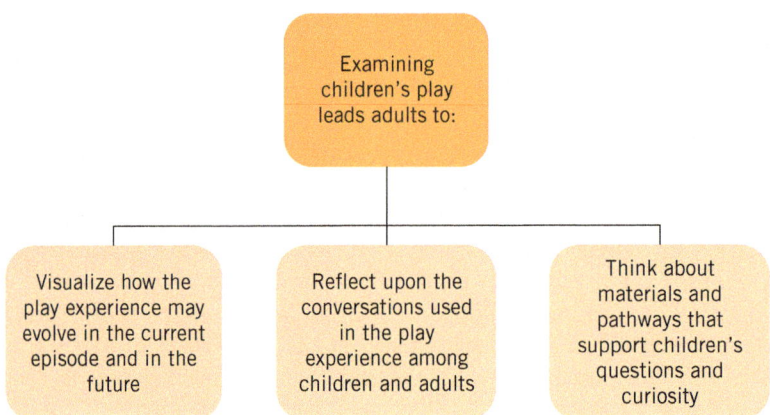

Figure 1.1 Why adults examine children's play.

childhood programming, and it is through play that children learn and develop. Early learning teachers observe children, examine the types of play that children participate in, and use their findings to support conversations with children and to expand play opportunities. As outlined in Figure 1.1, examining children's play, visualizing how it may evolve, and reflecting on what has been observed and heard sparks many questions, ideas, and pathways for early learning students, early learning teachers, and children. Play becomes part of the road map for programming. Observing children's play is discussed in depth in Chapter 3 and is a dominant theme that is presented in each of the upcoming chapters.

This chapter will introduce you to different perspectives about what play is and its significance in the lives of young children. Learning about the complexity of play will help you in understanding how a child's play becomes your guide for facilitating quality programming experiences—meeting the child's developmental needs, learning, and interests.

THE ORIGIN OF THE WORD *PLAY*

Scott (2008) suggests that the origin of the word *play* is unknown. It is thought that the English adopted the word *pleien*, meaning to "dance, leap for joy, and rejoice," from the Dutch in the later Middle Ages (c. fourteenth century). They translated it as *pleg(i)an*, which means "to exercise, or frolic." Throughout history, movement, and motion have been synonymous with the word *play*.

Johnson, Christie, and Wardle (2005) indicate that "the Greek words for play and education were the same (*paitheia*); distinguished aurally by whether the accent was on the second syllable (pie deé ah: education) or the last syllable (pie dee ah´: play)" (p. 3). Both words are derived from the Greek word for child, *pais*.

Defining Play

Discussions about play and learning, the definition of play, and the role of adults in children's play are essential tenets when we examine play environments in early learning programs. A vast amount of research clearly articulates that children in all cultures learn through play (Sandseter & Sando, 2016). It is through play that children's curiosity is triggered and that they acquire knowledge, skills, and abilities that become the foundation for lifelong learning and development. As identified by Guerrero, Hoffmann, and Munroe-Chandler (2016), children are engineered to play, and play is vital to their existence. Lifter, Mason, and Barton (2011) provide a unique perspective for us to consider. They suggest that there are inconsistencies in definitions and descriptions of play, largely a result of the varying conceptualizations that adults have of play. Chudacoff (2007) suggests that "articulating a single acceptable definition of play is almost impossible" (p. 1). Gleave and Cole-Hamilton (2012) concur that defining play is complex and is challenging due in part to the long-standing debate among social, policy, and academic groups. They indicate that further confusion about defining play is being influenced by the emergence of electronically based play combined with children being exposed to "structured play" sessions rather than them having the freedom to play where, when, and how they wish. As outlined in Figure 1.2, Gleave and Cole-Hamilton (2012) advocate for adults to view play as a crucial process of learning and development and understand its complexities.

"Children are engineered to play" (Guerrero, Hoffmann & Munroe-Chandler, 2016).

When we examine the literature on defining play, a clear distinction is made between work and play. The concept of play differs from the concept of work in that play is a self-chosen activity rather than prescribed. Play is a process rather than a predicted outcome or product (Association of Canadian Deans of Education [ACDE], 2016). Work has a defined intent and a prescribed outcome. Mark Twain (1876), in *The Adventures of Tom Sawyer*, said that "work consists of whatever a body is obliged to do" but that "play consists of whatever a body is not obliged to do" (p. 33). Work and play seem to be concepts in opposition. Jean Piaget (1923) argued that play is the work of the child. However, Maria Montessori believed that children prefer to work while they play. Montessori (1949) identified that work is part of civilization and that children are workers. By participating in work-related experiences, children engage in being able to explore and discover patterns of their own individuality.

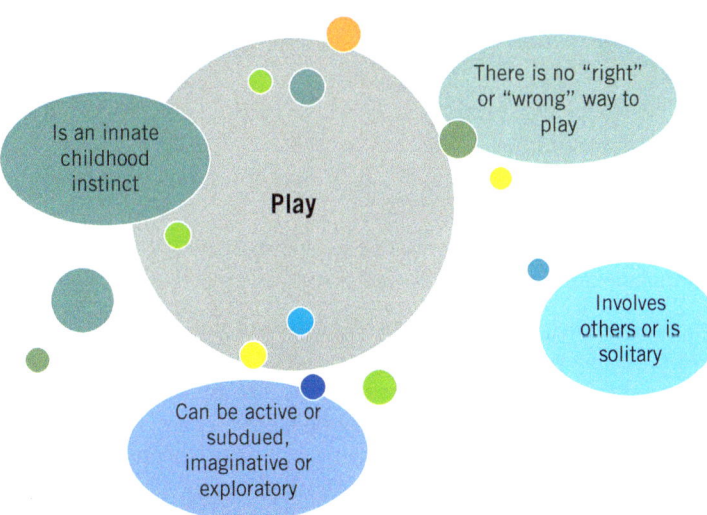

Figure 1.2 The complexities of play.

According to Froebel (1887), children learn through play. Piaget (1962) viewed play as a significant part of children's development. Smirnova and Riabkova (2016) indicate that "virtually all specialists today recognize the value of play for child development" (p. 41). They identify that the majority of educators, pediatricians, and neurophysiologists continue to cite new evidence that play is fundamental to children's development. They maintain that when children are deprived of play experiences, the absence is destructive to their normal development. Language, social, emotional, physical, and cognitive skills are highly connected to the play experiences, role models, and environments that children are exposed to in their early years. Children require play experiences in both indoor and outdoor environments (Dietze & Kashin, 2016).

There are many perspectives on what the term *play* means. As you explore the concept of play, it is helpful to examine it from the perspective of what is meant by **free play** and **prestructured play**.

Barnett and Owens (2015) suggest that it is difficult to choose one definition because it depends on the context. We need to think of play in broader terms—from building roadways in the sand or building elaborate block structures to rolling down hills or playing on a climbing structure. Rather than provide you with one specific definition, we invite you to examine the following six perspectives and determine if there is one that resonates with you or if there are parts of each of the statements that you support.

> **free play** Refers to a child's play experience that is intrinsically motivated, is unstructured, and has limited adult intervention (Santer & Griffiths, 2007).
>
> **prestructured play** Refers to play opportunities that are adult guided in an environment organized by adults (Weisberg, Hirsh-Pasek, & Golinkoff, 2013).

1. "The generally accepted definition of play would include three large categories: (1) sensori-motor play (large and small motor activity); (2) symbolic play, which involves representational abilities and includes the fantasy play of socio-dramatic play; and (3) construction play, which involves symbolic product formation" (Wolfgang, Stannard, & Jones, 2001, p. 2).

2. Play is a multidimensional, developmental (Sutton-Smith, 1997) activity expressed through a variety of forms and actions (Tannock, 2008).

3. "Play is the purest, the most spiritual, product of man at this stage and is at once the prefiguration and imitation of the total human life—of the inner, secret, natural life in man and in all things. It produces, therefore, joy, freedom, satisfaction, repose within and without, and peace with the world. The springs of all good rest within it and go out from it" (Froebel, 1887, p. 25).

4. "I believe that play is as fundamental a human disposition as loving and working" (Elkind, 2004, p. 36).

5. For educators from Reggio Emilia, Italy, whose preprimary schools have inspired others around the world, play is highly valued for its ability to promote development but none more so than the complex and long-term projects in which children and teachers become engaged (New, 1998).

6. Play is typically considered a pleasurable, spontaneous, non-goal–directed activity that can include anticipation, flow and surprise (Mardell et al., 2016).

There is no one perspective that encapsulates the importance, the breadth, or the complexities of play. As you examine the various tenets of play, you will gain insight into why play is pivotal to childhood for learning and development. Understanding the concept of play and the influence that adults have on a child's play is complicated. It requires early learning teachers to examine it from a variety of perspectives. As an approach to the concepts presented, we encourage you to think about the theory presented as well as your previous thoughts and experiences and to combine those areas of knowledge with the new information. We suggest that you engage in a reflective process as a way to help you synthesize your new learnings. We ask you to stop, think, discuss with others, and reflect.

> ## STOP ... THINK ... DISCUSS ... REFLECT
>
> When you examine the perspectives of play presented, what key components resonate with you? Why? If you had to choose two perspectives presented, which two would you choose? Why? Based on your perspective of play and what you have examined in this chapter, how do you define play? Why?

Smirnova and Riabkova (2016) suggest that contemporary early learning programs are replacing play experiences with play-related strategies, which include elements of instruction. When we think of instruction in early learning programs, it primarily refers to directions given by the adult to the children for completing a particular activity. The activity is intended to teach particular skills, such as counting, printing names, and word recognition (Smirnova & Riabkova, 2016). In essence, the intent of the activity is for children to acquire academic skills. For an activity to be considered play, the experience generally is child initiated and free of rules and objectives set by adults (Bergen, 2009). When adults try to label experiences as play but in reality have prescriptive requirements for the activity, as outlined earlier in the chapter, this becomes work, not play. For example, when early learning teachers engage with children in a game with flash cards, with the adult's purpose to have them memorize something depicted on each card, this is considered work, not play. Children quickly develop the skills to differentiate between pure play experiences that they initiate and work disguised as play that adults initiate.

As you read about play and begin to formulate your thoughts on what play means for you in your future role as an early learning teacher, you will note that there are national and international organizations, such as the International Play Association (Canada), ParticipACTION, and the Canadian Association for Young Children (CAYC), that

Photo 1.2 Children's play is stimulated by new experiences, materials, and the environment.

Used with Permission of Family Space Quinte, Inc.

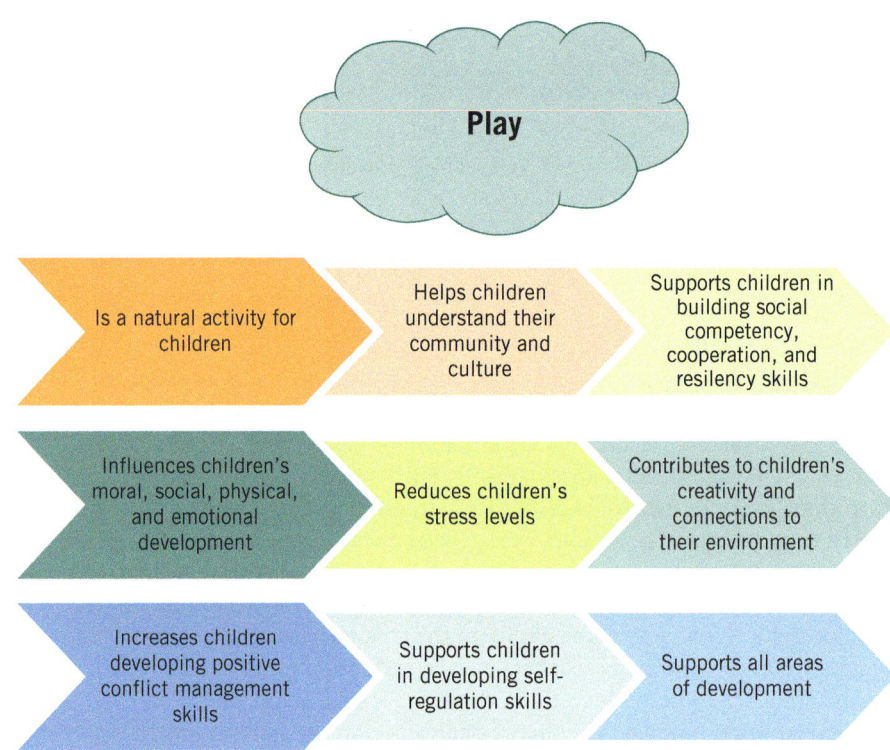

Figure 1.3 The value of children's play.

advocate for children to have the right to and opportunities for play to occur daily. In 2014, the International Play Association (IPA) made a Declaration on the Importance of Play. As part of that declaration, the IPA aims to:

- Protect the right to play by having time, freedom, and space to play in their own way
- Preserve the right to play by acknowledging that "play is a universal behaviour and the benefits to children and young people achieving their right to play are shared by all races and people around the world" (2014, p. 1)
- Promote the right to play by fostering and facilitating evidence gathering and exchange between international borders.

Throughout this text, the multiple facets of play are presented. Examine Figure 1.3 and then think about why the return to quality play experiences is being advocated and why early learning teachers value play.

Play is the way in which children gain new abilities, concepts, skills, and overall developmental attributes (Smirnova & Riabkova, 2016). Young children become highly motivated in the right play environment (Sandseter & Sando, 2016).

In this text, we highlight the United Nations Convention on the Rights of the Child, followed by some of the current societal issues that influence play, because both the United Nations international treaty and societal issues contribute to how students and early learning teachers formulate views and perspectives on play and its role in early learning environments. We encourage you to stretch your thinking about how children's development can positively or negatively be affected by their **play environment**. As you review this section, think about how you envision that our society and culture may contribute to, or erode, children's play.

play environment Refers to the total indoor and outdoor space, materials, conditions, people, and rules within the space where children may engage in play (Dietze & Kashin, 2017).

THE UNITED NATIONS CONVENTION ON THE RIGHTS OF THE CHILD

The UN Convention on the Rights of the Child is an international treaty that outlines universally accepted rights for children. The treaty provides countries such as Canada with a benchmark that is used to measure the treatment of children.

The UN Convention was officially approved by the United Nations in 1989. Canada ratified the Convention on the Rights of the Child on December 13, 1991. By ratifying the treaty, Canada made a commitment to comply with the articles of the Convention. This means that the Government of Canada made a commitment to protect and enhance the basic rights of children through its policies, programs, and services. Article 31 refers to child's play. Other articles of the treaty, discussed below, are interrelated with child's play.

Article 31 of the UN Convention states,

1. That every child has the right to rest and leisure, to engage in play and recreational activities appropriate to the age of the child, and to participate freely in cultural life and the arts.
2. That member governments shall respect and promote the right of the child to participate fully in cultural and artistic life and shall encourage the provision of appropriate and equal opportunities for cultural, artistic, recreational, and leisure activity.

Article 3 states that, in all actions concerning children, the best interests of the child shall be a primary consideration.

Article 12 indicates that the child has the right to express his or her views freely and have them considered.

Article 19 focuses on the prevention of child abuse and childhood injury. Adults have a responsibility to ensure that children have safe environments for their play episodes.

Photo 1.3 Play is the right of every child.

Used with Permission of Family Space Quinte, Inc.

Article 23 tells us that children with disabilities have the right to recreation and the fullest possible social integration and individual development.

Article 29 states that education should be directed toward a broad range of developmental areas, including the child's personality, talents, and mental and physical abilities.

Article 30 states that children of ethnocultural minorities or of indigenous origin have the right to their own culture. This includes their forms of play or recreation.

As outlined by the Public Health Agency of Canada (2016), children benefit from learning about the UN Convention on the Rights of the Child. This helps children to understand:

- What rights are, the responsibilities related to the rights, and how to support other children practice their rights.
- If others have violated their rights, what actions may be taken.
- To respect the rights of other children.
- That all children have rights under the Convention.

CURIOUS?

Add the words *The United Nations Convention on the Rights of the Child* to your search engine to obtain a PDF version of the Convention.

THE IMPORTANCE OF EXAMINING SOCIETAL CONCERNS AND CHILD'S PLAY

Societal concerns are issues that are facing society and that influence children's play. As identified in Figure 1.4, we highlight five societal concerns that are correlated with the state of children's play and active living. Early learning students and teachers are encouraged to make a commitment to promote play opportunities in a variety of environments. In so doing, children gain life benefits that can counteract the issues presented. As identified by Lee (2015), children's play emerges "akin to a state of mind, invariably related to issues of **autonomy**, **agency**, and **power**" (p. 241). Adults influence the quality of the play environments as well as the freedom that children have to play (Oppermann, Anders & Hachfeld, 2016). These elements contribute to children developing the foundation for a healthy lifestyle.

When children are given autonomy, they make decisions about their play independently. When children have a sense of agency, they feel in control of their play. Early learning students and teachers listen to and respect children's voices, recognizing that they are capable players in the play environment. If we make all the decisions for children, we are not empowering them to take control of their own play. When children are empowered, their learning and development is enhanced (Dietze & Kashin, 2016). Being aware of societal issues that influence children's play and ensuring that children have autonomy, agency, and power lead them to experiencing healthy development.

autonomy Refers to children being given independence or freedom to engage in play based on interests, environments, and resources.

agency Refers to children being in environments where they feel in control of things that happen around them and have the opportunity to have their voices heard in making choices about their play.

power Refers to the ability for children to engage in play by exercising control and acting on ideas, interests, and strategies without defined adult roles.

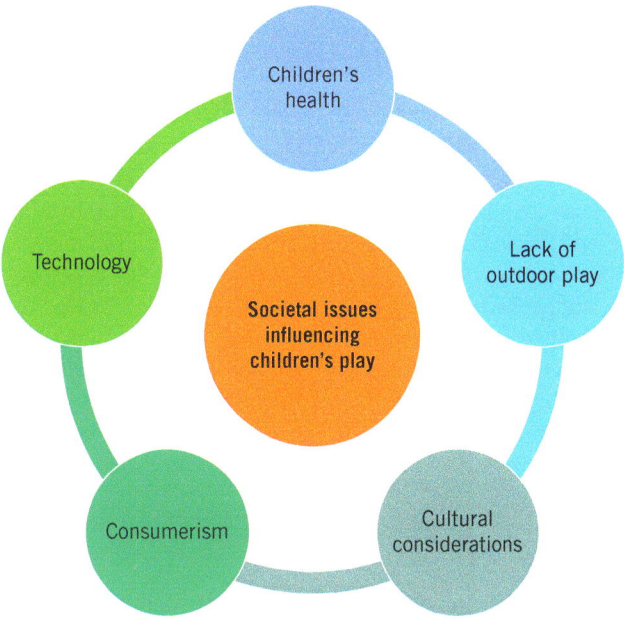

Figure 1.4 Societal issues influencing children's play.

Childhood Obesity

Many children living in Canada are considered overweight or obese due to defined health conditions, genetic dispositions, or environmental conditions. In fact, many experts, including Gotay and colleagues (2013) and Mann, Power, and MacLellan (2013), suggest that approximately 25 percent of Canadian children are overweight or obese. Gotay indicates that between 2003 and 2011, obesity rates in Canada increased from 22.3 to 25.3 percent. She notes that the Atlantic provinces and two of the territories, Nunavut and Northwest Territories, have the highest obesity rates in the country, with more than 30 percent of the population in these regions estimated to be considered obese. Table 1.1 provides an overview of facts to consider when examining the state of childhood obesity in Canada.

According to the Obesity Action Coalition (2016), children are classified as "obese" if their body mass index for age (BMI) percentile is greater than 95 percent. Children are classified as "overweight" if their BMI is greater than 85 percent and less than 95 percent.

Table 1.1 Facts about childhood obesity in Canada.

Facts to Consider
- "One-third of Canadians aged two to 17 are overweight or obese" (Peirson et al., 2015).
- "Research has demonstrated that excess weight puts children at risk for a range of preventable health problems, including type 2 diabetes, cardiovascular disease, joint problems and mental health issues" (Active Healthy Kids Canada, 2007, p. 13).
- Type 2 diabetes is most prevalent in African, Hispanic, Asian, South Asian, and Aboriginal ethnic groups (Canadian Diabetics Association, 2016).
- In Canada, 44 percent of children who are diagnosed with type 2 diabetes are of Aboriginal heritage (Canadian Diabetics Association, 2016).

> ## Body Mass Index (BMI)
>
> BMI is calculated by dividing an individual's weight in kilograms by the square of the individual's height in metres. For children, the BMI is age and sex specific. A child's weight status is determined using an age- and sex-specific percentile for BMI rather than the BMI categories used for adults. This, in part, is because children's body composition varies as they age and varies between boys and girls. Therefore, BMI levels for children are expressed relative to other children of the same age and sex. See additional information at Health Canada (https://www.canada.ca/en/health-canada/services/food-nutrition/healthy-eating/healthy-weights/canadian-guidelines-body-weight-classification-adults/body-mass-index-nomogram.html).

There are many factors that contribute to children becoming obese or overweight, including:

- An increased intake of energy-dense foods that are high in fat (World Health Organization [WHO], 2016).
- A decrease in physical activity due to the increasingly sedentary nature of children's play, lack of exposure to outdoor play experiences, and urban living conditions
- Food availability, food use, and food access (WHO, 2012).
- The complex relationships between physiology, individual behaviours, and environmental factors (National Aboriginal Health Organization, 2012).

Children with poor diets and lack of exercise who are overweight or obese are vulnerable to an array of health problems, including chronic diseases such as high blood pressure, type 2 diabetes, heart attack, joint problems, and mental health issues. For example, from 2009 to 2011, the Canadian Health Measures Survey (CHMS) results showed that 4 percent of Canadian children and youth have a blood pressure that is borderline or elevated.

All children living in Canada are influenced by their environments and role models. Appropriate role modelling, nutrition, and active play are vital to children and their wellness. For example, children with physically active role models and exposure to appropriate play spaces are more likely to engage in more active play activities, such as running, jumping, and climbing, than those who do not have active and encouraging role models who focus on keeping active. Children who have access to interesting play materials and resources in their play spaces will become intrigued and want to use them in their play (Dietze & Kashin, 2016). This, too, increases children's activity levels. Having unique resources increases children's sense of curiosity, play, and learning options, which in turn contributes to more physical movement (Dueck, 2016). Children exposed to peer and adult role models with active lifestyles during their early years are more likely to establish and continue this as a daily living practice (Ward et al., 2017).

Aboriginal Children and Obesity

Aboriginal communities are the fastest growing in Canada. According to Statistics Canada (2016), based on the National Household Survey, there were 1 400 685 people who had an Aboriginal identity in 2011, representing 4.3 percent of the total Canadian population. Aboriginal children ages 14 and under made up 28.0 percent of the total Aboriginal population and 7.0 percent of all children in Canada. By comparison, non-Aboriginal children ages 14 and under represented 16.5 percent of the total non-Aboriginal population. The largest numbers of Aboriginal people lived in Ontario and the western provinces (Manitoba, Saskatchewan, Alberta, and British Columbia). Aboriginal people made up the largest shares of the population of Nunavut and Northwest Territories.

Aboriginal Peoples (Indigenous Populations)

"A collective name for the original peoples of North America and their descendants. The Canadian Constitution recognizes three groups of Aboriginal peoples—Indians (First Nations), Métis and Inuit. These are three separate peoples with unique heritages, languages, cultural practices and spiritual beliefs" (Indigenous and Northern Affairs, 2016, p. 1).

According to the National Aboriginal Health Organization (NAHO, 2012), Canadian First Nations, Inuit, and Métis people have higher rates of obesity and diseases related to obesity such as diabetes, high blood pressure, and heart disease compared to Canadian non-Aboriginal children.

Willows, Hanley, and Delormier (2012) developed a socioecological framework as a way to illustrate and understand complex factors that could contribute to obesity among Aboriginal children. They suggest that **colonization** influences all levels of the model, as outlined in Figure 1.5.

colonization Refers to the action or process of establishing power and control over indigenous people and requiring them to assimilate into a new society.

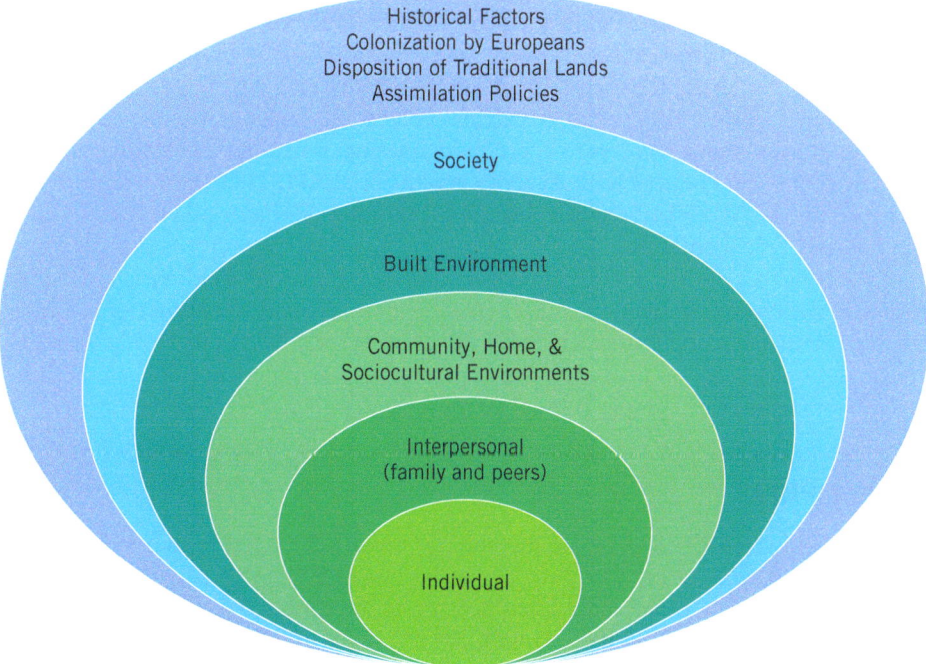

Figure 1.5 Socioecological framework to explain causes of obesity in the Aboriginal population.

The first sociological layer, *the individual*, refers to both the biological factors, such as age, sex, and genes, that may predispose a child to obesity and life circumstances, such as having a mother who is obese, having diabetes, or having been breastfed. Psychological factors such as self-efficacy and cultural identity highly influence a child's well-being. Children who embrace their Aboriginal culture and speak their Aboriginal language are generally healthier in all aspects of life.

The *interpersonal relationships* and interconnections among families and peers are identified as the second layer. In this layer, children's likelihood of becoming obese is strongly influenced by their families and peers. Generally, the role modelling that adults provide related to eating habits, food practices, and physical activity transfers to children. As outlined by the NAHO (2012), Aboriginal people have a higher rate of food insecurity than other Canadians. This results in many Aboriginal children consuming high-fat and low-nutrition food as their primary diet.

The third layer, *community, home, and sociocultural environments*, refers to the environmental influences, such as socioeconomic status, family organization, and adult education levels, that affect children's levels of obesity. For example, as identified by the NAHO (2012), there is a high incidence of Aboriginal children living with a lone parent or extended family members such as grandparents or other relatives. Lone-parent families generally have a higher rate of food insecurity, as do families living in geographically remote communities. Meanwhile, Aboriginal children living in families with hunters or fishers have a lower level of obesity due to the access to fish and game.

The *built environment* layer focuses on the attributes of the environment, such as those designed with outdoor play spaces for children and safe walking paths. Children benefit from living in communities where there is access to healthy foods and appropriate health care.

The *society* layer refers to the influence that local, provincial, and federal policies related to food, recreation, and environment have on children, families, and communities. Access to media, including messages about ideal body images and food, also influences individual children and family food and activity level experiences.

The final layer, *historical factors*, refers to the colonization by Europeans that led to Aboriginal people losing their traditional lands and way of life. The assimilation into the new society has contributed to Aboriginal people and communities experiencing a reduction in food security; access to appropriate housing, water, and healthy food; and a culturally competent environment. According to the NAHO (2012), these historical factors contribute to Aboriginal children having higher rates of obesity and related diseases than non-Aboriginal children.

As highlighted above, addressing obesity among Aboriginal children is a complex process. Early learning students and teachers seek to understand the impact of colonization, life experiences, and trauma (NAHO, 2012) on Aboriginal families and communities. Early learning teachers play a key role in promoting play experiences and establishing play environments that promote cultural competence for all children and families.

Outdoor Play

There are many reasons cited in the literature as to why there has been a reduction in the amount and types of outdoor play in which young children participate (Gleave & Cole-Hamilton, 2012). Some suggest it is because of the concerns adults have for childhood safety (Munroe & MacLellan-Mansell, 2013). Others indicate it is because children will be bullied while playing outdoors, and still others suggest it is because of parental desires to have children learn skills necessary for school (Wee & Anthamatten, 2014).

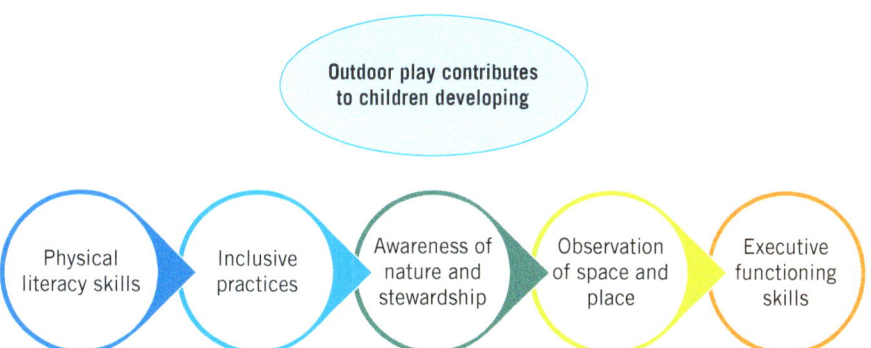

Figure 1.6 How outdoor play contributes to children's development.

Then there are those who express concern that the urban and rural play spaces are not suitable for children's play. There are many aspects of learning and development that children engage in during outdoor play. In addition to the areas of development outlined in Figure 1.6, it is through play that children develop talents; creative dispositions; language and communication skills; and social, emotional, cognitive, and physical motor skills. Acar (2013) articulates that "outdoor play spaces are the best play environments for children. These areas offer opportunities that are not found in indoor spaces" (p. 846). Outdoor play environments contribute significantly to all aspects of children's development.

For example, outdoor play stimulates children's social play because there is more space than indoors, the noise levels are less distracting outdoors, and there are more active play opportunities. The outdoor play environment is where children gain overall control over their bodies—a control that is essential to their total development.

Photo 1.4 All aspects of a child's development are influenced by outdoor play.
Used with Permission of Family Space Quinte, Inc.

Outdoor play influences children's physiological and psychological development. For example:

- Children labelled as having attention-deficit/hyperactivity disorder (ADHD) who are exposed to outdoor play experiences and natural settings have reduced ADHD symptoms and a related reduction of medications.
- Children's stress levels are reduced dramatically when in green spaces.
- Children who play outdoors on a regular basis have better distance vision than those who spend more time indoors.
- Children's social interactions are positive and occur with many peers.
- When children are given time to play outdoors, they experience comfort and a reduction in feelings of anxiety and boredom.

When children play outdoors, they gain exposure to light and sunshine, which are needed to nourish the human body (Hoel, Berwick, de Gruijl, & Holick, 2016). Children require sunlight to regulate their **circadian rhythms**, as these rhythms influence sleep patterns. Exposure to sunlight also influences the production of serotonin. Serotonin combined with vitamin D regulates moods and emotions. Healthy levels of serotonin are connected to children developing a feeling of happiness and security, whereas low levels of serotonin are related to children expressing impulsivity, aggression, depression, and anxiety behaviours (Kamal, Bener, & Ehlayel, 2014).

circadian rhythms Refers to the internal clock that regulates the sleep–wake cycle.

Children need the stimulation of the sun and light to nourish the human body (Hoel et al., 2016). Exposure to light decreases the heart rate, blood pressure, respiratory rate, blood sugar, and lactic acid in the blood following active movement. The active movement increases energy, strength, endurance, tolerance to stress, and the ability of the blood to absorb and carry oxygen (Hoel et al., 2016). These key body functions influence cognitive, physical, emotional, and social development.

Outdoor play contributes to children obtaining vitamin D. Vitamin D, which the body acquires from sunlight, helps to:

- Metabolize and absorb calcium and other minerals needed for physical and psychological development.
- Influence the production of the brain chemicals such as beta-endorphins and serotonin. These chemicals are directly related to emotional dispositions.
- Contribute to the neuromuscular function and immune function, including reducing inflammation (Groves et al., 2013).

Although there is sufficient research that identifies the importance of outdoor play to children's development, it continues to be one of the major deficiencies in many early learning programs (Dietze & Kashin, 2016; Munroe & MacLellan-Mansell, 2013). The Canadian Association for Young Children (CAYC) and ParticipACTION have created position statements on active play. These statements advocate for daily, active, outdoor play experiences that include children using their large muscle skills, experiencing the freedom of outdoors, and learning about their outdoor environments. Dietze and Kashin (2016) suggest that the outdoor environment and experiences are as important as indoor experiences. They indicate that "adults and environments that support children's development are those that provide materials, time and opportunities for children to explore and discover outdoors" (p. ii). As a future early learning teacher, you will play a significant role in responding to the growing body of evidence that aligns children's healthy development with contact in nature, with light, and with quality outdoor play experiences. You will read more about these components in Chapter 4, which is devoted specifically to outdoor play. We encourage you to think about outdoor play as an integral part of your role. Quality outdoor play experiences contribute to nourishing children's bodies and dispositions. The life practices established during the early years affect later life—children need to be exposed to outdoor play as part of their daily living routine.

Electronic Devices

Today's children have far less face-to-face play experiences with other children and their natural world than children did 40 years ago. There are many reasons for this, one of which is the exposure to electronic devices. For example, a study conducted by Common Sense Media (2013) suggests that "38% of children under the age of 2 have used a mobile device, compared to only 10% two years earlier" (p. 9). In some instances, adults provide children with access to computers and handheld devices as a way to entertain them or use it as a form of play

Electronic Devices

rather than providing the active play experiences that are essential for children. Others use electronic devices as a way to increase skills, such as literacy or numeracy (Given et al., 2016). There is great debate about the role that electronic devices should play in childhood. Parents, educators, and policymakers continue to examine the relationship, benefits, and ways in which technology can be mixed with children's play. At the same

Photo 1.5 There is controversy on whether children need electronic devices in their early years.
Used with Permission of Fiona Barton

The Importance of Examining Societal Concerns and Child's Play time, many advocates of play express concerns that electronic devices must not erode child's play; yet many parents are also suggesting that their children require access to electronic devices, as this is a resource that is part of children's learning. Think about how you use electronic devices. Do you agree with the newer research that supports children in having exposure to electronic devices in various circumstances (Dietze & Kashin, 2013)? Why or why not? How might access to the Internet or to digital cameras be used effectively in early learning programs?

Culture

Canada has one of the world's most diverse populations and has self-identified as a multicultural society (Canadian Heritage, 2007). Canada is one of the few countries with a national policy that focuses on respect for diversity, multiculturalism, and antiracism (Friendly & Prabhu, 2010).

There are many ways to describe culture. For example, Dietze (2006) suggests that "culture refers to the underlying beliefs, patterns of behaviour and assumptions of a group that are passed on from one generation to the next. Culture is developed from a society's key values" (p. 25). Wee and Anthamatten (2014) define children's culture of play as "activities that are shaped by a system of relationships that constitute the cultural context of their development" (p. 89). Early learning programs in Canada service families with differing beliefs and values on a variety of subjects, including the value of play, how play influences children's development, and how children learn foundational academic skills through play.

Early learning students and teachers come to early learning centres with their own sets of cultures and beliefs that influence their thinking about children's play. Wee and Anthamatten (2014) suggest that children's play is best understood when adults examine it from the children's perspectives and the cultures that children bring to the environment. They cite Pearce and colleagues (2009), and others, who emphasize the importance of viewing play as childcentric and relating children's play to their environment and culture. Wee and Anthamatten (2014) "consider children's play as a culture in its own right, with its own set of norms, behaviours, and preferences that are unique to a particular group of children, situated in a specific time and place" (p. 88). This reinforces the importance of early learning teachers developing partnerships with children and families and creating environments based on cues gained from the children.

Family beliefs, values, and culture and community assets contribute to the diversity of our Canadian society. Early childhood is the prime time for young children to learn about and develop positive thoughts, feelings, and respect for diversity (Friendly & Prabhu, 2010; Wee & Anthamatten, 2014). When early learning programs celebrate aspects of the various cultures or talents of children, they develop a disposition of acceptance and appreciation of all within the environment.

Early learning students and teachers benefit from viewing play as a facet of children's culture because it provides insight into:

- Where children play.
- How and what they play.
- Why they play as they do.

For example, think about children growing up in Indigenous communities and the cultural attributes within those communities. Battiste and Henderson (2009) characterize Indigenous views on learning as sacred, holistic, and a lifelong journey.

Photo 1.6 Some families prefer their children not to play outdoors in the Canadian winter climate, while others believe that it is essential for their child's development.

Used with Permission of Bora Kim

Values and approaches that inform socialization within many Indigenous families include:

- A recognition of children's varying abilities as gifts.
- Promotion of skills for living on the land.
- Respect for a child's spiritual life and contributions to the cultural life of the community.
- Transmission of a child's ancestral language.
- Building upon strengths more than compensating for weaknesses (Anderson & Ball, 2011).

Perspectives on the importance of children and play may differ from one region of the country to another, from one country to another, and from one family to another. For example, adults who have grown up in a country such as Norway, where the culture values outdoor life and freedom to explore, will have different perspectives on outdoor play during the winter months than parents who come from a warm climate and who have not had life experiences in colder temperatures and in weather conditions such as snow. Children from rural Canada and from farming communities have different play experiences than children from an urban environment. Families who have immigrated to Canada from Middle Eastern countries may exhibit different beliefs about child-rearing, family values, and the use of natural resources such as water than families who have immigrated from Europe, due to "lived experiences."

Play is influenced by a child's culture and environment. Early learning students and teachers examine each of the cultural attributes that children bring to the environment and determine how to best support each child and groups of children in their play. For example, in 2016, Vancouver had about 700 000 residents who speak languages other than English in their own homes. Chinese languages account for about 280 000 and Punjabi for 125 000 of these (City of Vancouver, 2016). This finding would be consistent among

cultural norms Refers to behavioural patterns or beliefs that are common among specific groups of people. Such behaviours and beliefs are generally learned from parents, extended families, peers, and other significant people in the child's life.

larger cities across Canada. This means that many children come to early learning programs with **cultural norms** that may include a first language different from the language used in the program. Early learning teachers work with families to collectively create a play environment that meets the needs of all children in the early learning environment.

Now we ask you to stop, think, discuss with others, and reflect on the issue of providing food in early learning centres as part of children's play experiences.

STOP ... THINK ... DISCUSS ... REFLECT

Think about an early learning teacher who has been examining the cultures of children in her program. She begins to question the challenges of providing children with corn, maize, beans, and vegetables to use in their play in the mud kitchen. She is concerned about whether it is acceptable for children to be given food for their play. How might families feel about this practice, particularly if they are struggling to provide food for their children? As this was being discussed at a staff meeting, another teacher suggested that this practice be considered from a cultural perspective. She gave the example that many children from a Mexican background may view corn as revered in traditional Mexican culture. West African families may view the practice of using food in play as wasteful. Overall, families who are modelling sustainable practices would view this practice as offensive because of the waste of food and its importance to daily living.

When you think about providing children with food in the mud kitchen, what is your perspective? Does the play value outweigh the potential waste? If families approach you about using food for play, how might you respond? Why? Should children's cultural backgrounds be considered in this situation? Would your position be different if the current children do not come from cultures that have particular beliefs about these foods? Based on what you have read about children, culture, and play, what values and beliefs would you like to include in your practice? Why?

Building on the work of Göncü and colleagues (1999), we have outlined principles and considerations that can guide early learning teachers when viewing how culture can influence children's play. Table 1.2 provides the principles and the interpretation of these six principles.

There is great benefit in early learning students and teachers learning about children's cultures. This helps you reach beyond your sphere of knowledge and contributes to you gaining insight into the relationship of culture and play. Networking with colleagues, families, and professionals in local communities and internationally is a valuable strategy to acquire an understanding of how children's cultural backgrounds influence their play and development and how the cultural attributes may be exhibited in play episodes.

Early learning teachers observe and listen to children during play. For example, children's conversations with their peers during dramatic play provide teachers with valuable insight into a child's cultural, family, and community celebrations and traditions (Smirnova & Riabkova, 2016). These insights guide early learning teachers in determining the types of materials and experiences that may trigger children's interest and expand their knowledge about play, culture, and problem solving.

Table 1.2 How early learning teachers view children, play, and culture.

Principle	Interpretation
The investment made for outdoor play space and equipment by local governments influences accessibility and availability for play within a community.	Communities that value children and their play make space and equipment available to families. Children living in lower-economic environments generally have fewer spaces to play or resources available for their play.
Structural designs of local play space influence how children and families access and use the space.	Children and adults with mobility restrictions are either included or excluded in local play space. Environmental barriers contribute to social barriers and social exclusion.
Children's life experiences and family cultures and beliefs are honoured in the play environments.	Children bring different life experiences to the play environments. Adults support children in their play, such as by supporting them in using sticks for a variety of play aspects, including using them as guns.
Adult behaviours toward children in their play episodes influence how children embrace and execute their play.	When adults communicate acceptance and support of children's play experiences, children are positively influenced. Conversely, if children feel negative vibes from adults, the play may be stopped and children may feel stressed.
Understanding children's play requires adults to view how children engage in and embrace play experiences.	If adults have preconceived ideas about children's play or culture, the depth and understanding of clearly seeing and understanding children's play is compromised.
Understanding children's play requires play to be examined, documented, and analyzed from a variety of perspectives.	When adults observe and listen to children during their play, there is an increased opportunity to view play from a holistic approach, including understanding how children bring life and family experiences into their play.

Photo 1.7 Children's family and their community culture influence their play opportunities.

Used with Permission of Family Space Quinte, Inc.

> **STOP … THINK … DISCUSS … REFLECT**
>
> Think about your childhood. Can you think of experiences with children from other cultures? Did you play only with children from cultures similar to your family's culture? Were you guided in playing based on cultural norms? Were there play experiences that you engaged in that your role models indicated were not appropriate? Why or why not?

Consumerism

Canadian children are exposed to a heavily commercialized media environment through television, the Internet, and the Web. Children today are considered digital natives (Thaichon, 2017). Recent research shows that:

- Six in ten children shop online (Thaichon, 2017).
- More than 41 percent of children use a mobile device to make general purchases (Ramasubbu, 2014).
- More than 58 percent of children experienced online purchases before the age of 12, and it is predicted that this will be 70 percent by 2018 (Thaichon, 2017).
- More than 28 percent of children between the ages of 3 and 4 use a tablet at home, with 12 percent using the tablet to go online (Given et al., 2016).

As toy and food companies increase their expenditures on advertising, the Canadian Paediatric Society is concerned about the impact of advertising on the lives of children. For example, according to Morrison (2010), four in five commercials advertising food on Canadian children's television are for foods that are high in undesirable nutrients, such as fast foods, soft drinks, candy, and presweetened cereals. The commercials for healthy food make up only 4 percent of the advertising shown on television.

According to Šramová (2014), the marketing strategies used for children aim to have the children put pressure on parents and grandparents in order to influence shopping behaviours and the products purchased. Advertising agencies focus on the infant to 3-year-old demographic because they are trying to get children to recognize their corporate logos and products (Nairn & Fine, 2008; Samova, 2013). Ideally, brand loyalties and consumer habits formed during childhood will be carried through to adulthood.

Toy advertising is generally children's first exposure to consumerism. Young children, because of their inability to distinguish fact from fiction, think that particular toys have the capability of doing many neat things because of the advertising presented. This is of concern, because children between 2 and 5 years of age do not have the cognitive ability to differentiate between a TV program and a commercial or between reality and fantasy. Although it has been more than 20 years since McNeal (1992) outlined the evolution of a child consumer, the relevance of his perspectives remains current today. He identified the process as outlined below.

- **Infancy to 2 years**—children accompany parents shopping, where all sorts of products are displayed. These children are usually placed in a shopping cart, and items are at their eye level.
- **Ages 2 to 3 years**—children accompany parents shopping and begin requesting items. They begin to make the connection between television advertising and store items. The more exposure to television they have, the more children begin to

express "wants." During this phase, children begin to use strategies such as whining, screaming, or tears to influence parents in providing them with desired items.

- **Ages 3 to 4 years**—children accompany parents shopping and begin selecting items that they desire. During this phase, they begin to exhibit a desire for specific brands of items. Children have made many connections—and they are able to express wants—to the stores where the products are available and to finding the items in the particular stores. This is defined as the stage at which a child expresses an understanding of the want–satisfaction process in a market-driven society.
- **Ages 4 to 5 years**—children accompany parents shopping and make independent purchases. This is the phase when children choose their products and take these products to the checkout counters.

Early learning teachers play a role in educating children about consumerism. They discourage children from using language such as "I want . . . I need" statements. They also try to reduce children's ideas that they require "material" things as part of their identity (Opree, Buijzen, van Reijmersdal, & Valkenburg, 2014). Rather, they support children in choosing and discussing materials that will provide them with an array of play options. Early learning teachers discuss with children (especially school-aged children) the intent of the advertising in relation to the characteristics of particular products. Over time, with appropriate adult guidance, children develop an understanding of media messages.

STOP ... THINK ... DISCUSS ... REFLECT

How does consumerism influence children's play? Why? What signs might you observe in an early learning program that would lead you to be concerned about consumerism and children? How might your consumerism influence children and families? Do consumerism and technology depend on the socioeconomic status of children and their families? Why or why not?

Poverty

In 2016, UNICEF ranked Canada as 17 out of 29 wealthy countries due in part to the number of children living in poverty in our country. In 2011, the Organisation for Economic Co-operation and Development (OECD) ranked Canada as 21 out of 27 countries for its poverty level. Canada ranks 15th in material well-being, 27th in health and safety, 14th in education, 16th in behaviours and risks, and 11th in housing and environment (Raphael, 2014).

Poverty can be defined in two ways. **Absolute poverty** is described as the deprivation of the basic goods and services needed to maintain a sustainable standard of physical well-being (Sarlo, 2013). As identified by Sarlo (2013), when individuals live in absolute poverty, they have the inability to access adequate food, shelter, and related daily necessities. **Relative poverty** refers to families that are worse off with fewer resources than other members of society (Sarlo, 2013).

Many media sources suggest that almost 1 in every 5 Canadian children, or 1 334 930 Canadian children, live in need (Kohut, 2015). Further:

- The rate of child poverty in Canada increased from 15.8 percent in 1989 to 19 percent in 2013.

absolute poverty The deprivation of the basic goods and services needed to maintain a sustainable standard of physical well-being.

relative poverty Refers to families that are worse off, with fewer resources, than other members of society.

- The poverty rate for Indigenous children is at nearly 40 percent.
- Fourteen percent of Canadian families with children live in poverty. This results in large numbers of Canadian children experiencing various forms of material and social deprivation, which in turn manifests a variety of adverse health outcomes (Adamson, 2013).
- One in seven Canadians using homeless shelters are children. Forty percent of food bank users are children (Raphael, 2014). This increases the potential for children to have higher rates of mental and physical health needs.
- Children living in either absolute or relative poverty have higher levels of a whole range of physical, mental, and social health problems (Lightman, Mitchell, & Wilson, 2008; Raphael, 2014).

Figure 1.7 outlines the child poverty levels by province. As outlined in the chart, Nova Scotia, Newfoundland and Labrador, British Columbia, and Manitoba have child poverty rates higher than the 8.2 percent national average, whereas New Brunswick and Prince Edward Island have rates of 3 percent or lower. Ontario is the only province that has a targeted focus on child poverty. Children new to Canada and Aboriginal families have a high risk for living in poverty (Statistics Canada, 2013).

As identified by the Public Health Agency of Canada (2016), living in poverty has a significant impact on children's levels of health, education, and behavioural attributes. The Public Health Agency suggests that children are influenced by the 12 key determinants of health, including the family income and social status, education and literacy levels of parents, physical and social environments, gender, and culture. The emphasis that adults place on children's play is influenced by these determinants. Access to play materials, peers, space, and positive role modelling are common factors that positively or negatively affect play experiences.

Poverty places stress on families. When parents have constant worries and stress about employment, housing, debt repayment, and the needs of their children, they have fewer human resources and less resiliency needed to nurture and support children (Chaudry & Wimer, 2016). This, in turn, reduces children's intuitive need to express curiosity, creativity, independence, and self-control. Excessive stress, regardless of its source, disrupts the neural pathways of a child's developing brain, which can cause lifelong problems (Chaudry & Wimer, 2016).

Statistics indicate that children in low-income families suffer a higher rate of accidents during their play (Public Health Agency of Canada, 2016). One of the reasons identified is that some of the neighbourhoods where families in poverty live have more

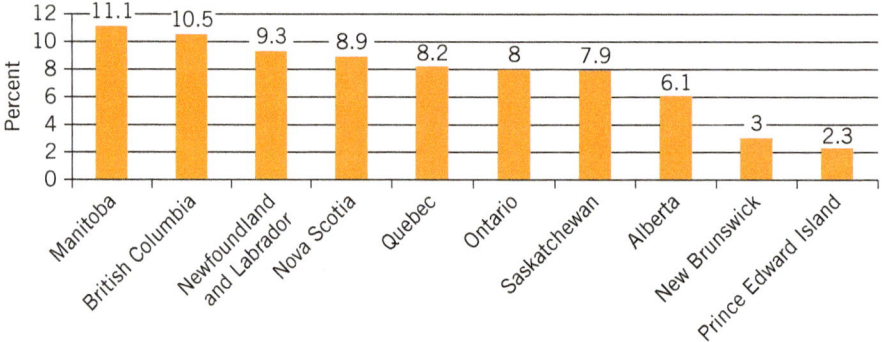

Figure 1.7 Child poverty rates by province.
(Source: Statistics Canada. [2013]. CANSIM 202-0802: Persons in low income families. Retrieved from http://www12.statcan.gc.ca/census-recensement/2013/dp-pd/index-eng.cfm).

safety issues compared to more affluent neighbourhoods, due to the lack of play materials and equipment. The lack of quality play materials and equipment may also contribute to the higher level of accidents. The simple story below, as presented in *Toward a Healthy Future: Second Report on the Health of Canadians* (2006), makes links between health, child development, family, and play.

> Why is Jason in the hospital?
>
> Because he has a bad infection in his leg.
>
> But why does he have an infection?
>
> Because he has a cut on his leg and it got infected.
>
> But why does he have a cut on his leg?
>
> Because he was playing in the junkyard next to his apartment building and there was some sharp, jagged steel there that he fell on.
>
> But why was he playing in a junkyard?
>
> Because his neighbourhood is kind of run down. A lot of kids
>
> play there and there is no one to supervise them.
>
> But why does he live in that neighbourhood?
>
> Because his parents can't afford a nicer place to live.
>
> But why can't his parents afford a nicer place to live?
>
> Because his Dad is unemployed and his Mom is sick.
>
> But why is his Dad unemployed?
>
> Because he doesn't have much education and he can't find a job.
>
> But why . . . ?

STOP ... THINK ... DISCUSS ... REFLECT

Think of a 4-year-old child who lives with her mother and three siblings ages 9 years, 3 years, and 18 months. They live in a two-bedroom apartment on the tenth floor of a high-rise block. How might this influence play? Is there room for the child to play? Is there room for movement? Will the child be able to keep materials in the environment so that she may return to the play in an hour or on the next day? If no, does that have any impact on the child's play and learning?

Now think about the outdoor experience. The children go to the play area, which is the parking lot at the apartment building. There is space for the children to run around, but they are required to move each time a car comes by. How does this affect play? Does the economic situation of the family influence the amount and type of play in which children participate?

BRAIN DEVELOPMENT

In recent years, early learning teachers have benefited from the brain-development research that has been conducted by researchers from a variety of disciplinary backgrounds, including neuroscience, psychology, and child development. Children's brains develop rapidly during the early years in response to genetics and their environment. The genes formulate the base for the development. The interaction between the genes and children's daily living experiences shape how the brain develops. In essence, the genes provide the initial structure for brain development; the experiences within their environments contribute to the overall shaping or development of the brain (Australian Early Development Census, 2014).

A child's brain is sculpted by the early experiences, which align with the development of the neural circuits known as the *synapses*. As identified by the National Childcare Accreditation Council (NCAC, 2007), "The architecture of the brain and skills are built in a hierarchical 'bottom-up' sequence. Foundations are therefore important, as higher level circuits are built on lower level circuits" (p. 8). Children who do not have opportunities to achieve a solid foundation at the lower level are more challenged in attaining higher-order skills because the lower-level circuits are not properly structured or wired.

By the time children reach age 3, they have about 1000 trillion brain connections or synapses. Through a pruning process, which is influenced by experiences and environments, as children reach adolescence the brain synapses number around 500 trillion and remain at this level through adulthood.

During the first four years of a child's life, the developing brain becomes organized based on the life experiences and environment that the child is exposed to and that form the foundation of the brain's architecture. Learning, behaviour, and health are built upon this foundation (Center on the Developing Child at Harvard University, 2016). Early cognitive neuroscience research shows that intervention changes the brain and changes behaviour. Researchers refer to this as "plastic"—the brain's plasticity is designed to respond to experience (Wasserman & Zambo, 2013). Perry (2004) indicates that neurons, neural systems, and the brain change in a "user-dependent" way. The "synaptic connections increase and strengthen through repetition, or wither through disuse" (p. 1). The brain adapts to the child's experiences. The richer the relationships and experiences are, the healthier are the synapses.

Children become a reflection of their environment (Perry, 2004). For example, if a child is exposed to environments that are rich with experiences, safe, and predictable, they "can grow to be self-regulating, thoughtful, and a productive member of family, community, and society" (Perry, 2004, p. 1). Conversely, if their world lacks supportive relationships, is chaotic, stressed, or bored, and lacks limited nutrition and stimulation, children are "more likely to become impulsive, aggressive, inattentive, and have difficulties with relationships" (p. 1). Adults have a major influence on the feeling, tone, and responsiveness that children experience in the environment. As outlined in Figure 1.8, optimal brain development is complex and is influenced by environmental conditions.

The Canadian Institute of Child Health (2008) indicates that there are four principles of brain development:

- The child's environment shapes the brain's wiring.
- A child experiences the outside world through the senses—seeing, hearing, smelling, touching, and tasting—which enables the brain to create or modify connections.
- The brain operates on a "use it or lose it" principle.
- Relationships with other people early in life are the major source of development of the emotional and social parts of the brain.

Children who are in environments that are consistent, enriched, and stimulating and that encourage creativity, exploration, and wonderment are in a position for optimal brain development. Examine the following play experience: Marley, Marti, and Megan decided, after reading the story of Elmer, to make an elephant out of boxes. They began this play process by discussing how they could make an elephant. They asked each other what they could use. Then, finding boxes, fabric pieces, and glue, they began to make an elephant.

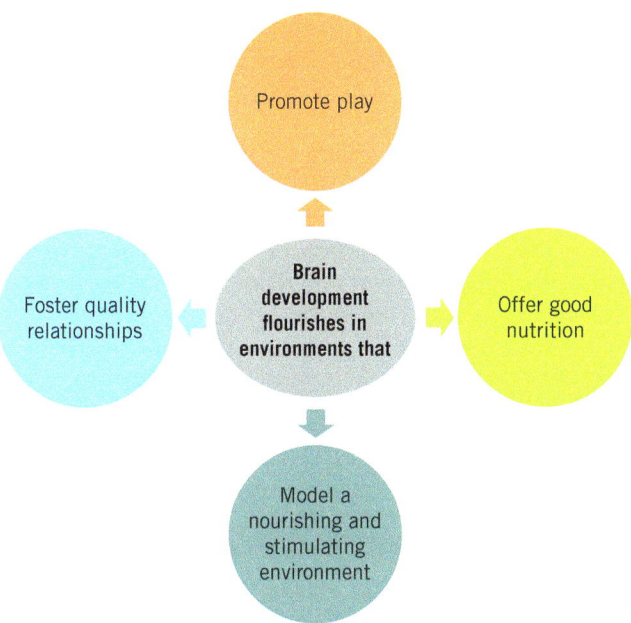

Figure 1.8 How children's brain development flourishes.

They had to determine how they were going to place the boxes. They engaged in dialogue that led to verbal negotiations among the children. They determined that they did not have anything to use for a trunk, and they did not know what they could use. This required them to think about elephant trunks and then explore the types of materials that could be used to achieve their desired trunk. They also returned to the storybook so that they could examine the elephant's trunk. In consultation with their early learning teacher, Suzanne, the children examined a variety of tubing, some of which were pliable and others of which were rigid. They looked at each piece to determine which would be most like an elephant's trunk. They decided that they needed to see a moving elephant so that they could watch how the trunk moves. This required the children and Suzanne to access videos about elephants on the Internet, as they did not have access to a place where they could observe a live elephant. Think about the learning that the children engaged in during this process. These types of play experiences have children using their brain capacity to engage in language, problem solving, socialization skills, resource identification, and physical activity.

When you think about children achieving optimal brain development opportunities, we ask that you reflect on play and adult–child relationships. Play environments are meant to be interactive and led by children. The environment is organized with interesting materials and options that will trigger children's curiosity and desire to play. Play that is child initiated and child directed is more likely to meet the needs of children than is adult-imposed play. Play is one of the best investments that can be made to support a child's brain development and growth potential (ACDE, 2016).

Add the words *Think, Feel, Act: Lessons from research about young children, positive relationships*, and *brain development* to your search engine to find a number of videos on this topic.

Observing children in their play helps early learning teachers to know the correct timing for offering new and stimulating experiences in the play environment (Dietze & Kashin, 2016). For example, when children stop playing with materials, use the materials in a repetitive way for long periods, or play in particular experience centres, adults take this as a cue that children may benefit from having new play options that are stimulating, and they add new challenges to their play.

In this section, we have examined the current issues that influence children's play. Understanding these issues is important because they provide you with the conceptual lens of why play is as essential today as it was from a historical perspective. Early learning students and teachers benefit from continuously examining how play is interwoven with child development. Understanding the theory and application of play is an essential skill that early learning teachers use in their daily practice and is needed for children to flourish.

AN OVERVIEW OF THE CLASSICAL, MODERN, AND CONTEMPORARY PERSPECTIVES ON PLAY

Students frequently ask educators why there is a need to examine the classical, modern, and contemporary perspectives on subjects such as play. Does it help early learning teachers to meet the needs of young children today? The simple answer is yes. Examining the varying beliefs about play helps students and early learning teachers to explore how the historical values, beliefs, and philosophies shape and influence practices today. The information guides us in questioning past practice, current practice, and future practice. This contributes to building new "knowledge." For example, Froebel determined that children learn through play and that the quality of play is enhanced in an outdoor environment. Why would play be enhanced outdoors? If true, can this outdoor environment be emulated indoors? Froebel's writings indicate that outdoor environments are rich with natural surroundings that stimulate children to interact with nature and their environment while contributing to their physical environment (Dietze, 2006; Ernst, 2014). The indoor environment sees children using more commercialized materials and cognitively related experiences, thus changing the play focus. With this new information and knowledge, how do we change our practice?

When examining theories, researchers usually classify them into three time frames. *Classical theories* are those that were prevalent in the nineteenth century through to World War I. *Modern theories* are those that evolved after World War I (Frost, Wortham, & Reifel, 2008; Scarlett & New, 2007). *Contemporary theories* are those that are currently being examined and debated. In Tables 1.3, 1.4, and 1.5 we present a brief overview of some of the more popular theorists, in chronological order, who have contributed to the literature on children's play. Each theorist has challenged previous perspectives and added new thinking and positions that lead us to ask more questions. This questioning process brings new thinking and learning to practice.

You may have studied the theorists presented in other courses and in other contexts. Ours is not an exhaustive listing; rather, we see it as an introduction to great thinkers. It is intended to whet your appetite. You may become intrigued with a particular philosopher or perspective. This may lead you to engage in further research. As you review the information that follows, we encourage you to think about what each perspective focuses on. Then we ask that you think about your beliefs and values in relation to the position presented. Think about what play is, what it looks like, why children play, and what your role is in children's play. Examine how each theorist has influenced early learning programs today. Determine whether one orientation best represents your current thought processes about children's play and learning.

Table 1.3 Classical theorists.

John Amos Comenius (1592–1670): The family, especially the mother, has the most influence on children's learning. Children should have access to organized education in the child's language.

Theory to Practice: Children require access to active learning, with reading being embedded in the play and learning experiences.

John Locke (1632–1704): Believed that children were born as blank tablets (Dietze, 2006) and that their life experiences determine who they are and who they become.

Theory to Practice: Children's play is observed to determine the child's interests. Play experiences are active, with acceptable role models. Environments are planned so that children are provided with pleasurable and successful opportunities.

Johann Heinrich Pestalozzi (1746–1827): Identified that children need to be given the freedom to choose their play materials from nature-based, sensory-rich environments. A natural environment provides children with the freedom to explore their natural surroundings, including plants, animals, and geography (Corbett, 1979). Children pass through developmental stages and they require opportunities to learn through trial and error.

Theory to Practice: Children require a balance of personal exploration and input or presentations from an adult (Frost, Wortham, & Reifel, 2012). This process triggers a child's curiosity in new directions and helps expand their life experiences.

Friedrich Wilhelm Froebel (1782–1852): Children require play-based environments in which there is a reciprocal relationship between God, humans, and nature (Wellhousen, 2002). Through observations, Froebel determined that children have an inherent need to play. This was seen as a radical discovery at that time in history (Maxim, 1993). Gardens were a major part of the children's learning environment, as this allowed children to acquire scientific principles of nature and contribute to sustaining living things (Brosterman, 1997).

Theory to Practice: Children learn best when their experiences are grounded in quality indoor and outdoor play opportunities. Children require opportunities to connect with nature and interact with specially designed materials, based on their interests.

Table 1.4 Modern theorists.

John Dewey (1859–1952): Children flourish in environments that "integrate with daily living, preserve social values including culture, and involve interacting with peers and adults. Children learn best by doing both physical and intellectual activities" (Dietze, 2006, p. 99).

Theory to Practice: Play experiences are planned according to children's needs, interests, and abilities. Children have the freedom to take an active role in determining the play. This occurs naturally with children when the environment is intriguing and not restricted by unnecessary rules.

Rudolph Steiner (1861–1925): The play experiences come from the children, as this is how children spark their sense of curiosity and become motivated to play and explore. Children lead the play experiences, while adults provide the conditions, such as the materials and opportunities.

Theory to Practice: Adults working with children invest time in developing relationships with children so that the play environment reflects the children's interests and needs. The learning environment includes music, arts, and drama in the play environment.

Maria Montessori (1870–1952): A child's play is his or her work. Children require opportunities to make choices in the materials they wish to use. The adult demonstrates to children the sequential steps in using the materials.

Theory to Practice: Play has more of a focus on adult–child interactions and less on child-initiated exploration. For example, if a child is interested in using the pink tower, which is a classic stacking apparatus, the adult first demonstrates to the child the process of carrying the cubes to the area and how the pink tower is built. Once the demonstration is complete, the child may pursue using the materials.

continues ▶

▶ *continues*

Abraham Maslow (1890–1970): Basic needs of food, safety and security, and belonging and love must be met before children are able to include others in their sphere.

Theory to Practice: Children require environments with adults who support them in developing a sense of "belonging" and self-esteem.

Lev Vygotsky (1896–1934): Play is a leading factor in development and is affected by one's community and culture. Group play is an essential venue for a child's social development because it is through play that children think about problems and solve them in new ways.

Theory to Practice: Young children benefit from mixed-age groups in their play because they gain new ideas, assistance, or opportunities to explore as children with different skills and experiences come together.

Jean Piaget (1896–1980): Adults facilitate or guide the process of hands-on play experiences that are rich in exploration, wonderment, and discovery. Children create knowledge by being in environments that encourage them to explore and construct knowledge rather than having adults provide it. Play experiences are extended across an environment rather than confined to specific play centres.

Theory to Practice: Play experiences move from simple to complex and are built and sequenced on previous experiences. Children have opportunities to repeat play experiences and exercise play experiences in all areas of the play environment. For example, if children express an interest in particular figurines in the block area, they have the freedom to take those figurines to the dramatic centre, the art area, or the garden.

Loris Malaguzzi (1896–1994): Culture, children, families, communities, and teachers are equal partners in learning, with play evolving in discovery-oriented environments (Henniger, 2002). Children are active participants in determining what their interests are and in their construction of learning. The learning environment is based on preparing the indoor and outdoor space. "The quality and aesthetics of materials, furnishings, and images (their "taste" or "flavor") help the child appreciate, love, respect, and take advantage of the environment" (Edwards & Gandini, 2015, p. 95). There is a balance between play and project work.

Theory to Practice: Using an emergent curriculum approach, the teacher carefully observes the children's interests, asks questions, and offers concrete learning experiences. Adults and children of mixed-age groups work together to choose and negotiate short- and long-term projects. During this process, the children's learning is documented, making it visible to be examined and used to provide direction for the next phase of play and learning experiences. A variety of media are used to document the child's learning, including conversations, observations, photographs, and two-dimensional or three-dimensional artistic representations.

Erik Erikson (1902–1994): Children's play supports the development of self-esteem. Through play, children learn how to manage their thoughts and feelings, without pressure from adults.

Theory to Practice: Children require access to peers and accessories such as those found in the dramatic centre. For example, a child who has just experienced one parent separating from the family unit may use play to act out feelings of loss, sadness, and anger that may be felt toward the parent who has left the home environment.

David Weikart (1931–2003): Children's play environments are structured so that children are active learners and planners. Children have hands-on experiences with materials and in environments that support them in planning, experiencing, and reviewing their activities and experiences. This is known as the plan, do, and review process.

Theory to Practice: Adults take on an active role in observing children and in posing questions that will extend children's thinking and trigger their sense of curiosity, which will advance their exploration and learning.

There are common themes among the theorists that include play being framed as:

- The natural way that a child learns.
- Requiring adults to provide opportunities for children to explore and discover.
- Children requiring a combination of spontaneous and guided experiences.

Early learning teachers use aspects of philosophical perspectives gained from these theorists as a foundation to determine how they will offer and execute play experiences for

Table 1.5 Contemporary theorists.

Jerome Bruner (1915–2016): Children's play is an active process in which they use past and current experiences and knowledge as a foundation to try new ideas, including trial and error situations, as a way to construct new knowledge.

Theory to Practice: The play materials and environment are organized to support children's interests and in a spiral manner so that children continually build upon what they have already discovered.

Howard Gardner (1943–): Children's play requires exposure to the nine different intelligences: linguistic, logical-mathematical, music, bodily-kinesthetic, spatial, interpersonal, intrapersonal, naturalistic, and existential.

Theory to Practice: Children are engaged in a variety of experiences that support all nine intelligences and that will appeal to their interests and learning styles.

and with children. For example, in one early learning program, the teachers gather with small groups of children each morning and afternoon. During the gathering, children discuss where they would like to begin their play and the resources required. At another early learning program, the teachers prepare the environment by placing specific materials in each of the experience centres that children may use for that particular day. The children make their choices of where they are going to play based on the materials available. Some early learning teachers may think that both of these approaches are acceptable. Others may argue that these approaches require further development. For example, they may suggest that gathering large groups of children for discussions only causes chaos for both children and teachers. They may think that it is better to set up environments that are safe and allow children to self-direct their places of play and types of play rather than having adult intervention. Students and early learning teachers examine the long-standing research and combine that with their beliefs and values to devise their practice and programming strategies.

TERMS THAT INFLUENCE EARLY LEARNING PLAY ENVIRONMENTS

As you examine this text, you will be exposed to many new terms. Here, we introduce you to three terms that support the theory of children's play.

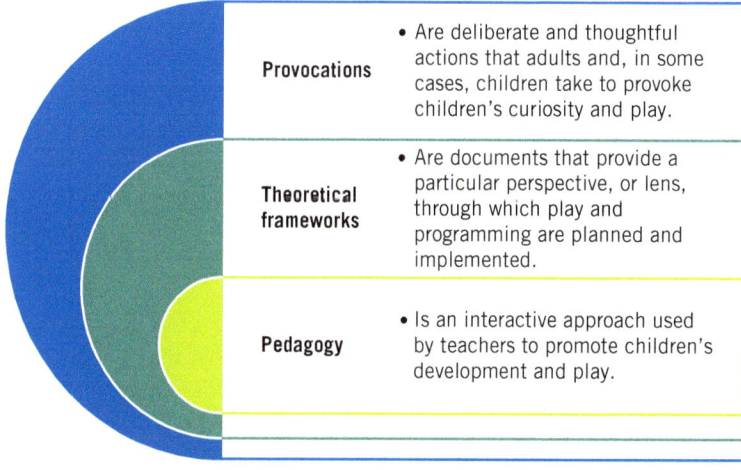

POSITION STATEMENTS ON CHILDREN'S PLAY

Two position statements related to children's play have been released in Canada over the past 10 years, as well as the Accord on Early Learning and Early Childhood Education. The first position statement, presented by the Canadian Association for Young Children (CAYC), articulated the CAYC's position on play for young children and school-aged children. Aspects of the statement follow.

CAYC believes the following about play for young children:

- Play is natural
- Play is essential for children
- Play is fun, exciting, adventurous, and open ended
- Play is creative and spontaneous
- Play is magical and complex
- Play is rewarding and stimulating
- Play is non-judgmental
- Play is directed by the children
- Play is full of choices and decision making opportunities
- Play is posing questions and hypothesizing
- Play is focused on the process and not on the product

CAYC believes play for school-age children is

- Natural
- Stimulating, invigorating, complex
- Exciting, adventurous, open-ended
- Self-directed, self-selected
- Multi-sensory
- Interactive
- Inquisitiveness, wonder, and joy
- Enjoyable and fun
- Endless possibilities
- Energetic and exuberant

Source: Canadian Association for Young Children. Used with permission.

CURIOUS?

Add the words *Canadian Association for Young Children* to your search engine to obtain a PDF version of its position statement on play.

The second position statement, *Position Statement on Active Outdoor Play*, was released in 2015. It was developed based on two systematic reviews that were conducted to examine the most up-to-date scientific evidence on the net effect of outdoor and risky active play, and it was interpreted by a group of Canadian experts representing 14 organizations with an interest in children's outdoor play. The statement includes recommendations for parents, educators, caregivers, health professionals, and various levels of government. This position statement provides early learning teachers with a valuable resource for their practice and in supporting families in understanding the benefits of active play.

Add the words *Position Statement on Active Outdoor Play (2015)* to your search engine to obtain a PDF version of the statement.

Add the words *Position Statement on Active Outdoor Play Process, International Journal of Environmental Research and Public Health* to your search engine to read about how the statement was developed.

The Accord on Early Learning and Early Childhood Education was developed by the Association of Canadian Deans of Education (2016). One of the key purposes of this accord is to address the uneven provision of quality early learning experiences of children across Canada. The accord is intended for members to advance a set of shared goals and principles pertaining to early learning and child care.

Add the words *Early Learning and Early Childhood Education Accord (2016)* to your search engine to obtain a PDF version of the accord.

SUMMARY

Chapter Preview

- Children's play is multifaceted and is directly linked to a child's development.

Defining Play

- There are many perspectives on what the term *play* means. It is challenging to articulate one definition that encompasses the breadth, depth, and complexities of the topic "play."

The United Nations Convention on the Rights of the Child

- Articles 31, 3, 12, and 23 outline the commitment that Canada has made to support children in having the right to play.

Societal Issues and Child's Play

- There are several societal issues that positively or negatively influence children's play.
- Many children living in Canada have been identified as obese or overweight. Children benefit from having role models who are engaged in active living principles and practise appropriate nutrition in their diet.

- Children who do not have adequate outdoor play experiences have a higher risk of not developing a variety of cognitive, social, emotional, and physical skills that are primarily gained from outdoor play.
- Children are being exposed to electronic devices. There are differing opinions on the relationship of children using electronic devices to play.
- By exposing children to different cultural practices during the early years, they develop positive values toward cultures and diversity.
- Children are now being exposed to consumerism through television, print, and the Internet.
- Poverty influences more than 1 million children living in Canada today. Families who deal with poverty have higher rates of anxiety, depression, and irritability than other families. These issues have a negative effect on children's play and development.

Brain Development

- Children's environments and experiences influence brain development. Children who are not exposed to a supportive, stimulating environment are at risk of their brain not developing to its fullest potential.
- Play experiences support brain development.

Classical, Modern, and Contemporary Perspectives on Play

- Each of the classical, modern, and contemporary theorists offer early learning professionals insight into the importance of play to child development. Some of the common themes include that play is a natural way for children to learn and that children require stimulating environments and a combination of spontaneous and guided experiences.

Position Statements on Play

- The CAYC has two distinct position statements on play—one for preschool children and the other for school-aged children. These two statements provide a framework for what the CAYC believes is important for children relative to play.
- The *Position Statement on Active Outdoor Play* provides recommendations for parents, educators, caregivers, health professionals, and various levels of government.

REVIEW QUESTIONS

1. Why is the concept of play important for early learning teachers? How do the complexities of play support early learning teachers in determining how to facilitate children's play?
2. What is the significance of the United Nations Convention on the Rights of the Child to early learning teachers and to children living in Canada?
3. What is meant by every child having the right to engage in play activities appropriate to their ages and cultural backgrounds?
4. Describe how the six societal issues outlined influence children's play, family dynamics, and the roles and responsibilities of early learning teachers.
5. Explain how classical, modern, and contemporary theorists influence early learning programs today.
6. Describe the similarities and differences among the CAYC position statements on play for young children and school-aged children and the *Position Statement on Active Outdoor Play*.

MAKING CONNECTIONS

Theory to Practice

1. What would the benefit be for early learning teachers to be familiar with the history of play? How can the historical perspective inform practice?
2. Visit an early learning setting and examine it in relation to the historical perspectives presented in this chapter. What areas would you examine to determine if there is a historical influence? What do you expect to see? Why? Once you have visited the setting, reflect on your findings. Are there areas where you were able to see clearly the connections of the historical underpinnings? Describe these findings.
3. What is meant by the notion that the historical information about play is a catalyst for helping early learning professionals to think critically about the depth and breadth of play?

DIGITAL PORTFOLIO ENTRIES

Many colleges, universities, and employers are emphasizing the benefits of students and professionals creating and maintaining a digital portfolio. At a basic level, early learning students create a portfolio to support them in having a place to explore, document, and share their ideas, perspectives, and questions about children, play, and learning. Active use of digital portfolios encourages a sense of lifelong learning by promoting reflective practices and discussions among colleagues. Developing digital portfolios help to transfer theory to practice and make sense of some of the complex concepts.

Potential entries for your digital portfolio include:

- My definition of children and play
- Theorists that resonate with my beliefs and values
- What I see missing from the position statements
- How I feel about children, families, and poverty
- Why I take a particular position on children's play and electronic devices

CURIOUS?

Add the words *Canadian health statistics* to your search engine to find out more about children's health.

Add the words *Health—Canada* to your search engine to obtain information on health, wellness, and nutrition.

Add the words *Child Poverty—Conference Board of Canada* to your search engine to obtain information on child poverty in Canada in comparison to other countries.

Add the words *Just the Facts Canada without poverty* to your search engine to get up-to-date information on poverty in Canada.

CHAPTER 2
The Process of Play

Rawpixel.com/Shutterstock

> " In play the child is always behaving beyond his age, above his usual everyday behaviour; in play he is, as it were, a head above himself. "
>
> —Lev Vygotsky (1978)

LEARNING OUTCOMES

After exploring this chapter you should be able to:

- Discuss the relationship of Urie Bronfenbrenner's ecological theory to children's play experiences.
- Examine what is meant by play, learning, intrinsic motivation, active engagement, and process rather than product.
- Outline common characteristics of play and phases in the play process.
- Describe how Piaget, Parten, Smilansky, and Seagoe classify play experiences.
- Explain how specified classical, modern, and contemporary theorists describe the purpose of play.
- Discuss the importance of creating play environments that reflect children's strengths.
- Describe four key roles that adults have in promoting child's play.

Sharing Stories of Practice

Every day, the children surprise me with their play experiences. Sometimes I observe children playing by themselves, and other days these same children are engaged in playing with groups of children. Last week, while we were outdoors, I noticed a group of children discussing something. Then Joma, who has just turned 4 years old, asked if she could bring one of the yellow chairs from the art area outdoors. We don't normally let the children take things from indoors out or outdoors in. I had some choices to make. I could say, "No, those chairs are for the indoors"; I could ask questions such as "Why do you need the chairs?" or "Is there something else in the yard that you could use instead of chairs?" or I could say "Yes" and let the play episode evolve.

The challenge that I have in working with children is that the decisions I make about what I think is best for the children or what they can or cannot do within the environment has such an influence on their play. I can either empower children to embrace their sense of curiosity or impede it. As I observe children more closely and listen to their play, I am trying to be more intentional in thinking about the types of open-ended questions I should ask. Sometimes I get so tense worrying that I may not be asking the right questions. I am beginning to appreciate how important it is to listen intently to the children. I am better able to support them with the needs and ideas that they express. Yes, over the past four years, I have worked hard to develop a relaxed style with the children. When children make a request for accessories, such as a chair, my answer is always "Of course." Then, I say to them, "Is there something I can do to help you incorporate this (chair) into your play?" I am always amazed that the children usually respond by saying "No" or "No, thank you." Of course, I observe the children in their play, and I participate when it is appropriate.

My mantra has become to provide children with the freedom to be, to encourage and embrace them in exploring their environment and incorporating into their play as many items and ideas as they wish from varying experience centres. The fewer restrictions adults place on the children, the richer their exploration and discoveries are through play. The more comfort that children feel within the environment, the more they will engage in quality play.

Danielle, ECE graduate, 2017

CHAPTER PREVIEW

We are living in a society in which children are increasingly experiencing more time indoors than outdoors and spending more time on tasks that prepare them for the school system (Sobel & Larimore, 2016). Their routines and schedules are adult controlled, which often disrupts the flow of children's play because of the pressures for them to stay on schedule (Ergler, Kearns & Witten, 2016). Children are moved through the day: they need to have a snack or get ready to go outdoors or come in for lunch based on time rather than need. We are asking children as young as toddlers to complete projects such as crafts. We are expecting children to complete academic school-type work such as learning the alphabet and numbers and learning how to print their names and cut with scissors rather than engage in play that supports their social and emotional development. If we continue to structure children's time and limit their play, as a society we are taking incredible risks that will influence children's overall development for life (Nicolopoulou, 2010; Sobel & Larimore, 2016). Play during the early years contributes to children's academic, social, artistic, and creative skills that should flow naturally from within; however, the quality of these skills is threatened because many children are in environments where rich play

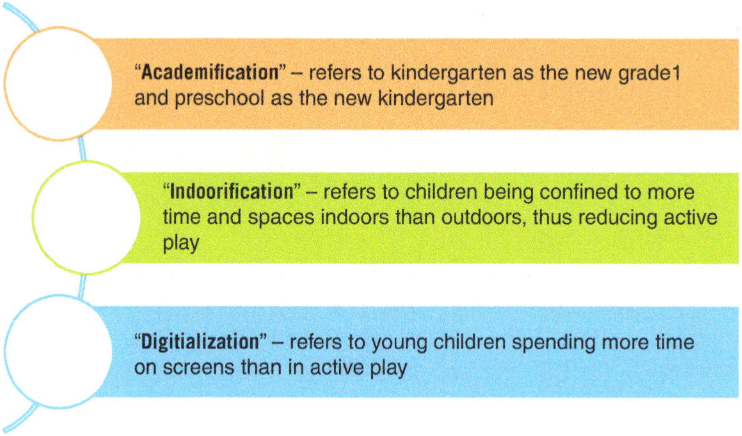

- **"Academification"** – refers to kindergarten as the new grade 1 and preschool as the new kindergarten

- **"Indoorification"** – refers to children being confined to more time and spaces indoors than outdoors, thus reducing active play

- **"Digitialization"** – refers to young children spending more time on screens than in active play

Figure 2.1 Trends contributing to the erosion of children's play.

experiences are limited. This influences every phase of a child's development (Sobel & Larimore, 2016).

Sobel and Larimore (2016) indicate that the pressure from parents and the way in which early learning teachers design curricula and experiences that focus on language, literacy, and numeracy outcomes rather than on play-based learning are contributing to play being eroded in the early years. For example, as outlined in Figure 2.1, they identify three disturbing trends in early childhood that are contributing to the erosion of play.

One of the key roles of early learning teachers is to constantly examine new research and different perspectives on the importance of play in the lives of children. As new findings are presented, our beliefs about child development and play may change as well

Photo 2.1 Play is the centre of children's lives.

Used with Permission of Bora Kim

as contribute to how we facilitate children's play. To understand play and its relationship to child development, we examine it from a variety of perspectives. The amount of time devoted to offering children *pure play experiences* is related to specific beliefs, values, roles, and goals for children. We continue to encourage early learning teachers to return play to the centre core of the child's life.

Play is a vital activity for children in all cultures (Massing, Kirova & Hennig, 2013). As identified in Chapter 1, each element of a child's development is influenced by play. Children's play experiences become more complex in environments that encourage and allow for exploration and risk-taking (Sandseter & Sando, 2016). The freedom to explore and take risks leads to children gaining a sense of success, especially when the play experiences are sequenced from simple to more complex (Sandseter & Sando, 2016).

Maja and Allie have been playmates since Allie moved to the neighbourhood six months ago. Their parents have been encouraging the girls to play together by arranging play dates for them when the children express an interest. During their last play date, Maja and Allie decided that they were going to play with the sand in the open sandpit. As Allie's mom, Maggie, observed the girls, she noticed the 3-year-olds talking back and forth, sharing sand accessories, giving each other ideas about what they could use for various things they were trying to create, and suggesting they try "this or that." Maggie realized that the girls had been playing in the sand area for more than 30 minutes. This was interesting to Maggie, because recently an early learning teacher at Allie's centre expressed concern about Allie's attention span. The teacher, Marissa, described Allie as flitting from one activity to another rather than engaging in play for extended periods. Marissa was concerned that Allie was not engaging in in-depth play experiences. This news was distressing for Maggie because she knows the importance of children developing concentration skills at an early age and how those skills are needed for today's marketplace. Maggie wondered about how she could encourage Allie to focus as she was doing today when she was at her program with Marissa.

STOP ... THINK ... REFLECT ... DISCUSS

Why might Allie have more concentration skills in the sand play environment than in other environments? What might be influencing her interest in the sand play? Why might her play experiences be different at the early learning and child-care centre? How might play experiences be expanded to support Allie's needs?

In this chapter, you will explore play concepts that support child development. The play process, components of play, play stages, the debate about process versus product, and the role of adults in child's play are among the topics discussed. A number of theoretical perspectives are presented as a way to help you begin to formulate your beliefs and philosophy about children and play.

CHILD'S PLAY: FROM AN ECOLOGICAL THEORY PERSPECTIVE

Early learning teachers recognize that play is one of the most important aspects of children's lives. Play is fundamental to all aspects of development (Goldstein, 2012). It is through play that cultural practices are explored and adopted into the child's being

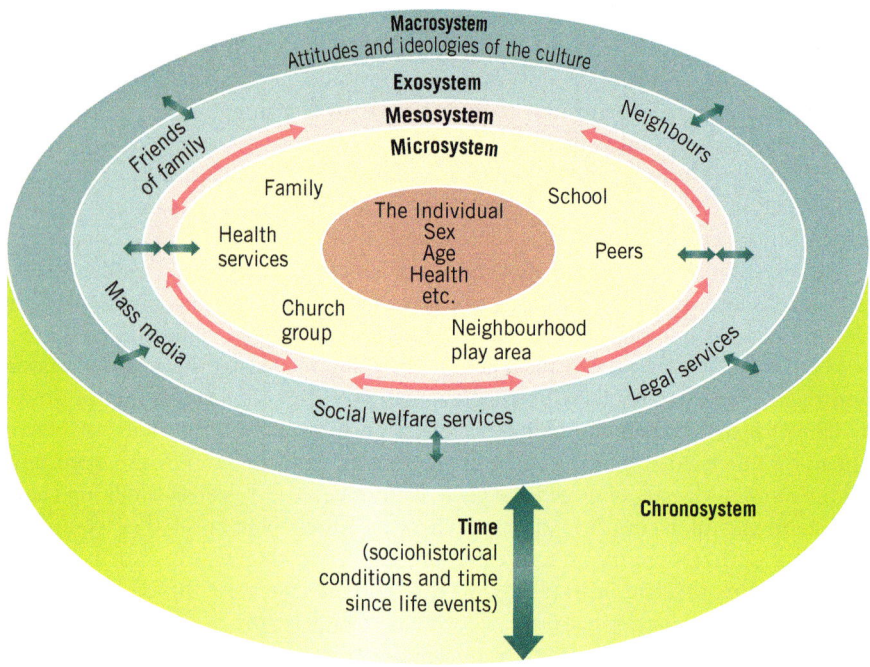

Figure 2.2 Bronfenbrenner's Ecological Systems

(Massing et al., 2013; Munroe & MacLellan-Mansell, 2013). A child's physical movement develops motor skills necessary for life (Ergler et al., 2016). Children who have consistent playmates enhance their opportunities to advance their social, self-regulation, moral, and emotional development. These developmental components are fundamental to children's personality development and the lifelong skills needed to deal with such things as bullying, stress management, and conflict resolution (Shanker, 2016). Children who develop positive self-esteem have an increased level of confidence and competence to try new things. Trying new things, exploring, figuring out, and discovering contribute to enhancing children's cognitive learning skills.

Urie Bronfenbrenner (1979) developed an influential theory of human development. This theory, known as **ecological theory**, helps us to examine how environmental influences contribute to a child's play experiences. His model outlines the relationship of children's environments and their interactions in play with human development. Figure 2.2 provides an outline of Bronfenbrenner's five major systems and how play is influenced by each part of the system.

Microsystem

This refers to the setting in which children live, including the home, early learning experiences, and the neighbourhood. The microsystem considers children's direct interactions with parents, peers, and early learning teachers as well as groups that apply to children's cultural context. Children are influenced by the position that the family and the community take toward play. If play experiences are encouraged, role modelled, and made available, children's development is positively influenced. Conversely, if play is not encouraged, there is a negative effect on children's development (Wessel, 2017).

ecological theory Bronfenbrenner's environmental system theory of development refers to a theoretical framework that emphasizes the relationship of environmental systems—microsystem, mesosystem, exosystem, macrosystem, and chronosystem.

Mesosystem

The mesosystem refers to the people and places outlined in the microsystem. For example, when we think of children in early learning centres, the mesosystem extends to include the beliefs, interactions, connections, and relationships among the parents, extended family members, early learning teachers, and children. Think about the early learning teacher who believes in children learning through play. In opposition, there is a group of parents who prefer to focus on academic preparation for their 3-year-old children. This leads to an imbalance and confusion for children and the early learning teacher. The imbalance may cause tension between the parents and the early learning centre, to the point that families choose to place their children in a more academically focused setting.

Exosystem

This system refers to experiences or influences from external people in social settings or forces. These systems generally have an indirect influence on children. For example, many provincial governments and territories have adopted new standards for playground apparatus. Because of the cost to upgrade the equipment, some early learning centres and community playgrounds have removed playground equipment. Government decisions may positively or negatively influence a child's access to having opportunities to engage in **healthy risk-taking play**.

Macrosystem

This system, in its broadest terms, examines the level of influence that occurs from cultural values and societal ideologies. As we think about this from a child's play perspective, the culture, society, and educational backgrounds of families influence the types of play and diversity of the play experiences extended to their children. For example, in some families, there is a belief that young children require play experiences. Parents make decisions about early learning experiences and settings based on that belief. Others may believe that in order for children to succeed, they must participate in academic learning rather than play. They in turn look for early learning experiences that focus on academic concepts. Or, think of the 3-year-old child who moves from a country such as Japan to a rural Saskatchewan farming community. This child may be one of the few children in the neighbourhood with a different ancestry, language, and customs. Early learning teachers' attitudes and understanding of cultural programming influence how this child integrates into the early learning environment and hence develops a feeling of belonging (Massing et al., 2013).

Chronosystem

This system focuses on the patterning of environmental events, transitions through the life process, and the time of events (Santrock, 2015). For example, preschool children who live in apartment buildings with limited or no access to outdoor play opportunities may experience a more sedentary lifestyle than those children who have access to a yard (Dietze & Kashin, 2016). The absence of rigorous play affects the development of the bone and muscle systems, which contributes to health issues later in life (Land & Danis, 2016). The lifestyle patterns such as active or sedentary activity established in early childhood influence children's lifestyles throughout the life cycle.

Bronfenbrenner's (1979) ecological model provides an important framework for understanding the relationship between play, environment, and child development. The social systems combined with family beliefs positively or negatively influence if, how, when, where, why, and for how long children play. It is beneficial for families and early

healthy risk-taking play Refers to play that involves risk of injury at the same time as it supports healthy development.

Photo 2.2 A child learning about puddles through senses.

Used with Permission of Family Space Quinte, Inc.

learning teachers to have thoughtful discussions about how playing during the early years contributes to learning for life. Look at Photos 2.2 and 2.3. What types of learning might the children gain from the play experiences? Think about the experimentation that children participate in. What kinds of new language might children be using?

When children are in environments that allow them to initiate and control their play, they learn through play. For example, look again at the children in Photos 2.2 and 2.3. Think about the types of discoveries the children are making and the new

Photo 2.3 Children exploring their environment.

Used with Permission of Open Air Learning.

information they are gathering, first through their own observations and, second, through those of their playmates. These types of play experiences and processes support children in trying things, thinking about processes, and reworking information that allows them to integrate the new information with previous knowledge. This interactive process becomes intrinsically motivating. It contributes to children developing an understanding of their environment, culture, and world (Siegel, 2016). Exploring and connecting with playmates and the environment are foundational for **self-regulation**, **executive functioning skills**, social competence, and **resilience**.

self-regulation Refers to "the ability to manage your own energy states, emotions, behaviours and attention, in ways that are socially acceptable and help achieve positive goals, such as maintaining good relationships, learning and maintaining wellbeing" (Shanker, 2016, p.1).

executive functioning skills Refers to a group of cognitive processes and capabilities that act in a coordinated way to contribute to the development of perception, emotion, thought, and action (McCloskey, 2016).

resilience Refers to the ability to adapt to life challenges such as adversity, trauma, stress, and feelings of anxiety and uncertainty (American Psychological Association, 2017).

CURIOUS?

Add the word *self-regulation* to your search engine to obtain more information on the work of Canadian Stuart Shanker on children and self-regulation.

COMPONENTS OF PLAY AND UNIQUE FEATURES OF PLAY

There are many theories and perspectives about how children and adults learn. As outlined in *How Does Learning Happen?* (Ontario Ministry of Education, 2014), children do not learn by being instructed in environments that teach a specific body of knowledge or a predetermined set of topics. Nor do they learn when they are expected to achieve a specific set of skills. The authors suggest that children learn through play, inquiry, and positive interaction within their environments. As outlined in Figure 2.3, the environments contribute to how children undertake the process of play and discovery.

Ecological Theory

Bronfenbrenner's environmental system theory of development refers to a theoretical framework that emphasizes the relationship of environmental factors and social context through the five environmental systems—microsystem, mesosystem, exosystem, macrosystem, and chronosystem. This perspective is especially emphasized within **constructionist theory**.

constructionist theory Refers to a theory about how humans learn and that new knowledge is constructed based on experience.

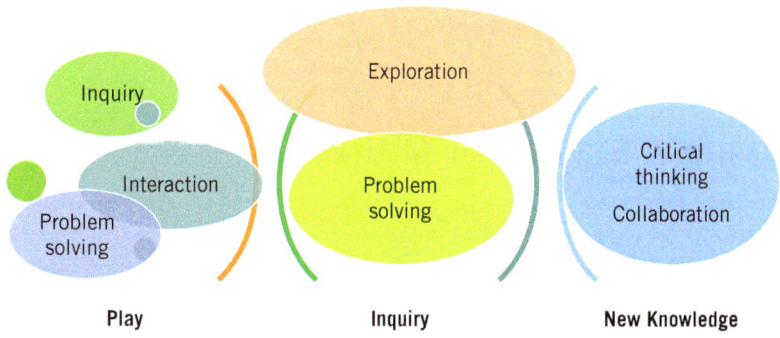

Figure 2.3 Children learn in environments that encourage play, inquiry, and new knowledge development.

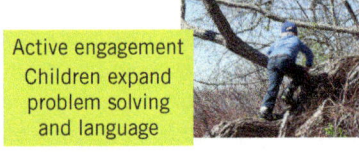
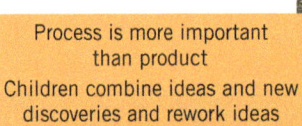

Figure 2.4 Unique features of play.
Source: Used with Permission of Family Space Quinte, Inc.

Children flourish in play environments where they are co-learners with peers; in some instances, adults and children become co-learners. Children gain more opportunities for their curiosity to be stimulated and to embrace active play when they:

- Interact about ideas, possibilities, strategies, and ways of knowing at strategic times during the active play process with peers and adults. Children are invested and engaged in their world of play.
- Share both the physical space and opportunities for play to be a social process (Vygotsky, 1978). The physical actions of play and the experiential experiences are combined with an internal process of thinking about what they are experiencing or discovering and reflecting transfers to learning.
- Have play environments that provide time, space, materials, and opportunities to ponder and tinker with ideas as individuals or in groups. The environments and the materials are rotated to provide a balance of familiarity and novelty for the play.

Early learning teachers work collectively to incorporate these components into their play environments.

Many theorists who have studied play and those theorists who have researched learning help us to understand some of the unique features of play (Monighan-Nourot, Scales, Van Hoorn, & Almy, 1987). As identified in Figure 2.4, we introduce you to the following three unique features:

- Play, learning, and **motivation.**
- Play, learning, and **active engagement.**
- Play, learning, and **process rather than product.**

Play, Learning, and Intrinsic Motivation

Play and intrinsic motivation are interrelated with spontaneous exploration and curiosity. More than 50 years ago, Bruner (1961) identified that there are three internal motivators that influence play and learning. These motivators remain current today. They are:

- Curiosity.
- Desire to show oneself and others what you know and what you are able to do.
- Striving toward a common goal with others.

Photo 2.4 Unique materials motivate children to explore and discover.

Used with Permission of Family Space Quinte, Inc.

Children are internally motivated in different ways. Children's intrinsic motivational levels are related to environmental conditions, including the exposure to play that the child has experienced. Internal motivation can be described as children engaging in a behaviour because it is personally rewarding and satisfying to them and is personally pleasurable rather than being done because of an external reward or pressures (Al-Dhamit & Kreishan, 2013; Cherry, 2016).

Intrinsic motivation is at the core of children's play, creativity, and the quality of their learning experiences (Al-Dhamit & Kreishan, 2013). During the early years, children develop intrinsic motivation influenced by the experiences, people, and materials within their environments and by the feeling of autonomy needed to try to learn by doing, making mistakes, and redesigning their ideas.

Internal motivation differs from extrinsic motivation. Extrinsic motivation involves children performing a behaviour or engaging in an activity in order to receive an external reward or to comply to avoid pressure from others or punishment. Children may adapt to environmental pressures and complete tasks as a strategy to obtain approval from others, especially if they believe that the activity is valued by the adults (Al-Dhamit & Kreishan, 2013).

Play and its contextual principles are driven by positive emotions, including social connectedness, motivation, and cognitive flexibility (Bai, Repetti, & Sperling, 2016).

When children feel comfortable in their play surroundings, they exhibit positive emotions, which in turn increase their spontaneity, sense of curiosity, and focus on their play task. Children's displays of emotion correlate with what they observe in their environments. If children are exposed regularly to adults who express negative emotions, such as anxiety and stress, over time this will detract from their positive motivational levels (Bai, Repetti, & Sperling, 2016; Santrock, 2015) and their interest in exploring learning opportunities. Think about infants. They try to grasp, throw, get to items, and scream and squeal as they encounter new objects (Oudeyer & Kaplan, 2007). Children will continue this zest for learning and exploring when the environment allows for it. Conversely, the will to play and learn becomes problematic in structured environments that confine children to specific activities or events. Infants and young children require opportunities for exploration of personal interests. When children are placed in environments that stifle their natural interests, spontaneous play and learning become jeopardized. This influences how they develop their self-regulation skills.

There are many ways to think about self-regulation. As identified earlier in the chapter, Shanker (2016) suggests that it is the cornerstone of development and is a central building block of early learning. He defines it as "the ability to manage your own energy states, emotions, behaviours and attention, in ways that are socially acceptable and help achieve positive goals, such as maintaining good relationships, learning and maintaining wellbeing" (Shanker, 2016, p. 1). Developing self-regulation is interconnected to developing attention skills, memory, cognitive flexibility, and the ability to interpret behaviour and social interactions. Children's abilities to exercise patience, persistence, flexibility, and curiosity; engage in exploratory play; and approach new experiences are dependent on the level of self-regulation and internal motivation developed. It is thought that behaviour such as bullying stems from a deficit in self-regulation, intrinsic motivation, and self-esteem (Shanker, 2016).

Shanker (2016) suggests that children's ability to self-regulate, including setting limits, influences their persistence and curiosity to explore, problem solve, and learn.

As identified in Figure 2.5, self-regulation and executive functioning skills are fostered when children experience environments that allow them to experience trial, errors, and success. The environment influences all of these factors.

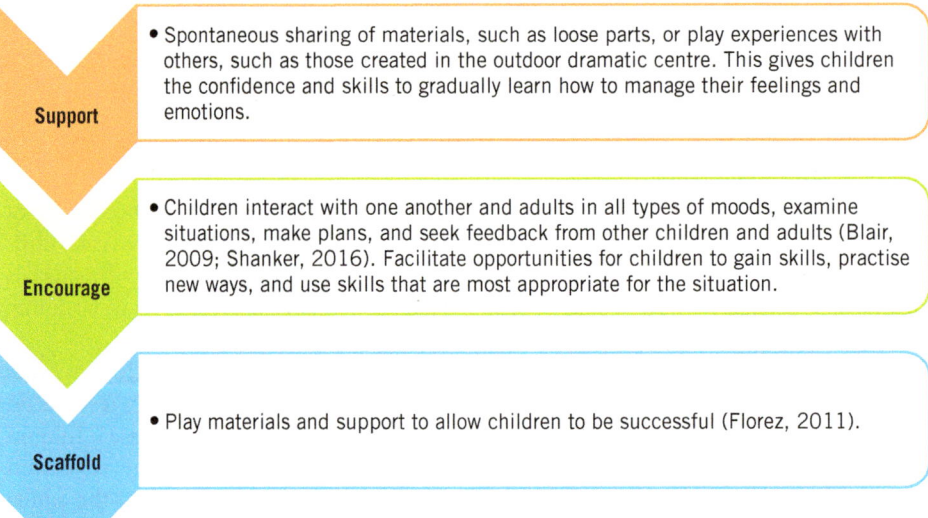

Figure 2.5 Self-regulation and executive functioning skills.

Photo 2.5 Children become internally motivated when they have stimulating environments.

Used with Permission of Kelly McPherson

Intrinsically motivating activities contribute to children exhibiting energy and the ability to and interest in taking new risks (Dietze & Kashin, 2016). Play ideas, directions of play, and the will to try new ideas are present with children who are intrinsically motivated. For example, think of children who observe construction workers using machinery to dig holes in their neighbourhood. Jacob, who has an interest in the large machines, observes the operator and the features of the machinery. Then, in his sand play, he replicates the sounds of the machine and the motions and movements of various parts of the machinery. Using the backhoe, he digs holes, he piles sand, and then he uses the grater to flatten the sand. He gets shovels and planks and uses them for other tasks. Jacob returns to this play for several days. Marley, the early learning teacher, offered resources such as a toolbox and construction books to expand the challenge while enhancing the play. Jacob knew so much more about the machinery than Marley did. He was able to tell her about tires, levers, and how the movement of the buckets occurs. Jacob's level of knowledge about graters was sparked by his interest rather than by the programming offered at the early learning centre.

Intrinsic motivation is affected by environmental conditions, challenges, curiosity, and fantasy (Dietze & Kashin, 2012; Shanker, 2016). Table 2.1 provides an overview of how these factors may look in an early learning and child-care setting.

STOP ... THINK ... DISCUSS ... REFLECT

How do early learning teachers know if children are being adequately stimulated and challenged? What are the roles of the adult and of the children in ensuring that they are being challenged, curious, and having the opportunity to participate in fantasy?

Table 2.1 Intrinsic motivators.

Factor	Description	Expanding Opportunities
Curiosity	**Curiosity** is stimulated by something in the child's environment that leads the child to have a desire to explore, discover, question, and wonder. Curiosity is foundational to developing new knowledge, skills, creative expression, and scientific inquiry.	■ Pose questions that require the child to think in new ways and reflect. ■ Make changes to the environment so that the child explores and makes new connections. ■ Provide new materials that will stimulate the child's cognitive curiosity and desire to explore and wonder. ■ Develop strategies that encourage children who are timid to explore areas of interest.
Challenge	**Challenge** is stimulated when children work with materials and activities that pose a continuously optimal level of difficulty (Malone & Lepper, 1987). Challenge expands exploration and learning.	■ Provide materials and experiences that support each child's personal interests. ■ Scaffold the activities so that as the child gains success, more advanced activities occur. ■ Provide feedback and encouragement.
Fantasy	**Fantasy** refers to the process of children using mental images of things and situations that are not actually present to stimulate their play. Fantasy extends children's creativity in their play. It helps children visualize what is possible.	■ Facilitate experiences that support the child in exploring the fantasy or imaginary context of play. ■ Discuss how the imaginary experiences may be in real life.

There is a relationship between satisfying basic needs, higher needs, and motivation. Maslow (1987) suggests that children have basic needs—food, safety/security, belonging/love, achievement/prestige, and aesthetic needs. Children must first satisfy their basic physiological needs before they are able to fully engage in higher levels of intrinsic motivation. All human behaviour, including that of young children, is motivated by attempts to satisfy human needs (Glasser, 1998).

One of the most challenging roles for early learning teachers is to create environments that support children feeling important, lovable, and that they can make decisions about their play. Children who are given the freedom to choose play experiences and execute them according to their ideas are, in essence, given the foundation to develop a strong sense of self. Providing children with encouragement and support to make choices is directly related to building intrinsic motivation, self-regulation, and executive functioning skills. Self-regulation is established when children are exposed to play experiences that encourage an individual child and groups of children to plan, revise, reflect, investigate, redesign, retry, and discuss their ideas with peers and adults (Shanker, 2016).

Intrinsic motivation and self-regulation is a scaffolding process. In the early phase of brain development, a neural platform for self-regulation occurs (Pascal, 2009). The more

Table 2.2 Common behavioural characteristics that children exhibit if executive functioning skills are not fully developed.

Skill	Behaviours That Suggest Executive Functioning Skills Require Further Development
Impulse control ■ Supports children in thinking before acting.	Children with this limited skill may blurt out inappropriate things or engage in unsafe behaviours, such as climbing too high for their skill set.
Emotional control ■ Supports children in identifying and managing feelings.	Children with limited emotional control may overreact to situations. They may become distraught when they are criticized or make mistakes.
Flexible thinking ■ Supports children in adjusting to new situations or dealing with the unexpected.	Children with more rigid behaviours may exhibit frustrations with sudden change or with different opinions.
Working memory ■ Supports children in maintaining key information needed for experiences or perspectives.	Children's underdeveloped memory skills lead to them having trouble remembering or following directions.
Self-monitoring ■ Supports children in evaluating and making adjustments as required for thinking or activities.	Children exhibit negative reactions to feedback or direction given to change behaviour.
Planning and prioritizing ■ Supports children in planning and prioritizing their ideas, intended goals, and ways to execute their plans.	Children with weak planning and prioritizing skills may feel challenged to identify how to sequence ideas and implement strategies.
Task initiation ■ Supports children in initiating ideas and taking actions that support their plans.	Children may become frustrated because they do not know where or how to start an idea or move from one phase of the idea to the next.
Organization ■ Supports children in keeping track of ideas and materials.	Children may have difficulty remembering their ideas, materials, or schedules.

positive life experiences a child has and the more nurturing that occurs, the stronger the self-regulation becomes. Building on the work of Morin (2016), we outline in Table 2.2 common behavioural characteristics that children exhibit when their executive functioning skills are not fully developed.

Play, Learning, and Active Engagement

Children are designed to climb, crawl, run, jump, swing, tumble, and twist. Active engagement in play is *children's work* during their early years. Play leads children to exhibit their zest for life and develop skills and abilities in language development, cooperation, sharing, problem solving, expansion of curiosity, and coordination of body skills (Ontario Ministry of Education, 2014). Active play supports children in developing skills to manage stress and to formulate a healthy lifestyle. The accord on Early Learning and Early Childhood Education (Association of Canadian Deans of Education [ACDE], 2016) indicates that early learning environments that offer children opportunities for

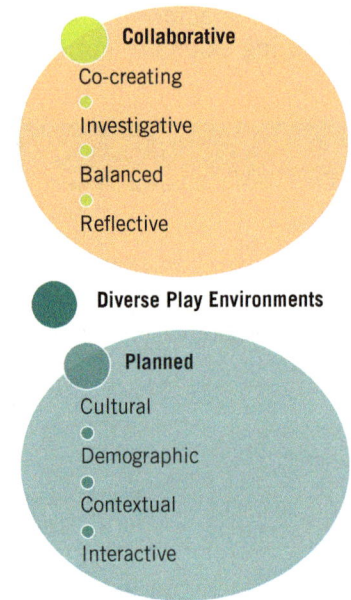

Figure 2.6 Characteristics of diverse play environments.

different types of informal and structured play contribute to "language, understanding, social competence, self-regulation, physical strength, imagination and creativity" (p. 9). As outlined in Figure 2.6, children thrive in environments that are diverse in opportunities and experiences.

During their early years, children require a balance of vigorous play and quieter activities. The combination of unique and innovative play experiences enhances children's "opportunities for full, balanced development of their abilities" (ACDE, 2016, p. 9). This reinforces why play is essential during the early years.

Play, Learning, and Play as Process Rather Than Product

process Refers to the experiences, risks, and reflections that children partake in to create and engage in a play episode.

product Refers to what is produced as a result of the process.

Children's play experiences should focus on the **process** of play rather than on the production of a **product**. For example, when we think of play and creativity, we know that creativity is generated from within the child (Hendrick & Weissman, 2007). Gardner (1993) argues that children's learning grows from children doing things, not just from imitating what they see others do. Children require opportunities to try new ideas, combine new ideas with current knowledge, and rethink how things were done and how they may be done differently. Salim, for example, is using a variety of materials. It is unclear what his intentions are. Salim has access to a variety of sticks, hoses, and related loose parts, so the opportunities are endless. This allows Salim to make choices about the materials he needs as his exploration evolves and his creation unfolds.

Mari has a different experience from Marine and her friends. She and the other 14 children are required by the end of the week to make a picture using the materials supplied by the early learning teacher. The early learning teacher embarks on having children produce products so that they have something to take home to their families on Friday. The objective of this is to share with families "work" that the children are completing. For families who want children to be able to print their names or numbers, these products can fulfill such needs.

Photo 2.6 Children's play evolves from the materials and the environment.

Used with Permission of Family Space Quinte, Inc.

Photo 2.7 An early learning teacher's philosophy influences children's play experiences.

Used with Permission of Family Space Quinte, Inc.

STOP ... THINK ... DISCUSS ... REFLECT

Think about children and learning. Consider the block structure that Salim created during his play. Then consider Marine's play. What are the differences in the experiences? Is one experience more play based than the other? Under what circumstances might both of these activities be considered learning through play experiences? In what context would Marine's activity be useful to his development? Why might some families be more enthusiastic about Marine's experience than Salim's? Why? How might you share the learning that Salim engaged in with the parents?

Two classic works provide further insight into the debate about process and product in early learning experiences. More than 40 years ago, Bruner, Sylva, and Genova (1976) suggested that "the essence of play is the dominance of means over ends" (p. 244). For early learning teachers who view play as the foundation for learning, process remains the essential ingredient for children's programming. Children need to be in control of their play. This requires them to have the freedom to engage in play, explore, and make mistakes without the feeling of failure (Sobel & Larimore, 2016). In essence, for a play process to evolve, it must be voluntary and self-initiated.

The second classic work is that of Helen Buckley. Her story, found in Box 2.1, helps us put the process-versus-product debate into context.

CURIOUS?

Add the words *The Little Boy by Helen Buckley* to your YouTube search engine to view a very powerful video on this story.

Box 2.1 The Little Boy

Once a little boy went to school.
He was quite a little boy
And it was quite a big school.
But when the little boy
Found that he could go to his room
By walking right in from the door outside
He was happy;
And the school did not seem
Quite so big anymore.

One morning
When the little boy had been in school awhile,
The teacher said:
"Today we are going to make a picture."
"Good!" thought the little boy.
He liked to make all kinds;
Lions and tigers,
Chickens and cows,
Trains and boats;
And he took out his box of crayons
And began to draw.

But the teacher said, "Wait!"
"It is not time to begin!"
And she waited until everyone looked ready.
"Now," said the teacher,
"We are going to make flowers."
"Good!" thought the little boy,
He liked to make beautiful ones
With his pink and orange and blue crayons.
But the teacher said "Wait!"
"And I will show you how."

And it was red, with a green stem.
"There," said the teacher,
"Now you may begin."

The little boy looked at his teacher's flower
Then he looked at his own flower.
He liked his flower better than the teacher's
But he did not say this.
He just turned his paper over,
And made a flower like the teacher's.
It was red, with a green stem.
On another day
When the little boy had opened
The door from the outside all by himself,
The teacher said:
"Today we are going to make something with clay."
"Good!" thought the little boy;
He liked clay.
He could make all kinds of things with clay:
Snakes and snowmen,
Elephants and mice,
Cars and trucks
And he began to pull and pinch
His ball of clay.

But the teacher said, "Wait!"
"It is not time to begin!"
And she waited until everyone looked ready.
"Now," said the teacher,
"We are going to make a dish."
"Good!" thought the little boy,
He liked to make dishes.

And he began to make some
That were all shapes and sizes.

But the teacher said "Wait!"
"And I will show you how."
And she showed everyone how to make
One deep dish.
"There," said the teacher,
"Now you may begin."

The little boy looked at the teacher's dish;
Then he looked at his own.
He liked his better than the teacher's
But he did not say this.
He just rolled his clay into a big ball again
And made a dish like the teacher's.
It was a deep dish.

And pretty soon
The little boy learned to wait,
And to watch
And to make things just like the teacher.
And pretty soon
He didn't make things of his own anymore.
Then it happened
That the little boy and his family
Moved to another house,
In another city,
And the little boy
Had to go to another school.
This school was even bigger
Than the other one.
And there was no door from the outside
Into his room.

He had to go up some big steps
And walk down a long hall
To get to his room.
And the very first day
He was there,
The teacher said:
"Today we are going to make a picture."
"Good!" thought the little boy.
And he waited for the teacher
To tell what to do.
But the teacher didn't say anything.
She just walked around the room.

When she came to the little boy
She asked, "Don't you want to make a picture?"
"Yes," said the little boy.
"What are we going to make?"
"I don't know until you make it," said the teacher.
"How shall I make it?" asked the little boy.
"Why, anyway you like," said the teacher.
"And any color?" asked the little boy.
"Any color," said the teacher.
"If everyone made the same picture,
And used the same colors,
How would I know who made what,
And which was which?"
"I don't know," said the little boy.
And he began to make pink and orange and blue flowers.

He liked his new school,
Even if it didn't have a door
Right in from the outside!

Helen Buckley, 1961

Source: The Little Boy by Helen Buckley 1961. Published in SchoolArts magazine, 1961, Davis Publications, Inc. Used with Permission.

STOP ... THINK ... DISCUSS ... REFLECT

What do you gain from the poem "The Little Boy"? What does this poem tell you about the roles of early learning teachers? How does adult role modelling affect a child's creativity and freedom to explore in play episodes? What strategies could an early learning teacher use to rekindle the self-directed exploratory characteristics that the little boy exhibited before being exposed to a product-orientated environment? Do you think that there might be circumstances in an early learning environment where product is emphasized as long as this is not to the detriment of process?

Figure 2.7 Seven common characteristics of play.

CHARACTERISTICS OF PLAY

Common characteristics of play are defined in the literature. As outlined in Figure 2.7 and below, becoming familiar with these characteristics helps early learning teachers understand the foundation of play and their roles and responsibilities in early learning programs.

Play is active (Ontario Ministry of Education, 2014)

Children explore, discover, experiment, become engaged, move their bodies, and make connections in environments using their bodies and materials. Active play increases children's senses, language acquisition, and interaction among peers. Children develop meaning, relevance, and the confidence to explore the "what if" possibilities.

As identified in Chapter 1, when children are involved in active play, their neural connections are enhanced, which contributes to situations, ideas, and skills becoming part of their long-term memory (ACDE, 2016). Conversely, when children are exposed to concepts and isolated facts that are irrelevant to them, the potential knowledge and experiences are less likely to be transferred to their long-term memory (Fromberg, 2002). Think of a group of children trying to figure out what they can use for a gas pump. First, they take long and short black pipes to the area. They try to attach a short pipe to a longer pipe to make a nozzle. They use this for a short period. It does not provide the children with the flexibility they require. Then, they discover a pliable hose—a vacuum hose. Suddenly, the play at the gas station takes on new meaning. Children gain knowledge about scientific principles such as hard, soft, flexible, and rigid and about the requirements needed for specific play interests. This is a much more effective way for children to learn than having adults tell or guide children with the required information.

Play is child initiated and focused (Ontario Ministry of Education, 2014; Sobel & Larimore, 2016)

Play episodes are much richer when play is child initiated and child focused than when it is adult planned and adult initiated. Children are intrinsically motivated in environments with adults who encourage them to have the freedom to choose materials and play topics. Marley is on the dramatic play platform in the garden. She thinks she would like to prepare for a wedding. She starts conversations with Tina, Tyla, and Jamill about the wedding. They decide they need chairs, flowers, and dresses. They also need to have food. Tyla asks the early learning teacher if snack time can happen at the wedding. The children develop a plan for how the wedding will occur and they determine the depth of the play experience. They use their previous knowledge and experiences about weddings to plan and embark on the play. If adults had tried to initiate this play, it probably would not have had the same richness as what the children brought forth. They execute the play based on their life experiences and vision.

Photo 2.8 Children learn by trial and error.
Used with Permission of Family Space Quinte, Inc.

Play is process oriented (Bruner, 1972)

Children require the freedom to play without adult-imposed structure. Children benefit from engaging in play experiences for the true pleasure of the experience rather than to achieve a finished product at the end. Such play experiences are richer in language, discovery, and movement than those that put pressure on children to produce a product. Children have total concentration on the play episode when it has been self-initiated. They gain a sense of success when play experiences and environments support active, meaningful learning with complex, challenging, and varied materials (Fromberg, 2002; Isenberg & Jalongo, 2001; Jensen, 1999; Moyles, 2014).

Play is symbolic and transformational

Children learn about life through play. They connect past experiences with their current world. They expand or take on new play endeavours by trying new ideas, reflecting on what worked and what did not, and developing their roles from simple to more complex. This requires children to "step outside the box" as they use their imagination to try new ideas. The use of creativity, spontaneity, and exploration advances a child's thinking process—"What if this happens?" or "If I try this, I wonder if"—which leads to a higher level of thinking. This contributes to the development of foundational skills necessary for critical thinking and problem solving.

Play is intrinsic (Sandseter & Sando, 2016)

Children engage in play when they are in the right environment, simply for the pleasure of the experience. If children get pleasure from the experience and the materials remain available, they may repeat the play again and again. During that process, they are refining their ideas and skills. Think of children at the beach making sand castles. If they like the sensorial feeling of the sand and water, they will build many castles, both for pleasure and to learn about adding more sophistication to their creations.

Play is rule governed (Vygotsky, 1978)

Rule governed refers to the structure of the rules that children impose on their play. Children engage in play based on their self-chosen rules. These rules are not like the rules of games; rather, they are the cognitive concepts that children decide on and use to guide their play. Think of children engaged in building a structure. Children use a defined process for the development of the structure. They ensure that the foundation is strong and then build upward.

Play is episodic

When in environments that support opportunities to return to play experiences or having time to embrace play, children will devise play episodes that have two or more parts. This is evident in children's dramatic play. Think about children who set up a flower shop in the dramatic centre. The first play episode may give children experience in setting up the shop. As their peers or adults engage in the fantasy play, the leaders of the play experience may increase the sophistication of the play by adding money exchange, wrapping flowers, or having a variety of flowers to purchase.

THE PLAY PROCESS

Toddler play is different from the play of preschoolers, which also differs from the play of infants or school-aged children (Jones & Reynolds, 2015). Children and their play constitute a progressive process, with each new phase building on previous learning and experiences (Dietze, 2006; Siraj-Blatchford, 2009). There are a number of developmental and environmental conditions that contribute to the progression of the play process. For example, a child's age and phase of development, combined with the materials and experiences provided, influence the play process and the level of engagement within the play experience. As children gain experience with the play materials, a play plateau is reached. If new stimulation is absent, the play progression is affected. Children require new play materials and opportunities so that they continuously achieve new skills, perfect skills, or modify skills. Children intuitively advance to the next level of play when they have had sufficient experiences at any given phase.

During childhood, we can expect children to experience all aspects of the first five phases in the play process. The sixth phase occurs during adulthood.

Phase I: Body Play

An infant's first exposure to play is with his or her body. Think of the infant who becomes intrigued by being able to move a hand one way or another, or discovering that sounds can be made. The infant will try to repeat the movement again and again. This process is how the child gains information (Driscoll & Nagel, 2005). Piaget (1962) identifies this body play as exploration. As infants explore their environments visually, through mouthing and their senses, they quickly begin to show preferences, such as for faces, patterns, and textures. When the infant has gained information through the exploration process, play begins. The infant repeats movements for the purpose of combining or reconfiguring information previously explored (Dietze, 2006).

Photo 2.9 The infant repeats movements for the purpose of combining or reconfiguring information previously explored.
Used with Permission of Fiona Barton

Phase II: Motoring Movement Play

As infants become more mobile through creeping, crawling, and toddling, their interest in play expands. They gain skills in being able to balance and coordinate body movements through the various movements that occur during play. The accomplishment of skills such as running, hopping, jumping, climbing, and rolling expands play options and advances skills in a variety of developmental domains.

Phase III: Imaginative Play

Between the ages of 3 and 4, children's play becomes more advanced by combining play with movement and peers. The freedom to move, run, jump, and climb has an expanded purpose (Driscoll & Nagel, 2005). During this phase, children become interested in determining how high their jumps can be or how to walk on one foot. Imaginative play evolves, usually triggered by experiences or observations that are made of other children in their environment. This phase provides early learning teachers and families with insight as to how children perceive their environments and the world. For example, after Jonathan's mother gave birth to a new sister, Jonathan spent many days in the dramatic centre playing mother and baby. At times, Jonathan spoke to the doll to tell her that she can go to someone else's home—she doesn't need to stay with Jonathan's family. At other times, Jonathan expressed caring, nurturing behaviours and loving dialogue toward the doll.

Photo 2.10 When the toddler has the opportunity to explore and gains more competence in his or her body movements, he or she will try new ideas and adventures.

Used with Permission of Family Space Quinte, Inc.

Photo 2.11 Children use imaginative play to make sense of their world.

Used with Permission of Family Space Quinte, Inc.

Phase IV: Intentional Imaginative Play

During this phase, between the ages of 4 and 6, the richness of fantasy play is enhanced. It is further expanded with school-aged children. Children use many objects or concepts within their environment as props in their play. Children develop sophisticated role playing. They use mental images to devise plans for objects and ideas that can be incorporated into the play episode. For example, children decide they want to be involved in catching a robber. As Jamie hears Matt and Mila discussing the robber play, Jamie decides that he will take on the role of the robber, using his tricycle as the getaway car. Jamie solicits help from Mandy. He and Mandy decide that she will hide the robber by getting on the back of the tricycle. They think this will help Jamie not to be visible. This play moves beyond imitating an act that was previously observed. Each child has a role in the play experience. Children became involved in the play because they were intrigued by the play.

During the imaginative phase of play, often children's cultural backgrounds, life experiences, and environments influence the depth and breadth of the play. Children who are active in their play have the ability to engage in a variety of roles. Their level of energy and their commitment to the play experience differ dramatically from that of children who have limited access to interesting play environments.

Phase V: Peer Play with Rules

Play among school-aged children moves from the innovative and imaginative play experienced by 4- to 6-year-olds, to a more structured play that is generally governed by rules. This phase sees children attracted to team-focused and competitive play. The spontaneous play seen in an earlier phase is replaced with materials and play that are specific to a predetermined end result.

Photo 2.12 School-aged children take risks in their play while following rules with peers.

Used with Permission of Beverlie Dietze

Phase VI: Adult Play

Play is a lifelong process. Through play, adults learn many valuable skills, including relationship skills, communication, innovation, problem solving, and visualization. Adult play generally occurs in competitive environments such as one's workplace or at social events. For example, think about the last social gathering you attended. Many there may have shared stories or reflected on experiences of the past. These processes support adults in constructing new knowledge or perceptions about issues and concepts through these exchanges (Dietze, 2006). Although play in adulthood differs from that in childhood, it remains an essential life experience to maintain life–work balance.

CLASSIFYING PLAY EXPERIENCES

The role models, environment, and materials available to them influence children's play. Theorists such as Piaget, Parten, Smilansky, and Seagoe categorize play stages and phases. These play stages and phases provide early learning teachers with a guideline to the progression of children's play and support them in planning the types of materials and opportunities available to the children. Table 2.3 provides a summary of the types of play stages, with examples.

Piaget's Stages of Play

As identified in Figure 2.8, Piaget (1970) suggests that children participate in three distinct stages of play. Each stage contributes to the child's cognitive-developmental domain.

1. **Functional/sensorimotor play (birth to age 2)** is marked by play that focuses on simple, repetitive muscle-like movements with people, objects, and sounds. Functional play is most prevalent among children to approximately the age of 2. It gradually

Photo 2.13 Children look and discover.

Used with Permission of Open Air Learning.

Table 2.3 Types of play stages.

Type of Play	Description	Example
Cognitive Play		
Functional/sensorimotor	Simple, repetitive muscle movements, with or without materials.	Infants throw block from high chair. Toddlers use a jack-in-the-box. Preschoolers repeat a pattern in a block structure. School-aged children figure out how something works.
Symbolic/dramatic	Objects used for props in play. Children take on roles such as being a firefighter.	Infants use blankets to disappear. Toddlers pretend to eat toys as a cookie. Preschoolers pretend by taking on roles such as a nurse. School-aged children take on sophisticated roles such as in plays.
Games with rules	Predetermined rules and consequences understood before the play begins.	Infants play pat-a-cake. Toddlers play peekaboo. Preschoolers play simple games. School-aged children play games with more challenges, rules, and competitiveness.
Construction play	Role play dominates play. Creativity and imagination combined with materials are used to construct items according to a predetermined plan.	Preschool children build a bridge for goats to cross. School-aged children use materials to create complex items, such as treehouses, for their play.
Social Play		
Solitary	Playing alone, without interaction with others. Use of materials is child's decision.	Infants play with toys but do not acknowledge others. Toddlers play beside other children but do not show an interest in other children. Preschoolers play by themselves with own materials. School-aged children play with materials on their own without peer contact.
Parallel	Playing independently or beside peers, but not with peers. The materials may be used in similar ways as peer. There is no sharing of materials during the play episode.	Toddlers play near others, without interaction. Preschoolers play beside others, using the materials in different ways and for different goals. School-aged children have a defined goal for the play. Are focused on achieving the goal on own.
Associative	Play occurs with other children. Materials are shared and playing together occurs. Being with other children is as important as the actual play.	Preschool children use the same materials but may not have the same goals in mind. School-aged children may have similar goals but try different strategies to achieve the goals.
Cooperative	Play with other children as part of a group. Collectively the children determine a common goal and work toward achieving the goal through negotiation, role assignment, and problem-solving interaction.	Older preschool and school-aged children determine the goal for the play, such as building a beach resort. Each child has roles and responsibilities in the planning and execution of the play.
Cooperative-competitive	Playing occurs as part of a team. The team works together to achieve winning results.	School-aged children become members of teams, usually sport teams. Each child has a role and works with team members to achieve results.
Unoccupied	No engagement in play.	Children will be in the environment but are not engaged in play. They appear to be thinking or reflecting.
Onlooker	Children observe other children or adults in their play.	Infants watch the activity in their environment. Toddlers observe other children with specific toys. Preschoolers observe groups of children in play. School-aged children observe individuals and teams in play.

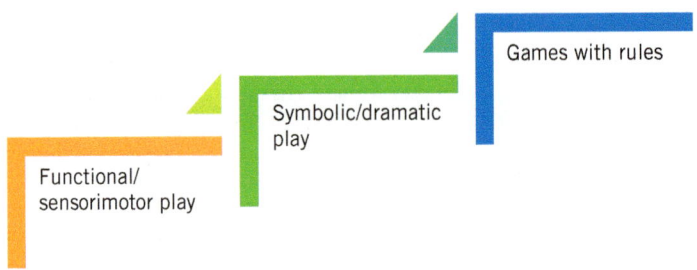

Figure 2.8 Piaget's stages of play development.

declines to about one-third of the play of preschoolers and less than one-sixth of play of school-aged children (Rubin, Fein, & Vandenberg, 1983). Some of the more common observable play examples are:

- A toddler stacking blocks and then unstacking them.
- A 3-year-old pulling a wagon with handles from the front and then pushing it from the back.
- A 4-year-old putting on a cape and repeating on several occasions, "I am superman."
- A 5-year-old creating structures with blocks, such as a bridge and a road with a specific pattern.
- A 7-year-old tracing marks in the sand.

2. **Symbolic/dramatic play (ages 2 to 7)** is marked by the onset of children expressing fantasy, using props, and taking on roles other than being children. Isenberg and Jalongo (2010) suggest that this play has three elements: props, plot, and roles. This phase is linked to the preoperational phase of development. As cognitive abilities advance, children expand the depth of their play by using objects, actions, and language in various ways. The children intentionally examine and determine the social roles that will be incorporated into their play. They make plans, create options, and express their feelings about how roles should be played out. Some examples of symbolic/dramatic play include the following:

- A toddler picks up wooden apples and pretends to eat them. As the play is advanced, the toddler may offer apples to other children or to a doll. This requires the child to have the cognitive skills to shift from a personal focus to focusing on others.
- A 3-year-old uses fingers as imaginary friends and talks with them as playmates.
- A 5-year-old becomes a pilot. The chairs are lined up for other children to sit on, and the child makes announcements about the flight.
- School-aged children become detectives, use secret codes, use written and verbal language to make up clues, and provide them to others to sort out the mystery.

Early learning teachers encourage symbolic play for many reasons. This play increases children's memory capacity (Bodrova & Leong, 2007; Newman, 1990) and provides a venue to acquire new ways of using language and vocabulary, while increasing language acquisition skills. Symbolic/dramatic play contributes to children's creative thinking and problem-solving skills, learning the importance of being flexible, and participating in inventive thinking (Ontario Ministry of Education, 2014).

As children become more involved in dramatic play (as you will read about in Chapter 9), the play generally includes two or more children. Children use their language skills to discuss the play episode and the direction the play will follow. This play is child to child rather than object oriented, as seen in symbolic play (Isenberg & Jalongo, 2010). Children exhibit social skills and use their knowledge and life experiences to think about the "what if" component of the play. This play may be extended for long periods of time or over several days. This extended play accommodates children trying new roles, refining roles, and adding new props based on group problem solving.

3. **Games with rules (school-aged children)** occur as children negotiate the rules before they engage in a play experience. As part of the process, children determine how to deal with the consequences if rules are broken. Children exhibit reciprocity and turn-taking in their play. Games with rules may include outdoor play games, such as street hockey and skipping games, or indoor games, including board, card, and computer games. This play period is consistent with the concrete operational phase of development. Children use more language skills, logic in their thinking, and advanced social skills, as this play requires negotiation skills as well as cooperative and competitive skills.

Smilansky's Contributions to the Stages of Play

Sarah Smilansky (1968) made two significant additions to Piaget's play stages. Children between 4 and 6 years of age participate in social/dramatic play that is complex and sophisticated. She labelled this as a constructive play stage and outlined six criteria for determining the level of the dramatic/sociodramatic play.

Constructive Play Stage (4 Years of Age and School Age)

This stage of play is determined by the level of sophistication of the social/dramatic play. The level of role playing, the use of and creativity with props, and the way in which children use their imagination with the materials to construct the play experience all contribute to the sophistication of that experience (Fehr & Russ, 2016). Children combine functional and symbolic play (Forman, 2005) into the play episode. This play exhibits a high level of problem solving and social interaction among the children.

Marshall, Megan, and Brittany visited a neighbourhood greenhouse. The children brought back many flowers and plants from the greenhouse to the early learning centre. They determined that they would like to turn the dramatic centre into a flower shop. They placed flowerpots on shelves, chose tall cups to use for vases, took large pieces of newsprint from the easel to use for wrapping flowers, and used ribbon and string from the creative area to wrap flower packages. The children took a rectangular block and used it for the debit and credit card machine. This type of play shows how children combine construction (making the flower shop) with symbolic play (visiting the greenhouse) and then incorporating their play experience to reflect what they saw in how they created their play environment (Isenberg & Jalongo, 2010). Constructive play is about children enjoying a process of experimenting and exhibiting a sense of "what will happen if I do this" rather than creating a specific product.

Early learning teachers observe both the level of construction play and the behaviours that are exhibited during dramatic play and, when appropriate, facilitate advanced play options.

Parten's Classifications of Social Play

Social play is essential for children. Social play leads children to develop skills such as sharing, turn-taking, group work, and cooperative skills. Mildred Parten (1932) examined play from a social behaviour perspective. Similar to Piaget, she identified that play progresses through a series of stages. It is interesting to note that although Parten correlated the phases of play with age ranges, more recent researchers describe Parten's phases of play as social descriptors rather than as phases of play. For example, Van Hoorn and colleagues (2007) suggest that children move back and forth in the cycles of play. Think of a 4-year-old child who is trying to figure out how to build a particular structure. This may require an environment that provides opportunities for solitary play experience because the child needs time to experiment, to think, and to try strategies. Once the child has figured out how to proceed, there is more opportunity to become a partner in an associative play experience.

1. **Solitary Play**—The child generally plays alone. There is limited or no interaction with other children or with the materials that other children are using. Solitary play is influenced by the context of the play. Solitary play assists children in working out ideas, thoughts, and strategies for their play. For some children, it is easier to try ideas on their own, master them, and then share their learning with other children (Hendrick & Wiseman, 2006).
2. **Parallel Play**—Children begin to either play independently or beside peers rather than with peers. Children may use similar materials and play in similar ways, but they do not play together or share materials.
3. **Associative Play**—Children begin to share play materials and participate in similar activities. Children enjoy being with other children as much as the play experience itself. This is often thought of as the "bridging" phase as children transition between parallel and cooperative play.
4. **Cooperative Play**—Children participate in group play. Children determine a common goal and then each child works toward meeting that goal. Cooperative play is more prevalent among school-aged children than in preschool environments because of the experience and maturity required to negotiate roles and responsibilities and work out strategies to complete a task. Cooperative play creates a bond with the group, and children gain a strong sense of belonging.

Parten (1932) also identified nonplaying as **unoccupied behaviour** time and **onlooker play**. However, according to Mayfield (2001), "Many contemporary researchers do not consider this to be a category of play, but rather a non-activity" (p. 268). What do you think of these two perspectives? Is one perspective more valid than the other? Why or why not?

Seagoe's Contributions to Play

Seagoe (1970) added to the body of literature on the social aspects of play. She identified that as children approach 7 to 9 years of age they participate in **cooperative-competitive play**. This involves play in which children focus on team sports and victory, such as soccer and hockey (Dietze, 2006).

The transition from one stage of play to another does not mean that children do not return to a previous stage. As each child engages in new play opportunities, new environments, and new playmates, there may be a change in the stage or phase exhibited. This is very common among children who move from one early learning centre to another. For example, Jamie (age 4) had been in the same early learning centre for three years. He had four "buddies" who he played with on a daily basis. These buddies also lived on the same street as he did. The children spent a great deal of time playing with one another (associative play) and were beginning to play as a group (cooperative play). When Jamie moved to a new neighbourhood, he played by himself (solitary play) for several weeks. Gradually,

unoccupied behaviour Time when children are not engaged in play; the children appear to be wandering in the play area without a defined purpose.

onlooker play Refers to children who observe other children or adults in play but do not become involved in the play. They may ask questions of the play participants. Children may use this strategy to learn about particular materials or to determine how they may participate in a play episode.

cooperative-competitive play Refers to play that occurs as part of a team. The group works together toward achieving their goal.

he began to play beside other children (parallel play) and then moved to associative play. As Jamie became more comfortable in the environment, he moved through the latter two phases more quickly than when he engaged in solitary play.

CHILDREN AND THE THEORIES OF PLAY

Both in Chapter 1 and in this chapter, we have discussed aspects of children's play in an effort to answer questions such as "What is play?" "Why do children play?" and "What are the theories and beliefs that guide researchers, educators, and parents in understanding the purpose of play?" Exploring theories helps bring clarity to our beliefs and perceptions.

Theories of Play

As discussed in Chapter 1, we are guided by the three groupings of theories: classical theories, modern theories, and contemporary theories. Each brings a perspective to the broad views of what play is.

Classical Theories

Classical theorists examine play through theories of surplus energy, recreation and relaxation, practice, and recapitulation (Ellis, 1973).

1. **Surplus energy theory.** This theory, identified by Friedrick Schiller and Herbert Spencer (Ellis, 1973), suggests that play is a mechanism to allow humans to burn off the excess energy that is not required for survival. When children are confined in their environment, they build excess energy. This causes children to become restless and unable to stay on task. Children need to expend the energy. This can best be achieved through active play experiences.
2. **Recreation/relaxation theory.** This theoretical base suggests that play is a mechanism to replenish energy after hard work has occurred. This is in direct opposition to surplus energy theory. When children engage in activities that are more cognitively focused or have been alternating between quiet and active play, active play or rest is needed to replenish the child's energy. This rejuvenation allows children to refocus on activities requiring concentration. Children benefit from being in environments that support a rotation of sedentary activity followed by active play.
3. **Practice theory.** Play is a mechanism whereby children practise adult roles and roles that are directly related to culture and community. Children will play the roles of significant people in their lives, such as their mother, father, or teacher, based on their observations.
4. **Recapitulation theory.** This theory differs from practice theory. Children engage in play that has them revisit the developmental stages their ancestors passed through. Children alleviate negative behaviours and develop correct processes that support current society.

Modern Theories

Modern theorists examine play from the perspective of why play exists and the consequences of play for the child (Frost, Wortham, & Reifel, 2008; Scarlett & New, 2007).

Psychoanalytic theory, cognitive-developmental theory, and sociocultural theory are included in the modern theories grouping.

1. **Psychoanalytic theory.** This theory, supported by the work of Freud and Erikson, examines how play enhances emotional release and esteem building as children gain mastery and understanding of their thoughts, bodies, and social etiquette. Through play, children act out feelings and work through areas of challenge using the following two mechanisms:

   Role switching. During play, children may switch roles as a way to suspend reality and engage in behaviours that allow them to be a recipient of a bad experience or take on the dominant role of executing the experience. For example, if a child has been disciplined by a parent, a child may take on the role of disciplining a doll. This level of activity provides the child with a feeling of power while transferring the negative feelings to the doll.

   Repetition. When a child has had a negative experience, the child will seek out play experiences that will allow the negative experience to be replayed many times. The child gradually assimilates the actions and feelings associated with the event. For example, if a child has had a negative experience in a hospital setting, through play, each segment of the experience is played out. Gradually, the child brings meaning to the experience.

2. **Cognitive-developmental theory.** This theory, supported by the work of Bruner, Piaget, and Sutton-Smith, views play as a venue for children to use materials and interact with people as a way to build their knowledge about the world in which they live. Children require time, flexibility, and the opportunity to practise new skills, test ideas, and amalgamate new ideas and information with previous knowledge and practices. Isenberg and Jalongo (2010) indicate that "because children focus on the process of play, they engage in multiple combinations of ideas and solutions that they use to solve relevant life problems" (p. 57). Quality play experiences provide young children with the "testing ground" needed to discover ideas and transfer findings to daily living.

   Bruner's theoretical construct indicates that there is a relationship between play and problem-solving abilities during childhood and later in life. In play, the means are as important as the end result because play promotes flexibility in solving real-life problems. The ability to problem solve provides a child with more behavioural options. There is a relationship between play and the development of **narrative modes of thinking**. Because children organize their knowledge in a sequential, narrative process, through verbal and logical play as well as social/dramatic play, they perfect their narrative thinking skills and abilities.

   Piaget's theory, as outlined earlier in the chapter, suggests that children engage in play experiences that correspond to their cognitive developmental levels. For learning through play to occur, children must engage in an **adaptation** process. This requires the child to incorporate new information into existing structures (known as assimilation) and to modify existing cognitive structures (known as accommodation).

   Sutton-Smith's theory reinforces that play influences cognitive development. Play is important to the child's behaviour, creativity, and problem-solving skills. Through play, a child prepares to develop skills needed in adulthood, such as flexibility skills.

3. **Neurobiological theory.** With the advancement of technology, researchers continue to gain new information about the organization and functional operations of the brain. The environment children are exposed to positively or negatively influence

narrative modes of thinking Refers to children figuring things out, learning by doing, making sense of ideas, and problem solving areas to gain new knowledge, and then expressing learning through their narratives or storytelling.

adaptation Refers to an organism's ability to modify its environment or to find ways to fit with the environment (Vasta, Miller, & Ellis, 2004).

brain development. Children flourish in environments that are nurturing, stimulating, and responsive to their needs and interests. Children exposed to environments lacking in stimulation or with inappropriate stimulation, such as ongoing stress, are less likely to reach their full potential.

Contemporary Theories

Contemporary theorists examine play in relation to current societal issues such as diversity, social justice, and the relative nature of truth and knowledge.

1. **Sociocultural theory.** This theory is dominated by the work of Goncu, Vygotsky, and Bronfenbrenner. Children learn about the social and cultural contexts, such as their social world, through their daily living experiences. Through play, children encounter problems and work through strategies that will support them in their problem solving.

   Vygotsky's (1978) zone of proximal development suggests that through play children stretch their boundaries to figure out situations and then construct knowledge.

   Bronfenbrenner indicates that children's development is influenced by both the person and the environment, which includes family, community, culture, and the broader society. The personal characteristics as well as the interaction among people and their environment contribute to the child's development.

   Goncu (Goncu, Mistry, & Mosier, 2000) and his colleagues examine child's play from both a cultural perspective and an interdisciplinary thinking process. Play behaviours are influenced by the economic, social, and political factors that are prevalent in larger cultures. The values and beliefs that adults have about play directly influence the quality of the play experiences that are extended to children.

2. **Critical educational theory.** This theoretical framework examines education from the social-political and cultural context. Critical theorists examine how play is influenced by gender, class, and race inequalities within society. Children's play and learning experiences should be linked to their cultural experiences, and children should have freedom and control over their learning. Adults facilitate opportunities for children to examine the inequalities that exist within their learning environment and in society in general.

   Each theoretical framework presented is based on play being a vital part of a child's life for optimal development, socially, cognitively, physically, and emotionally. This information causes early learning practitioners to think about values, beliefs, and philosophy about play.

> Vygotsky's (1978) zone of proximal development suggests that through play children stretch their boundaries to figure out situations and then construct knowledge.

PUTTING THE PLAY PROCESSES INTO PERSPECTIVE: BUILDING ON CHILDREN'S STRENGTHS

Throughout this chapter we have provided an introduction to play processes that children typically follow. However, not all children follow the processes in the same way. As outlined in Figure 2.9, there are many variables that influence how children play. For example, as identified by Szabó (2014), children with autism may not necessarily engage in spontaneous play; however, they may have extensive skills in creative object play. They may not necessarily engage in social-type play with peers but observe and adapt what they see to activities that give them comfort. Children with autism require role models who support them in developing their strengths. Often, this may mean teaching them ways to engage in particular situations.

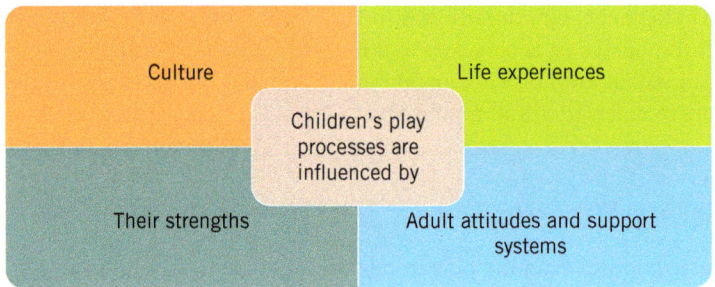

Figure 2.9 How children's play is influenced.

Children with developmental coordination disabilities are influenced by the environmental conditions of the play space (Dietze, 2013; Rosenblum, Waissman, & Diamond, 2017). If children have ample access to play spaces and adult support that focuses on their strengths, they gain skills to advance or adapt their skills.

Think about children who do not have fully developed speech. How might that influence their play? Or, consider children new to Canada who do not have the language needed to communicate with their peers. How does that influence children's play? Think about children with aggressive behavioural tendencies. How might that influence their play and the play of their peers? Think about children who have outdoor play experience with sticks and rocks or have snowball fights, and then when they participate in early learning programs that type of play is stopped. How might that influence their play? There are no definitive answers to any of these questions. The answers evolve from the observations that early learning teachers make and the communication that they have with children and families. Early learning teachers devise environments to support children to flourish.

We advocate that early learning teachers develop a program philosophy that focuses on the strengths and gifts that children bring to the environment. This approach allows every child to have their needs met without being centred out from other children. For example, if Jordan wishes to play in the dramatic centre but has a physical restriction of not being able to manoeuvre to put on dress-up clothes, the role of the early learning teacher is to help Jordan problem solve as to how he can put on the dress-up clothes. All children deserve access to an enriching play environment.

THE ROLES OF EARLY LEARNING TEACHERS IN PLAY

Throughout this text we will discuss the roles and responsibilities of early learning teachers in promoting play in the lives of young children. As a student teacher you may think that play is play; however, play is a very complex component of a child's life. Below, we outline five key roles of adults who have an interest in promoting children's play.

1. **Adults model positive attitudes toward play.** Adults model and exhibit a positive attitude toward both indoor and outdoor play, in each season. There is a balance between indoor and outdoor play throughout the year. There is a variety of active play experiences and materials that support each child's phase of development. The adult exposes children to play environments that meet established criteria for safety, risk, and challenge.

    Play opportunities that strive to be free of bias and exhibit respect for gender, race, culture, interest, and abilities are encouraged.

2. **Adults prepare appropriate environments.** Adults create equal opportunities for all children both indoors and outdoors. Children are provided with adequate options, intrigue, challenge, and freedom to explore, with limited adult intervention.

   Early learning teachers examine the ratio of children to materials. There are sufficient materials and equipment (but not an abundance of materials) that accommodate the number of children in the play area. The materials and experiences offer varying levels of interest and difficulty according to the strengths of individual children and groups of children. Early learning teachers ensure that there are not too many materials in the play space for children to choose from, because this reduces the need for them to invent new uses for materials. This inhibits them from looking at the possibilities that materials may offer, and it reduces the use of the child's wonderment and creativity.

   Both indoor and outdoor experiences provide children with interest/exploratory centres, space designated for physical movement activities, and places for children to pause and reflect or think about their next play experience. The play environments empower children to make choices and take safe risks as they explore the play possibilities.

3. **Adults observe and document children's play.** Conducting observations and environmental scanning, which is an ongoing process, provides early learning teachers with information about the child's interests, abilities, strengths, and opportunities for further learning and development. Early learning teachers make connections about the types of materials, skills, and interests that children have by reviewing ongoing observations and documentation. Observations provide insight into the types of materials that may support the play episode. When new play materials that add new dimensions or challenges are offered, children engage in new discoveries through exploration and problem solving. Further information on observations is provided in Chapter 3.

4. **Adults promote play and opportunities for expansive discoveries.** Children's play is rich in experience, creativity, and imagination when it is child initiated and reflective of the child's daily living experiences. Early learning teachers facilitate play by encouraging children to bring their interests and experiences to the play.

   One of the most challenging roles of early learning teachers is to examine child's play and find the appropriate balance of facilitating play, engaging in the play episode, and determining the benefits of modelling particular behaviours or skills through play. Environmental scanning and careful observations help adults to determine the most appropriate times and strategies to use to expand play opportunities and discoveries with children. When adults interrupt children's play, the benefits of the play experience to the development of the child's neural pathways *can* be inhibited. The child's neural pathways are influenced and advanced in their development as exploration, thinking skills, problem solving, and language expression occur during play episodes (ACDE, 2016).

5. **Adults promote play in and with nature.** The outdoor environment offers multiple possibilities for play with natural materials such as sticks and stones. In nature, children learn to take care of their surroundings and feel a sense of freedom not possible indoors. Early learning teachers understand the benefits and importance of outdoor play in nature and provide children with the time, space, and place to experience the joys and wonders of nature.

Adults' Participation in Child's Play

There are many perspectives on the role and level of involvement that adults should have in child's play. When appropriate, having children and adults participate in play provides opportunities for the play, communication, relationships, and learning to be expanded in new ways. Children benefit from taking charge of the play with the adult. Adults encourage this by asking the child to explain each of the roles in the play episode and ensuring that the child's performance or abilities are not judged. Student teachers and early learning teachers set aside their familiar roles and authority and follow the child's lead in the play. Adults avoid putting pressure on a child to succeed or do something the right way. They allow the play to unfold as the child wishes it to. Adults have important roles in child's play, from a coach to a partner to a facilitator. The cues come from observing children in their play and listening to the children.

Johnson, Christie, Yawkey, and Wardle (1987) identify three levels of adult participation in child's play experiences. They are parallel play, co-playing, and play tutoring.

Parallel play is described as adults playing beside the child, not with the child. The adult may use similar materials as the child. Adults exhibit this type of involvement when they wish to model positive play behaviours without intervening in the child's play episode with words or active involvement.

Co-playing is used to describe play episodes that include a child or group of children and an adult. The children control the play, thus determining the role that the adult will have. Co-playing provides the adult with an opportunity to role model particular skills and behaviours and introduces the children to new language and problem-solving techniques.

Play tutoring is the third level of adult participation when the adult participates with a child or group of children and takes charge of the play episode for a short period of time. This involvement occurs when the adult recognizes, through observation, the need to shift the play in new directions. This is of particular importance if a level of aggressive behaviour begins to develop or if the play has potential to hurt a child physically or emotionally.

Rosenblum, Waissman, and Diamond (2017) suggest that adults consider carefully when and how they become involved in children's play. The more adults become involved, the more intrusive and domineering the adults become in the play.

TERMS THAT INFLUENCE EARLY LEARNING PLAY ENVIRONMENTS

We conclude this chapter with three additional terms that support the theory of children's play.

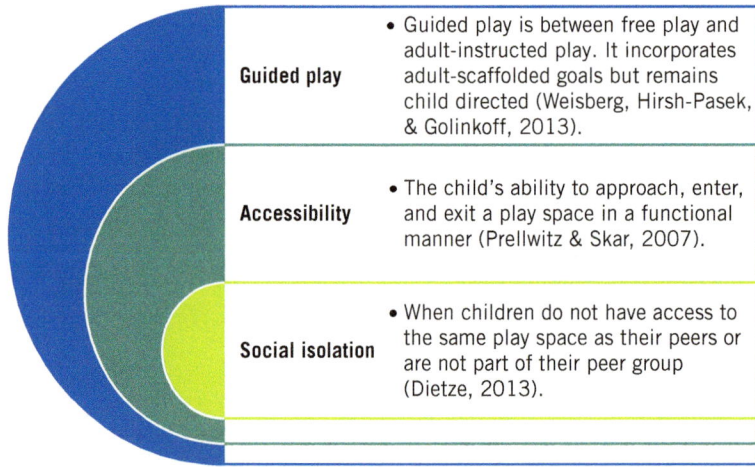

SUMMARY

Chapter Preview

- Children require opportunities to play. Children currently have little time to create play experiences. As a society, we are taking great risks by reducing children's play opportunities.

Child's Play from an Ecological Theory Perspective

- Urie Bronfenbrenner's ecological theory examines the relationship of how environmental influences contribute to a child's play experiences. There are five environmental systems: microsystem, mesosystem, exosystem, macrosystem, and chronosystem.

Components of Play and Unique Features of Play

- Play requires child and adult interaction, physical space, and individual and group experiences.
- Play has three unique features: intrinsic motivation, active engagement, and process rather than product.

Characteristics of Play

- There are seven common characteristics of play. They are that play needs to be active, child initiated and child focused, process oriented, episodic, rule governed, intrinsically motivated, and symbolic and transformational.

The Play Process

- Children advance through five phases in the play process: body play, motoring movement play, imaginative play, intentional imaginative play, and peer play with rules. The sixth phase of play occurs during adulthood.

Classifying Play Experiences

- Early learning teachers observe children's play and use information gained to plan an environment and experiences that support children's interests and strengths.
- Piaget identified three distinct stages of play: functional/sensorimotor, symbolic/dramatic, and games with rules.
- Smilansky identified that there is a construction play stage and the six criteria used to determine the level of dramatic/sociodramatic play.
- Parten outlined four stages of play from a social behaviour perspective. They are solitary, parallel, associative, and cooperative play. She also identified nonplaying as unoccupied behaviour time and onlooker's play.
- Seagoe identified cooperative-competitive play as a stage that occurs between 7 and 9 years of age. This involves children focusing on team sports and victory rather than on an individual's performance and success.

Children and Theories of Play

- There are three major groups of play theories. They are classical, modern, and contemporary.
- Classical theories focus on play from the surplus energy, recreation/relaxation, practice, and recapitulation perspectives.
- Modern theories examine play from the perspective of the consequences of play for the child and how it affects a child's development.
- Contemporary theories focus on the relationship of play to diversity and social justice relative to daily living and knowledge.

Putting the Play Processes into Perspective: Building on Children's Strengths

- Early learning teachers observe children with atypical developmental needs to determine the types of environmental play space and play material modifications needed to support their play and learning opportunities.

The Roles of Early Learning Teachers in Play

- Early learning teachers have many roles in supporting children's play. Four key roles are role modelling positive attitudes toward play, preparing appropriate environments, observing children in play, and promoting play and opportunities for expansive discoveries.
- Johnson, Christie, Yawkey, and Wardle (1987) indicate that there are three levels of adult participation in play. They are parallel play, co-playing, and play tutoring.

REVIEW QUESTIONS

1. How does Bronfenbrenner's ecological model of development help early learning teachers gain insight into the relationship of child development to play? Are there current macrosystem and chronosystem issues in your community that are affecting child's play? If so, how do early learning teachers and families address these issues?
2. What is the significance of child's play, learning, and motivation? How do early learning teachers and families address these components? What long-term challenges could occur if children do not gain the internal motivational attributes to engage in play?
3. Describe how the seven common characteristics of play guide early learning teachers and families in their work with children.
4. Outline the six phases of the play process. What do you envision the role of the early learning teacher to be at each phase? Is one phase more challenging than another? Why or why not?
5. Explain the key stages of play development as outlined by Piaget, Smilansky, Parten, and Seagoe. How do these stages influence the work of early learning teachers? How might play experiences differ in early learning environments with early learning teachers who do not have this knowledge?
6. What are the key features of the classical, modern, and contemporary perspectives on play? Describe their similarities and differences.

7. Why do early learning teachers create programs that support the strengths of children? How do early learning teachers accommodate all children in the play environment?
8. Describe four key roles that adults have in promoting child's play. Which are the most challenging? Why?

MAKING CONNECTIONS

Theory to Practice

1. You are working in an early learning centre. There is a 4-year-old boy who has been building the same type of skyscrapers for the past three weeks. If you made this observation, what recommendations do you have to handle this situation? Why?
2. In the chapter preview, we outlined a play episode with Maja and Allie. What knowledge have you gained from this chapter? Why might Allie have more concentration skills in the sand play environment than in other environments? What might be influencing Allie's interest in the sand play?
3. When you read the poem "The Little Boy," what information do you gain about the importance of environments supporting a process-oriented play environment rather than a product-oriented environment? How do early learning practitioners help parents understand the importance of these two concepts?
4. How do you envision a child's culture may affect imaginative play? Give specific examples. How would you support a child and family if their cultural perspectives do not include imaginative play options?

DIGITAL PORTFOLIO ENTRIES

Potential portfolio entries for your digital portfolio could include:

- When I think about children with disabilities and the theories of play, I wonder about …
- As an early learning teacher, how do I use all of the theory presented?
- When I envision children involved in their play, I now want to pay particular attention to … because ….
- If I get into an early learning program where the theory of play is misunderstood, what would that look like?
- I feel that I need to think of play in a particular way because ….

Add the words *nature-based play* to your search engine.

CHAPTER 3
Observing, Documenting, and Interpreting Children's Play

Rawpixel.com/Shutterstock

> ❝ Conflict is the gadfly of thought. It stirs us to observation and memory. It instigates to invention. It shocks us out of sheep-like passivity, and sets us at noting and contriving. ❞
>
> —John Dewey (1859–1952)

LEARNING OUTCOMES

After exploring this chapter you should be able to:

- Discuss how children's play contributes to their learning.
- Explain how observations contribute to children's play experiences.
- Outline how observation, documentation, interpretation, reflective practice, and authentic assessment support children's play, early learning teachers, and programming.
- Describe strategies that early learning teachers may use to acquire information about children that help them in understanding the whole child.
- Discuss documentation strategies that support early learning teachers in gaining information about individual children and groups of children during their play.
- Describe the types of discoveries that can be made through watching, listening, and discussing play with children.

Sharing Stories of Practice

I learned early in my studies and practice that there are different perspectives on the purpose, methods, and use of observations. I recall during my college days, one professor indicated that, without proper observational data, it was difficult to design an environment for children that supported their learning, interests, and phase of development. I remember at some of our placements we were required to plan activities specific to the observations made of children and that those activities were to focus on areas on which the children needed further development. If the experiences were not tied to observations, the activities were not to be implemented.

I think there has been a real shift in many early learning programs. For example, now we continue to observe children, but the observations are made to figure out children's interests, curiosity, competence, capacity, and strengths. If we build on these areas, children naturally become engaged in play and learning.

Learning to observe effectively is a process—and one that evolves and is refined as our knowledge about children and programming develops. My observational skills continued to develop not only through the ability to document what I see, using a variety of methods, but also through my ability to listen to children (their words and their actions) and to discuss my findings with colleagues, the children, and families. I then reflect on the discussions that have taken place, and my observations become more meaningful and pedagogical. Documenting children's play through the use of photos and video has been extremely helpful for me to be able to discuss and share with children and families stories about the experiences. Through this process, I have been able to make children's learning and development more visible. The discussions I have support the interpretations I make, which in turn lead to programming decisions that support children's further learning and development.

In essence, I believe that observations and documentation are similar to *painting* a picture or *weaving* a blanket. For me, I need to know the children and appreciate the vibrant rays that they each bring to the environment. Each discovery that children make changes the colours in the picture or the patterns in the blanket. I combine my observations, documentation, and conversations with children and families with my knowledge of child development, my philosophy about play and learning, and most importantly, what I hear the children say and see them do. This strategy allows me to appreciate the strengths that each child brings to my life on a daily basis rather than making judgments about what children can and cannot do.

Katrina, ECE graduate, 2017

CHAPTER PREVIEW

Play is the vehicle for children's learning (Cevher-Kalburan & Ivrendi, 2016). When children use blocks, they may compare size, shape, height, and weight; one-on-one relationships; and related mathematical concepts. They may create interesting patterns and build structures that exhibit intriguing architectural designs. They may use blocks as cellphones in the dramatic area or engage in social play, where they exhibit partnerships in play, cultural competencies, and language. As early learning teachers, how do we figure out what children know and what they are learning? Why is this important to us, to families, and to children? When we observe children at play, we see them negotiating with others, having conversations with peers and adults and trying new ideas, and we see their frustration levels. By combining this information, early learning teachers unlock how children's play influences their discoveries about their world and their learning.

Photo 3.1 Children observe and discover.

Used with Permission of Family Space Quinte, Inc.

Friedrich Froebel (1782–1852) was one of the early theorists to identify the importance of the role of adults guiding and supporting children in developing knowledge, skills, and abilities that are essential tenets for them to use throughout their lifespan. Early learning teachers examine the environment and observe and document how children use the materials and the environment and the depth and breadth of play they engage in. Early learning teachers develop effective observation skills and reflective practice strategies as a way to guide them in their work with children.

> "Observation is more than just passively seeing what is happening around us. It is about taking children seriously, hearing what they have to say, respecting their interpretations, and valuing their imagination and ideas, their unexpected theories and their explorations of feelings and viewpoints" (Fawcett & Watson, 2016, p. 14).

Observing children helps early learning teachers in creating inspiring and nurturing environments with and for children and families. How we support children in their environment influences their desire to learn and develop.

In early childhood education, child observation has a long history. It was originally associated with the child study movement that began with G. Stanley Hall in the United States in the late nineteenth century. According to Grieshaber and Hatch (2003), the original intent of observation was to collect data that would be used to provide the content of the curriculum. However, traditional observations that early learning teachers may be used to doing are meant to be objective. Observations in the past may have been mainly about assessing whether a child is conforming to a set of predetermined standards. Pedagogical documentation, by contrast, is focused on trying to see and understand what is going on in the pedagogical work and what the child is capable of without any predetermined framework of expectations and norms. Pedagogical documentation is child-centric and culturally appropriate rather than prescribed (Dietze & Kashin, 2017).

Observation methods of the past have had an accepted practice, with specific tools intended to gain information about the child's development. The information discovered becomes the framework for the types of experiences offered to children that would complement their next stage of development. Based on the understanding that the child's holistic development occurs across multiple domains, there is an increased interest in adopting a contemporary perspective on observation that includes documentation processes. Rather than observe to see discrete developmental milestones, there is a move toward considering the whole child. This perspective actually has its origins in the work of Johann Heinrich Pestalozzi, who emphasized that learning happens through the hands, the heart, and the mind (Elkind, 2015). In addition, that educational approach, as used in preprimary schools such as those in Reggio Emilia, Italy, practises a form of observation that includes documentation and interpretation (Dietze & Kashin, 2016). Many educators and researchers are suggesting that this practice, which is called *pedagogical documentation*, provides valuable insight that helps adults to learn about and understand each child and groups of children. Fawcett and Watson (2016) remind us that for observations and documentation to be effective, adults benefit from taking time to observe, make decisions, and look beyond what we have the tendency to look for. They suggest that early learning teachers take time to stop, watch intently, and examine what is seen from a variety of perspectives, rather than the perspective that is obvious.

In this chapter, we introduce information on both observations and pedagogical documentation. Early learning teachers benefit from having a combination of skills and knowledge about the purpose and use of observations and pedagogical documentation with colleagues, families, and children. Early learning teachers use their observations and documentation to inform their practice with children in a variety of ways. Observations and documentation become pedagogical when they influence teaching and learning. If pedagogy is the study of teaching and learning, and documentation serves as a record, then pedagogical documentation is the recording of the teaching and learning in a way that influences future teaching and learning. It is not a straightforward listing of daily events, but rather a study of those events as they relate to teaching and learning (Dietze & Kashin, 2017).

Planning play-based environments for young children requires early learning teachers to have knowledge about and genuine interest in each child. Understanding the child, child development, culture, families, pedagogy, and programming enhances the experiences and opportunities that adults extend to children, including the role of children in determining their play options and strategies for implementing their play episodes (Dietze & Kashin, 2016). As outlined in Figure 3.1, early learning teachers benefit from thinking about the strengths of children and how the environment and the children's role models influence their experiences. Early learning teachers are role models for children, and peers can be as well. Both can be referred to as the *more knowledgeable other* (MKO) who can

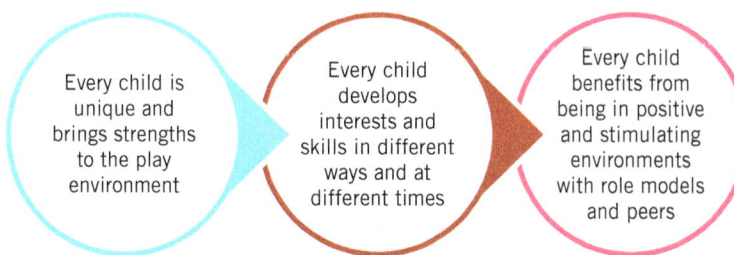

Figure 3.1 Views of children and environments.

zone of proximal development (ZPD) The difference between what a child can achieve on his or her own and what he or she can achieve with guidance and encouragement from a skilled partner (Dietze & Kashin, 2016).

help scaffold the child's learning across his or her **zone of proximal development (ZPD)** (Gadzikowski, 2013). With a view of the child as unique and full of potential, the play possibilities in the learning environment are enhanced.

Early learning teachers are encouraged to use a variety of ways of connecting with children so that the environment and program support their interests and opportunities for new learning.

STOP ... THINK ... REFLECT ... DISCUSS

Why might there be a movement in early learning programs to put more focus on the strengths of children than on areas requiring further development? What are the challenges for children and families if the focus is on areas where they are not strong? How might that change the environment and programming experiences offered to children?

CHILDREN AND LEARNING THROUGH PLAY

Play has long been recognized as the way children learn (Dewey, 1916/1944; Froebel, 1887; Hirsh-Pasek & Golinkoff, 2009; Ontario Ministry of Education, 2014, 2016; Whitebread, Basilio, Kuvalija, & Verma, 2012). Children's play is meant to provide them with the venue to try out ideas, experiment, try new ways, take risks, and reinvent ideas and ways of knowing (Kemple, Oh, Kenney, & Smith-Bonahue, 2016; Mardell et al., 2016). Mardell and colleagues (2016) suggest that there is an emerging model of playful learning that focuses on three overlapping categories: delight, wonder, and choice, as outlined in Figure 3.2. They suggest that this model examines the quality of children's experience "as they build understanding, knowledge, and skill" (p. 6). They argue that playful learning includes both subjective and objective dimensions and "indicators represent psychological states as well as observable behaviours. When all three categories are 'in play,' represented by the intersection of the circles, playful learning is most likely occurring" (p. 6). Playful learning offers new insight into how and why play is foundational for children's learning.

CURIOUS?

Add the words *towards a pedagogy of play* to your search engine to explore more information on this approach.

All children are different. From your experience, you may know some who are exuberant, leading them to be explorers and risk-takers, while others are introverted and reserved; children's emotions range from happy to sad, quiet to loud. Since each child is packaged differently, one of our roles as early learning teachers is to become partners

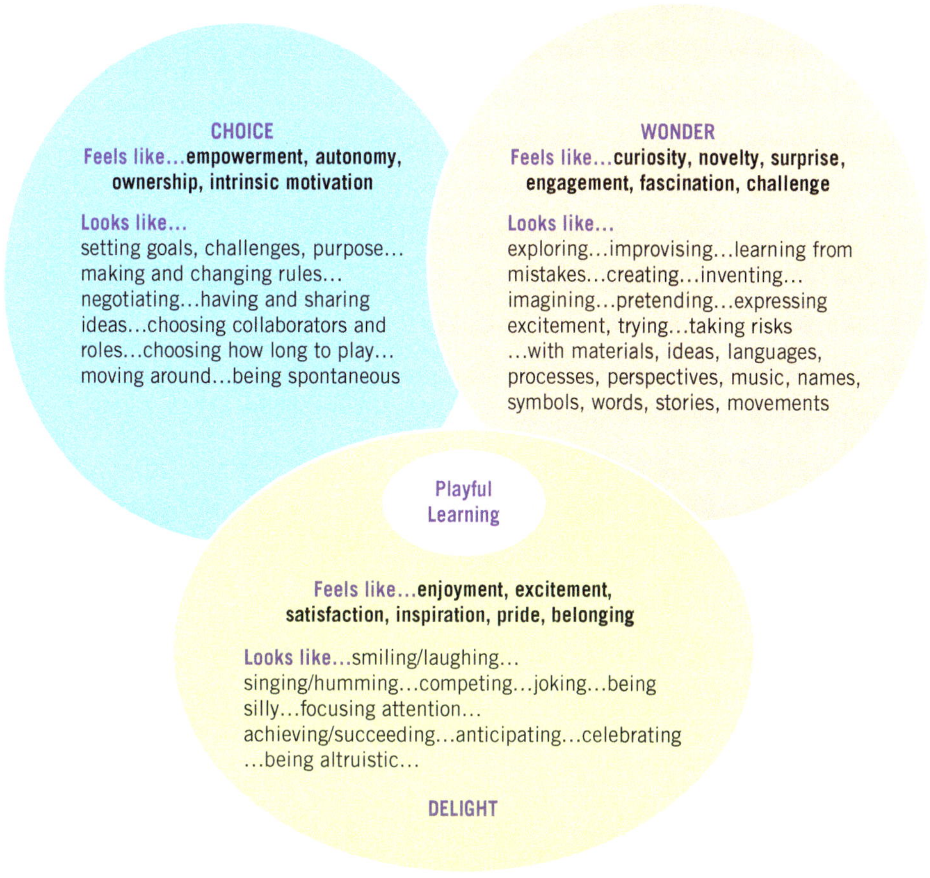

CHOICE
Feels like...empowerment, autonomy, ownership, intrinsic motivation

Looks like...
setting goals, challenges, purpose... making and changing rules... negotiating...having and sharing ideas...choosing collaborators and roles...choosing how long to play... moving around...being spontaneous

WONDER
Feels like...curiosity, novelty, surprise, engagement, fascination, challenge

Looks like...
exploring...improvising...learning from mistakes...creating...inventing... imagining...pretending...expressing excitement, trying...taking risks ...with materials, ideas, languages, processes, perspectives, music, names, symbols, words, stories, movements

Playful Learning

Feels like...enjoyment, excitement, satisfaction, inspiration, pride, belonging

Looks like...smiling/laughing... singing/humming...competing...joking...being silly...focusing attention... achieving/succeeding...anticipating...celebrating ...being altruistic...

DELIGHT

Figure 3.2 Elements of playful learning.
Source: Mardell, B., Wilson, D., Ryan, J., Ertel, K., Krechevsky, M., & Baker, M. (2016). Towards a Pedagogy of Play. Used with Permission.

with children as **co-inquirer** and **co-investigator** to support **co-construction**. Think about your role as trying to gather information to crack an important mystery or case. Each time you gain information about the child, more questions will evolve. This will lead to more observations and further investigations, providing more clues to the mystery of development. In essence, it is a continuous process. You are always trying to gain insight into children's play so that you can create an environmental framework that will support them in their quest to discover new knowledge.

Early learning teachers require knowledge about the relationship of child development to play, observations to play, and documentation to play, as it relates to children's play experiences and environments. These are knowledge touch points that are essential in your role as the architect, the person who creates diverse learning environments to support each child's strengths, abilities, and potential. Gathering information about children and being able to effectively use the information acquired from observations and discussions flourish when early learning teachers look at children's play from an inquiry or wonderment perspective. Think about what makes a child interested in blocks. Why do some children gravitate to the block area at a particular time each day? Is there a reason why Sammy and Jake find it so difficult to allow Markas into their play? Why does Markas have a need to play with Sammy and Jake? How do you

co-inquirer Refers to the people who have an interest in investigating a particular topic or idea.

co-investigator Refers to the process that two or more people (children or children and adults) use to investigate an area of interest and seek answers to their questions.

co-construction Defined as the generation of new knowledge by two or more people that neither would be able to generate alone (Damon, 1984; Rafal, 1996). Co-construction results in the partners in play internalizing the knowledge and using the knowledge independently and with others.

gain the information to get answers to these questions? There are many strategies that early learning teachers use to learn about an individual child and groups of children. In the next section, we introduce you to the key concepts that facilitate observation, documentation, interpretation, reflection, and assessment processes in early learning programs and in early learning teacher practices.

THE RELATIONSHIP OF OBSERVATION TO PLAY AND LEARNING

The work of Vygotsky and others helps us to understand how a child's perspective is merged and rooted in social behaviour (Li, Hestenes, & Wang, 2016). A child's environment directly influences curiosity levels and how the child learns, grows, and develops. "Play is culturally situated.... Furthermore, the meaning attached to involvement in these play-like activities is driven by cultural beliefs and practices developed and shaped within the ethos of parental socialization goals and expectations for children" (Roopnarine & Davidson, 2015, p. 231). In early learning environments, it is the combination of materials, experiences, language among children and adults, **cultural artifacts**, and the adults who are facilitators and coaches that stimulates a child's thoughts, experiences, and ultimately their play. The early learning environment and children's experiences are directly linked to an early learning teacher's knowledge and understanding of:

cultural artifacts Refers to things that humans create that provide information about their culture.

- Child development.
- Learning processes.
- Environmental design.
- The roles and responsibilities that adults exhibit in facilitating play and learning opportunities.

Children require environments where adults view play as a kaleidoscope—children playing with peers, engaging in creative and investigative work, participating in simple and complicated problem-solving activities—and where children are encouraged to take responsibility for their play choices and learning strategies (Sobel & Larimore, 2016). Knowing how children play, investigate, explore, and engage in peer-to-peer and child–adult relationships provides early learning teachers with insight and understanding into the whole child.

There are some experts, including Atherton and Nutbrown (2016), who encourage early learning teachers to create a play environment where children are encouraged to engage in a **thinking curriculum**. The purpose of a thinking curriculum is to support children in the development of flexible learning and problem solving (Aubrey, Ghent, & Kanira, 2012). The process supports children in developing an understanding of their world in conjunction with their experiences and emerging ideas, plans, and schemas. To facilitate this, children require environments that support problem solving and independent play and inquiry and access to materials that are stimulating and challenging (Aubrey, Ghent, & Kanira, 2012). Children's schema play focuses on the structure of children's thinking. It provides another lens from which to observe children's play. Schema play follows the theory that private aspects of children's minds are made public through actions, language, and representations. Athey (1991/2007) identified the following dynamic schemas that are discernible in actions:

thinking curriculum A curriculum that weaves the experiences and knowledge that children bring to the environment into new discoveries. Children connect the new discoveries with life experiences and transfer this knowledge to different settings or perspectives as required.

- Dynamic vertical.
- Dynamic back and forth.
- Dynamic circular.

- Going over and under.
- Going round a boundary.
- Going through a boundary.
- Containing and enveloping space.

In addition to examining the child's stage of development and schema play, adults use observations, discussions, and collaborative experiences with children, families, and colleagues to guide them in understanding their play partners and the types of play experiences that support new exploration opportunities relative to their zone of proximal development. Early learning teachers develop strategies that will allow them to consistently examine children's play and learning.

Another practice that supports early learning teachers in their observations and documentation of play is **inquiry-based learning**. This is similar to what is often referred to as emergent curriculum. The term *emergent curriculum* refers to an approach that emerges from the interests of the child and is socially constructed (Jones & Nimmo, 1994). Emergent curriculum is the umbrella term that incorporates project-based learning, inquiry, and Reggio Emilia–inspired teaching and learning. For educators in Reggio Emilia, teaching and learning becomes an art that is expressed through the use of *progettazione*, projected curriculum constructed with pedagogical documentation (Rinaldi, 1998).

Similar to a thinking curriculum, the foundation for inquiry-based learning and emergent curriculum evolves from early learning teachers and children working together to explore the questions, interests, and ideas that children either verbalize or exhibit. In inquiry-based environments, children increase their motivation, collaboration, social interaction, and innovation in thinking and in doing (Land & Danis, 2016; Natural Curiosity, 2011; Ontario Ministry of Education, 2013). Inquiry-based teaching and learning is a pedagogical approach. Pedagogy is how learning happens. A pedagogical approach is one that an early learning teacher will choose to guide and support them in creating children's play and learning environments. Pedagogy has a different meaning from the term *curriculum*. Curriculum refers to the content of the learning (Ontario Ministry of Education, 2014). For example, children may be interested in worms that they discovered in the playground after it rained. One pedagogical approach would be to offer children instruction so that they learn the facts about worms. In another environment, the early learning teacher would focus on an inquiry process; children would learn what is intriguing to them as they explore their wonder about worms. This pedagogical approach to play requires shared responsibility with teachers, children, and families in guiding the types of experiences and materials available within the environment. As outlined in Figure 3.3, early learning teachers have many roles in this approach, including observation and documentation.

inquiry-based learning
Learning that requires children to investigate, explore, search, pose questions, and decide about options. They test their ideas and refine their approaches as required. Children's knowledge is created from the processes they use to execute their ideas or solve problems when their ideas do not work. Inquiry-based learning aligns with a thinking curriculum approach in programming.

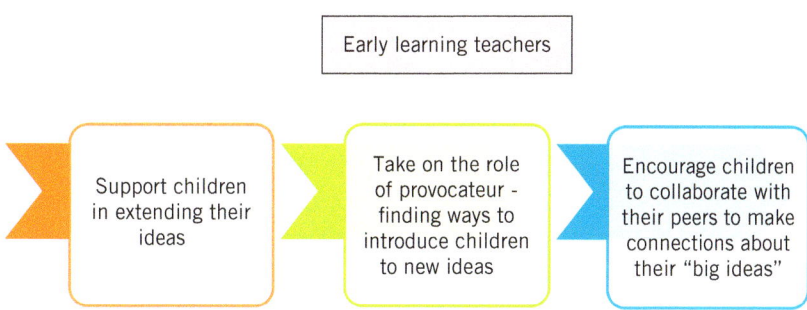

Figure 3.3 The role of early learning teachers in inquiry-based environments.

When early learning teachers take the role of "provocateur," they find creative ways to support children's initial curiosity and interest (Ontario Ministry of Education, 2013). In this process, early learning teachers model how to question, extend ideas, and carry out an investigation of children's ideas or theories. They are provoking learning often, with play provocations. During this process, early learning teachers are searching for the "**big ideas**" in children's play.

Observing and documenting children's ideas and play episodes provide children and adults with a lens that helps to visualize potential opportunities that may exist for children to pursue.

big ideas Ideas that expand the depth or breadth of thinking among children and early learning teachers, which leads to deep thinking (Dietze & Kashin, 2016).

Add the words *inquiry-based learning in early childhood education* to your search engine to obtain more information about this pedagogical approach.

Photo 3.2 Children flourish when they are surrounded by adults who allow them to look, think, explore, and examine their ideas for a thinking curriculum to evolve.

Used with Permission of Family Space Quinte, Inc.

Photo 3.3 Children benefit from different experiences and materials in their settings. This is how they expand the knowledge that they bring to the environment.

Used with Permission of Angela Roy

Photo 3.4 Children engage in a thinking curriculum when they explore their discoveries together with their peers.

Used with Permission of Angela Roy

Photo 3.5 A thinking curriculum evolves when children have time to explore their environments.

Used with Permission of Family Space Quinte, Inc.

OBSERVATION, DOCUMENTATION, AND INTERPRETATION: A TWENTY-FIRST-CENTURY APPROACH

Conducting observations as a way to develop an understanding about children is not new. In early learning programs, child observation strategies have long been practised as a guiding principle for program development. For example, in the late nineteenth century, G. Stanley Hall determined that child observations provided a scientific method for educators to understand children (Weber, 1984). Hall's premise for observing children in play settings was to collect data about each child so that the "true needs" of the child could be gained. On the basis of the data collected, Hall identified that "the data of child development should provide the content of the curriculum" (as cited in Weber, 1984, p. 49). Early learning teachers today consider how they use their observations to inform their practice.

Prior to the turn of the twenty-first century, observations were used to gain information "in order to build a more complete picture of [children]" (Perry, 1997, p. 27), often focusing on what they could and could not do. Now, early learning teachers use observations as only one part of their inquiry about the abilities and strengths that children bring to environments. They develop skills in conducting observation, documentation, interpretation, and reflective practice. These combined skills are embedded in the early learning teachers' practice because they contribute to informing them about the types of materials, experiences, and environments that will support child-centred, play-based programming (Dietze & Kashin, 2016).

Observation

Early learning teachers have many roles throughout the day—one of which includes observing children at play from a variety of perspectives. Observing is more than watching children play. Observing requires early learning teachers to have skills in (a) watching and observing, (b) documenting, (c) coaching, (d) facilitating, (e) reflecting, (f) planning, and (g) analyzing the observations with children, families, and colleagues so that appropriate play experiences or provocations may be offered.

Observation is a systematic process used to listen to and watch children in their play. Traditionally, the purpose of observation has been to gain information about a child's or group of children's stage of development compared with documented developmental norms or behaviours that are expected for a particular age group. Observations in early learning programs are considered informal; they are not diagnostic—meaning that it is not the role of the early learning teacher to diagnosis children. This limited view of observation is changing in the twenty-first century as more emphasis is being placed on the role of documentation and interpretation.

Observations may take many forms—from documentation to charting methods where early learning teachers check what they observe from predefined lists of behaviour. The information gained from observations is used to plan environments for children that build on their learning, ideas, theories, interests, and stage of development.

Early learning teachers conduct observations to gain insight into how:

- Children's play, their thinking processes, and the ways in which they try to make sense of their experiences and the world.
- To create environments that support children's sense of curiosity and wonderment, while expanding the complexity of experiences to positively challenge children.

Photo 3.6 Adults observe and listen to children as a way to gain insight into children's interests.
Used with Permission of Family Space Quinte, Inc.

- To share evidence-based examples of children's experiences and strengths with families, children, and colleagues.

As outlined in Figure 3.4, early learning teachers focus on the process of play rather than on the product that children produce during play.

Core questions that support early learning teachers' practice when observing children may include the following:

- To what areas of the play space do children gravitate?
- How do the children use the materials and their environment in their play?

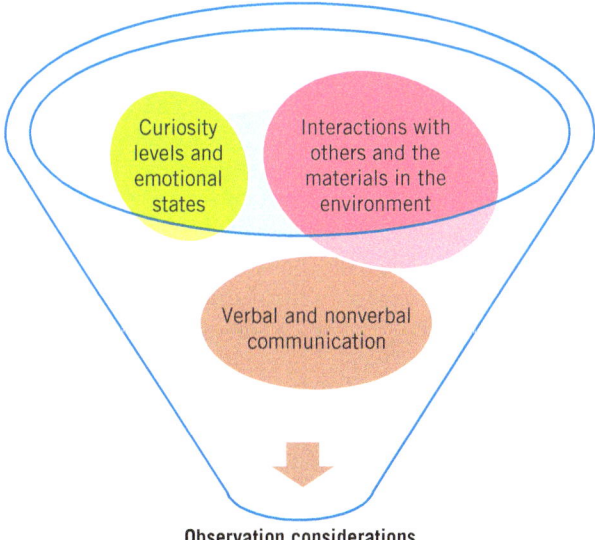

Observation considerations

Figure 3.4 Considerations that adults make when observing children.

Observation, Documentation, and Interpretation: A Twenty-First-Century Approach **85**

- Do children usually play alone or with peers?
- What types of ideas or inquiries do children appear to be exploring? What actions do the children exhibit that you lead you to this perspective?
- How long do children play and explore in an area? Do they return to the area after moving to another space?

Documentation

As we examine the current literature on documentation, it may seem as if this is a relatively new methodology and process for understanding children. However, more than 15 years ago, Alcock (2000) identified that researchers such as Susan Isaacs and Jean Piaget used a form of pedagogical documentation in their work with children. They used documentation as a "tool for studying and *understanding* the whole child within an open paradigm, where preconceived standards such as developmental norms did not frame the observations" (Alcock, 2000, p. 5). Now documentation is resurfacing in early learning programs.

Pedagogical documentation has now been reintroduced to early learning programs, due in part to the influence from the educators in Reggio Emilia, Italy. According to Wein (2011), the term *pedagogical documentation* was introduced by Dahlberg, Moss, and Pence (1999) and is often associated with the Reggio Emilia approach. "Pedagogical documentation has its origins in the innovative and, today, world-famous municipal early childhood services in the Northern Italian city of Reggio Emilia" (Dahlberg & Moss, 2005, p. 6). It is a complex process that many early learning teachers are embracing in practice throughout Canada.

When early learning teachers embed documentation in their practice, their pedagogy and curriculum decisions are clearly based on the real experiences and interests of children. This is complex because, as a process, it involves the interpretation of the documentation to discern meaning; therefore, it requires more than just recording events such as posting photos and noting "We went to the park today." Pedagogical documentation as a process takes time to examine and find meaning that supports children and families. Not all documentation is pedagogical. When an early learning teacher amasses a collection of observations that are shared via emails, panels, or bulletin boards/display boards either indoors or outdoors, there is ample opportunity for that documentation to become pedagogical. To be pedagogical, it requires interpretation from others and influences the direction of the curriculum and experiences that children may participate in (Dietze & Kashin, 2017).

As outlined by Fleet, Patterson, and Robertson (2012), pedagogical documentation "is not a real-time movie or a record of events, but a subjective set of frozen moments that provoke, inform, record, and provide opportunities for further thinking, wonder, able to be offered back to children for comment and reflection" (p. 7). Pedagogical documentation is a process whereby early learning teachers seek meaning about children's play experiences, both indoors and outdoors.

Early learning teachers who engage in the pedagogical process engage in:

- A process whereby meaning can be made.
- Making records of events in a way that represents the recording of these events as they intersect with people, places, and other events.
- Developing meaningful relationships in order to gain the depth of analysis required to create pedagogical documentation. Building relationships enhances the opportunities to gain a deeper understanding of the meaning of children's outdoor play experiences. This process allows for the creation of authentic relationships, which in turn can lead to authentic assessment (Dietze & Kashin, 2016).

The Reggio Emilia early childhood programs in Italy have provided educators, researchers, and teachers with new insights into working with children and families. "Reggio leaders understand that no theory is the absolute truth, but is just a starting point for further investigation and discussion" (Pence & Pacini-Ketchabaw, 2008, p. 247). Early learning teachers who are influenced by the Reggio Emilia approach find a need to "open up" their minds to a multitude of perspectives (Rinaldi, 2006) so that they do not become rigid in using one framework of thinking in their practice. Documentation is a way in which early learning teachers create a record of teaching and learning, making children's learning visible (Dietze & Kashin, 2016) and "generat[ing] new insights about teaching and learning" (Mardell et al., 2009, p. 1). Documentation assists early learning teachers, families, and children in seeing what children do in their play and how they learn from the various types of play that they engage in. Documentation provides an understanding of children's thinking and how the environment and experiences contribute to their learning. Documentation contributes to making children's learning visible, which in turn can act as a stimulus for children to expand their exploration and new options for discovery. Used in this way, documentation becomes pedagogical.

Documentation can be collected in many ways, including the following:

- Photos and video recordings of children and their early learning teachers.
- Artifacts, such as children's drawings, illustrations, writing samples, and printed communication.
- Printed summaries of children's planning for their play experiences and the execution of experiences.
- Children's use of language in their recall of experiences.
- Written observations that describe what you, as the early learning teacher, see or wonder about.

Not all children contribute to the collection of documentation in the same way. For example, early learning teachers who work with infants and toddlers think about and theorize about children's thinking. A key question to ask when observing younger children is, What might they be thinking during a particular play episode?

There are more core questions that guide early learning teachers' practice when determining if and what to document, which may include the following:

- Which play experiences will be documented?
- Why document this play experience?
- What form of collection will be used to make children's experiences visible (i.e., photos or video recordings)?
- Where and how will the documentation be shared with families, children, and colleagues?
- What will the role of children be in the preparation of the documentation, and why?
- How will the documentation be shared with families, and what is their role in contributing to the documentation?
- How are children encouraged to examine the documentation and use it to extend their learning?

Documentation is a process that encompasses what is to be reflected on, discussion points, and action that is generated from the documentation, as well as the reflective process, including what is seen; what is heard; and what interests, ideas, and theories the children generate. The reflective process brings together families, children, and early

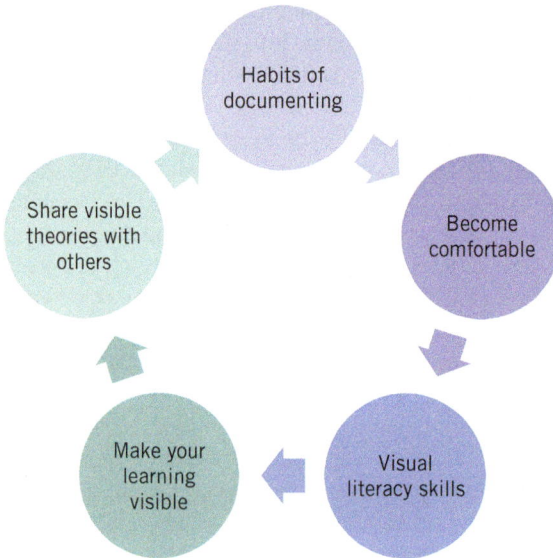

Figure 3.5 Documentation strategies.

learning teachers to engage in dialogue, exploration, questioning, and charting ideas for new directions. We encourage early learning teachers to develop the habit of documentation because of its benefits to children and programming. Wein (2011) suggests five strategies, as depicted in Figure 3.5.

Early learning teachers and students recognize that documentation is a learned process that takes time. At first, your documentation might be very descriptive, in that it recounts the experiences of the children. Over time, the more you share and open yourself up to the interpretations of others, you will develop your potential for expanding your documentation and capacity to go deeper with your interpretations and reflections. When documentation is shared, the visual aspects of the documentation are considered. Avoiding visual clutter will help you recognize how components of your documentation interact with each other, creating an aesthetically pleasing visual for the human eye to view. When documentation is viewed not only as a way to make the learning of children visible, but also as a way to grow and develop as an educator, this will help you conceptualize documentation. This is a process that makes your own learning visible. Documentation as a process requires time to interpret and theorize about children's learning and to make this visible. By sharing your theories and opening yourself up to the interpretations of others, your documentation reveals a greater depth of meaning. The number-one strategy is to get into the habit of documenting. Having access to tools for documenting is essential. Your documentation tools may include:

- Cameras
- Audio and video recordings
- Smartphones and tablets
- Computers
- Artifacts created by children
- Observation notes made by adults

Pedagogical documentation is a cyclical process that brings children and early learning teachers back to new beginning points (Pence & Pacini-Ketchabaw, 2008). Seeking to find meaning, early learning teachers read and reread documentation, look at the visuals, and try to identify whether what they are seeing aligns with an image of the child as being competent and capable in their play experiences. Pedagogical documentation calls for interpretation.

Interpretation

Pedagogical documentation without analysis is equivalent to a mere record (Fleet et al., 2012). By critically reflecting and analyzing interpretations, early learning teachers look for ways in which the documentation aligns with their provincial or territorial early childhood frameworks that guide programming. Early learning teachers consider different ways to share their documentation so that it can be viewed by others, including the children and their families. For example, as shown in Photo 3.7, the pedagogical documentation is positioned in the children's outdoor play environments near where the original play occurred. At other times, the documentation will be placed indoors. One of the benefits of sharing the documentation is that it becomes an invitation for early learning teachers to engage in the interpretation of others—children, colleagues, supervisors, and families. Early learning teachers celebrate the feedback and view it as part of the "in progress" process. Reflections and the interpretations of others can have a significant influence on moving both indoor and outdoor play programming forward in ways that reflect meaningful curriculum (Dietze & Kashin, 2017).

Core questions that guide early learning teachers' practice when engaging in the interpretation process may include the following:

- What do I see, and what does this mean for children and programming?
- What are children exploring and are there particular areas of the environment that may have triggered this play?

Photo 3.7 Documentation makes learning visible.

Used with Permission of Bora Kim

Photo 3.8 Children's interpretations provide insight into their living experiences and learning.
Used with Permission of Bora Kim

- Were there particular materials or experiences that may have influenced or extended children's play? What might support children in exploring further?
- Were there any surprises about how the children engaged in the learning or with the peers that they participated with?
- What might children need to have in their environment next to scaffold the play experience?
- What is powerful about the experiences I have observed and documented? What does it tell me about children's competence and capacity?

Reflective Practice

reflective practice A continuous process involving children, early learning teachers, and families reflecting on significant discoveries or experiences that occur during play episodes. Early learning teachers may coach children in looking at their experiences and making meaning of them by questioning and listening to children's perspectives.

Early learning teachers, children, and families revisit documentation often as part of a reflective process. Drawing from the work of Schön (1983), early learning **reflective practice** involves children and adults by thoughtfully considering the children's experiences in applying knowledge to practice. Reflective practice brings to light children's individual and group strengths, learning styles, and ways of knowing.

There are many reasons to incorporate reflective practice in our work. For example, the reflective process of a situation or experience changes over time. As we gain new knowledge and deeper meaning, our perspectives change. When we engage in a collaborative reflective practice, our thoughts and perspectives may change. This allows us to construct shared knowledge and gain new knowledge, meaning, and experiences. Reflective practice is now a vital part of early learning teachers' practice in gaining a sense of understanding the children from a holistic perspective rather than a skill-deficits perspective.

Core questions that guide early learning teachers' practice when engaging in the reflective process may include the following:

- What new learning has been identified?
- What new ideas and learning have been discovered?

- How do I use this new information to support children's play, experiences, and environment?
- What might I want to explore further with children, families, and colleagues?

The reflective process is also an integral aspect of early learning programming. There is no beginning and end; rather, it is cyclical and correlates with observation and documentation processes. For example, when children and early learning teachers have created documentation, the documentation is studied with the intention of figuring out triggers that lead to children's curiosity and sense of wonder being ignited. An understanding of what can be gleaned from the documentation is best achieved when early learning teachers, families, and children engage in dialogue, critique their perspectives, and engage in discourse. This is how rich meaning is formulated and can bring insight to the types of materials or experiences that would further enhance children's explorations and learning.

EXAMINING THE DIFFERENCE BETWEEN CHILD OBSERVATION AND PEDAGOGICAL DOCUMENTATION

There are differences between observation processes and documentation, as identified in Figure 3.6. Observations generally concentrate on one aspect of a child's play for a specific purpose. Observation data are generated so that the early learning teacher may gain insight into a child's developmental stage, thinking, ideas, theories, and interests. Documentation focuses on the process of learning and the interconnectedness among the child's ideas, partners in learning, and play. As well, documentation is used to view what the child brings to the environment as an individual rather than making a comparison of the child to others.

The seminal work of Dahlberg and colleagues (1999) helps us gain further insight into the difference between child observation and pedagogical documentation. They indicate,

> As we understand it, the purpose of "child observation" is to assess children's psychological development in relation to already predetermined categories produced from developmental psychology and which define what the normal child should be doing at a particular age. The focus in these observations is not children's learning processes, but more on the idea of classifying and

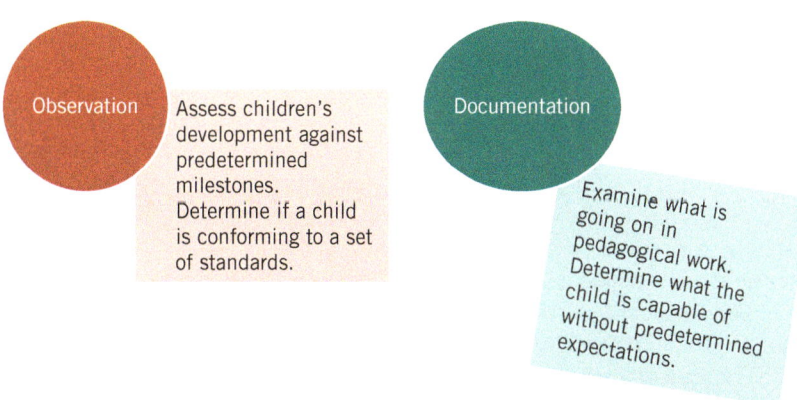

Figure 3.6 Differences between child observation and documentation.

categorizing children in relation to a general schema of developmental levels and stages . . . "Child observation" therefore is mainly about assessing whether a child is conforming to a set of standards. "Pedagogical documentation" by contrast is mainly about trying to see and understand what is going on in the pedagogical work and what the child is capable of without any predetermined framework of expectations and norms. (p. 146)

Dahlberg and Moss (2005), as cited in Pence and Pacini-Ketchabaw (2008), indicate that

> Documentation is not . . . "child observation" that assesses children's progress (usually in terms of development) against predetermined and normative categories . . . Instead, [Reggio Emilia educators] have shown how documentation, used in a critical way, can make us observant of the contingency of our constructions, and hence, make it possible to destabilise the meaning of that which we take for given and see as natural and true about the child . . . [Documentation] has helped [teachers] to refuse to codify children in prefabricated developmental categories, and hence they have been able to transgress the idea of a lacking and needy child. (p. 248)

In the preceding section, we introduced you to the traditional observation process, documentation, and pedagogical documentation. You play a significant role in working with children to document their play and learning and to have them revisit their learning and experiences on many occasions and in different parts of their indoor and outdoor environments.

Early learning teachers require skills in observing and in becoming a documenter—the documentation process communicates the important narratives about our work with young children and families. When we are transparent in communicating this valuable information, it helps both the children and early learning teachers to share with families the types of play experiences children engage in, how the learning occurs, and how children use one learning experience as a jump-off point to embark on new learning options. Developing documentation processes and reflective practice help to support early learning teachers in understanding children and being able to communicate with them through information sharing and questioning. These strategies lead children to collaborate with other peers and adults in ways that brings new options to their curiosity levels and motivation to embrace opportunities to engage in play.

AUTHENTIC ASSESSMENT

When documentation has meaningful content that depicts learning and development, early learning teachers share it with children, families, the community, and each other as a way to demonstrate children's competency and capacity. This is a form of assessment of children's learning, as it is visible, transparent, and meaningful. Using documentation for assessment is possible because the children's learning is visible. Observation notes that take the form of anecdotal or running records can be offered to external agencies if children require services to further enhance specified areas of development such as speech and language. It is important to remember that early learning teachers do not diagnosis the child. If necessary, an external agency may work with the families in that capacity.

When observation checklists have a set of predetermined standards, children can feel pressure to perform to meet these outcomes. Using these types of tools may reduce our need to listen to the children, to appreciate their strengths and interests, and to authentically view the contribution each child makes to the early learning environment.

Early learning teachers are now embracing using an **authentic assessment** process as a way to gain an understanding about children and the environments in which they play. Authentic assessment incorporates the information gleaned from ongoing observation, documentation, interpretation, and reflective practice. Authentic assessment incorporates what early learning teachers see, hear, and understand from children (Dietze & Kashin, 2016). Authentic assessment offers insight into children's learning, as it focuses on how children "create their own meaning and construct knowledge based on their own experience of the world combined with the new information they receive" (Howard, 2015, p. 1) and is based on evidence. Authentic learning in early learning programs is influenced by exposure to intriguing materials, experiences, collaborative knowledge, environmental conditions, and children's freedom to act on their sense of curiosity and need to explore (Dietze & Kashin, 2016; Howard, 2015).

> **authentic assessment** A process that early learning teachers establish with children and families to engage in ongoing observation, documentation, interpretation, and reflection of what they are seeing, hearing, and understanding from the children and the environment (Dietze & Kashin, 2016).

As outlined in Table 3.1, Dietze and Kashin (2016) indicate that traditional observation strategies and results differ significantly from authentic assessment. Similarly, Howard (2015) suggests that authentic assessment allows for multiple paths to demonstrate learning, depending on children's journeys of learning (Dietze & Kashin, 2016). As identified earlier, traditional observations are generally undertaken by early learning teachers when they have asked a child to "do" a particular activity. The teacher observes the child during the activity to determine what the child can and cannot do in relation to a set of predetermined developmental norms that have been established for children of similar ages. Authentic assessment differs significantly from traditional observation. In authentic assessment, early learning teachers take the lead from the children. They observe children as they use materials, engage in experiences, and embrace the options within the environments. The early learning teacher focuses on viewing children's strengths, skills, and processes used in their play.

Early learning teachers learn effective strategies for documenting children's experiences and bringing meaning to their learning. This includes ensuring that the strategies are "conducted in a natural environment; use multiple methods of gathering information; gather multiple types of information; involve families in the process and make a connection between the intent of the assessment process and the use of the information gained from the process" (Dietze & Kashin, 2016, p. 270). Authentic assessments embrace the joys and wonders that children bring to the environment.

Table 3.1 Differences between traditional observation and authentic assessment (Dietze & Kashin, 2016).

Traditional Observation	Authentic Assessment
Children are asked questions and are required to provide the correct response.	Children perform a task in a real-life situation as would normally occur during regular play opportunities.
Teachers determine what experiences will be observed, when and where.	Observations of real-life play occur.
Children are required to perform, recall, or recognize specific information or tasks.	Construction or application activities and experiences are observed.
Experiences and activities are teacher directed.	Experiences and activities are child centred and child initiated.
Teacher interpretations are identified and communicated with other adults.	Direct evidence is observed and assessed.

> **STOP ... THINK ... DISCUSS ... REFLECT**
>
> What does it mean to you when you read about becoming partners in play in early learning environments? As partners, who does the program planning? What is the role of an early learning teacher in being a partner? Is it the same as the role children have? Why or why not? How would your role with children be examined? Who would examine what you do in your role? What tools would be used to do this?

WAYS OF ACQUIRING INFORMATION TO SUPPORT STUDENT EARLY LEARNING TEACHERS IN UNDERSTANDING THE WHOLE CHILD

Early learning teachers have an important role in acquiring knowledge about the children in their care. Various aspects of each child's play are examined in order to develop an understanding of the whole child.

The following guidelines are intended to introduce you to strategies that will help you gain an understanding of children and that will support you in making positive connections with them in their play.

Photo 3.9 Understanding children's experiences and interests is important to early learning teachers.

Used with Permission of Bora Kim

Organize your observation tools

Develop a system to determine the type of observation you will conduct and how you will track your observations in a way that is efficient for you. These tools, combined with discussions with the child, early learning teachers, and families, guide you in planning experiences.

Develop purposeful observations

Observations have a purpose. Knowing the purpose of the observation helps early learning teachers and children to collect the information that will be useful in gaining insight into the question that triggered the observation. For example, if you are interested in observing a child new to the centre, for the purpose of determining the child's interests, would it be valid to observe the child on the first day and then determine what the child's interests, thinking, ideas, or theories are? Or, would it be reasonable for you to observe children on your first day working at the centre and then make statements of what the child's interests are? It would be unlikely that we could gather accurate information about children under such conditions. Neither of these cases would provide purposeful observations because of the conditions in which the observations were carried out. Observations are not useful if conducted under challenging conditions—either for children or for the early learning teachers.

Involve children and adults in observations

It is beneficial to have children as active participants in observations. Adults determine why the observation is being conducted and then determine the level of involvement of the children. For example, when appropriate, asking probing questions and listening to the children provides insight into what they say and think about their learning, their activities, their experiences, and their interests. Involving children also provides opportunities to discuss their vision for play and learning.

Examine information from varying perspectives

There are many ways to view children's play. Having more than one early learning teacher observe children at the same time provides an opportunity to acquire varying perspectives on the same situation. Think about children playing in the sandbox and three teachers conducting an observation. Most likely there will be aspects of the observations that differ. Through dialogue and reflection, you each gain new insight and understanding into individual children and groups of children.

Recognize what your biases and perceptions are

We all have biases and perceptions. As early learning teachers, it is important to be aware of the biases and perceptions that we bring to the environment. For example, if you determine that you do not like completing observations, this will influence what you see, the way in which you record your findings, and how you use the information gained from your observations. If you find yourself in a compromising position, such as if there is some aspect of a child's behaviour or personality that causes you discomfort, then it is important for you to develop a strategy to manage that bias so that the child is not negatively influenced by the situation. Children deserve the opportunity to play and learn in comfortable environments. Our personal life experiences, culture, and philosophical orientation toward working with children influence our observations.

Think of 3-year-old James. James has had a daily temper tantrum for the past week when his father drops him off at the centre. You observe the father being patient and offering words of comfort to James, yet James gets on the floor, kicks, and screams. You may think to yourself,

This child is "spoiled," and the father should not allow James to get away with this. Once we label the child as "spoiled," we have expressed our bias and reduced our ability to see the child with an objective lens. This has the potential to interfere with being able to see the strengths of the child and understand the needs that would support him in advancing his play.

Listen to the children

Listening to the children helps early learning teachers document useful information about children and their play. It is useful if the observer has the opportunity to record specific quotes from children's play. Read the play episode of Nabil on pages 103–104. Then think about how his direct quotes help provide insight into his knowledge of the use of a cellphone and of business etiquette, evidenced by his comment of "Nice doing business today."

Review documented observations many times to seek meaning

When early learning teachers review observations at different times, important details evolve that lead to making connections about children and their play. Think about 3-year-old Damian. In reviewing a video observation, you notice that he is using red and black play dough. You note that he extracts a piece of play dough from the large play dough ball with the thumb and forefinger on his right hand and then rolls it into a smaller ball. He alternates between the red and the black play dough. After reviewing the video three times, you notice that the more Damian used the play dough, the more efficient he became in the process. For example, instead of making one ball at a time, near the end he divided both the black and the red play dough into pieces. Then, he rolled all of the red play dough into balls and afterward rolled the black balls. This change in process led him to eliminate the movement back and forth from one end of the play dough table to the other. Although we can't determine from this observation whether Damian made the decision to change the process or if it just happened, it would be helpful to pose probing questions to Damian to gather his thought process on the play dough experience. If Damian does not answer your questions, it becomes your role to try to interpret what children's thought processes might be.

Examine children's play patterns and actions

By reviewing observations and documentation, early learning teachers and student teachers gain insight into the ways in which children approach problems and problem solving. For example, when children determine a strategy to figure something out to achieve the desired effect, generally they will proceed with confidence. However, if it does not unfold as they thought it might, there may be a pause or change of directions. This tells us that children have engaged in a different thinking pattern.

Think about Melissa, a 4-year-old child playing with connector blocks. According to your observation, Melissa has spent seven minutes picking up long connector tubes, placing the connectors on them, and trying to make them stay upright. Each time the structure fell, she rotated the connectors. She then stopped working with the blocks and walked away from the area. Melissa went to the block area and then returned. Why do you think Melissa left the area? Why might she have gone to the block area? What might she have gained from going to the block area? When Melissa returned, she tried a couple of new actions. In the end, she added long connector pipes and connectors both lengthwise and crosswise on the bottom portion of her structure. This gave her structure the stability that was needed.

Examine how children co-construct knowledge

We encourage children to play and learn together. As identified in Chapter 2, there are different levels of social play that children participate in. Children may collaborate with one another on a particular play project or several play experiences. Think about Maryellen and Mattie at the sand table. You heard Mattie indicate that she would like to make an underground tunnel between castles. As she began to dig out the sand, she made more of a roadway than a tunnel. Mattie then announced to Maryellen, "It is not working." They tried a couple of ways without success. Then Maryellen suggested they needed something for a base. Maryellen went to the block centre and brought back pipe pieces. They dug a hole, put the pipe in between the castles, and then covered it with sand. Mattie identified that they needed to scoop out the sand at both ends. Together, Mattie and Maryellen co-constructed knowledge that led them to figure out how to build the tunnel between the castles.

Early learning programs that use a **co-construction of knowledge** philosophical orientation will benefit from early learning teachers being participant observers. This allows the early learning teacher to participate in the play through discussions about play ideas, construction of ideas, and listening to the children's thoughts. The adult discovers possible future paths of interests and opportunities for learning.

co-construction of knowledge Refers to the social interactions that occur among children and adults in exploring information about a topic that leads to the creation of shared knowledge.

Examine how children express meaning and representation

One of the purposes of children's play is to help them bring meaning to their world. As you review the observations of Fritz and Gunter in the block centre, you note that both children are building structures. There is no verbal communication between the children as they build their structures. Fritz's structure has three levels to it, while Gunter's building has only one level. When Fritz's structure was complete, he said to Gunter, "Me, my Oma, and Opa live here." Gunter responds by saying, "Me live here, and my Oma and Opa live far away. They need a plane to see me." Later that day, the early learning teacher found out that Fritz, Gunter, and families had spent the weekend together with their grandparents. Gunter's grandparents returned to Germany on Monday. When children are able to express meaning and representation in a visual format, they begin to develop the skills to be able to verbally express their thoughts. Expressing cultural attributes and representations are interrelated to children being able to think about life experiences and bring meaning to their thoughts.

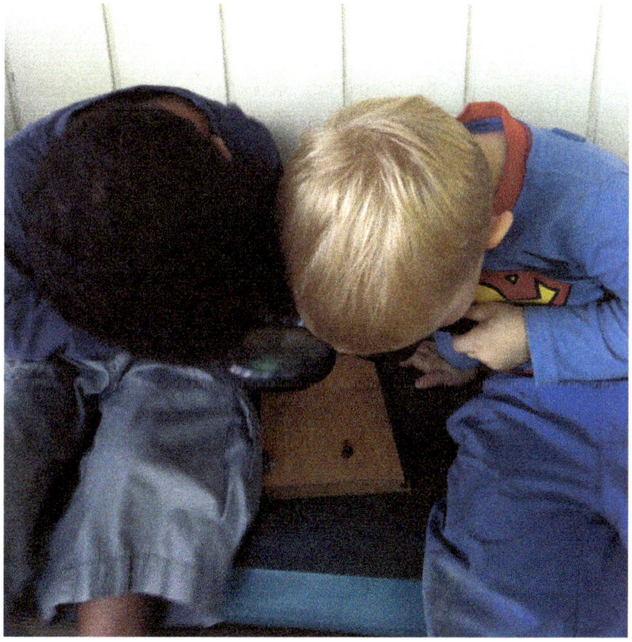

Photo 3.10 Co-constructing a play experience.

Used with Permission of Bora Kim

Examine the observations to determine the level of metacognition the child exhibits

metacognition Refers to having an awareness of our thinking about our thinking as it relates to how we embark on dealing with a problem or a situation. This includes how and what we think about our thinking processes in these situations.

When we think about **metacognition**, we are seeking insight into how children express knowledge about their thoughts, their thinking process, how they approach a task, how they problem solve, and what success is (Lee, Koh, Cai, & Quek, 2012). Shammin is 5 years old. You observe him and his buddy Matthew at the art centre. Shammin says to Matthew, "I don't like drawing faces. It's too hard. I can't get the eyes and the nose right." Matthew says, "I draw a circle, and then I put the nose in the centre of the page." As you review the children's comments, you realize that such a comment reveals that Shammin has evaluated his ability to make faces; he has also brought feelings from a past experience to his present situation. This illustrates how Shammin thinks about his abilities and how he has worked it through to be able to communicate his feelings and the challenges he has with producing a face. You also note that Matthew tries to help Shammin by sharing his process.

Examine children's play and determine if and how it should be documented

Children and early learning teachers benefit from documenting experiences and learning about what children engage in. As you observe children in their play, it is beneficial to determine if the play episode should be documented, and if so, why? What might the benefits be, and what would be the most effective way to document it?

When children or early learning teachers are able to document and share learning, it helps to tell stories of their learning. This is an important strategy that brings meaning and visibility of play to both the child and adults. Most often, documentation and storytelling provide insight into interests and potential direction that will bring forth further wonderment to the child.

Photo 3.11 Early learning teachers and children determine what aspects of their projects and their daily experiences they wish to document.

Used with Permission of Family Space Quinte, Inc.

DOCUMENTATION STRATEGIES

There are many documentation methods used by early learning teachers to gain information about an individual child and groups of children in their play.

Early learning teachers become skilled in using tools, documenting findings or insights, and discussing perspectives with colleagues, children, and families. In Table 3.2,

Table 3.2 Methods of documenting children's play and learning.

Strategy	How the Strategy Informs Practice
Portfolio The purpose of a portfolio is to be an active, living document that assists in planning potential experience centres and learning opportunities for an individual child and groups of children.	A portfolio is a family–child and early learning teacher document that is made up of a collection of observations, creative samples, pictures, anecdotes, recordings, and other artifacts that documents a child's experience while in the early learning centre. The portfolio records an array of experiences and achievements that informs how learning occurs through play. It supports children, early learning teachers, and families in capturing and understanding the child's experience. Early learning teachers and children collectively examine information to determine what learning is best to document and what strategy to use to document the learning episode. These are living documents that children have access to on a daily basis.
Photographs The purpose of photographs is to be able to capture particular moments in time. They support children, families, and early learning teachers in revisiting previous play and learning experiences. They may be incorporated into documentation displays.	Photographs provide a record of a specific action, interests, skills, and developmental levels. Photographs are a useful tool to help children recall experiences, reflect on experiences, and project how new experiences could evolve. Often photographs become valuable parts of stories of learning and may be transferred to a child's portfolio. When children have access to photographs instantaneously, they spontaneously describe activities and explanations about their play. This level of engagement is rich with information about their play and ideas going forward.
Brief Notes The purpose of a brief notation is a beginning strategy used in observation. They are also used to record important information that may be used to trigger other ideas or to examine specific information with children.	Early learning teachers record brief notes that depict an action or experience observed. These brief notes may be discussed with the children and families, included with photos, or placed in folders that are revisited periodically to piece together ideas and ways to add new meaning to children's environments. Early learning teachers may ask children specific questions about what they would like to do in the environment. Brief notes may be used to record this information and then used later to share with the children as part of a plan, do, review, and reflect process.
Video Recordings The purpose of video recordings is to capture a child's activity and actions exhibited during play. These recordings support teachers, children, and families in examining the same data and discussing their perceptions of what they see from various perspectives.	Similar to the portfolio, the video recording is a way to record data that illustrate child's play. It provides insight into the communication process among children and adults. The recordings provide insight into a sequence of events and help to understand attributes that an individual child and groups of children bring to the environment. The video recording offers early learning teachers and families a way to view children during play. Families are able to see how play contributes to development.
Learning Journals The purpose of the learning journal is for children, early learning teachers, and families to be able to record any information about their learning, their feelings, and their reflections. It may be done in word or pictorial format. This is a working, fluid document that may be public or private.	A learning journal is used to explore and record self-discoveries or to generate new ideas. Learning journals are often used to record experiences or events that include reflection and commentary.

 Do I have permission to take photos of or video the children?
If I don't, may I take photos if I don't show the child's face?
Source: Used with Permission of Family Space Quinte, Inc.

 How will I store the pictures or videos of the children? How will I discard of the pictures or vidoes of children?
Source: Used with Permission of Angela Roy

 Is it acceptable to use the photos or videos in other work outside the early learning program?
Source: Used with Permission of Angela Roy

 Do I own the video or photos of the children?
Source: Used with Permission of Angela Roy

Figure 3.7 Considerations made before taking photos or video of children.

we offer examples of documentation strategies. As part of developing your practice, we encourage you to try a number of strategies in order to gain an understanding of different ways and perspectives that help you to acquire information about an individual child and groups of children. Remember, documentation is intended to help you learn about children as you make connections to growth and development, ways of learning, children's interests, knowledge, diversity, curiosity triggers, abilities, and strengths.

Before exploring documentation strategies, many of which recommend the use of photographs or video, it is important to understand the responsibilities of early learning students and teachers when taking photos or videos of children. There are many reasons why families may not wish for their children to be photographed or videotaped. For example, in custody or abuse situations, children's lives may be compromised if the videos or photographs are released to the wrong people. Other families may want to control where and how documentation is used. Early learning teachers and student teachers honour these perspectives. In Figure 3.7, we outline core questions that you may wish to seek answers to before any photographs or video are captured.

Documentation is much richer when there is active involvement with the children rather than when teachers take on the role of directing children's play. When children and early learning teachers are partners in the play environment, there is less emphasis on early learning teachers viewing the child from a behavioural perspective or on comparing one child to another. Using a variety of documenting strategies is an inclusive practice that allows adults to look at situations and each child from multiple perspectives. This creates rich data that will help plan for children's experiences and our facilitation strategies with children.

Where Does Documentation Occur?

Documentation occurs in a variety of spaces that children use in their play. Each space provides different insights into children's play and strengths.

To acquire an understanding of the whole child, early learning teachers are encouraged to complete observations and documentation in both the indoor and the outdoor environments. Early learning teachers gain different information about the child *and* with the child, in the two settings. Although many observations and documentations are conducted indoors, we advocate that early learning teachers give equal consideration to both environments, as they are both important for children's development. There are many reasons to observe children during their outdoor play experiences, including the following:

- Outdoor play provides an opportunity to observe the physical literacy skills of children. Skills such as jumping, running, and climbing are less likely to be allowed indoors. This is an authentic environment for such activities where accurate observations may occur (Berg, 2015; Woolley & Lowe, 2013).
- The outdoor play environment allows children to exhibit different strengths or face new challenges from those observed indoors (Dietze & Kashin, 2016).
- Conducting observations outdoors communicates to colleagues and families the need for and the value and benefits of outdoor play to a child's development (Land & Danis, 2016).
- Children's outdoor play is different from indoor play. New interests are discovered in outdoor play (Li, Hestenes & Wang, 2016).
- Outdoor play contributes to experiences that support the child's overall developmental domains (Acar, 2014; Dietze & Kashin, 2016).

As we continue to support children in developing healthy, active lifestyles, the need for children to have access to and opportunities for outdoor play will only increase. Observing children outdoors is crucial to understanding their play interests and the types of materials and environments that support their exploration and discovery.

STOP ... THINK ... DISCUSS ... REFLECT

How might observations and documentation outdoors differ from that indoors? Do you think you get better information about a child from observing their play indoors or outdoors? What are the challenges of observing and documenting children's play outdoors? Why? How might the documentation process differ outdoors in the winter months compared to in the summer months? Why? Is the process different from that used in the spring? Why or why not?

DISCOVERING AND MAKING MEANING OF CHILDREN'S PLAY

There are a number of ways to get to know and understand children. It is a process that develops with time, experience, and guidance. The information outlined in Table 3.3 is intended to provide you with a starting point for ways to connect with children and discover information about them and their play.

STOP ... THINK ... DISCUSS ... REFLECT

Do you think that it is best to always plan what you are going to observe and document? Why or why not? What might you consider doing if you see a child engaging in a play experience that you have not seen before but do not have access to a camera to capture the experience? How do you gather the information and move it to a sharing process?

Table 3.3 A process for discovering information and understanding children and their play.

Preparation. What do I already know about this child? Is there specific information that I would like to try to discover about the child? What information is missing that would help me understand the child in more depth? How might I collaborate with the children, colleagues, and families to acquire the information?

The early learning teacher determines what information is known about the child and what may be helpful to understand the child more fully.

Selecting a strategy for gathering information. What strategies and resources are available that would help me capture the information that I seek? Why would one process be used over another?

The early learning teacher examines the various strategies available to determine which one is most efficient relative to the information being sought. Pertinent materials are prepared.

Gathering information. How will I gather the information? Where will I gather the information? What role will I play? What role will the children play? Is there a role for colleagues? If so, what is that role? How will I record the information?

The early learning teacher determines what strategy and resources to use to gather information about a child or children in their play. The strategy should support the type of information being sought.

Review of information. What can I glean from the information gathered? What new meaning have I acquired? How do my perceptions align or differ from my colleagues and the children? What connections can I make to my previous understanding of the child? What did I notice about the child that I have not previously noted? What did the child learn through play? How do I share the information with the children and families? What information from this process is valuable to communicate to the child, other teachers, and families? What is the best way to do so?

The early learning teacher examines the new perceptions and meaning acquired and discusses it with experienced practitioners to collectively interpret the data in terms of making connections, seeing themes, and examining gaps. Discussions assist in developing a program that is supportive of a child or group of children's needs and interests.

Sharing learning. What new meaning have I gained? How will it inform and guide my practice? What questions may help me clarify information with the child? What are some of the questions that I may seek to answer in my reflective process? Are there aspects of my information that I would like to move to story format for the child or with the child? What core questions may an experienced early learning teacher help me clarify? How do I isolate the new meaning or information gained that will help me in determining the types of experiences to provide an individual child and groups of children? How do I share the information with the various audiences?

The early learning teacher uses the results of the data analysis to guide one's practice, and in working with the child to determine the types of experiences that will support the child in being stretched just beyond their knowledge and skill level.

Reflective practice. How do I use the information gained to support the child or groups of children? How do I know if the new types of experiences that I wish to offer a child or children support their learning? How do I know that my perceptions are correct? Why do I feel that I am missing some aspect of information that would help me understand a particular child better? Why do I feel a disconnect? How does this new information and meaning developed inform my practice? What might I do differently next time?

The early learning teacher continues to seek out information that will answer questions and support a child or group of children. The teacher continuously seeks information and answers from the children, colleagues, families, and the environment to ensure that expanded play experiences contribute to new play episodes, learning, and development.

THE TYPES OF DISCOVERIES MADE THROUGH WATCHING, LISTENING, AND DISCUSSING PLAY WITH CHILDREN

Children are influenced by people, places, experiences, and environments. By watching, listening, and discussing play, early learning teachers may make many discoveries about a child. When early learning teachers examine play episodes from the perspective of a child's life experience, developmental milestones, and the environment, as outlined in Figure 3.8, new insight into the child—what they know, what their interests are, what is important to them, and their ways of knowing—is gained.

Figure 3.8 Life experiences, developmental milestones, and the environment influence children's learning and ways of knowing.

Read the play episode below. As you do, think about the type of information you can gain from observing such a play episode.

Nabil is an only child. His parents own a successful plumbing store. Nabil often plays "business" in the dramatic centre. Today Nabil comes to the dramatic centre with his briefcase and cellphone and sits down at the table that he is using as his desk. He announces to Mohammed, "We need to get the plumbing order in by noon today." Next, he goes into the briefcase and brings out a pad of paper. He reaches for his cellphone. As he begins to play with the pretend cellphone, his briefcase begins to slip off the table. He says to Mohammed, "Help!" As he catches the briefcase with his knee and hand, he turns to Mohammad and says, "That was close." After he rearranges the placement of the briefcase, he picks up the cellphone again. He presses numbers and then places the phone to his ear. He begins talking. Then he turns to Mohammad and appears to ask a question. The conversation between Mohammad and the person that Nabil is speaking with on the pretend phone is not audible to the early learning teacher. Mohammad sits at the chair with a pad of paper and crayon. Each time Nabil says something to him, there is movement of the crayon on the paper. As Nabil concludes the conversation, he says, "Nice doing business today."

He sets the phone down and turns to Mohammad: "Let's get some hoses, wrenches, and tape for our truck." Then, the two boys go to the block centre and begin using the large van trucks that have been placed in the area.

When early learning teachers observe play episodes such as that of Nabil and Mohammed, many important discoveries can be made. For example, reread the play episode and then think about the following questions.

Developmental Milestones

- What does Nabil learn as he plays?
- How does Nabil's play support his social, cognitive, and emotional development?
- What do we know about Mohammed from this play episode?
- Why might this play episode be important to Nabil and to Mohammed?

Life Experience

- What life experiences does Nabil bring to this play episode?
- How might Nabil's play be different from other children in his group?
- What life experience insight can be gained about Nabil and Mohammed from observing their play?
- What is the value of sharing this play episode with Nabil's parents?
- How can Nabil's parents help early learning practitioners gain information about their child?
- What learning is evident?
- How are role models affecting the play?

Environment

- How does this play setting contribute to Nabil's play?
- How can this setting further support Nabil's play? Why is it important to do so?
- How might additional material support the play for Nabil and Mohammad?
- What learning options could be extended?

Facilitating Play

- What strategies would be best to facilitate opportunities for Nabil and Mohammad to extend the play?
- How might early learning practitioners support Nabil's interests in the business play role?
- How might Mohammad's role change?
- How might the early learning practitioner engage in the play to extend it further?

Documenting Play

- How could you document this play?
- How might you get the children involved in documenting this play?
- What key elements of learning might you wish to explore with the children and document?
- How might the documentation inform practice?

All of these questions provide us with rich information that can help us to understand children and provide us with the impetus for the framework for program planning. When children participate in programs where a thorough examination of their play has not been conducted, potential play opportunities are missed (Mardell et al., 2016). Early learning teachers and children learn about play by examining what it is and what it could be.

TERMS THAT INFLUENCE EARLY LEARNING PLAY ENVIRONMENTS

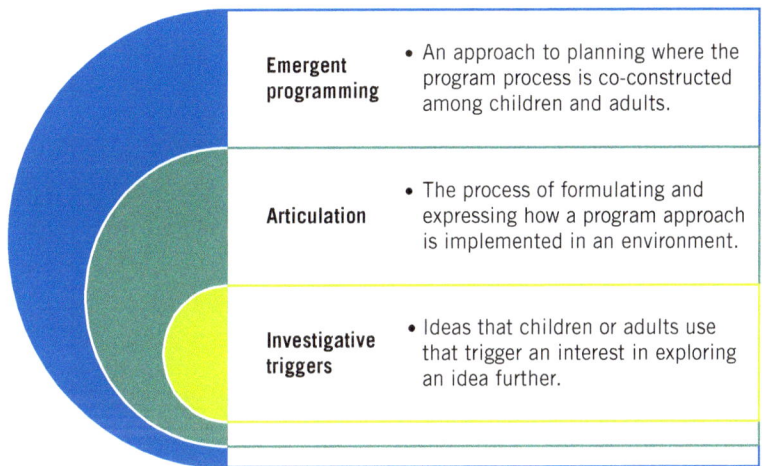

- **Emergent programming**: An approach to planning where the program process is co-constructed among children and adults.
- **Articulation**: The process of formulating and expressing how a program approach is implemented in an environment.
- **Investigative triggers**: Ideas that children or adults use that trigger an interest in exploring an idea further.

SUMMARY

Chapter Preview

- Play is the vehicle for children's learning.
- Observations, documentation, interpretations, and reflections support early learning teachers in examining children's play and learning.

Children and Learning through Play

- Playful learning focuses on children being in environments where they experience delight, wonder, and choice.
- Early learning teachers require knowledge about the relationship of child development to play, observations of play, and documentation of play as they relate to children's play experiences and environments.

Observation, Documentation, and Interpretation: A Twenty-First-Century Approach

- Observations were initially implemented to figure out the "true needs" of children and to determine the content of the curriculum.

- Observation is a systematic process used to listen to and watch children in their play. Early learning teachers conduct observations to gain insight into how children play, their thinking processes, and ways in which they try to make sense of their experiences and the world.
- When early learning teachers embed documentation into their practice, their pedagogy and curriculum decisions are based on the real experiences of children.
- Documentation is a process that encompasses what is to be reflected on, discussion points, and action that is generated from the documentation. A reflective process involves strategies used to examine, see, reflect, and understand a child's play and what the child is capable of.
- Pedagogical documentation without interpretation is considered a record. Reflection and analyzing interpretations influence moving indoor and outdoor play programming forward in ways that reflect meaningful curriculum.
- Reflective practice is used by early learning teachers to gain a sense of understanding the children from a holistic perspective rather than a skills deficits perspective.

Examining the Difference between Child Observation and Pedagogical Documentation

- Observations focus on one aspect of a child's play to gain insight into the developmental phase and interests.
- Pedagogical documentation focuses on the process of learning and interconnectedness between children's ideas, the environment, partners in play, and the play experiences. It includes interpretations and reflections of early learning teachers, children, and families.

Authentic Assessment

- Authentic assessment is a process that early learning teachers establish with children and families to engage in ongoing observation, documentation, interpretation, and reflection of what they are seeing, hearing, and understanding about children, their play, and the environment.

Ways of Acquiring Information to Support Student Practitioners Understanding the Whole Child

- There are many ways to gain information about children. These include organizing observation tools, involving children and adults in observations, examining information from varying perspectives, developing purposeful observations, and recognizing biases and perceptions. Listening to the children, reviewing observations to seek meaning, examining children's play patterns, examining how children co-construct knowledge, examining how children express meaning, determining how children exhibit metacognition, and determining how and what should be documented provide valuable insights about a child and groups of children for early learning practitioners.

Documentation Strategies

- Common documentation strategies include portfolio, photographs, brief notes, videotaping, and learning journals. Each strategy has its strengths, depending on the purpose of the documentation.

Where Does Documentation Occur?

- Documentation occurs in a variety of spaces that children use in their play.
- Outdoor play provides early learning teachers with uniquely different information about the child than what is gained from indoor play observations and documentation.

The Types of Discoveries Made through Watching, Listening, and Discussing Play with Children

- Early learning teachers make many discoveries about children and the environment by becoming familiar with the child's life experiences. Formulating questions and exploring the answers to them provides rich information about a child's developmental milestones, life experiences, environment, and ways to facilitate play.

REVIEW QUESTIONS

1. Describe what is meant by children requiring environments where adults view play as a kaleidoscope.
2. Describe the evolution of child observation and discuss why we are at the crossroads of redefining observation processes.
3. Explain the similarities and differences between observation and pedagogical documentation. Do early learning teachers benefit from knowing the principles of observation to engage in pedagogical documentation? Why or why not?
4. Why is it important for early learning teachers to acquire information about children in various ways? What are the dangers if only one or two methods are used? What are the benefits for early learning teachers in using one or two methods? Why?
5. There is a variety of observation and documentation tools available. How do early learning teachers determine which tool to use at any given time?
6. Why are observations and documentation processes carried out in both the indoor and the outdoor environments? What types of information might you gain from outdoors that would not be evident in an indoor environment?
7. Why might early learning teachers benefit from establishing a systematic process for discovering information and understanding children and their play? How does a process help student teachers focus on gathering useful data?
8. How do life experiences, developmental milestones, and the environment influence children's learning and ways of knowing? Why do early learning teachers consider these elements, examine play episodes, and then re-examine them?

MAKING CONNECTIONS

Theory to Practice

1. If you were working in an early learning environment and interested in exploring how observations and pedagogical documentation differ, what are the types of questions you would ask of your host teacher or field mentor? What do you envision the differences will look like? Is there

a difference in the role children play during observations and pedagogical documentation? If so, what are the differences? We outlined a play episode of Nabil and Mohammad. What information did you gain from that episode about each of the children? How would you prepare for their upcoming play experiences based on that episode? How would you involve parents? What learning story would you wish to tell? How would you get the children involved?

2. If you were asked to document a play episode in the dramatic centre for three days, what tools and process would you use? Why? Describe in detail.
3. Throughout this chapter, many questions have been posed for the early learning teacher to consider. How do such questions guide early learning teachers in their practice? Using the play episode of Nabil and Mohammad, answer the questions there, and then record your new learning about the children. You may want to use a reflective practice journal to write down your answers.

DIGITAL PORTFOLIO ENTRIES

Potential portfolio entries for your digital portfolio could include:

- When I think about getting families and children involved in documentation, I wonder about . . .
- As a student early learning teacher, I wonder what happens to children if I misinterpret my observations. How might families feel?
- I wonder how I will feel if I get to a centre that is focused on comparing one child's talents to another.
- I feel I need to learn more about observations, documentation, interpretations, reflections, and authentic assessment because . . .

CURIOUS?

Add the words *observation and documentation* to your search engine to find out more about how early learning teachers use the information in their practice.

Add the words *Reggio Emilia–inspired programs* to your search engine to learn more about how documentation is used in those programs.

CHAPTER 4
Outdoor and Nature Play: Unscripted and Unstructured

Rawpixel.com/Shutterstock

> "Must we always teach our children with books? Let them look at the mountains and the stars above. Let them look at the beauty of the waters and the trees and the flowers on earth. They will then begin to think, and to think is the beginning of real education."
>
> —David Polis

LEARNING OUTCOMES

After exploring this chapter you should be able to:

- Discuss three reasons why children living in Canada today may have limited outdoor play experiences.
- Explain why early learning teachers examine the historical perspectives on outdoor play, such as Froebel's perspective, to influence outdoor play today.
- Explain why and how outdoor play is important to children's development, health, and wellness.
- Explain how children's adult role models influence their outdoor play experience.
- Discuss what challenging, risky, and adventurous play and their benefits to children's problem solving, socialization, and critical thinking skills mean.
- Explain the types of considerations that early learning teachers may consider when examining outdoor play space for infants, toddlers, preschoolers, and school-aged children.
- Describe what is meant by loose parts and how they influence outdoor play.
- Give examples of the types of roles early learning teachers have in planning and implementing outdoor play.

Sharing Stories of Practice

When I became a student in an early childhood education diploma course, I was determined that I was going to become skillful in programming. I practised creating activities for children that could be implemented indoors. I felt that during outdoor play early learning teachers used the time to have a coffee break while the children "run off their energy." With their energies depleted, the children would settle down indoors to focus on the important learning parts of their program. During my first placement, I always volunteered to clean up or set up for new activities while the children were outdoors. I hated the thought of having to go outdoors. I didn't have the right clothes. More importantly, I considered this important work because I was supporting children's learning by preparing the indoor environment for their return.

During my second placement, I was assigned to an early learning program where the children had at least four hours of outdoor play each day. When I found this out, I dreaded starting this placement! Knowing that I had to complete the practicum, I reluctantly continued. After the first day of observing the staff and children in the outdoor environment, I knew I had to change my approach and develop a more positive outlook. I began to reflect on my attitude about outdoor play, and I engaged in some self-talk, as I needed to develop some coping strategies. Eight weeks was a long placement! At first, I kept thinking that supervising outdoor play was not what I had envisioned when I started in early childhood education.

Now, I can tell you it was the best placement that I had because I began to see the merit of outdoor play for children and staff. Over time, I recognized the different attitudes and abilities that children exhibit when they are playing outdoors. I noticed in my observations that children were more spontaneous and energized outdoors than they were indoors. I enjoyed the children's laughter, and I realized there was very little fighting—rather, children played together. I also began to appreciate that there were fewer rules for the children to remember—they could run, or hop, or glide. They could climb, jump, and squeal with excitement; they could dig in the dirt; they could explore the puddles; and they could use blocks, tricycles, wagons, books, boards, and pipes to create play options. Their play was rich with creativity, language, physical activity, and partnership. They seemed busy and content.

I learned that outdoor play is influenced by the attitudes of early learning teachers and the space that is available to children. When early learning teachers embrace outdoor play, they listen to the children, offer programming that supports the play interests and options of the children, and document play episodes that contribute to children reflecting on their play, discussing their play, and imagining how to expand the play. Developing an effective outdoor play experience is as challenging as planning for the indoor portion of the program. The rewards are significant. And yes, I learned that outdoor play is not a time for early learning teachers to take a step back and have a coffee break. It is a time to observe, facilitate, discuss, and play with the children.

Amaz, ECE graduate, 2017

CHAPTER PREVIEW

As you begin to review this chapter, you may be thinking about when you grew up playing with mud and rocks at the brook or climbing up to a treehouse. You may reflect on the amount of time you spent being outdoors. It may have been for most of the day, with some of that time being supervised, while other times were unsupervised in the neighbourhood with groups of children. Or, it could have been in your backyard where you played by yourself and with your siblings for hours. For some of you, outdoor play may have taken place in parks with supervision or while you attended an early learning program. Do you envision that children today have those same types of experiences? Why or why not? Why and how might children's experiences today differ from those 15 years ago and 30 years ago?

Many children living in Canada who participate in early learning programs today have limited outdoor play opportunities or experiences (Carsley et al., 2017). This, combined with the reduction of unstructured outdoor playtime, changes the scope and breadth of children's play experiences (Carsley et al., 2017). These changes have an influence on their development. For example, since World War II, a large percentage of our population has settled in urban areas. In many parts of Canada, urban areas offer limited access to natural outdoor play spaces for children. The increased access to technology and the concern for the security and safety of children have reduced the freedom of play extended to children (Beets et al., 2014). Many kindergarten and school-aged children are in school settings that are removing outdoor recess for gym activities or reducing the amount of time allocated for outdoor play in favour of more academic experiences (Sobel & Larimore, 2016). As well, many before and after school programs do not have an outdoor play component or have limited time requirements (Beets et al., 2014).

It is estimated that 70 percent of 3- to 4-year-olds across Canada obtain at least 180 minutes of physical activity daily. However, only 7 percent of 5- to 11-year-olds living in Canada meet the recommended guidelines of 60 minutes of moderate to vigorous activity daily (ParticipACTION, 2015). On average, young children under 5 years of age spend less than 10 hours per week playing outdoors, versus 20 to 30 hours per week in sedentary activities. This lack of active play negatively affects children's health, wellness, and development (Berg, 2015; Chiao, Li, & Seligman, 2016). As identified in Chapter 1, there has been an increase in type 2 diabetes and heart disease among children. These health and lifestyle issues follow children into their adulthood.

At the same time, we have growing numbers of children who are involved in structured activities such as swimming and gymnastics. Although these activities are beneficial, when children have a significant amount of structured time, it reduces their opportunities to participate in open-ended, self-initiated **free play**. Children require time and the freedom to participate in play, as this contributes to them developing **tinkering** skills, problem-solving options, and **critical thinking skills**. These are directly related to the development of self-esteem, self-confidence and competence and self-regulation skills (Berg, 2015; Li, Hestenes & Wang, 2016).

Expanding children's access to and opportunities for outdoor play is essential. This requires early learning teachers to acquire knowledge about and skills in planning for and facilitating outdoor play programming. Early learning teachers who expand their knowledge about outdoor play increase their comfort levels about its importance, and they will expand their strategies for facilitating quality outdoor play options.

This chapter focuses on the various elements of outdoor play, including ways to facilitate outdoor play so that children are offered a wide spectrum of experiences to support their identified interests, as well as their cognitive, social, emotional, and physical development.

As you review this chapter, think about Johah, a 3-year-old child, wanting to make a structure using plywood pieces, long boards, and cedar blocks in the outdoor play area. Think about why this outdoor play experience may be important to him. Why does Johah benefit from the freedom to build his structure outdoors? What type of learning might Johah engage in from a math and science perspective? How? Would Johah use different types of language outdoors than indoors? How might building structures be different from constructing them indoors? How might the weather influence the play experience? Why? These are all valuable questions that we hope you will gain insight into as you explore this chapter.

free play Refers to child-directed play that is intrinsically motivated, with a goal that may not have external rules or structure (Lawson Foundation, 2017).

tinkering Active engagement and manipulation with materials or experiences that children create to figure out ideas and answers to questions (Dietze, 2016).

critical thinking skills Refers to a process children use to figure things out by conceptualizing ideas, applying ideas into action, and evaluating results or information gathered from the experience or the observation.

THE COMPLEXITIES OF OUTDOOR PLAY AND EARLY LEARNING PROGRAMS

Children's play is complex. Outdoor play adds additional complexity to early learning programs because of the space, materials, and environmental attributes. As research continues to evolve, consistent themes outline the benefits of outdoor play to children's wellness and development. Early learning teachers and students are being encouraged to examine its complexity and determine how outdoor play helps children learn new perspectives and understand the basis of their experimentation. As well, early learning teachers note how outdoor play contributes to children developing a meaningful relationship with and respect for their peers, adults, and the environment.

Although early learning teachers may have a desire to expand the scope of outdoor play opportunities for children, many societal issues contribute to access to outdoor play actually being reduced. Family values and cultural beliefs are shifting toward the promotion of academic preparedness (Belknap & Hazler, 2014; Smirnova & Riabkova, 2016). The excessive use of TV and technology (Levin, 2015) and the feeling of the need to protect children in their neighbourhoods (Belknap & Hazler, 2014) are also contributing to the reduction of children's access to outdoor play.

Shifting the current perspectives and discourse on outdoor play requires early learning teachers and students to discuss how as a society we have allowed children's access and outdoor play opportunities to be eroded, despite it being a right of children. As outlined in Figure 4.1, Dietze and Kashin (2017) identified that early learning teachers

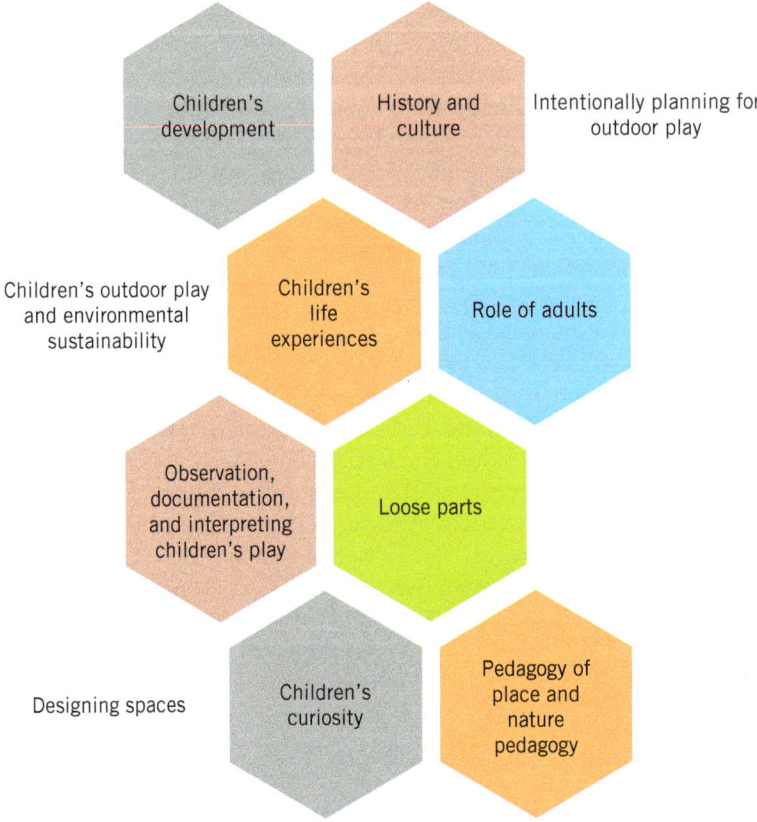

Figure 4.1 The depth and breadth of outdoor play.

and students benefit from exploring the depth and breadth of outdoor play from a variety of perspectives. It is not as simple as having the children "go outdoors to play." We draw upon the historical perspectives of outdoor play to support how lessons learned from history, previous research, ideologies, and current research can influence positive practices today.

To fully understand the complexities of outdoor play, we provide a brief introduction on its many aspects. We encourage early learning teachers to continue researching and exploring outdoor play from both a child's perspective and the role of the adult.

HISTORICAL PERSPECTIVE ON OUTDOOR PLAY

As identified in the previous chapters, theorists including Piaget, Montessori, Dewey, Rousseau, and Froebel have long recognized the value of play and outdoor play. For example, Froebel believed that children require time to play in gardens. He suggested that outdoor play brings a depth and breadth to learning that is not emulated in other settings. For Froebel, outdoor play is essential for the child's whole development, not just physical development (Berg, 2015).

Froebel determined that outdoor play is a place where children find natural places to play—this includes trees and tree trunks for climbing or for imaginative play, gardens for scientific concepts such as germination, water sources such as brooks, and areas of grass for games. Froebel advocated for outdoor play environments to have natural elements and free-flowing materials (Solly, 2015).

In the 1880s, piles of sand were placed in public parks in Berlin, Germany. This was the beginning of the Sandgarten (sand garden) movement. By 1897, sand play became a valuable part of childhood. G. Stanley Hall noted that sand play benefited young children and school-aged children, from both a developmental and a psychological perspective (Lane, 2014).

Photo 4.1 The power of sand play.

Used with Permission of Angela Roy

Photo 4.2 Materials for dramatic play.
Used with Permission of Family Space Quinte, Inc.

In the early 1900s, many early childhood programs across North America began to recognize the importance of outdoor play. Froebel's outdoor play blueprint became the standard model that programs worked to achieve. Over time, educators advocated for additional open-ended props and play experiences to be incorporated into the child's outdoor play experience (Bruce, 2012). These included items such as

- Carts, wagons, playhouses, and related materials for dramatic play.
- Woodworking.
- Cardboard boxes.
- Balls, ladders, and sand piles (Bruce, 2012).

As nursery schools evolved in the 1920s, the importance of outdoor play in programs was further expanded (Frost, 1992). Similar to Froebel and the kindergarten movement, the nursery school movement emphasized the relationship of outdoor play to child development. Nursery school programs known for their quality ensured that there were natural grassy areas, places for dramatic play, trees, contact with animals, and commercially prepared climbing and play apparatus available. Frost (1992) identified that "the total array of materials and certain program practices were impressive" (p. 118) for that time in history.

In the late 1940s and early 1950s, nursery schools and kindergartens began to pave areas for wheeled toys. Shelters were added for use in times of inclement weather. At the same time, safety issues became a focus, leading programs to add soft surfaces under equipment, restricting the height of climbing apparatus, and offering a variety of soft and hard play surfaces (Johnson, Christie, & Wardle, 2005).

Until the early 1950s, playground equipment was generally made from steel, iron, or wood. The equipment included swings, rope swings, sliding surfaces, teeter-totters, and monkey bars. Most equipment was set in concrete or asphalt, with no other ground cover. At the same time, health care professionals began recording data on children's playground injuries. This led to some cities and municipalities examining the conditions of their playgrounds. This triggered new playground designs across North America (Moore, 2006).

In the 1960s, manufacturers devised new features in playground equipment. During this period, known as the "novelty era," play structures were created to exhibit various fantasy characters, animals, or related societal experiences such as nautical and rocket themes. Swings, slides, and climbers remained popular. From a manufacturing perspective, the look of the structure became more important than the child development features or the versatility for play (Moore, 2006).

During the 1970s and 1980s, there was a resurgence of wooden play equipment. The structures combined physical play features by incorporating swivel swings, tires, slides, and climbing apparatuses with dramatic play areas by adding hiding places and shapes to the architecture, such as castles and ships. The structure, combined with sand piles, tricycle paths, and space for materials with **loose parts**, became the standard. These play works were intended to provide rich play experiences for children (Moore, 2006).

As outlined by Parachute (2017), a Canadian organization dedicated to preventing injuries and saving lives, falls are the leading cause of injury-related deaths and hospitalizations in Canada. For children between the ages of 0 and 6, falling is part of their development as they learn to walk, climb, run, and jump. Despite its importance, the latest statistics identified that "nearly 5000 children from birth to 9 years were admitted to a hospital and over 165,000 visited an emergency department as a result of a fall" (Parachute, 2017, p. 1). The majority of falls by children between the ages of 5 and 9 years of age occur at playgrounds. The most common medical diagnoses are fractures, followed by soft-tissue injuries and lacerations.

loose parts A term coined by architect Simon Nicholson (1971), described as natural or synthetic materials or objects that children have access to and that support them in engaging in creativity and imagination in their play.

CURIOUS?

Add the words *Parachute Preventing Injuries – Saving Lives* to your search engine to find out more information about childhood injuries across Canada.

In the early 1990s, the first set of playground safety standards was developed by the Canadian Standards Association (CSA). These standards are known as CAN/CSA-Z614-07. The nationally recognized standards are voluntary guidelines that provide detailed information about items such as materials, installation, equipment, surfacing, and specifications for different types of equipment (Canadian Standards Association, 2014). The standards are continuously updated and are applied to public park playgrounds, school grounds, and early childhood learning centres. Some provinces, such as Ontario, require early learning and child-care centres to meet the CSA standards before an operating licence is issued (Ontario Ministry of Education, 2014).

Table 4.1 provides an overview of the breadth of the information and standards for play spaces as outlined by the CSA. Further information on the CSA standards is found in the final section of the chapter. In addition to being aware of CSA standards,

Photo 4.3 Public parks.
Used with Permission of Beverlie Dietze

early learning teachers benefit from checking their provincial or territorial guidelines to determine the recommended outdoor play time required daily, the minimum types and standards of the equipment for outdoor play, and the maintenance regime required for equipment and outside play spaces.

Add the words *CSA standards* to your search engine to obtain more information on the standards that are recommended for outdoor play equipment.

Search for outdoor play standards for your province or territory to find out information on specific guidelines for outdoor play requirements.

Table 4.1 Aspects of CSA guidelines.

Materials and specifications for play equipment
Playground installation
Surfacing for under play areas
Play space layout
Maintenance
Guidelines for including water features in children's play spaces
Making play spaces more accessible to children with special needs

Photo 4.4 Movable and flexible materials offer variety to play.
Used with Permission of Bora Kim

In the early 2000s, many public parks across Canada had simplistic climbing apparatus with appropriate ground surfacing installed that may or may not have included teeter-totters. Now, as many early learning programs focus on increasing opportunities to expand outdoor play, they are replacing stationary climbers with natural materials such as tree stumps, logs, boards, trees, rocks, and related loose parts (Dietze & Kim, 2014). These changes are positively influencing the types of outdoor play experiences children are engaging in (Acar, 2013).

OUTDOOR PLAY FOR TODAY AND TOMORROW

When the environment is rich with opportunity and stimulating, children find outdoor play fascinating. The more open-ended experiences that children engage in, the richer the opportunity for diverse development and learning is (Acar, 2013). Early learning teachers who wish to use the outdoor play environment as a place for children to muck about and discover new ideas and connections with the place, space, and people view outdoor play through a new lens, seeing it as an extraordinary opportunity for children to embrace life and learning (Dietze & Kashin, 2016). Outdoor play is critical to the development of healthy children (ParticipACTION, 2015). The next generation of early learning teachers and student teachers will influence how outdoor play becomes embedded in the lives of children.

THE IMPORTANCE OF OUTDOOR PLAY TO CHILD DEVELOPMENT

Outdoor play has many benefits to children's social, emotional, physical, spiritual, and cognitive development (Berg, 2015; Li et al., 2014). For example, through outdoor play, children enhance skills such as exploring, risk-taking, language development, social competence, fine and gross motor development, creativity, imagination, problem solving, and thinking skills, all of which are connected to later academic skills (Shanker, 2016). Outdoor play enriches children's language and is often a venue where they use a different vocabulary from the indoor setting. Children learn about their natural environment (Mardell et al., 2016). Outdoor play provides a backdrop for formulating informal networks, exploring cultural identity, and building learning communities (Sobel & Larimore, 2016). Think about how outdoor play contributes to children's desire to explore, wonder, and embrace discovery and learning. What kinds of outdoor play experiences would contribute to children learning about shape identification, patterning, one-to-one correspondence, number sense, sequencing of events, and knowledge of prepositions. How are emotional skills enhanced through the outdoor play?

The Association of Canadian Deans of Education (2016) has developed principles to guide early learning teachers in programming and environmental considerations. They reinforce the importance of adults focusing on the "whole child." Adults have an ethical responsibility to foster transformative and supportive environments that contribute to the well-being of children. Rich outdoor play experiences contribute to each of the developmental domains (Tremblay et al., 2015).

Outdoor play is a natural place for children to make connections with peers and adults (Ontario Ministry of Education, 2014) and to learn from one another. Early learning teachers plan for and assess outdoor play space to ensure that all children have equal access to an array of play experiences (Dietze, 2013). It is not acceptable for children or family members with disabilities to be segregated at any time, especially during outdoor play (Dietze, 2013). Outdoor play is for all children and should be accessible to all children. Early learning teachers and student teachers are encouraged to view outdoor play spaces as inclusive places for all children. "Instead of highlighting differences between children in a negative way, a good outdoor play environment can absorb and support diverse play behaviours. Inclusive environments are those in which it is possible to play in varied ways that … can accommodate children's different ways of being and expressing themselves" (Casey, 2011). Without equal access to outdoor play, children may be at a disadvantage in terms of developing a number of core skills, including peer play and communication and teamwork (Smirnova & Riabkova, 2016).

Outdoor play is clearly linked to child development (ParticipACTION, 2015). Figure 4.2 provides a sampling of the skills children gain from outdoor play (Banning & Sullivan, 2011; Shanker, 2016; Sobel & Larimore, 2016). Further discussion of the relationship of outdoor play to children's development follows.

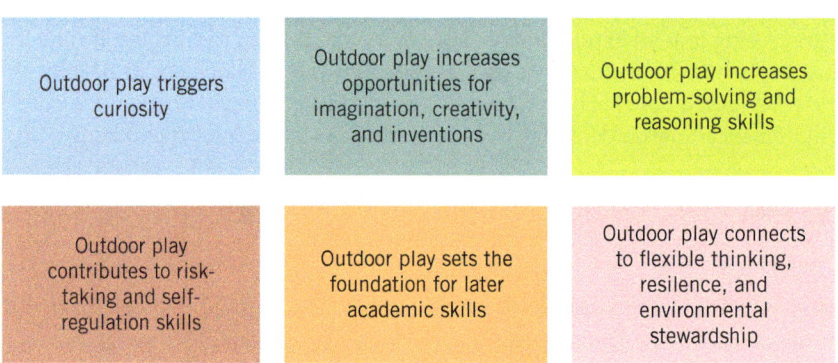

Figure 4.2 Skills children gain from outdoor play.

Cognitive Development

Studies indicate that children who actively participate in play, including outdoor play, are advanced in cognitive development, score higher on tests of imagination and creativity, and have an enhanced ability to think inventively (Shanker, 2016; Sobel & Larimore, 2016). These findings are aligned with Piaget's (1962) perspective that play is vital to cognitive development. Through outdoor play, children practise skills that they have observed and acquired in nonplay situations. Play episodes allow children to assimilate the information that they gather and then, by using it in play, make sense of it.

Photo 4.5 Outdoor play and child development are closely linked.
Used with Permission of Angela Roy

Aimie, who is 4 years old, and her family have just experienced the death of their pet cat named Mussie. Today, when Aimie entered the outdoor play area, she began playing a game she called "Kitty Kitty." This play had Aimie walking on her hands and knees. She moved toward children and adults, meowing. She tried to jump up on children's laps. She attempted to curl up and have a catnap. She announced to the children and the early learning teachers: "I'm dead." Aimie repeated this play daily for more than a week. Then, as quickly as the play idea began, it was replaced by an intense interest in butterflies that she observed in the garden. Aimie needed the time, the support of her early learning teachers, and the play experience to be able to work through the loss of her pet. This type of cognitive problem solving contributes to children developing **executive functioning** (Magar, Phillips, & Hosie, 2008; Shanker, 2016). Children create new knowledge that is then transferable to other lived experiences (Zamani, 2012). These play episodes further support children in learning how to negotiate with peers and advance their understanding of scientific concepts such as life cycles (Flannigan, 2015).

executive functioning Refers to the mental processes children use in planning, focusing on ideas, filtering distractions, and controlling impulses.

CURIOUS?

Add the words *executive functioning* to your search engine to obtain more information on why executive functioning is important for children's development.

Social Development

Smilansky (1968) outlined in her seminal work that play helps children to develop socially. Generally, children's play becomes more social as children get older. For example, 3-year-old children may play together in groups of two or three. By the time they become school-aged, their play groups may expand to five or more children playing together. When outdoor environments are rich with sociodramatic play opportunities (dramatic play that involves more than one player), their social skills—including cooperation, negotiation, sharing, problem solving, self-regulation, and appreciation of another's play efforts—are enhanced (Gleave & Cole-Hamilton, 2012). Children who have access to quality outdoor play settings develop observation skills and the ability to see things and situations "through others' eyes. They develop ways of sharing, helping, cooperating, and empathizing" (Flannigan, 2015). These become lifelong skills.

Generally, there is less structure during the outdoor play portion of the program than what is experienced indoors (Dietze & Kashin, 2017). Early learning teachers support and encourage children in developing the various skills needed to sustain play episodes (Payler, Georgeson, & Wong, 2016). They also help children learn to express themselves and their emotions in socially acceptable ways. This is the beginning phase when children develop turn-taking skills and exhibit flexibility toward ideas and behaviours that other children express (Payler et al., 2016). Outdoor play environments are generally more relaxing and unstructured, contributing to children extending networking skills with peers who they may not necessarily connect with indoors (Flannigan, 2015).

Emotional Development

Children express their feelings through play—it is their natural way to communicate. The more limited a child's vocabulary and understanding of emotions, the higher the need for play (Payler, Georgeson, & Wong, 2016). Self-initiated play helps children "play out" their experiences and express their feelings (Shanker, 2016). Outdoor environments provide the setting for vigorous play to occur and for relationship connections to be made among children and adults.

Outdoor play spaces that offer children natural materials and connections with the space and place support their emotional needs. They are places where children may explore new ideas, express new thoughts, and try new expressions and feelings that may not be tried in the indoor environment. These experiences contribute to their development of executive functioning and **self-regulation skills**.

Physical Development and Movement

Children's **physical literacy** skills influences all facets of their development. Children's movement is related to their competence, their self-esteem, the quality of their interactions with others, their knowledge about their environment and their world (Bilton, 2002; Gallahue, 1993; Physical & Health Education in Canada, 2013), and their ability to embrace their environment.

Due in part to the reduction in children's outdoor play, there is a growing number of children across Canada experiencing **motor illiteracy**. Children who are not active outdoor play consumers do not develop a proficiency in motor skills necessary to support active play (Tremblay et al., 2015). This can become a lifetime issue that influences a variety of physical development requirements such as skeletal and muscular development. As you will read later in the chapter, motor development is directly related to children's levels of participation in safe risk experiences and injury prevention (Physical & Health Education Canada, 2013). Ideally, as outlined in Figure 4.3, the outdoor play environments are rich with opportunities for children to develop and refine a variety of basic movement skills (Flannigan, 2015; Gallahue, 1993; Poest, Williams, Witt, & Attwood, 1990).

The movement skills and abilities acquired during the early years provide the foundation for attitudes toward active living principles throughout life (Physical & Health Education Canada, 2013). Young children who do not master the required physical developmental milestones are less often active, play less on large playground equipment, and spend less time interacting socially with peers. As well, they experience a higher

self-regulation skills Refers to "the ability to manage your own energy states, emotions, behaviours and attention, in ways that are socially acceptable and help achieve positive goals, such as maintaining good relationships, learning and maintaining wellbeing" (Shanker, 2016, p. 1).

physical literacy "Moving with competence and confidence in a wide variety of physical activities in multiple environments that benefit the healthy development of the whole person" (Physical & Health Education Canada, 2013, p. 1).

motor illiteracy Refers to children not having developed the motor skills needed to support the required body movements necessary for various active play experiences.

Figure 4.3 Outdoor play and basic movement skills.

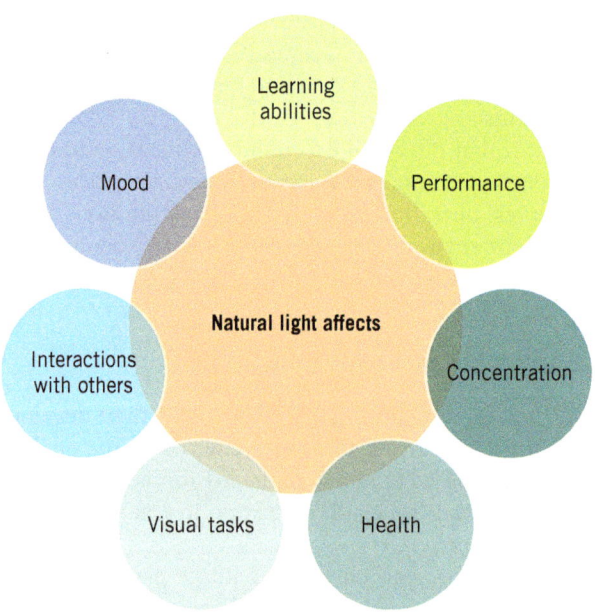

Figure 4.4 How natural light affects development.

incidence of serious diseases, injury, and social issues (Tremblay et al., 2015; Flannigan, 2015; Gleave & Cole-Hamilton, 2012).

Children who do not have sufficient outdoor play experiences generally have poorer connections to the environment, less ability in motor tasks, lower levels of physical activity, a reduction in self-regulation skills and ability to deal with stressful or traumatic situations and events, poorer ability to access and manage risk, and poorer social skills (Pacini-Ketchabaw & Nxumalo, 2015; Shanker, 2016; Smirnova & Riabkova, 2016). Early learning teachers have a core responsibility to develop opportunities for children to participate in active movement individually and with their peers.

Outdoor Play and Exposure to Natural Light

There are many studies now being conducted to determine the benefits of children being exposed to natural light during outdoor play. As outlined in Figure 4.4, Katerina (2012) indicated that exposure to natural light affects all aspects of children's development. Lack of exposure to light influences the natural body system functions, such as children's sleeping and eating patterns, because of the circadian rhythms. The circadian rhythms release, among other hormones, the hormones that are responsible for memory (Katerina, 2012).

CURIOUS?

Add any of the words in Figure 4.4 together with *outdoor play* in your search engine to obtain more information on how natural light influences children's development and dispositions.

Lack of exposure to natural light has many ramifications for children, as noted in Figure 4.4, because the human body is nourished directly by the stimulation of sunlight. As an example, one area of concern is that when children do not have regular outdoor exposure, they are at risk of acquiring diseases due to vitamin D deficiency. According to Statistics Canada (2017), approximately 11 percent of children between the ages of 3 and 5 are classified as having a vitamin D deficiency. Exposure to sunlight helps the body to synthesize and absorb vitamin D. Vitamin D influences bone growth and maintenance. It also helps the body to absorb calcium and phosphorus. If children have low levels of vitamin D, they are at risk for diseases such as rickets, a condition whereby they experience soft bones and skeletal deformities. This disease increases the risk for fractures.

STOP ... THINK ... DISCUSS ... REFLECT

There are many perspectives about the ways in which sunscreen should be used with children, and the types of sunscreen that should be used. It is important to protect children's skin from the sun. If children need exposure to the sun for vitamin D absorption, is there ever a time of the day when children do not go outdoors with sunscreen on? Who decides this and how? What happens if an early learning program has one policy and families have different beliefs about this?

Another area of children's health that is being affected by outdoor play is myopia or children's nearsightedness. According to Turbert (2014), current eye research suggests that children who spend time outdoors with eye protection have better eyesight than their peers. He claims that, in one study, findings indicated that for each hour children speed outdoors per week, their risk of being nearsighted dropped by 2 percent.

Developing an Appreciation for Outdoor Play

Nurturing children during the early years is an important role of early learning teachers and early learning students. How early learning teachers support children in having access to and opportunities for outdoor play influences how children develop, think, and engage in outdoor play. For example, children who are exposed to adult role models who exhibit an appreciation for the outdoor environment have a higher probability of developing an interest in outdoor play, which in turn increases children's connections to their environment and environmental stewardship. Research in ecopsychology and evolutionary psychology disciplines suggests that humans have an affinity for outdoor play (Nordic Council of Ministers, 2014). Evolutionary psychologists use the term *biophilia*, which refers to an innate, hereditary emotional attraction that humans have to nature. It means that we are born with genetic coding and instincts that require us to participate in the outdoor environment (Nordic Council of Ministers, 2014).

Early learning teachers are in a position to positively influence children in developing an appreciation for outdoor play and our environment. Early learning teachers are most effective when they become highly skilled, with a deep knowledge and understanding of how outdoor play supports and influences child development, environmental stewardship, and lifelong health and wellness practices (Jacobi-Vessels, 2013).

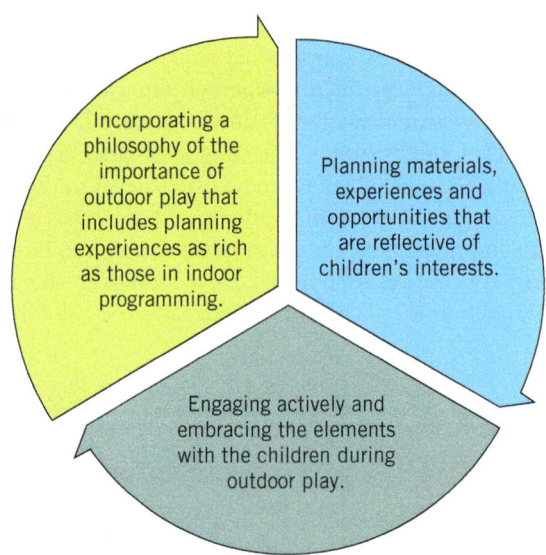

Figure 4.5 Ways in which adults role model and embrace outdoor play.

As identified in Figure 4.5, children thrive in outdoor play environments with adults who role model the joy and wonderment that can occur outdoors (Jacobi-Vessels, 2013). Adults provide children with many materials and experiences. The experiences differ from those indoors and include diverse opportunities for children to explore and discover in a safe but challenging environment. While outdoors, children also require opportunities for solitude and wonderment. The freedom to play and explore thoughts and feelings, although complicated, allows children to have a sense of choice and become self-motivated and self-regulated, spontaneous, and imaginative based on their interests rather than on adult-imposed perspectives. Early experiences within a **natural play space** contribute to the development of positive feelings about the outdoor environment, nature, science, other children, and the world around them (Derr & Kellert, 2013).

As identified at the beginning of this chapter, Froebel believed that children require a garden as part of their environment. The garden is where the children and nature meld together, creating an appreciation for play and nature. Gardens support children in gaining a sense of observation and respect that is difficult to emulate in other settings. Despite their importance, over time, gardens have been removed or separated from playgrounds, each having a different focus. Early learning teachers and children benefit from realigning these elements of the outdoor play space.

Appropriate play spaces contribute to children learning about their natural world. For example, they can learn about the food chain by growing fruits and vegetables. Children learn about insects that are attracted to the fruits and vegetables. This allows children to scaffold and connect their learning about the relationship of ladybugs eating aphids or birds eating particular insects. Children learn about butterflies and hummingbirds in outdoor environments that have bushes that attract them. Sunflowers bring an array of birds such as goldfinches and chickadees. Children have an affinity for tall grasses, trees, tunnels, butterflies, sunflowers, and natural loose parts. When children have outdoor play environments that hold their interests, they also extend the play options and the opportunities for creativity and spontaneity (Sobel, 2014).

natural play spaces Spaces that provide children with play zones that combine natural areas, locally appropriate plants, and environmental features such as slopes and surfaces that trigger children's interest in exploring the characteristics and wonderment of the natural world.

Photo 4.6 Children have infinite opportunities for play in nature.
Used with Permission of Family Space Quinte, Inc.

Children's Outdoor Play: Risky, Challenging, and Adventurous

Children benefit from outdoor environments that invite them to engage in invigorating experiences and that challenge them to think about what they wish to do, what their skills are, and how they might accomplish their goal. Invigorating play experiences contribute to children learning about their world, tinkering with materials, and testing out their ideas. They reflect upon successes and mistakes and how to use the assets within the environment (Dietze & Kashin, 2016; Pye, 2013). To accomplish all of these goals, children must be surrounded by adults who embrace their freedom to explore and pursue active play. The *Canadian Position Statement on Active Outdoor Play* (Herrington & Pickett, 2015) states that "access to active play in nature and outdoors—with its risks—is essential for healthy child development, and that opportunities for self-directed play outdoors should be increased in all settings" (p. 1). Why, if it is so important for children, are we as a society struggling to support children in engaging in this play?

Researchers, educators, policymakers, and early learning teachers are at a crossroads in determining how to classify play that requires a high level of competence, problem solving, and activity (Waite, Wickett, & Huggins, 2014). Is it risky play? Is it purely play, or should we label it challenging and adventurous play? Sandseter (2016) suggests that from an injury-prevention perspective, the term *risky play* best describes the characteristics of the play. Yet one of the reasons why the term *risk-taking* is being challenged is because of its negative connotation. In fact, from the perspective of children, child development, and outdoor play, risk-taking is a necessity. Children learn about new skills, try new ideas, and achieve new knowledge and skills by taking risks. Children who do not have opportunities to engage in play with risk-taking are living in a world that is inhibiting their development—children need challenges (Heppell, 2013).

| Challenging play refers to something that children create that involves excitement and adventure. Children decide if they will take the risk. | Adventurous play refers to children being adventurous by taking opportunities to explore and test their own capacities, to manage risk, and to grow in their capacity, resourcefulness, and resilience. | Risky play refers to children engaging in thrilling and exciting experiences that involves a potential risk of injury, but more importantly, offers them opportunities for challenge, testing limits, exploring boundaries, and learning about managing risks. |

Figure 4.6 Definitions of challenging, adventurous, and risky play.

CURIOUS?

Add the words *risky play* and *outdoor play* to your search engine to obtain more information on the various definitions of and perspectives on risky play.

As outlined in Figure 4.6, many researchers—including Solly (2015); Frost, Wortham, and Reifel (2012); and Sandseter (2007)—have contributed to the discussions on the language and definitions of play that has an element of risk, challenge, and hazard.

One of the challenges of risky, challenging, or adventurous play is the concern that children will be hurt. As a result, many early learning teachers and families focus on reducing children's opportunities to engage in this play for the sake of safety. Risk-taking play is also being overshadowed by strict provincial and territorial standards and regulations that are being put in place to reduce childhood injury, despite the need for children to engage in healthy risk-taking opportunities (Cevher-Kalburan & Ivrendi, 2016; Heppell, 2013; Sandseter & Kennair, 2011). Some advocates suggest that these constraints limit early learning teachers in being able to provide a balance of healthy freedom and exploratory opportunities to young children (Cevher-Kalburan & Ivrendi, 2016). The more restrictions there are, the more detrimental it is to children's learning and well-being. Early learning teachers are required to adhere to standards, while still offering children risk-taking opportunities.

Often *risk* and *hazards* are viewed as synonymous terms. Early learning teachers benefit from understanding the differences between risk and a hazard. In a working document created by the Lawson Foundation (2017), "Risk is the possibility of gaining or losing something of value, with an intentional interaction with uncertainty and probably. Risk is subjective and can vary from person to person. Hazard is the potential source of harm or danger" (p. 5). A hazard may be one that is not obvious to children; they may not see it or be able to predict the end result, such as walking on a broken railing.

Photo 4.7 Children and risky, challenging adventure play.
Used with Permission of Angela Roy

As presented in Table 4.2, Frost and colleagues (2012) identified three hazard levels to be considered in environmental design and **risk management** plans for early learning programs. Whether early learning teachers decide to call the play risky, adventurous, or challenging, they examine how play spaces can be designed so that children have graduated play experiences that increase the level and complexity of the play. This scaffolding process helps children gain confidence, success, and problem-solving skills (Dietze & Kashin, 2016). Outdoor play must be thought of in healthy terms—providing children with the opportunity to discover, be adventurous, and build confidence in using their bodies—rather than as a possibility of injury. This can be achieved by managing safe risk opportunities.

risk management Refers to a process that early learning teachers use to examine the environment in an effort to reduce potential hazards within children's environments.

Table 4.2 Levels of hazards.

Level 1—Limited Hazard	Level 2—Moderate Hazard	Level 3—Extreme Hazard
Conditions that lead to minor injuries, such as scraped knees.	Conditions that cause serious injury, such as a broken leg.	Conditions that cause permanent disability or loss of life.

Source: Data from Frost, Wortham, and Reifel (2012).

The Importance of Outdoor Play to Child Development   127

Safe risk does not equate to nonchallenging play equipment, materials, or experiences. There are implications when the play space becomes hazard-free and sterile. Children may become bored, lose interest in play, or engage in negative behavioural activities as a way to add excitement to the play. Children will find ways to make their environment more challenging, often by taking inappropriate risks (Wilkinson, 2015), using equipment in inappropriate ways, and exhibiting behaviour toward peers that may not normally be exhibited. For example, children will jump from one place to another on the equipment or go backwards on sliding apparatus as a way to add interest to their play. These child-initiated challenges become hazardous (Wilkinson, 2015) and contribute to unnecessary accidents.

As part of due diligence, early learning teachers develop strategies to minimize and manage risk by conducting risk–benefit assessments. These assessments are intended to identify benefits of particular play and levels of hazards. Prior to children entering the outdoor play space, early learning teachers conduct a visual inspection of the space to examine it for potential risks such as fallen logs and branches or snow or ice that could slide from buildings. Any area of concern is documented and shared with administrators. The process assists early learning teachers in identifying the potential risk for injury and making informed decisions about how to proceed with play, without danger to children. Table 4.3 provides a sample of a risk assessment document. Early learning teachers develop ways to manage risk in play rather than eliminate it, as safe risk is essential for

Table 4.3 Risk assessment document.

Subject of Assessment: Painted stick activity
Assessor: **Date:**
Description of Activity, Location, Tools, Equipment
Children will use vegetable peelers to "whittle" the sticks free of bark at both ends. They will then paint the ends in rainbow colours. They will be used to create geometric shapes and for walking outdoors.
How Will the Children Benefit from This Play Opportunity?
■ Children will use vegetable peelers to "whittle" the sticks free of bark.
■ Children will learn safety tips and precautions needed to whittle with knives. The sticks with the sharp points offer them versatility in their play.
■ Children will feel challenged and build confidence because adults are allowing them to use this type of equipment and create materials for their play.
Possible Hazards and Risks
■ Children may receive cuts. The sharp edges may have an element of danger if children run with the sticks and fall.
Measures to Reduce Risk—Severity or Likelihood
■ Provide children with safety gloves.
■ Discuss safety with children and model the correct positioning for whittling.
■ Discuss strategies for carrying and using sticks safety.
Precedents or Comparisons
■ I have observed this activity with a similar age group. Children were reminded of the importance of following the safety guidelines before they engaged in the activity. There were no incidents.
Judgment
■ I feel that the benefit the children acquire from the activity outweighs the risk. It does not pose a life-threatening experience. At worst, it would be considered a limited hazard.

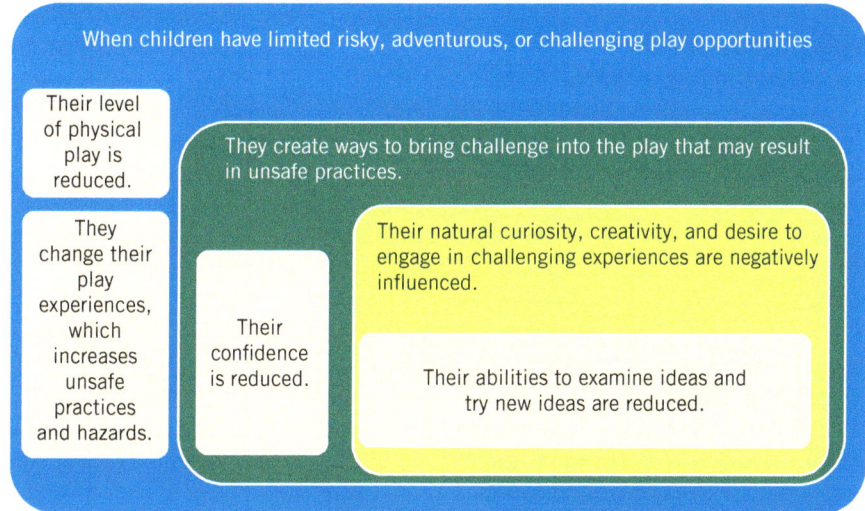

Figure 4.7 Why risky, adventurous, challenging play is essential.

the child's optimal health and development. Ultimately, the outdoor play environment provides appropriate levels of risk, while also encouraging creativity, challenge, and new learning options.

Finally, as Figure 4.7 illustrates, children miss key learning opportunities when the risky, adventurous, challenging outdoor play is removed from their environments on an ongoing basis.

STOP ... THINK ... DISCUSS ... REFLECT

How can early learning teachers meet the safety requirements that govern outdoor play equipment and still provide children with opportunities for physical challenge and risk-taking play? What are the issues for children if they do not have opportunities to participate in physical activities that require risk, adventure, or challenge? Is there a long-term implication for their development? If so, what is it?

Planning Outdoor Play Spaces

The outdoor play space and play opportunities are important features needed for children to engage in ideas, exploration, and a sense of wonderment (Berris & Miller, 2011). Preparing an outdoor environment that is stimulating, challenging, and a safe place to play is difficult to accomplish without understanding how environmental factors contribute to children's play, learning, and their connections to place and space.

Outdoor play spaces are designed to offer children different play experiences with a balance of skills and concepts to promote active movement, exploration of the unknown, experiences with unpredictable events, and new discoveries. Early learning teachers prepare the outdoor play space in similar ways to the indoor play experiences. There is versatility within the space, coupled with natural elements, equipment, and materials that stimulate children's senses, curiosity, opportunities for intrigue, interests, and abilities (Dietze & Kim, 2014). These attributes help children flourish in outdoor play spaces.

The outdoor play environment correlates with the experimentation that children will engage in, which in turn is intended to contribute to their expansion of or reconfiguration of their knowledge base. The theoretical principles of child development, the interests and exploration styles of children, and the related level of developmental milestones of children become pivotal in creating effective play spaces. As a programming process, early learning teachers ensure that there are opportunities for children to have both solo play and group free-flowing play experiences (Ernst, 2014b; Sobel & Larimore, 2016).

Similar to the indoor environment, the outdoor play space flows from one area to the next. It is open-ended, versatile, and as simple as possible. Versatile space helps children to use their imaginations and to make the space "theirs." Quality outdoor play spaces are measured for their openness and diversity rather than their physical attractiveness. As outlined in Figure 4.8, early learning teachers consider environmental aesthetics and each of the components illustrated.

According to Carson (1998), children benefit in outdoor play spaces that offer them opportunities to discover the joys and mystery of their world. She believed that children's sense of wonderment flourishes when they can listen to the winds, observe the trees and the flowers, and feel the rain and snow. She encouraged early learning teachers to create environments that offered a variety of experiences and were "awe-inspiring."

Dietze and Kim (2014) identified that outdoor play environmental designs focus on key elements of nature and early learning curriculum. Each will be described.

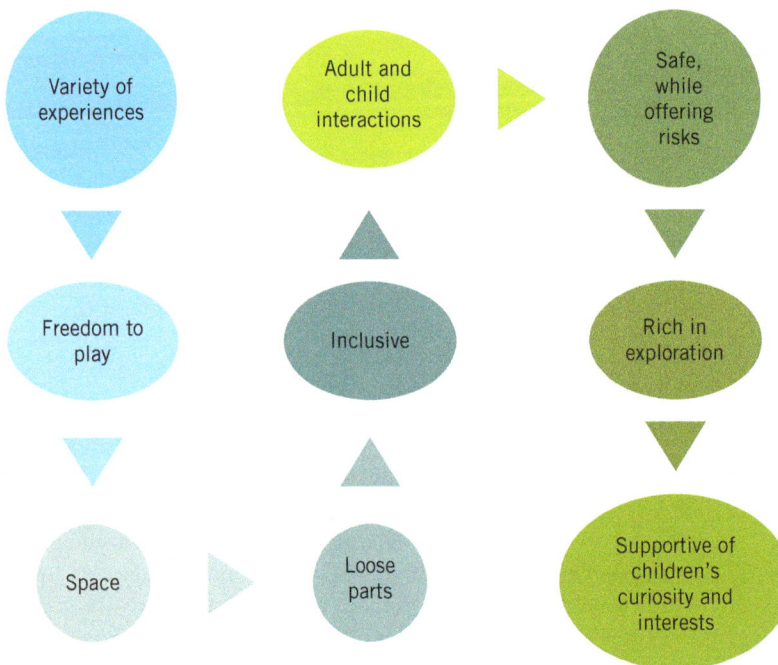

Figure 4.8 Consideration of outdoor play space.

Nature and Physical Movement Zones

The nature zone includes trees, grasses, water, boulders, gardens, and plants. This is an ideal location to include mounds of earth for the children to climb on or to dig in. Children have options to combine items with water and natural items such as mud, leaves, feathers, and rocks in their play. These zones provide opportunities for both quiet and active play.

Experiential Play Zones

These zones are designed to support more active experiences, including construction activities, dramatic play, mud play, language and literacy, math and science, and new play possibilities. Many types of materials are combined in this area to support the development of adventure play. For example, boards, planks, wheelbarrows, dirt, rocks, and cedar blocks may trigger children to create ramps, bridges, and roads.

Active Play Zones

These zones include opportunities for children to run, jump, and use tricycles, wheeled toys, and games. This area has a variety of ground surfaces—hard surfaces for the wheeled toys, grassy areas for rough and tumble play, and a combination of surfaces for pathways.

Quiet Learning and Affinity Play Zones

These zones are usually protected from the weather elements and are used for experiences such as project ideas, reading, tinkering, storytelling, and creative arts experiences. They provide an individual child and small groups of children space to engage in their play. Tables, blankets, benches, baskets of materials, and lawn chairs may be available to

Photo 4.8 Children benefit from having places to dig and explore in their environments.
Used with Permission of Bora Kim

support children in their play options. Children are provided with a place to engage in solo play or less active experiences with peers.

Rich outdoor play environments have materials such as:

- Sand and water.
- Trees, bushes, flowers, and long grasses.
- Places and features to sit in, on, or under; lean against; and provide shelter and shade.
- Places that offer privacy and views.
- Structures, equipment, and materials that can be changed.
- Loose parts.
- Props for dramatic play and construction.
- Materials that support children in adding to permanent structures.
- Apparatus that encourage children to roll, run, and climb.

Think about children and outdoor play. If children do not have access to these types of spaces, what outdoor play opportunities might they be missing?

CURIOUS?

Add the words *Seven Cs* to your search engine to obtain another perspective on ways to make outdoor play space inviting for children.

PLAY SPACES FOR INFANTS, TODDLERS, PRESCHOOLERS, AND SCHOOL-AGED CHILDREN

Depending on the provincial and territorial early childhood regulations, many early learning and child-care programs divide their outdoor play spaces into at least three areas: one for infants and toddlers, one for preschool children, and one for school-aged children. Each of these age groups benefit from their outdoor play space reflecting their social, emotional, cognitive, and physical needs.

The infant and toddler space is designed to accommodate a wide range of movements. Frost (1992) advocated for infants to have confined space, which is "gentle for crawling, kind for falling and cool for sitting" (p. 260). The space ensures opportunities to accommodate the emerging developmental attributes of sitting, crawling and standing, toddling, and walking. A combination of hard and soft surfaces is necessary to support the varying motor developments.

Play spaces provide a variety of materials intended to stimulate children's senses. Different ground textures such as grass, chimes blowing in the wind, and soft music support sensory development. Grass, blankets, and mats are useful surfaces for crawling experiences. Early learning teachers incorporate novelty and challenge into the infant and toddler environment on a gradual basis. Too much stimulation may have a negative effect on children. Infants need time to learn about the world around them by exploring sounds, sights, smells, and textures gradually.

As toddlers become more confident with their mobility skills, they require space that allows them to be active in toddling, jumping, running, and darting. Toddlers benefit from

Photo 4.9 Children will engage in adventure play when they have time, space, peers, and materials that trigger their curiosity.
Used with Permission of Family Space Quinte, Inc.

environments that provide them with the freedom to explore without impeding the needs of infants or older preschoolers. As children gain confidence in their motor movements and with the adults in their environment, they expand their scope of the play space. Toddlers require

- Easy access to places to dig or jump, such as sand areas.
- Open areas to run through, roll in, or hop in, such as grass and tall grass plants.
- Hard surfaces for pull and ride-on toys, such as asphalt.
- Places to rest, such as a covered area.
- Places with inclines so they can crawl up them or run or roll down them, such as hills.

Preschool children further expand the use of their play space. Preschool children require

- Areas for equipment such as swings, climbers, and balance beams.
- Areas to explore the natural environment, such as trees, insects, gardens, and animals.
- Places for running, rolling, and playing games, such as large grassy areas.
- Hard surfaces for tricycles, wagons, constructive play, and dramatic play, such as asphalt and wooden platforms.
- Space to separate active play and quiet play.
- Places with inclines for active movement, such as hills.

School-aged children benefit from outdoor space that allows them to roam, play, and connect with peers. Open space helps school-aged children to engage in active play (Oke & Middle, 2016).

School-aged children require

- Space for challenging physical activities, such as open space that accommodates competitive games, skateboarding, and various types of exercise.
- Space that allows them to socialize with their friends, such as picnic tables, benches, and space under a tree.
- Space to hang out.

Early learning teachers continuously examine the physical space and resources available to determine how the environment supports the outdoor play desires of the various groups of children. Effective outdoor play spaces reduce conflicts among children and minimize safety risks.

Examining the Use of Play Space

It is challenging to predict how children will use a play space because there are many influences that contribute to how the play space is used. For example, children's imagination, life experiences, space availability, the play surface, the play space design, the materials, and the attitudes and adult role models all influence how play space is used. Each child's level of risk-taking (as discussed in the previous section), willingness to take risks, interactions with other children, and ability to explore the environment also contribute to how the play space is used.

Children prefer integrated outdoor play spaces to those that have isolated experience centres (Friedberg & Berkeley, 1970; Jennings & Carlisle, 2013; Mason, 1982) or those that are all open. Jennings and Carlisle (2013) indicated that, based on study completed with children, children require space that has the following common elements:

- Action and adventure—ability for play such as climbing and exploring.
- Opportunities to be creative—ability to build forts or dens, use sand, and develop temporary ideas.
- Traditional play—ability to have space to play ball games and use various equipment.
- Aesthetics and nature—access to trees and plants, public art, and related pleasing items.
- Function and access—access to water and toilets and the overall play space.

The organization of the play space either helps or hinders the flow of play. For example, if children have access to a play stage and block centre with various materials, as well as a tricycle path, dramatic play is more likely than if the play stage is a distance from the blocks and tricycle path. The closer the proximity of defined centres and materials, the more likely children will integrate a combination of materials, ideas, equipment, and play options. When integration occurs, there is a higher potential for play that includes rich dialogue, new play partners, creativity, and new knowledge development to evolve (Dietze & Kim, 2014).

Analyzing Play Spaces

The play space design influences children's social play behaviour. As outlined in Table 4.4, when the play space meets the needs of children, they engage in positive social play. Conversely, when the play space requires some adjustments or is not meeting the needs of children, negative behaviour becomes evident. Early learning teachers observe children's play to watch

Table 4.4 How play space influences children's behaviours.

Evidence of Positively Engaged Social Play	Evidence of Negatively Engaged Social Play
Social conversation	Arguing
Cooperative play	Object possessiveness
Child-initiated play	Unilateral decisions
Sharing of materials	Aggressiveness toward others and with materials
Friendly, caring play	Aggressive play

for signs of behaviours that could lead to negative behaviours, such as wandering, rough play, or aggressive play. These are important clues that identify that adjustments to the play space are needed.

The arrangement of outdoor play space considers play as being symbolic, free flowing, and fluid. The outdoor space offers children opportunities to create, play on structured equipment, recreate, and restructure play spaces.

There are a number of variables that early learning teachers consider when arranging materials and experiences and maintaining fluidity in the play space. These considerations include but are not limited to:

- The terrain, including the slope and water runoff areas.
- The sun, shade, and areas where children are protected from rain and wind.
- Ground surfaces, including asphalt, sand, grass, and required gravel.
- Visual supervision.
- The safe risk elements.
- Storage of materials.
- The garden space.

How children wish to use the space (Dietze, 2006) is also considered. Box 4.1 provides a guide for early learning teachers to consider when examining children's play space.

More than 40 years ago, Kritchevsky, Prescott, and Walling (1977) analyzed play spaces by considering the complexity and variety of play units (Wellhousen, 2002) made available to children. They identified that insufficient materials or lack of stimulating play options adds to disruptive behaviour. Their process for analyzing space continues to be used in many early learning programs today.

Box 4.1   Examining children's play spaces.

Where do children go to do the following?
- Be up high or be down low
- Dig worms
- Plant flowers
- Build a wooden structure
- Observe friends rolling balls
- Yell
- Be alone
- Play with only three children
- Use boards to practise balance
- Play in the leaves

A **play unit** is described as a single unit item that allows items to be incorporated into the play. The unit may or may not have defined boundaries. For example, a sandbox with only sand would be considered to have a visible boundary, whereas a dramatic stage near the blocks and playhouse may have fewer boundaries.

Complexity refers to "the extent to which [the play units] contain potential for active manipulation and alteration by children" (Kritchevsky, Prescott, & Walling, 1977, p. 11). Early learning teachers examine the complexity of the play unit, as this guides the number of children who may potentially use the area and how it may be set up for play experiences.

A **simple play unit** generally has a defined use, such as a swing or a tricycle. A simple play unit may become complex by adding materials that will advance the play opportunities (Kritchevsky et al., 1977). For example, by adding a tent and picnic baskets, dramatic play may be stimulated or enhanced.

A **complex unit** allows children the opportunity to engage in play with two or more play support materials, such as a water table with rubber ducks or a cash register with pots of flowers.

A **super complex unit** is considered a play area that accommodates one or more play materials, such as adding tables, cellphones, order pads, and a computer keyboard to the playhouse.

Potential units refer to empty spaces found within identified boundaries. These spaces provide children with opportunities to use the space to meet their play requirements.

Each play space is assessed for its complexity and assigned a corresponding value rating. Simple units are given a value rating of 1, complex play units have a value of 4, and super complex units have a value of 8. The complexity of the play unit of each area is determined. Then, the assigned values are totalled and divided by the number of children playing during the play episode. The goal is to have at least 2.5 play spaces available per child, per day. These play spaces offer children opportunities for intrigue and curiosity with the variety of materials and play option potentials.

Table 4.5 provides an overview of how the play space may be analyzed to determine if there are sufficient play spaces available for the number of children in the environment.

Assume that you have 16 preschool-aged children. Your current playground choices have a total value of 42. This value is then divided by the number of children playing in the environment (16 children). This indicates that there are 2.6 spaces

Table 4.5 Analyzing play space.

Play Unit	Complexity Rating	Value
One sandbox with vehicles, cones, plastic tubing, buckets, and sieves	Super complex	8
One drama platform with tables and chairs and prop boxes	Super complex	8
Three swings	Simple	3
One adventure play area with slide, gates, and lookout	Complex	4
One bicycle path with six tricycles	Simple	6
One bench under the tree	Simple	1
A set of cedar blocks of varying sizes with plywood strips and accessories	Super complex	8
One basket of balls of various sizes	Complex	4
Total		42

> **Box 4.2   How to calculate outdoor play space materials.**

Sample of how to calculate outdoor play space

1. Identify the number of:
   - Simple units (× 1)
   - Complex units (× 4)
   - Super units (× 8)

2. Calculate the total number of play spaces (based on the totals in calculations above).

3. Identify the number of children usually playing in the outdoor play spaces.

4. Calculate the complexity of the play relative to the environment by dividing the total number of play spaces by the number of children in the environment.

available for each child. Think about what additions could be made to the play space that would provide children with a variety of play experiences and challenge, while increasing the play spaces for each child to a minimum of three spaces. For example, Brent wanted to increase the complexity of the play environment. He felt that his group of 4-year-olds needed to have an equal ratio of complex and super complex units. In his plan, he was thinking about Brittany, who uses a wheelchair for mobility, and her excitement about watching the wheelchair athletes during the Olympics. Brent determined that if he added a small basketball hoop, balls, a parachute, pillowcases, and three child-sized wheelchairs (borrowed from a local supplier) and created roller paths with masking tape for children in the wheelchairs, new play options would be created. These additions would offer both complex and super complex units for the children. Children's creativity, imagination, and experience in diversity would also be enhanced. The more opportunities children have to wonder, be curious, and make connections with their environment and the people in that environment, the more their creative thinking and appreciation of others is enhanced (Kemple, Oh, Kenney, & Smith-Bonahue, 2016; Sutterby, Frost, & Frost, 2006; Tovey, 2007). Box 4.2 provides a sample of how the calculations are completed.

The purpose of analyzing the play space is to determine if there are sufficient play spaces, the complexity of the materials and play spaces, and how the play spaces support the children's expressed interests.

CHOOSING MATERIALS FOR OUTDOOR PLAY: WHY LOOSE PARTS

Children require outdoor play environments that have open-ended materials and **loose parts** as standard materials. The more open-ended the materials, the more flexibility and divergent thoughts children express (Kable, 2013). As outlined earlier in the chapter, loose parts, a term coined by architect Simon Nicholson (1971), refers to natural or synthetic materials or objects that give children choices in their play and will empower creativity. Because loose parts lack structure, they offer children endless possibilities to use their imagination and engage in creative play and new discovery.

Loose parts may be used as a singular material or combined with other materials. There are a number of loose parts materials that complement outdoor play. For example, in a natural play area, water, sand, dirt, sticks, branches, leaves, tree stumps, pine cones, feathers, and stones provide children with numerous play options. Other loose parts may

> **loose parts** Materials that can be moved, redesigned, put together, and taken apart in a variety of ways.

include items such as a variety of balls, hoops, straw, parachutes, blankets, buckets, cups, hoses, digging tools, boxes, shovels, brushes, wind chimes, baskets, kites, and plastic pipes.

Loose parts support children in using them to initiate or maintain dramatic play episodes (Beloglovsky & Daly, 2015). For example, children who have access to a realistic pirate ship, as well as loose parts, participate in dramatic play more often than children who only have the shape of the play equipment (Beloglovsky & Daly, 2015) to stimulate play. "In any environment, both the degree of inventiveness and creativity and the possibilities of discovery are directly proportional to the number and kind of variables in it" (Nicholson, 1971, p. 39). Loose parts, large and small, spark children's curiosity.

Four important reasons for incorporating loose parts into play environments include:

1. Loose parts encourage children to create their play options within the environment.
2. Loose parts expand the play options that increase the variability of the play and the potential for active movement.
3. Loose parts support children in being able to use materials with success and reflective of their interest.
4. Loose parts stimulate children's play, thus increasing appropriate play behaviours (Dietze & Kashin, 2016).

Early learning teachers encourage children to use materials from the various play spaces. This diverse use of materials helps children make learning connections and think about how materials can be used as a variety of props. Children who integrate loose parts within their play express an increased use of creativity and flexibility needed for discovery learning.

STOP ... THINK ... DISCUSS ... REFLECT

You are in an early learning centre that has a structured outdoor play space. Children have access to ride-on toys, climbers, and a sandbox. You are interested in adding loose parts to the environment. How will you discuss this with your cooperating teacher? How will you decide what loose parts to introduce to the children first? How do you envision the children will respond? Do you think it is best that early learning student teachers try these ideas as a student or perhaps wait until you are on staff at a facility? Why or why not?

ACTIVE OUTDOOR AND CONSTRUCTIVE PLAY EXPERIENCE AREAS

Preschool and school-aged children are drawn to constructive play opportunities. Constructive play gives children a sense of being able to determine how their play will evolve and how they can control it. The constructive play area is designed to offer flexibility to accommodate the needs of an individual child and groups of children. Constructive play areas encompass a variety of materials, including sand, water, and vehicle play. Woodworking, blocks, art, and science experience centres add great value to outdoor play (Ramani, Zippert, Schweitzer, & Pan, 2014). Materials are changed on a regular basis to offer a sense of intrigue and flexibility in their usage.

Blocks

As you will read in Chapter 6, hollow blocks, planks, crates, cedar solid blocks, and related accessories are essential outdoor play materials. Blocks support children in developing a range of skills, abilities, and interests. For example, when blocks are combined with resources such as outdoor magazines, road signs, masking tape, construction hats, and vests, children will often incorporate these items into their play, such as in creating forts or fancy walls. These structures have the potential to become the backdrop for imaginative play episodes that may include rough and tumble play, rescue play, or acting out fairy tales.

Woodworking

Another important outdoor constructive play centre is the woodworking centre. Although this is an area that many early learning teachers and student teachers question, the benefits are numerous. It is interrelated to block construction, scientific principles, and the expression of creativity. Working with real materials suggests to some that there is an increased risk for injury. Sandseter (2016) is among the advocates of children having these types of experiences on a regular basis. Rules need to be established, such as ensuring that safety goggles are worn, that adult supervision is provided when tools are being used, and that the tools are returned to their specified holding place once the children have used them. Woodworking offers children experiences in following a design, pattern, or model. Children require appropriate wood and tools in order for the play to be positive and constructive.

Art

Children's art takes on new dimensions and processes when completed in the outdoor environment. Three contributing factors to this are:

- The natural light, giving children a realistic view of colours and textures.
- The natural environment offering a sense of calmness.
- The freedom to use messier materials such as clay and sculpturing materials.

Children are intuitively attracted to objects such as sticks, acorns, and leaves. Often children will incorporate these natural materials into their art experiences. Their creative processes and problem-solving skills are uniquely different when they are using flat surfaces with the wind blowing, on the grass or a rock, or up against a fence or building from those in traditional methods such as at easels or tabletops.

Discovery and Science

Outdoor play provides children with a natural introduction to science and discovery principles. Children require a variety of hands-on experiences that support them in discovering scientific principles such as weight, temperature, gravity, buoyance, and strength. As identified earlier in the chapter, a garden is an essential element of outdoor play. Children learn about vegetation, germination, growth cycles, the importance of sun and rain, and harvesting. They gain information on outdoor creatures such as worms, snakes, toads, and rabbits. Children also require access to unique materials such as measurement tools, bicycle pumps and tires, a variety of hoses, clamps, and tools for taking things apart. Combining art materials such as paint and clay with science props supports children in making connections such as the shading of colours and how rainbows and light shadows are made.

Photo 4.10 Children experiment with their play differently when indoors and when outdoors.

Used with Permission of Angela Roy

Sociodramatic Play

Similar to other outdoor play experiences, the composition and arrangement of materials may foster or hinder dramatic play. The traditional playground space with climbing apparatus does not facilitate dramatic play (Cloward Drown & Christensen, 2014). Materials, time, and space are needed to spark dramatic play.

Outdoor sociodramatic play offers young children a combination of imaginative and active play. Playhouses, tents, forts, dramatic play platforms, canopies, and related accessories provide children with the opportunities to create symbolic play episodes. Dramatic play requires props—if not, the play area may have high levels of aggression and conflict because children wish to play, but there are not sufficient resources to support a role in the play. The more loose parts available, the better the dramatic play opportunities, as children may manipulate and incorporate various loose parts into their play (Beloglovsky & Daly, 2015).

Movable materials contribute significantly to supporting children in active movement. For example, slides, fire poles, clatter bridges, large planks, tables and chairs, ride-on toys, and materials such as umbrellas, boots, and dress-up clothes support active movement and dramatic play. Dramatic play platforms, forts, and panels also add unique opportunities for dramatic play to evolve.

Adding materials in various parts of the play area may stimulate sociodramatic play. For example, you may place dolls that may be washed near the water table with towels, brushes, and clothes in a nearby basket. You may place a restaurant sign and tables and chairs near the tricycle path. These invitations become play triggers, which help children connect with their peers and participate in sociodramatic play.

Early learning teachers examine the outdoor environment to ensure that there are locally appropriate and culturally relevant materials available to the children. For example, if an early learning centre is located in an area such as a fishing village along the Atlantic or Pacific Ocean, children benefit from having realistic materials such as nets, traps, rope, and perhaps even a boat to use in their play. Or, if you are in an environment that is rich with a natural play space, children require opportunities to design an authentic dramatic play space rather than having adults place plastic items such as houses or forts in them. We want children to learn with authentic materials and experiences.

Games with Rules

Games are sequenced in a way that supports children's skill sets and is correlated with their interests and capabilities. Children require games to move from simple to complex. For example, the first phase of game playing with rules would include Simon Says or Follow the Leader. More complicated games such as Duck, Duck, Goose follow, because children need to be able to follow two or more instructions in the game progression. Generally, games that have one instruction are the first to be introduced, then those with two and three instructions, and so on. Games are considered the highest level of cognitive play (Piaget, 1962). School-aged children are ready for complicated games with many more rules.

The Roles of Early Learning Teachers in Outdoor Play

The role of early learning teachers is multifaceted. Figure 4.9 provides an overview of the scope of the roles and responsibilities as they relate to outdoor play. Each is described below.

Early Learning Teachers' Attitudes and Abilities

Studies suggest that there are significant changes in early learning teachers' attitudes and abilities after participating in specialized studies in outdoor play (Ernst, 2014a). Some of the changes include posing more in-depth questions, extending opportunities for children's knowledge base to be enhanced, and providing encouragement to the total group of children. Early learning teachers who are comfortable with outdoor play generally exhibit

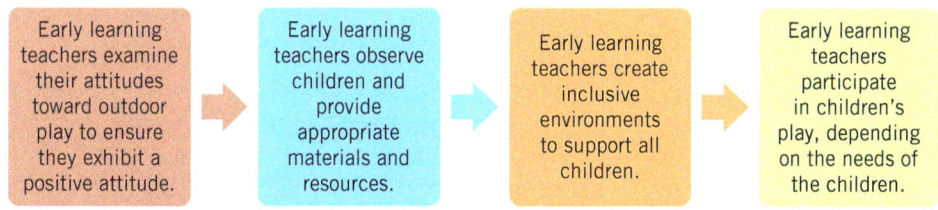

Figure 4.9 Roles of early learning teachers in outdoor play.

> **Box 4.3 Strategies to support early learning practitioners in facilitating outdoor play.**
>
> **Ten Strategies for Facilitating Children's Play Outdoors**
>
> - Provide long, uninterrupted play periods (40 to 60 minutes).
> - Provide opportunities for indoor and outdoor play to flow between the two areas.
> - Provide a variety of open-ended, loose parts materials with stationary materials.
> - Provide opportunities for challenging, safe-risk play to evolve in play.
> - Encourage the play to flow from the children.
> - Provide all children with equal access to rich play experiences.
> - Become partners in play at the appropriate times.
> - Pose questions and make comments that will facilitate discussion and wonderment with an individual child or groups of children.
> - Observe and document children's play and provide materials that will scaffold and expand learning opportunities.
> - Reflect on children's outdoor play experiences and how they support children's learning.

more smiling and positive contact with the children, and they offer more types of play experiences and time for outdoor play (Bilton, 2014).

The attitude of the early learning teachers directly relates to the quality of the play experiences, the access to and opportunities for outdoor play, and the duration of outdoor play time (Kemple et al., 2016). Early learning teachers are role models. Therefore, it is essential that we think about outdoor play as a healthy experience, no matter what the weather is (Bilton, 2014). This requires children and adults to have the correct clothing for cold and inclement weather. Think about the learning that occurs when children have opportunities to be in the rain, wind, or snow. How do they respond when they discover the toad or the rainbow or feel snowflakes hitting their faces? Box 4.3 provides strategies to support the early learning teachers in facilitating outdoor play.

Program Schedules for Outdoor Play

There are many perspectives on how to structure the outdoor portion of early learning programs. Children require access to outdoor play that provides them with large blocks of time that span 30 to 60 minutes (ParticipACTION, 2015). When children have sufficient play time, they are able to engage in complex, integrated experiences. Short play periods result in children abandoning their group dramatizations or constructive play just when they begin to get deeply involved in a particular play experience (Sobel & Larimore, 2016). If children are required to disrupt their play on a continuous basis, they generally abandon more sophisticated forms of play. They will settle for surface play that can be completed in short periods of time. This reduces children's abilities to experience the many attributes of play, such as persistence, negotiation, problem solving, planning, and cooperative play (Bilton, 2014). Children who are given time to play advance the complexity of the play, which in turn makes play more productive (Duhn, 2012).

Early Learning Teacher's Facilitation Roles

Children benefit most when early learning teachers offer facilitation strategies that meet the needs of the children. The most effective strategies are teacher-supported involvement, child-initiated exploration, and teacher–child-guided discovery opportunities.

Early learning teacher–supported involvement refers to short- and long-term experiences or projects that the children and practitioner engage in. The early learning teacher's role focuses on supporting children in gaining information through questioning, describing, modelling, repeating, or imitating actions (Pacini-Ketchabaw & Prochner, 2013). These actions support children in exploring new experiences and in learning from one another. For example, early learning teachers may offer children warm-up experiences at the onset of outdoor play. This supports children's muscle and motor development, and it sets the tone for feeling psychologically secure. Or, the teacher may take the children indoors for five minutes during a winter's day for a quick story and warm-up and then return them to the outdoors.

Child-initiated exploration refers to the area of concentration for exploration and activities that a child initiates or participates in. When the environment meets the needs of a child and groups of children, a variety of approaches will be explored through trial and error, and ultimately problem solving, to master the challenge. For example, a child who serendipitously discovers how a sand mould works may be motivated to use other materials to see if a similar pattern occurs from the initial mould.

When outdoor environments provide a range of materials and experiences for play, children's observational skills become more attuned to their play space. This increases children's abilities to build on their observations, experiences, and depth of dialogue with other children and adults. Children's observational skills are thought to be enhanced in outdoor play because of their freedom to explore, the open space in which to explore, the reduction of noise levels, and the distractions caused by classroom stimuli (Munroe & MacLellan-Mansell, 2013).

Photo 4.11 Children observe things in their play environments.

Used with Permission of Angela Roy

Photo 4.12 Children discover many science and mathematical concepts through their outdoor play experiences.

Used with Permission of Angela Roy

Early learning teacher–child-guided discovery is described as experiences that the teacher and child initiate. The partners in play use questions and suggestions to formulate the foundation for discovery. For example, the child may ask the teacher, "Can you roll down the hill just like me?" or the early learning teacher may pose questions or offer a sequence of suggestions that will support the child in learning how to walk on tiptoes backwards. The early learning teacher may guide or model certain behaviours when the play becomes frustrating for children or if a child requires further information in order to proceed with the play.

As identified earlier in the chapter, outdoor play is paramount for children in constructing knowledge. Young children acquire more opportunities to experience outdoor play with early learning teachers who collaborate with them in their exploration, experimentation, and manipulation of the environment. This allows children to build on what they know. Through child-to-child and adult-to-child interactions and active experimentation, children discover new knowledge, skills, abilities, and interests.

OBSERVING AND DOCUMENTING CHILDREN'S PLAY OUTDOORS

Children's use of space, time, and materials and their types of play episodes differ between indoor and outdoor environments. Early learning teachers conduct observation and documentation outdoors that contribute to them learning about children's interests, capabilities, and interests and allow them to give children a voice in their environment. For example, through observation, early learning teachers may gain insight about children's social interactions, cognitive and language abilities, motor skills, and emotional development. As well, early learning teachers may acquire information that identifies the differing strengths of children, allows them to plan for future play experiences and materials, or allows them to obtain an overall perspective on the varying interests that evolve in the outdoor play environment.

The outdoor play environment requires a level of monitoring and observation that differs from indoors because of the increased potential for hazards, more rigorous exploration, and safety concerns. Early learning teachers examine children's behaviours, the quality and the quantity of the play, and the level of physical play. Understanding the relationship between children and the environment is gained by watching, listening, and engaging in play. This requires early learning teachers to

- Develop skills in recognizing the developmental and individual variations in play.
- Complete an assessment on the risk and hazard potential of play experiences.
- Identify children's levels of competence and independence (Munroe & MacLellan-Mansell, 2013).
- Observe the social interactions among children.

Children expand their quality of play experiences when they are the decision makers, such as when they are able to choose where to play, what to play, and with whom to play. Early learning teachers may need to support children who wish to join in a play episode, modify behaviour, or assist in negotiating a disagreement. They scan play episodes to determine when and how to intervene in children's play so that it is a positive experience for children.

Watching and listening to children guides early learning teachers in identifying individual and group needs and interests that may be incorporated into the play space. For example, children from rural communities may use space differently—they are used to having large spaces to play. They use more space and their play generally consists of more vigorous gross motor play than the play of urban children. Children living in apartments may have only designated playgrounds in which to play. Children from different cultural backgrounds may use space and materials differently. For example, children who come from countries where water is scarce may have had role models who helped them learn to conserve water. These children may find it difficult to use water in play experiences.

As identified in Chapter 3, there are many observation and documentation strategies that may be used by early learning teachers. Strategies are chosen depending on the information that you are trying to obtain. For example, early learning teachers are interested in knowing how children use the play space. Table 4.6 provides an example of how space use may be examined.

As you think about observations, documentation, and outdoor play, keep in mind that the purpose of observations and documentation is to provide you with insight into children's strengths, interests, and capabilities. Observations allow the early learning teacher to view children's interests and opportunities to scaffold experiences from simple to more complex. Observation and documentation help adults manage the outdoor play environment. Through observation and documentation, early learning teachers become

Table 4.6 Observing how children use outdoor play space.

Area of Observation	Child I	Child II
What play spaces are used?		
What play zones are used?		
What types of equipment and materials does each child use?		
What type of play is each child engaging in—solitary, parallel, associative, cooperative?		
In what situations does the child initiate play? When is there a need for an adult to encourage one of the children?		
What is the duration of the play experience in the various play zones?		
How does the child exhibit creativity in using the materials and equipment?		
What risk-taking and problem-solving techniques are evident?		

familiar with their understanding of their role during the outdoor play experiences and become attuned to how children create play when given the freedom, space, tools, and materials to do so.

CURIOUS?

Add the words *documenting and observing children's outdoor play* to your search engine to obtain further information on strategies to consider.

Examining the Environment for Health and Safety Issues

As much as we want children to have the freedom to play and explore, we need to take the necessary precautions to ensure that the play space supports children being safe. The Canadian Standards Association (CSA) provides early learning teachers with guidelines for creating safe play spaces. Early learning teachers ensure:

- Proper child-to-adult ratios and supervision as a vital component of outdoor play.
- Ongoing maintenance of the play space, equipment, and surfacing.
- Opportunities for children to engage in risky, adventurous, challenging play.
- Appropriate shelter for the children is available and that precautions, such as applying sunscreen appropriately, are taken.
- Plants in the play space are nontoxic and safe for children to have access to.
- Safety checks of equipment and materials are completed as per standards.

Early learning student teachers benefit from becoming familiar with provincial or territorial ministry guidelines and standards for licensing or approving early learning programs in their jurisdiction. This information informs practice, as it helps us become familiar with the required standards of practice that must be adhered to. Table 4.7 provides an example of standard 11.2.7 for equipment, facilities, and surfaces as outlined by the CSA.

Table 4.7 Standards for equipment, facilities, and surfaces as outlined by the CSA.

Item	Precautions
Access	Check for missing or broken rungs, steps, or treads; loosened or missing planks; splinters in handholds; and blocked exits.
Crush points	Check for broken covers exposing crush points and exposed mechanisms.
Decay, deterioration	Check for rust, cracks, decay or rot, heavy wear, and evidence of insect attacks.
Drainage	Check for plugged drain holes; drain holes in tires, equipment, or hollow components. Special attention should be paid to heavy-use areas such as those under swings and slide exit regions.
Edges	Check for protrusions, sharp points, or sharp edges.
Emergency equipment	Ensure that the telephone is in working order, emergency numbers are up to date, and emergency access is not blocked.
Enclosures and fences	Check the enclosures and fences are not broken, tilted, or otherwise damaged.
Equipment protective surfacing	Check for obstacles in equipment protective surfacing zones.
Foundations	Check that foundations are not eroded, beginning to rot, loose in ground, or exposed.
Guards, handrails	Check for missing, bent, broken, loosened, burnt, or wobbly guards and handrails.
Hardware	Check for loosened, missing, bent, worn, or open hooks or rings; protruding nails or hardware; and missing protective caps.
Lead paint	Use non-lead-based paints in all new equipment and when repainting existing equipment to eliminate the risk of childhood lead poisoning from playground equipment.
Lubrication	Check for noisy or squeaky motion.
Moving parts	Check for worn bearings, jammed or nonfunctioning equipment, lack of lubrication, excessive motion, noisy motion, missing protective pieces, or loose spring castings.
Needles	Remove needles in a safe manner. Do not handle them directly; use a tool such as pliers. Contact local authorities for disposal of needles.
Other general hazards	Check for potential clothing entanglement hazards and open S-hooks. Check for trip hazards, such as exposed footings on anchoring devices, or rocks, roots, or any other environmental obstacles in the play area. Children should remove helmets, other than those worn for medical reasons, prior to play on equipment. Remove all ropes and skipping ropes tied to equipment.
Other surfaces	Check for uneven, worn, poorly drained, or otherwise damaged surfaces.
Other surfaces and pathways	Check for worn patches, holes, and cracks.
Park furnishings	Check for broken, unturned, or otherwise damaged furnishings.
Plastics, fibreglass, rubber	Check for splitting, cracking, breaking, discoloration, scorching or burnt areas, abrasion, or wear.

continues ▶

▶ *continues*

Protective surfacing	Check for compacted, eroded, unsanitary, or littered surfacing; surfacing that has been displaced to an ineffective level; and surfacing that is not extensive enough to cover the recommended area.
Roads, sidewalks, and pathways	Check for unevenness, frost damage, and poor drainage.
Ropes, cables	Check for worn spots, fraying, vandalism, degradation, deteriorating joints and splicing, insecure attachments, and ropes or skipping ropes tied to equipment.
Sand facilities	Check for rancid sand, signs of stained clothing or skin, debris, insufficient sand, and need for raking. Check that the lid is in good condition. Change sand at least once a year in areas where there is a high incidence of animal excrement deposits.
Seats	Check for missing, damaged, or loosened seats; sharp edges or corners and insecure fittings or attachments.
Site	Remove foreign objects such as nails, glass, ponding water, sharp objects, litter and syringes, and any entanglements such as scarves, skipping ropes, shoelaces, and belts.
Structure	Check for bending, warping, scorching, cracking, loosening, breaking, distortion, vandalism, uneven surfaces, splintered or decaying wood, corroded or damaged metal, exposed footings, and unstable anchoring of equipment.
Supervision	Determine volume of use relative to maintenance costs, costs of vandalism, success of measures to reduce injuries.
Surface finishes	Check for missing protective coats, splinters, and initial signs of rust or corrosion.
Water facilities	Check for leaks, clogged drains, improper drainage, debris, and growths. Check for nonfunctioning water sprayers on other components.

As identified by the CSA in *Children's Playspaces and Equipment Standards* (April 2014), a number of plants are not appropriate for children's play space. The plants that are appropriate require regular inspection for sharp edges, broken branches, and pest infestation. As a general rule of thumb, the CSA identifies that any plant with white berries should be avoided. Early learning programs become familiar with the plants that are not suitable for play spaces.

Another important area that early learning student teachers become familiar with is toxic fungi. For example, all mushrooms that appear in the play space should be removed for safety reasons. The *Amanita virosa* (Destroying Angel) mushroom is responsible for the majority of fungus poisonings in Canada. This mushroom (the cap, gills, and stem) is white and must be removed immediately from the play space.

CURIOUS?

Add the words *Universal Design Principles* and *CSA* to your search engine to gain further information on making space accessible to children with disabilities.

TERMS THAT INFLUENCE EARLY LEARNING PLAY ENVIRONMENTS

We conclude this chapter with three additional terms that support the theory of children's play. These terms have been taken or adapted from a working document of the Lawson Foundation (2017) on terminology.

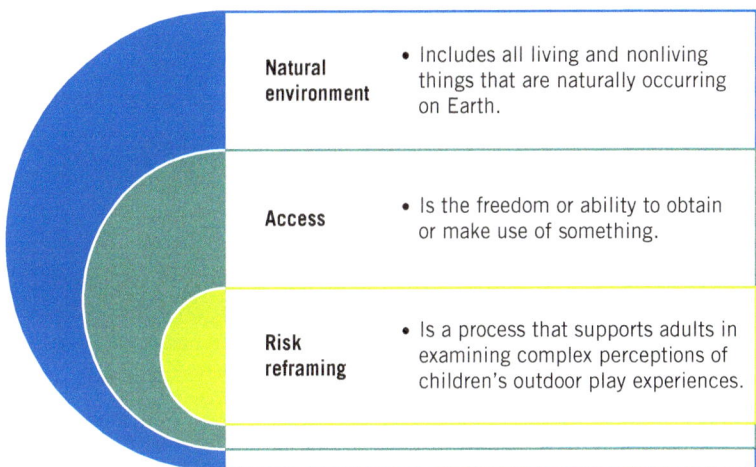

Natural environment	• Includes all living and nonliving things that are naturally occurring on Earth.
Access	• Is the freedom or ability to obtain or make use of something.
Risk reframing	• Is a process that supports adults in examining complex perceptions of children's outdoor play experiences.

SUMMARY

Chapter Preview

- Outdoor play is an essential component of childhood. Early learning teachers require knowledge about and experience in planning and facilitating outdoor play to support children's interests, strengths, and development.

The Complexities of Outdoor Play and Early Learning Programs

- Children's play is complex. Outdoor play directly links with children's wellness and development.
- Early learning teachers examine outdoor play from a historical and cultural perspective and in terms of children's life experiences, environmental sustainability, loose parts, children's curiosity, pedagogy of place and nature pedagogy, and the role of adults.

Historical Perspective of Outdoor Play

- Outdoor play has long been recognized as an important component in the lives of children.
- Froebel and the nursery school movement in the 1920s identified that outdoor play cannot be emulated in other settings. It is essential for a child's whole development.
- Standard play equipment has evolved over the decades, ranging from steel, iron, plastic, to wood. In response to the number of childhood injuries, the Canadian Standards Association developed a set of playground safety standards in the early 1990s.

The Importance of Outdoor Play to Child Development

- Outdoor play enhances a child's cognitive, social, spiritual, emotional, and physical skills, including exploration, risk-taking, language development, social competence, fine and gross motor development, creativity, imagination, and thinking skills, all of which support later academic performance.

Outdoor Play and Exposure to Natural Light

- Exposure to natural light during outdoor play has many benefits for children, as it affects all aspects of their development. Lack of light influences many natural body system functions.

Developing an Appreciation for Outdoor Play

- Children who are exposed to adult role models with an interest in nature, the environment, and outdoor play have a higher probability of developing an interest in outdoor play and the environment, including plants, animals, and environmental sustainability components. The importance of outdoor play is now recognized by a variety of experts in disciplines such as education, health, psychology, and ecology.

Children's Outdoor Play—Risky, Challenging, and Adventurous

- There is debate about whether to call play risky, challenging, and adventurous, or just play. Whatever the terminology, this play is complex and is an important component of outdoor play, as it allows children to learn about new skills, try new ideas, and achieve new knowledge and skills through risk-taking. This play is different from hazardous or unsafe play.

Planning Outdoor Play Spaces

- Early learning teachers examine space to ensure that it is accessible for all children, that it addresses the environmental conditions, and that there are defined play zones. The space offers children variety and opportunities to follow their curiosity and interests.

Play Spaces for Infants, Toddlers, Preschoolers, and School-Aged Children

- Play spaces are generally arranged to support the interests and developmental needs of each age group. Different space requirements are recommended for each of the age ranges to accommodate their interests, strengths, and opportunities to expand curiosity and active play.

Examining the Use of Play Space

- How children use play space is influenced by a number of factors, including their imagination, life experiences, space availability, materials within the space, play space attributes, and adult role models.

Analyzing Play Spaces

- There are a number of ways to examine the effectiveness and versatility of play space. Children's behaviours, duration of the play, the use of materials, how the space is used, and the materials used provide useful insight into the effectiveness of the space.

Choosing Materials for Outdoor Play: Why Loose Parts

- Loose parts are singular materials or combined materials that children use in a variety of ways. Loose parts can stimulate variability in children's play and their learning.
- Loose parts encourage creativity, expand play options, support a child's developmental level, and stimulate children in their play.

Active Outdoor Play Experience Areas

- Outdoor play experiences differ from indoor play experiences. The motor and social skills, sensory skills, types of activities, and interaction among children are some of the more notable differences between the two settings.
- Early learning teachers devise active play opportunities with experience areas such as construction, blocks, woodworking, art, discovery and science, sociodramatics, and games with rules.

The Roles of Early Learning Teachers

- Early learning teachers exhibit various roles, depending on the needs and interests of the children. These roles include teacher-supported involvement, child-initiated exploration, and teacher–child-guided discovery.

Observing and Documenting Children's Play Outdoors

- Observing children's play outdoors provides early learning teachers with insight into children's interests, strengths, and capabilities, most often differing from the indoor environment.
- The early learning environment and experiences extended to children must adhere to appropriate health and safety concerns.

REVIEW QUESTIONS

1. Describe how the novelty era of play structures affected child's play. What were the benefits of the play structures? How did they negatively influence the child's outdoor play?
2. Why is it important for early learning practitioners to be familiar with the Canadian Standards Association guidelines for children's play spaces?
3. Describe some of the challenges that children face in their daily living if they do not acquire sufficient outdoor play experiences.
4. How does the role of the adult affect a child's outdoor play experiences and appreciation for outdoor play?
5. Describe risk-taking and outline why it is an important component of outdoor play and a child's development.
6. Describe seven factors that should be considered when planning children's outdoor play space. Discuss how play space differs for infants, toddlers, preschoolers, and school-aged children.
7. Why is it necessary for early learning practitioners to analyze play space? What are some strategies that may be used to accomplish this?

8. What types of experience centres are effective for children to have in their outdoor environment? Why?
9. Describe five key roles of an early learning practitioner in preparing the outdoor play space and in facilitating play.

MAKING CONNECTIONS

Theory to Practice

1. Visit an early learning outdoor play setting. Examine the space to determine whether a child who uses a walker will have the same access to the play experiences as children who have independent mobility. What changes might you recommend to support the child in having equal play opportunities? Why?
2. Visit an early learning program. Using the seven considerations for examining space and the potential experience areas outlined in this chapter, examine the play space. Are there areas of the play space that may need attention? If so, what areas? How might you change the space to support advancing the use of the play space? How might you increase the opportunities for additional experience areas to be incorporated into the play space?
3. Using the model for examining the complexity and variety of play units as outlined by Kritchevsky, Prescott, and Walling (1977), examine a play space to determine if there are sufficient play spaces available for children in the setting. Make recommendations based on whether there is a need for simple, complex, or super complex units. Justify the reasons for your recommendations.
4. You are required to set up an information documentation panel for parents on the importance of risky, adventurous, challenging outdoor play. What would you highlight? Why? How would you document examples of children engaging in play that is risk-taking rather than unsafe?

DIGITAL PORTFOLIO ENTRIES

Potential portfolio entries for your digital portfolio could include:

- When I think about children and outdoor play I wonder about . . .
- As an early learning student teacher, how do I align my vision about outdoor play with an early learning program's approach?
- When I envision setting up outdoor play experiences, I think about . . .
- I think loose parts . . .
- I wonder about how indoor play and outdoor play . . .

CURIOUS?

Add the words *children's outdoor play and its importance* to your search engine and review the results.

CHAPTER 5
Planning Play Spaces

Rawpixel.com/Shutterstock

> **"** The most effective kind of education is that a child should play amongst lovely things. **"**
>
> —Plato (427–347 BC)

LEARNING OUTCOMES

After exploring this chapter you should be able to:

- Discuss how children's play influences play space requirements.
- Outline how children's play is affected by environmental conditions.
- Discuss how play spaces influence children's learning, health, and wellness.
- Describe characteristics of responsive play space environments.
- Discuss how design features of responsive play spaces support children's play.
- Outline traditional physical play space considerations that early learning teachers use to guide their work with children and space designs.
- Discuss how play spaces affect children's behaviour.

Sharing Stories of Practice

When I began studying early childhood education I was required to create floor plans showing how I would organize play spaces for the children. I examined a number of floor plans that were included in our textbooks. This provided me with insight into thinking about space features such as wet and dry, and quiet and noisy areas. I learned that there were government regulations for early learning centres that required a minimum space for each child for both indoor and outdoor play spaces.

During my 10 years in the field, I have learned so much about how space and the presentation of the space influences children's play, socialization, and experiences.

I have learned that when children's environments are organized, neat, and aesthetically pleasing, the children are calmer, they respect the environment more, and there is more positive energy within the space. Children and staff who are exposed to cluttered environments appear more hyper; the noise level is higher; and children spend less time exploring play options. These observations have led me to focus on creating an appropriate feeling tone within the room and on the fact that children have many opportunities to determine where, when, and how to devise their play space. In fact, I like to think that by deviating from the traditional placements of learning centres, children will stretch play opportunities across the play environment rather than being restricted to the specified area.

My advice to students and new early learning teachers is to look at space options, materials, and interests of the children. There may not be a specific floor plan that should remain constant. Dynamic spaces and places that children create bring new stimulation to staff and children.

Wigwan, ECE graduate, 2017

CHAPTER PREVIEW

Throughout this book we outline information on programming components that support quality play experiences for children. The program planning that children and early learning teachers engage in is important to the success of each play episode. The environmental attributes of the play space are also linked to where and how children take the play episode, which in turn contributes to the success of the play experience. Ideally, the environmental conditions offer children a feeling of comfort, a sense of curiosity, and a desire to explore potential play options. It is the early learning teacher, the children, and the environmental conditions that collectively contribute to the quality, duration, and depth of the play experience.

As Wigwan identified in the chapter's "Sharing Stories of Practice," the **feeling tone** of the environment is as important as the placement of the experience centres. Early learning teachers plan environments that create the context for play, provide children with opportunities to initiate play, stimulate new ideas and levels of curiosity, and encourage children to take risks (Dietze, 2006; Ludlow, 2012). This requires early learning teachers to be attentive to the environment on a daily basis (Azhari, Qamaruzaman, Bajunid, & Hassan, 2015).

As you begin to observe play spaces and children in play spaces, it is beneficial to observe a variety of different environments. Each environment will provide insight into how children use the space and the feeling tone experienced when in the space. Some environments will make you feel alive and well; others may contribute to you feeling agitated and unsettled or give you a sense of overstimulation (Stankovic et al., 2015). Still other environments may have a calming effect that triggers you to want to explore new things. As you think about children in early childhood programs, remember that

feeling tone Refers to how positive, comfortable, and engaging the atmosphere is among teachers, peers, and families.

many children spend up to 40 hours per week in that space. This is more time than they spend awake in their home environments. This leads us to explore core questions in this chapter, such as, Are there places and spaces that offer children more comfort for playing and learning than other places? Are there places that appear to contribute to children feeling more alert than other places? If there is clutter in the space, how does that influence children and their play? Do children act differently when there is order and routine rather than a free-flowing schedule? What space appears to offer children a sense of calmness, and what are the spaces that may increase them feeling agitated or less calm? These environmental questions will affect each child and early learning teacher differently. Early learning teachers consider each environmental attribute carefully when planning for the play space with children and colleagues.

This chapter does not specifically address how experience centres should be placed in an early childhood environment. Experience centres, also called learning centres, are areas in the learning environment with particular focuses such as dramatic play or blocks. There are many ways to arrange these areas, depending on space availability and the philosophy of both the program and the early learning teachers. This chapter introduces you to principles that guide early learning teachers in play space design. We also present an array of environmental attributes that influence children's play. These environmental attributes require careful consideration, as they are foundational to creating quality play spaces for young children.

CHILDREN'S PLAY

As identified in Chapter 2, there are varying types of children's play that early learning teachers observe and plan space around from both an environmental and a play perspective. The types of play—*sensorimotor play*, *symbolic play*, and *construction play*—combined with the children's interests, learning, and phases of development sets the stage for planning play spaces (Azhari et al., 2015).

Let's take a few minutes to reexamine the characteristics of sensorimotor, symbolic, and construction play from a planning play space perspective. Children engage in these

Photo 5.1 Children's play is influenced by their environment and the people in the environment.
Used with Permission of Bora Kim

types of play in stages, moving from sensorimotor to symbolic to construction play (Frost, Wortham, & Reifel, 2012). As children's life experiences expand, there is a shift in the types of play and the duration of each type of play. The more children are exposed to rich play experiences and environments, the more advanced their play becomes (Frost, 2012).

In Wolfgang and Wolfgang's (1992) seminal work, they suggested that children between the ages of 1 and 2 years spend approximately 80 percent of their play in sensorimotor play, while the remaining 20 percent is spent in symbolic play. Children between the ages of 2 and 3 years spend about 50 percent of their play in sensorimotor play, 25 percent in symbolic play, and 25 percent in construction play. Children 3 to 4 years of age reduce their sensorimotor play to approximately 30 percent, and there is an increase to approximately 40 percent symbolic play and 30 percent construction play. Children between the ages of 4 and 5 years spend approximately 25 percent in sensorimotor play, 20 percent in symbolic play, and 55 percent in construction play (Hanline, 1999). Children between the ages of 6 and 12 years spend most of their play in construction play. These phases of play guide early learning teachers in examining and designing play space that supports productive, quality play.

Sensorimotor Play

During the first phase of life to approximately age 18 months, children learn through their senses and interaction with people and things in the environment. Children's play spaces offer opportunities for repetition of sensory motor acts, many of which involve repetition of an action involving their bodies. Children flourish in environments that provide opportunities for their play and include materials such as pushing and pulling toys, grasping and shaking items, and materials that require them to engage in trial-and-error experimentations. Children require intimate play spaces, yet they also need sufficient space so that they may exhibit their need for autonomy.

Symbolic Play

This phase of play is characterized by children using their imagination and role-playing to transform people, items, or events into various items or uses depending on the interactive play episode with adults and peers (Hobson, Hobson, Cheung, & Calo, 2015). Children expand the types of symbolic play based on their developmental phases and life experiences. They begin with something that is familiar to them and that requires a real-life object (Hobson et al, 2015). For example, a child may pick up the cellphone and pretend to speak to mommy. The child may use items interchangeably as props, such as using a block for a bottle with doll play and then using it for stacking. As children progress in their play, they include various props and engagement with playmates (Adamson, Bakeman, Deckner, & Nelson, 2012).

microsymbolic play Refers to children using child-sized materials that are replicas of objects, such as a child's tea set or a doctor's kit.

macrosymbolic play Refers to children assuming pretend roles such as being a firefighter.

Children exhibit both **microsymbolic play** and **macrosymbolic play**. Children require a variety of play spaces and materials in the environment that are familiar daily living items.

Add the words *microsymbolic* and *macrosymbolic* to your search engine to find out more information about these two concepts.

Photo 5.2 Play environments influence children's experiences.
Used with Permission of Bora Kim

Construction Play

During this phase of play development, children begin to express an idea or construct items that represent ideas that they have previously observed, with various materials. Hanline (1999) indicated that construction play requires children to have access to both **fluid materials** and **structured materials** in their play space. Construction play progresses in phases. Each phase requires children to have access to more time and more play space. For example, children first engage in play that focuses on mastering defined processes, such as stacking blocks, then move gradually to constructing realistic items, such as a sand structure, a block structure of a castle, or a picture that expresses a life experience, such as children playing on logs at a playground.

Play spaces are examined from the perspective of creating them, improving them, and ensuring that they are inclusive play spaces. To ensure that play experiences will be stimulating and advance children's learning opportunities, play spaces reflect their interests and needs. Each play space decision is positively or negatively weaved into play experiences, including the relationships with people, materials, expectations, and routines (Callaghan, 2013).

fluid materials Refer to those materials that change in shape or by their use offer children opportunities to create items that can be altered in shape and form (Hanline, 1999). Examples of fluid materials include play dough, sand, water, paint, and paper.

structured materials Materials with predetermined characteristics that influence or guide the child in how to use the materials in construction. Blocks, puzzles, and climbing apparatus are classified as structured materials.

THE ENVIRONMENT AS THE THIRD TEACHER

In many early learning environments, the phrase "the environment as the third teacher" is associated with Reggio Emilia and Reggio-inspired programs. In fact, researchers from a wide range of disciplines, including early childhood education, adult education, psychology, and architectural design, are emphasizing the importance of examining both the physical space and the social space (Fraser, 2012) for children, families, and early learning teachers. The Reggio Emilia approach suggests that there are three educators within a play space at any one time: the teacher, the child, and the environment. It is during childhood, when given the freedom to explore, that children use the environment in unique and innovative ways (Strong-Wilson & Ellis, 2007). The environments created

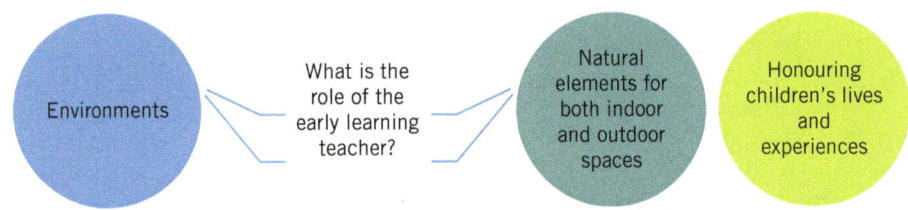

Figure 5.1 Considerations made when designing environments as third teachers.

The educators of Reggio Emilia characterize the environment as the third teacher. The first teachers are families and educators (Kuh, 2014). The environment has the power to organize, promote relationships, and teach (Ontario Ministry of Education, 2014). Gandini (1994) speaks for Reggio educators when she describes space as an "aquarium that mirrors the ideas, values, attitudes and cultures of the people who live in it" (p. 149).

for children can either enhance or impede children's desire to act on their curiosity and opportunities for learning.

As outlined in *How Does Learning Happen? Ontario's pedagogy for the early years* (Ontario Ministry of Education, 2014), the environment is where children's learning takes place. Children's indoor and outdoor spaces are intended to "mirror the ideas, values, attitudes, and cultures of those who use the space" (p. 20). Early learning and student teachers benefit from looking at both the indoor and the outdoor space to visualize it from the perspective of children. For example, what might 3-year-old children see at their eye level? How might the materials be placed and displayed so that children have the freedom to self-select them and discuss their findings with their peers? What might the artifacts communicate? As you review the remaining sections of this chapter, think about early learning environments that you have observed. If you had an opportunity to change them, how might you do so and why? How might changes influence new and valuable playing opportunities for children? What role would you encourage the children to have in creating the space?

The educators of Reggio Emilia encourage early learning teachers to carefully and consistently examine the space and the messages that it sends to children and families (Strong-Wilson & Ellis, 2007). As we think about the skills, knowledge, attitudes, and abilities that support children in reaching their full potential, early learning teachers play an important role in creating environments that foster these diverse skills. Figure 5.1 provides an overview of the complexity of the considerations that early learning teachers make when intentionally designing children's environments as third teachers. Early learning spaces, whether indoors or outdoors, are created to draw children to engage in the space and place.

CHILDREN'S PLACES

Children's play is directly influenced by environmental conditions. "Beauty is the voice that calls the child[ren] to engage with the materials and elevates [them] to a higher level of grace and courtesy as [they] interact in [their environment]" (Haskins, 2012, p. 34). Early learning teachers and children observe, engage, and determine how and what speaks to them in the space. Early learning teachers understand the difference between children's places of play and places for children to play (Strong-Wilson & Ellis, 2007).

STOP ... THINK ... DISCUSS ... REFLECT

What do we mean by children's place to play and places for children to play? How do these differences influence the planning process associated with creating children's environments?

Photo 5.3 Children's places are planned with care, comfort, and attention to aesthetics.

Used with Permission of Fox Hollow Child Care Centre

Think about early learning play spaces as places that bring children, ideas, other people, and resources together. The way in which the play space is presented to children is aligned with their abilities to function effectively within it. Adults who are concerned about children's places to play create play spaces that offer them a sense of belonging and give them permission and opportunities to build upon their curiosity. The play space supports children and families in having a feeling of mutual respect and comfort with others in the play space. The adult–child and child-to-child interactions are nurturing and supportive (Li, Quinones, & Ridgway, 2016).

Early learning teachers consider a number of principles and perspectives when planning children's play spaces (Azhari et al., 2015). Position statements, program statements (as required in Ontario), curricula, and theoretical frameworks and philosophies guide how environments are designed to support children in their play. Figure 5.2 offers an overview of perspectives that early learning teachers consider.

Think about children who are digging in the outdoor sandpit. You notice that other children are frequently walking along the edge of the sandpit to get to the tricycles. This may result in children in the sandpit play becoming upset with their peers who are trying to get to the tricycles. By placing a divider between the sandpit and the tricycles, the early learning teacher creates an environment that is responsive to the needs of children. Not only does the divider stop children from being distracted in the sandpit zone, it also reduces the amount of intervention for redirection needed between the adults and children. As well, it reduces a potential safety issue. Now, think about children who are consistently running out of floor space for their block construction. By rearranging the block centre so that there is adequate space, early learning teachers support children in being able to use the blocks in more creative ways. Without adequate space, children will not be able to embrace or expand on their ideas. This reduces children's desire to explore and make new discoveries (Hinkley, Carson, & Hesketh, 2015).

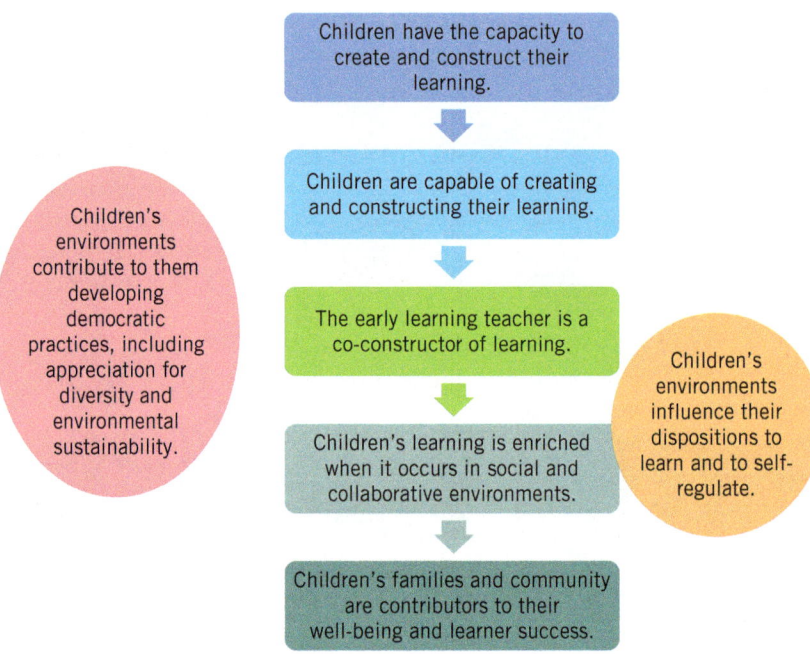

Figure 5.2 Overview of perspectives for consideration.

STOP ... THINK ... DISCUSS ... REFLECT

Think about children who do not have adequate space for their play, such as for their block construction. How does this detract from their opportunities to explore and discover? What scientific and mathematical principles might children not experience because of the lack of space?

Play spaces that are responsive to the children's needs require early learning teachers to observe and engage in teachable moments as they become evident (Poole, 2016). For example, when children express an interest in digging for worms, teachers ensure that they engage in dialogue with the children about their discoveries and provide resources that they may require for their exploration. As well, they may further support the children's explorations by placing books about worms and a magnifying glass outdoors. Such resources, when thoughtfully placed, increase children's desire to look closely at the worms and compare their findings.

As illustrated in the examples above, early learning environments are designed to support children's play, senses, and discoveries. The play space and play options provide children with a variety of materials that facilitate many types of play and experiences (La Paro & Gloeckler, 2016). Early learning teachers plan play space that reflects how children learn. As identified by Ludlow (2012), children embrace environments with

> a predominance of hands on, open-ended materials such as various lengths and types of wood, junk materials, natural materials, fabric and clay. These materials allow children to productively investigate, experiment, problem solve and test hypotheses without close adult supervision. (p. 22)

When the environment is appropriate, children will exhibit their natural curiosity and playful attributes. More than 13 years ago, Greenman (2005) made a valuable contribution to environmental design that remains true today. He suggested that "childhood is when human beings should fall in love with the world and all its untidy and sometimes scary complexity, delights, and mysteries" (p. 2). He identified that if we reduce play options and the freedom for children to play, we are removing the meandering, the sense of journey, and the exploration "along the way"—all of which are essential parts to children's desire to explore, play, and discover (p. 2). Think about early learning environments that you have observed or participated in. Do they currently provide children with the ability and the freedom to meander, to have a sense of journey, and to explore "along the way," or are they places with clear schedules and routines that must followed? How do we build these characteristics into children's places today?

STOP ... THINK ... DISCUSS ... REFLECT

If it is important for children to have the ability and freedom to meander and explore along the way, why do early learning programs have schedules and timelines that early learning teachers adhere to? What do we need to do to change the attitudes about schedules? How do we build in time for children to explore along the way?

Early learning environments are essentially the children's home away from home; therefore, children's play spaces are ideally designed to offer them a safe, caring, and nourishing place to be in and to facilitate play. Ideally, the play space provides opportunities for children to be free to explore their environment and be comfortable within the space so that they may engage in play to the fullest. The play space is reflective of children's lived experiences, interests, and cultures. The aesthetic presentations of materials, furniture, and resources are positioned in ways that trigger children to engage, innovate, discover, and support them in their quest to satisfy their curiosity (Dietze & Kashin, 2016; Ludlow, 2012).

Play space is not made up of fixed components; rather, it is fluid and emerges and changes with children's input and interests. Examining and adjusting play space is a continuous process that accommodates children's needs. Much of the research indicates that early learning environments honour children when they:

- Are appropriate for children.
- Offer freedom and flexibility to support children to explore, experiment, and engage in play.
- Build a sense of community, diversity, social justice, respect, and trust among the individual child, groups of children, and adults within the play space.
- Are smaller spaces with cozy spaces combined with sufficient space and freedom to move and are versatile to support various play opportunities.
- Foster a sense of ownership of the environment.

As we think about children and their play, early learning environments incorporate the components outlined in Figure 5.3 on the following premises.

1. Children require spaces that facilitate opportunities to engage in a variety of experiences that build upon their sense of wonderment, exploration, and lived experiences.

Photo 5.4 Children will re-create play spaces to support their play ideas.
Used with Permission of Family Space Quinte, Inc.

Children flourish in environments that are stimulating. Stimulating environments lead children to want to explore and experience new and innovative opportunities. Children engage in play and with play partners in environments where they are able to connect with nature and natural resources. Children benefit from exposure to water, sand, things that move, things that they may dump and pour, and things that will allow them to create, build, and take apart (Stankovic et al., 2015).

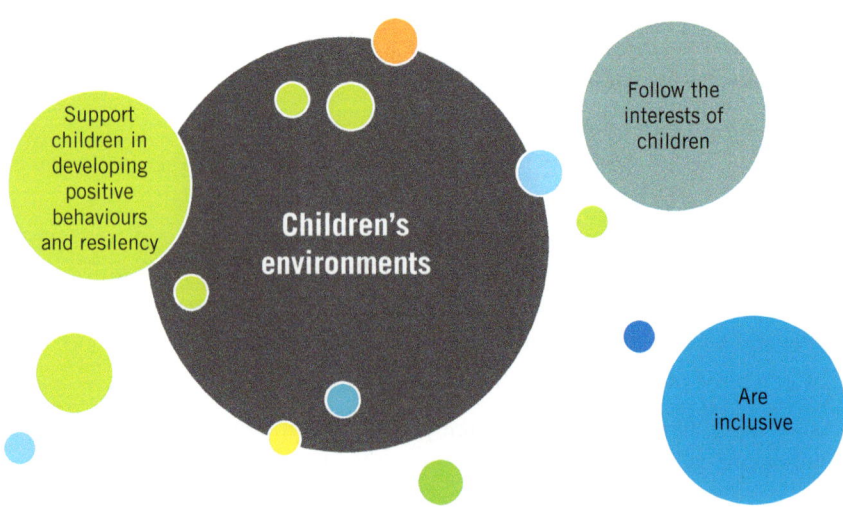

Figure 5.3 Children's environments support children in many ways.

2. Children are free to play within all aspects of the space. Ideally, the environment offers children many options for quiet and active play and individual and group play. There are a variety of natural materials that trigger exploration and play engagement (Dietze & Kim, 2014).

3. Children have appropriate adult role models. The adults are experienced in coaching aspects of play and discovery that lead children to develop confidence and competence in their play, problem solving, and play engagement. Early learning teachers offer a variety of materials and resources, probing questions, dialogue, and documentation in their practices with children. This contributes to children developing their play from simple to complex and from surface to deep learning opportunities (Connors, 2016).

4. Children's environments extend beyond the early learning space. Children use community space as another place for play. Early learning teachers offer children access to resources and seek out resources that will enhance the children's play and learning experiences. Children benefit from learning about our culturally diverse populations. They expand their knowledge and curiosity when they are provided with options to use and embrace space in the community in which they live (Connors, 2016).

5. Children's play spaces incorporate daily living responsibilities into the environment. They, like adults, flourish when they are assigned tasks to support daily living in the environment. Caring for plants, caring for their environment, and understanding principles of recycling and reusing help children incorporate these skills into their play. This is foundational for environmental stewardship.

CHARACTERISTICS OF RESPONSIVE PLAY SPACE ENVIRONMENTS

In this section, we introduce additional characteristics and considerations that early learning teachers think about when creating a responsive play space for children, as outlined in Figure 5.4. These are in addition to the considerations needed for the overall physical play space arrangement. These components may seem less important to early learning teachers than the actual placement of the materials, but research suggests that they are as important as the physical play space design.

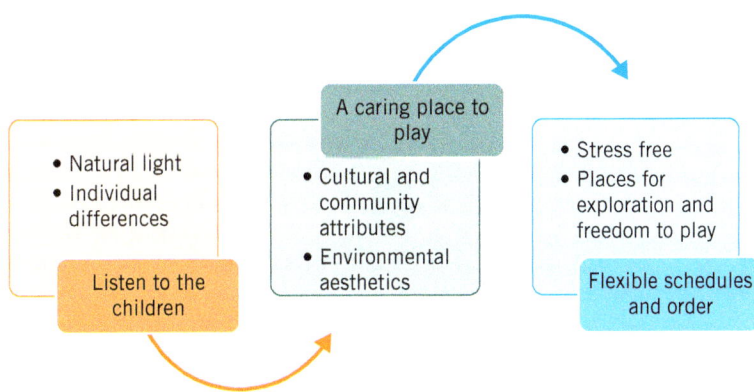

Figure 5.4 Characteristics of responsive play spaces.

CURIOUS?

Add the words *responsive environments* to your search engine to find out more information about what this means and how it influences space design for children.

Feeling Tone

Early learning teachers examine both the play space and the overall feeling tone within the space because together these two factors influence children's play and engagement within the environment. The feeling tone is interrelated to the behaviours that children exhibit and the relationships among children and adults. The feeling tone also influences who children play with and how the materials are used, which contributes to the depth and breadth of the play experiences (Stankovic et al., 2015). As outlined in Figures 5.5 and 5.6 feeling tones are influenced by many physical and human aspects. Early learning teachers benefit from thinking about and responding to the questions posed in the figures below.

Environments that exhibit appropriate feeling tones show evidence of happy, active children. Throughout the environment, there is a humming sound of children engaged in play. Early learning teachers monitor the noise levels and the types of noise levels because excessive or ongoing noise can affect children's hearing and learning permanently (Li et al., 2016; Werner, Linting, Vermeer, & Van IJzendoorn, 2015).

Think about children being exposed to yelling and screaming among children or early learning teachers using loud voices as a child management strategy. Such noise negatively influences the feeling tone of the play space. This type of noise level impedes

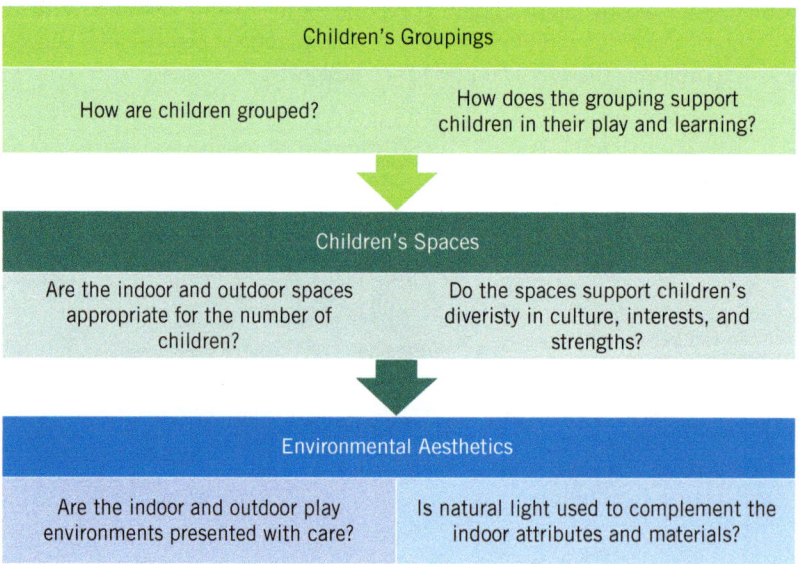

Figure 5.5 How children's groupings influence the feeling tone of the environment.

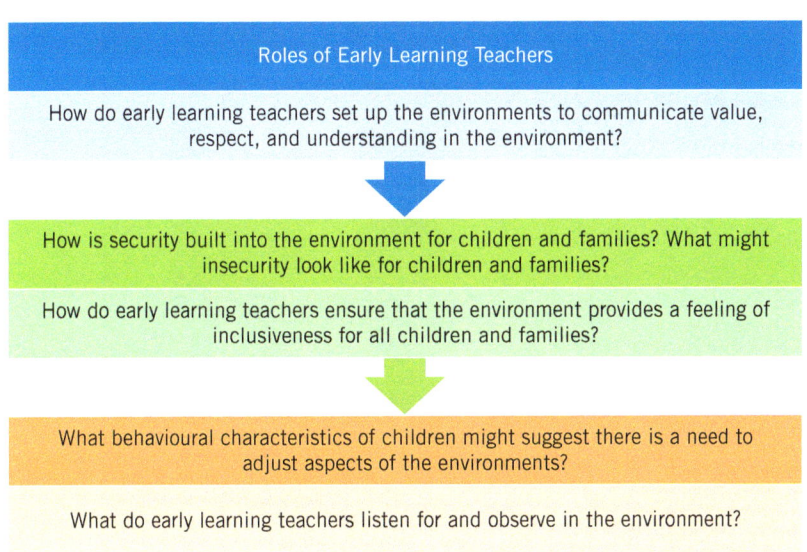

Figure 5.6 How the role of early learning teachers influences the feeling tone of the environment.

children's abilities to effectively focus or have the desire to engage in play because they are not able to concentrate in the play space (Li et al., 2016).

The feeling tone is built on many factors. As you review the upcoming sections and as you reflect on the environments you have observed for children, think about how environments can support or detract from children having a safe, nurturing place to play and to grow.

Listening to the Children

As early learning teachers prepare play spaces, they listen to the children during their play, observe children's play processes, and consider their interests. This helps early learning teachers to gain insight into a child's point of view about materials, spaces, and interests. By listening to the children, early learning teachers match their observations and insights with their understanding of children's strengths and interests (Batemen, 2013; Houen, Danby, Farrell, & Thorpe, 2016). For example, when you listen to the play of 4-year-olds in the block centre, you may hear them using construction terms and wearing hats that depict their role in the construction, such as a white hat for the supervisor. This information tells you that the children are ready to use or produce pictorial or written signs in their play for their structures. Or, you may observe younger children playing with materials that are familiar to them, such as a particular car, truck, or doll. This reinforces the need for children to have access to materials they are familiar with and the need to add new materials on a gradual basis (Siraj & Asani, 2015).

Listening to the children helps early learning teachers to evaluate the quality and quantity of the conversations among the children, staff, and families. They also acquire information about how adults listen to the children. For example, many early learning teachers are eager to listen to the children so that they gain insight into their thinking and lived experiences. This information becomes foundational in formulating questions to provoke and challenge children's thinking in new ways. Such processes lead children to create new ideas and learning. Listening to children and families builds a sense of

Photo 5.5 New materials add new dimensions to children's level of exploration and experimentation.

Used with Permission of Fox Hollow Child Care Centre

a community of play and learning, while also creating a context in which early learning teachers become more thoughtful and intentional in their environmental designs (La Paro & Gloeckler, 2016).

A Caring Place to Play

Children require caring places to play. Children and their families come to early learning programs with different family stories and backgrounds. Early learning teachers are cognizant of the varying cultures, beliefs, and values that each family brings to the play space. Some values may differ from our personal beliefs or our professional practice (Romero, García, & Jiménez, 2015).

The needs of families and communities continue to evolve. What one family or group of families requires today may differ significantly in six months or a year. Early learning teachers respond to the changing needs of families and children. For example, you may be exposed to a centre where a large proportion of families require services until after 6:00 p.m., or you may have a large group of children whose first language is not English.

Based on the family population, policies and procedures may need to be developed or revised to support the needs of the families. Some centres examine their family dynamics and hire staff that will complement the family demographics.

Ideally, early learning centres are places for children and families to connect. This increases the life experiences of the children and the overall connectedness among children, staff, and families. For example, think about the possibilities if one of the parents in the centre is an artist. She agrees to share some of her expertise with the children. As the artist works with the children to explore colour, she recognizes the incredible works of art that the children have created. She, the children, and staff decide to have a gallery showing of the children's work. This extends a learning branch of the children's life experiences in new directions. Or, think of the family trying to start a new life in this country. For many, the early learning centre is one of the first safe places in the community that they become connected with.

Creating caring environments takes time, acceptance of families, and space. For example, a place that welcomes families and empowers families to be part of the early learning place to play ensures that there is space that allows for family interactions. Displays of documentation that depict the children's play and learning are available as a way to make the learning visible and to have families interpret what they see in the documentation. A caring place to play connects and engages families in the program.

Inviting Engagement in Environments with Provocations

Early learning teachers and families collectively contribute to offering children interesting items that may spark their curiosity or wonderment in new ways. These items may include items from nature, photographs, various artifacts, or documented experiences. **Provocations** are placed in both indoor and outdoor environments in various places where the children will discover them. They will want to respond to this arrangement of provocative materials. Provocations, when intriguing, expand children's desire to engage in their environments and take their thinking and play experiences to new levels of exploration. Think about what might happen if children found large sticks, rope, tape and lights, and flowing fabric in the outdoor space? How might that intrigue them to engage in play? What might they explore?

Early learning teachers consider how to incorporate provocations into children's spaces, based on children's expressed interests. Provocations can take many forms. They could include:

- **Items from nature:** Present an array of locally appropriate items such as seashells, pine cones, leaves, moss, wildflowers, or fresh flowers from a garden.
- **Photos of children engaged in play:** Create a display of photos from children's previous play and display them near where the play occurred.
- **Experiences:** Offer picnic baskets that have many surprises within them and that are taken to a local space for an outdoor snack or lunch.
- **Resources:** Provide children with unique resources such as books, art materials, or construction materials that reflect children's expressed interests.
- **Unique materials:** Offer a variety of unique materials or artifacts that children may not have experienced.

Provocations are meant to guide or trigger children's desire to explore and extend their play. Early learning teachers observe if, how, and when children are drawn to the provocations. After several days, if they have not intrigued children, they might be placed in other areas of the play space or removed from the space.

provocations "The deliberate and thoughtful actions taken by adults, or in some cases children, to provoke or extend children's sense of wonder and thinking, such as by adding displays or materials that may attract children to areas of the environment" (Dietze & Kashin, 2016, p. 206).

Photo 5.6 Provocations are intended to trigger a new or deeper sense of exploration.
Used with Permission of Family Space Quinte, Inc.

Environmental Aesthetics

<u>environmental aesthetics</u>
Focuses on how individuals experience their world through their senses by incorporating their environmental perceptions and their aesthetic preferences in environments, cultures, and seasons (Carlson, 2002).

Environmental aesthetics is a subfield of aesthetics and environmental philosophy (Brady, 2009). Environmental aesthetics includes the physical and social space as well as the natural objects and processes within the environment (Brady, 2009; Carlson, 2002) as opposed to artworks. The space focuses on "the ways in which humans experience the world through their senses" (Carlson, 2002, p. 1). For children, environmental aesthetics includes how their perceptions and aesthetic preferences are experienced. Children learn through their five senses. This means that their environments need to include materials and things that they may touch, smell, taste, see, and hear. This reinforces the importance of early learning teachers exposing children to nature, art, culture, community, and people within the community.

Discussion about the aesthetics of the environment is not new to the early learning field. For example, Dewey (1956/1999) indicated that children require environments that provide "conversation . . . inquiry . . . making things . . . and artistic expression" (p. 47). He further identified that children require "large grounds, gardens, and green house." He advocated for children to have "open air" interiors with a variety of workspaces and the feeling of a "well-furnished home" (Upitis, 2005, p. 8). One way to achieve this is for early learning environments to provide children with natural products such as tables and chairs made of wood, rather than the popular coloured plastic furniture found in many early learning play spaces today.

Malaguzzi (1991) indicated that play space aesthetics has a major influence on children's comfort and security within their play space. Malaguzzi further emphasized the importance of early learning teachers paying attention to the play space aesthetics "because of its power to organize, promote pleasant relationships between people of different ages, create a handsome environment, promote choices and activity and its potential for sparking all kinds of social, affective, and cognitive learning" (p. 6). This means that early learning teachers critically examine the play space environments to ensure that what is in the environment has meaning to the children and that what is displayed is attractively presented. When the environment is meaningful and well organized, it acts like another adult in the room, providing support and encouragement to children's play experiences.

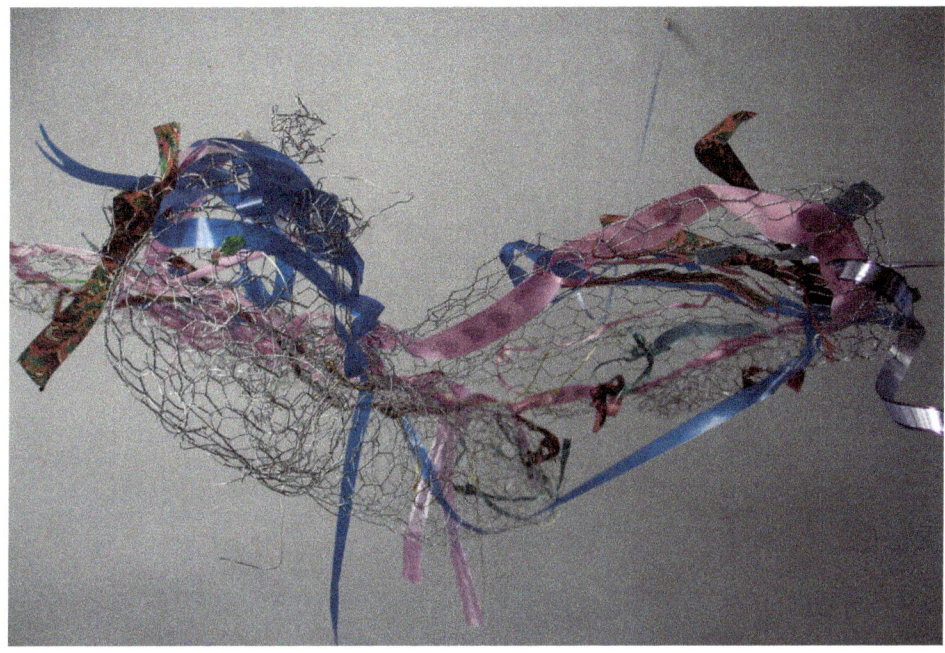

Photo 5.7 Children and adults collectively determine how to create interesting displays in their play spaces.
Used with Permission of Fox Hollow Child Care Centre

Aesthetic appreciation and presentation mean different things to different people. Each family and individual within a family develops his or her own approach to aesthetic appeal. Research continues to help early learning teachers link the connection of the presentation of the environment to children's behaviour, resiliency, learning, and comfort within the environment. When the aesthetic environment is correct, there is an increased level of sensory and perceptual activity (Stankovic et al., 2015).

Environments may influence children either positively or negatively. Visual stimulation is a key influencer in children's learning. Ishai, Ungerleider, Martin, Schouten, and Haxby (1999) determined that the way in which a child's brain deals with visual stimulation is directly related to learning. They explain that the circuitry in the brain's visual system responds to each visual stimulus that children are exposed to. The more stimuli within the environment, the more the brain must process. The brain requires oxygen to process the images through the circuits. When children are exposed to cluttered environments, the brain uses energy to suppress the images. The more cluttered the environment, the more energy the brain requires to block out the stimuli (Stankovic et al., 2015). When children use their energy for this purpose, it increases children's activity levels and often leads to behaviours such as biting, hitting, and pushing. Environments that bring natural light and nature into play spaces and reduce visual chaos and clutter generally experience less overactivity by the children.

Children's ability to concentrate and focus on play may be impeded in environments where huge amounts of information are found on the walls or hanging from the ceilings (Stankovic et al., 2015). For example, if you enter a play space where many pieces of children's art are placed on bulletin boards at the adult eye level, with tape or tacks and with no semblance of order, you immediately may gain an uncomfortable, closed-in feeling. This discomfort is a result of the presentation within the environment. Quality play spaces replace the commercial images, the permanent murals, and the overabundance of "stuff" in the environment because these images take valuable oxygen and energy away from the children's opportunity to use them for playing and learning. It is much healthier

Photo 5.8 A child's environment incorporates community and culture outdoors.

Used with Permission of Diane Kashin

for children to experience natural light, the acoustics, furnishings, and materials that enhance the aesthetic attributes of the space.

Aesthetic appreciation requires a balance of minimalism, natural products, and a sense of coziness. The materials and the aesthetic touches must have meaning for the children. Early learning environments are child friendly and not overstimulating for the child. They do not project either too much clutter or too much sterility. Our experience tells us that children should be exposed to beautiful things.

Photo 5.9 A child's environment incorporates community and culture indoors.

Used with Permission of Fox Hollow Child Care Centre

Natural light affects

- Learning abilities
- Concentration
- Academic performance
- Health
- Mood
- Ability to interact with people

Figure 5.7 How natural light affects children.

Natural Light

There are many advantages for children and adults to being exposed to natural light in both their indoor and their outdoor play spaces. Natural light helps children concentrate; it keeps them focused and less distracted; and it improves academic performance and leads to improved attendance (Hathaway, 1995; Plympton, Conway, & Epstein, 2000; Reicher, 2000; Stankovic et al., 2015).

There is a relationship between light and physical well-being, health, and wellness (Hinkley et al., 2015). A number of studies suggest that exposure to poor lighting or fluorescent lighting is linked to hyperactivity and decreased productivity (Harmon, 1951; Liberman, 1990; Ott, 1976). As outlined in Figure 5.7, natural light affects many aspects of children's development. Katerina (2012) indicated that some studies suggest that children's language; social, emotional, and academic performance; and physical development progress more rapidly in outdoor play spaces than in indoor play spaces, due to increased access to natural light. Early learning teachers examine ways to implement strategies that will expose children to adequate natural light throughout our changing seasons.

Add the words *natural light* to your search engine to find out more information about the importance of light to children's health and wellness.

Stress-Free

How children feel in the environment influences the intensity level and the quality of the play experience. Early learning teachers strive to create stress-free environments. When the environments are free from stressful feelings, children become more engaged in their experimentation and thinking. They also become more curious, which leads them to explore more ideas or things.

Stress occurs in environments when there is an imbalance between the demands on individuals or groups and human resources (Evans & Wachs, 2010). Creating a stress-free environment for young children today is imperative, as many of our children live in stressful home environments due to situations such as family relationships and dynamics, economic conditions, parental careers, or intergenerational responsibilities.

There are many stressors hidden within children's environments. Two prevalent stressors are poor diets and noise pollution (Klatte, Bergström, & Lachmann, 2013). These factors influence how children use the play space.

- **Poor diet.** Children who are exposed to an overabundance of convenience food or to a diet that does not meet Canada's Food Guide may lack proper nutrition. This may contribute to children experiencing mood swings, having a lack of energy, and not having the resiliency to deal with stressful situations (Otten, Hirsh, & Lim, 2017).
- **Noise pollution.** Some children are negatively affected by the noise in their play environments. Noise pollution is caused by many factors (e.g., too many children in a play space, the busyness of the environment, the adult–child interactions, constant music, distracting noises from various toys). Noise pollution has the potential to decrease the energy levels of adults and children and their ability to concentrate on exploring new learning opportunities. Children from noisy environments may suffer ill effects from noise pollution, which include less cognitive growth, delayed language skills, increased anxiety, decreased quality of sleep, and impaired resiliency (Klatte et al., 2013; Werner et al., 2015).

When early learning teachers note that the noise level is escalating and the children are beginning to disengage in their play, steps are taken immediately to reduce the noise level. There are many ways to achieve this. Early learning teachers may wish to circulate among the children and speak softly to the children. The teacher may engage in one-on-one dialogue with children who appear restless. Different play areas may be suggested, or new materials that offer children new exploration may be presented. The objective is to change the noise level and find ways to have children re-engage in play.

Early learning environments are designed to positively influence children's play and behaviour. When the environment meets the needs of children, there is a reduction in aggressive or negative behaviours (Li et al., 2016). The more comfortable children are in the play space environment and with the people in the play space, the more likely it is that prosocial behaviours will be exhibited (Stankovic et al., 2015). Stress-free environments support children feeling physically and psychologically safe and free from fear and chaos (Boss, 2001; Werner et al., 2015). When children do not feel safe and secure, anxiety levels increase. Over time, they may exhibit the **fight-or-flight response** to other children, adults, and the environment (Werner et al., 2015). Children may try to find a place in the environment with fewer visual or auditory distractions. They may also look for places that they find cozy and tight as a way to feel protected.

fight-or-flight response
Refers to a built-in defence mechanism, designed to protect us, that triggers psychological and physical changes to our bodies when in a specific danger.

REFLECTS CULTURAL AND COMMUNITY ATTRIBUTES

Similar to children gaining a sense about aesthetically pleasing spaces and beautiful things in their environment, quality play spaces provide exposure to culture- and community-specific items such as art, books, and artifacts. Early learning teachers encourage families to bring culture-specific materials for the children to explore. The early learning teacher creates opportunities for children to gain knowledge and experience with the cultural items in the correct context.

STOP ... THINK ... DISCUSS ... REFLECT

What might be some community culture attributes and traditions that you would expose children to? What might families bring to the children's play environment?

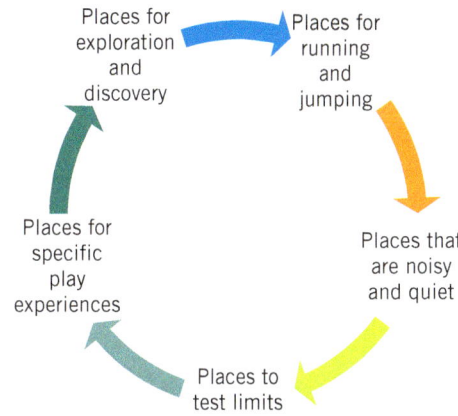

Figure 5.8 Spaces children require in their early learning environments.

Places for Exploration and Freedom to Play

Creating early learning play spaces that provide children with opportunities to explore and freedom to play requires discussion among the children, early learning teachers, and families. Arranging the furnishings and assigning storage constitute two small aspects of the overall needs of children. More important is looking at the needs of children. As outlined in Figure 5.8, children require an array of flexible spaces.

In the upcoming chapters, we will introduce you to overviews of dramatic play, art, science and math, language and literacy, music and movement, and outdoor play. As you review those chapters, think about how each of those curriculum areas requires places for exploration and freedom to play.

Photo 5.10 Children's play is richest when it is hands on.

Used with Permission of Family Space Quinte, Inc.

Reflects Cultural and Community Attributes

Photo 5.11 Children require a variety of play spaces.
Used with Permission of Bora Kim

Experience-based, hands-on learning evolves in play spaces where children may choose what they wish to engage in and with. The environmental attributes are designed to support the children's planned and spontaneous creativity, movement, and expansive play. Think about children going into an art studio. What would they see? What would they feel? And what would they experience? Or, if the children have opportunities to have a garden in their play space, what experiences will that provide them with? What are children missing in the world of play if a garden is not part of the play space?

Children require access to unique and innovative spaces both indoors and outdoors. The environment reflects the children's interests, while offering them new options for exploration and learning. For example, there are places for children to engage in scientific explorations, such as with kaleidoscopes, stained glass, sensory materials from their natural environment, and magnifying glasses. There are flexible indoor and outdoor spaces to use natural products such as clay, paint, and paper (Azhari et al., 2015). Children require places to dig, to pour, and to "muck" about—to be free to explore the properties of mud, water, and sand. Children need room to climb, run, throw, jump, roll, and use their bodies in interesting ways.

FLEXIBLE SCHEDULES AND ORDER

A sense of security occurs for children in environments that reflect the needs of children and are familiar and predictable. Children require places that provide **ordered time** and space. How the day is structured influences the depth and breadth of play and exploration. Early learning teachers organize the time with the children to establish a balance of the rhythms of children's needs and the predictable programming structure. Children's schedules, similar to the play space, require flexibility, not rigidity, so that their needs and interests may be accommodated. For example, in order for children to have the freedom to play, flexibility is required in their daily routine. When children become absorbed in

ordered time Refers to an established framework that early learning practitioners and children follow to support children to anticipate the sequence and predictability of their daily routine.

Table 5.1 Environmental order perspectives and practices.

Perspective	Practice
Children become independent and competent in the space.	Materials are positioned so that children have access to them and may obtain what is needed when required.
	Pictorial and printed signs support children in knowing where to return materials.
Environment changes to reflect children's interests.	As children's sense of curiosity wanes, new materials or play space changes occur to add new stimulation or opportunities for children's exploration and discovery.
Aesthetic appreciation is emphasized.	Materials are displayed so that children are drawn to them and they want to interact with them.
	Children's displays are positioned within the environment, with consideration for message, size, and colours.
Physical space is designed to support inclusive practices.	The play spaces and materials within the play space are clearly positioned with adequate pathways that support all children accessing them.
	Spaces are available that allow children to move from large groups to places on their own.
	Visual cues about the space may be provided to support children with autism or communication disabilities.
Children's curiosity is sparked with provocations.	Displays and materials are positioned at children's levels and are reflective of their interests.
	The displays and materials are rotated to support new options for exploration.
	Displays and materials reflect children's backgrounds and diversity among cultures and families.
Celebrate children's diversity in daily routines.	Early learning teachers examine the needs of children and adjust environmental conditions to create a calming and pleasant environment.

building a large box sculpture, the early learning teacher observes the children's intensity in the activity. Then a judgment call is made, based on what is best for the children. Is it more important to allow the children to continue to be engaged in the structure or to stop the play so that the children may return to the indoor environment for a group experience?

Building on Greenman's (2005) work, Dietze and Kashin (2017) examined schedules and order from an environmental perspective. As outlined in Table 5.1, they suggest that environmental order is struck to support children's needs and be reflective of the program philosophy.

STOP ... THINK ... DISCUSS ... REFLECT

Is it really necessary for early learning teachers to examine each of the responsive components outlined? If so, how do early learning teachers gain sufficient knowledge and skills to be able to effectively carry out this task? How much of this is related to one's philosophy? Are we asking early learning teachers to engage in so many "other responsibilities" that there is no time for play?

CHARACTERISTICS OF EFFECTIVE PLAY SPACE ENVIRONMENTS

The Physical Environment

The physical play space influences the quality of children's play experience. Early learning teachers invest a significant amount of time in planning an environment that will promote quality play experiences and the interpersonal relationships among children and adults, in the indoor and outdoor play spaces. For example, when planning the play space, early learning teachers consider the space, the place, the play options, and the materials that will complement each child's chronological age, skills, strengths, and interests. If the materials are not correct or if the environment is not carefully planned, important play opportunities that support the various types of play may be jeopardized. As you examine this section, we ask that you consider how play space can accommodate fluid and structured play materials; child-initiated and adult-guided experiences; the required indoor and outdoor versatility; and the sensorimotor, symbolic, and construction play options.

There are varying perspectives on the amount of space and number of play centres that should be made available to children. Generally, provincial and territorial governments outline the minimum requirements of play space for both the indoor and the outdoor environments. It is important to understand that these are minimal standards rather than ideal guidelines. Think about how the recommended space might differ from a minimal standard. More than 40 years ago, Kritchevsky and colleagues (1969) indicated that the most effective play spaces for children incorporate a minimum of 2.5 play spaces in each play zone per child. This means that for each group of eight children, there would be 20 different play spaces available. You may initially think that this is an overabundance of play space. However, as you develop knowledge about and observe children at play, you will discover that the various experience centres, such as blocks, science, literacy, art, music, physical play, math, and dramatic play, are all very important in children's play. Generally, in child-centred play environments, children will extend their play to two or three play spaces at any one time; they may change play spaces a minimum of four times in any 60-minute period. The younger the child, the more frequent the change in play episodes. One of the most effective ways for early learning student teachers to become familiar with how children use space is through dedicated observations and documentations.

Early learning teachers consider many areas when planning play space (Azhari et al., 2015). As you read about each of the considerations that follow, think about how they could influence play if one or more of the items are not considered fully.

Space

Planning for and providing interesting play spaces and materials for young children require careful observation and planning by the early learning teacher and children so that their various needs are met, including opportunities for their social, emotional, cognitive, and physical development to flourish. For example, teachers ensure that space for infants is bright and that adequate floor space and materials are available to stimulate them to begin to roll, creep, crawl, stand, and use their language capabilities. Early learning teachers provide additional space to toddlers to accommodate their needs for toddling, walking and balancing, pouring, dumping, and filling objects. Limited, defined spaces are created. The preschool child has additional space needs. The number of places to play and the array of materials are increased both indoors and outdoors. There is a need to accommodate space for advanced rough-and-tumble play, gross motor play with tricycles

Table 5.2 Perspectives on play space and children's play.

1. How does the play space support child's play?
2. What play space considerations are used to guide our practice?
3. What role do children have in designing the play space?
4. Are children required to play in specific play spaces for specified times each day, or may they play in places of their choosing until they have completed their play episode?
5. How does the play space support the versatility that children require to develop creative play experiences?
6. How does the play space support or detract from positive play engagement?
7. How does the play space help children to be competent in their play?
8. How active and engaged are children in the play space?
9. How does the play space accommodate inclusive play practices?

and bicycles, and overall running. The school-aged space accommodates larger groups of children and reflects their interests, which include group activities.

As outlined in Table 5.2, early learning teachers are constantly examining the play spaces, both indoors and outdoors, to determine how they are meeting the interests of the children, the children's changing needs, the materials needed, and the new opportunities for exploration that either the children or the adults wish to incorporate into the environment.

The environmental design influences the opportunities for adult–child connections. Well-designed space ensures that children have space to play collectively and independently. There are places for the children to have discussions with adults and other children. There are places for both group and individual dialogue, such as in cozy corners, window seats, benches, and near the garden space.

Design Considerations for Effective Play Spaces

As outlined throughout this chapter, early learning teachers have a significant role in creating a responsive, effective play space that accommodates the needs and interests of the children. For example, early learning teachers who take an interest in the outdoor environment are more likely to encourage children to engage in the variety of risk-taking play options that are possible in the outdoor play space. Teachers who are passionate about the outdoor environment are more likely to encourage children to explore, wonder, and appreciate the natural learning opportunities during their outdoor play (Dietze & Kashin, 2017). They interconnect the outdoor environment and indoor experiences by incorporating opportunities for the children to explore information about plants, water, surfaces, ice, flowers, trees, and other natural learning options at the early learning centre.

Dietze & Kim (2014) identified nine design features (see Figure 5.9) of a responsive play space that early learning teachers and children use.

Green Space

The green space area is where children have an opportunity to engage in a quiet and serene experience or in active, gross motor play. It provides children with a calming effect, and it rejuvenates their ability to be resilient in play spaces where there are noise, stimuli, and other children. When children have opportunities to engage in long periods of active play, it facilitates gross motor development and reduces stress and tension. Green space increases the quality of the air that children are exposed to. Ideally, green spaces provide

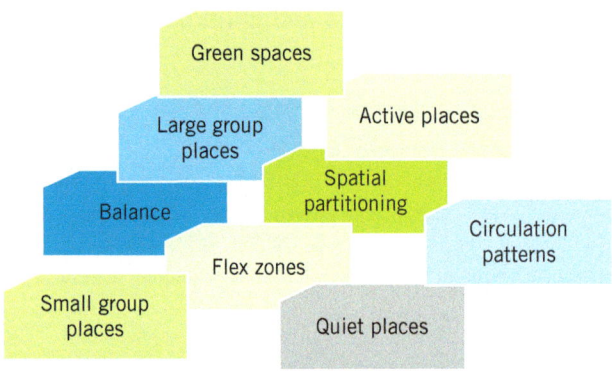

Figure 5.9 Design features of a responsive play space.

children with opportunities to play among trees, grasses, gardens, and other natural materials such as rocks and water. Early learning teachers and children benefit from the green space being visible from the indoor environment. Green space and nature collectively enhance children's social and psychological well-being, which in turn has the potential to trigger wonderment, curiosity, and new play options.

Quiet Places

Quiet places provide children with a place to pause, reflect, reconnect, rejuvenate their energy, or plan the next areas of interest that they wish to explore. Quiet places accommodate children wishing to work on a project on their own or to listen to music or review a favourite book. Quiet places are located in both the indoor and the outdoor play spaces. They are cozy places where the child may observe other children play, and these places may accommodate up to three children at any one time.

Active Places

Children require active places to play indoors and outdoors. Active places attract children wishing to play together. The children come together to decide about the theme of their play, their roles, and how the play will be executed. Active places facilitate children connecting, networking, observing the skills of others, and engaging in group play. Active play spaces may be louder than other parts of the early learning environment, and they are places where exuberant play is most prominent.

Small-Group Places

These are located in both the indoor and the outdoor spaces. They are used by small groups of children for a variety of play and exploratory experiences. Such a space may allow children to gather to hear a story, to engage in a focused project or discovery, or to document previous play experiences. Early learning teachers may use the small group places to display provocations and interesting items that children may wish to explore. Small group places provide children with a sense of security and belonging. They are often the spaces where children new to the centre will feel most comfortable until they adjust to their play space surroundings.

Large-Group Places

Early learning teachers and larger groups of children may come together periodically to engage in dialogue or group experiences. Large-group places are usually located both indoors and outdoors. Large-group places offer the flexibility to be used by the children for a variety of play experiences, such as dramatic play, when they are not being used for group activities.

Flex Zones

Flex zones located in both the indoor and the outdoor play spaces are designed to be child friendly, and their use is primarily guided by children. Flex zones allow children to use the same space in different ways and for different purposes. The furnishings in a flex zone are designed so that children may move the pieces as required. Early learning teachers provide freedom to the children so that they may use the space in very different ways from one day to the next, as a flex zone is intended to offer children the vision of what can be and how they can actualize that vision.

Circulation Patterns

Circulation patterns are essential components of play space. The patterns provide children with opportunities to move from one play area to another without purposely disrupting the play of other children. The circulation patterns are inclusive for all children. They are wide passages so that the children may move their bodies and their play materials with ease. As children move from one play area to the next, there may be times when they choose to pause along the circulation path to observe, think, or determine their next destination. The indoor circulation patterns try to accommodate children having access to the natural light and green space. This has a calming effect, and it also helps children regain a play focus.

Spatial Partitioning

Spatial partitioning is used to clearly define space for children and is of particular importance in play spaces that have an open-concept design. When spatial partitioning is done effectively, children are able to self-regulate how the space is intended to be used. This process allows children to competently move within the play space. More exploratory play occurs; peer interaction is facilitated; and positive child behaviour occurs because children intuitively know the boundaries.

Balance

Indoor and outdoor play spaces require a contrast between their elements. As early learning teachers and children create their play space, they are encouraged to have discussions about placing items that are thick and thin together and combining items that are hard and soft, open and enclosed, long and short, dark and light, and thin and wide. As identified by Dietze (2006), by "juxtaposing different shapes within the overall space, action or lack of action occurs" (p. 158). Generally, in early learning room designs, the larger spaces flow from the centre of the room. The smaller spaces flow from the periphery. Most often, the smaller spaces attract the children; this may be due to the feeling of security that they provide.

Traditional Physical Play Space Considerations

Previously, we introduced you to a number of considerations that early learning teachers use to guide them in working with children and space designs. Below are 10 additional considerations that early learning teachers use in preparing environments for children's play.

1. Safety and accessibility for all children guide the play space design.
2. Indoor and outdoor spaces are given equal consideration in all four seasons. When appropriate, children move between the indoor and outdoor areas freely.

3. The materials are placed in well-defined spaces both indoors and outdoors. The complexity of the materials is scaffolded from simple to more complex.
4. Provisions for environmental conditions, such as ozone ratings in the summer and colder temperatures in the winter, are made.
5. The play space has a combination of defined and open space, which supports children in engaging in active and quiet play. The space offers children a sense of security.
6. The play areas and pathways are designed so that children may stop and observe the materials available in the centre or the play that is taking place. The pathways are organized to support children in moving around the play space without disrupting other children's play.
7. The play areas are placed so that early learning teachers have visual access to the play space for observing children and their play.
8. The children's documentation of their play is displayed in visually attractive ways in both the indoor and the outdoor play spaces. Other materials displayed are chosen based on the meaning that they have for the children.
9. The indoor and outdoor storage units display materials clearly and attractively. They are designed to provide children with independent access to the materials. Other storage within the environment allows for unused materials to be placed and rotated as required.
10. The play spaces are arranged by wet, dry, noisy, and quiet designations (see Figure 5.10).

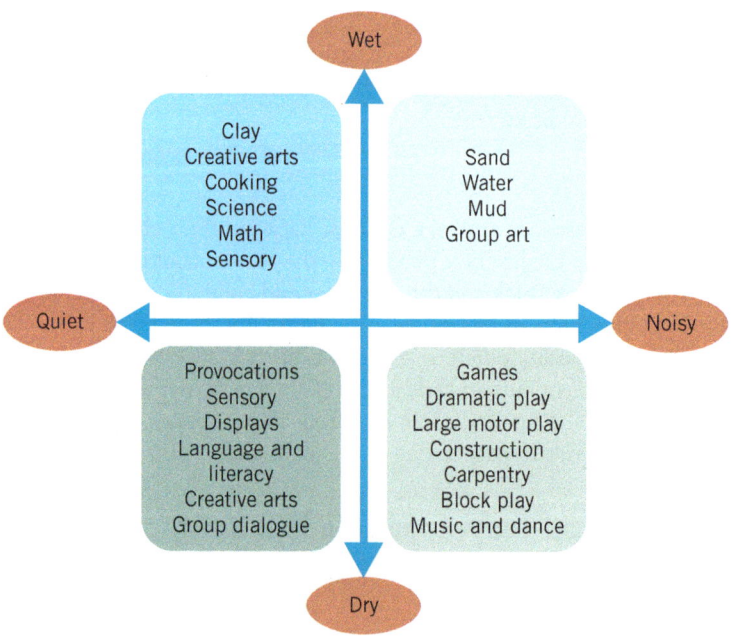

Figure 5.10 Play space designations.

Adapted from Dietze, B. (2006). Foundations of early childhood education: Learning environments and child care in Canada. Toronto, Page 159, ON: Pearson. Reprinted with permission by Pearson Canada Inc.

HOW PLAY SPACES AFFECT CHILDREN'S BEHAVIOUR

As Table 5.3 illustrates, children are affected by the aesthetics of their play space and the people in their play space. "Children and adults tell us how the room should be by their behavior" (Greenman, 1988, p. 136). Children are naturally good, but when the environment does not meet their needs, they become anxious, feel overwhelmed, or experience psychological discomfort. Think of the 3- and 4-year-old children who have high activity levels. These children function best in large spaces and in environments where they may engage in physical activity and play—most often elements of the outdoor portion of the program. When early learning teachers have expectations that these children will participate in indoor, small-spaced play experience for long periods of time, the children will react with behaviours that are not conducive to creating a harmonious play environment. It will take these high-energy children time to adjust to their environment. Or, think of children who have a low tolerance for noise and clutter. If the play space has music playing constantly, if children and adults speak in loud voices, and if the walls and the play space project a sense of clutter, these children experience disequilibrium. Over time, children adjust to the play space in their own way; however, if the environmental conditions are not correct, it can impede their energy levels, ability to problem solve, and ability to cope with the daily living behaviours required in early learning places.

The interactions among children, families, and early learning teachers are influenced by the feeling tone or psychological comfort within the play space. Play spaces that have

Table 5.3 How environmental conditions affect children's behaviour.

Response to Environmental Conditions	Impact on Children
Anxiety	■ Causes distraction and lack of concentration
	■ Reduces ability to spend time on task.
	■ Changes children's brain functions, including processing mechanisms, coding processes, and memory function.
	■ Impedes intensity of the play experience.
	■ Reduces ability to be creative.
	■ Reduces social networking skills and prosocial behaviour.
Feeling overwhelmed	■ Impedes ability to complete tasks or engage in discovery learning.
	■ Reduces attention span in play.
	■ Interferes with child's use of imagery.
	■ Causes the child to be easily distracted.
	■ Increases agitation, leading to negative behaviour such as biting, hitting, and kicking.
Psychological discomfort	■ Reduces verbal interactions, language acquisition, and vocabulary expansion.
	■ Reduces social interaction and social networking.
	■ Reduces tolerance for adapting to environmental conditions.
	■ Reduces tolerance for cultural, gender, family, or atypical development differences.

Adapted from Dietze, B. (2006). Foundations of early childhood education: Learning environments and child care in Canada. Toronto, Page 159, ON: Pearson. Reprinted with permission by Pearson Canada Inc.

a sense of warmth, caring, and nurturing attributes contribute to an environment in which the interactions are richer, language acquisition is stronger, and children are able to verbally communicate their interests, needs, and discoveries. Children who do not gain a sense of comfort in their play space are more prone to exhibit inappropriate social interactions such as hitting, biting, or kicking. They may also regress in controlling their bodily functions, leading to wetting or defecating accidents.

The play space environment is intended to build respect among children and adults (Houen et al., 2016). When the environment is planned to support the needs, interests, and strengths of children, adults, and families, there will be greater respect for differences in areas such as culture, family units, skills, and talents. The early learning teacher ensures that children and families have opportunities to use and experience materials, resources, and learning options that celebrate the diverse society that children and families bring to the play space. For example, early learning teachers ensure that children who use a wheelchair for mobility may be as self-sufficient in having access to displays and materials as other children. Children who come from cultures that have different traditions and objects have opportunities to share these in the play space.

Early learning spaces are intended to offer children opportunities to play, learn, experience, revise, wonder, reflect, discover, question, connect new information, create, and discuss their experiences (Dietze & Kim, 2014). To achieve these goals, early learning environments are rich in ideas, values, and aesthetics. The early learning teacher values and encourages children to explore the environment, using their five senses. This contributes to children exhibiting a quest for knowledge. They will invent things in their play; they will make new connections between what they know, what they thought, and what they now have discovered. When the environment does not have the correct balance of aesthetics, space, interactions, and acceptance of diversity, children's behavioural patterns and learning processes differ markedly from the ones just mentioned. Early learning teachers have a major responsibility to plan and implement play space environments that meet the needs of all children.

TERMS THAT INFLUENCE EARLY LEARNING PLAY ENVIRONMENTS

We conclude this chapter with three additional terms that support the theory of children's play. These terms are used when examining space and with children in their play.

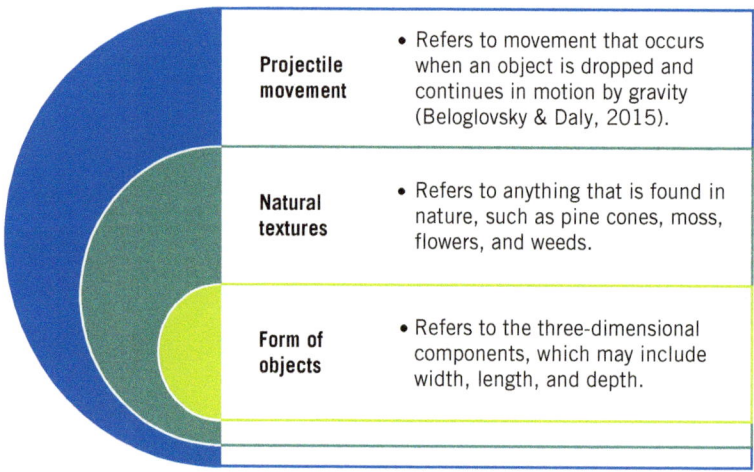

SUMMARY

Chapter Preview

- Early learning space is linked to children's engagement in and the quality of their play.
- The environmental considerations are as important as the floor plan.

Children's Play

- Each type of play requires various space allocations, resources, and materials to support the play.
- Children engage in sensorimotor, symbolic, and construction play. Children benefit from having exposure to fluid and structured materials.

The Environment as the Third Teacher

- The environment is viewed as a third teacher because it speaks to the children about what they can do within it.

Children's Places

- Play spaces are designed to be responsive to the children's needs and interests so that they may engage in many types of play and experiences.
- Play space is not made up of fixed components; rather, it is fluid and emerges based on children's life experiences.
- Learning environments are created to offer children a variety of experiences; freedom to play; opportunities for exploration, role modelling, and learning; exposure to adults, children, and neighbourhoods; and opportunities to incorporate daily living responsibilities into the environment.

Characteristics of Responsive Play Space Environments

- Early learning teachers are guided by examining the following: assessing the feeling tone; listening to the children; developing a caring place to play; inviting engagement in environments with provocations, environmental aesthetics, natural light, stress-free environments, cultural and community attributes, places for exploration and freedom to play, flexible schedules and order, and individual differences.

Characteristics of Effective Play Space Environments

- Early learning teachers consider the space and the following design features: green space, quiet places, active places, small group places, large group places, flex zones, circulation patterns, spatial partitioning, and balance.

How Play Spaces Affect Children's Behaviour

- Children's behaviour can be positively or negatively affected by the play space.
- The interactions among children, families, and early learning teachers are influenced by the feeling tone or psychological comfort within the play space. When the play space is not conducive to the needs of children, they may exhibit signs of anxiety, feeling overwhelmed, or psychological discomfort.

MAKING CONNECTIONS

Theory to Practice

1. You are working in an environment that you determine has a significant amount of clutter in it. How would you approach your colleagues to discuss this topic? What information would you highlight about clutter and children's learning? Why? What recommendations would you be prepared to share?

2. You have been asked to rearrange one of the play spaces in the early learning setting. How would you proceed in this? What research would you conduct? How? What areas from this chapter would you incorporate into your plan? Why? How?

3. Visit an early learning centre. Using the wet–dry, quiet–noisy guidelines, examine the placement of the experience centres according to this guide. Would you recommend moving any of the centres? If so, why? How might your recommendations support noise reduction, behavioural issues, and play engagement?

4. Is there a place for cartoon-like characters in the early learning environment? Why or why not?

DIGITAL PORTFOLIO ENTRIES

Potential portfolio entries for your digital portfolio could include:

- When I think about how the environment influences children's play, I wonder about. . .
- As an early learning student, I wonder about how I can influence children's spaces because. . .
- When I look at indoor and outdoor space. . .
- I think about space now. . .

CURIOUS?

Add the words *children's indoor and outdoor spaces* to your search engine and review the results.

CHAPTER 6
Loose Parts and Children's Play

> "The spontaneous power of the child, his demand for self-expression, can not by any possibility be suppressed."
>
> —John Dewey (1859–1952)

LEARNING OUTCOMES

- Define what is meant by loose parts and the theory of loose parts.
- Explain how loose parts support children's curiosity, exploratory experiences, and new knowledge creation.
- Describe how children playing with loose parts contributes to them developing schemas, assimilation and accommodation strategies, and varying play experiences.
- Outline the role of early learning teachers in creating environments and promoting children's play with loose parts.
- Examine the types of strategies that early learning teachers use in the outdoor environment to support children in having access to and gaining benefits from loose parts.

Sharing Stories of Practice

When my colleagues came back from a workshop, they started discussing what they had learned about loose parts and how they could incorporate loose parts into the environment. As I listened to them for the first few days, I really did not know what they were talking about. Then, as I took more time to listen, I realized that they were discussing the types of materials that could be brought into the environment that would offer children new play experiences. It became clear to me that "loose parts" were different from toys. Sara told me that one of the key distinctions between loose parts and toys is that loose parts can be used in multiple ways and in various play episodes.

As a staff, we began thinking about the types of loose parts that we could offer the children. We became so intrigued by how children's play changed when we provided an array of loose parts. We noted that many of the children began combining cardboard boxes with items such as grass and pine cones. Some children used little tree discs they called cookies for making patterns and then jumped from one large tree slab to the other. Other children became intrigued with sticks—thick ones and thin ones, long ones and short ones.

Over the past several months I have learned so much about how loose parts provide us with so many opportunities to trigger children's curiosities and imaginations. I like to think about the space where I place the loose parts because my observations suggest that this influences whether children are drawn to them. I also have learned that had my colleagues not participated in the professional development workshop, we may not have engaged in offering children these materials.

My advice to students and new early learning teachers is that they should never stop learning. Because research approaches to working with children and programming strategies evolve, and you could miss out on something as amazing as loose parts!

Carla, ECE graduate, 2015

CHAPTER PREVIEW

Creating effective and engaging play environments is a complex process. The materials, the environmental conditions, and the other children and adults within the environment influence children's play. As identified by Dietze and Kashin (2016), the more open-ended the materials in the indoor and outdoor spaces are, the more opportunity there will be for children to become motivated to embark on exploring new ideas and play combinations. **Loose parts** lack a defined purpose and structure. With experience, children can learn that loose parts may be used in a variety of ways in their play episodes.

Loose parts offer children many learning options. These include:

- Creativity and creative thinking by combining materials that have differing principles and purposes.
- Expansion of mathematical, science, language, and literacy concepts.
- Conservation of materials, especially if original product was created without a glued or turned process.
- Environmental sustainability by experiencing how materials for one purpose may be repurposed.
- Creative and divergent thinking and problem-solving skills.

loose parts Open-ended materials that may to be used alone or with other materials, without specific directions.

This chapter provides an overview of the benefits of loose parts to children's development and play. The role of the early learning teacher is outlined. Early learning teachers not only facilitate and support loose parts play but also collect loose parts from multiple sources.

As you begin to explore the concept of loose parts, think about the materials that can be classified as loose parts, how loose parts support children in their play, and why early learning students and teachers are adopting this concept in early learning programming. Think about the indoor and outdoor play environments that you have experienced with children. What types of loose parts do you recall seeing? How did children use them in their play? Should children find the loose parts in their environment, or is it best for early learning teachers to place them in the environment? Then think about how loose parts bring meaning to and new options for children in their play.

UNDERSTANDING THE CONCEPT OF LOOSE PARTS

The term *open-ended* is connected to loose parts (Ryan et al., 2012). Open-ended materials, or loose parts, in early learning environments offer children opportunities to engage in unique play experiences that support their curiosity and life experiences. Although the term *loose parts* was not coined until 1971, by the British landscape architect Simon Nicholson, loose parts had their first pedagogical foundations during the 1800s. Friedrich Froebel is often associated with recognizing the importance of children having open-ended, hands-on materials. The "gifts" were made of varying forms of wooden, geometrically shaped parts, providing children with materials that encouraged them to combine cognitive attributes with aesthetics and object manipulation (Sutton, 2011).

Similar to Froebel, Maria Montessori believed that children required hand-sized materials. She, too, created apparatus that were used with the children as learning props to stimulate sensory perception and investigation. Children were encouraged to use the materials in innovative ways as part of their self-directed inquiry and deep-thinking processes (Daniels & Gamper, 2011; Follari, 2014).

Piaget's (1952) developmental theory stressed that children learn by experimentation with and exploration of materials on an individual basis and with peers and adults. He emphasized that children required the open-ended materials for true creativity, risk-taking, and problem solving to occur. Piaget emphasized that environments influence how children create and draw mental maps that they construct and build upon. Children require new opportunities and experiences to continue to adjust and accommodate new ideas, perspectives, and learning. Early learning teachers and student teachers have a critical role in offering children environments that provide them with time and opportunities to expand their options for play.

Nicholson (1971) identified the need to develop a theory of loose parts, due in part to the environments that adults were creating for children. He was concerned that adults presented children with materials and resources that had defined purposes. This meant that children did not need to use their imaginations or tap into their creative ideas or problem-solving options. These types of environments, combined with the materials, deprived children of crucial play and learning experiences that required them to engage in creative thinking and problem-solving processes. He therefore determined that there needed to be an explicit theory for loose parts. The tenets of the theory were based on children environments, requiring that "both the degree of inventiveness and creativity, and the possibility of discovery, are directly proportional to the number and kind of variables in it" (Nicholson, 1971, p. 39). Nicholson was clear that toys within children's environments differ from loose parts. Children require an array of open-ended materials that support their play, enrich their environments, and scaffold their play to new thinking and learning (Ryan et al., 2012).

Nicholson believed that children who have access to loose parts in their play environment are empowered to think, design, create, and engage in experiential learning. Loose parts contribute to children expressing flexible and divergent thinking while building upon exploration of new ideas, perspectives, and skills that contribute to fundamental skills necessary for later academic performance. He further suggested that loose parts provide children with play experiences that help them make connections and gain knowledge about concepts such as gravity, sound, language, and teamwork. Think about environments that have hills within the play space. Now combine this affordance with cylinders and balls. How might the environment influence how children use the balls and cylinders?

TAKING A SPECIAL LOOK

Go to https://ojs.lboro.ac.uk/SDEC/article/view/1204 for further information on Nicholson and loose parts.

STOP ... THINK ... DISCUSS ... REFLECT

What might stop early learning teachers from offering children loose parts in their environments?

According to Nicholson (1971), to be classified as a loose part, the materials must be movable so that they can be redesigned, put together, and taken apart in a variety of ways. Sutton (2011) expanded on Nicholson's definition of loose parts. Sutton suggested that loose parts be defined as:

> Any collection of fully movable elements that inspire a [child] to pick up, re-arrange or create new configurations, even realities, one piece or multiple pieces at a time. Loose parts require the hand and the mind to work in concert; they are catalysts to inquiry. Loose parts are the flexible edge of an inviting open-ended interactive environment that allows participants to make an imprint of their intention. Experiences with loose parts provide a profound yet playful way for children to form associations between learning and pleasure. (p. 409)

Nicholson (1971) suggested that loose parts support both creative and noncreative children. When children have access to a variety of loose parts, in any given day they may be drawn to the same materials but use them in different ways. This contributes to children manipulating the loose parts and thinking about how they could use the materials to accomplish a particular objective. As outlined in Photos 6.1, 6.2, and 6.3, one child may use tree cookies in very different ways, depending on the types of materials available to support varying types of experiences (Houser, Roach, Stone, Turner, & Kirk, 2016).

Photo 6.1 Children combine loose parts for matching and mathematical concepts.

Used with Permission of Diane Kashin

Photo 6.2 Children combine loose parts with other loose parts to support their play ideas.

Used with Permission of Elizabeth Hicks

Photo 6.3 Tree cookies are used as a foundation to examine snow and ice.

Used with Permission of Elizabeth Hicks

CLASSIFICATION OF LOOSE PARTS

Loose parts are generally categorized into two types: natural and synthetic. *Natural loose parts* are defined as materials that are nature related, such as acorns and flowers, pine cones and stones, and leaves and seeds. The availability of natural loose parts may be seasonal, as with icicles and snow, piles of leaves, and seashells. *Synthetic loose parts* refers to materials that are purchased, recycled, or repurposed, such as aluminum foil, fabric scraps, rope, plumber pipe, bricks, and cardboard boxes.

Natural and synthetic loose parts have common elements. As outlined in Figure 6.1, to be considered a loose part, the materials must provide children with opportunities to adapt, control, change, and manipulate. As outlined in Figures 6.2 and 6.3, natural and synthetic loose parts differ in their characteristics. Each type of loose part offers children options for their play.

Loose parts are chosen to support children's ideas, creativity, and imagination in their play. As outlined in Figure 6.4, loose parts have value to children in a number of ways.

Loose parts do not have a defined purpose; rather, their purpose is undefined, resulting in children viewing their potential to be used in their creative play and new options for play (Mincemoyer, 2016). Loose parts offer children opportunities to engage in divergent, creative, and flexible thinking. These thinking processes are essential for children's

Figure 6.1 What loose parts provide children.

Photo 6.4 Natural loose parts.
Used with Permission of Bora Kim

Photo 6.5 Synthetic loose parts.
Used with Permission of Diane Kashin

Classification of Loose Parts 191

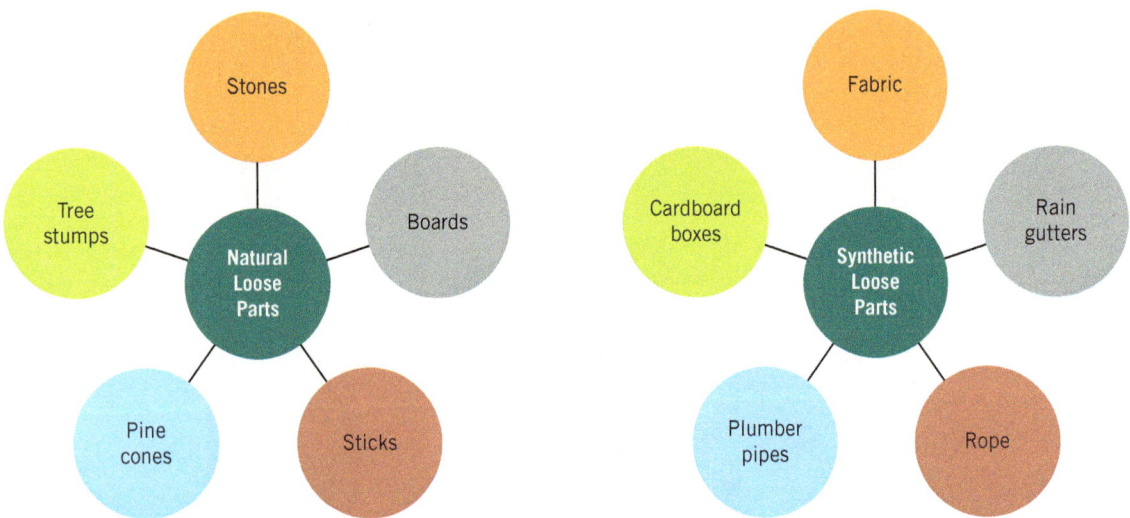

Figure 6.2 Examples of natural loose parts.

Figure 6.3 Examples of synthetic loose parts.

later academic performance and life development (Fisch & McLeod, 2012). Divergent and flexible thinking leads children to examine possibilities and make connections between their current knowledge and ideas and new ideas and discoveries. "Divergent thinking evolves because loose parts are open-ended and offer children materials that do not dictate a particular way in which the materials are to be used" (Russ & Wallace, 2013, p. 16). Loose parts offer children "ways to transform things into whatever they mentally imagine" (McClintic, 2014, p. 1). Loose parts add to children's opportunities to be messy and free to explore.

Loose parts can range from simple, natural materials, such as pieces of wood or small stones, seeds, or plant pods, to construction materials, such as pieces of wood, plumber pipe, and rain gutters. Some loose parts are found in the outdoor environment and others are gathered from a variety of sources and then placed in children's indoor and outdoor environments. Loose parts are flexible, engaging, and endless (Staempfli, 2009; Zamani, 2012) and provide children with a creative way to explore their world and their ideas (McClintic, 2014; Yavuz, 2016).

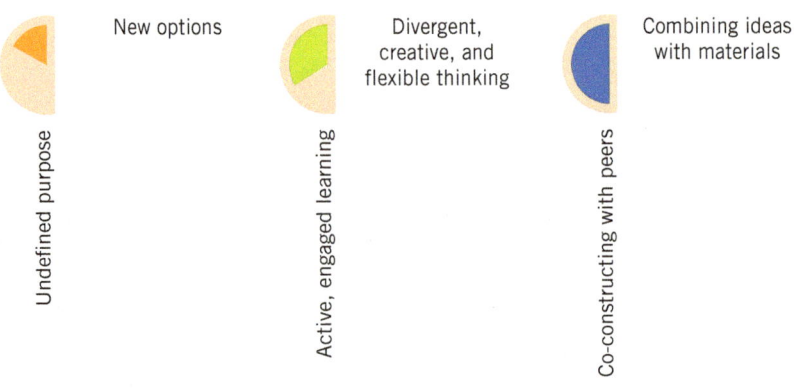

Figure 6.4 Values of loose parts.

> **STOP ... THINK ... DISCUSS ... REFLECT**
>
> Think about what types of materials you would classify as loose parts and why. How might loose parts change children's play options? How might loose parts add to children's imagination, creativity, intrigue, and challenge during outdoor play?

EXAMINING THE THEORY OF LOOSE PARTS

Loose parts is more than just a term that is prevalent in early learning programs today. Understanding the theory of loose parts is a beginning process for early learning students and beginning teachers. Early learning teachers and programs that embrace the theory of loose parts do so by:

- Ensuring that the loose parts chosen for the environment are reflective of children's interests.
- Scaffolding the materials to challenge children to explore new play and learning opportunities.
- Planning the play space to accommodate loose parts.
- Encouraging children to play freely with their peers and create or implement the impossible with the loose parts.
- Consistently reflecting on how these materials can have high impact on children's development (Beloglovsky & Daly, 2015; Topal & Gandini, 1999).

Children who have exposure to a variety of loose parts engage in an array of unique play experiences. These experiences influence their overall depth and breadth of play and subsequent growth and development. The more variety, challenge, and options children are presented with, the more they engage in higher levels of thinking and problem solving.

Nicholson (1971) identified that the theory of loose parts is founded on children being given open-ended materials to be used alone or with other materials and without specific directions. The materials may be moved, carried, combined, redesigned, lined up, taken apart, and put back together in multiple ways. The materials and the environmental attributes offer children numerous opportunities to be creative and to build upon their past experiences with new ideas. Nicholson (1971) theorized that the richness of an environment depends on the opportunity it allows for people to interact with it and make connections with previous and new experiences.

As early learning student teachers think about how to support children's play experiences, they apply a **thinking lens** to their practice that is grounded in a theoretical perspective. Ideally, that lens embraces children having numerous experiential learning opportunities with materials that have multiple uses and require minimal, if any, teacher intervention or instruction (Curtis & Carter, 2007).

thinking lens A thinking lens refers to a reflective process that is used by early learning teachers and student teachers "to think deeply and reflect on practice in a way that makes it meaningful and responsive to children's curiosity, learning, and development" (Dietze & Kashin, 2016, p. 212).

> **TAKING A SPECIAL LOOK**
>
> Add the words *thinking lens* to your search engine to find out more information about what a thinking lens means as an early learning teacher practice.

Thinking deeply about the theory of loose parts helps early learning students and teachers to understand the complexities of these materials and how they are foundational for children's learning and development in the early years. John Dewey made significant contributions to educational theories. As identified by Cuffaro (1995), Dewey identified that

> the materials we choose to bring into our [outdoor] classrooms reveal the choices we have made about knowledge and what we think is important to know. How children are invited to use the materials indicates the role they shall have in their learning. Materials are the text of early childhood classrooms. Unlike books filled with facts and printed with words, materials are more like outlines. They offer openings and pathways by and through which children may enter the world of knowledge. Materials become the tools with which children give form to and express their understanding of the world and the meanings they have constructed. (p. 33)

Early learning students and teachers are encouraged to embed theory in their practice. Loose parts provide children with many options to change, expand, create, and gain new knowledge from their play. Think about how loose parts support children's cognitive, social, emotional, language, and physical development. What kinds of new words might children experience through their play with loose parts? In the next section, we introduce you to the concept of intelligent materials. As you review that section, think about how loose parts become intelligent materials.

INTELLIGENT MATERIALS

Intelligent materials are those materials that Malaguzzi (2001) identified as being open-ended, creative resources that support children in sparking their curiosity and expressing their creativity. Malaguzzi suggested that the more the material can do, and the more flexible it is, the more intelligent it can become with children, because the attributes of the materials determine the potential and depth of learning that may occur (Dietze & Kashin, 2016).

Early learning teachers and student teachers are encouraged to view materials from a sensorial perspective as well as in terms of how the materials speak to the children (Gandini, 2005). When children have opportunities to engage with and manipulate materials, they begin to determine the possibilities of what can happen with them and how they can incorporate them into their play. "As children use their minds and hands to act on a material using gestures and tools to begin to acquire skills, experience, strategies, and rules, structures are developed within the child that can be considered a sort of alphabet or grammar" (Gandini, 2005, p. 13). Children, when given time and unique materials, will discover the **"language of the materials"** through their experimentation, trial and error, repetition, and observations of how other children and adults approach the use of the materials. As children use the materials, they are "acquiring knowledge about the material itself" (Gandini, 2005, p. 14). Examine Photo 6.6. How might the materials pictured speak to the children? Think about how children can gather intelligent materials from their outdoor environments. How do the items in the photo offer children different ways of thinking? Why?

Early learning teachers create environments that are rich with materials that support children in being expressive, while also acquiring knowledge and skills as they design their play episodes. There are many ways in which early learning teachers can think about the materials that they place in environments. The questions below, as outlined by

language of the materials
In the preprimary schools of Reggio Emilia, it is believed that children can express themselves in a hundred languages and a hundred more. Materials offer children opportunities to express themselves and speak to the children as they build, bend, shape, and construct. Materials have languages of their own (Edwards, Gandini, & Forman, 1998).

Photo 6.6 Materials that can speak to children.

Used with Permission of Diane Kashin

Dietze & Kashin (2016), help early learning teachers to choose materials that are open-ended, versatile, and rich in play options.

- Will the materials be used in many ways, or does the material dictate a particular use?
- Will many children use the material, or does the material have limited usage?
- Does the material lend itself to a variety of different kinds of explorations?
- How could the materials be introduced to the children to allow for the greatest number of possibilities?
- Is the material suited for outdoor exploration? Why? (p. 216).

CHILDREN'S PLAY AND DEVELOPMENT WITH LOOSE PARTS

Observing children being introduced to loose parts generally reveals that they are curious about them (Epstein, 2014). As identified by Flannigan (2015), when children become interested in loose parts, they begin the process of exploration and discovery. This contributes to them learning about some attributes of the loose parts, which in turn increases the ways in which they physically manipulate the objects. Children's curiosity about the openness and the potential of unfamiliar loose part objects extends their play exploration and play episodes (Houser et al., 2016; McClintic, 2014).

Children exposed to varying types of loose parts outdoors make connections about the relationships between changes in their play actions and changes with the materials (Flannigan, 2015; Neill, 2013). The more exposure children have to loose parts, the more they develop an understanding of how playing with materials can affect how the materials may be used (McClintic, 2014). As children discover this knowledge, it helps them in creating new ways of using and reshaping the materials, according to their interests and needs for their play episode (Drew & Nell, 2015). Think about children and sticks. One day, sticks may be used as part of den making, especially if fabric is nearby. Another day, children may use the sticks to sketch in the mud. Then, watch as children combine sticks with a walk. How might they be used? These differing uses reinforce how loose parts in both indoor and outdoor environments contribute to varying types of play emerging (Yavuz, 2016). Early learning teachers correlate the availability of loose parts to the types of play children participate in. This approach supports inquiry-based and emergent curriculum programming processes (Mincemoyer, 2016).

Children's environments are intended to be places where children develop skills such as divergent thinking, language, abstract thought, physical literacy, and problem solving. Early learning teachers plan for and identify ways in which children's curiosity can be triggered through a variety of materials, ideas, and discussions (Daly & Beloglovsky, 2015). Observations of children's play environments confirm that they often gravitate to open-ended play materials such as loose parts. Loose parts stimulate them to be creative, experiment, and gain a sense of accomplishment (Beloglovsky & Daly, 2015).

Loose parts in early learning programs are chosen with intentionality. They support and encourage diversity in children's play. Loose parts:

- Support children's development, culture, and diversity.
- Complement children's interests in particular areas.
- Trigger children's curiosity in new ways.
- Expand children's exploratory experience or new knowledge development.
- Connect peers with a common interest to create ideas and play options (Beloglovsky & Daly, 2015).

Many theorists, including Piaget (1952), Vygotsky (1967), and Dewey (1903), identified that children require environments that promote activity and are experiential

Table 6.1 How loose parts support developmental domains.

Developmental Domain	Example of Loose Parts in Play	Type of Development
Physical development	Using tree stumps and tree cookies for obstacle courses	Children gain gross and fine motor skills. They learn about spatial awareness, how to use their bodies within the space, how to balance, how to move within the space, and how to manipulate their bodies to do what they wish to achieve.
Social-emotional development	Creating dens with sticks and fabric	Children gain a sense of inclusiveness, a sense of belonging through group processes, and a sense of individual success. They learn about taking risks, problem solving, negotiating, compromising, a sense of power and control, and planning strategies among peers. The open-ended materials offer children opportunities to develop confidence because there is no right or wrong.
Cognitive development	Creating a stage with planks, sticks, fabric, and bricks	Children engage in mathematical and scientific principles as they classify the items needed to construct the stage. They think critically about what they want the stage to look like, the size of the stage, and how to use the materials to create their concepts. As they create the stage, they manipulate the materials, use previous experience, and integrate new learning. New words and meanings evolve as the characteristics of the loose parts are discovered.

with materials and resources that can be manipulated. Experiential learning encourages children to combine current knowledge with new experiences to create new discoveries and learning. Loose parts are ideal in supporting all aspects of children's development. Examples of how loose parts support children's development are illustrated in Table 6.1.

Loose parts are introduced, added to, removed, and combined with other materials. Ideally, children have access to the loose parts as they require them, rather than needing an adult to obtain the materials. Natural surroundings provide children with a wide spectrum of loose parts that introduce them to unique patterns and sequences that are not found with synthetic materials. Think about the pine cone, with its varying shape, or the patterns on plant leaves. What is the sensory presentation that children experience when examining tree bark? How are these loose parts different from plastic?

CHILDREN'S PLAY AND SCHEMAS WITH LOOSE PARTS

Jean Piaget (1952) made significant contributions to helping early learning teachers understand the cognitive development of children. He suggested that the way to process and build upon knowledge occurs through schemas, assimilation, and accommodation. As outlined below, loose parts provide opportunities to engage in play that supports these cognitive processes.

- **Schemas.** *Schemas* are the mental and physical actions or patterns used to organize the understanding of a concept or idea. They are the basic building blocks of thinking (Woolfolk, 1987). Schemas may be discrete and specific or sequential and detailed. For example, children may have experienced the use of tree cookies outdoors only as paths on which they jump from one to the next. They may believe that tree cookies have no other purpose.

- **Assimilation.** *Assimilation* refers to adding new information to an existing schema in an effort to better understand a process or idea. When children see tree stumps, they classify them within the category of tree cookies.

- **Accommodation.** *Accommodation* refers to changing ideas or concepts to include new knowledge. As children have new experiences with tree stumps or observe other children rolling them or using them in combination with other loose parts such as rocks, they will absorb this information and modify their previously existing schema to include this new information that may then become part of their play. Children's experiences with tree stumps and tree cookies help them to identify similarities and differences. They then adapt their previous thinking with their new learning.

As children gain new life experiences, cognitive development proceeds, new schemas are developed, and existing schemas become better organized and adapted to the environment. In essence, the process of assimilation involves organizing existing schemas to better understand events in the external world, whereas accommodation involves changing pre-existing schemas to adapt to a new situation or to new ideas and knowledge gained. Loose parts support children in engaging in a variety of experiences that lead to advancing new schemas.

As identified in Chapter 2, Piaget defined the several stages of cognitive development as sensorimotor (ages 0 to 2), preoperational (ages 2 to 7), concrete operational (ages 7 to 11), and formal operational (age 12 to adulthood). Starting with children in the preoperational stage, during the play process they engage in a variety of activities that are identified as "play schemas." These types of schemas are described below (Harper, 2004).

- **Orientation**—refers to children exploring space and their environment from different perspectives, such as by hanging upside down from a climber or standing on a table to acquire different points of view.
- **Positioning**—refers to the process and detail that children use in positioning the materials that they use, such as lining up toys or positioning similar items together in a particular way.
- **Connection**—refers to joining pieces of materials together, such as the process used in block building or disconnecting or destructing items that have been built (e.g., sand castles).
- **Trajectory**—refers to the urge to climb, pour, throw, and drop things. Children may use their bodies in diagonal, vertical, or horizontal movements in the process.
- **Enclosure**—refers to the process that children use to create structures that enclose items such as building fences to place animals behind.
- **Enveloping**—Children wrap things or their bodies in various ways and with various materials.
- **Core and radial schema**—refers to the process of children creating shapes, such as drawing circles or drawing a circle with lines resembling items such as the sun.
- **Rotation**—refers to the process of circular motion, such as spinning motions.
- **Transporting**—refers to children moving objects from one place to another.

Early learning teachers observe children's play to determine the types of schemas that they are exhibiting. This information is used when choosing loose parts for the environment that complement each of the schemas and build upon children's preferred play schemas.

CHOOSING LOOSE PARTS FOR EARLY LEARNING ENVIRONMENTS

Appropriate play space and materials contribute to children learning about their natural world. For example, when children have access to the right loose parts, they engage longer in a play episode and often will repeat the play as a way to work out or refine their new ideas (Beloglovsky & Daly, 2015). Think of children using large rocks to create bridges for their toy vehicles to drive under. Having a variety of sizes and shapes of rocks available contributes to children scaffolding and connecting their learning of bridge building from their block experiences to rocks. When children have access to flat rocks and large stacking rocks, their play options are extended, as are their opportunities for creativity, spontaneity, problem solving, and critical thinking. Early learning teachers choose loose parts with intent based on their observations of and discussions with children and on the interests of children.

Early learning teachers determine criteria that they use to choose loose parts. Ideally, this is based on their beliefs in and value of the importance of loose parts to children's play, the program philosophy, and strategies used for curriculum planning and implementation. As outlined in Figure 6.5, early learning teachers benefit from considering the flexibility, adaptability, availability, and sustainability of and the children's competence with the loose parts being considered for the early learning environment.

Dietze & Kashin (2016) identified the meaning of each of the categories and related core questions for each of the considerations outlined in Figure 6.5. The questions are intended to support early learning teachers and student teachers in their quest to

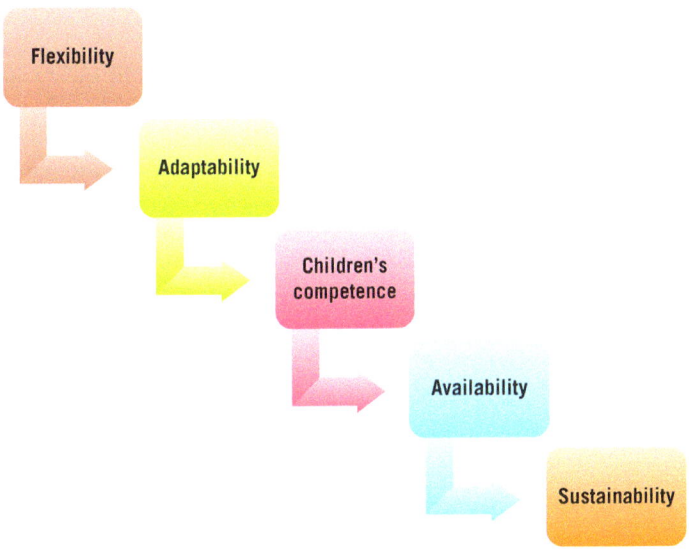

Figure 6.5 Considerations for choosing loose parts.

intentionally provide children with materials that are reflective of their curiosity, previous play, and opportunities to expand and challenge new options for discovery. Each category is described below.

- **Flexibility.** *Flexibility* refers to the flexibility of the item. How flexible is it? For example, how might fabric be used in the dramatic outdoor play area, and how might it be used differently in the construction area to change the play experience?
- **Adaptability.** *Adaptability* refers to how the item can be used and reused in different ways. How might the same item be used in different ways and in different forms? For example, how might plumber pipes be used near the water area, and how might that change if there is an area with marbles or balls?
- **Children's competence.** *Children's competence* refers to the ease with which children may use the loose parts. Can they manipulate the material, or do they require teacher support? For example, how easily can the children move the large rocks from one area of the playground to another? Are the rocks the right size for the children's strength and experience in using them? Is it safe to allow the children access to the rocks?
- **Availability.** *Availability* refers to the availability of the item. Is it something that can be gathered, replenished, and reused easily, or is there limited access to the material? For example, how easy is it to replenish pine cones versus large cardboard boxes? How does the availability influence when and how the children have access to the loose parts?
- **Sustainability.** *Sustainability* refers to the durability of the loose part. Can it remain in the environment over several days, or must it be stored after each play episode? For example, what is the durability of plumber pipes as opposed to fabric cushions? How does the sustainability influence children's play from one day to the next and the extension of play episodes? Can they build on the play from the previous day, or must they start over?

Loose Parts Outdoors and Indoors

Early learning programs provide children with loose parts in both their indoor and their outdoor environments. Generally, the types of loose parts found in the indoor environment support children in their math, science, language, and dramatic play explorations (Epstein, 2014). The loose parts outdoors generally differ in size, with many contributing to more physical literacy (McClintic, 2014).

There are varying beliefs about the purpose of outdoor play, one of which is that outdoor play is a time for children to have free play. In many early learning centres, the outdoor play curriculum is not planned as it is indoors (McClintic, 2014), although the planning process is expanding and becoming visible in high-quality early learning programs (Epstein, 2014). As early learning teachers place more emphasis on outdoor play experiences for children, there is growing interest in how open-ended materials such as loose parts can support diverse play options.

As early learning teachers and student teachers expand the options for children's outdoor play environments, it is necessary to determine the types of loose parts that are made available to children. Similar to the indoor environments, outdoor play spaces can be divided into zones (Dietze & Kim, 2014). With each play zone, such as the construction zone, early learning teachers and student teachers ensure that there are loose parts that complement the potential play options; in the construction zone, these could include boards, pylons, hammers, nails, saws, clamps, string, rope, sticks, bricks, and other related materials. This approach is extended across the outdoor play zones.

Outdoor play environments with loose parts stimulate a wide range of play types, including dramatic, constructive play (Änggård, 2011; Ridgers, Knowles, & Sayers, 2012) and creative play, and promotes inclusive play among children. Think about how loose parts could contribute to a variety of play types during the early years. How might loose parts influence dramatic play, constructive play, creative play, social play, and inclusive play? Table 6.2 provides examples of loose parts. Examine each example and determine which you envision in the outdoor environment and in the indoor environment. Why?

Table 6.2 Types of loose parts.

Loose Parts	Loose Parts	Loose Parts
Food tubs	Recycled tires	Wooden planks
Plastic bottles	Rain gutters	Tin cans
Stones and pebbles	Wooden crates	Cardboard rolls or tubes
Small twigs	Large chains and rope	Shells
Leaves	Sand and gravel	Sticks
Seeds	Stumps and tree cookies	Pails
Old street signs	Landscape netting	Brushes
Pine cones	Hay bales	Ribbon
PVC pipe	Buttons and beads	Tarps
Large branches	Driftwood	Moving dolly
Fabric	Spools	Wheels
Pylons	Laundry baskets	Pallets

THE VALUE OF LOOSE PARTS IN COMPARISON TO FIXED EQUIPMENT OUTDOORS

Loose parts add incredible value to children's play. Their value is much more substantive than that of fixed equipment or apparatus, which has defined uses and purposes, in supporting children's various play experiences and learning. Studies suggest that children prefer using items such as stones, boxes, stumps, tree cookies, and boards rather than stationary outdoor play equipment (Flannigan, 2015; Moore, 1990). The more children can choose what to play with and how to manipulate the materials and move the loose parts, the more tinkering, exploration, and problem solving occurs; these actions are necessary in establishing higher-level and deeper thinking skills (Epstein, 2014). Environments with open-ended loose parts that are readily accessible increase children's opportunities to design their own play options either individually or collaboratively. "Materials that can be moved, manipulated, and changed feed developmental needs" (Nicolson & Shipstead, 2002, p. 352). The materials and play experiences influence how children establish patterns for thinking, drawing upon previous experiences, and engaging in new ideas and life experiences.

There are a variety of loose parts suitable for early learning environments. A major benefit of placing loose parts in environments is that they can trigger children's curiosity. Later in the chapter, you will see examples of loose parts. As you review them, think about how they might trigger children's curiosity.

Now, think about the differences in play value of fixed and movable equipment, such as climbers and tricycles, to the play value of loose parts. Table 6.3 outlines differences between fixed equipment and loose parts.

Children exposed to play environments with loose parts benefit in a variety of ways, especially if the loose parts are available freely and not adult dominated (Ridgers et al., 2012; Staempfli, 2009). Figure 6.6 illustrates further benefits that children experience from having access to loose parts.

Children who have exposure to environments where loose parts are added and changed regularly have higher levels of play that challenges them (Nell, Drew, & Bush,

Table 6.3 Differences between fixed equipment and loose parts.

Fixed Equipment	Loose Parts
Tends to focus on gross motor play such as climbing, spinning, and jumping.	Provide opportunities for children to design and redesign the materials to support their play episode.
Limited opportunities for children to incorporate ideas into the usage of the equipment.	Accommodate all types of play and children's skills.
Becomes boring over time as the thrill of trying new ideas is limited by the stationary nature of the equipment.	Support children in building, dismantling, manipulating, incorporating, and repurposing materials as required for the play experience.
Limits peer and social play because of the equipment having limited movement capacity.	Encourage active, creative, and imaginative play with peers.
Low maintenance.	Require maintenance and storage.
Focuses on building children's physical competence.	Increase skills and competence in social, emotional, physical, and cognitive domains.
Limited need for children to think, ponder, and explore options.	Require thinking and problem-solving skills to incorporate loose parts into play episode.

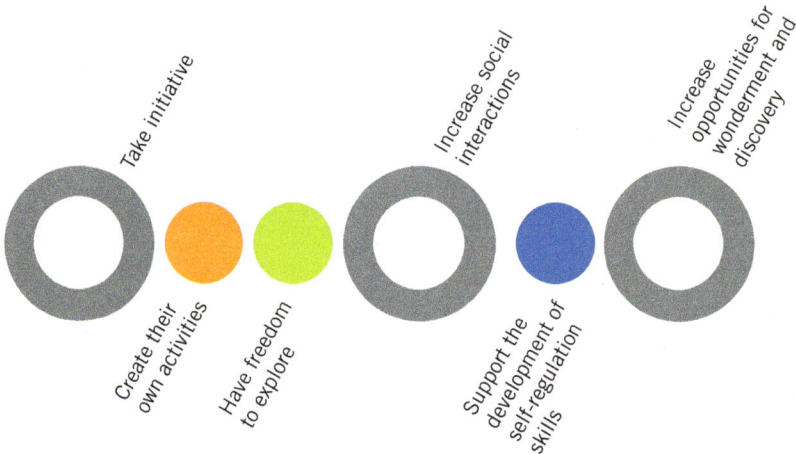

Figure 6.6 Benefits of loose parts.

2013). Programming with loose parts sets the stage for children to have the freedom to think, explore, and implement self-regulation skills (Beloglovsky & Daly, 2015). For example, children are able to use loose parts to construct complex play episodes individually or among their peers (Zamani, 2012). The intensity of the play differs dramatically in imaginative thinking and learning with loose parts compared to preformed materials.

LOOSE PARTS, TINKERING, AND THE MAKER MOVEMENT

Martinez and Stager (2014) indicated that "the impulse to create is one of the most basic human drives" (p. 1). This is related to children's curiosity. Children satisfy their curiosity in a number of ways; one is through the process of questioning, and another is through **tinkering** with loose parts or ideas. For example, curious children may tinker with trying to determine how to make a den or a shelter. They may explore questions such as where the ideal place is to build a shelter. Is it in open space or near a tree? How might they get the poles to stand up? How might they get the branches to stay on the shelter?

Tinkering is part of the **maker movement**. This process supports children in exploring, in experimenting and engaging with materials in ways that offer new options, and ultimately in learning through trial and error. When children are given the time; the place; materials that they can combine, assemble, take apart, and create with; and adult endorsement to tinker, they become immersed in experimentation and discovery (Martinez & Stager, 2014). Tinkering increases their desire to expand additional explorations. These actions are necessary for deep, constructive learning to occur.

What Tinkering in Play Looks Like

Dietze and Kashin (2016) identified that the level of tinkering that children engage in correlates with learning features within the environment. Table 6.4 outlines what tinkering may look in play environments that are rich with loose parts and supportive adults.

When children have opportunities to tinker and subsequently become makers of their ideas, they move their ideas to the creation of products that they are interested in making. No matter who the children are, the process of tinkering and the making of the

tinkering An active engagement with and manipulation of materials or experiences that children perform to figure out ideas and answers to questions.

maker movement Involves providing a space with raw materials and opportunities for children to engage in exploring and creating projects that are complex and meaningful to them.

Photo 6.7 A maker space.
Used with Permission of Diane Kashin

product support communication, collaboration, critical thinking, problem solving, decision making, and using materials in nonpredictable ways and in ways not anticipated by adults (Martinez & Stager, 2014).

Tinkering and the Hawkins theory of messing about have commonalities. Hawkins (2000) identified that adults need time to play with and explore materials in order to gain insight into the potential experiences and learning that may be generated from the materials. The experimentation process helps both children and adults to determine what happens when different materials are combined together—what are the possibilities? Adults benefit from the "messing about" process, as it helps them to identify the depth of concepts that children might experience, such as balance and velocity. Knowing the potential that the materials have in children's play supports adults in scaffolding the material so that children have success.

Hawkins (2000) encouraged educators to "mess about" so that children's learning may be supported to the fullest. He indicated that early learning teachers will be challenged to support aspects of children's learning unless there has been a process of exploring and appreciating how simple materials of children's play are related and how they can add value to children's play experiences. Further information about Hawkins's perspectives on materials is provided in Chapter 11.

Table 6.4 The process of tinkering.

Learning Feature	Children	Environment
Engagement	Children become interested in spaces, places, or materials. They put things together, move items, take things apart, reflect on their experience, and start over again. They invest large amounts of time in the materials and their ideas. Children combine different types of materials in their exploration. Children observe others with the same material and then try their ideas. Children ask questions of their peers or adults about the materials they are using.	Variety of materials, including recyclables, loose parts, and familiar and unfamiliar materials that trigger curiosity and inquiry. Places and spaces for tinkering to occur. Adults who use open-ended questions to expand children's thinking.
Social partnerships	Children seek support and engage with others to gain the new ideas needed to support their tinkering or their work and to develop other new ideas. Children request help from others to solve a problem. Children invite others to work with them on a particular idea.	Adults who offer children role modelling and opportunities for discussion, debate, and expansion of flexible thinking. Peers who support their peers, encouraged by adults.
Resourcefulness	Children set individual goals and ideas. Children create a purposeful plan in examining their idea, material, or goal. Children take risks with their ideas and with exploring new materials or ways of combining previous knowledge with new ideas and intentions. Children figure out when they are stuck and what resources they can draw upon to move their thinking in a new direction. Children develop their own questions and construct new ideas.	Documentation through pictures or stories that capture the experiences and sequence of exploration. Addition of new materials or language that will trigger further curiosity and tinkering. Adults who observe and listen to the children and offer input when required. Multiple pathways are encouraged.
Belonging and well-being	Children feel a sense of belonging as they contribute to the sharing of the tinkering experience. Children feel successful in the open-endedness of the experience and in their opportunities for expression. Children and their families can contribute to the collection of materials for tinkering, encouraging a sense of belonging.	Materials that support a broad range of development and skill are included. Through scaffolding, adults and peers offer opportunities for children to be challenged while continuing to learn and develop.
Creativity and expression	Children's opportunity for creativity supports their artistic expression. Children express themselves in multiple languages.	Different ways to create inventions, contraptions, machines, and art are offered.
Actualizing discoveries	Children share how to do something with others. Children apply their knowledge in new situations.	Documentation is continuous, and children's learning is celebrated.

CURIOUS?

Add the words *tinkering* and *maker movement* to your search engine to find out more information about the importance of these concepts to children's learning.

CHILDREN'S PLAY TYPES AND LEARNING THAT EVOLVE WITH LOOSE PARTS

Often, early learning teachers and student teachers choose loose parts for the harmonious, safe play they believe children should experience. Taking this approach may mean that loose parts such as sticks are eliminated from the array of materials provided in the environment, primarily because early learning teachers have concerns about weapon or gun play. Yet there are many positive reasons why children benefit from having access to sticks as part of their loose parts materials. For example, listen to the conversations that children have when engaged in weapon play. Children will take turns being the *good guys* and the *bad guys*. This contributes to children learning about morality—they learn about what is right and wrong and good and bad. Weapon play leads children to take on roles to "save" people, and they become the heroes in the play episode, such as when re-enacting the role of a police officer catching the "bad guy." These are positive attributes of play. Early learning teachers who make available loose parts that align with children's play episodes are helping children work through fears, gain insight from different perspectives, and learn how to treat their peers in kind and caring ways.

Dramatic Play

Dramatic play supports children in exhibiting an imaginary role or when they use objects, such as loose parts, to represent an imaginary idea (Mincemoyer, 2013). Loose parts contribute to dramatic play, especially outdoors, due in part to the unstructured nature and flexibility of the materials. The more flexible the materials, the more options children have to exercise imaginary play that is influenced by the materials. For example, when children have access to white sheets, the potential for children to create play that includes goblins is increased. Neill (2013) identified that children in outdoor environments with a variety of loose parts have more dramatic play than those in play spaces that either do not have loose parts or in which loose parts are limited in scope and flexibility.

Photo 6.8 Children are drawn to natural loose parts such as water.

Used with Permission of Bora Kim

Photo 6.9 Children's dramatic play with loose parts.

Used with Permission of Diane Kashin

Constructive Play

Constructive play is goal oriented by definition and involves the use of materials that may be manipulated to create something (Flannigan, 2015; Zamani, 2012). Construction play generally includes at least two actions with loose parts, such as stacking, rearranging, assembling, disassembling, drawing, and creating (Szekely, 2015). Constructive play with loose parts is strongly influenced by the materials and the roles of adults. Environments that are free from adult goals support children in leading their play. This freedom contributes to children constructing items needed for the play by using their own control and creativity, without dictation from an external source such as adults (Ridgers et al., 2012; Schwartz & Luckenbill, 2012). Constructive play with loose parts increases children's expression of ideas and opinions to others through the use of language, role modelling, and observations. Having a variety of loose parts in the environment contributes to children exhibiting skills such as negotiating, sharing, and self-regulation. Through loose parts and constructive play, children increase their knowledge about space, scale, and complexity (Maxwell, Mitchell, & Evans, 2008), all of which are foundational skills necessary for later mathematical and scientific academic knowledge.

Social Play

One of the main features of loose parts is that they offer children less structure in terms of what they can play with and interact with (Drew & Nell, 2015). The openness and flexibility of loose parts encourage children to engage in higher levels of social interaction and peer play (Oncu, 2015). The increase in social interaction

Photo 6.10 Loose parts and constructive play.

Used with Permission of Diane Kashin

that naturally occurs with children using loose parts contributes to them developing the skills needed to relate to other people by understanding different points of views, values, ideas, and ways of doing tasks and by sharing in the play process (Gleave & Cole-Hamilton, 2012).

Play environments with loose parts support children in being able to invent and play in an imaginary world. Open-ended loose parts encourage children with various skill levels to plan for and manoeuvre their play options. Children are less likely to be alienated or bullied for using an object in an inappropriate way, because open-ended materials have no "right" or "wrong" attached to them (Drew & Nell, 2015).

Creative Play

When children are exposed to play spaces with intriguing loose parts, unstructured play evolves. Unique and different loose parts contribute to children being required to continuously use their creativity and imaginations to construct spaces and objects that fit their interests (Flannigan, 2015).

Photo 6.11 Social play.
Used with Permission of Diane Kashin

Photo 6.12 Loose parts add to children's creative play ideas and actions.
Used with Permission of Bora Kim

EARLY LEARNING TEACHERS, PLAY, AND LOOSE PARTS

Early learning teachers influence the exposure to and depth of play experiences that children have with loose parts (Flannigan, 2015). The teacher's disposition and how the space is presented influences the loose parts that the children will use and how they will interact with the people and materials within the environment (Beloglovsky & Daly, 2015). The early learning teacher's beliefs about play, such as the structure of play, the amount of time spent, and how much direction to give about the use of loose parts, positively or negatively affect children's play experiences.

STOP ... THINK ... DISCUSS ... REFLECT

When you think about making loose parts available in the outdoor environment, what considerations do you take into account? How do these considerations differ for indoor environments?

Early learning teachers and student teachers consistently observe children to become aware of those who use loose parts in their play and those who appear to have no interest in them. Findings from the observations of children are used to examine the environment to determine how the space and placement or availability of the loose parts influence their play. As outlined in Figure 6.7, early learning teachers provide a mix of familiar and novel materials as well as time so that children scaffold their play and test new options. Finally, the attitudes, engagement, and roles of the early learning teachers are discussed to determine how the adults engage, construct, model, and support children's experiences with loose parts. The more comfortable adults are with tinkering and using loose parts, the more likely such play will be extended to children (Szekely, 2015).

Think about children exploring loose parts. Are there times when the early learning teacher acts as a direct coach, such as by demonstrating how the loose parts could be used? Are there times when the early learning teacher stands back, observes the children, and

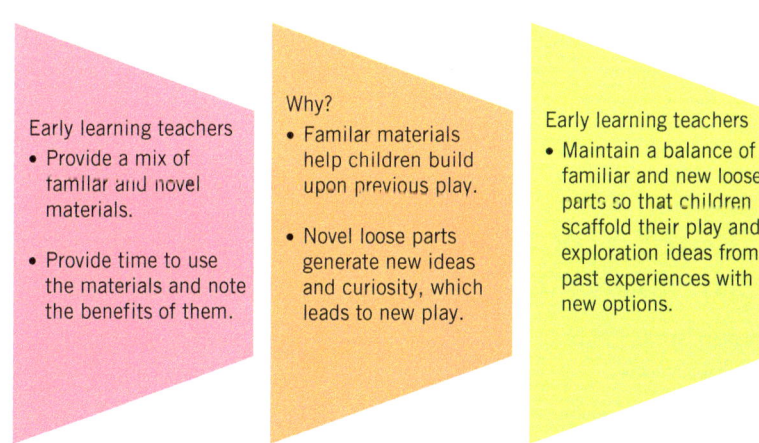

Figure 6.7 The roles of early learning teachers.

Photo 6.13 Teachers support children in using loose parts that surface in their environments.

Used with Permission of Bora Kim

provides information only if asked for by the children? Do the complexities of the loose parts dictate the role of the early learning teacher?

Children's use of loose parts is influenced by what materials are available, where they are placed in the environment, and the discussions that occur among children and adults. The observations that teachers make and how they scaffold the types of loose parts available influence if and how children move their thinking and discoveries to higher levels of learning.

TAKING A SPECIAL LOOK

Add the words *how early learning teachers support children with loose parts* to your search engine to find YouTube videos that provide further information on roles of early learning teachers.

STRATEGIES FOR ENHANCING THE USE OF LOOSE PARTS IN EARLY LEARNING ENVIRONMENTS

In this section, we offer you strategies for enhancing children's opportunities and experiences with loose parts.

Strategy 1. Develop observation skills to determine when children require assistance or could benefit from either new loose parts being added or some loose parts being removed.

Four children, Marla, Jacq, Kaleb, and Devi, have been using plumber pipes with connectors, pails, sponges, and water. They have been making various designs with the pipes and then pouring water into them. Marla and Kaleb decided yesterday to hold the plumber pipes in the air before pouring the water. They noted that the water did not flow as it had when they had the pipes on the ground. The children had long conversations about why the water would not come out. Kaleb and Devi tried to manipulate the pipes in different ways and suddenly had the experience of the water coming out. Marla tried again without success.

Today, in my role as an early learning student teacher, I am going to add rain gutters and balls to the area. I am thinking that if Marla could see the water flow in the rain gutter and position it to have the water flow where she wants it, she may then be able to transfer that new learning to the plumber pipes.

Strategy 2. Examine the loose parts for risk-taking opportunities and hazards.
Yesterday I noted that the children were climbing on the tree stump. They were laughing and screaming with glee. Then I noted that three children were hauling boards over to it. I decided that I would stand back to see how they were going to use the boards with the tree stump. Jomi started to angle the board against one part of the tree stump and then climb up the board. As a student teacher, I became uncomfortable with that play. Suddenly, I realized that I needed to look closely at this play to determine if it supports the children's need for risk or if there is a high level of hazard associated with the activity. I realized that I needed to discuss with the early learning teacher the risk-taking and hazards process. I realized that I need to examine the strength of the board, the placement of the board, and the supports that exist when children get to the top. If this is a hazard, how do I support children in their play? What strategies could we could put in place to support their play?

Strategy 3. Role model attributes of loose parts for the children.
Last week a dad brought us 18 shiny wheel rims. They are really neat. I placed them near our mount, thinking the children would want to roll them down the hill. Although I had many ideas about how they could be used, the children did not seem interested in them. I decided that I would place a large rope in the middle of the hill and then ask the children to predict if I could use enough energy to push the rims to reach the yellow rope. When I posed the question to a group of children, they said, "Try it." So, I did, and then new play opportunities began for the children. They ran up and down the hill moving the rope, they attached the rope to the rims to haul them back up the hill, they had rim races, and the imaginative play continues.

Strategy 4. Examine how the placement of loose parts influences the play options.
We have a gigantic tree in our play space. The children primarily play under it in the fall when the leaves are on the ground. I would like to see if I can stimulate the children to incorporate the tree into their play throughout the seasons. Tomorrow I am going to see how the children respond to loose parts near the tree. I am going to place lightweight fabric that blows nicely in the wind, large sticks, climbing blocks, string, duct tape, and wire. I am going to place one stick into the ground and then place a piece of the fabric over it. I wonder what the children will do. Will children be attracted to the area? If so, which children? Will they want to build a den? If so, how will they proceed?

Strategy 5. Trigger children's curiosity to use loose parts to extend their play.
I have been observing the children in our centre and note that some use a variety of loose parts in their play and others do not. I am concerned about three children because their play is primarily focused on riding their trikes around the loop. I have never seen them use any loose parts. I think that if they would become interested in them, it may increase their play options, their social interactions, and the diversity of their play. I wonder if

I put large boxes with their names on them and a street address near the trike track, that might spark their play in new ways. Maybe they will use the boxes as their houses and the trikes as cars. I can imagine how that could increase the types of play that they engage in.

Strategy 6. Provide a variety of loose parts to extend play and creativity.

Children's creativity and play can be so diverse outdoors. I have noticed that three children are intrigued by the baskets of moss, twigs, seeds, dried flowers, and grass stems. I saw three children taking the items from the baskets and incorporating them into their mud play creations. I saw Mallie using the flower pods at the easel for paintbrushes. Tomorrow, I am going to add shiny buttons and ribbon to see if they trigger other types of creativity.

Early learning teachers listen to and observe the children and then plan the environment accordingly. They seek ways to trigger children's play in new ways. Investigative triggers evolve as children and adults become interested in new ideas with loose parts. Early learning teachers benefit from thinking about how they can provide children with loose parts that will support their play while contributing to developing new knowledge and ways of knowing. Early learning teachers examine how individual loose parts combined with other loose parts can become an investigational trigger for children. Think about the loose parts listed below. What types of play might be triggered when children combine these items? Where might you place these items in the play space? What other types of loose parts combined may trigger ideas for children's play?

Pebbles and cardboard tubes = ?	Cardboard boxes and tubes = ?
Branches and fabric = ?	Rocks and bricks = ?
Large stones and boards = ?	Pine cones and clay = ?
Plywood and milk crates = ?	Tree cookies and fabric = ?
Tree cookies and blankets = ?	Seashells and scarves = ?
Water and ice blocks = ?	Glass stones and mud = ?
Umbrellas and fabric = ?	Cardboard boxes and books = ?

STOP ... THINK ... DISCUSS ... REFLECT

Why do you intentionally add loose parts combinations as an investigative trigger strategy? How might you proceed to create more investigative triggers in your environment?

TERMS THAT INFLUENCE EARLY LEARNING PLAY ENVIRONMENTS

We conclude this chapter by introducing three additional terms that support the theory of children's play. These terms are used when examining children's potential learning experiences.

Epistemology	• Refers to describing what is known and how it became known.
Small world play	• Refers to creating and acting out scenarios in a miniature scene with small figures and objects.
Affinity spaces	• Refers to spaces in which two or more children can engage in experimental play based on common goals.

SUMMARY

Chapter Preview

- Loose parts offer children many learning options, including creativity and creative thinking, divergent thinking, and expansion of mathematical, science, language, and literacy concepts, as well as an introduction to environmental sustainability practices.

Understanding the Concept of Loose Parts

- Open-ended materials, or loose parts, in early learning environments offer children opportunities to engage in unique play experiences that support their curiosity and life experiences. Although the term *loose parts* was not coined until 1971, by British architect Simon Nicholson, loose parts had their pedagogical foundation during the 1800s, with Friedrich Froebel.
- Loose parts contribute to children expressing flexible and divergent thinking, while building upon exploration of new ideas, perspectives, and skills that contribute to fundamental skills necessary for later academic performance.

Classification of Loose Parts

- Loose parts are generally categorized into two types: natural and synthetic. Natural loose parts are defined as those materials that are nature related, and synthetic loose parts refer to materials that are purchased, recycled, or repurposed.

Examining the Theory of Loose Parts

- Loose parts play a prominent role in children's play environments. The more variety, challenges, and options children are presented with, the more they engage in higher levels of thinking and problem solving. The most effective environments with loose parts are those in which the theory of loose parts is prevalent in early learning practices.

Intelligent Materials

- Intelligent materials are those materials that Malaguzzi (2001) identified as being open-ended, creative resources that support children in sparking their curiosity and expressing their creativity.
- Early learning teachers and student teachers view materials from a sensorial perspective as well as in terms of how the materials speak to the children (Gandini, 2005). When children have opportunities to engage with and manipulate materials, they begin to determine the possibilities of what can happen with them and how they can incorporate them into their play.

Children's Play and Development with Loose Parts

- When children become interested in loose parts, they begin the process of exploration and discovery. This contributes to them learning about some attributes of the loose parts, which in turn increases the ways in which they physically manipulate the objects.
- Children exposed to varying types of loose parts outdoors make connections about the relationships between changes in their play actions and changes with the materials (Flannigan, 2015).

Children's Play and Schemas with Loose Parts

- Schemas are the mental and physical actions or patterns used to organize the understanding of a concept or idea. Assimilation refers to adding new information to an existing schema in an effort to better understand a process or idea. Accommodation refers to changing ideas or concepts to include new knowledge. As children have new experiences or observe other children, they will absorb this information and modify their previously existing schemas to include this new information, which may then become part of their play.

Choosing Loose Parts for Early Learning Environments

- Appropriate play space and materials contribute to children learning about their natural world. Early learning teachers choose loose parts with intent based on their observations, discussions with children, and the interests of children.
- Early learning teachers determine criteria that they use to choose loose parts. Ideally, these criteria are based on teachers' beliefs and values of the importance of loose parts to children's play, the program philosophy, and strategies used for curriculum planning and implementation.

The Value of Loose Parts in Comparison to Fixed Equipment Outdoors

- Loose parts are much more substantive in supporting children's development, play, and learning than is fixed equipment or apparatus that has defined uses and purposes.
- The more children can choose what to play with, how to manipulate the materials, and how to move the loose parts, the more tinkering, exploration, and problem solving occur. These actions are necessary in establishing higher and deeper thinking skills (Dietze & Kashin, 2016).

Loose Parts, Tinkering, and the Maker Movement

- Children satisfy their curiosity in a number of ways, one of which is the process of questioning and another of which is tinkering with loose parts or ideas.
- Tinkering with ideas supports children in exploring, experimenting, and engaging with materials in ways that offer new options, and ultimately in learning through trial and error. The process of tinkering increases their desire to expand additional explorations. These actions are necessary for deep, constructive learning to occur.

Children's Play Types and Learning That Evolve with Loose Parts

- Play environments with loose parts stimulate a wide range of play types, including dramatic, constructive play (Änggård, 2011; Ridgers et al., 2012), and creative play, and promote inclusive play among children.

Early Learning Teachers, Play, and Loose Parts

- Early learning teachers influence the exposure to and depth of play experiences that children have with loose parts (Flannigan, 2015). The teacher's disposition and how the outdoor play space is presented defines the loose parts that the children will use and how they will interact with the people and materials within the environment (Canning, 2010).
- The early learning teacher's beliefs about play, such as the structure of play, the amount of time spent, and how much direction to give about the use of loose parts, positively or negatively affect children's play experiences.

Strategies for Enhancing the Use of Loose Parts in Early Learning Environments

- There are six strategies that enhance children's opportunities and experiences with loose parts. They are (1) develop observation skills to determine when children require assistance or could benefit from either new loose parts being added or some loose parts being removed; (2) examine the loose parts for risk-taking opportunities and hazards; (3) model attributes of loose parts for the children; (4) examine how the placement of loose parts influences the play options; (5) trigger children's curiosity to use loose parts to extend their play; and (6) provide a variety of loose parts to extend play and creativity.

REVIEW QUESTIONS

1. Describe the characteristics of loose parts and what is required for an item to be classified as a loose part.
2. Explain the evolution of loose parts in children's play, including when the term was coined and by whom.
3. Outline reasons why early learning teachers place loose parts in the indoor and outdoor environments.
4. Explain how loose parts contribute to children's development.
5. Describe the role of early learning teachers in creating and promoting the use of loose parts in children's environments.

MAKING CONNECTIONS

Theory to Practice

1. Visualize your ideal play space with loose parts for children. What types of loose parts do you envision being in that space? Why?
2. Many early learning centres place loose parts, especially those from nature, in the indoor environment. How do you envision you could encourage colleagues to support maintaining the loose parts in the outdoor environment? How do you envision the experience will be for the children? Will it be different from the experience indoors? If so, how?
3. Imagine that you are required to prepare a presentation for parents on the importance of loose parts for children's development. How would you present the information? What key messaging would you wish to share with the parents? Why? What role would children have in the presentation?
4. Examine your early learning centre. Then, visualize how and from where you could acquire unique and innovative loose parts for the environment. What role would children have in participating in sourcing and repurposing the loose parts for their play?

DIGITAL PORTFOLIO ENTRIES

POTENTIAL PORTFOLIO ENTRIES FOR YOUR DIGITAL PORTFOLIO COULD INCLUDE THE FOLLOWING:

- When I think of loose parts, I wonder about. . .
- As an early learning student, what is my role in introducing loose parts to children in early learning programs?
- When I examine the use of loose parts in my field placement, I can think of these ways to improve it:. . .
- I think that loose parts add . . . to children's play because. . .

TAKING A SPECIAL LOOK

Do a library search for this article, http://www.abcee.org/sites/abcee.org/files/Loose%20parts%20manual.pdf, or for this: https://www.fix.com/blog/get-children-playing-outside/.

CHAPTER 7
Art and Play

Rawpixel.com/Shutterstock

> " Every child is an artist, the problem is staying an artist when you grow up. "
>
> —Pablo Picasso (1881–1973)

LEARNING OUTCOMES

After exploring this chapter you should be able to:

- Describe why Dewey, Froebel, Steiner, and Malaguzzi advocate for art experiences in early learning programs.
- Examine how art influences a child's physical, social, emotional, and cognitive development and supports creativity and problem solving.
- Discuss the benefits of children being exposed to both the principles of design and the elements of art in early learning programs.
- Describe the four principles that support children in developing their visual language through art experiences.
- Explain the stages of children's drawing and use of clay
- Describe why children's art is more than the production of a product.
- Examine common strategies used for encouraging creativity with art experiences.
- Describe common types of open-ended art materials.
- Examine seven early learning teacher characteristics that benefit children in the arts.

Sharing Stories of Practice

When I began my ECE studies, I realized that I had had very limited memories of enjoying art in my early years. When I think of art, I reflect back to a time in grade 1 when the art director for the school district visited our rural school. I think he was probably there to offer us some enrichment. I recall that he stood over me trying to guide me to draw a gingerbread man. I don't believe I accomplished the task to his standards. The experience has stayed with me and has become a guiding force in how I support children in their art. I do not want children to feel the same way I did that day. I was embarrassed and ashamed. I truly believe that children require experiences that allow them to create whatever they desire. It is not fair to try to guide a child to represent something the way the adult wishes it to look. Providing children with models of or precut materials for what they should produce is not part of my practice.

As an early learning teacher for more than eight years, I continue to find that one of the biggest challenges in my practice is working with colleagues who prefer to cut shapes for children, prepare craft products, and call it art, or who wish for children to collectively sit at the art table and complete a "look-alike, teacher-led" project. Art and crafts are so different, yet they seem to be thought of as one and the same by some early learning teachers.

I believe that art expression must evolve from within. Our role as early learning teachers is to provide an array of art materials in various sections of the early learning environment that will trigger children's interest in experimenting with them. Art may be a solitary experience or group activity, as long as the group evolves from the children. If children choose to create "look-alikes," so be it, but it is not something that, as an early learning practitioner, I am going to specifically prepare for.

I encourage new early learning teachers to view art as an incredible creative thinking process for the children. It must be representative of the child's thoughts, feelings, and experiences to be truly creative.

Cheree, ECE graduate, 2016

CHAPTER PREVIEW

Historically, art has been a major component of early learning programs. Dewey, Steiner, and Froebel all discussed the importance of art to the development of the whole child. The educators in Reggio Emilia, Italy, also place a high value on art experiences (Vecchi, 2010). However, since the late twentieth century and during the first 15 years of the twenty-first century, the wide spectrum of art experiences for young children has continuously been reduced and replaced with activities that have a more academic focus (Christakis, 2016). This attitudinal shift in programming is influenced by families and early learning teachers. Christakis (2016) determined that art for children should be offered for art's sake and that it is an essential ingredient to a well-rounded education. Art is an expression of one's self. It is a curriculum area that should not be up for debate; rather, it is beneficial to view art as a learning domain, similar to critical thinking and number sense. Academic preparation occurs in the school system. Play, including art, is the foundation of early learning programs.

Early learning teachers are under pressure to focus on programs and experiences that will enhance a child's literacy and numeracy skills (Buis, 2014; Christakis, 2016). Although we agree that these skills are important, it is a disconcerting phenomenon because, increasingly, children have fewer opportunities to participate in spontaneous

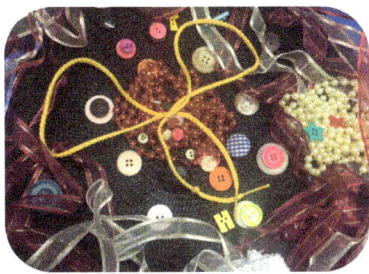
ART: Stimulates Memory

ART: Enhances Symbolic Communication

ART: Promotes Relationships

ART: Provides a Venue for Building Competence and Self-Esteem

Figure 7.1 Art touches on all aspects of children's development.
Used with Permission of Diane Kashin

play and creative discovery. Art play has a pivotal role in a children's development, including language and literature. Exposure to art enhances children's verbal and nonverbal expression, cognitive and physical development, social and emotional skills, creativity, and problem-solving attributes (Isenberg & Jalongo, 2013). Think about the process of art and the new words that children may learn. *Curve, symmetry, asymmetrical,* and *translucent* are among the words that complement children's art processes.

As outlined in Figure 7.1, art touches all aspects of children's development. Art stimulates memory, enhances symbolic communication, promotes relationships, and provides a venue for building competence and self-esteem. Art is one of the most natural components of play. These attributes support children in developing innate talents and a level of sophisticated play experiences that cultivate curiosity and develop self-identity (Englebright Fox & Schirrmacher, 2014).

When art is integrated appropriately, children are given a venue to express themselves visually in ways that they may not be able to do verbally. Art and the expression of creativity provide young children with a medium that supports their development of independence, confidence, pride, and self-expression. Early learning teachers offer children opportunities to see things from a different and new perspective. Children require changes to their environments so that new ideas are generated. When children have exposure to the same art activities and materials daily, their minds and creativity begin to stagnate, which contributes to them losing their zest for exploration and curiosity.

Photo 7.1 Self-portraits.
Used with Permission of Diane Kashin

This chapter introduces you to what is meant by "the arts." It explores how art provides richness in children's development, including how it positively influences their whole development. A discussion of the importance of open-ended materials and of the process and product debate also occurs. We highlight the role that early learning teachers have in facilitating opportunities for children to be exposed to art experiences that support their interests and capabilities.

DEFINING ART

There are many ways to define art. Pear Cohen and Gainer (1984) defined art as "the conscious efforts of human beings to express their ideas and feelings about themselves and their world by arranging colours, shapes, lines, sounds, movements, and other sensory phenomena" (p. 17). Cornett and Smithrim (2001) described art as the "means of thinking through our senses . . . Art is hands-on and tangible. We touch materials to make art and manipulate colour, line and shape . . . the symbols used in art are also thinking tools. These sensory-rich symbols form a special language . . ." (p. 137). For children, according to Bentley (2013), art is not limited to a specific area in the learning environment.

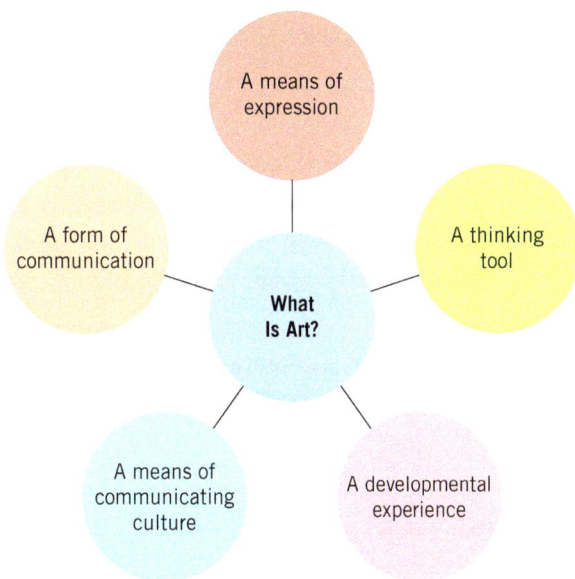

Figure 7.2 What is art?

It is boundless. "For the young child, art is a way of solving problems, conceptualizing the world, and creating new possibilities" (Bentley, 2013, p .3). The artistic practices of children exist fluidly and often continue spontaneously throughout their lives. Children are inclined to create art anywhere, including on walls!

According to Lowenfeld and Brittain (1987), art is primarily a means of expression. Lowenfeld and Brittain's work on children's art is seminal. They defined art as "meaningful communication with the self as children select and organize parts of their environment into a new whole" (p. 34). As you read the definitions presented, you will note that art is more than an easel with paint at it. We view it as exploration, discovery, and a creative process that helps children make sense of their world.

As identified in Figure 7.2, art contributes to a child's communication processes, organizational skills, and self-expression. It is a process that contributes to the development of the "whole child."

STOP ... THINK ... DISCUSS ... REFLECT

What types of art experiences do you remember from your childhood? Was there one particular art medium that you enjoyed? If so, do you know why you enjoyed it? Was there a medium that you found challenging? If so, do you know why?

Educational Approaches Influencing the Visual Arts in Early Childhood Programs

Understanding the importance of art to the development of young children is a process that has been challenged throughout history. For example, prior to the early 1920s, many adults, including educators, viewed children's art as clumsy and without personal creativity. It was viewed as a version of adult art. As educators and philosophers expanded their knowledge about children and learning, they recognized that there was a connection between art and child development (Isenberg & Jalongo, 2013).

Key philosophers, including John Dewey, Friedrich Froebel, Rudolf Steiner, and Loris Malaguzzi, identified art as a pivotal point in the experiences that children require.

John Dewey

In the 1920s, when John Dewey began to examine education, he took an interest in redefining the importance of art to the development of children. He indicated that children must be viewed as active learners. Children have a need for inquiry. Their creative energies are essential in helping them figure out who they are and bring meaning to their world around them. He suggested that a school setting be an expansion of their family and community. He advocated for adults to help children participate in group experiences, problem solving, and collaborative learning. In *Art as Experience*, Dewey indicated, "A beholder must create his own experience. And his creation must include relations comparable to those which the original producer underwent . . . Without an act of re-creation, the object is not perceived as a work of art" (Dewey, 1934, p. 54). Dewey's work on art and education has influenced generations of children and teachers.

As other educators examined Dewey's approach, a progressive movement in education for young children evolved. Art experiences began to have prominence as a tenet in new programs for young children. It was noted that, given the correct experimental environments, children had the ability to be creative, engage in self-expression, and be authentic through their expression of art. Chapman (1978) suggested that Dewey's influence helped educators recognize that a child's self-expression is essential for maturity to occur. Children require experiences that would help them clarify their ideas from both an individual and a group perspective. This generated opportunities for children to create murals and charts and use puppet shows as a means of communication and expression—all of which are a form of art. At the time, this was a radical approach. It continues to be important—free-flowing art experiences are essential in early learning programs.

Friedrich Froebel

As identified in earlier chapters, Friedrich Froebel believed that children learn best through play. "Children in the Froebel Kindergarten are not 'schooled', they are developed. The aim is not merely mastery of content, but the nourishment of the whole child—physically, mentally, emotionally, socially, and spiritually" (Corbett, 1979, p. 17). Froebel emphasized that the nourishment of the whole child is best realized in an environment that is play-based, because play provides children with transforming power (Elkind, 2015). This power process is necessary for children to explore their creative and imaginative abilities (Corbett, 1979).

Froebel advocated for young children to have stimulating, creative activities in all aspects of the program. Creative activity is the foundation for learning. Each child's creative expression comes from within, and each child, when given the materials, the environment, and encouragement, can be creative in his or her own way (Joyce, 2012).

Froebel developed 10 "Gifts" for children to use in their play environment. These gifts consist of colourful wooden balls, rings, geometrical shapes, cubes, and tablets. The "Occupations" are the art activities. The Gifts and Occupations complement each other. Through play with the Gifts, children explore solids, surfaces, lines, and points. This exploration corresponds to the Occupations through the active manipulation of clay, plasticine, play dough, wood carving, woodwork, papier mâché, sand, snow, or rocks. Further, Occupations include art activities such as painting, colouring, drawing, weaving, paper folding, sewing, and collage (Corbett, 1979). Froebel insisted that if children did not have exposure to art materials, they would not develop to their fullest potential.

The Waldorf Approach

Rudolf Steiner (1861–1925) was the founder of the Waldorf approach, which has gained international attention. With an emphasis on creative play, Waldorf schools are often described as arts-based (Nordlund, 2013). Steiner saw the child as being of three parts—body, soul, and spirit (Ullrich, 2014). In the Waldorf approach, play is seen as "a creative construction of one's own knowledge of the world and one's place in it. When creating art, we essentially play: translate and construct our world, create new things, and take risks with the unknown" (Nordlund, 2013, pp. 16–17). Art is seen as a way of knowing and is an integral part of the approach developed by Rudolf Steiner. He believed that the whole child must be nurtured. This can best be realized when young children are involved in creative play and healthy work activities. Creative play experiences require children to use their imaginations through the manipulation of open-ended materials such as blocks, puppets, painting, drawing tools, clay, and working with articles from nature (Nordlund, 2013). The healthy work activities refer to daily chores such as sweeping, wiping tables, and assisting in the upkeep of the environment.

The Waldorf program exposes children to a wide range of artistic activities, such as watercolour painting, drawing, colouring with beeswax crayons, modelling, puppetry, gardening, storytelling, and playing musical instruments (Nordlund, 2013). These visual and tactile arts are integrated in programming from preschool to high school. "Waldorf education is known for its intentional use of art and **aesthetic experience**" (Grella, 2015, p. ii). According to Nordlund (2013), the climate within Waldorf schools supports arts integration. There are no arts disciplines versus non-arts disciplines dispositions. The disciplines such as math, science, language, and literacy coexist. There is also a strong element of dramatic play.

aesthetic experience Refers to an experience in which your senses are operating at their peak.

CURIOUS?

Add the words *Waldorf school images* to your search engine. Examine the photos you find. Can you describe how what you see reflects a climate that supports an aesthetic experience?

Loris Malaguzzi

As identified in earlier chapters, the Reggio Emilia preprimary schools evolved from a small community in north-central Italy, under the vision and guidance of educator Loris Malaguzzi (Fraser, 2012). The Reggio Emilia approach is based on the belief that children are competent, intelligent, curious, and social beings (Fraser, 2012). Children are seen as having rights and these rights include expression in 100 languages (Ontario Ministry of Education, 2014).

This approach provides children with opportunities to develop inquiry skills and to deepen their curiosity for learning through expression involving multiple media. For example, children would be invited to draw, paint, sculpt, sketch, construct, dance, and move to represent their learning (Fraser, 2012). Relationships are essential to children's experiences with the arts. These include relationships with others and relationships with artistic media. Through the process of documentation, early learning teachers observe, record, and collect artifacts during children's experiences in order to determine the path and scaffolding process for the curriculum. Often, long-term inquiries or projects result from the process that begins with pedagogical documentation. However, early learning teachers benefit from being open to the emergent quality of the curriculum. Malaguzzi (1994) suggested,

> We need to be open to what takes place and able to change our plans and go with what might grow at that very moment both inside the child and inside ourselves. Each one of us needs to be able to play with the things that are coming out of the world of children. Each one of us needs to have curiosity, and we need to be able to try something new based on the ideas that we collect from the children as they go along. (p. 3)

While the Reggio Emilia preprimary schools use project work, the *project approach* is a set of teaching strategies that enable teachers to guide children through in-depth studies of real-world topics (Katz & Chard, 2012). The two approaches are similar in that children are involved in **project-based** learning. John Dewey was one of the first to suggest that project-based learning was ideal. The role of the early learning teacher is to support children through their inquiry (Alfonso, 2017). Projects unfold in an emergent way and often involve children's opportunities for artistic expression during their project work (Katz & Chard, 2012).

Reggio Emilia schools emphasize the importance of art by ensuring that there is an *atelier* (art studio) adjacent to each classroom and an *atelierista* (art teacher) to support children in their work. The *atelierista* specializes in the visual arts and assists the teaching team and children as they relate to the materials. In the *atelier*, children will find an array of open-ended materials that include a variety of paints and brushes and a wide selection of paper, drawing tools, clay, wood, coloured glass, bits of mirrors, and natural materials. Children use the materials to express symbolic representation and communication, whereas teachers use the arts as a way to understand each child's thinking. The collaboration among the teachers, the children, and the environment strengthens the depth and breadth of the visual arts experiences (Vecchi, 2010).

The Reggio Emilia environments position visual arts as a pivotal element to programming. Art experiences are intended to trigger children's curiosity, which leads them to explore new options in new domains, either individually or with peers. This exploration, combined with the interactions among children and adults, leads children to discover in-depth knowledge and skills about areas of interest that may otherwise be neglected. As outlined in Chapter 5, Reggio Emilia and Reggio-inspired programs view the environment as a "third teacher." Care is taken in the preparation of the environment because it acts as a third teacher (Fraser, 2012). There is an underlying order and beauty in the design and organization. All of the early learning space has an identity and purpose, is rich in potential to engage in it and to communicate, and is valued and cared for by children and adults (Dietze & Kashin, 2016).

Recognizing the importance of art to the development of young children, plants, natural light, and the children's own artwork are prevalent in the environment. The environment offers a sense of order and intrigue for each child. Commercial posters are not part

---

project-based approach
Children and early childhood teachers design projects that explore concepts and principles that support the topic of interest. The projects provoke children's thinking, inquiry, wonderment, skills, and collective knowledge. A project may be for a short period of time or extend over several weeks, depending on the complexity of the project, the authentic questions that evolve, and the resources available to maintain children's interest and intrigue in the topic.

Photo 7.2 A mural in a preschool classroom.
Used with Permission of Diane Kashin

of a core Reggio-inspired environment. When children's art becomes the focal point of an environment rather than commercially prepared materials, the children's environment becomes a learning incubator for them. Children's own art increases their curiosity and sense of wonderment. It may lead children to expand on previous work and try new ideas.

Early learning teachers constantly examine the art medium's potential to determine how it may support children's interest and influence their development. When early learning teachers engage in this exploratory process, they are less likely to provide children with inappropriate art experiences.

Art and Child Development

As you explore the benefits and contributions that art makes to a child's development, you will note that we emphasize the need for art experiences to be open-ended and **process-based**. Why? Open-ended, process-based experiences support children's creativity and development. The types of materials and opportunities extended to children influence how they express their own thoughts and ideas about how things look to them in their

process-based art Refers to experiences that are open-ended without step-by-step instructions, a sample for the children to follow, or a right and wrong way to create art.

Photo 7.3 Transient art.

Used with Permission of Diane Kashin

transient art Refers to art that is movable and nonpermanent. It invites children to manipulate and create with loose parts in a process-oriented way.

world. Children gain a sense of success from open-ended materials because there is no one right way to do something and no need to specifically produce something. Consider the environmental benefits when children engage in **transient art**, where there is no pressure to produce. By providing empty frames, mats, or other platforms and multiple loose parts without glue or paint, children create without consuming the materials, and the materials can be used another day.

This freedom to explore contributes to motivating children to have independence, confidence, and an interest in taking risks to try new experiences. At the same time, we learn from the work of the educators at Reggio Emilia that teachers can help children to learn basic artistic techniques if done in a natural and authentic way. Consider a child who is trying to affix two balls of clay. The early learning teacher scaffolds the learning by working with the child to determine what happens when small amounts of water are applied to the structure. Art is not something taught outside of the experience, and it is more than just technique. Art contributes to the child's development in all of the developmental domains.

CURIOUS?

Add the words *process art in early childhood education* to your search engine. Examine the images you find and investigate some of the links. What can you learn about process art?

Physical Development

Young children learn through motor experiences and sensory exploration (Englebright Fox & Schirmacher, 2014). Art experiences contribute to the development of both fine and gross motor skills. For example, gross motor development is influenced when children use paint or clay. When children paint at an easel, they use their entire arms and upper torso as they make large, sweeping motions with their brush (Englebright Fox & Schirrmacher, 2014). The wider the brush, the more movement the child must exert. Like painting, clay is also valuable for gross motor development. When children tear, roll, twist, or flatten clay, they are using their entire arms and hands. Generally, these types of experiences allow children to gain control of the gross motor muscles prior to perfecting fine motor development.

There are many ways in which children develop fine motor skills through art experiences. The most popular art activities that contribute to fine motor development include cutting with scissors, making collages, painting, and drawing. Art activities also contribute to children developing the hand and finger muscles that are needed to hold a pencil, manipulate a computer mouse, or make other related fine motor movements. Through observation, pedagogical documentation, and listening to the children, early learning teachers gain insight into how their physical development is progressing. Through observation, early learning teachers learn about children's thinking patterns and how children examine and understand what they see and experience in their environment.

Cognitive Development

During the early years, a child's brain is making neural connections at a rapid rate. Ideally, children's play that includes movement, language, drawing, and related forms of art contributes to all of their senses being engaged. This supports the wiring of the brain processes needed for successful learning. There is a strong connection between art, thinking, and what the child knows (Eisner, 1976). Art serves as a manifestation of a child's thinking. By looking at children's art, you will gain insight into what they know about the world and how they choose to represent what they know (Englebright Fox & Schirmacher, 2014).

Art contributes to the development of essential thinking and learning skills such as pattern recognition and development, mental representations of what they observe or imagine in their world, and symbolic and metaphorical representations. Children and adults create symbols of their experiences in order to think about them, problem solve, and make sense of experiences. This symbolization process is necessary for thought to take place (Bjorklund & Causey, 2017). Drawing is a way in which children can represent what they know about the world. It illustrates how they choose to translate ideas and experiences into a visual language. This is their way of *thinking out loud*.

When children are exposed to visual arts materials at an early age, their problem-solving skills and abilities emerge. Problem-solving skills become apparent as children use symbols to represent their ideas in art and as they begin to develop rules about how they work with the materials. For example, when children work in specific sequences (drawing head, eyes, nose, and then mouth) and have specific rules about space and location of elements in their drawings, a problem-solving process is being used. Similarly, when children work with paints and modelling materials, they explore the attributes of the materials. This leads them to discover cause and effect, balance, symmetry, solidity and fluidity, and concentration and dilution (Barnes, 2015). As children use art materials, they discover that ideas can take form.

SHAPE: Examine two-dimensional shapes such as circles and squares.

FORM: Examine how three-dimensional enclosures use space.

LINE: Examine how lines can be made on paper and how different tools produce different lines.

SPACE: Examine how the illusion of space is created through light and shadow.

COLOUR: Examine the colours so that they can be named. Explore the intensity of colour.

TEXTURE: Examine the surface quality and their attributes.

SPATIAL CONCEPTS: Examine right, left, up, down, beside, through, over, and under.

Figure 7.3 Elements of art.

As identified in Figures 7.3 and 7.4, children require a variety of art experiences in order to learn about the concepts of the elements of art and the principles of design. While children experiment, discover, and create, they are scaffolding their knowledge about art.

When children engage in art experiences, they explore the principles of design. For example, when they repeat marks on a paper and create a flow in their design, they are

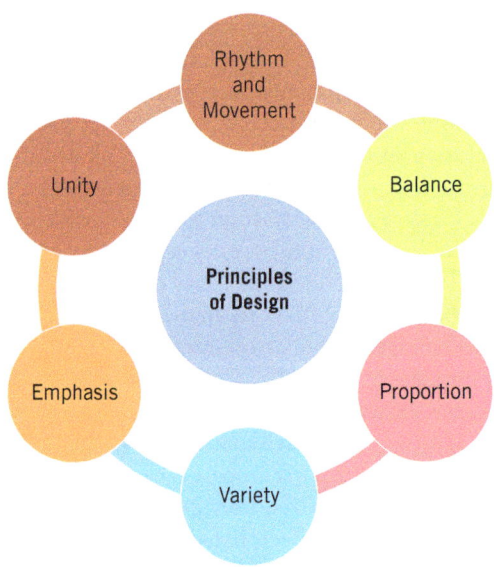

Figure 7.4 Principles of design.

exhibiting the principle of *rhythm and movement*. When children play with *balance* in their art, they are discovering symmetry and asymmetry. The results that come from the use of different and contrasting elements illustrate the principle of *variety*. Playing with *emphasis* will make something stand out, such as placing dark beside light or large next to small. Considering how all aspects of a child's creation work together is following the principle of *unity*.

The concepts that children learn during the preschool years are crucial to later cognitive development (Englebright Fox & Schirrmacher, 2014). According to Piaget, "The acquisition of cognitive skills relies on the nonverbal operations of manipulating, sorting, constructing, interpreting shapes and symbols, and appreciating different points of view" (Pear Cohen & Gainer, 1984, p. 89). Active involvement with art materials develops and strengthens these skills.

Social Development

Learning through play requires young children to be involved in observation and interaction with others in the environment. Children observe something, try to recreate what is seen, and match their vision with reality. Environments in which children are encouraged to manipulate and interact with materials (Jones & Reynolds, 2015) allow them to learn about themselves and others. Children express their uniqueness by making a personal statement through art, but art is rarely a solitary endeavour (Englebright Fox & Schirrmacher, 2014). Art experiences allow children to observe the uniqueness of others and to develop an understanding of the individuals within their social environment. For example, when children are engaged in art, they develop the prosocial skills of sharing materials, taking turns, and interacting positively with others. These socialization skills are necessary for relationship building, interpersonal communication, and civic life.

Art introduces children to social and cultural constructs. For example, children learn about other cultures when they see and share artifacts, such as various forms of drawing and painting, pottery, jewellery, and related items from their family and culture. This is one way in which children build an appreciation for diversity and accept other cultural and social perspectives (Isenberg & Jalongo, 2013). As children explore artifacts and have discussions about them, they share information that supports them in becoming valuable members of a learning community.

When children are in art-supportive environments, they build self-esteem. If encouraged appropriately, children take pride in the works of art they create. Art also contributes to children developing their problem-solving skills, especially when children are challenged with experiences such as three-dimensional problems that are inherent in sculpting experiences or when they have paint that is more runny than thick.

Emotional Development

Social and emotional development are influenced by childhood experiences (Dowling, 2014). Kostelnik and colleagues (2016) indicate that self-concept has three dimensions: competence, worth, and control. As identified in Table 7.1, each of these dimensions has

Table 7.1 Dimensions of self-concept.

Competence	Worth	Control
Believe that you can accomplish a task.	Know your sense of belonging.	Feel that you can influence events within your environment.

Photo 7.4 Observing and painting.

Used with Permission of Mona Fakhry

a positive or negative impact on a child's artwork. For example, the child who is encouraged and believes that a rainbow similar to the one seen coming toward the early learning centre can be created will more likely have the ability to try to re-create the rainbow, compared to the child who says he or she is making a rainbow and has the early learning practitioner respond, "It doesn't look like a rainbow to me." When children are in a caring, nurturing environment, they view art as an emotionally pleasurable experience.

Art is a venue that allows children to express their feelings, fantasies, fears, and frustrations (Englebright Fox & Schirrmacher, 2014). Art can be viewed as an emotional outlet that allows children to release inner feelings (Isbell & Raines, 2012). It also enhances a child's self-image and feelings about the self. Children who are exposed to a variety of open-ended art materials are encouraged to be creative, use originality, and express individuality. The stronger the sense of self-identity, the more likely children are to develop skills used to cooperate in solving disputes over objects, playing games, and solving simple problems (Berk, 2013). Art experiences provide the motivation for the development of the whole child: physical, social, emotional, and cognitive development. Based on this reality, quality art experiences continue to be emphasized in early learning programs.

Figure 7.5 provides an overview of how art and creativity support children in developing self-regulation skills. When early learning teachers examine the area in which art is presented to children, they look for the arrangement of materials to encourage children's access to and learning how to care for the materials. Children benefit from learning how to wash paintbrushes, store glue, put lids on markers, and put away materials on a shelf. Taking care of materials serves to support children in conserving them so that they have enough for their creations, without using too much. Early learning teachers have an important role in modelling how to keep the art area tidy so that it is ready for the next

Figure 7.5 Strategies for supporting self-regulation in the art area.

child wishing to use it. At the same time, early learning teachers encourage and support children in learning how to keep the materials and art area clean and tidy.

Principles of Children Developing Their Visual Language through Art Experiences

As identified earlier in the chapter, children's art experiences contribute to them gaining a sense about both the elements of art and the principles of design. Children also benefit from developing their **visual language**. Children use their visual language to communicate ideas and to make sense of their world. As children experience art they follow a sequential process that takes time.

Principle 1: Children follow a sequential process in creating art.
Influence on programming: Children require time and experience to explore and practise various skills and techniques used to accomplish tasks such as drawing or creating with clay. (See section titled "Stages of Clay Development.") When adults rush children to draw or produce items before they are ready to do so, there is the potential that they may not adequately develop the foundational skills needed to engage in more complicated art experiences (Isenberg & Jalongo, 2010).

Principle 2: Children's visual language evolves from their thinking and experience.
Influence on programming: Children require open-ended art materials and time to explore them. This helps children develop ways to express their thoughts and feelings. Through art, young children work through and make creations that reflect their thinking patterns, how they bring meaning to their world (Goodenough, 1956; Kellogg, 1979), and the environment in which they live. This means that, many times, the work that children share with adults may not be a recognizable object. Early learning teachers observe how children work with the materials and then use effective discussion points to stimulate dialogue that is intended to advance their inquisitive exploratory options.

Principle 3: Children's visual language is influenced by their environments and their experiences.
Influence on programming: Children's learning is influenced by the context of what they know (Isenberg & Jalongo, 2010; Lowenfeld & Brittain, 1982). Children flourish when the experiences are sequenced from simple to more complex.

visual language A process whereby a child communicates an idea through the use of art media such as pictures and images, shapes, structures, and words as a way to make sense of the world.

Photo 7.5 Painting at the easel.

Used with Permission of Angela Roy

Each child's brain assimilates new information or processes based on previous knowledge (Isenberg & Jalongo, 2010). Children explore their environment based on life experiences and the exposure to new learning opportunities. If children do not have "newness" in their environments, their level of curiosity and wonderment is compromised. This directly affects their level of exploration.

Principle 4: Children's exploration and experiences in art are positively influenced by a guide or facilitator.

Influence on programming: There are times when children "get stuck" at a particular juncture, which inhibits them from moving forward. When this occurs, early learning teachers offer assistance and guidance in the form of questioning, demonstrating a particular technique, or researching an idea or process with an individual child or groups of children. It is important that this be a guiding process rather than simply provision of predetermined models or ideas to the children.

To facilitate children's art experiences, early learning students and teachers require knowledge about the stages of artistic development. When knowledgeable about these predictable sequences, materials, time, and support can be given for children to move through these stages.

STAGES OF CHILDREN'S ARTWORK

Viktor Lowenfeld (1978) connected intellectual growth, psychosocial stages of development that fall into predictable age groups, and stages of development in children's drawings. Similar to Lowenfeld, Brown (1984), and Stokrocki (1988) provided insight into the common progression, or stages, of clay making that children progress through. Each of the stages will be outlined.

Table 7.2 Stages of scribbling.

> Disorder scribble—uncontrolled markings that could be bold or light, thick or thin, depending on the mood of the child. There is little or no control over motor activity.
>
> Longitudinal scribble—controlled, repetitive motions and movements. There is a visual awareness of the lines.
>
> Circular scribble—expanded exploration of controlled motions that demonstrates the ability to create more complex forms.
>
> Naming—the child begins to tell stories about the scribble. The child is moving toward using imaginative thinking to represent his or her world.

Stages of Children's Drawing

Scribble Stage (2 to 4 years of age)

This scribbling stage begins as disordered scribbles. As children gain more experience and practice, the marks become orderly. Then children begin to name the scribbles, and forms and shapes are evident. See Table 7.2.

Pre-Schematic Stage (3 to 4 years of age)

During this phase, children begin to draw the human figure. The figure generally has a circle and two lines that are used for the legs. This is often referred to as a tadpole drawing. Occasionally, children will include a rectangle shape for the body. It appears as though the

Photo 7.6 Ethan's drawing.
Used with Permission of Diane Kashin

child has little understanding of space, as the objects are placed in a haphazard position. As children gain more experience, other forms develop, some of which are very complex. They seek out ways to represent ideas and items in their environment. The children's thinking process becomes more evident.

Schematic Stage (5 to 7 years of age)

Children increase their use of symbols. Their drawings are referred to as X-ray drawings because the picture is being seen from both the inside and the outside. For example, if a child draws a child on a bicycle, both legs are shown to the front, even though we should see only one of the child's legs. The sky may not meet the ground at the horizon. There is an increase in details such as hands and figures and special effects such as glasses or jewellery. There is also an exaggeration between figures, such as the human being taller than the house or the flowers being taller than the person.

The Gang Stage: The Dawning Realism (8 to 10 years of age)

During this phase, children's art becomes increasingly more realistic and is expressed with more detail for individual parts. Dawning realism becomes the objective. Space is discovered and is depicted with overlapping objects, and the use of both small and large objects is evident. The human is depicted as a girl, a boy, a woman, or a man with details that often depict "stiffness" in the representation. Three-dimensional effects are achieved. Children also experiment with shading and colour combinations. During this phase, children begin to compare their work, and they also become more critical of it. They try to conform to the level of their peers (Donley, 1987).

Stages of Clay Development

Brown (1984) and Stokrocki (1988) conducted three significant studies to acquire information on the stages of clay making that children engage in. Note that Brown used the same titles for the stages as Lowenfeld (1947) did for the stages of drawing.

Scribbling (3 to 4 years of age)

During this phase, children make coils, snakes, and mud pies (Brown, 1975). As children gain more experience, they progress from making flat objects to upright creations, such as snow people. There are limited details on their creations. Children often create items while verbalizing what they are making. For example, as Martina took a ball of clay, she explained, "I am making an ice castle with a chapel for my mummy's wedding." Children begin to exhibit seriation by making simple "cookie forms" and connecting them.

Pre-Schematic (4 to 5 years of age)

During this phase, there are more recognizable forms. Children use the clay as a palate for drawing. The head has eyes, a mouth, and limbs that are attached.

Schematic (5 to 8 years of age)

Children exhibit new skills during this phase. Objects may now be in standing positions, tilted positions, or a combination of both. People sculptures include necks, hair, fingers, and so on. Animals have prominent features as well. For example, cats will have tails and elephants will have trunks. Children make letters to write their name or the names of important people in their lives.

Photo 7.7 A clay creature.
Used with Permission of Diane Kashin

Dawning Realism (9 to 11 years of age)

During this phase, children concentrate on facial features, patterns, sexual characteristics, and special effects such as hats and a scarf. Clay forms look realistic.

The stages presented for drawing and clay are guidelines only. Some children may progress through the stages more quickly than others. Some children may overlap between more than one stage at any given time. You may find some children who prefer painting to clay, and vice versa.

Although these stages are used as guidelines, early learning teachers benefit from examining each of the children's artwork and use the findings as a guide to devise programming experiences that will enhance experiences and challenges that will lead children to explore more techniques and ideas, leading them to make new discoveries. This provides early learning teachers with an overview of children's strengths and how they are progressing. Many children with learning challenges may have advanced creative and visual talents in drawing.

At each stage of development, early learning teachers gain insight into a child's perception about the world he or she lives in. For example, the use of colour, materials, and the art medium provide information about children's sense of self-worth and self-expression (Englebright Fox & Schirrmacher, 2014).

THE PROCESS OF ART AND THE PRODUCT

Children's art is more than the production of something recognizable to the adult or a specific product—art is a process. Our role as early learning teachers is to support young children engaged in exploring and creating a painting that evolves from them mixing colours rather than using only the three paint colours placed at the easel. We become more intrigued by how children make a sculpture that combines play dough and sticks than by a creation that can be clearly labelled as an item, such as a cup. In essence, it is the *process of exploring and creating*, rather than a finished, recognizable product, that is important to us. Open-ended art experiences require children to use their imagination and their abilities. This is how they explore the "what ifs." These are keys to nurturing creativity.

Just as there are ways to encourage creativity, there are also some practices that discourage creativity. For example, when children are given precut shapes to create a specific item such as a rabbit, or pictures to paste onto a paper bag for a puppet, these items become "dictated art." Jenkins (1986) indicated that such experiences lead children to lose their creativity, sensitivity, self-confidence, and freeflow or independent thinking. These types of assembly tasks lead children to become conformists and perfectionists as they try to meet the expectations of completing the task to the required standard. Think back to the story of *The Little Boy* highlighted in Chapter 2. Clearly, dictated art affected that little boy's creativity.

STOP ... THINK ... DISCUSS ... REFLECT

What are your early recollections about art? Did you experience process art or dictated art? Were you told what to do like the little boy in the poem? Think about how your early experiences have affected how you feel about art now. Did you try to create something perfect to match a sample given? Imagine if children fail in their attempts to replicate a model and then feel like a failure. How will that affect their view of themselves as artists?

Similar to the assembly tasks outlined above, colouring books and sheets of paper with lines on them for colouring negatively affect a child's opportunity for creativity. These products do not support a child's individual expression or emotional release. Fill-in art is often "doing without thinking" and promotes mindless obedience to authority, rather than

Photo 7.8 A wall of dictated art.

Used with Permission of Diane Kashin

creative problem solving. The sense of achievement and pride that should come from art is lacking in dictated art (Christakis, 2016).

Cornett and Smithrim (2001) indicated that "dictated art" could frustrate children's development. When children are not involved in a creative problem-solving process, they are not stimulated or encouraged to engage in higher-order thinking. We encourage higher-order thinking because it advances children's ideas, perspectives, and opportunities to explore in new ways. We suggest that early learning students and teachers resist mindless "dictated art" that involves a directed craft, as it stands in opposition to creativity and art.

One of the key purposes of providing children with art experiences is for them to learn to express their feelings and ideas; it is not to have children duplicate adult ideas. If you have chosen the experience for the children and you want them to follow particular directions in order to produce a particular product, you will spend most of your time reminding them about the instructions. In the end, you may be disappointed with the results and resort to trying to fix their creations in order to duplicate the craft. Children require the freedom to engage in appropriate art process experiences that are fluid in nature. This will lead them to intertwine art, play, and real-life experiences. For example, Matt, since the age of 3, has exhibited an interest in vehicles. He carries cars in his pockets, he draws cars, and he makes the sounds of the car engines. Often, his play is vehicle related, as identified in the scenario that follows.

While making trucks from cardboard boxes, Matt was joined by Justyn, Patrick, and Mohammad. They each made the trucks using the boxes, a paper punch to make holes, string to attach the boxes, and a knife and scissors to cut out doors to the cab. Two of the children discussed painting the trucks but decided that they needed to "get on the road." As they started to push their trucks on the floor, out of the art area, Matt yelled, "I need gas." Jamie, who had been standing on the sidelines, immediately said, "My gas station is open." Quickly, the children pulled into the pretend gas station with their vehicles. As Matt's tank was filled, he turned to Mohammad and said, "I'm hungry . . . Let's pull in at the Pizza House." The children proceeded to the play dough table, where a small group of children were making pizzas with the play dough. The truck drivers said, "We want pizza to go." Archie responded by saying, "You got it. Will that be with cheese?" This illustrates how art influences play and how play influences art. Early learning teachers encourage the overlap between the play and art processes because this interconnectivity allows children to explore ideas, see things in new ways, and make their own reality.

It is common practice for children to have recurring themes in their art and their play. For example, as identified earlier, Matt has a keen interest in vehicles. For him, vehicles are prominent in his drawings, in his stories, with clay, and in the sand. Each time he draws a vehicle, there are different details. It is as though he is trying to perfect one aspect of the reproduction. In one drawing, he drew lines that he identified as roads. Weeks later, his drawings had roads with curves. And some more weeks later, his drawings illustrated roads with curves, a truck, and dots on the windshield that he identified as snow. When children combine art and play, they are developing the conceptual framework that supports them in expanding their abstract and higher-order thinking. This higher order of thinking provides children with resourceful options for learning.

The following questions help guide student early learning teachers in determining whether potential experiences are creative art experiences or dictated art experiences.

1. Is the early learning teacher preparing precut pieces, patterns, or models? This implies that the children are required to produce a product, even though early learning teachers suggest that the children may create whatever they wish.
2. Will each child's work be original or look nearly identical to another child's creation? Do early learning teachers need to "fix" the child's work? When a child's art looks like

another, originality and creativity have been stifled. Such experiences become "busy work" rather than art. If an early learning teacher fixes a child's work, it undermines the child's self-esteem and confidence.

3. Are children given the choice of when to engage in art experiences, or are they required to participate in the art experience at an assigned time? If children are required to come together for art in a group, or if they must complete an art activity over a specified period of time, this is not art. If art experiences are designed to be used as display pieces for parents, this is not art; rather, it is a marketing strategy for parents.

4. Are you offering children products such as food items to use as creative materials? Children require authentic art products. When children are given items such as macaroni, beans, or finger-painting experiences with pudding, early learning teachers are sending children mixed messages. First, artists do not generally use these types of products to express creativity. Second, it says to children that it is okay to play with food.

5. Are early learning teachers offering art experiences that may be completed in only one way? If so, this implies that a structured product is necessary.

6. Are the art materials and experiences offered at one interest centre indoors? If so, this implies that art is a solitary activity rather than one that spans across play. It also indicates that indoor programming is more important than outdoor programming. This reduces the opportunity for children to incorporate natural items from their environment into their creative experiences.

STOP ... THINK ... DISCUSS ... REFLECT

Think about being an early learning student doing a field placement. The centre is using a theme of *101 Dalmatians*. The book has been read, the movie has been shown, and there are many photos of Dalmatians in the play space. Because a group of children seemed interested in the photos of the dogs, you thought it would be neat to provide children with cut-out paper shapes of Dalmatians, black crayons, black tissue paper, and black and white construction paper.

Is this an activity that should be offered to children? Why or why not? What are the potential impacts on children? Are the impacts positive or negative? Why? Are there other ways to support the children's interests in the dogs?

STRATEGIES FOR ENCOURAGING CREATIVITY WITH ART EXPERIENCES

Early learning teachers are continuously incorporating ways to support and encourage a child's creativity with art experiences. There are many strategies that support creativity, such as

- Encouraging children to examine possibilities, think about options, and solve problems in creative ways. Encourage children to take risks and make mistakes. Support growth by providing idea options for the children to consider.
- Providing children with an array of materials and choices for exploration both through their senses and by the questions that the early learning practitioner poses.

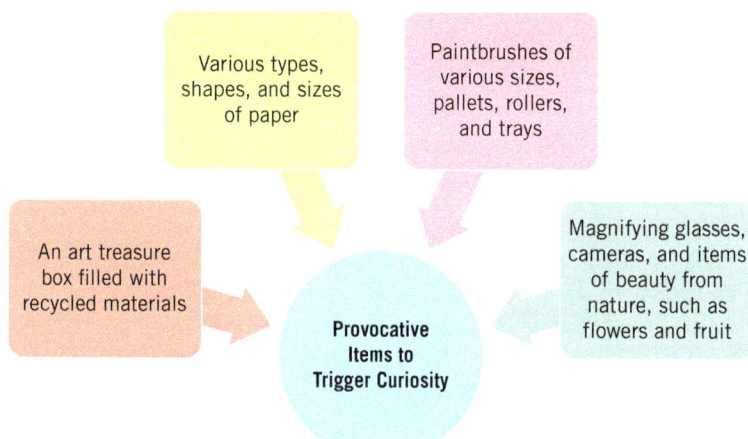

Figure 7.6 Provocative items to trigger curiosity.

- Providing children with an environment that has established routines that support and encourage children to think and explore without adult direction.
- Providing children with opportunities to observe, explore, and experience aspects of other cultures relative to their life experiences.
- Creating changes to the indoor and outdoor early learning environment so that children are stimulated to explore their environment in new ways.
- Encouraging children in ways that help them build their skills and expand their sense of accomplishment and experimentation.
- Displaying children's artwork at their eye level, in an aesthetically pleasing format.
- Offering art experiences in both the indoor and the outdoor play environments.

Figure 7.6 provides ideas for materials that will trigger creativity.

TYPES OF OPEN-ENDED ART MATERIALS

Early learning teachers examine materials to gain an understanding of the core attributes that each material has. This helps early learning teachers and student teachers explore how children may potentially use the materials, and it guides the questioning process used to advance their thinking skills and exploration of materials. For example, Mattie and Akik were at the easel. There were jars of red, blue, yellow, white, and black paint available. Suddenly, Akik said, "Mattie, I made pink!" Mattie asked, "How did you do it?" Akik said, "I don't know?" Brent, the early learning teacher, heard the conversation and walked over to Akik to ask, "Akik, what paint colours did you use—did you use any yellow?" Akik thought for a moment, looked at the colours on his page, and then said, "No, I did not use yellow—red and white make pink." Then Mattie said, "I am going to try it. Yes, it does!" Then Brent asked, "What happens if you add another colour, such as yellow, to it? What colour do you think you will create?" Other children gathered around to watch as Mattie and Akik mixed different colours. Brent wondered aloud about what would happen when they mixed other colours. Children observing made a prediction, as did Akik and Mattie. Then they proceeded to see the results.

The example above illustrates how open-ended experiences lead children to discovery learning or hands-on learning. One child made a discovery about what happens when you mix two colours: a new colour is formed. Then other children participated in the discovery. The children learned by doing. These types of experiences are foundational in early learning programs. There are many types of open-ended materials to have in an early learning environment, such as the following:

- **Potter's clay:** Clay offers children opportunities to be creative while providing a release for energy and stress. Clay requires children to pull, push, squeeze, and punch it. These actions support the child's fine motor development. Popular accessories used with clay include rolling pins, various containers, dull knives, and sticks.
- **Paint:** Painting is one of the most popular activities that support children in exploring colours, patterns, and art forms. Children benefit from having painting activities occur on a variety of surfaces and places, such as at an easel, on the floor, on a tabletop, in a sandbox, and on a plywood fence. The paint needs to vary in colour, texture, and thickness. Children benefit from using several shades of the same colour. Painting instruments include paintbrushes of different thicknesses, paint rollers, straw, cotton balls, cotton swabs, sponges, feathers, and string; all of these provide unique experiences for the children.
- **Sand:** Sand provides children with an unstructured medium. Sand exploration supports children in mixing, pouring, stacking, moulding, sifting, and combining. Sand tools include buckets, cups, sifters, moulds, vehicles, pipe pieces, and boards. This medium supports children in creating art sculpture. Dry paint added to sand expands the opportunities for creativity.
- **Chalk:** Chalk has many uses. Children benefit most when they have large surfaces to use the chalk on, such as driveways or surfaces that may be washed off.
- **Crayons:** Similar to chalk, crayons support children in exploring line and drawing formation. Tools such as textured surfaces under paper or over paper, screens, and corrugated cardboard offer children intrigue with the crayons.
- **Materials for collage:** A variety of materials and bases are presented for collage. Collage activities lead children to examine the qualities of design, colours, textures, and forms that the materials exhibit. Materials that have similar qualities and those that are unique and different offer curiosity triggers. Collage bases may include scraps of wood, trays, discarded mat boards, and cardboard. Fabric pieces that are soft, stiff, and netlike are also provided.
- **Paper:** A variety of paper, including tissue, construction, corrugated, fancy doilies, and specialty papers, is made available. Boxes of all sizes and shapes are present, as are rolls of paper and paper cylinders.

Figure 7.7 outlines ways to display materials to trigger curiosity.

When art materials are displayed at the children's eye level, creativity and accessibility are encouraged. If the shelves are movable, this allows for changes to the environment that are intended to stimulate new discoveries. Sorting materials by colour will support children's understanding of colour and help them in the tidying-up process. By sequencing materials from simple to complex, early learning teachers are supporting children's artistic development and feelings of success. When early learning teachers clean and maintain the art area, the aesthetic appeal will support children's curiosity and creativity. Adding new materials and interesting objects to the art area will increase curiosity. Imagine children seeing a bowl of exotic fruit on the table in the art area. How might this trigger their curiosity?

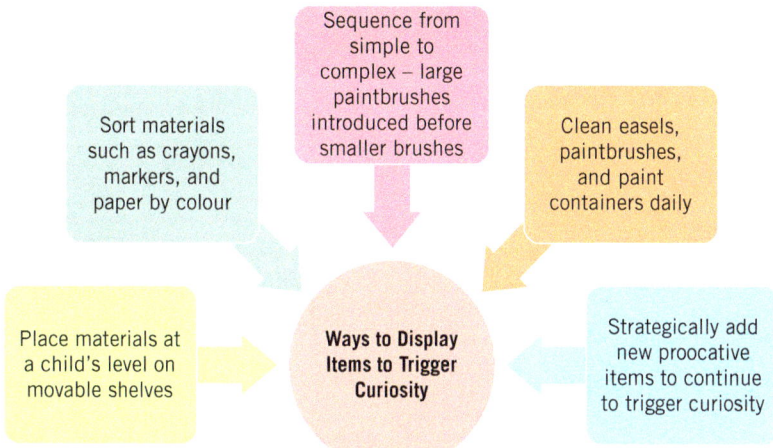

Figure 7.7 Ways to display items to trigger curiosity.

Children's curiosity can be triggered when early learning teachers recognize that art does not have to be confined to a particular area and that there is great potential for art experiences outdoors. Nature provides a bounty of loose materials that can be used for transient art experiences. The ground becomes the canvas for art that is considered *ephemeral* or landscape art. Ephemeral art is that which lasts a short time and is transitory.

Photo 7.9 Landscape art.
Used with Permission of Diane Kashin

Photo 7.10 A tree face.
Used with Permission of Diane Kashin

CURIOUS?

Add the words *ephemeral art* and *ephemeral artists* to your search engine. Look specifically for images. What inspiration can you take from these images for art experiences that can be implemented with children?

STOP ... THINK ... DISCUSS ... REFLECT

Examine the photo of the tree embellished with clay and found materials to represent a face (Photo 7.10). This experience took place during a morning spent in the forest. What will happen to the tree after the children return to their centre? What makes clay the ideal material for ephemeral art?

THE ROLE OF EARLY LEARNING TEACHERS IN ART EXPERIENCES

The quality of the art experiences and the strategies used to support children in their quest with art experiences must be of high quality and developmentally appropriate (Eckhoff, 2008). Children benefit most from early learning teachers who have an interest in art and know that art experiences may span across the early learning program and occur in both indoor and outdoor environments.

As early learning teachers and student teachers, we need to be concerned about building our knowledge levels about the arts. Why? Because our knowledge levels or lack of knowledge influences the types of art experiences children are exposed to. Understanding the core elements of art requires early learning teachers to explore materials, to play with these materials, and to make discoveries about these materials. Early learning students and teachers benefit from practising playing (Nell, Drew, & Bush, 2013). Similarly, children flourish in environments that provide them with opportunities for art experiences, aesthetic experiences, and encounters with art. Children also benefit when their teachers engage in observations, reflection, and dialogue to support children in their construction of art-based knowledge (Cremin, Glauert, Craft, Compton, & Stylianidou, 2015).

Throughout your studies, you are gaining new knowledge and skills that are intended to help you develop a working philosophy. Your philosophy guides you in your observations, your interactions with children and adults, how you prepare the environment, how you embrace the sense of curiosity that each child brings to the environment, and what you believe about professional development and lifelong learning opportunities. Thinking about art and its presentation to children is directly related to your beliefs about how children learn.

STOP ... THINK ... DISCUSS ... REFLECT

When you think about children and art experiences, what do you wish them to gain from the experiences you provide? Why? How do you envision your philosophical beliefs about art experiences supporting the needs of children? Are there conflicts between your beliefs and the ideas presented in this chapter? If so, how might those conflicts be resolved? What are the impacts on children when there are conflicts in philosophy and programming?

There are many strategies to support you in exploring your philosophy about art and young children. What we believe about play, learning, and the arts influences the early learning environments. Hermon and Prentice (2003) encouraged teachers to incorporate each of the following into their art programming practice: enable, empower, engage, and extend. Figure 7.8 describes what is meant by each of these powerful words.

The following suggestions will help you think about what you believe about the arts. The framework is intended to further enhance your understanding and an appreciation for the arts with young children.

1. Children Require Early Learning Teachers Who View Themselves as Embracing Play, Creativity, and Art

Children require early learning teachers who gain knowledge and skills about art and play. Meaningful art activities are extended to children. There are opportunities to combine art with other play experiences. Early learning teachers offer children various types of stimulus, time, and materials that will create an environment to fuel creativity.

Five core questions help you determine how you view yourself as a creative early learning teacher: What are my beliefs about children and art? What types of open-ended

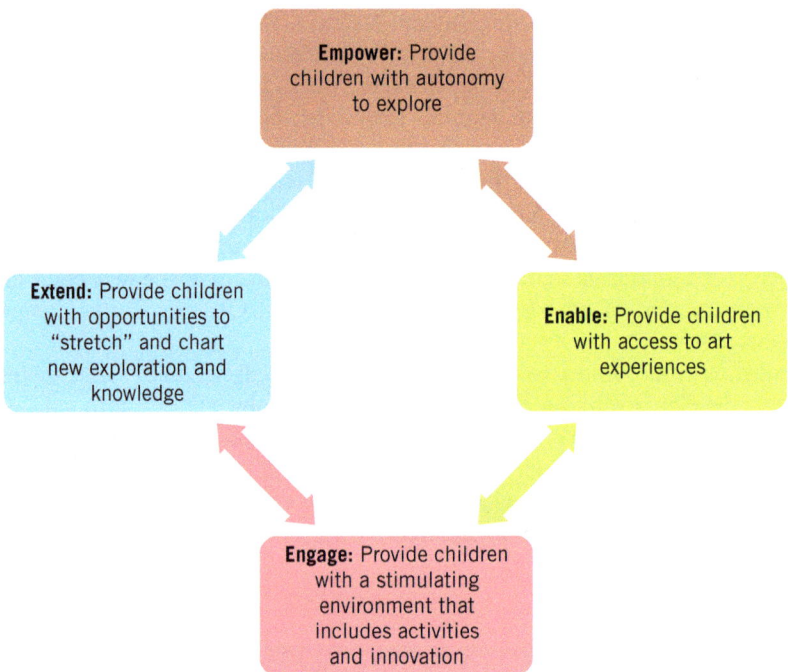

Figure 7.8 Herman and Prentice's powerful words for art programming practice.

opportunities should I provide children? How will I encourage and support children who exhibit an interest in art? How do I personally view my creative talents? How will my attitudes affect the children?

Early learning teachers who gain a sense of their philosophical orientation are more likely to model appropriate attitudes toward art and play. They show respect for the interesting ideas that children create, and they have the ability to ask probing and "what if" questions that help children move to a deeper level of thinking and exploration.

2. Children Require Early Learning Teachers Who Have an Understanding of the Elements of the Materials

Early learning teachers who develop an understanding of the technical information of the materials used by children are better able to discuss ideas with the children and plan potential learning opportunities. For example, how are soft, gentle colours such as light blue and pink made versus harsher colours such as brown and black? What are the primary and secondary colours, and how do they blend? What are the differences between newsprint and glossy paper? What is the best paper for the various media? How will these paper choices affect a child's work? What is the difference between plasticine and potter's clay? What is the difference between white clay and red clay? Why would you use one over the other? What are the safety concerns of the paints and the various materials that may be introduced to children? How do the various paintbrushes affect a creation? Knowing information about the materials builds the early learning teachers' confidence in their program planning and facilitation skills with children.

3. Children Require Early Learning Teachers Who Know When to Be Supportive and When to Allow Children to Be Free and to Problem Solve the Area of Challenge

When children explore new materials that they do not have any experience with, they may become frustrated; this interferes with their creativity and play. Early learning teachers, through observation, are able to see signs of concern or frustration building. Technical guidance is offered when required, recognizing that it is proffered without imposing our ideas on the children.

Another area of support that children benefit from is them having enough *time* to engage in experiences and with sufficient materials to support exploration. For example, think back to Matt, Mohammad, and Justyn. Consider what would have occurred had the children not been given enough time to make their vehicles and then exercise the play episode of requiring gas and having pizza.

4. Children Require a Learning Environment with a Variety of Materials and Places to Use the Materials

Early learning teachers view the environment as a safe place for children to explore, experiment, and create new knowledge. Creativity is enhanced when children have access to a variety of materials, plenty of materials, space, and opportunities to use the materials. Children gravitate to play spaces that are aesthetically pleasing. Carefully arranged art materials help children exercise independence and self-regulation. Children must not be rushed so that other children can be accommodated.

When we think of variety, we need to think beyond the materials that are presented. Using a variety of spaces in the play space allows children to observe different ideas, possibilities, and material attributes. For example, in an observation conducted with eight 4-year-old children who had access to a variety of materials, including pipes and wooden pieces, the creativity differed significantly among the children who used the materials outdoors and those who used them indoors. Children using the materials outdoors made life-sized creations that were built in upright positions, and they incorporated a variety of materials into their creations. The children using the materials indoors used smaller pieces; the creations were flat; and only three types of materials were incorporated into their designs (Dietze & Kashin, 2016).

5. Children Benefit from Early Learning Teachers Who Encourage Children to Discuss Their Creations

When children discuss their art experiences and those of other children and professional artists, they begin to develop an art-focused and self-focused vocabulary. They connect vocabulary related to the medium. For example, when Brent was discussing the clay experience with 4-year-old Marti, he was amazed to hear Marti say that he began by using a slab, then he had to pinch the clay, and then he rolled it. He said he was not going to fire his sculpture today. The language expressed by Marti is commonly used among potters. Marti has mastered the language at this very young age because of exposure to it and having the language context.

Early learning teachers and children record the information that the children share. Throughout discussions, there is an emphasis on the process rather than the product.

Early learning teachers take their lead from the children. For example, if the child says, "I made very thick lines," the early learning teacher may expand on that idea and ask, "How did you make those thick lines?" If appropriate, discussion may also occur on how to make thin lines or how curved lines may be created.

6. Children Benefit from Early Learning Teachers Who Observe Children and Engage in Documentation

Observing children using art materials provides the early learning teacher with insight into the child's interests and skill levels. For example, knowing the children's pincer grasp ability will help early learning teachers determine which sizes of brushes are most appropriate for them to gain success. As children are first introduced to brushes, these need to be large-handled brushes. Children who have a more developed pincer grasp will use both large and small brushes. Children who you notice are intrigued by sculpturing would be offered materials such as potter's clay, plasticine, and play dough. The tools are chosen based on children's strengths, interests, and opportunities for new discoveries.

7. Children Require Early Learning Teachers to Have Rich Dialogue with Them about Their Art Creations

Children's art experiences and creativity are dependent on materials, the environment, the facilitation, and the time allocated for creative expression. Early learning teachers focus on advancing a child's confidence to explore new materials and methods. Dialogue between the early learning teacher and the children must be correct. The questions posed by the adult are intended to lead children to think about what was done and what possibilities exist. The questions are open-ended and nonjudgmental and stimulate intrigue. As identified in other chapters, it is challenging to develop questions that encompass intrigue, problem solving, wonderment, and potential new directions for exploration. Student teachers require practice in observing children's art and in formulating questions that advance children's thinking, exploration, and learning. In Figure 7.9, conversational ideas are outlined.

8. Children Benefit from Early Learning Teachers Who Know about the Relationship of Art to Child Development

Jalongo (1999) indicated that if early learning teachers are not being exposed to "educationally worthwhile art experiences" in their college or university programs, they must be available through professional development opportunities. "If the arts mission of early childhood education must be to provide high-quality arts experiences for all children . . . then, professional development in the arts is not a frill, it is a necessity" (Jalongo, 1999, pp. 206–207). As Krishnamurti (2000) stated, "Education can be transformed only by transforming the educator. Throughout the world, it is becoming more and more evident that the educator needs educating. It is not a question of educating the child, but rather the educator" (p. 60). Spending time experiencing art and learning about the principles and elements of art will support early learning teachers in supporting children.

Early learning teachers require access to ongoing professional learning so that they continue to gain an understanding of the relationship of visual arts to child development and of the design and delivery of appropriate visual arts experiences for children during their early years. Children are more likely to explore the medium when the materials and the environment allow for fluidity.

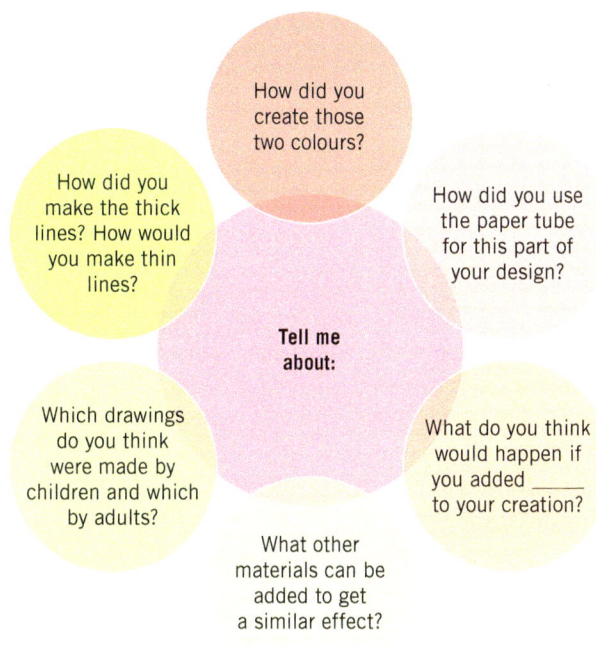

Figure 7.9 Conversational strategies for discussing children's art.

Early learning teachers have a key role in expanding their knowledge and skills about the benefits of art experiences. The more the teachers know about the creative process, materials, and the development of an environment that supports the arts, the more likely children are to integrate art into their daily living.

TERMS THAT INFLUENCE EARLY LEARNING PLAY ENVIRONMENTS

We conclude this chapter with three additional terms that support the theory of children's play. These terms are used when examining space and with children in their play.

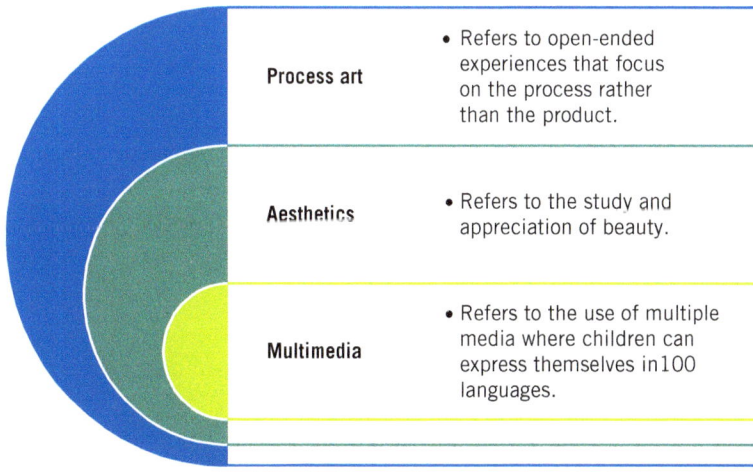

SUMMARY

Chapter Preview

- Research indicates that art enhances a child's creativity; problem-solving skills; language skills; and cognitive, social, emotional, and physical developmental domains. Yet many early learning programs have a focus on academic instruction rather than art.

Defining Art

- There are many ways to define art. Art is a means of expression, a form of communication, a developmental activity, and a way to understand culture and community. It is interconnected to the development of the "whole child."

Educational Approaches Influencing the Visual Arts in Early Childhood Programs

- Educators and philosophers, including John Dewey, Friedrich Froebel, Rudolf Steiner, and Loris Malaguzzi, identified the benefits of young children participating in early learning experiences with art as a core focus. They suggest that children who are not exposed to developmentally appropriate art experiences will not develop to their fullest potential.

Art and Child Development

- Open-ended art experiences facilitate children gaining a sense of success because they create as they desire, rather than needing to produce a specific product.
- Art advances the child's fine and gross motor development.
- Art is deeply cognitive, as many mental processes occur throughout the thinking and problem-solving activities, many of which are essential for later academic learning, such as pattern recognition and development.
- Art provides children with the venue to develop social and cultural constructs. Children develop their self-identity, competence, worth, and control through their interactions with art experiences. Art helps children to develop and release their ideas and feelings.
- Children develop their visual language through art experiences in environments that recognize that children follow a sequential process in creating art; that it evolves from their thinking and experience; and that it is influenced by their environments, experiences, and their guides or facilitators.

Stages of Children's Drawing

- Lowenfeld identifies four stages of drawing that children pursue. They are scribble, pre-schematic, schematic, and the gang stage.
- Brown and Stokrocki use the same classifications as Lowenfeld to identify the stages of clay development.

The Process of Art versus the Product

- The process that the child engages in to create something is more important than producing a recognizable product.
- Open-ended art experiences require young children to use their imagination and curiosity.

- Precut shapes and structured art activities are known as "dictated art"—these types of activities negatively affect the flow of independent thinking and learning.

Strategies for Encouraging Creativity with Art Experiences

- Children require environments that have established routines, have art experiences both indoors and outdoors, display artwork at the child's level, provide children with encouragement, have faith in the children's abilities, and encourage children to take risks and make mistakes.

Types of Open-Ended Art Materials

- The more common open-ended materials include potter's clay, paint, sand, chalk, crayons, materials for collage making, and paper.

The Role of Early Learning Teachers in Art Experiences

- Early learning teachers benefit from determining their philosophy as it relates to the arts. Herman and Prentice suggest that early learning teachers incorporate *enable, empower, engage,* and *extend* into their practice.
- Children benefit from early learning teachers who view themselves as embracing play, creativity, and art; understand the elements of the materials; know how to support and when to let the children problem solve; provide a variety of materials and places to use the materials; encourage and discuss the children's creations; consistently observe children; and understand the importance of art to child development.

REVIEW QUESTIONS

1. Describe how art experiences contribute to a young child's development.
2. Explain why Dewey, Froebel, Steiner, and Malaguzzi advocate for children to have access to a variety of art experiences in their early years.
3. Discuss how art experiences support children in learning about the elements and principles of design.
4. Outline the four principles of children developing their visual language through art experiences.
5. Highlight the stages of children's artwork and clay work.
6. Describe the debate among educators on process versus product related to children's art.
7. Outline ways in which early learning teachers may encourage creativity with art experiences.
8. Discuss a minimum of seven roles that early learning teachers have in providing art experiences for young children.

MAKING CONNECTIONS

Theory to Practice

1. Visualize your ideal play space for children using art materials. In what ways do you think your philosophy about how children learn and your thoughts on process versus product influence your view of the ideal space for children's art?

2. There are many early learning centres that establish an art centre for the children in the indoor environment. How might you move the art experience to the outdoor environment? How do you envision the experience will be for the children? Will it be different from that indoors? If so, how? What different practices would you need to think about if your art centre was outdoors? How might the materials differ? Why?
3. Imagine that you are required to prepare a presentation for parents on the importance of art for young children. How would you present the information? What key messaging would you wish to share with the parents? Why? What role would children have in the presentation?
4. Examine your early learning centre. Then visualize how you would incorporate art experiences into one of the experience centres. How would you set it up? Why? What considerations are required? How would you encourage the children to combine the two experience centre play opportunities?

DIGITAL PORTFOLIO ENTRIES

Potential portfolio entries for your digital portfolio could include:

- Why I think process art as opposed to product art is important for children's development
- As an early learning student, I wonder about how I can increase my comfort level and knowledge about art.
- When I examine the art area in my field placement, I can think of these ways to improve: . . .
- I think art is as important to children as other critical areas such as math and science because . . .

CURIOUS?

Find and read this article: Why Typical Preschool Crafts Are a Total Waste of Time (http://nymag.com/scienceofus/2016/04/why-typical-preschool-crafts-are-a-total-waste-of-time.html).

CHAPTER 8
Blocks and Child's Play

Rawpixel.com/Shutterstock

> "The freest child is the child who is most interested in what he is doing, and at whose hand are the materials for his work or play."
>
> —Caroline Pratt (1867–1954)

LEARNING OUTCOMES

After exploring this chapter you should be able to:

- Define block play.
- Discuss the historical perspectives of block play.
- Compare Reifel and Greenfield's stages of block play with Hirsch's stages of block play.
- Explain what is meant by table blocks and floor blocks.
- Discuss how block play supports child development, creativity, and children with disabilities.
- Discuss the various roles that an early learning practitioner has in facilitating block play.

Sharing Stories of Practice

Four years ago, I graduated from an early childhood education program at a local college. During my studies I had terrific field placements that provided me with insight into how theory translates to practice. As I participated in the field placements, I found myself developing an interest in the block area. I always seemed to gravitate to that area, so naturally so I began watching the children there. Soon I gained confidence to ask children questions about their structures. I completed a number of observations and took photos of children and their structures. Then I used a video camera to further document the structures that the children were making. Like many of the children, I became hooked on block play. I believe that, as a result of my interest and enthusiasm for this play, I invested time and listened to the children as they created and recreated with the blocks. As I learned from the children, I was better able to add new, innovative materials, such as large planks, cedar blocks, and flexible and rigid pipes of various dimensions that supported their play. I was always intrigued to see what the children would do with the new materials and how they would extend their sense of exploration and learning.

Over the four years of working with children, I have learned that blocks are a versatile medium that may be used by infants, toddlers, preschool, and school-aged children. I have also learned that children need time, space, and unique materials to support their expansion of ideas and opportunities to maintain their structures so that they may work on them over time. As an early learning teacher, I have a responsibility to thoroughly review how children use the materials and to visualize with them . . . what will happen . . . or I wonder about . . . or if you do this . . . what do you think may happen?

My advice to early learning students and teachers who are just beginning their careers is to develop areas of passion and share that passion and enthusiasm with the children, because your passion will become positively contagious. When this occurs, there is no predicting what the children are capable of doing with their blocks and support materials.

Avril, ECE graduate, 2013

CHAPTER PREVIEW

Many early learning programs have blocks among the materials for children to choose from. However, as identified by Tepylo, Moss, and Stephenson (2015), if blocks are available, they are often located in out-of-the-way places, such as in corners or areas with limited light. In some centres, blocks may not be present, due in part to the cost or the trend to make the spaces look more like school classrooms (Hansel, 2015).

Blocks are one of the simplest yet most important play materials that we can offer children. The play value in blocks contributes to children's whole development. Children learn skills and knowledge through block play that set the foundation for later academic studies, such as science, math, and problem-solving skills. For some children, block play leads them to engage in careers such as architecture, construction, and design.

Let's think about block play. What do children gain from these materials? Think about how block play:

- Enhances children's understanding of patterning, objects, forms, systems, and designs
- Allows children to recreate the world around them

- Supports children in having a free flow of creativity in terms of using their imaginations to design, construct, recreate, and expand their creations
- Contributes to children developing many skills, including sorting, grouping, comparing, arranging, making decisions, cooperating and role playing (Koralek, 2015)
- Expands children's understanding of social communication, literacy, physical science, language, art, mathematics, creativity, and problem-solving techniques (Hansel, 2015)

In early learning programs where blocks are available to young children, many early learning teachers may not fully be familiar with the value that they contribute to children (Hansel, 2015; Luckenbill & Schallock, 2015; Tepylo et al., 2015). Many young children are provided with worksheets or other academic tasks to "teach" children math, literacy, or social studies concepts (Sobel & Larimore, 2016) rather than with concrete materials, such as blocks. Paper-and-pencil tasks are not considered appropriate or effective because preschoolers and children in kindergarten are in the preoperational or concrete-operational stage of cognitive development. Children learn best when they are exposed to hands-on, experiential learning and free-flowing materials, such as blocks (Christenson & James, 2015). Children who are provided with blocks and block-building experiences gain skills and concepts more quickly and with more enthusiasm for learning than if they are required to do so in a structured "teacher-led" process (Ramani, Zippert, Schweitzer, & Pan, 2014).

Children require access to blocks in both the indoor and the outdoor environments. Both spaces offer unique opportunities for creative experimentation. The use of different materials, the social interaction, and the development that is inherent in both of these settings offer children different types of problem-solving techniques that are needed to execute block play. For example, using blocks outdoors invites children to experiment with building materials such as crates, rocks, logs, sticks, and bricks that aren't easily negotiated indoors. The structures that children create may be longer and wider, and accessories such as ride-on toys and the natural environment may be integrated into the structures. School-aged children, when given the opportunity, expand their block building to include a variety of elaborate structures.

As you explore this chapter, you will discover how block play provides children with the opportunity to develop a variety of skills and abilities that are transferable to other learning domains. Early learning teachers and student teachers have an important role in continuing to examine strategies that will advance the use of block play with children.

DEFINING BLOCK PLAY

Many perspectives are used to define block play. For example, Cohen and Uhry (2007) defined it as "any time a child manipulates proportional wooden [or related product material] blocks, using actions and/or language to represent realistic or imaginary experiences" (p. 302). Ness and Farenga (2016) suggested from an analytical framework that the terms *blocks* and *block play* are too generic and lack clarity and specificity. They determined that block play be redefined as **"visual-spatial construction play objects"** (p. 202). They maintained that visual-spatial construction objects include blocks such as standard wood, plastic, and foam blocks; bricks; and planks. Although these definitions vary considerably, they both acknowledge that blocks are used for construction and are necessary in children's play environments.

visual-spatial construction play objects "[D]efined as materials that [children] use when they imagine and construct something in their world" (Ness & Farenga, 2016, p. 202).

> **STOP ... THINK ... DISCUSS ... REFLECT**
>
> Do you think that block play should be redefined? Why or why not?

THE HISTORICAL PERSPECTIVE OF BLOCKS

Beginning in the 1700s

Children and blocks are not a new phenomenon. Block building appears to have evolved simultaneously with the movement toward establishing a child-centred culture in the late 1700s. Philosophers and educators, including John Locke, Richard Lovell Edgeworth, Frederich Froebel, Maria Montessori, and Caroline Pratt, recognized the importance of young children having materials that would support them in using their imaginations and creative abilities (Provenzo & Brett, 1983). Their contributions to block history is detailed below.

Friedrich Froebel

Froebel (1782–1852) introduced the first systematic use of blocks as part of children's early learning experiences. He believed that blocks were an educational material that would lead the child to increase his or her understanding of her world.

As part of Froebel's block system, he created "gifts" known as the wooden sphere, a cube, and a cylinder. He ensured that the sphere, with its rounded sides, was opposite to the cube. The cylinder had the roundness of the sphere and the clearly defined edges of the cube.

According to Provenzo and Brett (1983), Froebel described the use of building blocks using the "gifts" in the following way:

> The material for building in the beginning should consist of a number of wooden blocks whose base is always one inch square and whose length varies from one to twelve inches. If, then, we take twelve pieces of each length, two sets—e.g., the pieces one and eleven, the pieces two and ten inches long, etc.—will always make up a layer an inch thick and covering one foot of square surface; so that all the pieces, together with a few larger pieces, occupy a space of somewhat more than half a cubic foot. It is best to keep these in a box that has exactly these dimensions; such a box may be used in many ways in instruction, as will appear in the progress of a [child's] development. (p. 12)

Froebel suggested that blocks were the foundation materials to support children in acquiring the skills to distinguish, name, and classify (Wright, 1957). He designed a block system consisting of four specific cubes. Each of the cubes contributed to children being able to build complicated structures that supported their creativity while advancing their knowledge about classification, balance, and related architectural, scientific, and mathematical principles. For example, the cube (known as the third of eight gifts) was divided equally down the middle. This allowed children, through their play, to engage with the blocks having eight equal parts, which would lead them to discover the principles of size and the internal and external characteristics of cubes.

The next cube in the series (known as the fourth gift) is split four times, which allows children to have oblong bricks or blocks. The next cube (known as the fifth gift) is made out of 27 cubes. These cubes can be subdivided into half and quarter triangle forms.

The sixth cube (known as the sixth gift) consists of 27 oblong blocks, 3 being divided lengthwise and 6 being divided across (Provenzo & Brett, 1983).

As the kindergarten movement spread to North America in the 1850s, programs were sponsored by charities in local communities and linked to the settlement movement. Over time, they became part of the school system. The educational ideas of Froebel became foundational to the programming (Brosterman, 1997). The use of blocks evolved to be an important part of children's play experiences. Educators examined ways to bring blocks into both indoor and outdoor environments as part of the core experiences and curriculum (Brosterman, 1997).

CURIOUS?

Add the words *kindergarten movement* to your search engine to find out more about the kindergarten movement in Canada. Examine when kindergartens were established in your area.

Late-Nineteenth-Century Block Systems

Richter Building Blocks

As society moved to understand and accept the importance of play, the use of blocks became a significant component of childhood. The Richter Building Block systems were created out of wood, cardboard, and related materials. Many of these initial block systems, such as the *nesting blocks* and *alphabet blocks*, remain prevalent today. The nesting blocks continue to support children in classifying colours and sizes and concepts such as large, larger, largest, small, smaller, and smallest. These types of blocks will be explained further later in the chapter in the section titled "Table Blocks."

The Twentieth Century

Maria Montessori

During the twentieth century, there was a societal development that focused on the development of programs that supported the academic and play attributes of young children. Maria Montessori (1870–1952), a medical doctor and Italian educator, recognized that block play was an important component of educational programs for young children.

Montessori believed that children needed to be exposed to a series of didactic materials. She suggested that these materials helped children develop their inner self. When children are comfortable with their inner self, they have increased skills and abilities to observe their world, make decisions about their world, and express their thought processes. Concentration skills are further enhanced.

Like Froebel, Montessori created a set of structured block materials that graduated from simple to more complex. The *pink tower*, consisting of 10 pink wooden cubes, was designed to be sequenced from 10 centimetres to 1 centimetre. As part of their learning, children were guided to examine each of the cubes and then place them from largest to smallest, or in descending order, to create a tower.

Another popular Montessori block apparatus is the *brown stairs*. These 10 oblong blocks provide children with the opportunity to examine the blocks and position them from thickest to thinnest, or by ascending or descending order. The objective is to construct them to resemble a set of stairs.

The *color rods* add to the block construction apparatus that is prevalent in an environment following Montessori principles. These are graduated oblong rods that are intended to be placed in ascending order by children.

Montessori apparatus is designed with specific learning outcomes. These outcomes support children in gaining the knowledge and skills that are fundamental constructs of math, science, and literacy.

Caroline Pratt

Caroline Pratt, an American educator during the late 1800s, is known for her philosophical orientation of *learning from the children*. She identified the importance of block play during the early years, suggesting that "a child playing on his nursery floor, constructing an entire railroad system out of blocks and odd boxes he had salvaged from the wastepaper basket, taught me that the play impulse in children is a work impulse" (Provenzo & Brett, 1983, p. 27). Children flourish in environments that provide them with materials that allow them to design their play experiences based on their imaginations.

Flexible, open-ended materials that have multiple uses position children to engage in play that does not require adult intervention. Children require blocks that include a variety of sizes, pillars, wheels, and rods because the different shapes and dimensions provide children with unlimited play opportunities. For example, a simple oblong block becomes the foundation for a house, a slide in the park, a race car, and so on.

In the early 1900s, Caroline Pratt made one of the most significant contributions to children's play when she created *unit blocks*. They consist of a set of hardwood, natural blocks that are in proportions of 1:2:4—half as high as they are wide and twice as long as they are wide. We will explore unit blocks further in the section titled "Floor Blocks."

CURIOUS?

Add the words *Caroline Pratt* and *block building* to your search engine to explore how Pratt contributed to the theory and application of block play.

Ole Christiansen

Ole Christiansen founded the LEGO toy company in 1934. In 1955, LEGO released the brightly coloured plastic studded and interlocking LEGO bricks. In 1969, LEGO launched Duplo construction blocks. These blocks, twice the size, length, and width of LEGO bricks, were intentionally developed for children under the age of 5. Today, LEGO continues to develop blocks and accessories.

Walter Drew

Walter Drew developed Dr. Drew's Blocks in 1978. These are small blocks of the same size and shape and are generally used for tabletop building projects.

Karl Oppen

Karl Oppen invented Tree Blocks in 1995. These blocks, also known as tree cookies, are created from reclaimed and recycled wood cut into slices. They are more often discussed as loose parts than as blocks.

> **STOP ... THINK ... DISCUSS ... REFLECT**
>
> How does the historical perspective on block building influence our perspective on making blocks available to children today? Is there a relationship to early learning today? Why or why not? How important is it for early learning teachers to consider how blocks were used historically when thinking about how to use them with children today?

The Stages of Block Play

There have been a number of studies conducted that suggest children progress through sequential stages in their block play. For example, Gesell (1940) examined how young children play with blocks in his work related to maturational timetables. His findings suggested that infants and toddlers to approximately 18 months of age use a block as a single unit rather than for constructing anything. As children move toward the 24-month-old range, they begin to place blocks in a row and make simple towers. Three-year-olds experiment with vertical and horizontal construction. Four-year-olds engage in more sophisticated construction, using a two-dimensional approach. As children gain more information on architectural,

Photo 8.1 Blocks provide children with opportunities to engage in architectural design while gaining mathematical skills.
Used with Permission of Diane Kashin

mathematical, and scientific principles, their constructions exhibit further intricacies. This is particularly evident in school-aged children's construction. This age group increases the level of detail in the structures and the types of secondary materials integrated into the structures.

The complexity of children's block play increases as children gain more experience with the blocks (Hansel, 2015). Block play supports children in incorporating both spatial relationships and symbolism into their representations (Nath & Szücs, 2014). More than 35 years ago, Reifel and Greenfield (1982) suggested that early learning teachers assess the symbolism and the spatial complexity of the structures created by children in the block area. They recommended that teachers use the following guidelines.

The symbolism consists of three levels:

0 = children use blocks simply as blocks

1 = children use blocks to represent a real-world object such as a car

2 = children use blocks to represent roles of people or things in imaginative play (e.g., a circus)

Through observation, early learning teachers examine spatial complexity by looking at the level of detail and the represented dimensions that children use to integrate blocks into their play (Tepylo et al., 2015). Adults determine how children use blocks to identify ways in which they can advance children's growth opportunities with blocks through adult guidance and with potentially new play options (Ramani et al., 2014).

Hirsch (1996) also outlined stages of block building that children engage in. As shown in Table 8.1, Hirsch indicated that children pass through seven stages in block building.

Table 8.1 Stages of block building.

Stage I: Carrying
Children carry blocks around, but they are not used for construction. Children typically gather blocks and dump them. This is the beginning of children exploring concepts such as more, less, thin, thick, large, and small. This helps the young toddler to refine fine and gross motor skills.
Stage II: Rows and Stacks
Children begin to place blocks in rows or vertical stacks. Repetition is visible. This is a time when toddlers repetitively make stacks and towers. Over time, they take more risks, and their stacks and towers become more imaginative.
Stage III: Bridging
Children's structures begin to have two blocks with a space between them, spanned or connected by a third block. During this phase, children use problem-solving skills to explore spatial relationships. They examine ways to support two blocks and join them together with a third block.
Stage IV: Enclosures
Children's structures now exhibit using blocks to enclose a space. Enclosures require children to look at space, connections, patterning, and internal and external positioning. Children repeat and refine the process as they experiment with joined enclosures and consider how the varying shapes and sizes of blocks affect their enclosures.
Stage V: Decorative Patterns
Children express competencies with block building and now take risks and express more imaginative attributes, including defined symmetry, in their construction. They discover how spatial relationships influence their building.
Stage VI: Naming Structures for Enactment
Children name the structure, based on what they have attempted to create, such as skyscraper, space station, zoo, and so on. These structures are complex, with bridges, enclosures, towers, and complicated designs.
Stage VII: Resembling or Naming for Play
Children reproduce and construct structures based on their daily life experiences. The names of the structures correspond to their intended functions. Children may express what they intend to build prior to acquiring the blocks to start construction.

Table 8.2 Typical skills developed and the types of blocks children use at each phase of block building.

Age	Skills	Recommended Blocks
Infant to 12 months	Transfers blocks from one hand to the other. Dumps blocks from containers. Puts blocks in mouth.	Small wooden blocks that may be washed Foam blocks covered in fabric that may be washed
Toddler (12 to 24 months)	Carries blocks to a variety of areas. Puts blocks in containers. Dumps blocks. Begins to stack blocks.	Small wooden washable blocks Washable blocks covered in fabric. Brick blocks made from cardboard Smaller tree blocks
Pre-preschooler and preschooler (24 to 48 months)	Makes rows, towers, bridges, and enclosures. Names simple structures. Begins to form patterns. Discusses what is being built.	Unit blocks Hollow blocks Planks Cedar blocks Cardboard blocks Accessories Tree blocks
Kindergarten (48 to 60 months)	Incorporates rows, towers, bridges, enclosures, and special forms and items such as ramps, doors, and gates into structures. Incorporates literacy skills by adding signs and maps to work. Buildings are sophisticated and built over several play episodes. Uses plans and ideas from other sources such as the Internet.	Unit blocks Hollow blocks Planks Plywood Cardboard blocks Cedar blocks Tree blocks Accessories
School age (older than 5 years)	Uses a variety of blocks with accessories. Incorporates several types of accessories into the structure. Draws out or discusses with peers a plan for the complex structures. Usually incorporates more than one structure into the overall construction. Each child may be assigned a specific role in the construction phase.	Unit blocks Hollow blocks Planks Plywood Tree blocks and stumps Accessories

Early learning teachers examine how children use blocks and discuss with them the types of interests they have in creating block structures. This provides insight and information that assists in ensuring that the appropriate blocks and accessories are provided to reflect the children's interests (Christenson & James, 2015).

The more children engage in block play, the more complex their play becomes. As outlined in Table 8.2, each phase of block play contributes to how children use the blocks in their play.

Photo 8.2 Children learn mathematical and scientific principles through block building.

Used with Permission of Angela Roy

TYPES OF BLOCKS

As you begin to examine early learning environments, you will note that there are a number of different types of blocks, although they are primarily divided into two categories: tabletop blocks and floor blocks. Tabletop blocks are generally used by one child or by two children who choose to work together. The floor blocks, much larger in size, generally attract two or more children to work together to create a particular structure. Tabletop blocks, although versatile, are generally used more as indoor blocks, whereas floor blocks are used in both indoor and outdoor spaces.

As you explore the different types of blocks available to children, you will become familiar with which blocks are best suited specifically to the block area, those that are more useful in the manipulative area, those that are specific for indoor use, and those that offer intrigue to children in both indoor and outdoor environments. Examining the different types of blocks and discussing with children and colleagues the potential types of play that may occur with the blocks helps you visualize the types of accessories that may be added. This also helps in generating ideas to support children using blocks in their play to their full potential.

Table Blocks

These are often small, coloured blocks that come in a variety of sizes. In addition to other developmental domains, they support children's fine motor development. Table blocks may include unique shapes that trigger children's curiosity (Christenson & James, 2015). Children use these blocks most frequently on a tabletop or small carpet. Table blocks are usually used on a flat surface. Children often spread their structures out rather than building their structure up high.

Picture and Alphabet Blocks

Picture and alphabet blocks date back to the seventeenth century. They continue to be some of the first blocks provided to children. These cube blocks have pictures or letters on each of their sides.

Parquetry Blocks

These blocks are straight-edged geometric shapes such as triangles, squares, rectangles, and diamonds. Children generally use these flat blocks for creating patterns.

Bristle Blocks

These blocks come in rectangles, oblongs, squares, and circle shapes. They have bristles on each of their sides and they interlock. Children create structures by sticking them together in various configurations. Because of the way they can be positioned and angled, these blocks provide children with more flexible possibilities for creating unique block structures than do traditional blocks.

Duplo® Blocks

Duplo blocks are used with toddlers because they are larger blocks. They are easy for a toddler to manipulate. These blocks contribute to children gaining skills at grasping, stacking, and experiencing the concept of pulling apart and putting back together.

Foam Blocks

These blocks are usually introduced to toddlers. They are easy for toddlers to carry and stack.

Floor Blocks

Floor blocks are large blocks that come in a variety of sizes. They are generally made from wood and are sturdy. Because of their size, children use these blocks to build replicas of buildings, enclosures, and structures that may be used for a number of purposes.

Unit Blocks

Unit blocks are made of carefully finished hardwood. Their lengths are based on a single unit, and other blocks are based on two, three, and four times that unit. The blocks are made with precision so that children may combine three half-units to match one three-unit block. Unit block sets include the unit blocks, pillars, angles, and ramps that may be large and flat. The versatility of unit blocks supports children in gaining foundational skills in mathematics and science and gives them the flexibility to create with patterns and designs.

Tree Blocks

These blocks are made from recycled wood. Their depth and thickness are dependent on how individuals choose to slice them. Tree blocks are used in block play either horizontally or vertically and may be used flat or on their side.

Hollow Blocks

These blocks offer children a different type of play experience from that of unit blocks, due in part to their increased size. These blocks bring versatility to children's play because large structures may be constructed. The size of the blocks requires children to use large motor manipulation when picking them up and using them in their construction. Often, two children will manoeuvre the blocks together to the construction area, or children will put them in wagons to transport them. Hollow blocks, similar to unit blocks, are built in mathematical proportion. There is a half square, a double square, and a half double square. Typical sets of hollow blocks include ramps as well as long and short boards.

Cardboard Bricks

These blocks are large, lightweight, and easy to stack. Children use them as they venture into building bridges and enclosures.

> **STOP ... THINK ... DISCUSS ... REFLECT**
>
> Some early learning environments may not have access to the commercial blocks that have been described above. What alternative materials could be provided to children to support them in creating structures?

Photo 8.3 A child concentrates on building a specific structure with her blocks.

Used with Permission of Angela Roy

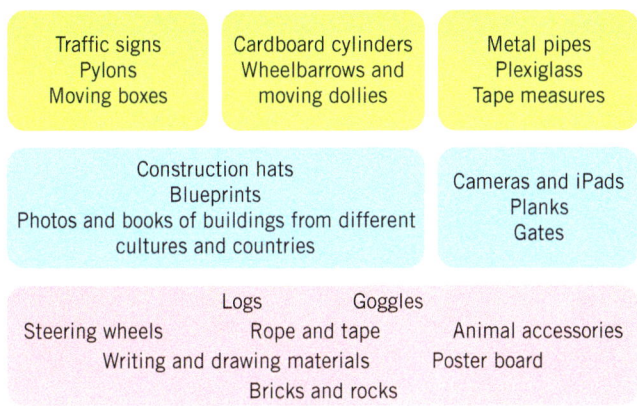

Figure 8.1 Accessories for block play.

LOOSE PARTS AND ACCESSORIES

As identified in Figure 8.1, block play is enriched when children have access to blocks and accessories. Early learning teachers and children choose accessories based on the expressed interests of children. The accessories encourage the children to move from simple to more complex play. The accessories trigger children to participate in more problem-solving skills, language, cooperation, and creativity as their play becomes more complex. They also contribute to more imaginative play among children, which in turn leads them to play out family roles, occupations, and community events.

STOP ... THINK ... DISCUSS ... REFLECT

Assume that you have a child who has expressed an interest in clocks and in using tape measures. How do you support the child in exploring these concepts in the block area? What types of props might you add to the area? What thought-provoking questions might you use with the child to gain new information on the child's knowledge level and depth of interest? How would you document your findings?

HOW BLOCKS SUPPORT GREAT LEARNING OPPORTUNITIES FOR CHILDREN

Many theorists, including Froebel, emphasized the importance of blocks in relation to children's play and development (Tepylo et al., 2015). Block building helps children to construct their context related to later life and academic skills such as mathematics and daily living (Petersen & Levine, 2014). For example, when children build roadways out of blocks and use vehicles to travel along them, they are playing out their life observations of how adults drive on the road. Building paths or forts or using blocks as cars provides children with strategies to gain an understanding of mathematical and scientific principles as well as their world.

Photo 8.4 Children use blocks and accessories in various ways.

Used with Permission of Angela Roy

spatial reasoning Includes the understanding of "structuring the space; noticing and describing shape, location, orientation, movement, and spatial relations" (Tepylo et al., 2015, p. 18).

There are many initiatives occurring in early learning programs that focus on twenty-first-century skills as they relate to science, technology, engineering, arts, and mathematics (STEAM) (Hunter-Doniger, 2016). Blocks provide children with opportunities to plan, experiment, measure, problem solve, and predict ideas and solutions. These skills support children in developing new ways of thinking and in looking at problems and solutions in nontraditional ways. Block play helps children to practise and consolidate skills and to develop flexible and abstract thinking capabilities and **spatial reasoning** (Lindeman & Anderson, 2015; Piaget, 1962; Vygotsky, 1976). Using imagination, taking risks to try new approaches to block building, and being challenged to use previous strategies or processes in new ways further enhances twenty-first-century skills.

CURIOUS?

Add the words *twenty-first-century skills in early childhood education* and *block play* to your search engine to learn more about how block play contributes to those identified skills.

zone of proximal development Refers to "the distance between the actual developmental level as determined by independent problem-solving and the level of potential development as determined through problem-solving under adult guidance or in collaboration with more capable peers" (Vygotsky, 1978, p. 86).

Exposing children to blocks supports Vygotsky's concept of children engaging in activities that support children's **zone of proximal development**. Think about 4-year-old Natioka, who has been using blocks at an early learning centre for two years. She has developed skills in planning, drawing plans, and building complicated structures. She can build enclosures, has the ability to build large structures with bridges and towers that exhibit symmetry, and has the language skills to tell stories about her structures. She also reproduces parts of her stories in pictorial and written formats. Recently, 4-year-old Inika

Photo 8.5 Co-construction of knowledge occurs during block play.

Used with Permission of Angela Roy

came to the centre. This is her first exposure to an early learning program. It appears as though she has had limited experience using blocks. Over several weeks, Inika watches Natioka and gradually asks her if she can play. Natioka welcomes Inika to play with her. Within two months, Inika develops skills and competence in using the blocks. She mimics the language descriptors used by Natioka and uses construction strategies similar to those modelled by Natioka. Inika, bringing some technology skills to play, now uses the camera and iPad to document the structures. As Wandnita, the early learning teacher, reviewed the block construction and the pictorial documentation that Inika presented, she was reminded of how, through the block play of the past two weeks, these children constructed knowledge about science, mathematical principles, language, technology, and social skills. They collectively solved problems and shared knowledge, which added to their block-building capabilities. Both children were stretched to incorporate new accessories and knowledge building into their play.

As outlined in Table 8.3, children who participate in quality block play experiences develop knowledge and skills that are foundational for understanding language, science, and math concepts and processes. Block play contributes to children building confidence in working individually and in groups, which is essential for later social and academic settings. When children use blocks in pretend play, they are enhancing the use of their imaginations more than when they participate in other experience centres such as the dramatic play area, because blocks are an open-ended, less structured material (Hansel, 2015). As outlined by Hansel (2015), through the use of blocks, children develop skills that are later beneficial to engineers, designers, architects, and artists. She cites Golbeck (2005), who indicated that when children play with blocks "they solve problems in spatial visualization, spatial orientation, planning and problem solving, and implicit measurement" (p. 80). As you will note in the next section, blocks contribute to children's development and learning in social, cognitive, emotional, and physical domains. For many early learning teachers, it is helpful to become familiar with how block play supports each of the domains and then transfer that knowledge to the development of the whole child. Early learning teachers

Table 8.3 Concepts gained through block play.

Cognitive/Language	Creativity
Emergent Concepts	**Emergent Concepts**
Use of symbols as a communication tool.	Use of imagination and pretend play.
Comparison and matching of the same and different concepts.	Understanding of symmetrical principles.
Vocabulary development through interpreting pictures and making up stories.	Relationship of creating pictures and designs to the production of structures.
Relationship of symbols and labels to words and reading.	Use of problem-solving skills to advance discovery and results.
Oral language development through exposure to new words.	Discovery of the results that occur when two or more mediums are used together.
Understanding of principles such as estimation; distance; patterning; comparing sizes, shapes, and numbers; seriation; and mapping (mathematics concepts).	Use of design, representation, balance, and stability concepts.
Understanding of concepts such as matching, comparing, balancing, the impact of weight and height, inclined plane, gravity, negative space, and balance (science concepts).	Expansion of divergent thinking.
	Use of mixed media.
	Strategies and results of combining blocks with loose parts.
Relationship of creating a plan prior to construction of the end product.	
Understanding the concepts of combining math, science, and technology principles with production.	
Offering children of dual language opportunities to express themselves and exhibit their learning in their languages and cultural experiences.	
Social/Emotional	**Physical**
Emergent Concepts	**Emergent Concepts**
Understanding how culture and community are represented in play.	Understanding spatial relationships.
Sharing space, resources, knowledge, and skills.	Experiencing visual perception/discrimination skills such as stacking, dropping, grasping, lifting, and swaying.
Practising negotiation and leadership skills.	
Forming friendships.	Understanding body awareness and how the left and right sides of the body move as one.
Examining roles and responsibilities, including gender roles and adult–child roles.	Developing eye–hand coordination and fine and gross motor control.
Expressing feelings and communicating them through words.	
Releasing stress/regression in meaningful ways.	
Developing an appreciation of aesthetic principles.	
Developing feelings of autonomy.	

combine the knowledge of developmental domains with their observations and vision of what children are interested in and capable of achieving.

In addition to the areas outlined in Table 8.3, as outlined in Figure 8.2, block play contributes to children's language, math, science and engineering, and creativity and arts learning. Each area will be discussed below.

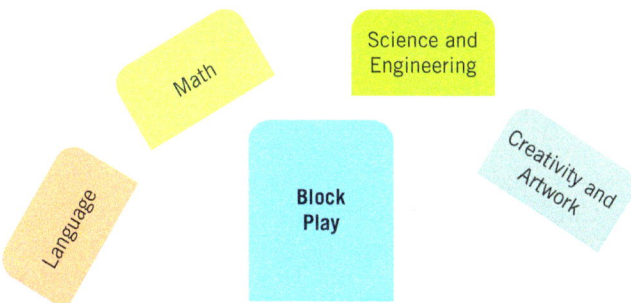

Figure 8.2 How block play contributes to children's learning.

Blocks and Cognitive Development

Block play can be the catalyst for children to expand their sense of math, science, and language skills. For example, as children use blocks, their skills of sorting and classifying are integral to the structure they create (Koralek, 2015). When children create a structure, they develop the ability to select and group blocks according to shape, size, weight, and use. As they become more experienced, their classification skills expand to include the relationship of size to balance, area, volume, and ordinal and cardinal numbers. They match blocks with the same attributes, and they estimate the number of blocks required for their construction. This leads children to acquire counting and numeration skills. The classification and comparison skills support children in creating patterns and graphs, as well as in acquiring spatial and measurement skills (Worth, 1990). This requires children to think, experiment, communicate, problem solve, and strategize.

Blocks and the Affective Domain

We think of the affective domain as the domain of the internal emotions and feelings. The process of block play contributes to children developing affective attributes of socially appropriate behaviours and attitudes, self-development, creativity, esteem, and motivation.

Block play and the affective domain can be aligned effectively. Block play nurtures a child's imagination and creativity. When children create from *their inner child*, the process and the product differ from when they create from a more structured experience. Blocks, with their open-ended characteristics, provide children with the flexibility to try new strategies and ideas. These applications lead children to discover the possibilities of the blocks as well as to explore feelings and roles. Children gain a sense of their feelings and working out those feelings, similar to when they participate in dramatic play. For example, think of a child who has just returned home from spending three days in a hospital setting. By recreating the hospital with its emergency entrance and having ambulances for props, the child can work out feelings of being afraid, lonely, and unwell. Or, think of Marquette, who has just returned from being on an airplane. Having airplanes as accessories and providing a variety of blocks may lead Marquette to create an airport experience.

Blocks and Physical Skills

Block play helps children develop physically. Blocks contribute to the child's gross and fine motor skills, as well as to eye–hand coordination. Fine motor and eye–hand coordination skills are precursors to being able to formulate the letters in handwriting. The physical skills developed through block play support later physical development milestones.

Think about a group of children building a structure using hollow blocks. What might children discover if they place the hollow blocks by height rather than by width? Children may learn that they can build their structures taller and more quickly than if they lay the hollow blocks flat. What happens when children add ramps to their structures? They learn about velocity. And what do children learn if they drop blocks from the top when standing on a staircase versus if they drop them when using them for construction? Children begin to experiment with the concepts of speed and distance (Rogers & Russo, 2003). When children take photos of objects and use them as a guide, they are transferring imagery to production. This requires the child to visualize and use problem-solving skills, creativity, and critical-thinking skills along with the attributes of the blocks.

Block Play and Language Development

Block play is rich with language development. Both language and reading skills are practised in block play. When children make signs for their structures, they discover the relationship of letters and words as symbols. As children create interesting structures, new language is acquired, including disciplinary vocabulary such as that related to architecture or engineering (Christenson & James, 2015). For example, both Jana and Janelle will be celebrating their fourth birthday in the upcoming weeks. As they participate in building a tall structure, Anita notices the girls using words such as *uneven*, *tipsy*, *collapse*, *balance*, *span*, *expansion*, and *shattered*. Anita is amazed at how their vocabulary has expanded and how their sentence structure has evolved to include five to eight words. As children engage in block play and are encouraged by adults to share information about their structures, more descriptive language is used (Hansel, 2015). Open-ended materials such as blocks support children in collaborative play and peer talk, which contributes to further expansion of the use and comprehension of language (Ramani et al., 2014).

Rogers and Russo (2003) indicated that the language used during block play helps children "describe the actions that they are performing (present), predicts ideas or expectations of what will occur (future), and recapitulates what has been done (past)" (p. 18). Generally, children communicate with others as their construction takes form. Often, the dialogue will focus on what, why, and how they build (Nell, Drew, & Bush, 2013). This communication process helps children use scientific and mathematical terms such as *height*, *weight*, *width*, *big*, *bigger*, *biggest*, *length*, *thick*, *pattern*, and so on. This contributes to children constructing the language related to math and science principles (Lee, Collins, & Winkelman, 2015). Figure 8.3 illustrates ways in which early learning teachers can facilitate language development through block play.

The early learning teacher extends children's language skills by facilitating or coaching children to document their play episodes. Using a digital camera to capture photos of children's structures and having the children tell their stories helps them to connect words, objects, construction, and pictures to storylines. As children's play with blocks becomes more sophisticated, their language expands to reflect the complexity of their structures. Early learning teachers encourage children who require additional opportunities to strengthen their vocabulary, expressive language, and social interactions with peers to engage in block play. The open-endedness of blocks supports children in creating structures and using the related language that is meaningful and comfortable for them. As they observe other children and develop confidence in their block play, they expand their skills in social and language development (Hansel, 2015).

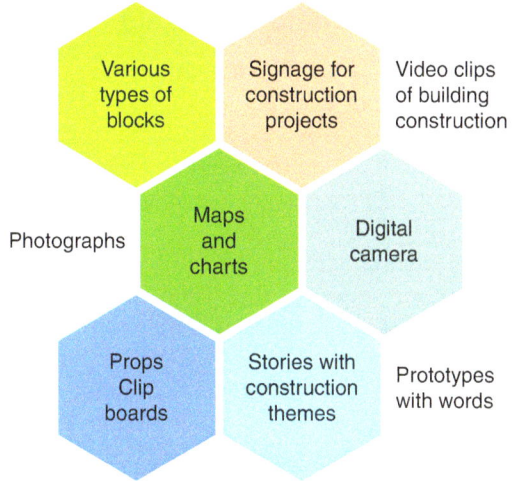

Figure 8.3 Resources that contribute to language and literacy with blocks.

Block Building and Math

Block building introduces children to the foundations of mathematics. When children are exposed to blocks, even during the phase of free exploration, they engage in mathematical actions, expressing mathematical terms, discovering mathematical concepts, and relating objects to their personal life experiences (Newcombe, Levine, & Mix, 2015). Children begin to understand the relationships of counting, comparing, measuring, width, height, and reasoning during their play (Oostermeijer, Boonen, & Jolles, 2014), as well as geometry and spatial relations. Block building improves children's spatial skills, which are necessary for complex mathematical problem solving in middle and high school years (Verdine et al., 2014).

Children's mathematical understanding is enhanced when they have hands-on experiences with blocks. The building process requires children to exhibit higher levels of thinking skills, and they make more complex mathematical conclusions than are achieved through paper-and-pencil tasks (Oostermeijer et al., 2014). As children use blocks, they classify them according to their needs. This contributes to children beginning the process of adding and subtracting and understanding the differences between two- and three-dimensional shapes (Hansel, 2015).

Early learning teachers encourage children to describe their block-building process using words such as *next to*, *parallel*, *behind*, and *horizontal to*. This supports children in learning about directions, positions, and characteristics of space from a horizontal and vertical perspective. Mathematical skills are strengthened with the introduction of architecture skills. When children become interested in the shapes and sizes that they see in buildings, they can transfer such information to their block play. As outlined by Hansel (2015), when children make

> connections with shapes in the environment, such as doors being rectangles and windows being arched, [it] encourages children's in-depth understanding of geometric shapes in mathematics. These experiences offer children a reference for building block structures. (p. 48)

Early learning teachers and student teachers think about ways in which they can design the environment so that children become intrigued with blocks and use them in a variety of ways in their play, while incorporating mathematical concepts in the process.

Block Building, Science, and Engineering

Early learning students and teachers introduce children to science and engineering principles in a number of ways. For example, block play offers children opportunities to learn about scientific principles such as motion, stability, gravity, structure, and the natural world. As part of the block-building process, children intuitively engage in design technology as they figure out solutions to their construction challenges and problems (Lindeman & Anderson, 2015).

Early learning teachers offer children support in seeking answers to their inquiries, such as what angles are necessary for ramps that will contribute to the speed with which cars move on those ramps. Think about children building structures with various shapes and types of blocks. How might discussions about form, shape, and function lead children to expand their knowledge and skills about design? Now think about how children solve block-building problems through a defined process. For example, Amy wants to build an enclosure that is three blocks high. As she uses blocks of different weight, her enclosures collapse. Through trial and error, she decides to switch the blocks on the bottom for larger ones. Eventually, she succeeds through experiential learning. As part of the process,

Photo 8.6 Block play offers the foundations for math and science.

Used with Permission of Angela Roy

her early learning teacher supported her through discussions and reflections. Lindeman (2013) suggested that children be encouraged to think about the following engineering-type questions:

- Why is something happening, and how can I create what I am trying to do?
- What types of materials will I need in relation to what my idea is?
- Which materials will work best and why?

Children benefit from having books with unique buildings and access to technology such as a digital camera to document their structures either during the construction or when the construction is considered complete. This offers children opportunities to reflect on the building process, study their structure, and determine whether they would like to rebuild or redesign it (Lindeman & Anderson, 2015).

STOP ... THINK ... DISCUSS ... REFLECT

Think about children engaged in block play. What do children produce with blocks? How do they begin the process? Why do you think they use particular materials? How do children build? How might they achieve building their intended structure? What is the role of the early learning teacher and why?

Block Play, Creativity, and the Arts

Block play enhances creativity, the arts, and design processes. As children construct with the blocks, they are creating or recreating something that they have seen or imagined. Creativity requires children to try a variety of thinking patterns that connect previous experiences to a new idea or a new way of manipulating blocks (Lee et al., 2015).

Early learning teachers and student teachers support children's creativity and the arts with blocks by visualizing with the children as many new and creative ideas as possible. When children have a variety of blocks and props, they are motivated to look beyond their usual use of the blocks. Newness requires children to look for new solutions. The more solutions and creative ideas the children generate, the more likely it is that new, interesting solutions will be developed. This advances the types of learning experiences that children will pursue. The more freedom and time that children have to explore their ideas, the more likely they are to take risks to try their thoughts and rethink their ideas to reach their ultimate goal (Ramani et al., 2014).

It is not unusual for children to have periods when they build and rebuild the structure again and again. This could occur in part because children are trying to perfect a process, or they could be "stuck" in terms of trying to generate new ideas. When early learning teachers observe that the block play is stagnating, they work with the children to spark new ideas. They may offer new materials, become play partners, or ask other children to assist them in building a particular structure. They may also share with the children documentation that exhibits the structure that the children have been reconstructing again and again to have them talk about it, tell stories about the structure, and then pose *what if* questions. The important part is that early learning teachers examine and reflect on how they may stimulate children to move beyond the plateau, into a phase of new block-building creativity and discovery. Early learning teachers may further stimulate children's block building by discussing construction opportunities in different play spaces and different play episodes (Murphy, 2014; Nell et al., 2013). Think about how children and early learning teachers may discover an interesting building in their neighbourhood. Children may proceed to paint that building and then recreate it in the block area. Similarly, children may engage in piling sand and making unique patterns in the sandbox. Early learning teachers may plant a seed with the children about how they could use the blocks to build a fence around the sand pile. These types of experiences support the arts, language, literacy, science, and math being integrated into children's play (Lindeman, 2013).

Block Play and Gender

There is controversy in the literature on whether block play is dominated by one gender over the other. According to Casey, Pezaris, and Bassi (2012), early learning teachers have identified that boys show a greater interest than girls in using blocks in their play. Despite this, they identified that there is no evidence to suggest that boys have greater competency in block building. Tokarz (2008) suggested that girls use blocks in ways similar to dramatic play, where they develop socialization and nurturing skills. Many of the creations may focus on houses or community spaces. Tokarz contrasts this with boys, who generally create new and elaborate structures that illustrate elements of innovation. These findings align with anecdotal perspectives expressed by some early learning teachers. There is a perception that the block centre attracts more boys than girls. However, the block area requires blocks and accessories that reflect the interest of both genders, so that all children will have equal interest in the area.

Blocks and Inclusive Practice

Children who do not have typical developmental patterns may play less often than others (Barton, 2015). Early learning teachers examine the strengths and skills of children to ensure that various blocks are available that are "appropriate for children at different ages and developmental levels" (Guyton, 2011, p. 52). Children will use blocks in different ways, depending on their skills and interests and the resources available (Luckenbill & Schallock, 2015). As identified earlier in this chapter, block play generates opportunities for all children to engage in social interaction, creativity, problem solving, and language development. Quality block experiences for all children require attention to children's strengths, space, time, and materials.

A number of strategies may be implemented in the environment to support children with differing strengths, without singling them out. For example, if building space is an issue, by placing large pieces of painted plywood in areas, the space that may be used for building is defined. Arranging blocks that are within easy reach and are displayed with cues to support children returning them to the shelves is important in managing the block environment. Early learning teachers facilitate block play in ways that connect the children to the materials, their peers, and play options.

THE ROLE OF EARLY LEARNING TEACHERS IN BLOCK PLAY

Block play is an important aspect of the early learning environment. Early learning teachers and student teachers have many roles and responsibilities in preparing the environment for block play and facilitating the play experiences. Similar to other areas of early learning experiences, children require play environments that allow them to have the freedom to

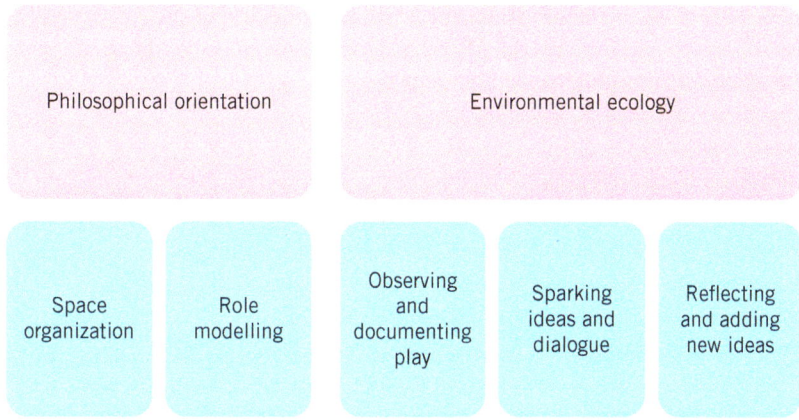

Figure 8.4 Roles and responsibilities of early learning teachers in block play.

explore, based on their interests, skills, and ideas. Early learning teachers who advance their knowledge and professional attention to the benefits of block play are better able to offer children a learning environment that will support their play. Let's look at some of the key roles that early learning teachers engage in when facilitating play opportunities with blocks and accessories. Figure 8.4 provides a snapshot of the roles and responsibilities that early learning teachers may participate in with children and block play.

Determining One's Philosophical Perspective

One of the most important practices that early learning student teachers embark on is trying to figure out how their interactions with and decisions about children with whom they are working influence chidren's play, their desire to try new things, and their motivational levels to engage in new learning opportunities. A core question that is beneficial when thinking about children and block play is, "How can I foster children's play, thinking, exploration, and visualization through block play?"

The influence that early learning teachers have on children's learning can be significant. For example, Piaget (1971/1974) identified that children develop relationships, such as logico-mathematical ones, when they *think*, to understand problems such as design features or space and design options (Tepylo et al., 2015). Thinking means supporting the children in being able "to make mental relationships about objects, people, and events" (Kamii, Miyakawa, & Kato, 2004, p. 56). Blocks support this complex area of thinking.

Student teachers benefit from investing time in getting to know the children's dispositions, their strengths, and the ways to support them in play. This helps them focus on the children's needs and identify strategies that may encourage them to advance the complexities of their block play. For example, think of Mallia, who is building a tower. She has tried to get the blocks to stay piled one on top of the other. Each time Mallia attempts to add a new block, she needs to think about where to place it: Does it go in the middle or to one side? Does it go to the front or to the back? As part of this process, Mallia participated in a physical-knowledge activity as she tried to figure out how to produce the desired result. If you were supporting Mallia, what would your role be in this? You may tell Mallia that if she places the block in a certain position her tower will remain standing or, conversely, fall, or you may ask her, "What is it you need to do to make the tower stand in the way in which you would like it to?" If your philosophical orientation is to support children in the development of thinking, which of the two strategies would you wish to transfer to your practice? Why is it important to think about the relationship of your philosophical orientation to block play?

> ### STOP ... THINK ... DISCUSS ... REFLECT
>
> There are five children working together to build a large structure. How high will you allow the children to build it? Are there dangers that need to be considered? Is there a way that children can build the structure as high as they want? What happens if adults curtail their desire to build high?

The responses from early learning teachers influence the richness of the play episode, as illustrated with Alukik and Equik. Alukik and Equik spent a considerable time in the block area. Using hollow blocks for the foundation and unit blocks for the remaining structure, they created a large structure that has a tower at each corner. When Alukik had difficulty getting her final blocks on the top, she announced to Equik that she was going to use a hollow block to stand on so she could reach the top. Equik quickly indicated that he was tall and he did not need a block. As Alukik moved the hollow block into position, Equik tried to put his rectangle block on top. He announced that he did it by himself.

As Alukik continued to stand on the hollow block so that other blocks could be added, Equik soon said, "My tower is bigger than yours." Then Alukik added more blocks and said, "Mine is bigger now." As the two children continued to add blocks, Equik's additions became more difficult. As he stretched to add another block, his tower swayed. And as he added another block, it swayed again. Equik took a few minutes to observe Alukik's success, then announced that he, too, was going to use a hollow block to stand on.

The early learning teacher, Anita, approached the children. The children announced, "We're making our towers the largest they can be without falling." Anita replied, "This is interesting, but you must not stand on the hollow blocks." Although safety rules are essential in early childhood environments, Anita missed a **teachable moment**. There are a number of other approaches she could have used to redirect the play and engage the children in discussions about their structures. For example, she could have suggested that the children come off the hollow blocks and look at the different shapes of the blocks they used. She could have redirected them to obtain a large plank each, so that they could measure the structures with their feet flat on the floor. Or, she could have asked them to stand by their towers so that she could measure them against the tower and take photos of it. Any one of these strategies would have had the potential to enhance the play and, at the same time, guide them to use safe building practices.

teachable moment Refers to an unplanned opportunity that evolves when an adult or child can share about an experience, idea, or concept that expands learning.

The Early Learning Environment

Environmental factors influence children's interest in and use of blocks in their play. Providing children with the right environment and adequate time to work on projects that extend beyond one play episode is essential (Lindeman & Anderson, 2015). Children's depth of play is expanded when structures remain standing for long periods of time and

Photo 8.7 Children need opportunities to use blocks in a variety of ways in their play and experimentation.
Used with Permission of Family Space Quinte, Inc.

when they have opportunities to showcase them to adults and peers. When children have options to return to the structures or receive feedback on them, they experience cycles of planning, reflecting, making changes, researching, and developing new ideas to incorporate into the structure (Durham, 2015). This allows children to review documentation and visualize what could be and how they may change the structure to reflect new ideas.

Block play generally attracts three to four children to engage in the play. This can create vigorous, social, and loud play. At times, there may be children who benefit from having time to explore and build with blocks on their own. This requires early learning practitioners to be aware of children who benefit from this solitary play and determine how this may occur without other children interfering with the solo play. The environmental design must be flexible enough to accommodate both solitary and group play. Children may require spots away from the block area, such as under a table, inside a large box, or in a quiet area in the playground, to rethink their ideas or the process for their play.

Photo 8.8 Children may require quiet places for block play.

Used with Permission of Bora Kim

> ### STOP ... THINK ... DISCUSS ... REFLECT
>
> Do you think that block play is found in every culture? If so, is it always with wooden blocks? Why might some cultures, such as Japan, provide children with large blocks that require two or more children to move them?

Organizing the Space

The physical space allocated for block play influences the depth and breadth of children's play. When children move materials between experience centres and mix the use of materials, they test and produce more innovative play ideas. Block play requires space and materials if our goal is to have children participate in play that promotes divergent thinking.

Placing the blocks in space that is not being fully used is ideal for expanding block play (Durham, 2015). Also placing the blocks near other centres that can cross-pollinate ideas has many advantages, including increasing the interchange among centres (Epstein, 2014). When blocks are placed in a creative discovery zone, symbolic thinking skills are used. This is an ideal strategy that promotes children combining creative ideas and the problem-solving skills of visual arts with scientific and mathematical concepts. For example, young children who have an opportunity to use the block and dramatic area may engage in block building that builds roads to apartment buildings or castles. Some of the blocks may be used to create furniture. Children may incorporate props such as dolls and vehicles into their structural designs.

Children benefit from having blocks and related resources presented in ways that are orderly and accessible. Initially, children may require reminders on their roles and responsibilities in the block centre (Murphy, 2014).

There are a number of factors that early learning teachers consider when preparing the block play area. Table 8.4 provides guidelines that support early learning student teachers in organizing block play space.

Table 8.4 Environmental considerations for block play.

Location for Block Play	Displaying Blocks
■ The blocks are positioned in areas that get limited traffic and are three-sided. ■ Placing blocks in space with corners both indoors and outdoors supports children in playing longer. ■ The space provides opportunities to build structures up and patterns out (such as roadways and train rails). ■ The space allows for children to make reasonable noise. ■ The space allows children to keep their block structures up for long periods of time.	■ The blocks are displayed on low, open shelves. ■ Shelves may have block shape templates affixed to them as a way to assist children in locating and replacing the blocks. ■ Larger blocks are placed on the bottom shelves to help stabilize the shelving unit. ■ The storage shelves support children in exhibiting independence during the building and disassembling phase. ■ Matching and sorting are encouraged.
Block Accessories	**Quantity of Blocks**
■ A combination of open, see-through containers and shelving is used for accessories as a way to support children thinking about opportunities. ■ Popular props and accessories are displayed.	■ At least 100 blocks for children under 3 years of age. ■ At least 200 blocks for children 3 years of age. ■ At least 300 blocks for children 4 years of age. ■ At least 500 blocks for children over 4 years of age.

Observing and Documenting Children's Block Play

Observing children during block play helps early learning teachers and student teachers to view when and how children use blocks in their play. For example, observing a group of children building a playhouse may provide insight into their level of problem solving, how they predict the types and quantity of blocks required, how they plan for constructing the structure, and the roles and responsibilities that each child takes on. Observations familiarize us with the environmental conditions that support children in being able to effectively participate in quality play. Table 8.5 provides examples of children's behaviours that may alert early learning teachers that children require adult support.

Early learning students and teachers gain insight into children's interests and strengths through observation and documentation. For example, some children engage in block play as a social experience outdoors, whereas others prefer to use blocks as a solitary play episode indoors. Some children gravitate to the unit blocks, whereas others prefer the tabletop blocks. Early learning teachers gather information about how the children use the blocks from a building perspective as well as a tactile and sensory experience.

Observations provide early learning teachers with information about children's knowledge and skills about block play. By listening to the children and observing their play, adults are able to determine the most appropriate time to facilitate or support a play episode. For example, if children express an interest in trains, you may provide train props and pose cognitively challenging, open-ended questions that will help them build a particular item, such as a train station or train tracks. As you observe and support the children through play, you note the types of blocks that the children use. Are they the unit blocks, the tabletop blocks, soft blocks, or cardboard blocks? Are there props involved? If so, how are they used? Who do children play with in the block area? Are they

Table 8.5 Examples of children's behaviour observed in block play.

Observation	Role of Facilitator
The noise level in the block area starts to escalate.	The facilitator becomes part of the play with one or two children. A soft voice is used with the children. This encourages the children to use their softer voices and to listen to one another more attentively.
A child begins to interfere with the structure of others, or the play becomes destructive and unsafe.	The facilitator becomes part of the play by encouraging the child who is interfering with others to refocus on adding to the structure or developing a structure with the facilitator. Guidance to other areas of the play area may be required.
A child becomes tense or begins to cry.	The facilitator examines areas that may be contributing to the child's stress. Open-ended questions are used as a strategy to refocus the child. Comfort strategies and dialogue are used with the child. The facilitator may suggest that the child expand the play by using the video camera or graphs for documenting the structure.
A child begins to lose focus on the structure.	The facilitator has dialogue with the child about the structure. Open-ended questions are used as a strategy to expand the play. If the child appears to have lost interest, the facilitator works with the child to move to another area of interest.
Children begin to argue.	The facilitator listens to the dialogue to determine if it is animated discussion or children arguing. The facilitator may offer open-ended questions that will bridge the opinions expressed by the children. The facilitator helps children use critical-thinking skills while building on their socialization strengths.
Children say, "We need help."	The facilitator asks the children to put into words how they *identify* the problem. Discuss the problem. Using open-ended questions, help the children *brainstorm* possible solutions. Advance children's thinking by having them examine the advantages and disadvantages of possible solutions before selecting the one that they use. Support the children in *implementing* the solution. Help the children verbalize their evaluation of the solution. Did it work? Why? If it did not work, why not? (Miller, 1993).

generally the same children? Do you need to pose open-ended questions to advance the play? Are there special materials that may lead children to new discoveries? Or, are there ways in which you and other children may become involved to reduce frustrations in the play? These questions are important, as they guide our practice in acquiring information about children, which leads to offering materials and experiences that support them in their play. Early learning teachers determine the opportune moments to expand play experiences and trigger new investigations and learning.

As identified in Chapter 3, observations and documentation are important practices of early learning teachers. These provide information that gives us a more holistic view of what children know about block building and how problem-solving and creative-thinking processes are used during block play. The type of observation methods and tools used are chosen based on the early learning teacher's style and the purpose of the observation. The examples below are data collection samples of methods used by early learning practitioners. The process of collecting data and using the information effectively is a developmental process that is influenced by a personal philosophy as well as the early learning centre or classroom philosophy.

Anecdotal records provide a brief description or "word picture" of the event (Cartwright & Cartwright, 1974). These records are generated from direct observation. They describe the

Table 8.6 Sample checklist or rubric for stages of block play.

Child's Name: Sara, 3.5 years of age						
Carrying Blocks	Rows and Stacks	Bridging	Enclosures	Decorative Patterns	Naming Structures	Resembling or Naming for Play
		09/16 Took six blocks to make bridge over roadway. Had people figures walk over the bridge.	09/17 Used 24 blocks to make a corral for horses outside of the barn.			

behaviour observed. For example, Marick entered the block area at approximately 9:15 a.m. He went to the block shelf and obtained a container of table blocks. He took all of the red rectangle blocks and laid them on their edge. Then he placed them to make a rectangle enclosure. Andrew approached Marick to ask if he could play with him; Marick said no and returned to building an enclosure inside the existing enclosure. All of the blocks used for the inside enclosure were blue. Marick started another enclosure outside the original enclosure. He was focused on his structure. Other children approached him wanting to play, but he kept building.

Checklists or rubrics provide an overview of a child's skill level compared with that of typical developmental profiles of children of a similar age. Table 8.6 provides an example of how a checklist supports understanding a child's level of development, by recording the specific example observed.

This observation identifies that Sara has an interest in walking across bridges and in horses, barns, and corrals. If an early learning teacher added *Lincoln-type blocks* (long, loglike connecting blocks) to Sara's choices, this may lead Sara to build a corral that combines open space with enclosures. Books about barns and bridges may also spark some additional block-building experiments.

Conversational notes are a strategy frequently employed in Reggio-inspired settings (Cadwell, 1997). These notes are acquired from discussions that early learning teachers have with a child or groups of children about their block structures, including the processes used to create these structures. The notes may be recorded and placed with digital documentation. An example of a conversational note is given below:

> I was observing Mila, Ben, Sara, and Maggie in the block area. Ben and Sara went to the dramatic centre and brought back binoculars, plants, and boots to the block area. As the four children were participating in conversation, I approached them and asked, "What's happening in this area of construction?" They said they were building a path to the forest. So, I started asking questions that related to the path and the props that the children had brought to the area. I wonder why you wish to have binoculars in the forest. Mila described how binoculars help you see things that are far away. Then I asked, "What kinds of things do you think you will see in the forest?" Ben and Sara said they would see little animals like rabbits and groundhogs and little white flowers, while Mila and Maggie said that this time of year they would be looking for big bears and deer and all the trees that are green.

This conversation provides insight into the children's knowledge about the forest. It helps early learning teachers and students determine the interests that children have and how additional props may expand the depth of the play experiences.

Digital documentation provides photos or videos taken at each phase of the project or investigation. The documentation is dated and used with children to facilitate discussions, help them identify their knowledge and skills of block building, and tell stories about what they see. Early learning teachers and students may also use the documentation to acquire further information about the child.

Role Modelling

Early learning teachers are role models to the children in the block area. It is through encouragement and experimentation that children gain the sense that it is acceptable to try new ideas. For example, the early learning teacher monitors negotiations, poses thought-provoking, open-ended questions that will support children in problem solving, and makes comments such as "How does this . . ." or "Explain to me . . ." or "Tell me about. . . ." These types of comments enhance problem-solving skills while supporting thinking in divergent ways. This facilitation strategy also supports children in the process of building rather than focusing on the defined product.

Early learning teachers play an important role in working with children who may not use the block area as much as other children, by inviting them to become partners in building a structure. This can begin by stacking a couple of blocks and then inviting other children to come to the area. The purpose is for children who do not use the block area to gain success. This requires you to be an encourager, guide, and partner in play. You listen to the children and, most importantly, support their ideas. If the children's ideas do not work, the mistake is turned into a learning opportunity. Through open-ended questions and discussion, the early learning teacher and student teacher help children analyze why an idea may not have worked and what they could do differently next time. As children become engaged in the structure, you gradually move away from the area.

Early learning teachers and student teachers guide children who exhibit signs of unsafe building practice, become destructive with the blocks or other children, or use the blocks inappropriately. One of the most effective strategies to change behaviour is for the early learning teacher to become involved in the play directly with the child. This may take on two formats. The first is to have dialogue about how you can help

Photo 8.9 Early learning teachers support children in their play by deciding how the environment is presented.

Used with Permission of Family Space Quinte, Inc.

with the construction and the types of blocks that are being used, and ask questions such as "What would happen if . . . ?" as a way to refocus the child. The second strategy is to share with children, through words or body language, your interest in block play.

Starting Dialogue with Children about Block Play

Many factors contribute to children's success and experience with blocks. Dialogue among the children and with early learning teacher is one of the most influential activities that contributes to children taking risks in the block area (Epstein, 2014; Nell et al., 2013). In quality programs, the involvement with the children, the verbal exchanges, and the interactions among children and adults are evident. It takes practice to facilitate discussion with children while using the blocks. Box 8.1 provides some phrases that may be used to start a conversational exchange between children and early learning teachers.

STOP ... THINK ... DISCUSS ... REFLECT

Marti and Hunter are using blocks. Marti sees that Hunter is building a structure that she thinks she could go in and out of. She wants to make one, too. Marti starts by getting long boards and some of the cedar blocks. Her blocks tumble. Two early learning teachers take different approaches to responding to Marti.

Donna responds: You need to take your cedar blocks and place them on their side into the shape of a square. Then you need to place cedar blocks at each corner to put your planks on.

David responds: I am not sure how to build your structure. Tell me what you are thinking as your strategy. How do you think your strategy will work?

Box 8.1 Phrases for starting conversations during block play.

Tell me (about)
- The block shapes that you are using . . .
- The blocks on top of or beside . . .
- How you got the blocks underneath the . . .
- How you made the space for the trucks to go under the bridge . . .
- Why you used the squares and triangles in this part of your construction . . .
- What will happen if you take your hand away . . . Will the structure stay standing or fall?
- Your structure . . .
- How people get inside your structure . . .
- What happens if two cars try to pass on the roadway . . .
- How many steps the prince needs to climb to get into the building . . .
- How you balanced the planks . . .
- How I can help you use the plank to . . .
- The problem with . . .
- What happens when . . .

Block play requires experimentation and discovery learning that occurs through trial and error. Which of the responses do you prefer? Which leads children to further problem solving, exploration, and discovery? Why?

Reflection and Development

Block play is essential for young children because it contributes to a variety of domains. Early learning teachers continuously seek out new knowledge and strategies that will help them facilitate meaningful block play with children. When teachers observe that the children are building similar structures and not taking risks to create more elaborate structures, there is a need to examine the environment, the materials, and the interaction among children and adults. Often, by reviewing documentation of the children's play, early learning teachers gain insight into what strategies may support children in trying new adventures.

When early learning teachers find themselves offering children the same types of props and blocks, or when children's creativity in the block area wanes, it is essential to participate in further reflection and seek out ways to bring new opportunities into the environment. Early learning teachers' stagnation reduces the potential for children to embrace block play. Collaboration among early learning teachers and student teachers helps to facilitate new directions for the play experiences.

TERMS THAT INFLUENCE EARLY LEARNING PLAY ENVIRONMENTS

We conclude this chapter with three additional terms that support the theory of children's play. These terms are used when examining children's potential learning experiences.

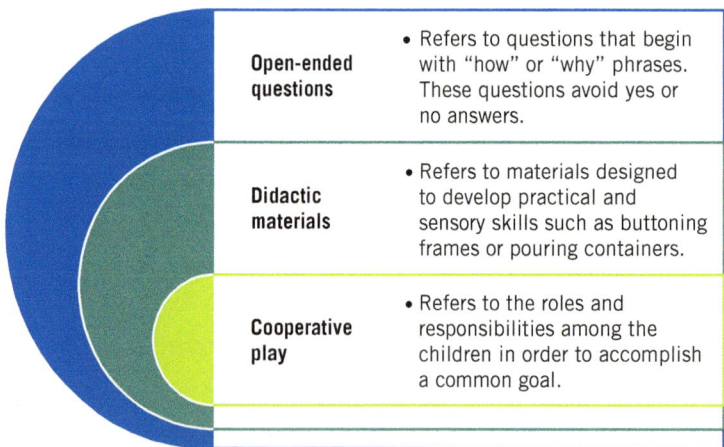

SUMMARY

Chapter Preview

- Block play provides children with a variety of skills and abilities that are transferable to other learning domains. These concrete materials support children in acquiring knowledge about math, literacy, and science principles more effectively than paper-and-pencil worksheets.

Defining Block Play

- There are many perspectives on block play. Some suggest it refers to children manipulating blocks by handling them, stacking them, and using actions and language to represent realistic or imaginative play. A newer perspective is that it needs to be redefined as "visual-spatial construction play objects."

The Historical Perspectives of Blocks

- Children and blocks are not a new phenomenon. They evolved at the same time as a child-centred culture during the late 1700s.
- Philosophers and educators, including Froebel, Montessori, and Pratt, have contributed to understanding the importance of play in early learning environments.

The Stages of Block Play

- Reifel and Greenfield provide a three-level evaluation process to assess the symbolism and spatial complexity used by children in the block area, while Hirsch outlines seven stages of block building. They are carrying, rows and stacks, bridging, enclosures, decorative patterns, naming structures for enactment, and resembling or naming for play.

Types of Blocks

- Blocks fall into two categories: table blocks and floor blocks.
- Early learning teachers provide children with a variety of blocks, spaces, and accessories.

How Blocks Support Great Learning Opportunities for Children

- Block play contributes to children developing twenty-first-century skills, including mathematics, science, and language development, as well as their physical and affective domain.
- Empirical research indicates that there is inconclusive information to suggest that block play is dominated by one gender.
- Children with varying strengths benefit from resources and space being organized so that they may use the blocks with ease, without being singled out from other children.

The Role of Early Learning Teacher in Block Play

- Early learning teachers' roles include determining one's philosophical perspective, examining the learning environment and ecology, organizing space, observing children's play, role modelling, engaging in dialogue with the children, and participating in training and development.

REVIEW QUESTIONS

1. Why is block play an important programming area for early learning teachers to know about? How does block play inform your work with children?
2. What is the significance of examining the historical perspectives of block play? How does it influence your approach to block play with children today?

3. Reifel and Greenfield, as well as Hirsch, indicate that there are stages to block play. What are those stages, and how do you use that knowledge in your work with children?
4. Describe the types of blocks that would be considered table blocks and those that would be considered floor blocks. How does each category influence children's block play?
5. Block play contributes to the development of children in a variety of ways. Describe how block play supports child development, the arts, creativity, and problem-solving skills.
6. How can early learning teachers ensure that children with disabilities have access to block play without being singled out by other children?
7. Describe the key roles that early learning teachers have in facilitating block play.

MAKING CONNECTIONS

Theory to Practice

1. You have been asked to reorganize the block centre that will be used with a group of 3- and 4-year-olds. Based on the information you have gained from this chapter, what key attributes would you include in the centre?
2. How would you ensure that children have an opportunity to use blocks in the outdoor environment? What would need to be considered in having a block centre outdoors?
3. What would you need to consider if you were setting up a block centre in an after-school program for 5- to 7-year-old children? How might it differ from one for 3- and 4-year-old children?
4. Documentation is an important part of block play. How do you envision gathering documentation from the block play? What will you do with the documentation? How does it inform your practice?

DIGITAL PORTFOLIO ENTRIES

Potential portfolio entries for your digital portfolio could include the following:

- When I think about block play, I wonder about . . .
- I see my role now as . . .
- When I examine blocks and accessories I want to . . .
- I think I want to promote block play by . . .

CURIOUS?

Add *children and block play* to your search engine to obtain further information on the importance of block play during the early years.

CHAPTER 9
Dramatic Play

Rawpixel.com/Shutterstock

> " Almost all creativity involves purposeful play. "
>
> —Abraham Maslow (1908–1970)

LEARNING OUTCOMES

After exploring this chapter you should be able to:

- Discuss the importance of dramatic play to children's development and relate it to the theories and perspectives of Vygotsky, Erikson, Piaget, Gardner, and Similansky.

- Define dramatic play and explain its scope.

- Describe the role of early learning teachers in supporting and scaffolding children's dramatic play experiences.

- Explain the types of dramatic play, including gun and superhero play.

Sharing Stories of Practice

As a college student, I thought that dramatic play only took place in the "house" centre. I learned that you could change the "house" centre into something else, such as a doctor's office. I stopped children from taking play dough into the housekeeping area and putting it in pots and pans to make pretend food. I told them that play dough belonged at the play dough table. Then one day I arrived late to work and saw that the children were collectively and collaboratively moving the furniture from the dramatic play area to across the room. I was so shocked that I was speechless and did not jump to stop the children. Instead, I listened to their conversation. They were talking about "moving day," and as they brought the furniture to the carpeted area they discussed and negotiated where each piece would be placed. That was a turning point in my practice. The children and I decided to leave the furniture where it was and set the new space as a store. Now children could buy their groceries, go home, and put them away. The whole room changed that day, and I, too, changed as I discovered that dramatic play is everywhere!

Jema, ECE graduate, 2016

CHAPTER PREVIEW

Dramatic play is one of the most important forms of play (Smilansky & Shefatya, 1990). It is a common activity of young children that should be in all early learning programs. Children will engage in dramatic play spontaneously, and it supports them in combining their ideas and thoughts to bring meaning to their world.

Think back to your own early childhood experiences. Did you like to play house? Did you enjoy playing "cops and robbers"? You may have liked to play "school" or "race cars."

Photo 9.1 Driving a horse trailer.

Used with Permission of Gill Robertson

Can you recall a time when you lined up your dolls or stuffed animals and then taught them a lesson? This may reflect your earliest image of a teacher! Can you recall driving your small cars and trucks on pretend roads? This may have been your introduction to developing an interest in vehicles. You may not have known it at the time, but you were learning while you were playing. In this chapter we introduce you to theories, stages, and types of dramatic play. You will gain insight into how early learning teachers encourage dramatic play. You will learn why dramatic play is important play and a learning experience that children require in their early years.

Theoretical frameworks provide students and early learning teachers with a foundation from which to explore one's thoughts and beliefs. The theories of dramatic play are very important for you to consider as you read this chapter. Think about what you are reading and relate it to your own experiences as a child and now as a student teacher. Think about what you believe about children and play and about if and how dramatic play aligns with your values and beliefs.

THEORETICAL FOUNDATION

Dramatic play and social play are interconnected. As outlined in Figure 9.1, we introduce four long-standing theories that have made significant contributions to the understanding of the relationship between dramatic play and social development and one emerging theory.

Erik Erikson (1963) stressed the relationship between dramatic play and children's ability to learn about the social world. Play facilitates children's understanding of cultural and social norms and provides an avenue for learning social skills. Erikson maintained that there is a relationship between dramatic play and wider society. Through play, children integrate acceptable social and cultural norms into their own personalities. Erikson and Piaget believed that children who have exposure to rich play experiences become socially competent (Frost, Wortham, & Reifel, 2012).

For Piaget, play provides children with opportunities to develop social competence through interactions. Children learn to be social as they play out different ideas and perspectives. When engaged in dramatic play, children start to make sense of their world. In Piagetian theory, children assimilate concepts and ideas, practise, and expand on their ideas during play with others. Play interactions contribute to children developing perspective-taking, especially when they take on the role of others while role-playing (Robertson, 2016). They begin to understand that other players have perspectives different from their own. Piagetian perspectives focus on stages of cognitive development. During the preschool years, dramatic play is characterized as imitation of reality. In dramatic play, "children develop play themes and carry them out by playing different roles"

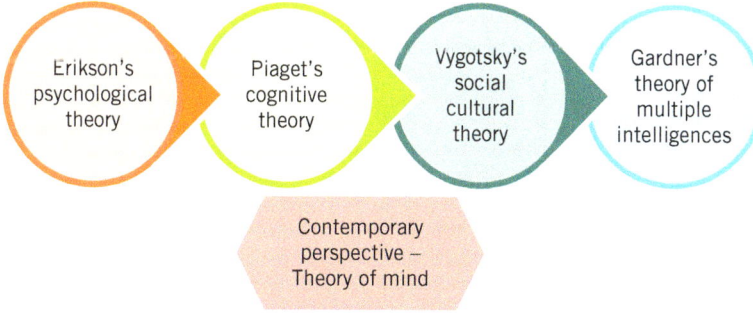

Figure 9.1 Theoretical foundations that influence dramatic play.

(Frost et al., 2012, p. 138). According to Piaget's stage theory of cognitive development, dramatic play is an important feature during ages 4 through 7. Between the ages of 7 and 12, symbolic play declines and is replaced by games with rules.

Vygotsky's sociocultural theory views play as a significant venue in helping children to separate fantasy from reality, to control impulses, and to follow social rules. Dramatic play is vital for the acquisition of social and cognitive skills. Vygotsky (1976) focused on functions of play rather than on stages of play. He suggested that representational play and make-believe play emerges at the end of toddlerhood, develops in the early years, and evolves into games with rules (Frost et al., 2012). Children learn to choose between courses of action when engaged in pretend play. They learn to control their impulses as they subject themselves to the rules of play (Bodrova, Germeroth, & Leong, 2013).

Experiences with dramatic play tap into three kinds of intelligences, as espoused by Gardner (1993) in his theory of multiple intelligences. Gardner's multiple intelligence theory suggests that children, like adults, depend on different areas of their brain in different situations, at different times, and for different reasons. "Each type of intelligence involves cognitive skills and variations occur in children in each type of intelligence" (Frost et al., 2012, p. 186). For example, when children act out stories, situations, and ideas, they use their bodily-kinesthetic intelligence to express themselves. They do this through gesture, voice, and movement. They use interpersonal intelligence to work cooperatively to determine how to dramatize a story or to interact with an audience; they use intrapersonal intelligence to assess their own feelings and mood. They can do this through role play and pantomime. Table 9.1 lists the three types of intelligences and relates the theory to practice with examples.

Table 9.1 Multiple intelligences and dramatic play.

Intelligence	Examples in Practice	Theory to Practice
Bodily-Kinesthetic		
The ability to use the body to express thoughts and feelings and to problem solve. The ability to use hands to handle objects skillfully.	Role play Acting out stories Pantomime Dramatic play Dance and movement	A concrete, hands-on, specific, and personal way for children to develop abstract and representational skills.
Interpersonal		
The ability to distinguish the intentions, moods, and feelings of others by being sensitive to voice, gesture, and facial expressions. The ability to respond sensitively to others' feelings and moods.	Improvisation Pantomime Role play Pretend Puppets	An opportunity to explore feelings, moods, and points of view of others and to respond to them.
Intrapersonal		
The ability to detect one's own moods, needs, and desires and to look both inward and outward.	Dramatic play Pantomime Improvisation Readers theatre Puppets	A socially acceptable way for children to reflect on and explore their own feelings and to test out their feelings and emotions as well as their responses to others.

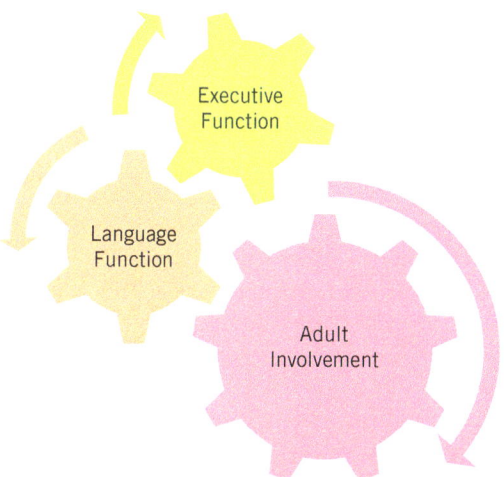

Figure 9.2 Factors influencing ToM.

Theory of mind (ToM) is the ability to ascribe mental states to oneself and to others. This is essential for social interaction. The early development of a child's ToM can be supported through dramatic play with voluntary social role-taking with others. When children negotiate the theme of their play and the role of each child, they are developing this ability. Researchers suggest that the positive effect of dramatic play on ToM is dependent on a number of factors, as depicted in Figure 9.2 (Qu, Shen, Chee, & Chen, 2015).

Qu, Shen, Chee, and Chen (2015) conducted research with kindergarten-aged children and found that their language and executive function were positively affected by their involvement with dramatic play, especially when supported by adults with knowledge and training in ToM. Theory of mind offers early learning students and teachers another perspective on dramatic play.

theory of mind (ToM) Refers to the ability to attribute "mental states such as beliefs, knowledge, and intentions to oneself and others" so as to understand and predict the behaviour of oneself and others (Qu et al., 2015, p. 716).

Photo 9.2 Making breakfast with loose parts.
Used with Permission of Gill Robertson

Theoretical Foundation

Early learning teachers examine dramatic play from a broad perspective. We begin by examining core definitions for dramatic play. You will note that there are interchangeable terms related to this area of development. These definitions are intended to help you think about the depth and complexity of dramatic play and introduce you to the expansive possibilities of programming in this area.

WHAT IS DRAMATIC PLAY?

Dramatic play is also known by terms such as *pretend play*, *imaginative play*, *symbolic play*, *make-believe play*, and *sociodramatic play*. The terms may vary, but they all refer to a type of play that involves pretending or using symbols to stand in for that which is real. For example, when a child acts like a puppy and another child takes on the role of the dog owner, they are pretending. When the dog's owner spontaneously produces a block to represent the dog's water bowl, a symbol representing something real is being exhibited. Figure 9.3 illustrates the scope of dramatic play.

Dramatic play connects to the whole child and contributes to multiple developmental domains. For example, puppets are an example of a prop that encourages pretend play. While using a puppet, all areas of children's development can be engaged. Small muscles manipulate the puppet to make the mouth move—that is fine motor development. Expressive language occurs when children make the puppet speak. Deciding how the puppet will interact with other puppets gives children control over their play—this is important for emotional development. As two puppets speak to each other, children are practising their social skills.

Dramatic play also offers children a forum for cognitive development, as it helps them create a mental picture or schema of events. If children decide to take the dolls shopping, they are developing a mental picture of what it means to shop. After repeated experience, the schema becomes complex. Once the mental picture of shopping is created, it contributes to children understanding future real experiences. This helps them develop **higher-order thinking** (Robertson, 2016).

Vygotsky (2004) suggested that dramatic play involves the creative "ability to combine elements to produce a structure, to combine the old in new ways" (p. 12). According to Robertson (2016), Vygotsky maintained that "children are not reproducing events that

higher-order thinking Often involves taxonomies that suggest that there are levels of thinking (Dietze & Kashin, 2016).

Figure 9.3 The scope of dramatic play.

they have seen or heard; rather, they are making creative re-workings of what they know about the world and the meaning that it has for the child" (p. 3). Children use their imagination as they develop the cognitive processes required for problem solving, reflective thinking, self-regulation, attention, and perspective-taking (Karpov, 2014). These areas of development reinforce why early learning students and teachers promote dramatic play.

The more experience that children have with dramatic play, the higher the level of play exhibited. During the beginning stages of dramatic play, children most often take on the roles of those who are meaningful in their lives: mommies, daddies, doctors, storekeepers, and so on. If a child takes on a role alone, he or she is engaging in dramatic play. If a child takes on a role with others, they are engaging in sociodramatic play. Whether it is with another child or an adult, the dramatic play becomes social play when the other person also takes on a role. This level of play requires the ability to transform objects and actions symbolically. The play is enhanced when there is dialogue and negotiation; it involves role-taking, script knowledge, and improvisation (Robertson, 2016).

In the transcript in Box 9.1, three children are playing hairstylist. They decide to play out a scene together, taking on roles of hairstylists and customers. They are not using real props or even realistic toy props. They are using other objects for the scissors and mousse.

These children are 4 and 5 years old. They have had many experiences with dramatic play, and their enactment is more symbolic than what it would have been when they were toddlers. They are skillful and proficient in their dramatic play enactments. They work well together. You could say that they are **master players**.

> **master players** Refers to children who are skilled in representing experiences symbolically in their self-initiated improvisational dramatic play.

Characteristics of Dramatic Play

As children gain more experience with dramatic play, it becomes more complex. You will observe variations of breadth and depth of play within each age group. For example, some children provide a leadership role for other children during play (Robertson, 2016). Jones and Reynolds (2011) refer to these children as master players. The children in the aforementioned scenario had the skills of master players as they self-initiated the experience and represented the play symbolically.

Prior to advancing to this level of sociodramatic play, master players learned their craft when as toddlers, or even in some cases as infants, they used symbolism in their solitary play. Between the ages of 8 and 12 months, children develop memory skills and begin to

---

Box 9.1 A transcript of a play episode.

Anthony:	It's a hair salon here! We're doing the hair salon.
Joey:	Is that mousse?
Anthony:	Yeah!
Joey:	I'm going to be scared of it!
Anthony:	Oh, you want me to do your hair? It's for boys, too; I can give you a haircut.
Rebecca:	No, I'll make you look like a Backstreet Boy.
Anthony:	These are not real scissors.
Rebecca:	Okay, ready to put your cap on?
Anthony:	No wait, we don't have real water in here.

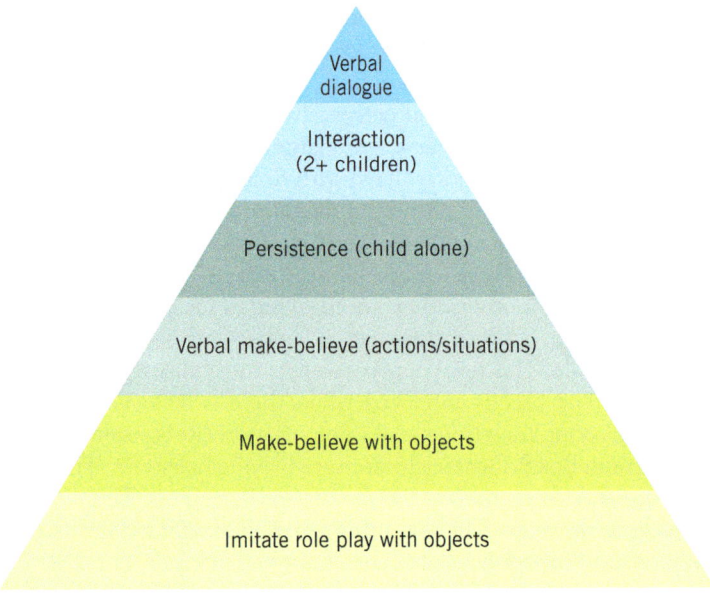

Figure 9.4 Criteria of dramatic play.

play symbolically. To play symbolically means that the child is able to represent objects mentally and engage in pretend actions. Toddlers can do this by themselves. Preschool children are able to play with others in symbolic ways. Children of kindergarten age become so skilled in their dramatic play enactments that they are seen as master players, enacting scenes that are more exotic than the previously described store, house, or doctor's office. School-aged children take dramatic play to a new level of sophistication. Generally, they re-enact components of shows from television or movies. Their props are more realistic, and they take on the roles of characters in books and in actions (Frost et al., 2012).

As identified in Figure 9.4, Smilanksy (1968) characterized six criteria of dramatic play, as described in Chapter 2. The first is *imitative role play*, and this criterion, along with the second, *make-believe play*, involves children and objects; the third, *verbal make-believe*, involves actions and situations, and the fourth criterion, *persistence in role play*, involves children playing alone; the last two are the criterion of *interaction*, where there are at least two players within the context of a play episode, and the criterion of *verbal communication*, where there is dialogue between children (Smilanksy & Shefatya, 1990).

As with other areas of development, children progress through stages. The more experience children have with dramatic play, the more involved and interactive it becomes. To become mature master players, children require environments and materials that offer various types of dramatic play opportunities. Having the right materials and environment, combined with adults who encourage and facilitate dramatic play opportunities, increases the sophistication of children's dramatic play experiences.

Stages of Dramatic Play Development

Toddlers are engaging in dramatic play when they move from "mastering simple acts of putting on their clothes or brushing their hair to applying these acts to their dolls and stuffed animals" (Bodrova & Leong, 2012, p. 29). Eventually they will go from being "toy oriented" to "people oriented" in their play. Imagine a child playing with a spoon and pretending to eat.

At this stage, the play is about the spoon. As the child becomes experienced in dramatic play, she feeds her favourite doll while pretending to be the "mommy." "At this later stage, the play is no longer about the spoon and not even about a specific doll—it is about the relationship between mother and daughter" (Bodrova & Leong, 2012, p. 29). Focusing on six critical elements of dramatic play that Bodrova and Leong (2012) have created, the acronym PRoPELS is used by adults as a support to propel children to new heights in their dramatic play.

Plan—when children think ahead about what they are going to do in their dramatic play.

Roles—when children take on the actions, language, and expressions associated with a role.

Props—when children use objects (real, symbolic, and imaginary) in their play.

Extended time frame—when children play for longer periods of time. As they develop, children's dramatic play goes from a few minutes to play sessions that can extend over several days.

Language—what do children say when they are in the act of dramatic play? Language is used to develop a scenario or coordinate the actions of different players. Language is also associated with the speech connected to a particular role.

Scenario—what is the scenario that children are acting out, including the sequence of scripts and the interactions between roles?

Bodrova and Leong (2012) identified five stages of dramatic play connected to these essential elements, as featured in Table 9.2.

Table 9.2 Stages of dramatic play.

Stages	Plan	Roles	Props	Time Frame	Language	Scenario
First Scripts	No plans.	No roles.	Plays with objects as objects.	Explores objects during play time.	Uses little language.	Does not create scenario, but can copy teacher or follow directions if script is simple and repetitive.
Roles in Action	No plans.	Acts first before deciding on roles. No rules revealed.	Objects as props. Action with prop leads to role.	Scenarios last a few minutes.	Language describes actions.	Created scenario limited and stereotypical.
Roles with Rules and Beginning Scenarios	Plans roles.	Has rules, but they can be changed.	Needs props for roles.	Scenarios last 10 to 15 minutes.	Language describes roles.	Plays familiar scripts and accepts new script ideas.
Mature Roles, Planned Scenarios, and Symbolic Props	Plans in advance.	Complex and multiple roles.	Uses symbolic and pretend props.	Scenarios can last an hour and, with support, over days.	Language describes actions and roles and uses role speech.	Describing unfolding scenarios that overlap and can change with input.
Dramatization, Multiple Themes, Multiple Roles, and Director's Play	Plans elaborate themes and scenarios.	Can play multiple roles at the same time.	Doesn't need a prop to pretend. Objects can even have roles.	Scenarios last a day or longer. Play can be interrupted and started again.	Language use to delineate scenarios, roles, and action. Can use knowledge from books in language.	Can coordinate a series of scenarios that can change. Themes and stories can come from books.

Without support from adults, not all children will move to more advanced stages of dramatic play. Toddlers usually play with objects as objects. Even a preschooler can continue to be object oriented in their play. To help, early learning teachers can support higher levels of play in children. Preschool children can create more imaginative and make-believe situations, such as preparing meals for a family or taking care of a baby (Isenberg & Jalongo, 2015). By age 4, children are capable of engaging in "mature" or "high-level" pretend play. This usually involves sustained pretend scenarios, multiple roles, and symbolic use of props. They become particularly adept at enactment and are master players. School-aged children are able to structure their pretending for presentation to an audience. Usually the more formal aspects of the dramatic arts—acting, directing, scene and costume design, playwriting, and stage management—are left to adolescents and young adults.

Enactment occurs when children adopt actions, feelings, thoughts, and behaviours of people in particular situations. This ability emerges around age 3 and signals children's developing imaginations. According to Isenberg and Jalongo (2015), enactment in early learning occurs in three forms: (1) informal drama, (2) story or interpretive drama, and (3) formal or scripted drama. During *informal dramatic play*, children spontaneously enact roles and behaviour of familiar people or characters. Little preparation time is needed, and simple, familiar props are the only materials necessary. With *story or interpretive drama*, some rehearsal is necessary and therefore some preparation time is required. Simple props are necessary. In *formal or scripted drama*, memorization of a script is required and extensive preparation time is necessary. In the first two types of enactment, children have an active role. In formal or scripted drama, the role of the children is passive, and they must rehearse as directed. This latter type of enactment is not considered developmentally appropriate for the early learning settings, as it is product oriented and focuses on technique rather than spontaneous self-expression.

Photo 9.3 Cooking our dinner.
Used with Permission of Gill Robertson

CURIOUS?

Conduct a search on the Internet to look for dramatic play using open-ended materials. Why do you think it is important to use these types of materials rather than purchasing expensive costumes?

Experiences for Children in Dramatic Play across Ages

Early learning teachers incorporate dramatic play every day for all children regardless of their age and interests. Building dramatic play skills begins in toddlers and advances throughout childhood. Early learning teachers scaffold the dramatic play experiences with children according to their ages, stages, and interest in dramatic play. For instance, given the skills necessary to participate in staged performances, school-aged children are given more ownership in their dramatic play experiences. Older children make their own decisions about roles to take and stories to enact.

Trister-Dodge, Colker, and Heroman (2014) suggested that when preschool children are engaged in dramatic play, there is a beginning level and an advanced level. At the beginning level of role playing, children imitate the familiar—mommy, daddy, baby, and pets. As children become more advanced, they select roles from the outside world, such as doctors, police officers, and firefighters. When children begin the first level of using props, they generally use real objects or replicas of objects. Advanced-level players use any object as a prop (e.g., a block stands in for a phone). Children at advanced levels also sustain their dramatic play experiences, whereas those at beginning levels may engage only fleetingly. As children advance in their dramatic play, their verbal communication increases and is related to the play theme. At this stage, children are constantly discussing roles. They are interacting cooperatively, whereas the beginning player often engages in solitary play and verbalizes around the use of props—"I had that doll first."

After reading about the complexities of dramatic play and how rich the experiences gained through it can be for children, you might be surprised to learn that dramatic play has been discouraged and replaced with academic preparation for younger children (Association of Canadian Deans of Education [ACDE], 2016). As outlined by Paley (1986), for children, "fantasy play is their ever dependable pathway to knowledge and certainty" (p. viii). As you read on, there will be further evidence of the importance of dramatic play in the lives of young children.

The Importance of Dramatic Play

In dramatic play, children use a number of developmental attributes, including cognitive, language, and social skills, in carrying out a play theme or event. The work of Bergen (2002) is seminal in the study of children's pretend play. According to Bergen, children engage in role-taking (e.g., parent-child), script knowledge, and improvisation using the strategies of joint planning, negotiation, problem solving, and goal seeking.

When children simulate the identity or characteristics of another person, they are taking on a role (Kovačević, 2016). Examine the child in Photo 9.4. What role is the child taking on? On the surface, it may appear that she is assuming the role of a mother

Photo 9.4 Dress up with open-ended materials.

Used with Permission of Gill Robertson

with a baby. According to her early learning teacher, the child was involved in making her own clothing with the scarves. She became a beautiful princess superhero with a puppy helper (the doll).

STOP ... THINK ... DISCUSS ... REFLECT

Children's dramatic play can be complex. This is a reminder not to underestimate the sophistication that children bring to their experiences. What types of open-ended materials could you offer to children to support their dramatic play experiences?

Bergen (2002) suggested that there are many connections between cognitive competence and high-quality pretend play. Many cognitive strategies, such as joint planning, negotiation, problem solving, and goal seeking, are exhibited during dramatic play, which Bergen identified.

If children lack opportunities to experience such play, their long-term capacities related to metacognition, problem solving, and social cognition, as well as to academic areas such as literacy, mathematics, and science, may be diminished. These complex and multidimensional skills involving many areas of the brain are most likely to thrive in an atmosphere rich in high-quality pretend play. (p. 5)

Dramatic play enhances children's emotional development. Unlike adults, children generally are not able to verbalize their feelings. They experience similar feelings to adults; however, they express their feelings through play. Children feel safe in play. According to Sigmund Freud (1856–1939), play can be cathartic. Children may use play to reduce anxiety and understand traumatic experiences. They may recreate an unpleasant experience over and over to assimilate it and thereby reduce the intensity of the associated feelings. Sociodramatic play supports emotional development. Children also use play to express positive feelings of joy and contentment. Children who have aggressive or negative feelings are able to develop a sense of mastery and control during their sociodramatic play. Sociodramatic play helps children acquire a greater feeling of power, a sense of happiness, and positive feelings of self (Frost et al., 2012).

As identified in Chapter 2, there continues to be a great deal of research conducted on *self-regulation* in early childhood education. According to a seminal study by Bodrova and Leong (1996), a key ingredient to developing self-regulation is play; specifically, *mature* dramatic play. This level of play is complex. It may include extended make-believe scenarios involving multiple children and last for hours, or even days. Throughout the play experience, children practise skills in both self-regulation and being regulated. Children, through dramatic play, gain skills in controlling their emotional and cognitive impulses. It becomes part of their **executive function**.

executive function An umbrella term for self-regulatory skills, which are the set of cognitive operations and strategies necessary for regulating behaviour (Berk & Meyers, 2013).

Photo 9.5 Playing spies.
Used with Permission of Gill Robertson

Learning to be both the regulator and the object of regulation is important to the development of higher mental functions. Vygotskian theory proposes that other-regulation precedes self-regulation. Children learn to regulate the behaviour of others before they can regulate themselves (Bodrova & Leong, 1996). Vygotsky maintained that at 4 or 5 years of age, a child's ability to play creatively with other children is a better gauge of future academic success than any other indicator, including vocabulary, counting skills, or knowledge of the alphabet (Bodrova & Leong, 2009). Vygotsky is quoted in the *New York Times* article "Can the Right Kinds of Play Teach Self-Control?" as saying that dramatic play "is the training ground where children learn to regulate themselves, to conquer their own unruly minds" (Tough, 2009, p. 5). According to Vygotsky, children are guided by the basic rules of dramatic play, which involve taking on a role and sticking to the role. When children follow the rules of make-believe and push one another to follow those rules, Vygotsky identified that children develop important habits of self-control (Tough, 2009).

According to Russell (2015), the potential to develop executive function skills is innate, but the level of competence achieved depends on the practice children have with the three specific processes known as inhibitory control or self-regulation, working memory, and cognitive flexibility.

CURIOUS?

Read more about how early learning teachers can support children's executive function by searching the Internet using the words "Supporting Play and Executive Function".

Variations in Sociodramatic Play

Robertson (2016) cites Bodrova and Leong (2015) and others to suggest that dramatic play is on the decline and that the reason for this is limited adult understanding about its importance. In a study conducted comparing the dramatic play behaviour of 101 children ages 4 to 6 years using the levels described by Smilansky (1968) (see Figure 9.3), the findings indicated that adult involvement has an impact. Without support from adults, there can be variations in children's dramatic play opportunities and experiences.

Just as there are differences in children's social development, there are variations in children's social play. Studies have shown that variations in sociodramatic play can be explained by parenting style, child-care quality, attitudes of early learning teachers, children's temperaments, and socioeconomic differences. Families who encourage and model pretend play give their children a chance to practise playing. As well, when children have access to peers and play activities, they gain skills at developing prosocial behaviours with their playmates. On the other hand, families who do not provide young children with mentoring or opportunities for social play inhibit them from acquiring the background to engage in advanced social play. Similar to family roles, early learning teachers can positively or negatively affect children becoming socially competent in their play. When children have positive role models who support dramatic play, they gain skills in executing dramatic play and, in turn, become more socially competent. Socially competent children are more skilled in understanding the play cues exhibited by peers and can engage in higher levels of fantasy play (Frost et al., 2012).

Often, in low-quality early learning programs, there is a lack of complex social play interactions (Frost et al., 2012). There are a number of reasons that account for this correlation, including an absence of equipment, furniture, props, and an environment that would support and provoke children's dramatic play. Another reason may be the attitude of the adults in the environment. Attitudinal barriers largely derive from the value that early learning teachers place on play. Early learning teachers may be under pressure to provide a more academically oriented and less play-based curriculum. This often results in children being exposed to more teacher-directed academic instruction (ACDE, 2016) rather than having the freedom to learn through play.

Some research suggests that children from lower-income families engage in less and poorer-quality sociodramatic play. This is due in part to their not having as many play opportunities (Frost et al., 2012) as other children. Yet studies indicate that children from all socioeconomic levels respond well to opportunities for sociodramatic play. Not only do they learn prosocial behaviours but their language performance also improves. Dramatic play can be an equalizer for all children regardless of gender, culture, and background. It is important for early learning teachers to encourage dramatic play for these reasons.

THE ROLE OF THE EARLY LEARNING TEACHER

An adult's participation in dramatic play provides a scaffold to raise children's social interaction to a higher level. An adult's involvement may also extend the length of the interaction (Robertson, 2016). The more time that children engage in sociodramatic play, the more likely is their opportunity to evolve to master players. The work of Davidson (1996) has contributed to the understanding of the role of adults in dramatic play. An early learning teacher's involvement in dramatic play communicates approval and support for the children's pretend play. When children see that an early learning teacher is excited about the pretend play, it becomes a stimulus for them and triggers other children to become involved. If the adult takes on a role that supports the children's play, it illustrates to children that pretend play is a fun and valuable activity (Davidson, 1996).

Prairie (2013) suggested that early learning teachers could use knowledge gained through observing children's play to choose whether and how to be involved or not in children's dramatic play episodes. Teachers encourage children to discuss and plan ways in which they can build on previous episodes. "Teachers can implement curriculum that emerges from play themes, which in turn feeds into children's creation of richer thematic scenes" (Prairie, 2013, p. 65). Children can be asked to share their reflections about the play. This can lead to a deeper understanding of their own theme. "Often times children lack background knowledge to build their scenarios. Even to play common themes . . . often children require more knowledge of the setting, roles, and actions associated with these roles" (Bodrova, 2008, p. 364). Prairie (2013) outlined the following ways for adults to support children's dramatic play.

> **Plan**—collaboratively plan for future dramatic play experiences with children and other early learning teachers.
>
> **Participate**—participate in children's dramatic play episodes by commenting during play or taking on roles. The more an adult follows the child's lead, the less likely the adult's presence will disrupt the flow of the play. With intentionality, adults can make suggestions that children are free to reject, such as "Do you think the baby might need a blanket?"

Nonplayer participation—in this role, the teacher discusses and makes suggestions but does not take on a role.

Taking a role within the play—by taking on a role, the teacher communicates directly in character but is careful not to control the play.

The most essential task for early learning teachers is that they take on some form of involvement, such as an observer, a documenter, or the roles suggested by Prairie (2013). Unfortunately, in some early learning settings, the early learning teachers may not become involved in the dramatic play episodes. They may choose to become involved only when children are having trouble maintaining their play smoothly. They may intervene to tell children to play more quietly, to reduce the number of children in the area, or to remind children to use materials correctly. This type of negative intervention sends a message to the children that adults do not like or approve of this play (Davidson, 1996).

The stages of play as introduced by Parten (1932) and featured in Chapter 2 have been examined from the perspective of the role of the early learning teacher by Davidson (1996), who assigned specific adult roles for each stage. These will support adults in making decisions about their role in children's dramatic play experiences. Table 9.3 provides an overview of these roles and a description of the enactment you might see during dramatic play.

For solitary play, early learning teachers can help individual children to re-enact complex stories. This play may be more elaborate than when done with peers because children can devote total concentration to the development and creation of the story without having to negotiate ideas with others. With 2-year-olds who are just beginning to develop parallel play, early learning teachers provide many duplicates of the same materials, because in parallel play the main form of interaction is doing the same thing next to a peer.

When children are involved in associative play, early learning teachers promote the play by using themes that allow for a combination of some interaction and independent play. For example, playing store is a theme that encourages this balance. Paying for purchases requires some interaction. The independent play occurs when children select what they wish to purchase (Davidson, 1996).

An airplane-themed dramatic play area produces more cooperative play. The early learning teacher encourages the children who are acting as the pilots to talk to the children who are acting as the air traffic controllers. If the early learning teacher and children turn the dramatic play area into a fire station, a map area is set up for the dispatchers to direct the drivers to the fires. A beauty salon offers different stations, including a waiting area, a shampoo station, a cutting and styling station, and an area for manicures and pedicures.

Table 9.3 The role of the early learning teacher in dramatic play.

Type of Play	Children's Enactment	Role of the Early Learning Teacher
Solitary Play	Stories	Express enjoyment. Provide space.
Parallel Play	Object play	Provide multiple sets of the same object.
Associative Play	Scenarios—independent and interactive	Provide materials and themes that allow for a balance of interaction and independence.
Cooperative Play	Scenarios with multiple roles	Help children to negotiate roles. Support children in finding the necessary materials to enhance the complexity of the play theme.

The adult may explain the roles to the children, support them in negotiating the direction of the play, and assist in resolution if conflicts arise (Davidson, 1996).

As you read about different *themed dramatic play areas*, be careful not to confuse this concept term with the term *theme* used in program planning. In the case of program planning, the term *theme* usually means a broad concept or topic such as "seasons" or "animals" and is often based around holidays. These themes are usually teacher directed and teacher owned, and involve planning the children's experiences in advance with limited or no input from the children. Often, these themes have questionable meaningfulness for the children. For example, holiday themes run the risk of being little more than a convenient backdrop for classroom decorations and craft displays. Young children usually come away from such experiences without having expanded their concepts or increased their skills across the curriculum (Isenberg & Jalongo, 2015). It is suggested that the key to programming should be an emphasis on meaning making. A meaningful programming experience is relevant to children. Children need to be involved in the programming process, and the experiences extended to children must reflect the various learning styles and interests of the children. Since themes are often short-lived (one week in duration), there is also potential for a lack of depth (Dietze & Kashin, 2016).

CURIOUS?

Do an Internet search for *meaning making in dramatic play*, and read the first three articles that appear. What have you learned about dramatic play through this activity?

Dramatic play concept themes differ from the thematic approach to programming employed by some early learning teachers. When an early learning teacher sets up the dramatic play centre based on the emergent curriculum concept, children have input on how the dramatic play evolves, diverging along new paths as choices and connections are made, and the play is always open to new possibilities that may not have been thought of during the initial planning process (Dietze & Kashin, 2016). The early learning teacher responds to the children's exploration of the theme by adding props and making connections to other areas of the indoor and outdoor play spaces.

OBSERVATION AND DOCUMENTATION

When children are playing in the dramatic play area, the priority for the teacher or student is to observe the play in order to know how to facilitate, expand, and support it. How do you know what props or themes to incorporate in the children's dramatic play experiences? The only way you will know is by first carefully observing their play, by listening to the children and documenting key play episodes. Begin by observing children in the dramatic play centre prior to transforming the centre by using a different theme and adding new materials or props. There are a number of observation tools available to assist you. You may wish to begin by using a basic observation technique and then analyze what you have written. The questions in Table 9.4 help teachers to further reflect on the types of roles and experiences that children may be engaged in.

Table 9.4 Types of questions to support examining dramatic play.

- What types of play are the children engaging in?
- Are there any children in an onlooker role?
- What roles are the children engaged in?
- What roles are the teachers exhibiting?
- What types of props are the children using?
- Are children using the props that are in the environment?
- Do the props reflect the type of play that is evolving?
- Is there any evidence of metacommunication?
- What materials are needed to encourage scaffolding to the next level of play?
- What role could you take during this future play episode?
- How might you document the upcoming play episode, and how might you use the documentation with the children to further expand their opportunities?

After your observation and analysis are completed, it is beneficial for you and the children to set up a dramatic play centre that may take the children's play experiences in new directions. This leads you to begin the cycle again—observe, reflect, analyze, and program plan.

Planning and Facilitating Dramatic Play

When planning for and facilitating dramatic play, early learning teachers consider the interests, dramatic themes, and props that are familiar to children and those that will add a new level of curiosity and exploratory opportunities. Children who are beginning players, rather than the master players described earlier, find it easier to pretend around familiar themes. Davidson (1996) suggested that the same is true for adults who are beginning players. If early learning teachers are not experienced in facilitating dramatic play, it makes sense to begin with a familiar theme, such as playing house. If a child tries to enter the dramatic play centre while other children are playing house, it is a comfortable starting point for the early learning teacher to generate the role the newcomer can take (Davidson, 1996). The early learning teacher may suggest alternative scenarios if conflict arises because of the familiarity with the theme. As adults and children become more skilled at dramatic play, the themes chosen can become more complex and exotic.

Some children have difficulty entering into dramatic play enactments with their peers. For example, children with language delays generally have more difficulty than others when trying to enter or initiate play. These children become the watchers of others until they build the problem-solving skills and self-confidence to figure out how to enter the play. Parten (1932) identified that, at this phase, the child is at the beginning of a continuum of social participation in play. She suggested that the child is taking on an onlooker role. The early learning teacher assists children to move along this continuum through solitary, parallel, associative, and group play.

Children who have not yet developed the necessary cognitive and language skills to analyze a social play situation may try to enter the play of others, but their interactive behaviour may be inappropriate. The adult's role in this circumstance is to facilitate positive peer interaction so that children who are watching learn how to approach and enter

Photo 9.6 Engaging in dramatic play.

Used with Permission of Gail Molenar

the play with the group. By setting up opportunities for interaction and giving a socially isolated child a specific role to play, the early learning teacher extends the potential for the child to join in the play using appropriate sociable behaviours.

Setting up an interaction in the dramatic play centre to encourage social play involves knowing what topical themes to offer, selecting and arranging appropriate props, keeping the area neat, and ensuring there is time and space for play. Davidson (1996) referred to this role as a stage manager. The early learning teacher as *stage manager* provides background experiences, such as books, trips, group discussions, or classroom visitors, which can serve as a prompt for dramatic play. In addition to stage manager, Davidson (1996) identified possible adults roles that may include being *players* or participants in the play or *mediators* who help children to resolve conflicts and misunderstandings. The early learning teacher may assume the role of *interpreter* and help children to understand other children's points of view. As a *social director*, the early learning teacher supports children who are onlookers to find a role. The early learning teacher also becomes the observer and documenter of the children's dramatic play episodes.

Photo 9.7 Baking in a homemade oven.

Used with Permission of Gill Robertson

There are so many reasons to actively promote and support children's dramatic play. Prairie (2013) suggested that early learning teachers could intentionally plan the time and space for dramatic play. This will enhance social and cognitive skills that emerge in sociodramatic play, contributing to children's later success in school. Sometimes it is essential to look beyond the dramatic play centre to see how and where children pretend because, when given the opportunity, pretend play takes place anywhere and everywhere! Children will engage in pretend play outside, in the block centre, when using manipulatives, or even "as they look through a pretzel at snack, pretending it is a pair of glasses" (Davidson, 1996, p. 70). By observing children when they pretend and by transcribing their dialogue, early learning teachers become aware of the children's level of dramatic play. This guides us in determining ways to scaffold the children's experiences. Once the nature of the children's play is identified, you can make meaningful programming decisions, which may include introducing children to specific types of dramatic play such as story play, pantomime, puppets, story drama, and early teacher theatre.

Types of Dramatic Play

Story Play

A young child's sense of story and drama is closely connected to dramatic play. Story play is suitable for preschoolers to school-aged children. Paley (1981) identified that when children share their own stories by acting them out, they "feel that they are playing together inside a story" (p. 167). For example, in the *Boy Who Would Be a Helicopter*, Paley (1990) described the experience of Jason, a child who is an outsider or onlooker in the classroom. Jason eventually becomes the inspiration for a technique Paley developed to build on the children's sense of story and drama called *story acting*. As Paley (2001) demonstrated in *In Mrs. Tully's Room*, very young children can participate. There is a connection between this technique and the constructivist theory approach because the experience begins with the children's own stories and dramatizations. The children construct their own knowledge by making meaning and representing their stories. Children also learn to be part of an audience and to perform for an audience. The technique is summarized as follows:

- The child initiates by telling a story.
- The adult writes the story down exactly as dictated by the child, who becomes the author.
- The children in the classroom take on the parts of the characters in the story.
- The author may pick the part that he or she wants to play.
- Additions and revisions to the story may be made in process if parts are unclear or incomplete.
- Only the author has the right to make changes in the story.

Older children document their own stories and collaborate with others to create jointly composed stories and dramatizations. Through these experiences, children develop a sense of story. Children discover that a story has a beginning, a middle, and an end and that it has a setting and a plot. There are characters in stories, including the main character or protagonist. Usually, the plot involves some sort of conflict or problem that the protagonist has to overcome (Waite-Stupiansky, 1997). Creating an environment for storytelling is a gift an early learning teacher or student can give to children, as it enhances their development in so many areas.

Pantomime

During pantomime experiences, children do not speak; instead, they communicate through gesture or movement. They express themselves by "miming." In pantomime, children communicate ideas, feelings, and actions—without using words. Pantomimes are the starting point for creative drama. They help children to feel comfortable using their bodies to express themselves. Because pantomimes begin with physical experiences, they make concepts more concrete. Pantomimes are particularly useful for children in the early learning centre whose first language is not English. Pantomimes are also valuable for children who have speech or hearing problems or who are very shy (Isenberg & Jalongo, 2015). Some appropriate mime activities for children include the following:

- Acting out a familiar nursery rhyme.
- Showing what it is like to ride a bike or climb on the jungle gym.
- Being a character or an animal in a favourite song. "I'm a Little Teapot" is a good example of a song to mime to.
- Modelling familiar actions like brushing teeth, washing hands, or eating lunch. The early learning teacher can mime the action, and the children guess the action and then mime it as well.
- Imagining that they are animals performing specific actions, such as a lion stalking through the jungle looking for food or a kitten lapping up some milk or a wiggling worm (Isenberg & Jalongo, 2015).

Puppets

The word *puppet* is derived from the Latin word for doll. However, puppets are much more than dolls—they are powerful teaching and learning tools that invite children to explore their imaginations and share their imaginings with others. They are a natural prop for toddlers, preschoolers, kindergarteners, and school-aged children. Puppets offer children opportunities to exhibit creativity, imagination, and self-expression (Isenberg & Jalongo, 2015). Jalongo (2000) described four reasons for using puppets in the early learning environment:

1. *Puppets improve communication skills.* Children often will talk to or through a puppet when they feel uncomfortable talking to another person.
2. *Puppets speak a universal language.* Children with hearing problems or limited English can watch a puppet play and usually can infer the meaning of the performance.
3. *Puppets encourage cooperation.* Coordinating one's puppet's behaviour with that of other children's puppets helps children to work together.
4. *Puppets help to integrate curriculum.* Learning in all of the developmental domains can be explored through puppetry.

Children may experiment with puppets that are provided or make their own. Children are encouraged to have their puppets vary the pitch of their voice and make a variety of sounds, such as animals growling or chirping. Children can be involved in discussing what puppets can be used for. For example, puppets can be used for creating a puppet show, talking with one another, or retelling a story (Isenberg & Jalongo, 2015).

Introducing a mirror so that the children can see the puppet's movements and gestures help children learn the art of puppetry (Isenberg & Jalongo, 2015). Younger children find it easiest to use puppets that have moving mouths, so that it makes sense to add dialogue if they choose to do so (Hunt & Renfro, 1982). Creating a puppet centre with puppet-making materials such as fabric, paper plates and bags, recycled buttons, yarn, and sticks may trigger an interest in children creating their own puppets.

Puppets also provide early learning teachers with an opportunity to discuss with children the limits of and responsibility for puppet use. For example, puppets thrown carelessly in a corner of a room can send a message to children that caring for the puppets is not important. This could lead to children throwing the puppets around or using them for "hand-to-hand" combat. Puppets are important props and therefore require careful consideration when displayed and when being stored.

Story Drama

Sometimes referred to as story retelling, story drama is a type of interpretive drama based on the re-enactment of familiar stories, poems, or fables. Often, story drama involves a facilitator-led group experience, with children creating scenes from familiar literature that use both dialogue and movement. Story drama is used in the early learning environment as a way to support children in understanding the structure of a story and how language affects others. For early learning teachers, it offers a natural and authentic way to promote literacy learning. Research shows that enacting stories improves reading comprehension and promotes speaking, listening, critical thinking, and creative reading skills. It heightens children's interest in reading and enables children to experience the feelings and behaviours of others (Isenberg & Jalongo, 2015).

Teacher Theatre

Curtis and Carter (2007) described another dramatic play strategy called teacher theatre. By using stories and props to convey ideas, early learning teachers coach children in grasping certain concepts. "Stories captivate children's attention, and playing out the details with dramatic play and props helps them internalize the concepts and strategies" (Curtis & Carter, 2007, p. 132). The topics for teacher theatre can be chosen in response to a particular or recurring interpersonal issue that is happening among the children. For example, using three rubber dinosaurs, an early learning teacher demonstrates to children the issue of excluding others from play. The children suggest ideas and solutions to help the protagonists in the story solve their problems. By early learning teachers and children acting out the situation, the children involved revisit their problems and receive some coaching without feeling singled out or criticized (Curtis & Carter, 2007).

Curtis and Carter (2007) identified that "whenever children are invited to pretend, they seem to be able to access skills and concepts that are more difficult for them to grasp when they are in the middle of a real situation" (p. 134). Teacher theatre coaches children to think constructively about social problems. The issues being conveyed are one step removed from the emotion and intensity of their own play. Stop and think about teacher theatre. What theory are you bringing to the environment if you give children an opportunity to constructively think and discuss social problems? Reflect on a situation that you might act out with another student or teacher. What are the skills you need to employ in order to do this? Write the skills out and share your responses with a classmate. You may try to simulate teacher theatre during class with pairs of students acting out potential real situations such as bullying, issues around sharing or inclusion, separation anxiety, and so on.

Tools of the Mind

Tough (2009) described a Tools of the Mind classroom where "every morning, before embarking on the day's make-believe play, each child takes a coloured marker and a printed form called a play plan and draws or writes his declaration for the day's play: 'I am going to drive the choo-choo train'; 'I am going to make a sand castle'; 'I am going to take the dollies to the beach'" (p. 6). In a Tools of the Mind program, it is important at the beginning of the day for children to be coached on dramatic play. This is called Make-Believe Play Practice—with the early learning teacher leading children in a step-by-step process. For instance, the example of coaching a child to feed a baby doll is used: "I'm pretending my baby is crying. Is yours? What should we say?" (Tough, 2009, p. 6). As children progress to kindergarten, they carry around a clipboard with the day's activities on it, and on each Friday, children have a 5- to 10-minute "learning conference" with their early learning teacher that is viewed as a mini–performance review. The children discuss what they accomplished in the week, where they fell short, and what skills they want to work on. Tough suggested that these practices reinforce habits of self-control using pretend play.

According to Bodrova and Leong (1996), when children are engaged in dramatic play scenarios, the early learning teacher's suggestions and guidance are most important when any of the following things happen:

- Children do not talk to each other.
- Children exclude a specific child.
- Few roles emerge.
- Children do not pretend.

- Children do not use objects to stand for other objects.
- Play is fleeting, lasting only for two to three minutes.

Early learning teachers do not discipline children for not playing well in the dramatic play centre. Rather, their role is to guide play more directly by suggesting how to include other children, proposing a "plot" or roles, asking questions, or even coaching specific children. It may include role-playing with children to practise cooperation and conflict management skills. Children practise the social skill of joint decision making and negotiating. These skills help children become better prepared to handle conflicts when they arise, reducing the need for the early learning teacher to intervene. Through role play, children confront conflicts. These conflicts can be both internal and external to the story. Either way, children become more experienced at conflict resolution. In the transcript in Box 9.2, three preschool disagreements are quickly resolved.

Box 9.2 Solving conflicts.

Sam:	No, look, we need one, two, three.
Sarah:	No, no, let me!
Sam:	And one for you, and the baby, one for you.
Sarah:	No, no!
Sam:	This is gross, let's play water table.
Sarah:	No, no! Wait, wait!
Sam:	I get to play house.
Sarah:	Okay, okay, put some tea in here.
Sam:	Done. No, maybe a little more. Hey, Sarah, we need water in here.
Sarah:	Is this finished?
Sam:	It's finished. More, more, more,
Lily:	Sarah, Sarah, let's go to get more coffee.
Sam:	It's a treat. Ta da!
Lily:	The baby needs a small spoon. I'm going to get some. Dad, don't do that.
Sam:	But I need a lot!
Sarah:	I did give you lots.
Sam:	Let me do it. Everybody does it by themselves!
Sarah:	Stop. Stop, I said!
Sam:	It's my idea.
Sarah:	You want me to put more water?
Sam:	Yeah, put more water, please.
Sarah:	You want me give you a cup?
Sam:	Yeah. Uh, could I have some more, please? A lot more, could I have the whole thing, please?
Sarah:	I've got more!

When early learning teachers view dramatic play as an opportunity to enhance learning during the experience, they create and encourage simulations that children can learn from. For example, in the scenario outlined in Box 9.2, the children were able to solve their own problems during the play. Early learning teachers need to know what materials to provide and ideas to present that will give children the opportunity to practise negotiation, problem solving, and collaboration skills. You could refer to this as a provocation for dramatic play.

Provocations for Dramatic Play

Educators from Reggio Emilia, Italy, focus on provocation as a way of helping children to think more deeply or broadly about a topic, question, or issue. As described by Gandini (1998), **provocation** is something that arrives by surprise.

Chaillé (2008) described provocation as "an intentional sparking of interest" (p. 63). A provocation can be as simple as reading a book that might spark an interest to dramatize an event described in the book. There are many possible provocations for dramatic play in the early learning environment, including the much overlooked treasure chest of dress-up clothing and early learning teacher-created prop boxes that are built around topics. Table 9.5 provides suggestions for the contents of five prop boxes focused on dramatic play. These types of boxes are offered on a rotating basis or in response to children's expressed interests.

provocation A means for provoking further action. A provocation can be anything that arrives by surprise and sparks interest, such as a collection of interesting scarves or pieces of materials that children find by surprise in the dramatic play centre one morning.

Setting Up for Dramatic Play

Dramatic play centres are recommended in all early learning settings. Children require both a permanent space designated for dramatic play and a flexible space that may be converted as play ideas evolve. Space constraints make it difficult for most early learning settings to include more than one area devoted to dramatic play; however, think of the possibilities for children to extend and expand their experiences. Dramatic play options occur indoors and outdoors.

The "House" is the central theme in children's dramatic play, and very often you will hear the dramatic play centre referred to as the housekeeping area. This is because playing house is a familiar family theme for all children. Early learning teachers provide familiar

Table 9.5 Prop boxes.

Prop Box 1: The Office—Stapler, tape, old cellphones, computer keyboards, computer monitors, paper, pencils, pens, paper clips, stickie notes.

Prop Box 2: A Flower and Fruit Stand—Flowers, vegetables, fruits, boxes, crates, bags, table for display, cash register, play money, credit cards, chalkboard to list prices, baskets for carrying produce once purchased.

Prop Box 3: A Bakery—Cookie sheets, muffin tins, play dough, oven, telephone, labels, chalkboard for prices, cash register, play money, credit cards, beads for decorations, cookbooks, blocks for display cases.

Prop Box 4: Dining Out—Aprons, chef's hat, menus, tablecloths, silverware, dishes, play food, chalkboard and chalk for "specials," order pads and pencils, cash register, play money, credit cards, telephones.

Prop Box 5: The Shoe Store—Shoes and boxes, foot measure, tape measure, rules, socks, telephones, receipt book, price labels, cash register, play money, credit cards.

props and storylines on this topic and other topics based on the children's interests. Ideally, the concept theme areas represented by the prop boxes listed in Table 9.5 would be in addition to a specific "house" area. Can you imagine children playing house and then going to the bank for money to purchase a new pair of shoes at the shoe store? The house centre, if it remains static, becomes a symbol of lost opportunities for children when this is their only exposure to dramatic play.

The house centre is set up to encourage and invite children to engage in various types of play. Davidson (1996) suggested some guidelines that should be considered when arranging the house area. These guidelines can be transferred to other types of dramatic play areas.

> **Allow Enough Space.** Children require enough space to move around easily; however, the area should not be so large as to complicate negotiations over roles, props, and the direction of the play. The larger the group, the harder this becomes. Having two areas that accommodate smaller groups works best.
>
> **Clearly Define the Space.** The furniture in the dramatic centre (i.e., fridge, stove, and sink), along with the backs of shelves from adjacent areas should be used to define and enclose the space. Clearly defining the space decreases disruptions from children not currently in the area. If possible, the dramatic play centre should be beside the block centre, as children often use the two together.
>
> **Provide Dress-Up Clothing.** Since dressing up is an integral part of pretend playing for children, there should be a variety of clothes for both boys and girls. Ethnic and cultural clothing is included. Consideration is given to how easily the children may independently put on the clothes and take them off. Clothing with Velcro fasteners, large buttons, elastic waists, and pre-tied ties will give children a sense of independence.
>
> **Provide Props.** Props often set the direction of the play. Too few props will create disputes, and too many will result in dumping and clutter. Younger children require realistic props. As the children get older, less-realistic props will allow for more creative use of materials.

If the early learning environment has space, the house area can have more than one room, or the house area can be set up in addition to another area in the environment so that children may expand their play, such as shopping in a grocery store. They will have a place to put the groceries once these are purchased. It provides more room for pretending and can accommodate a large number of children at a time. Early learning teachers recognize that at times children will need to extend their play beyond the designated play space. Children will assume, pretend, and take on roles readily in the outdoor environment.

Time to Play

Finding time for children to play in the day's schedule is extremely important. Children need ample time to plan, carry out, and sustain their dramatic activity (Isenberg & Jalongo, 2015). The role of the early learning teacher is to ensure that the schedule for the day allows for long periods of play. Christie and Wardle (1992) conducted a study on 4- and 5-year-olds' play behaviour and found that the length of the play period affected the amount and maturity of play. How much time is adequate? Frost, Wortham, and Reifel (2001) suggested that at least one hour of uninterrupted free play is recommended in a daily schedule, and even that may not be adequate. Some "children spend 45 minutes to an hour planning their play—designing play sets, negotiating roles, and discussing themes" (p. 301).

STOP ... THINK ... DISCUSS ... REFLECT

Why do you think that some early learning teachers stop children's dramatic play experiences so that the children may move to the next scheduled activity? Is it more beneficial to keep children on a timed schedule than to allow the play to continue? Why or why not? What are the advantages of allowing the play to continue? What are the disadvantages?

WEAVING DRAMATIC PLAY INTO THE EARLY LEARNING ENVIRONMENT

Pretend play can occur in all parts of the early learning environment and at all times of the day. The types of materials provided will influence the direction and quality of pretend play. For example, when children are pouring water into pots at the water table and shaping "cakes" from sand at the sand table, they are pretending to be cooking. Adding boats to the water table, the children pretend that they are sailing on the seas. Including dump trucks in the sand table could trigger children to pretend that they are construction workers.

In the outdoor setting, larger equipment such as playhouses, slides, climbers, boxes, sticks, and hollow blocks will prompt children to develop themes involving not only the ever popular house but also pirate ships, secret hideouts, and camping trips (Davidson, 1996). Science and dramatic play intermingle when children are encouraged to act out seasonal changes with their bodies (Isenberg & Jalongo, 2015). Children have fun pretending to be babies and illustrating with their bodies their own growth and development from an infant who crawls and cries to someone who can run, jump, and ride a tricycle. Art materials lend themselves to dramatic play in two significant ways. First, children can create stories to accompany their pictures and they can act them out. Second, children can construct props to be used in their pretend play (Davidson, 1996).

If children need a sign to add to the gas station that they have created in the block centre, they can create their own from art materials made readily available. By providing children with access to props, pretend play may be extended into various areas of the play space. For example, imagine children who have blankets and dolls and create beds for their babies from blocks. Including access to signs will integrate literacy into the play. Using other written-language props, such as maps, tickets, magazines, or letters, will support a print-rich environment that promotes dramatic play, language, and literacy. Books can be used for both building and pretending.

When writing experiences are associated with dramatic play, they become more meaningful than if children are given lessons or seatwork in which they practise their letters. The connection between emerging literacy and dramatic play is significant. For example, when children set up a restaurant and take orders from printed menus as a waiter and customer, they are writing within a meaningful context. Meaning is given to literacy learning. Through play, literacy becomes an enjoyable and satisfying experience for young children. Whenever children are exposed to an environment that makes use of everyday written language, such as taking orders, filling out forms, making shopping lists, or jotting down appointments, dramatic play will encourage literacy development (Galda & Pellegrini, 2015).

It is during dramatic play situations that fantasy and collaborative storytelling can spontaneously occur. Children practise using language during play. By describing other worlds, events, and characters, they begin to *decontextualize* language and learn to assume multiple perspectives (Ahn & Filipenko, 2007). It is through this play that children are most likely to expand their language skills or engage in pretend reading or writing.

Guns, War Play, and Superheroes

It is very uncommon to find toy weapons in early learning settings. Given the opportunity, predominately boys will fashion guns from blocks, Legos, sticks, or other construction material. Children use guns and weapons to carry out fantasy play. The research does not suggest that this type of play leads to aggression and violence, but early learning teachers are generally uncomfortable with the play and tend to ban children from using items as guns (Frost et al., 2012). Here is an opportunity for you to reflect on a perspective that you may not have considered before. Think about children who come from families with parents who are involved in the military, police, or conservation professions, who are required to use guns as part of their jobs. Or think about children who have parents who engage in hunting as a sport. Think of children who immigrate with their families from war-torn countries and how they might need to play out their experiences. Guns may be part of children's lives. Are we disrespecting these children's play if we ban guns from the environment?

STOP ... THINK ... DISCUSS ... REFLECT

Do you think that sticks and guns should be part of children's play in early learning programs? What happens if you see the value in this play but some families do not? What is your role?

An early learning teacher can spend a great deal of energy trying to enforce a ban on gun play and restricting superhero play, as it is natural that children will use play guns and weapons to enact superhero scenarios. Is it so terrible for children to engage in superhero play, even if it involves gun play? Many long-time teachers will tell you that even when you ban guns, children will be inventive at making their play more acceptable to adults—for example, "*This isn't a gun, it is a laser camera*" (Barnes, 2008). Early learning teachers are cognizant that their values and beliefs about weapons such as guns must not interfere with children's play.

Superhero play is a form of dramatic play in which children use figurines, costumes, or other props as accessories to imitate the superheroes they admire. Children are drawn to the power, strength, and special attributes of superheroes. It gives them a sense of feeling in charge of their world. It provides children with a safe way to achieve a sense of power and play out violence that they may have observed, whether it be on television or in their own homes. There are positive attributes to this type of play. It is active, creative, and empowering. Having clear guidelines about appropriate behaviour will support superhero play in a positive way. This is different from aggressive behaviour. Children should know that aggressive behaviour is unacceptable and that everyone needs to feel safe.

Despite recognizing that children have engaged in superhero play for centuries, it is one area that causes discomfort for many early learning teachers. Superhero play, pretend fighting, chase games, and rescue games are the areas of dramatic play that early learning teachers restrict most (Storli & Sandseter, 2015). De-Souza and Radell (2011) identified

Photo 9.8 Sticks as guns in outdoor play.

Used with Permission of Gill Robertson

that the notion that "bad play" will evolve from superhero play is an adult-imposed interpretation. They determined, in conversations with children, that superheroes are those who "save people," "find your pet" "help you," and "save cats, like firefighters do" (p. 27). The children also suggested being that, in being a superhero, a cape is important. Examining superhero play from children's perspectives reinforces the importance of early learning teachers being guided by children's ideas and perspectives. For example, think about having such discussions with children. How might this provide children and teachers with opportunities to think critically about how superhero play is a venue for caring for peers and others? Superhero play has the potential for children to expand their social and emotional development through the creation of superhero play episodes that may include helping others, such as by rescuing them from particular dangers. Think of children who may have experienced an accident, a loss of a pet, a new family member, or an illness. Then think about the role that superhero play may have in supporting children working through those experiences from their perspective.

In the same way they do with other types of dramatic play, early learning teachers engage with the children. They may ask core questions, such as "Do you think people can really fly?" or "Do you think that firefighters are really that rough with people when they are saving them?" Early learning teachers role model the ways in which true superheroes are kind and caring individuals. This approach helps early learning teachers gradually bring superhero play into children's environments.

TERMS THAT INFLUENCE EARLY LEARNING PLAY ENVIRONMENTS

We conclude this chapter with three additional terms that support the theory of children's play. These terms are used when examining space and with children in their play.

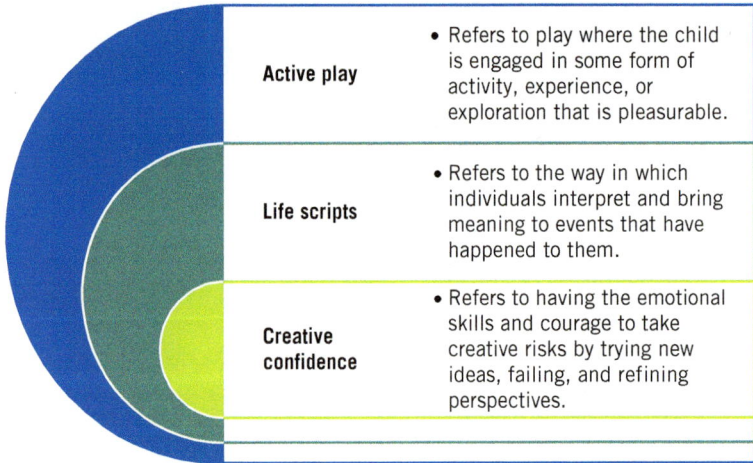

Active play	• Refers to play where the child is engaged in some form of activity, experience, or exploration that is pleasurable.
Life scripts	• Refers to the way in which individuals interpret and bring meaning to events that have happened to them.
Creative confidence	• Refers to having the emotional skills and courage to take creative risks by trying new ideas, failing, and refining perspectives.

SUMMARY

Chapter Preview

■ Dramatic play is one of the most important forms of play for young children.

Theoretical Frameworks

■ Theoretical frameworks provide students and early learning teachers with a foundation to explore one's thoughts and beliefs. Piaget, Vygotsky, Erikson, and Gardner's theories are lenses through which to view dramatic play as it relates to child development.

What Is Dramatic Play?

■ Dramatic play is known as pretend play, imaginative play, symbolic play, make-believe play, and sociodramatic play. All refer to a type of play that involves pretending or using symbols to stand in for that which is real.
■ Dramatic play is an important developmental experience as it relates to multiple domains.

- When children take on a role alone, they are engaging in dramatic play; with others, it becomes sociodramatic play and requires the ability to transform objects and actions symbolically. With experience, children develop their dramatic play skills, eventually becoming master players.

Characteristics of Dramatic Play

- The complexity of dramatic play varies across the ages. There are variations of breadth and depth of dramatic play within each age group.
- Smilansky (1968) characterized six criteria of dramatic play: *Imitative role play* and *make-believe play*, which are in regard to children and objects; *verbal make-believe*, regarding actions and situations; *persistence in role play*, involving children playing alone; *interaction*, with at least two players; and *verbal communication*, where there is dialogue among children.

Stages of Dramatic Play Development

- With experience, dramatic play becomes more complex. Toddlers have the ability to enact events. Preschoolers add complexity to the play. By age 4, children are capable of sustained pretend scenarios, multiple roles, and symbolic use of props. School-aged children are ready for an audience.
- Enactment occurs when children adopt the actions, feelings, thoughts, and behaviours of people in particular situations. According to Isenberg and Jalongo (2001), enactment in early learning occurs in three forms: (1) informal drama, (2) story or interpretive drama, and (3) formal or scripted drama.
- Theatre is a more structured form of dramatic play or creative drama. It fits Smilansky's definition of "games with rules."

Experiences for Children in Dramatic Play across the Ages

- Trister-Dodge, Colker, and Heroman (2014) identified that there is a beginning level and an advanced level when preschool children are engaged in dramatic play involving role playing and the use of props.

The Importance of Dramatic Play

- There is a connection between cognitive competence and high-quality pretend play. Cognitive strategies exhibited during dramatic play include joint planning, negotiation, problem solving, and goal seeking. Dramatic play can provide opportunities to challenge the social norms that may be marginalizing children.
- Dramatic play is the key ingredient in developing self-regulation, as it requires children to gain skills controlling their emotional and cognitive impulses. It becomes part of a child's executive function.

Variations in Dramatic Play

- Studies have shown that variations in sociodramatic play can be explained by parenting style, child-care quality, attitudes of early learning teachers, and socioeconomic differences. There is also a correlation between low-quality early learning and child-care centres and a lack of complex social play interactions.

- Dramatic play can be an equalizer for all children regardless of gender, culture, and background. It is important for early learning teachers to encourage dramatic play for these reasons.

The Role of the Early Learning Teacher

- An adult's participation in dramatic play can provide a scaffold to raise children's social interaction to a higher level. Early learning teachers and students become involved in children's dramatic play beyond just intervening because of children's play issues. Teachers are facilitators of play, and they ensure that there are space, props, and time set aside for the purpose of expanding children's development.
- Early learning teachers use observation tools and pedagogical documentation to encourage reflection and discussion about dramatic play with children. Early learning teachers ask thoughtful questions to support children in provoking creative thinking.
- For solitary play, early learning teachers can help individual children re-enact complex stories. With 2-year-olds beginning to develop their parallel play, early learning teachers provide duplicates of materials. When children are involved in associative play, the play can be promoted by the use of themes that allow for some interaction as well as independent play

Observation and Documentation

- When children are engaging in dramatic play, early learning teachers or students observe and document the play in order to know how to facilitate, expand, and support the play further.

Planning and Facilitating Dramatic Play

- When planning for and facilitating dramatic play, consider the interests, dramatic themes, and props familiar to children and those that will trigger curiosity and add new exploratory opportunities. If conflicts arise, suggest alternative scenarios.
- Adults assist children in moving through solitary, parallel, associative, and group play.
- There are multiple roles for the early learning teacher to take in dramatic play, including stage manager, player or participant in the play, mediator, interpreter, social director, observer, and documenter.

Types of Dramatic Play

- Early learning teachers and students make meaningful programming decisions, which may include introducing children to specific types of dramatic play such as story play, pantomime, puppets, story drama, and early teacher theatre, as well as to a specific program titled "Tools of the Mind," based on Vygotsky's theories.

Provocations for Dramatic Play

- Provocation is a means for provoking further action. A provocation can be anything that arrives by surprise and sparks interest, such as a collection of interesting scarves or pieces of materials, which children find by surprise in the environment. Early learning teachers use prop boxes to provide provocation for dramatic play.

Setting Up for Dramatic Play

- Children require both a permanent space designated for dramatic play and a flexible space that may be converted as play ideas evolve in both indoor and outdoor environments.
- The "House" is the central theme in children's dramatic play. In setting up housekeeping-themed dramatic play, early learning teachers allow enough space, make sure the space is clearly defined, and provide dress-up clothing and props.

Time to Play

- Finding the time for children to play in the day's schedule is extremely important. Children need ample time to plan, carry out, and sustain their dramatic activity.
- The role of the early learning teacher is to ensure that there is at least one hour of uninterrupted free play in the schedule for dramatic play.

Weaving Dramatic Play into the Early Learning Environment

- Pretend play can occur in all parts of the early learning environment and at all times of the day. The types of materials provided will influence the type of pretend play.
- Dramatic play connects to art, math, science, blocks, language, literacy, music, and movement. Dramatic play occurs both outdoors and indoors.
- Dramatic play offers children opportunities to use symbolic representation: the ability to use one thing to represent another. It is during dramatic play situations that fantasy and collaborative storytelling can spontaneously occur.

Guns, War Play, and Superheroes

- Children use guns and weapons to carry out fantasy play. The research does not suggest that this type of play leads to aggression and violence. Early learning teachers are generally uncomfortable with and tend to ban this type of play.
- Superhero play is a form of dramatic play in which children use figurines, costumes, or other props as accessories to imitate the superheroes they admire. Children are drawn to the power, strength, and special attributes of superheroes.
- There are positive attributes to superhero play. It is active, creative, and empowering. Having clear guidelines about appropriate behaviour will support superhero play in a positive way and increase opportunities for children to feel safe and engage in this play.

REVIEW QUESTIONS

1. Explain the theories of Piaget, Erikson, Vygotsky, and Gardner as they relate to dramatic play.
2. What are the interchangeable terms for dramatic play? What does having so many terms tell you about dramatic play?
3. Explain the stages of dramatic play, beginning with a young toddler and continuing to school-aged children. Relate each stage to the criteria developed by Smilansky.
4. Why is dramatic play known as an equalizer for all children regardless of gender, culture, and background?

5. Give examples of how your dramatic play can be woven into other areas of the early learning program.
6. Discuss the pros and cons of war play and superhero play.

MAKING CONNECTIONS

Theory to Practice

1. Relate the concept of self-regulation to Vygotsky's theory about dramatic play. Can you find any further research that supports a focus on executive function in early learning? In Ontario, for example, the curriculum developed for the implementation of full-day learning for 4- and 5-year-olds pays particular attention to self-regulation.
2. The next time you spend the day in an early learning classroom, check the schedule. How much time is given to dramatic play? What do you think can be done with the schedule to encourage longer periods of play?
3. There are many Internet articles and magazines aimed at parents of young children. Write a short article for parents on the importance of dramatic play as it relates to child development. What do you need to remember when you are communicating with parents? Style, length, language? Remember to consider how your article appears visually.

DIGITAL PORTFOLIO ENTRIES

Potential portfolio entries for your digital portfolio could include the following:

- When I think about the importance of dramatic play, I wonder about . . .
- As an early learning student, I wonder about how I can influence children's dramatic play because . . .
- When I look at dramatic play centres, I think . . .
- Now when I think about superhero and gun play, I believe . . .

CURIOUS?

Do a library search to seek information on how dramatic play supports math, science, and technology in early learning programs.

CHAPTER 10
Language, Emergent Literacy, and Play

> " Do not . . . keep children to their studies by compulsion but by play. "
>
> —Plato (427–347 BC)

LEARNING OUTCOMES

After exploring this chapter you should be able to:

- Define language development and emergent literacy.
- Explain the stages of language and literacy development and the reasons why children communicate.
- Describe how children's play is interconnected with the development of language and literacy skills.
- Explain the theoretical foundation of language, emergent literacy, and play.
- Describe the roles of early learning teachers related to language and literacy.
- Discuss the role of the environment to children's language development and emerging literacy skills.

Sharing Stories of Practice

I have worked in early childhood education for many years. Often, parents have asked, "What is my child learning?" Then I ask them in response, "What do you want them to learn?" They tell me, "I want them to learn their ABCs." This is where I have had difficulty reconciling what I learned in college with the realities of my practice. In college, I learned that children's social and emotional development is important. I learned that my role is to facilitate play. Teaching the ABCs is the role of teachers in the school system. This never felt right to me but neither did incorporating the formalized, structured instructional strategies used in later school years. As I began to incorporate a literacy-rich environment in my practice, I was amazed by the evidence I observed every day of children learning the real meanings of letters, sounds, and words through their play. When I took pictures of the children in the process of learning, collected their work samples, and created documentation, I could finally tell and show parents with confidence that their children were learning their ABCs!

Susan, ECE graduate, 2017

CHAPTER PREVIEW

Can you imagine a world without language? Language is everywhere. Children are exposed to language in their homes, schools, and communities. Language acquisition and literacy skills are essential developmental milestones for children (Genishi & Dyson, 2015). Through play, children acquire language and develop literacy skills. Language development and play are crucial to development "because they affect subsequent development in cognition, academic achievement, social competence, and positive peer relationships" (Conner, Kelly-Vance, Ryalls, & Friehe, 2014, p. 221). Play is often the motivator for children to expand their language knowledge and practise their literacy skills (Ewing, Callow, & Rushton, 2016).

Young children use and learn language in a variety of ways. For example, the simple acts of exploring sounds, inventing language, and using symbols when playing leads to them becoming familiar with words and meanings. Language is essential for communication. Children require various forms of communication to have their basic physical needs met and for the human function of socializing (Yule, 2014). For example, when children begin making sounds while pointing at a cup of water, they are communicating their needs. Rather than handing them a cup, an early learning teaching can verbalize the children's desires. This is a way to support language development. Children learn to speak what they hear.

From the first babbles of an infant to the complex sentences of a 4- or 5-year-old, early learning teachers have important roles in supporting the development of children's language skills. Understanding that play is a method for learning language is a significant component of the role. Another important component to children's language development is the early learning environment (Follari, 2015). When the environment is rich with play, children will take an incredible journey that sees babbles evolve into a vocabulary of at least 5000 words by the age of 5 (Asaridou, Demir-Lira, Goldin-Meadow, & Small, 2016). Early learning teachers require an understanding of the relationship of appropriate play experiences and programming options to support literate behaviours, language development, and literacy skills.

Photo 10.1 A 6-month-old child "reading" a book.
Used with Permission of Jordana Rapuch

Children are motivated to learn when their curiosity is aroused and they are exposed to new and exciting things in their environment. Scientists call this **novelty preference**. This is how the very young child's cognitive system processes information. Once a child has mastery of all the information an object or event has to offer, he or she is motivated to keep learning. Paying attention to something novel allows the acquisition of additional information in a short amount of time (Ostroff, 2012). Early learning students and teachers recognize the relationship of novelty preference to new objects, events, and children's budding curiosity. For example, children are never too young to be exposed to books. Books support language and literacy development as well as novelty preference.

This chapter introduces you to language development and literacy processes. You will gain insight into the significance of children recognizing their first letter of the alphabet or printing their name for the first time. You will be introduced to the connections between children understanding the sounds of a letter and reproducing marks for print. You will be able to reflect on the important role of play in the learning of language. You will also examine how the early learning teacher's use of language supports children as they develop theirs.

As you explore the chapter, we ask that you think about the questions that follow. What can you do to inspire children to want to learn to read and write? How do language and literacy concepts in a playful environment motivate children? How might children want to learn about new words, reading, and writing? What are the best strategies for children to learn to read and write? Would you want someone to instruct you on how to

novelty preference A child's way of processing information based on novel objects and events. It develops into childhood curiosity and the desire to explore (Ostroff, 2012).

Chapter Preview **321**

read and write? Or, would you want to discover reading and writing and language concepts while playing within a literacy-rich environment?

THEORETICAL FRAMEWORKS

Theoretical frameworks of language development provide early learning students and teachers with a foundation from which to explore thoughts and beliefs. These in turn influence our practice. You will find it beneficial to think about your knowledge and beliefs about language and literacy at this point, and then revisit your ideas after you have reviewed this chapter. In Figure 10.1, we introduce you to three theories that have influenced how adults work with children in supporting language and literacy. B. F. Skinner, Noam Chomsky, and Lev Vygotsky have provided the theoretical foundation upon which early learning students and teachers can build their practice.

A number of theorists have been connected to behaviourism. Perhaps the best known is B. F. Skinner (1957), who initiated the behaviourist theory of language development and the idea of **operant conditioning** (Frost, Wortham, & Reifel, 2012). Behaviourism suggests that as the child progresses from infancy, adults reinforce the child each time the most correct form of language to say words is expressed. For example, a child may be given a treat each time the word *kitty* is verbalized correctly. Teachers who follow this theory suggest that children learn language through imitation. This requires adults to create an environment in which children are conditioned or rewarded each time they use correct language forms, including imitating adult language (Frost et al., 2012).

Noam Chomsky (Lees & Chomsky, 1957) developed the nativist theory based on the understanding that children take charge of learning language innately based on a biological system he called **language acquisition device (LAD)**. The LAD contains a set of rules common to all languages. Children use these rules as they develop their language (Frost et al., 2012, p. 105).

Higher mental functions, such as memory, attention, and self-regulation, occur in the context of shared tasks between individuals. Thinking begins on the interpersonal or social plane before it is internalized as intrapersonal knowledge. The active and creative roles of individuals further influence language development. Vygotsky indicates that children are part of a social construct, actively experiencing and internalizing the environment, making meaning of it, and in turn influencing it, just as the social situation influences

operant conditioning Built on the work of Ivan Pavlov, Skinner's theory of operant conditioning is based on the premise that reinforced behaviours will tend to continue, while those that are punished or are not reinforced gradually end.

language acquisition device (LAD) The term Chomsky used to refer to the system of language that children are born with in their brains. The LAD contains a set of rules that is common to all languages. Children use these rules to understand their native language (Frost et al., 2012).

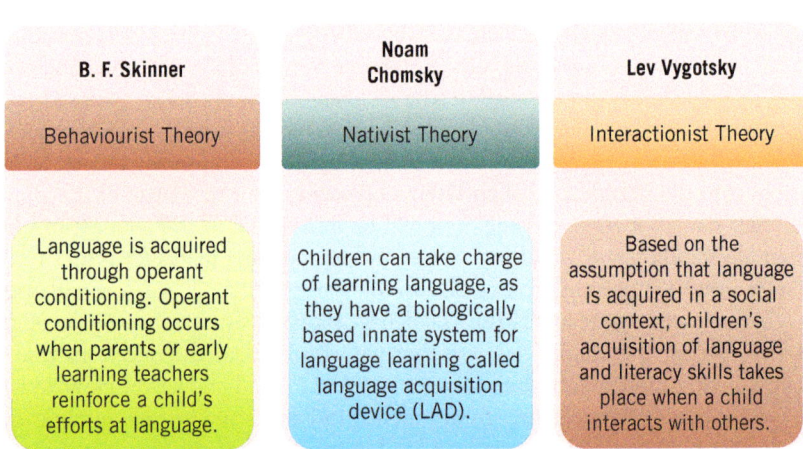

Figure 10.1 Theories and theorists on language acquisition.

children. Vygotsky's view of the way that social, individual, and creative growth are intertwined helps us further understand his idea of the *zone of proximal development* (Kashin, 2009). The term **scaffolding** (Wood, Bruner, & Ross, 1976) describes the transition from interpersonal to intrapersonal knowledge. Through *scaffolding*, learners are able to cross the zone of proximal development: "The distance between the actual developmental level as determined by independent problem solving and the level of potential development as determined through problem solving under adult guidance or in collaboration with more capable peers" (Vygotsky, 1978, p. 86).

scaffolding A fundamental principle of nature whereby one concept is built upon a previous learning structure, thereby ensuring its stable integration into the child's knowledge or skill base (Dietze, 2006).

STOP ... THINK ... DISCUSS ... REFLECT

How do you think children acquire language? How do you think children learn to read and write? The answers to these questions form your current beliefs about language and literacy. Now relate your answers to play. How do you value play as a vehicle for language and literacy learning? Is play part of your values and beliefs? It will be helpful to write down your answers and save them. Share your answers with a classmate and continue to reflect on your values and beliefs as you review this chapter. At the end of the chapter, you may want to stop and consider whether you have changed or adjusted any of your values and beliefs.

CURIOUS?

Do an Internet search for information on how to teach reading in the early years. Have you discovered different perspectives and views on how children learn to read?

FROM THEORY TO TRENDS

Throughout the decades, we are able to trace certain types of language learning methods that have become trendy. In the past 60 years, there have been shifts back and forth between whole language approaches to reading and writing and the phonic approach. For example, Flesch (1955) proposed that the best way to teach children to read was through a phonic or direct instruction approach. At the time, a whole-word method was dominant in schools. There continues to be debate among educators and the media about the merits of both approaches. The disagreements on how to teach reading have been characterized as the phonics debate (Pressley & Allington, 2014). These approaches reflect different underlying philosophies and stress different skills. The two methods are featured in Figure 10.2.

Today, the research in early literacy provides new approaches and understandings that differ from the tenets of either traditional phonics or whole language philosophies (Cecil, 2017). Now early learning teachers are encouraged to look beyond the restrictions of the traditional approaches. Using research evidence on language and literacy development, teachers are now creating clearer and more purposeful programming and experiential experiences for children based on interests, capabilities, developmental needs, and milestones (Pressley & Allington, 2014). Children benefit most in environments where experiences are customized to meet the individual needs and strengths of children, rather

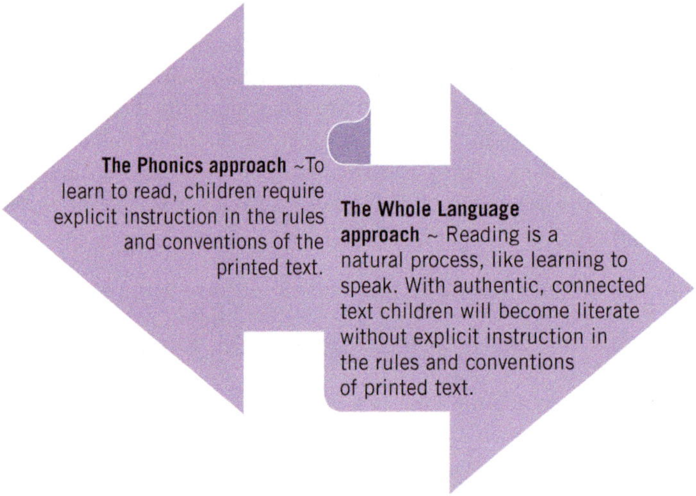

The Phonics approach ~To learn to read, children require explicit instruction in the rules and conventions of the printed text.

The Whole Language approach ~ Reading is a natural process, like learning to speak. With authentic, connected text children will become literate without explicit instruction in the rules and conventions of printed text.

Figure 10.2 Approaches to literacy.

than where activities are implemented based on a particular philosophy or approach. Similar to other programming areas, early learning teachers observe children, examine development phases, engage in discussion with children, and respond with appropriate materials and experiences that will support their developmental phase and interests during play (Jones & Reynolds, 2015). This approach values both the children's and the early learning teacher's input and suggests that individuals, whether they are adults or children, have substantial influence on what happens in the environment and how they execute their learning options. Examine Photo 10.2 to view how a child's interest in bridge building is supported by materials and a resource book.

Photo 10.2 A preschool child building bridges.
Used with Permission of Shannon Terrana

The scope of language and literacy research and knowledge for children is immense. We begin by examining core definitions for language and literacy. These definitions are intended to help you think about the complexity of language and literacy development and introduce you to the breadth of this area of programming.

DEFINING LANGUAGE DEVELOPMENT

Researchers and educators define language development in a variety of ways. Broadly defined, language development is viewed as the process by which children come to understand and communicate language during early childhood. Language is speech, the written symbols for speech, or any other means of communication. Language development follows a predictable sequence. It requires individuals to engage in communication strategies (Bates, 2014).

Language development is categorized in terms of receptive and expressive language. **Receptive language** is the ability to listen and understand the spoken, signed, or written word. **Expressive language** is the ability to communicate or to use language. It is what a child says or signs. This eventually includes what the child prints. Expressive language is also referred to as productive language. Usually, receptive language develops faster than expressive language (Chambers, Cheung, & Slavin, 2016).

receptive language The ability to listen and understand the spoken, signed, or written word.

expressive language The ability to communicate or to use language.

DEFINING LITERACY DEVELOPMENT

Literacy is commonly defined as the ability to read and write the printed text that represents spoken language—that is, to be literate (Kucer, 2014). **Emergent literacy** refers to the earliest signs of interest in and abilities related to reading and writing (Whitehurst & Lonigan, 1998). These early signs of literacy are the precursors of literacy development; they precede conventional reading and writing (Mayer & Trezek, 2015).

Learning to become literate is a gradual process that begins at birth and continues throughout life. Literacy is continually evolving through interactions with others and the environment. Although the sequence of literacy development follows the same general pattern, individual rates of growth may vary depending on life experiences and cognitive processes. "Children cannot become literate alone. They need the help of others to claim their own unique literacy" (McVicker, 2007, p. 18), and early learning teachers along with parents can rise to this challenge. Play is a key factor in developing language and literacy skills.

literacy The ability to read and write the printed text that represents spoken language.

emergent literacy The earliest signs of interest in and abilities related to reading and writing.

Play and Language

Oral language is identified as the process used in developing communication skills and in facilitating both early reading and writing skills (Shanahan, 2016). Early learning teachers have a major role in providing learning environments that promote interpersonal communication among children and adults. The role modelling that occurs through body language, conversations, and print format in the various experience or learning centres and during play episodes helps children to connect oral language, reading, print, and play to daily living.

Vygotsky made the connections between play, early learning experiences, and language development. Language development requires children to have experiences that unite thoughts with language through inner speech. **Inner speech** is described as the silent speech that becomes part of our thought processes (Bruner, 1976). This internal process is influenced by children's social network and psychological state. As children

oral language The process used in developing communication skills and in facilitating both early reading and writing skills.

inner speech The silent speech that becomes part of our thought processes.

Photo 10.3 Discovering letters in the outdoor environment.

Used with Permission of Gill Robertson

engage in play, an internalization process contributes to many facets of speech development (Vygotsky, 1980). For example, when we observe children talking to themselves, they might be working out a problem, developing a plan, or trying to figure out how something works. This process helps children to self-regulate their thoughts and actions. In essence, children are expressing literate behaviours that assist them in developing the framework for literacy development. Play and life experiences, including social skills and family and adult interactions, add to the opportunities that children have for language and literacy skills to evolve.

Play experiences are essential for literate behaviours to develop. The examples below illustrate how children's play and language are connected.

1. Play provides children with the venue to express themselves in specific play experiences or as they explore an element of their environment. For example, Martin is trying to figure out how to build a tower that will be stable. He says, "If I place this big board on the block and then put smaller blocks on it, maybe my tower will stay." He is talking through possible solutions.

2. Play, such as solitary, parallel, and cooperative play, supports children in developing language, literacy, and communication skills. For example, in the sand area, Melinda

Photo 10.4 Drawing letters in the mud.

Used with Permission of Gill Robertson

and Max are using pails and shovels. Melinda fills hers and uses a wooden spoon to compact the sand. Max watches and then says, "Why do you want the sand to stick in the pail?" Melinda responds, "I don't know." Then a few minutes later she says, "I think it makes a pattern."

3. Unique play experiences help children incorporate new language into the play, which may further expand the quality and complexity of the play experience. For example, as Melinda thinks about the pail and the sand and as she tries to remove the sand from the pail, she realizes that it is compacted. She then says to Max, "Look what I did." Max and she then use other types of containers to get different shapes. With each success, they giggle. When they have four different shapes, Max says, "What will we make?" Melinda says, "Let's make a tower with a turret and a bridge that goes up and down."

4. Play leads children to explore and discover new knowledge, reframe information, or confirm knowledge, including language and literacy skills. For example, Mia, a 4-year-old from China, is learning English. Her peers help her with the pronunciation of words and matching words with objects.

Later in the chapter, we examine the role of the early learning teacher in supporting children with their language and literacy development. Children require early childhood environments and play experiences that create and support opportunities for them to establish literate behaviours and make the interconnections of play to communication and language and to culture and community.

Characteristics of Language Development

Language development is a complex process. It is a gradual, sequential process. Early learning teachers influence a child's vocabulary development and communication process through role modelling. They facilitate development through the play and language opportunities

Photo 10.5 Print in the environment.

Used with Permission of Diane Kashin

extended to children throughout the day. Children's language development flourishes in environments where language and literacy experiences are integrated into every aspect of the day's programming and experiences. In the block centre, for example, early learning teachers provide paper, magazines, signs, and tools for writing signs. This approach supports children in linking play and learning to language and literacy development.

Language development includes the development of grammar, vocabulary, and pragmatics. Understanding the framework of each of these components helps early learning teachers to incorporate language experiences into programming that reflects the developmental milestones common among each of the age groups and the interests of individual children.

Grammar

By the age of 2, toddlers typically speak in two-word utterances, mostly composed of nouns and verbs with some adjectives and adverbs. For example, "Me go." By the age of 5, a typical sentence can contain four or five words. For example, "I want to eat carrots." As children begin to use longer sentences, they demonstrate that they know grammatical rules, such as the use of plurals, possession, and tense in nouns and verbs. These are considered the rules of **morphology**, which involves the structure of words. As children learn the order of words in a sentence, they are learning **syntax**. Morphology and syntax rules relate to the understanding of sounds and grammar of language. A third system of rules in language development is **semantics**. Semantics involves the meaning of words and vocabulary development (Frost et al., 2012).

Vocabulary

When children are in stimulating play environments that offer challenge and new opportunities for exploration and are rich with language, they will acquire vocabulary at an astonishing rate of an average of five new words per day. As words are added to their vocabulary, children make basic assumptions about a word's meaning. Children use the words and hear them used in different contexts. Then they refine their understanding of the meaning of a word (Berk, 2013). For example, Katie, age 3, said to her mother one day, "The butterfly was astonishingly beautiful." Such vocabulary at the age of 3 is unusual. The exposure to butterflies and language had a significant influence on Katie's vocabulary.

Pragmatics

The pragmatics of language refers to the rules for carrying out a conversation or communicating. Young children learn the rules of conversation, such as eye contact and taking turns, from their role models. By the age of 4, children have learned acceptable ways to communicate in their language community. They are able to adapt their language to different situations (Frost et al., 2012).

morphology The study and structure of the form of words, including the use of plurals, possession, and tense in nouns and verbs (Frost et al., 2012).

syntax Refers to a set of grammatical rules that includes word order and use of inflections. Children learn to ask questions and to make negative statements (Santrock, 2010).

semantics Involves the knowledge of meanings of words demonstrated through an expanding vocabulary (Frost et al., 2012).

Photo 10.6 Adapting language to different situations.

Used with Permission of Amanda Benton

Early learning teachers can take guidance from children's varying stages of language and literacy development to support their language and literacy acquisition. According to Kostelnik, Soderman, and Whiren (2011), children's development hinges on their:

- Neurological maturity;
- Language exposure;
- Interactions with others;
- Focus on print;
- Engaging in new opportunities to apply language learning.

The connection between language and literacy acquisition is complex, requiring early learning students and teachers to be aware of the stages of oral language, as this is the foundation to becoming fully literate. Adapted from Feeney, Moravcik, and Nolte (2013), Table 10.1 details the stages of language development.

Stages of Language Development

After 5 years of age, children's ability to use language increases rapidly, including:

- Reaching a vocabulary of 40 000 words by grade 5;
- Understanding grammar by age 6;
- Becoming adept at pragmatic uses of language—they choose words, modify sentences, or change voice inflections to fit the listener in a particular situation (i.e., simpler words and shorter sentences when talking to a younger sibling, code switching when speaking to an adult—e.g., inserting the word *please*) (Tough, 2012).

Table 10.1 Stages of language development.

From Birth	**Sounds**	Making and responding to sounds. Crying, gurgling, and cooing.
By 12 months	**Babbling**	Engaging in pseudo-language, babbling to mimic the language that they hear.
By 24 months	**Holophrases**	Holophrases are when first words stand in for a variety of meaningful sentences. The child says *car* while looking out the window; he means *Look at the car outside*. Children use holophrases to increase their expressive language. Receptive language or understanding words may be more developed.
Between 18 and 24 months	**Two-Word Sentences**	Two words are used to express ideas that relate, such as *cat sleeping* or *drink milk*. At this age, vocabulary could include 300 words.
After 24 months	**Telegraphic Sentences**	Short and simple sentences. *Where daddy go? Me push truck.*
From age 3 to 4	**Joined Sentences**	Related sentences are joined, expressing ideas about time and spatial relationships. Adult forms of language are used, such as *Let's read this story*. Vocabulary increases to nearly 1000 words.

When children enter middle childhood, teachers continue to have a responsibility to encourage language and literacy skills. Ongoing language development is crucial because it is the basis for social interactions. Early learning teachers incorporate many opportunities for children to interact with others, including shared reading, role playing, discussions, and storytelling. However, not all children will be equally amenable to holding conversations. Some children are more social than others.

CHILDREN'S CONVERSATIONAL ROLES

According to Weitzman and Greenberg (2002), there are four conversational styles typical of young children that will help early learning students and teachers "appreciate which children are likely to need more encouragement to initiate and interact:

1. The Socialable Child—initiates and responds with ease.
2. The Reluctant Child—seldom initiates but responds when he or she "warms up" and feels comfortable.
3. The Child with His or Her Own Agenda—plays alone, initiates only when he or she needs something (if this style is persistent, it may be indicative of a social-pragmatic disorder).
4. The Passive Child—seldom responds or initiates (persistent passivity can be indicative of a developmental delay) (Justice, 2006, pp. 144–145).

Understanding conversational styles helps you gain insight into why some children communicate naturally and why others find it difficult to do so. Children's conversational styles guide the early learning teacher in how to approach each child. This guides early learning teachers in determining which strategies will be most effective in facilitating language experiences among individual children and with groups of children.

OBSERVING, WAITING, AND LISTENING (THE HANEN CENTRE OWL STRATEGY)

You will note throughout this text that we advocate for observation and use of pedagogical documentation to be a consistent practice for early learning teachers. Observing, waiting, and listening (OWL) is a strategy rather than an observation tool. Early learning students and teachers can employ the OWL strategy as a way to support children in reaching their fullest potential for conversations. *Observing* means paying close attention to children so that you can gain insight into the interests of individual children and what they are trying to tell you. *Waiting* is a powerful tool because it gives children an opportunity to initiate and to take control of their role in the conversation. *Listening* means paying close attention to what children are saying so that you can respond appropriately (Weitzman & Greenberg, 2002). Sometimes teachers are too quick to respond to children's actions with a question, and often it is a testing question, such as "What colour is it?" When the objective is to enhance conversation, testing questions can be a conversation stopper. Early learning teachers are encouraged to adopt the strategy of *observe, wait,* and *listen* and to watch children closely to determine their interests. Then the teacher is able to effectively focus comments or questions on those interests. Sometimes by just pausing (waiting) before speaking, children will have an opportunity to speak and will tell you their interests and aspirations.

CURIOUS?

Do an Internet search for *The Hanen Centre—Speech and Language Development for Children* to find out more about this organization and what it does.

Language Skills and Play

As identified by Susan in Sharing Stories of Practice at the beginning of the chapter, early learning teachers are often asked by parents how language and literacy skills are acquired if the children are *only* playing all day rather than receiving specific lessons and instructions. One of the key roles for early learning teachers is to provide families with meaningful examples of how children use drawings, scribbling, pretend writing, storytelling, and invented spelling in their play as precursors to the more formalized language and literacy skills that will be acquired in school settings. Early learning teachers describe the scaffolding process of language development and discuss the need for children to have a foundation in the use of language gained through tangible, concrete play before they are able to produce words in the printed format. When children are exposed to experiences that offer them a sense of curiosity and intrigue, such experiences motivate them in their play, which enhances their competencies in their communication strategies during play episodes.

Children, Play, and Communication Skills

During spontaneous and guided play, children are communicating. They are involved in interaction among the people in their presence and in gathering information. Weitzman and Greenberg (2002) identified that children have seven reasons to communicate throughout their play processes:

1. To make a request of another person.
2. To protest something, such as complaining or rejecting something.
3. To greet or to say good-bye.
4. To respond to another person's words or conversation.
5. To seek information, such as to ask a question.
6. To verbalize thinking, planning, or problem solving.
7. To express feelings, ideas, or perspectives.

Halliday (1975) called this process "learning how to mean," as children discover that what they say translates to what can be done. Children use communication to meet a variety of goals. For example, they communicate to think, to plan, and to problem solve. During pretend play, these communication strategies are evident because of the varying roles that children engage in. When children use language to plan a storyline for their dramatic play, they are using **metacommunication**, which is communicating about communication (Matteoni, 2013).

Each of the seven communication areas is important for children to practise during their play because these areas formulate the foundation for their communication abilities and their abilities to express social and emotional attributes.

metacommunication When children communicate about how an interaction will take place. They constantly negotiate what and how they are playing, how they will continue to play, and often even interpretations of past play events (Sawyer, 1997).

Children Learn Purposeful Verbal Interaction During Play

While children are playing, they use language. They ask for materials. They express ideas or ask questions of others. For example, when children are role-playing during dramatic play, they plan the play, manage the play, problem solve, and maintain the play by verbal explanations, discussions, or commands. This process illustrates highly developed language (Isenberg & Jalongo, 2014). Children learn verbal language best when the experience is meaningful and purposeful, such as in sociodramatic play. Play is a meaningful context in which to embed language opportunities.

Children Learn to Play with Language

Children use language during play, and they play with language. As children develop, language play becomes more complex. Younger children playfully experiment with words, syllables, sounds, and grammatical structure. School-aged children joke, make riddles, and use jump-rope rhymes as part of their play with language. These forms of language play require the ability to explore the phonological, syntactic, and semantic rules of language (Isenberg & Jalongo, 2014). The words and meanings children learn depend on their experiences and the language they hear. As children's vocabularies expand, they require many opportunities to use words (Richards & Rodgers, 2014). As a result, early learning teachers develop opportunities to expose children to more complicated language and to use it as required.

Characteristics of Literacy Development

Play in the early years significantly influences children's literacy skills. Developmentally appropriate play experiences support children in gaining extraordinary powers that are essential foundational skills needed for later reading and writing. For example, sociodramatic play and literacy require children to use cognitive processes such as imaging, categorizing, and problem solving (Smith, Cowie, & Blades, 2015). These cognitive processes are foundational to literacy development. As you examine the next section, think about your role as an early learning teacher or student. Explore your thoughts about literacy, and reflect on how the early learning environments that you have been exposed to have supported literacy practices. What aspects of literacy stand out for you? What additions might you recommend?

Literacy development is related to language development. Children initially communicate most often through oral language. When children gain the ability to read and write, it extends their possibilities to transmit and receive information. From a development perspective, children are first exposed to print and written language through books. Initially, children are unable to interpret words in print or to print using adult forms of the alphabet or to use standard spelling. As children become familiar with books and print in their environments (home and early learning settings), as well as oral language, they make connections among pictures, print, and language, while being exposed to the principles needed to become literate. Children gradually understand that the print, not just the pictures, gives meaning to books. They begin to recognize print, as well as the spacing between words, and learn that individual letters are used to form words (Frost et al., 2012). Think about the excitement of children when they begin to recognize their names or produce their names on their artwork. When this occurs, it is a signal that a new phase of language and literacy development is unfolding.

In 1966, New Zealand researcher Marie Clay introduced the term *emergent* to describe what children know about reading and writing before they begin to read and

Photo 10.7 Producing names in artwork.

Used with Permission of Diane Kashin

write in the conventional way. Clay created the Reading Recovery Program, a well-established intervention scheme for children with reading difficulties. The program identifies those having difficulty with reading early in their school career. The work of Marie Clay affirmed the importance of the preschool years in the development of literacy skills. The more exposure younger children have to books and print, the less likely it is that they will need intervention. However, Clay reminded early learning teachers that some children need extra resources and supportive interventions from teachers to progress to the stage of self-managed learning. The key to Clay's suggestion for intervention is that it is supportive and that an adult helps to *scaffold* children's learning and development (Gibson & Moss, 2016).

Stages of Literacy Development

Stage theorists suggest that children progress through stages as they develop literacy skills. Skebo and colleagues (2013) suggested that there are five stages of literacy development over our lifespan, as outlined in Figure 10.3. Early learning teachers focus on Stage 0, or the pre-reading stage, from birth to 6 years of age. During this time, children have the capacity, when exposed to print, to learn **graphemes** and memorize labels and signs in the environment. The decoding stage, or Stage 1 (ages 6 to 7 years), includes the development of letter–sound correspondence rules and the use of the **alphabetic principle**. In Stage 3, ages 10 to 12 years, children are able to use reading as a tool for learning new information. In Stage 4, ages 14 to 18 years, reading is refined, and there is an ability to comprehend complex information. The final stage occurs in college and beyond, with the attainment of adult reading skills.

graphemes Letters that represent a sound.

alphabetic principle The understanding that letters represent sounds that form words.

334 Chapter 10 Language, Emergent Literacy, and Play

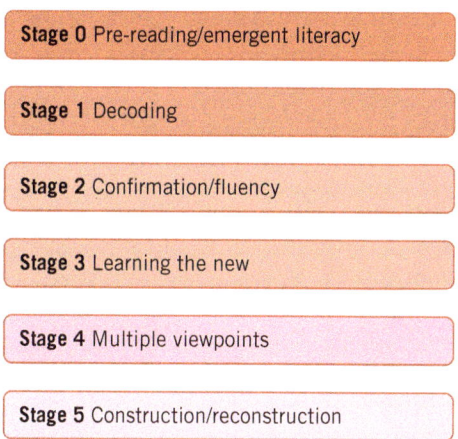

Figure 10.3 Stages of literacy development.

The Importance of Child Participation in Emerging Literacy

Children learn to construct meaning and comprehend text from exposure to books. Families and early learning teachers who read aloud to children are supporting emerging literacy. The way children respond to being read to provides adults with information on how to scaffold the language and literacy experiences for optimal development. How children respond when listening to books becomes more and more complex and varied as they get older. McVicker (2007) identified three modes of reader response for preschoolers. They are:

1. **Imitation:** of language, language patterns, action, emotion, art, peers, literacy behaviours, and story.
2. **Imagination:** predicting, pretending, and creating props.
3. **Interaction:** group talk, questions, agreements and arguments, empathy talk, literacy talk, idea sharing, and role playing.

McVicker (2007) described seven modes of reader for school-aged children. They are:

1. **Listening behaviour:** stretching to see, spontaneous laughter, chanting repetitive phrases, and nudging closer to the book.
2. **Contact with books:** browsing and choosing, attention to books, and proximity of books.
3. **Impulse to share:** reading together, telling about a book, sharing discoveries, and sharing connections.
4. **Action and drama:** echoing the actions, dramatic play, and reader's theatre.
5. **Making things:** visual representation, constructions, cooking, and musical response.
6. **Oral response:** retelling/storytelling, prompted responses, and literature discussions.
7. **Written response:** literature, response journals, and answers to teacher prompts.

It is important to understand that "children's development is uneven" and that "many preschoolers also use some of the seven modes described for 5 to 12 year old children" (McVicker, 2007, p. 20).

Photo 10.8 A school-aged child makes a sign.

Used with Permission of Diane Kashin

LITERACY SKILLS AND PLAY

Most children's first attempts at reading and writing will occur during sociodramatic play if appropriate reading and writing tools are present. Imagine setting up the dramatic play area with grocery story flyers, pictures of food with written labels, and paper and pencils to create shopping lists. Children practise reading and writing through their play in the "grocery store." According to Isenberg and Jalongo (2014), their play can reveal the following literacy understandings:

1. **Interest in stories, knowledge of story structure, and story comprehension.** When children show eagerness to hear stories read aloud and retell the stories in their own versions, they are demonstrating interest in stories. When they retell a story and it has characters, a plot, a setting, goals, and conflict, they show knowledge of story structure. Opportunities to act out the stories contribute to children developing or expanding their story comprehension skills.

2. **Understanding fantasy in books.** During dramatic play, children can enter the play world "as if" they were another character. When children develop the ability to transform oneself in play, it enables them to enter the fantasy world of books (Isenberg & Jalongo, 2014). This leads children to be exposed to *decontextualized* language. The benefit of supporting children in engaging in decontextualized language experiences is that it facilitates children experiencing the here and now and moving into the imaginary world of fantasy.
3. **Symbolic representation.** As children reinvent or create their own versions of stories, it helps them to understand the world around them. Through play, children represent their understandings symbolically. They are able to represent their knowledge (Isenberg & Jalongo, 2014).

STOP ... THINK ... DISCUSS .... REFLECT

Think about your role as a storyteller. What strengths do you have? What kinds of silly stories might you create to spark children's interest in storytelling? If you have never done this before, how do you develop that skill?

NARRATIVES OR STORYTELLING

A narrative is the telling of a story. Between the ages of 3 and 4, children begin to develop their narrative skills. Narratives are thought to form from oral language to literacy. Stories require more complex language skills than are needed for daily conversations. Children begin to tell stories by recounting personal experiences. Stadler and Ward (2005) identified five levels that children go through in the development of narratives.

1. **Labelling:** Giving labels to people and objects is a necessary stage for the development of narratives.
2. **Listing:** Children move from labelling to listing when their story focuses on a list of things, such as a character's actions.
3. **Connecting:** At this stage, the character's actions are linked to a central topic or to certain events.
4. **Sequencing:** Once a child is able to use correct temporal sequencing and cause and effect, he or she has moved from connecting to sequencing.
5. **Narrating:** This stage combines all of the components of the previous stages, but now the child's story has a predictable beginning and end. Plots are more developed.

Early learning teachers can encourage narrative development in children through the use of props as catalysts for storytelling; examples of such props are pictures, sequences of pictures, wordless picture books, puppets, blocks and other constructive play materials, dramatic play props, and drawing and painting (Stadler & Ward, 2005).

Vivian Paley is famous for telling stories of her practice as a kindergarten teacher, where she encouraged children to tell and act out their own narratives. She has written books on the topic, including *In Mrs. Tully's Room*, which illustrates that children as young as 2 years of age are capable of enacting their own stories. Her book *A Child's Work* explores the importance of fantasy play in the growth and development of young children.

Fantasy play is the work of children. It is through this type of play that they learn. Paley (2004) illustrated that it is not only important to provide children with opportunities to tell and enact stories but also important to understand that when teachers listen and try to make sense of the children's stories, they too are joining in an experience that scaffolds learning. Paley refers to Vygotsky's perspective, which indicates that children rise above their average behaviour in fantasy play and that teachers develop alongside as they encourage storytelling and dramatic play in their classrooms (Paley, 2004).

CURIOUS?

Do an Internet search for *Vivian Paley* to learn more about her work with children and storytelling.

Variations in Language and Literacy Development

While language and literacy development follows a predictable sequence, not all children will progress through the stages at the same rate. The variations are due to many factors, such as motivation, culture, gender, developmental delays, family background, and the children's family language. Early learning teachers become familiar with each of these areas so that they can work with individual children and their families in appropriate ways.

Motivation

The research indicates that there are critical content areas for early literacy: oral language comprehension, phonological awareness, and print knowledge. Another critical factor that is emerging is referred to as dispositions. A disposition is defined as a tendency to exhibit frequently, consciously, and voluntarily a pattern of behaviour that is directed to a broad goal (Georgeson & Campbell-Barr, 2015). For example, if the goal is early literacy, the assumption is that children require the motivation to read and write. Print motivation is the frequency of requests for shared reading and engagement in print-related activities, such as pretend writing (Carroll, 2013). Early learning teachers cultivate children's disposition to early literacy by creating environments that model literacy principles and practices. This would include facilitating, reinforcing, and becoming aware of "teachable moments" such as the following:

- Willingness to listen to stories;
- Desire to be read to;
- Curiosity about words and letters;
- Exploration of print forms;
- Playfulness with words;
- Enjoyment of songs, poems, rhymes, jingles, books, and dramatic play.

Culture

Children enter early learning environments with different family structures and cultures. Many families living in Canada today speak languages other than English or French in the home environment. As a result, children may enter early learning programs with vast differences in their language skills (Frost et al., 2012). Regardless of children's cultural background or first language, early learning teachers embrace and respect the diverse language skills that children and their families present.

How many different languages are spoken by children and their families in Canada? Do an Internet search to find out. Keep searching to find out the illiteracy rates in Canada. Do they look different between provinces and territories?

Early learning teachers appreciate that young children need to develop proficiency in their family language as well as in English or French. While some children are *bilingual* or even *multilingual*, speaking more than one language has many benefits for all children (Ellis, 2015). Early learning teachers and children celebrate the various cultural backgrounds and reach out to involve all families in their programs. This partnership not only supports the children but also helps families and teachers in developing strategies to facilitate each stage of language development that children are learning. Preschool children may become frustrated because of their limited communication skills in a particular language. Often they will exhibit their frustration through unacceptable behaviours such as biting, bullying, and temper tantrums. Early learning teachers understand this and provide children with relevant support.

Exposing children to the various languages spoken by their peers is an effective strategy in modelling an atmosphere of respect and appreciation of cultural diversity. Early learning teachers acknowledge the social nature of language. This means that children will want to communicate with their peers. School-aged children not only will want to learn the language but also will be striving to gain cultural knowledge.

English Language Learners

The term *English language learners (ELLs)* is used to identify children whose family language is not English and who are learning English as a second or third language. When working with children whose first language is not English, it is important to provide them with input that is comprehensible and above their level of competence. This method of scaffolding is an important technique when working with ELLs because it advances children's ability to figure out words and their meanings in various contexts. Early learning teachers, through observations, offer experiences that build on the strengths of each child. The environment reflects the languages and cultures of the children present. Children are encouraged to continue to develop their first language at the same time that they develop a second language (Ellis, 2015).

Family

The family is the earliest learning environment that children are exposed to. Families play a crucial role in children's early learning experiences, including building strong language and literacy skills. Of all the influences on children's language growth, families are the most important. The environments that families provide, combined with their attitudes toward learning language and literacy skills, make a substantial contribution

family literacy Home literacy experiences that help children and all families to develop literacy skills.

to the children's development (Fernald & Weisleder, 2015). Early learning teachers are encouraged to promote **family literacy**, as this contributes to providing children with the optimal emerging literacy development opportunities.

> ### STOP ... THINK ... DISCUSS ... REFLECT
>
> How do you envision you could support families in expanding literacy opportunities for their children? What community resources are available to support families?

Other Variations

Researchers who have studied familial and cultural differences in the language that children hear indicate that mothers speak with daughters more than with sons (Johnson, Caskey, Rand, Tucker, & Vohr, 2014). This suggests that there are gender variations in language development. Middle-class families use more elaborate language with their children than do families from lower socioeconomic environments. This means that there can be socioeconomic variations in language development. Families generally speak more to first-born children than to later-born children and multiple-birth children. This suggests that there can be birth-order variations in language development (Frost et al., 2012). Research helps early learning teachers understand variations in language and literacy.

Photo 10.9 An opportunity to play with letters.

Used with Permission of Diane Kashin

THE ROLES OF EARLY LEARNING TEACHERS

As with other aspects of play and learning, early learning teachers have a variety of important roles to execute in order to support children's language and literacy experiences and opportunities. Early learning teachers are important role models for children. Because language and literacy skills are being developed at an incredible pace during the early years and are influenced by the adults in the children's lives, early learning teachers must exhibit appropriate language skills. As you examine the upcoming section, you will note the influence that you, the environment, and the experiences within the environment have on children developing foundational language and literacy skills.

Early Learning Teacher Interactions

Weitzman and Greenberg (2002) identified seven different "teacher roles" related to the development of language and literacy. The way in which early learning teachers interact with children is likely to vary, depending on environments and situations.

1. **The director role.** In this role, the early learning teacher maintains tight control over the children and their activities. The focus is on making suggestions, giving directions, and asking questions. The adult behaviour tells children that they are not expected to initiate, just to respond as directed. While an early learning teacher needs to direct children some of the time, if this is the predominant role, it makes it very difficult for children to be spontaneous and to play an active role in interactions.
2. **The entertainer role.** In this role, the early learning teacher is playful and fun to be with. The teacher typically does most of the talking and playing, giving children few opportunities to get actively involved in the interaction.
3. **The timekeeper role.** In this role, the early learning teacher rushes through activities and routines in order to stay on schedule. Busy schedules are a fact of life, but this role can and does result in very limited interactions.
4. **The too-quiet teacher role.** In this role, the early learning teacher sits with the children but hardly interacts with them, even when they initiate dialogue.
5. **The helper role.** In this role, the early learning teacher thinks that children will not be able to express thoughts, so the adult speaks for a child or groups of children or offers help before children have shown any need for it. This may reflect an early learning teacher's desire to help children or to reduce frustration. It may result in children having less confidence in being able to communicate verbally.
6. **The cheerleader role.** In this role, the early learning teacher gives children a lot of praise and gets very excited when they accomplish a task, large or small. Words of encouragement such as "Good" or "Good job!" are often expressed. Positive reinforcement is evident. Children seem to get pleasure from praise. The disadvantage of praise is that children can become too dependent on it and may not develop their own motivation to learn new skills or take on new challenges. In addition, cheerleaders often end the conversation with their praise—the interaction seldom continues after the child has been praised.
7. **The responsive partner role.** In this role, the early learning teacher is tuned in to the children's abilities, needs, and interests. The adult responds with warmth and interest to children, which encourages them to take an active part in interactions, both with the adult and with their peers.

The experiences that an early learning teacher provides to encourage language and literacy development are as important as how the teacher responds to children's words and stories. The more opportunities that children have to speak in the environment, especially with adults, the more extensive and advanced their vocabulary will be when they enter kindergarten. Children need to progress from *learning to talk* to *talking to learn*—the latter is dependent on the ability to use **decontextualized language**, which is language removed from the here and now. An example of a here-and-now context is a teacher speaking to children about a snack. An example of the use of decontextualized language is an adult sharing a storybook with children. Here, children have the opportunity to use language in more complex and abstract ways not connected to their current context. Written language is also decontextualized—that is, the sender and receiver of a written communication usually do not share the same space (Roskos, Christie, & Richgeis, 2003).

Early learning teachers encourage interaction and provide information when they share books with children. As a student, it is beneficial to take every opportunity you can to read to children. Reading aloud is one of the most successful strategies for promoting emergent literacy skills among preschool-aged children. Small group interactive reading improves children's vocabulary and print awareness and, in some cases, emerging writing skills (Sim, Berthelsen, Walker, Nicholson, & Fielding-Barnsley, 2014).

> **decontextualized language**
> Abstract language that is removed from the here and now (Rowe, 2013). For example, talking about an event in the future with a child is decontextualized language.

STOP ... THINK ... DISCUSS ... REFLECT

If small-group interactive reading was successful in improving children's vocabulary, print awareness, and emerging writing skills, do you think a large-group reading activity would be equally as successful? Imagine reading to a group of four preschool children. Now imagine reading to a group of 24.

Students and early learning teachers encourage interaction and provide information by asking children questions. There are two common types of questions we use when conversing with children: closed questions and open-ended questions.

Closed Questions:

- Require a nonverbal response or a one- or two-word answer from children;
- Tend to have right or wrong answers;
- Are ones to which adults already know the answers;
- Require a "quick" response;
- Focus on facts and similarity in thinking;
- Ask for information and focus on labelling or naming;
- Require the child to recall something from memory.

Open-Ended Questions:

- Promote multiword, multiphrase responses from children;
- Have more than one correct answer;
- Are questions to which adults do not know what children's answers might be;
- Allow children time to formulate and collect their thoughts;
- Focus on ideas and originality in thinking;

- Ask for reasoning;
- Focus on thinking and problem solving;
- Require the children to use their imagination.

Which type of questions do you think are preferable? Many students are guided to use open-ended questions to encourage children's language. However, early learning teachers strive to establish natural conversations with children. Sometimes it is acceptable to ask a closed question within the context of a back-and-forth dialogue. Perhaps preferable to both the closed question and the open-ended question is the *cognitively challenging* or *thought-provoking question*. Instead of asking a child, "What shape is the structure?" ask the child to tell you what the structure is. When the child replies that it is "a house," ask, "Who lives in the house?" When a child holds up a shell to an ear, the conversation is in jeopardy of ending when closed questions are asked, such as, "What do you hear?" Continue the conversation by provoking children's thinking, such as by asking, "How did the sound of the ocean get into the shell?" These types of questions challenge children to think deeply. When you test children's knowledge and ask questions such as "What colour is it?" or "What shape is it?" children will have their comfort reduced in the environment. They will feel as though they are always being tested. An early learning environment that supports language and literacy development encourages conversations to occur during play and provides opportunities to support these experiences with print.

THE EARLY LEARNING ENVIRONMENT

Adding literacy-rich areas to the play environment improves children's phonological awareness. Increasing the amount of environmental print in the play space facilitates the likelihood of children engaging in literacy-related play activities (Markussen-Brown et al., 2017). However, there is a need to find balance with print materials. When the environment becomes saturated with print materials, it will detract from children's abilities to engage with the print. Early literacy experiences are embedded in the basic experiences of early learning—these include reading aloud, group time, small-group activities, adult–child conversations, and play. When early learning teachers partner with children in their play experiences, there are opportunities to enrich literacy. A literacy-enriched play environment exposes children to valuable print experiences and lets them practise narrative skills (Niranjanan, 2016).

Creating a Community Culture for Language and Literacy

How can you create a community culture in an early learning environment that supports language and literacy? Consider the following principles to support a literacy-rich environment:

- Reading and writing are tools. Adults and children read and write to accomplish many goals. Reading and writing are incorporated in activities throughout the day. When literacy is seen as a tool, it becomes an integral part of life, not just an isolated skill to be taught.
- Children learn about written language by being in an environment where it is used. Adults model their use of written language for the children in their care. Seeing the power of written language encourages children to want to have this power.
- Children are provided with opportunities to experiment with print.
- Children need to see that written symbols can communicate and can stretch their knowledge and that they can gain meaning from these symbols.

- The environment and the programming schedule provide time, space, and materials to children, and the adults respond to them as members of the literate community.
- Children are provided with opportunities to share their writing and ideas with each other.
- Children are exposed to free-flowing child-initiated and child-directed activities, rather than a structured program.
- Children are encouraged to link symbols having meaning in order to comprehend the meaning of letters and words.
- Children are given the opportunity to read and use pictorial symbols in the early learning environment so that they can become confident in their ability to interpret symbols.

Observations

An early learning teacher observes children experiencing language and literacy throughout the day. A good way for early learning student teachers to begin to learn about language and literacy is through books. Can you remember a particular book from your own childhood? From Dr. Seuss to Robert Munsch—we probably all have books that resonate within each of us. What is your favourite book? What draws you to that book? What questions do you have about the story? Did you ever wonder about the story, about what happened to the characters after the book is finished? Did the story make you think? Books can be wonders. Books can be provocative—they can make you think, question, speculate, predict, and theorize. Introduce a small group of children to your favourite book. Create a schematic map or web with the children about what they wonder about the book. Give the children opportunities to draw their theories. Then record their ideas, questions, and theories to create a documentation panel that illustrates children's learning through reading and related activities.

When choosing books to read to children, consider these guidelines:

1. Select books that you enjoy. Children know when you are reading something you do not like (because you lack enthusiasm). Starting with your favourite childhood story is one way to ensure that you are enthusiastic about reading the book.
2. Choose a book with appropriate content for the children. Ensure that children can identify with at least some parts of the book and its characters.
3. Analyze books for unfavourable racial stereotypes and sexism.
4. Consider the length of the text (not too long), the illustrations (bright, colourful), the size (big enough for everyone to see in a group setting), and the content (is it too complex, can children "participate" in the story?).
5. Consider the author's style. Is it enjoyable? Is the vocabulary clear? Are the phrases memorable? Look for repetition and rhyme in the story. Consider the climax and end of the book. Do these exist? Are they satisfying? Is there humour in the book?
6. Pick a book with educational value. Be sure that the book expands children's knowledge in some way (new vocabulary, new understanding).
7. Examine the illustrations in the book to ensure that they match the text. Do they coordinate with the text and explain what is happening in the story?

Reading to children can be a most enjoyable experience for an adult, but it can also be challenging. How do you hold the book so that a group of children can see the illustrations? Often it is preferable to hold the book in front of you and read upside down. This is a skill that requires practice. During the reading of the story, you can also pause when illustrations appear and slowly move the book so that it scans the whole group. This way, you may not hear the children exclaim over and over, "I can't see!"

Add the words *reading to young children* to a search engine. What have you learned from this search?

The Dramatic Play Centre

Literacy-related play has its roots in the theories of Piaget (1952) and Vygotsky (1978), who both suggest that children learn through play. Dramatic play has been of interest to literacy researchers (Campbell, Torr, & Cologan, 2014). Dramatic play fosters communication, conversational skills, turn-taking, and perspective-taking as well as the skills of social problem solving, persuading, negotiating, compromising, and cooperating. Play requires complex communication skills. Children must be able to communicate and understand the message: *this is play*. A great deal of child-initiated play involves acting out life experiences. These experiences often involve printing, drawing, "reading," and "writing." When a group of children engage in play, it almost always requires speech. Children use speech to direct the play and act out these life situations. When we consider these simple aspects of play, it begins to become evident that language is a key part of play and that play is a key part of language development.

Children are eager to talk to one another so that they can choose characters and settings ("Let's play house in the kitchen centre. I'm the mommy!"). Language is used to establish roles and direct action. As the children take on different roles, they experiment with the language that fits the role. Communication is used to assign roles, define objects, and define action. Children become very adept at moving in and out of roles; first they are the director and then they are actors. Eventually, the children will become such good communicators that they direct play without leaving their acting role.

Written language is a system of symbols, and so is dramatic play. Children use objects and symbols to represent the things they are imagining. This practice with symbols is a good basis for later language development. Finally, dramatic play is child directed, allowing all children to move at their own pace. This means that children are able to participate comfortably at their own level of literacy. Below is a list of items that may be included in dramatic play centres to encourage language and literacy:

- Note pads for doctor's prescriptions or grocery lists;
- Phone message pads for executive assistants and notebooks for waiters and waitresses;
- Maps, tickets, letters, and blueprints in the block centre and books;
- Clothing, tools, and utensils to spark dramatic play.

Writing and Book Centres

Experience centres can be set up that have a specific language and literacy focus. Provide ample tools for printing and writing. Label bookshelves and equipment. Help children make their own books. Encourage children to "write" notes, lists, or letters to one another,

Photo 10.10 Opportunities to print outdoors.

Used with Permission of Diane Kashin

the early learning teachers, and their families. Provide writing materials and print in different forms: iPads, coupons, magazines, resource books, and so on. Include paper supplies, such as envelopes, in your writing centre that will encourage the children to communicate in print.

Shared Group Reading with Children

Reading with children is important for their language development. The smaller the group, the more likely the early learning teacher will be able to interact with the children and provide information to scaffold children's learning. However, many early learning teachers use the commonly referred to "circle" experience as the only time to read to children. These group experiences are often uncomfortable for children if they are forced to sit for long periods of time. "Reading aloud with children is a time-honored and effective way to introduce books and promote literacy skills" (McVicker, 2007, p. 19). Reading to children is most successful when early learning teachers and students read to smaller groups of children, as well as to individual children, as much as possible throughout the day's schedule.

The Art Centre

Children love to talk about their artwork. Asking them to describe what they have drawn or painted is a way to encourage children to use language. When children are creating their artwork, they are also practising fine motor skills that are necessary to develop their ability to print. All types of art materials support language and literacy development. Offer children a variety of art forms, techniques, and materials, and make resources readily available to use. Children can describe to you the materials they are using or the picture or structure they have created. Consider transcribing the children's stories about their art. Have books about art and artists available for children in the environment.

Math and Science

When writing materials are added to math and science experience centres, it is easy to make literacy connections. Early learning teachers label materials and provide resource books and reference materials. Cooking is a great way for children to practise language, math, and science skills. The use of recipe cards with both pictures and words provides children with the opportunity to see how the printed word connects to a concrete object. There are many cookbooks geared toward young children. These can be displayed near the cooking area. Teachers and children may also create cookbooks. Materials can be labelled with both printed words and diagrams. As children observe nature (plants, animals) and perform experiments with materials, they can graph growth and changes.

Blocks

When reading and writing materials are introduced in block play, children's language and literacy development is enhanced. Children can make signs and labels for their structures. When drawing materials are provided, they can sketch their structures. Blocks enhance literacy development because children can practise symbolic representation—the blocks can become whatever children require them to be. Children can use blocks, boxes, and other materials to create structures that represent a fantasy world. Ask children to tell the story of the world they created. Books about buildings and building things and architectural magazines add print to the block centre.

Outdoor Play

Outdoor play provides opportunities for children to use language playfully as they run, jump, climb, and explore. Encourage children to describe their actions expressively. Add materials to the outdoor environment to encourage exploration. Consider bringing traditional indoor activities such as reading, writing, and drawing materials outdoors. Add new types of materials to the environment. This enhances vocabulary development.

Music and Movement

Children learn language and develop literacy skills by listening to music, moving to music, and creating their own music. Offer children a variety of instruments and materials to make instruments. When songs have accompanying movements, children learn to connect the words of the song to the movement, much like making the connection between the words of a book and the illustrations.

SETTING UP A LITERACY-RICH ENVIRONMENT

When designing areas in the early learning environment that promote language and literacy, early learning teachers examine where to place a potential experience devoted to reading in the play environment. The library or reading centre is generally placed in an area that is visually and physically accessible and is partitioned from the rest of the room to encourage quiet exploration of books and other print materials. The area could have a rug, pillows, and a rocking chair (to encourage adults and children to share books). Bookshelves are used for storing books, and a system to organize the books, such as by genre or reading level, is evident. Generally, five to eight books per child are available, and there is a variety of books to represent different reading levels and interests, such as big books, board books, and chapter books for older children. These could include picture books, poetry, informational or resource books, biographies, magazines, newspapers, and brochures. Felt boards with story characters and puppets enhance the reading experience. Books and print material are rotated so that children do not become bored by the same resources. Ideally, a library centre has multiple copies of the same book. This encourages shared reading among children. Children benefit when there are opportunities for them to check books out and record books that they have expressed an interest in (Bailey-White & Stewart, 2016).

To encourage literacy knowledge and skills, a writing centre is recommended. The writing centre includes writing posters and bulletin boards for the children to display their creations. There is a variety of writing utensils, such as pens, pencils, crayons, markers, and coloured pencils. Writing materials include paper in all sizes and types, booklets, and pads. Materials for writing stories and making them into books, as well as folders in which to place writing samples, are made available. A message board or mailboxes, as you find in many Reggio-inspired classrooms, are known to encourage the children to write (Fraser & Gestwicki, 2002). Computers and tablets are other tools that support children in writing stories and exploring various forms of language and literacy.

The early learning play space has literacy materials in all centres. Materials are changed often to reflect the children's interest and to spark their curiosity. For example, in the science centre, there will be books on the current project topic, and in the music area, there will be posters of songs related to that topic. All centres offer environmental print, such as signs, webs, charts, and graphs related to the project topic. Every centre has appropriate books, magazines and newspapers; writing utensils; and a variety of papers and clipboards to make the writing process more mobile.

TERMS THAT INFLUENCE EARLY LEARNING PLAY ENVIRONMENTS

Here, we introduce you to three terms that support the theory of children's play.

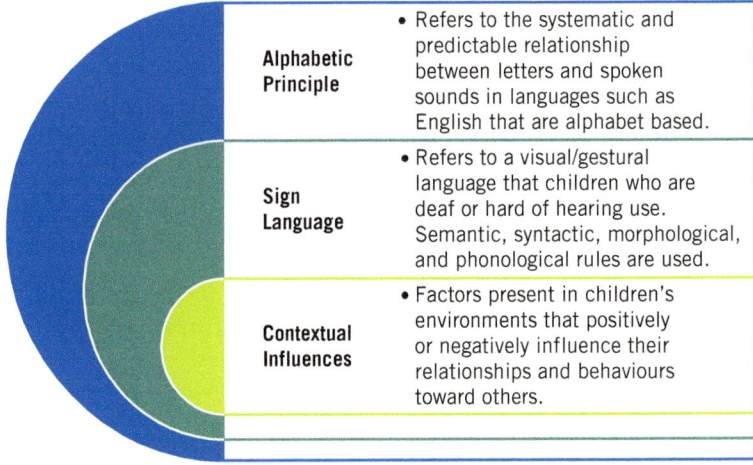

CURIOUS?

Do an image search for *literacy provocations in the early years*. Review the images and describe what you see. Can you see how these types of experiences would be play-based?

SUMMARY

Chapter Preview

- Language is everywhere. Children are exposed to language in their homes, schools, and communities. Language and the corresponding literacy skills are essential developmental milestones that affect a child's lifelong cognitive, social, and emotional attributes.
- Early learning teachers and families have important roles to play in supporting young children to use language in a variety of ways.

Theoretical Frameworks

- The three common theoretical frameworks that influence the work associated with language and literacy development that adults do with children are behaviourist theory (B. F. Skinner), nativist theory (Noam Chomsky), and interactionist theory (Lev Vygotsky).
- According to the theories of Vygotsky, through *scaffolding*, learners are able to cross the zone of proximal development.

From Theory to Trends

- Generally, there are two approaches to reading: phonics and whole language. The trend has been that these are the only two approaches. Debate continues over which method is preferable.
- Today, research on early literacy is providing new approaches and understanding that differ from the tenets of both traditional phonics and whole-language philosophies.
- Early learning teachers are being encouraged to base their choice of approach on observation of children and to respond with appropriate materials and experiences that support the child's developmental phase and interests.

Defining Language

- Language development is categorized as receptive and expressive language. Receptive language is the ability to listen and understand the spoken, signed, or written word. Expressive language is the ability to communicate or to use language; this includes what a child says or signs and eventually what the child writes.

Defining Literacy Development

- Literacy is commonly defined as the ability to read and write the *printed* text that represents spoken language—to be literate.
- Literacy is continually evolving through interactions with others and the environment. While the sequence of literacy development follows the same general pattern, individual rates of growth may vary depending on life experiences and cognitive processes.

Play and Language

- Oral language is identified as the process used in facilitating both early reading and writing skills.
- Literate behaviours are the precursors to more specific literacy skills. Literate behaviours are methods of communication used, either verbal or nonverbal, that help the child to identify needs or interests.
- Play experiences are essential for literate behaviours to develop because they provide children with the venue to express themselves. Play supports children in developing language, literacy, and communication skills, and play experiences help children to incorporate new language into the play. Play and knowledge are also closely aligned.

Characteristics of Language Development

- Language includes the development of grammar, vocabulary, and pragmatics. When children use longer sentences, they begin to demonstrate grammatical rules such as plurals, possession, and tense in nouns and verbs.
- When children are in stimulating play environments, they will acquire vocabulary at an astonishing rate of an average of five new words per day.
- The pragmatics of language refers to the rules for carrying out a conversation or to communicate. Children learn acceptable ways to converse and are able to adapt to different situations.

Children's Conversational Roles

- There are four conversational roles for children. They can be sociable, reluctant, a child with own agenda, or passive.
- A child's conversational style guides the early learning practitioner in how to approach the child. It helps us to determine what will be most effective in facilitating language experiences among individual children and with groups of children.

Observing, Waiting, and Listening (the OWL strategy)

- The OWL strategy can help children reach their fullest potential for conversations. Observing means paying close attention to the child to ascertain the child's interest and what he or she is trying to tell you. Waiting involves pausing so that the child has an opportunity to initiate and take control of their role in the conversation. Listening means paying close attention to what the child is saying to respond appropriately.

Language Skills and Play

- During spontaneous and guided play, children are communicating. Children have seven reasons to communicate throughout their play processes: to make a request; to protest; to greet or to take leave; to respond to another; to ask for information; to think and plan; and to share feelings, ideas, or interests.
- When children use language to plan a storyline and assign roles, they are using meta-communication, which is communication about communication.
- While children are playing, they use language. They ask for materials. They express ideas or ask questions of others. Children learn purposeful verbal interaction during play.

Characteristics of Literacy Development

- Children initially communicate most often through oral language. When children do gain the ability to read and write, it extends their possibilities to transmit and receive information.
- Children are first exposed to print and our written language through books. By building on oral language development with books and environmental print, young children are exposed to the principles needed to become literate.
- Initially, when children are exposed to books, they are unable to interpret words in print or to write using adult forms of the alphabet or to use standard spelling. With exposure, they make the connections between print and language.
- Children progress through stages as they develop literacy skills.

The Importance of Child Participation in Emerging Literacy

- The way children respond to being read to offers parents and early learning teachers opportunities to scaffold language and literacy development. Reader response becomes more and varied as they get older. McVicker (2007) identified three ways that preschoolers and seven ways that school-aged children respond when listening to books.

Literacy Skills and Play

- Most children's first attempts at reading and writing occur during sociodramatic play where the appropriate reading and writing tools are present. Their play can reveal the following literacy understandings: (1) interest in stories, knowledge of story structure, and story comprehension; (2) understanding fantasy in books; and (3) symbolic representation.

Narratives or Storytelling

- A narrative is the telling of a story. By age 3 or 4, children begin to develop their narrative skills. Narratives are thought to form from oral language to literacy. Stories require more complex language skills than are needed for daily conversations.
- Children go through five levels in the development of narratives: labelling, listing, connecting, sequencing, and, finally, narrating.

Variations in Language and Literacy Development

- While language and literacy development follow a predictable sequence, not all children will progress through the stages at the same rate. The variations are due to many factors, such as motivation, culture, gender, developmental delays, family background, socioeconomic levels, birth order, and whether English is the child's native language.

The Roles of Early Learning Teachers

- There are seven different "teacher roles" related to the development of language and literacy. The way an early learning teacher interacts with a child is likely to vary, depending on the child and situation. These roles have been identified as the director, the entertainer, the timekeeper, the too-quiet teacher, the helper, the cheerleader, and the responsive partner. The final role, that of responsive partner, is the most effective in supporting children's language development.
- The more opportunities children have to speak in the environment, especially with adults, the more extensive and advanced their vocabulary will be when they enter kindergarten. Children progress from *learning to talk* to *talking to learn*; the latter is dependent on the ability to use decontextualized language, which is language removed from the here and now.
- Closed, open-ended, cognitively challenging or thought-provoking questions are all questioning techniques that early learning teachers use with children. Each technique encourages different responses and language.

The Early Learning Environment

- Adding literacy-rich areas to the child's play environment improves children's phonological awareness. Increasing the amount of environmental print in the play space increases the likelihood of children engaging in literacy-related play activities. Early literacy experiences are embedded in the basic activities of early learning—these include reading aloud, group time, small-group activities, adult–child conversations, and play.
- An early learning practitioner should be able to observe children experiencing language and literacy every minute of every day. A good way for an early learning student practitioner to begin to learn about language and literacy is through books.

REVIEW QUESTIONS

1. Explain the importance of oral language development.
2. What is the difference between literacy and emergent literacy?
3. Outline the relationship of play to language and literacy development.
4. If a child that you are working with is not engaging in conversation with others, how would you scaffold the child's oral language development?
5. Describe the stages of language development.
6. Name and describe the three theories of language acquisition. Why do you think that at least one of these views is controversial?

7. Describe the three stages of reader's response in preschoolers and the seven stages in school-aged children.
8. What guidelines are used when choosing a book to read to children?
9. Give three examples each of closed, open-ended, and thought-provoking or cognitively challenging questions.
10. What is meant by decontextualized knowledge?

MAKING CONNECTIONS

Theory to Practice

1. Look at the description of the teacher's roles in this chapter. Do you see yourself in one of these roles? How about others you have observed in early learning classrooms? Write a few paragraphs to reflect on the roles you have seen both in yourself and in others.
2. Can you remember your favourite book as a child? Do you still have it? If not, see if you can find a copy in the library or purchase it from a local bookstore. Think about why it is meaningful to you. Share your favourite book with your classmates or colleagues and discuss why you have chosen this book. Reflect on whether this book would be suitable to share with the children you are currently working with. If it isn't, reflect on why. Record the names of the books that were shared. You now have a list of book titles to add to your own personal library.
3. Try to visualize the last early learning environment you spent time in. Was the environment set up to encourage language and literacy? If your answer is yes, write down the ways in which it supported language and literacy. If your answer is no, write down what could have been done differently in the environment.

DIGITAL PORTFOLIO ENTRIES

Below are two possible digital portfolio entries to support your knowledge and experience of the relationship between language, literacy, and play.

- Create a plan for introducing a small group of children to a book. Spend some time choosing an appropriate book, read it, and make a list of questions you would ask during the experience. Take photos of the book experience and upload them to your portfolio.
- Visit a program and consider the environmental print. Would you consider it a language-rich environment? Why or why not?

CHAPTER 11

Math and Science and Play

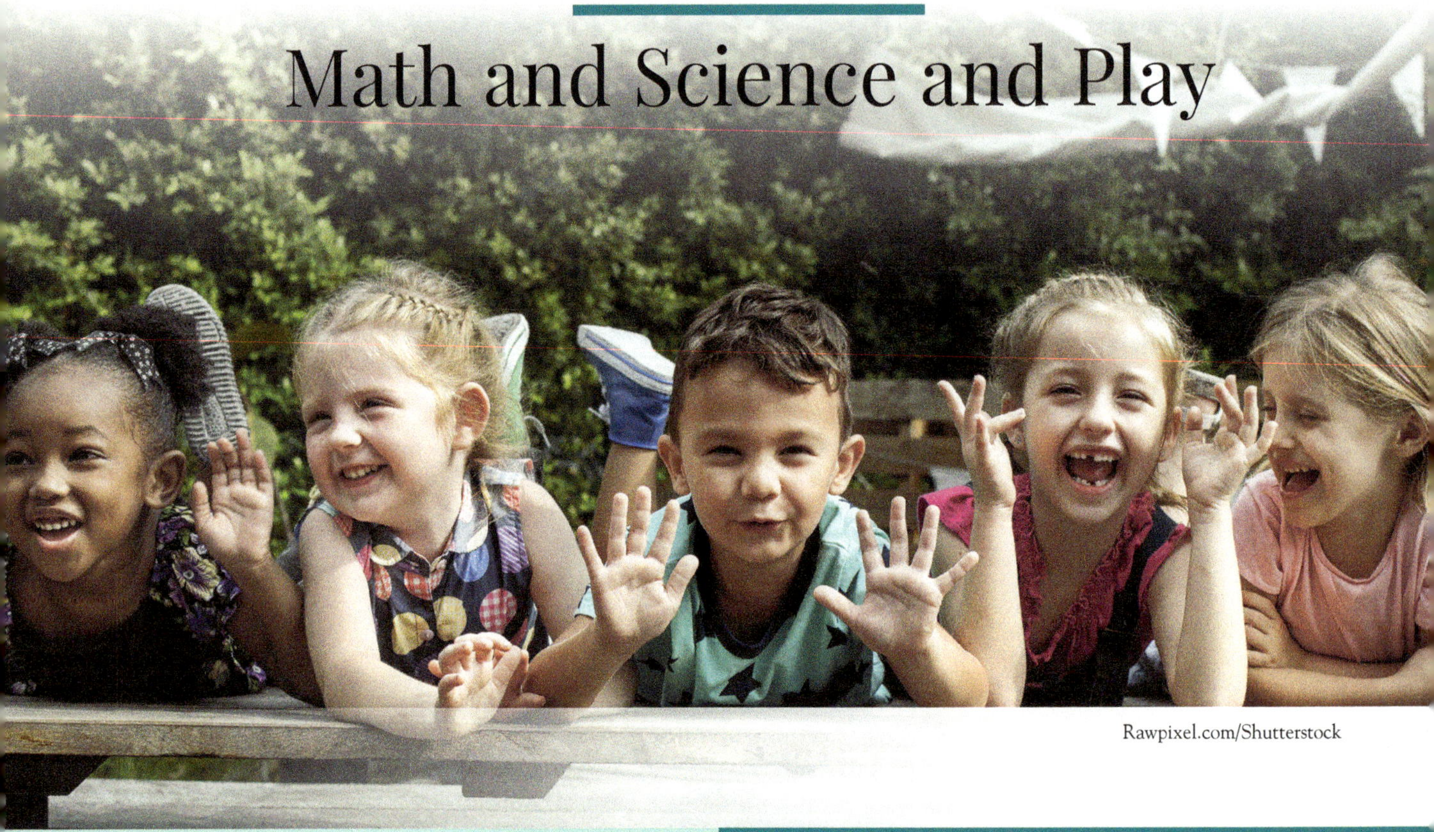

Rawpixel.com/Shutterstock

> Imagination is more important than knowledge.
>
> —Albert Einstein (1879–1955)

LEARNING OUTCOMES

After exploring this chapter you should be able to:

- Describe how math and science principles relate to children's development, play, and later academics skills.
- Explain the relationship of math and science concepts to experiential play and learning.
- Outline what is meant by wonderment with young children.
- Describe how the processes of the scientific method relate to children's play.
- Identify the role of early learning teachers in planning and facilitating math and science experiences.

Sharing Stories of Practice

I always hated math and found science difficult in school. I don't remember talking much about either subject when I studied early childhood education. I feel strongly about professional learning, and I have been taking workshops for years on the areas that really fascinate me, but to be honest, I have largely ignored math and science experiences in my programming. Yes, I put out math manipulatives every day and I have a small discovery centre in the play space that I change seasonally, but that is about all.

I know this is not enough. I am secure enough in my abilities as an early learning teacher, but I admit that I need to change some of my practices in order to better address all areas of children's learning. I need to overcome my negative disposition to math and science, as it reduces my ability to observe and enhance children's opportunities. I know there is potential to expand this area. It is up to me.

Fariba, ECE graduate, 2015

CHAPTER PREVIEW

Do you think that math and science as content areas belong in early learning programming? It has been our experience that these programming topics are often overlooked in the early years, due in part to early learning teachers having some level of discomfort with the principles of math and science experiences that are foundational in children's play during the early years. Why do you think this might be? Might it be something to do with how students and teachers feel about math and science? Perhaps, it is because early learning teachers associate math and science with the difficulties they experienced with these subjects while in secondary school. Some may view these as academic areas that are best left for children to learn when they enter their formal school experience.

Math and science experiences during the early years offer young children powerful ways of knowing about the world. The earlier that children have opportunities to explore and discover the array of math and science principles and topics, the better prepared they will be for more formal study in later years. During the early years, math and science principles are embedded into many of the play options for children. For example, as children engage in jumping, the early learning teacher and children may measure the distance that they jumped. Or, the children, using a scale, may decide which item is heavier or learn what sinks and what floats. Math and science experiences do not have to be rigid or formal; rather, they can be discussed and encouraged during the play process when **teachable moments** become evident. When an early learning teacher provides play possibilities for children, math and science concepts will naturally occur. Seizing on these moments, there will be many learning opportunities for children to engage in.

Math and science experiences during the early years differ from the curriculum presented in formalized academic programming. In early childhood programs, math and science constructs are discovered through their hands-on exploration and discovery play experiences. Young children, when given the opportunity, will naturally engage in thoughtful and challenging mathematical concepts and scientific theory. It is the process of experiencing science and mathematics concepts, rather than specific content,

teachable moment First popularized by Havighurst (1952), a teachable moment is about the timing of learning. Epstein (2009) suggests that to seize the moment, early learning teachers can be intentional about the experiences they provide for children.

that offers the foundational skills needed to achieve more complex academic outcomes. In essence, through play children will learn about scientific and mathematical concepts and transfer their learning to other real-life experiences. Think of the children using blocks and planks for construction. Through this play, children learn about measurement, balance, formulas, symmetry, weight, height, and inclines. These concepts are foundational skills used to predict and problem solve more advanced math and science experiences. If children are not afforded the opportunities to gain these principles during their early years, through hands-on experiences, it will influence their ability to grasp the concepts as part of an abstract thinking process.

As identified earlier in the text, there is an increasing demand for academic-focused early childhood curricula, which researchers identify as the "academic pushdown." Not only is this prevalent in kindergarten programs, but early learning teachers are also feeling the pressure to replace play with more academic-type work (Genishi & Dyson, 2014, p. 230). Efforts to increase science and mathematics learning in young children coincide with a push toward incorporating academic programming into early learning settings. As well, there is a trend to support specific **STEM** subjects - science, technology, engineering, and math- at a younger age as a way to address the perceived knowledge gaps that children are exhibiting in their later years (Tippett & Milford, 2017).

STEM An interdisciplinary approach to learning that involves real-world experiences through which children can apply science, technology, engineering, and mathematics in a context that makes connections between science, technology, engineering, and math (Tippett & Milford, 2017).

With an increasing emphasis on STEM at the preschool level, early learning teachers and administrators question how "these STEM standards fit with developmentally appropriate practice and the needs of young learners" (Christenson & James, 2015, p. 26). Advocates of play, including Dietze and Kashin (2016), suggest that early learning teachers examine ways in which they can incorporate scientific and mathematical learning opportunities for children through play. Foundational concepts are best learned through play.

Early learning teachers who plan structured experiences that children are required to complete do not contribute to these children learning math and science concepts; rather, for some children, the pressure to learn teacher-defined concepts reduces their desire to explore and gain the valuable learning that evolves from experiential play and learning (Charlesworth, 2015). It is through children having opportunities to play with science and math concepts and engage in the sense of wonderment and discovery that they discover skills and concepts that they will transfer to other experiences. Science and math concepts require a discovery-based environment embedded in the context of play. In fact, science and math experiences often overlap (Charlesworth, 2015). Consider Photo 11.1, which depicts a child creating with tubes and funnels. How are math and science coming together in this experience?

This chapter focuses on the theoretical concepts of math and science in early learning environments. We introduce you to the importance of including such experiences in early learning environments and outline the connection between math and science to play and children's development. The theories support the learning of math and science through play. Once again, as we have seen in other chapters, theories influence our practice.

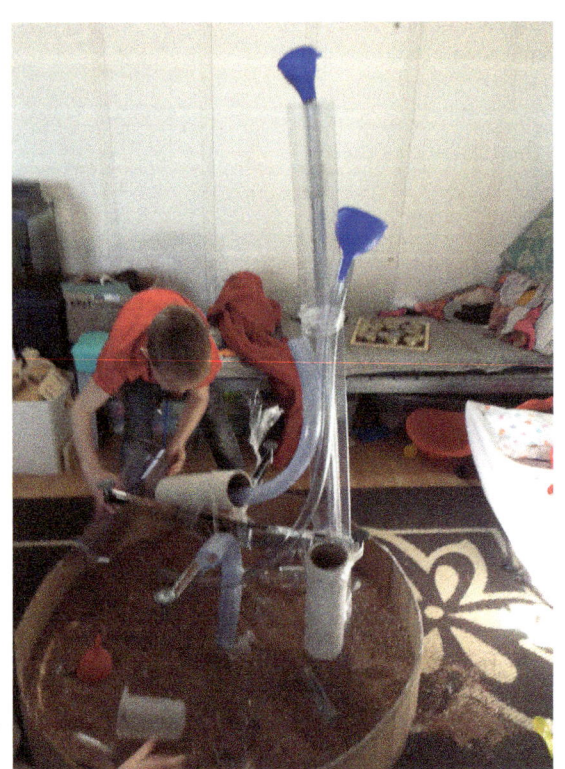

Photo 11.1 Science and math concepts come together in one play experience.

Used with Permission of Gill Robertson

THEORETICAL FOUNDATION

The experiences that children have with math and science during their early years are fundamental to later learning. Our understanding of how and when this development takes place has been influenced by theories of concept development put forth by Jean Piaget and Lev Vygotsky. These theories support a constructivist approach, which places the emphasis on children as intellectual explorers who make their own discoveries and construct knowledge based on their life experiences with people, places, and objects (Charlesworth, 2015). According to Piaget's theory, children acquire knowledge through their interactions with the environment. Piaget distinguished between three types of knowledge (Kamii, 2016), as featured in Figure 11.1.

When children are learning about objects in the environment and the object characteristics, such as colour, weight, size, texture, and other elements central to the object's physicality, they do it by acting on and with the object (Charlesworth, 2015). Consider the experience children may have with different sphere-shaped objects such as balls and globes. By interacting with these objects, children discover that the ball bounces but the globe does not; however, both objects can roll.

During this experience with the balls and globes, children gain logical-mathematical knowledge to make sense of the world. When the balls and globes are divided into categories, children are engaging in classification. When they count the balls and globes, they may discover that there are more balls than globes. This is known as logical-mathematical knowledge (Charlesworth, 2015). Then children discover that the bouncing spheres are called balls and the nonbouncing, rolling spheres are called globes. This type of knowledge is called social-conventional knowledge, and it includes information created by people, such as rules for behaviour in various social situations (Charlesworth, 2015) and, in this case, the proper names for objects (balls and globes) that children interact with.

The three types of knowledge are not easily separated from each other. Just about every learning experience uses physical, logical-mathematical, and social-conventional knowledge. Understanding the way Piaget classified knowledge helps us to facilitate and plan math and science discovery opportunities for children. Providing children with experiences that enhance one type of knowledge increases their opportunities to develop all three types of knowledge (Charlesworth, 2015).

Similar to Piaget, Lev Vygotsky was a cognitive development theorist. Unlike Piaget, Vygotsky placed more emphasis on the role of the adult or more mature peer as an influence on children's cognitive and emotional development. Whereas Piaget placed emphasis on children as intellectual explorers making their own discoveries and constructing knowledge independently, Vygotsky promoted a more social context for constructivism, suggesting, "It is through others that we develop into ourselves" (Vygotsky, 1981, p. 181). This suggests that, according to Vygotskian tradition, children's interests, depth of discoveries, and desire to expand math and science knowledge are influenced by others and can be scaffolded to higher levels.

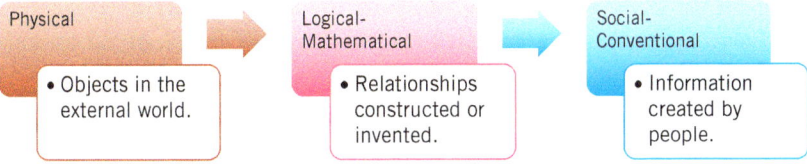

Figure 11.1 Three types of knowledge.

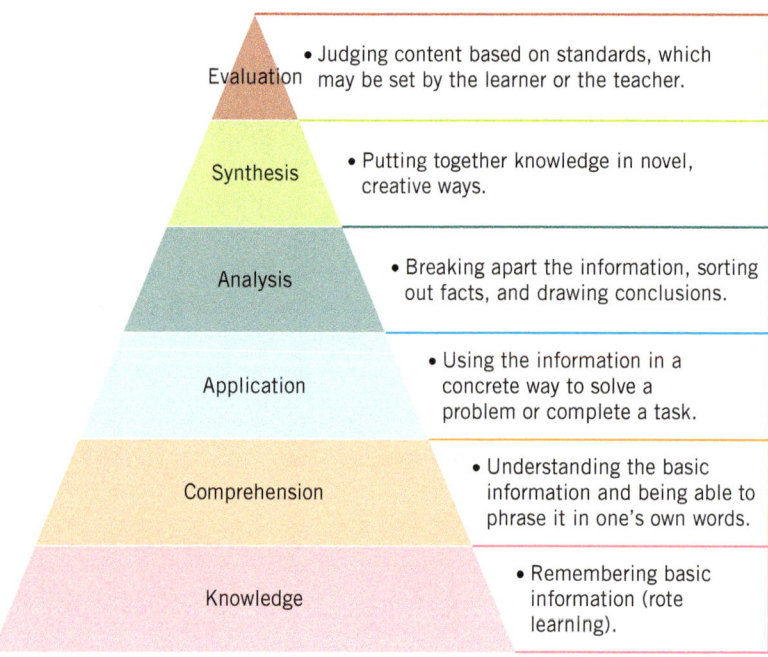

Figure 11.2 Bloom's taxonomy.

Higher levels of learning coincide with higher-order thinking skills. Benjamin Bloom (1956) identified six levels of higher-order thinking that form a hierarchy, from lowest to highest. Each higher level requires all of the thinking skills needed at the lower levels (Jacovina, McNamara, & Allen, 2015). Social constructivists who identify with the theories of Vygotsky could consider these levels when focusing on scaffolding children's development across Vygotsky's zone of proximal development, as described in Chapter 2. The six levels appear in Figure 11.2.

Since Bloom's original hierarchy of higher-order thinking was published, in the 1990s, a student of Dr. Bloom's recommended changing the names of the six categories from noun to verb forms and rearranging them (Krathwohl, 2002). Presenting the taxonomy as a pyramid suggests that in order to address higher levels of thinking, it is recommended that learning be scaffolded from simple to more complex. For twenty-first-century teaching and learning, creativity is at the forefront. Now there are recommendations that the pyramid be flipped. The pinnacle of the triangle is creativity (Wright, 2012), due in part to how one's creativity influences thinking, innovation, and problem solving. From this point, children learn to evaluate, analyze, and apply their thinking, which builds their understanding of concepts that they then draw upon later. Open-ended experiences and materials support critical and creative thinking in math and science as well as in other critical learning areas. Figure 11.3 depicts the new categories and illustrates that when Bloom's taxonomy is flipped, it supports the core concepts associated with twenty-first-century skills.

Early learning teachers are encouraged to use probing questioning techniques with children that will align and support the scaffolding process. This will contribute to creative experiences and knowledge building. Bloom's taxonomy of higher-order thinking reinforces the importance of developing skills in questioning. Consider focusing on levels 2 to 6, as level 1 calls for memorization, which is the lowest level of higher-order thinking. Rather than asking knowledge questions that are focused on rote learning, if children can

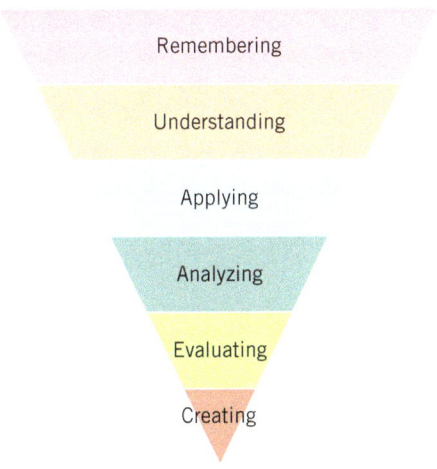

Figure 11.3 Flipping Bloom's taxonomy.

produce the correct answer, it is recommended that they be given opportunities to discover and create their knowledge. Ideally, children are naturally curious about the world and want to find out as much as they can about it. This means that they need to discover the answers to their questions rather than have adults give them these answers. The more opportunities children have to manipulate objects, discover, and do (Charlesworth, 2015), the better their foundational math and science skills will be.

Consider the image of three children counting snails in Photo 11.2. Imagine that the children came inside and were asked to sit in a circle formation for a group meeting.

Photo 11.2 Counting snails in nature.
Used with Permission of Amanda Benton

The early learning teacher wanted them to share their experience with the other children, so she asked them, "What did you find outside?" When the children answered in unison, "Snails!" the teacher replied, "How many snails did you find?" followed by "What colour were the snails?" At that point, the children could not remember, and one replied, "One hundred!" Then they responded, "Brown." In this example, the focus was on remembering, and the children could not recall the exact number. However, they were able to identify the correct colour of the snails, but how is this important? The questions were testing them. Testing and play-based learning are not congruent. Now, imagine a different scenario.

While still outside, the children were invited to draw the snails on a piece of paper attached to a clipboard. The children counted the snails on the log and then counted the snails that they had drawn. Once they were satisfied that the numbers matched, they took the clipboard inside. One of the children wanted to take the snails indoors, but after they discussed this, the early learning teacher asked the children if they could create snails from clay. With the clay, the children recreated their images of the snails. Once they had the correct number, they lined them up in a row. The early learning teacher then asked if they would like to build a home for their "snails." As they created a structure with blocks, she asked whether the home would be big enough for all of the snails. She wondered if all of the snails would fit inside. How many rooms will they need? Will some of the snails live outside the structure? Such experiences support children in beginning to use mathematical language and apply their understanding of number concepts and spatial relationships in their experiences. At the end of the day, because they started with creating, the children were able to recall the number of snails they discovered outdoors!

Math and science are critical areas that are considered essential in helping children to form "lower-resource communities" (Clements & Sarama, 2014, p. 1). David Hawkins (1983), an influential scientist, philosopher, and mathematician, believed that math and science are great equalizers, as they have the opportunity to narrow the achievement gap between children from different socioeconomic backgrounds. What children experience and learn about math concepts by the time they enter kindergarten predicts later mathematics achievements (Clements & Sarama, 2014). As a result, early learning teachers develop innovative strategies for children to experience math and science in their play environments (Piasta, Pelatti, & Miller, 2014).

Young children have the capacity for scientific thinking and learning. Scientific skills such as "observing, describing, comparing, questioning, predicting, experimenting, reflecting, and cooperating" are core concepts that are evident in environments for children during the early years. "Such skills are critical for continued academic success" (Piasta et al., 2014, p. 446). Given their importance, how much time during the course of a day of play is given to math and science?

Despite the importance of math and science, Piasta and colleagues (2014) determined that, as content areas, math and science are emphasized less than other areas during the early years and that there are considerable differences in the amount and kinds of opportunities that are offered or discussed. As you will read further in this chapter, early learning students and teachers are encouraged to examine the scope of math and science and how it aligns with the other areas of play and learning concepts. We begin by examining core definitions for these topical areas. These definitions are intended to help you think about the complexity of children's development as it relates to math and science. The definitions help to make the interconnection with play. You will learn that in order to optimize development in math and science, you need to think carefully about how to apply this knowledge to practice.

DEFINING SCIENCE, MATHEMATICS, AND SCIENTIFIC INQUIRY

Many complex definitions are available for both math and science. From an early learning perspective, science, simply put, refers to a system for acquiring and maintaining a body of knowledge about things, people, and the environment. Acquiring knowledge requires a system that involves processes, content, and concepts. It involves observation and experimentation to continually refine, extend, and revise that body of knowledge. The processes through which knowledge is gained are known as scientific inquiry. The knowledge that comes as a result of **scientific inquiry** helps to explain the world around us (Worth, 2010).

Historically, science has been a male-dominated field of study (Tolley, 2014). However, research has indicated that all children love science! When children engage in science experiences, they "enjoy observations and thinking about nature." They are involved with a "strong presence, and are engaged and absorbed in experimental and creative activities" (Broström, 2015, p. 109). Children gain competence in the processes of science while participating in meaningful scientific activities (Charlesworth, 2015). Concurrently, children develop an understanding of scientific concepts—the "big ideas" in science. Scientific content includes the facts of science, and while these are still a basic part of science education, they are not its primary goal (Hoorn, Nourot, Scales, & Alward, 2011).

scientific inquiry The process of questioning, predicting, investigating, analyzing, explaining, and communicating in order to learn about the world (McLean, Jones, & Schaper, 2015).

Using a search engine, look for images of scientists. Do the images you see match the stereotype you may have visualized in your mind's eye? Do you think these images are changing over time?

Mathematics, or arithmetic for some, is a subject in the school system that may not necessarily seem to have a relationship to the outside world (Clements & Sarama, 2014). According to Counsell and colleagues (2015), mathematics is a language of science. To describe the world, mathematical language is necessary. The world exists three dimensionally and needs to be described in spatial terms. Measurement is critical to describe the world (Counsell et al., 2015). Math and science intersect every day!

Science is about the knowledge and study of the world. It is based on one's observation and experimentation rather than on how it has been traditionally taught by memorizing terms and following step-by-step instructions (Counsell et al., 2015). Is this how you remember learning science? If your learning involved memorization, how much of the content do you remember now?

Providing science and mathematical experiences for children within a play-based learning environment is not difficult. When math and science are seen through a constructivist lens, children play with materials, play with ideas, and play with language as they build knowledge. Constructivism is a way of coming to know one's world, scientifically through observing, predicting, and analyzing and mathematically by establishing meaning and relationships using number, measurement, shape, line, and form (Charlesworth, 2015).

Photo 11.3 Making a fishing rod.

Used with Permission of Gill Robertson

Some students and teachers are comfortable providing math and science experiences because they recognize the potential that everyday materials and objects can bring to children's experiences. Others feel that they are complicated and abstract subjects and not as important as other experiences. However, if provided in a way that connects to children's play, math and science explorations become real, meaningful, and authentic. Math happens everywhere and every day, as depicted in Photo 11.3. Here, a child is making a fishing rod that required careful consideration of its length and diameter. Being able to recognize such dimensions is an important skill that transfers to more complex math and science principles.

The Importance of Math and Science

Continued professional learning is essential. David Hawkins spent most of his life providing professional development to teachers that illustrated the importance of math and science experiences for young children (Lehmann-Haupt, 2002). He emphasized the need for math and science to be experiential and to be introduced in the early years. Hawkins worked closely with his wife, Frances, an early childhood educator, to develop a relationship with the Boulder Journey School in Colorado. They recognized that in order to enhance and promote math and science experiences, there was a need for adults working with children, including early learning teachers and teachers in the school systems, to acquire opportunities to explore and experiment with materials and math and science principles that are inherent in the everyday lives of children (Kellogg, 2010). When adults experiment with materials, they are better able to understand and support children's learning. Hawkins (1974) referred to this process as *messing about*.

Hawkins (1974) identified three phases of learning in math and science. These phases are not ordered numerically because they do not always happen sequentially. He used mnemonic signs to label the phases. We feature the three phases of messing about in Figure 11.4.

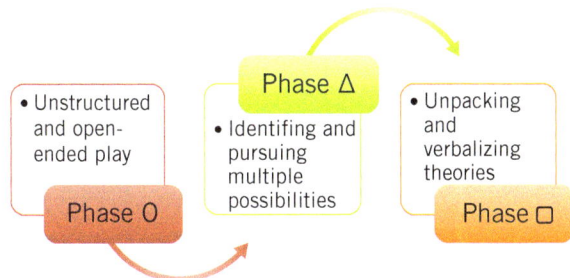

Figure 11.4 The theory of messing about.

Hawkins (1974) theorized that the time devoted to unstructured and open-ended play was key to messing about. He said that this time should be "much greater in amount than commonly allowed, which should be devoted to free and unguided exploratory" play (Hawkins, 1974, p. 1). During this phase, children use materials to construct, test, probe, and experiment. This type of exploring is, according to Hawkins (1974), "the essence of creativity. (p. 3)" These processes are where math and science learning begins and where, through experiences, children deepen their learning and develop their own theories. Children and adults can mess about with materials, ideas, or situations.

David and Frances Hawkins advocated for early learning programs to have a variety of materials available for teachers and children to use for messing about. Table 11.1

Table 11.1 Materials for messing about.

Plants	Small tubs	Funnels
Ropes	String	Hardware
Water	Tires	Shovels
Dirt	Sieves	Utensils
Bottles	Squeeze droppers	Air pumps
Popsicle sticks	Ice cube trays	Tinker toys
Test tubes	Electronics	Lumber
Flashlights	Screwdrivers	Clay
Large tubs	Metal materials	Pulleys
Wood	Clothespins	Levers
Hammers	Rubber stoppers	Batteries
Nails	Measuring cups	Wood scraps
Rulers	Seeds	Pot lids
Wire	Squirt bottles	Sticks
Pipe cleaners	Buckets	Glasses
Paper cups	Coloured water	Unit blocks
Sand	Pegboards	Magnets
Rocks	Large tubes	Tree cookies
Beads	Small tubes	LED lights

CURIOUS?

Search for the Boulder Journey School on the Internet to learn more about this inspiring program. Search for Hawkins Centers of Learning to learn more about Frances and David Hawkins.

introduces you to that list of materials. As you review the list, imagine the types of messing about that could occur. Then, think about what types of math and science learning may evolve when children have opportunities to engage with these materials.

Children require a variety of materials in their play to influence their discoveries about and understanding of mathematical and scientific concepts. Adults, who understand the unlimited possibilities of materials, are better able to provide children with opportunities to explore, discover, and create. Scientists know that in order to learn science, you have to experience science. Van Hoorn and colleagues (2011) believed that science opportunities in the early years should be similar to those of scientists involved in doing science. That means that, during play, children are more likely to become interested in science when they are in environments with early learning teachers who exhibit a sense of curiosity and zest for exploring and discovering. This is similar for mathematics. Copley (2010) suggested that to understand mathematics is to do mathematics. It is through play-based spaces and environments that children begin to construct their understandings of basic mathematical concepts (Van Hoorn et al., 2011). In early learning settings, it is the early learning teacher's role to create environments that make math and science come to life.

STOP ... THINK ... DISCUSS ... REFLECT

Pick 10 items from the list in Table 11.1. Can you think of how you would present these items to children to encourage exploration and discovery through their play? Discuss your list and related ideas for math or science experiences with another student in the class. What have you learned about math and science by sharing your ideas? How do you envision transferring your math and science knowledge to your work with children?

Concept Development in Science and Mathematics

Concepts are the building blocks of knowledge. They allow children to organize and categorize information (Charlesworth, 2015). Concepts help children to organize their world, serving as a mental filing cabinet. As information is discovered and organized, through the learning process children will file similar concepts together. Categories are formed by observing and identifying the similarities and differences of objects and ideas. During the early years, children actively engage in acquiring fundamental concepts and in learning fundamental process skills. Manipulating materials and being creative and innovative encourage children to engage in processes that lead them to apply their newly

Photo 11.4 Ropes, buckets, pulleys, and levers for messing about.

Used with Permission of Diane Kashin

acquired knowledge about concepts in various ways and in different situations. By being involved in the process of math and science, children expand their current knowledge, skills, and abilities about specific concepts; transfer their knowledge to different ideas; and develop new ideas (Charlesworth, 2015).

Science, Mathematics, and Development

Concept growth and development begins as early as infancy. Gopnick, Meltzoff, and Kuhl (2001), in *Scientist in the Crib*, refer to an infant as "the most powerful learning machine in the universe" (p. 1). "The development of mathematical abilities begins when life begins"

Photo 11.5 Climbing to great heights.

Used with Permission of Steph Connor

(Clements & Sarama, 2014, p. 4). Babies explore the world with their senses: looking, touching, smelling, hearing, and tasting. Children are born curious and intuitively strive to learn more about their world (Hyson & Tomlinson, 2014). As children learn to crawl, to stand, and to walk, they gain the freedom to discover on their own and to learn to think for themselves. Very early on, they begin to learn ideas about *size*. For example, as they hold and examine objects, they discover their larger size relative to what they are holding. When they go over, under, and into large objects, they see their size as smaller. Infants learn about *weight* when they are unable to lift items of the same size. They learn about *shape* when they notice that some things stay put and others roll away. Babies first look, then they move. This process contributes to them discovering *space*. Some spaces are big and some are small. They learn *time sequence* when they wake up and feel wet and hungry. They cry, they are changed, and then they are fed. Next, they play, get tired, and go to sleep.

As toddlers, children sort things by putting them in piles—of the same colour, the same size, the same shape, or with the same use. They are developing classification skills. When they pile blocks into tall structures and watch them tumble down, they are practising the concept of cause and effect. The solitary tall structure becomes many small parts again. When they pay for food in an imaginary store, they are learning about money concepts and adding and subtracting concepts. When they pretend to cook imaginary food, they are measuring imaginary flour, salt, and milk. When they set the table in their play kitchen, they are practising the concept of one-to-one correspondence. These types of opportunities are essential as part of children's free exploration and discovery as a basis for learning foundational skills related to math, science, language, and environments (Charlesworth, 2015).

As children grow older, they begin to understand more abstract, relational concepts such as ideas about motion, light and shadows, changes, and relative position (Van Hoorn et al., 2011). They acquire these fundamental concepts through active involvement with their environment. Children learn that cows, pigs, cats, and dogs are animals. Eventually, they subdivide the animals into categories such as those that can be pets and those that are usually not. Children learn that the forest is full of trees. Eventually, they subdivide the trees into those that lose their leaves in the winter and those that do not.

LEARNING SCIENCE AND MATH THROUGH PLAY

Children have an innate curiosity about the world around them. The world around them is a world of natural wonder and mathematics! Math and science connect easily to other areas of learning, including art, literature, technology, and engineering, when children have the opportunity to play with and among the wonders of nature (Ahlskog-Björkman & Björklund, 2016). As outlined in Figure 11.5, children will be motivated to learn about science and math concepts when they are given opportunities for hands-on experiences that are multifaceted. Children will want to learn about science and math when they have a sense of **agency**.

Children with early learning teachers who support them and are involved in their learning through play benefit from having many opportunities that scaffold learning. Scaffolding is a metaphor that refers to the ways in which adults or more sophisticated

agency When children have a sense of agency, they make choices and decisions that influence events and affect their world (Gowrie South Australia, 2015).

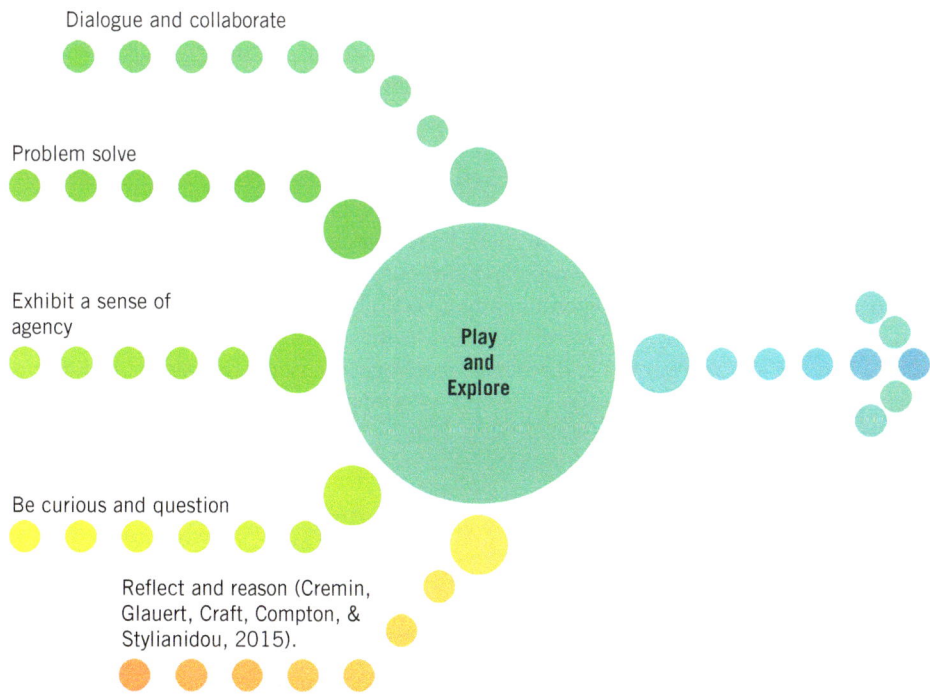

Figure 11.5 Play and exploration to support math and science learning.

Photo 11.6 Finding the math in nature.

Used with Permission of Diane Kashin

peers extend support for children as they learn. Imagine the scaffolding you would see at a construction site and consider this quote:

> Analogous to the way that scaffolding is built to just the needed level when constructing a building and then removed when the building is complete, educators engage in scaffolding by providing the necessary level and type of support that is well timed to the children's needs. (Zurek, Torquati & Acar, 2014, p. 28)

Now imagine a scenario where children have been invited to examine seashells while playing with sand. During this hands-on experience, children may respond to their curiosity about the spiral pattern in the shells by recreating it in the sand. An adult who is familiar with the **Fibonacci sequence** can point out how the spiral pattern grows bigger and then follow up by introducing children to a book about Leonard Fibonacci, who as a young boy in medieval Italy discovered how this mathematical sequence repeats itself in nature. Later, the early learning teacher may encourage and support children in finding more evidence of the Fibonacci sequence and more opportunities to create spirals with other materials such as clay.

Fibonacci sequence Refers to a pattern of numbers in which each successive number is the sum of the previous. This sequence can be seen in many examples in nature (Moomaw, 2013).

CURIOUS?

Do an Internet search to find books and articles about *Leonardo Fibonacci*, and consider how these can motivate children's math and science experiences, using Fibonacci as inspiration.

Table 11.2 Bruner's modes of representation.

Enactive representation	Action-based	Invite children to act on (play with) objects.
Iconic representation	Image-based	Invite children to play with pictures of objects.
Symbolic representation	Language-based	Children play with numerals, operational signs, letters, and words.

The term *scaffolding* is associated with Vygotsky's (1978) zone of proximal development that was coined by Jerome Bruner (1957). Bruner supported the importance of constructivism as opposed to behaviourism (Greenfield, 2016). He advocated for children to be active rather than passive learners. To help children with concept attainment, early learning teachers use Jerome Bruner's (1966) modes of knowledge representation as they work with children at their cognitive developmental levels, as illustrated in Table 11.2.

The first mode of representation involves encoding action-based information, such as a baby remembering the experience of shaking a rattle and storing that experience in memory. As an adult, you can think of this kind of representation, such as when you use a keyboard. It is a motor task that you may find difficult to describe pictorially or symbolically. In the next mode of representation, information is stored in the form of images. The final mode of representation appears after age 7. This is when information is stored in the form of code or symbol (Bruner, 1966). These modes of representation, as outlined by Bruner, reinforce the importance of children playing with concrete materials and objects in the early years.

PLAYING WITH SCIENCE IS TO CELEBRATE WONDER

Children are scientists at play (Sharifnia et al., 2015). When children make mud pies for baking or construct worm playgrounds, they are conducting playful experiments. Children are natural wonderers; they are full of wonder. They approach life with an openness and eagerness to know and to experience. Early learning teachers play a key role in supporting children's natural sense of wonder, as humans are innately curious beings. From birth, babies have an instinct for inquiry. As children develop their curiosity, it can become insatiable (Chiarotto, 2011).

Visit http://www.naturalcuriosity.ca/ to learn more about the inquiry approach and how it supports children's natural curiosity about nature.

One of the most important roles that early learning teachers have is to encourage and support children's wonder. This means giving children an opportunity to explore and discover scientific and mathematical concepts. "Wondering is one of the professional missions of childhood, and children don't hesitate to wonder out loud. Why? How? Where? When? As early learning teachers we may often feel the impulse to simply respond with answers" (Ross, 2000, p. 12). This response will not encourage children to discover and construct their own knowledge based on their wonder.

It is sometimes difficult for adults to break away from the need to provide children with the right answers. This might relate to early learning teachers' own experiences as young learners and what they have come to view as being the role of the educator. In early childhood environments, there is no question that focusing on rote learning limits children's quest for knowledge and their learning. What would be the purpose of giving children the right answer? Is it so they could try to remember the answer and recite it to their parents? Rather than memorizing the right answer, early learning teachers challenge children to speculate, make predictions, and create theories. This skill serves them far better over time than any soon-to-be-forgotten answer from a teacher (Kashin, 2009). If you can simply affirm that you share the children's curiosity and sense of wonder, it is better than trying to give them answers.

Wilson (2010) has advocated for adults to recognize and honour children's way of knowing and strive to keep the children's and their own sense of wonder alive. If children are placed in structured environments, without the freedom to explore, their desire to wonder will dissipate over time. Visualize a group of young children playing in a pile of leaves. They will be engaged with their whole bodies, laughing with exuberance and joy. Adults are more likely to respond to a pile of leaves with thoughts about what comes next. They may spend little time immersing themselves in the moment and in the sensory experiences of the collection of leaves. Most likely, the adults are thinking about all the raking they have to do. According to Wilson (2010), children relate to the world based more on wonder, whereas adults' sense of wonder dissipates over time. Imagine the possibilities when adults restore their sense of wonder and learn alongside children!

Photo 11.7 A sense of wonder.

Used with Permission of Bekki Bradshaw

As children discover the wonders of the world, ideally early learning teachers encourage them to look closely and to notice details about what they are seeing (Rubin, 2013). Using tools such as tape measures and magnifiers, children are encouraged to stop and notice the sizes, shapes, and things in their environments. Rubin (2013) identified these as **moments of science**. With their early learning teachers, children observe, notice, and look for evidence to answer their own questions using the scientific method.

> **moments of science** Refers to using an inquiry approach. Early learning teachers respond to everyday moments of looking closely at nature rather than following a script and focusing on the right answers. Moments of science are about supporting children to engage in scientific inquiry (Rubin, 2013).

THE SCIENTIFIC METHOD FOR YOUNG CHILDREN

Science is about exploration and inquiry. Early learning teachers encourage children to engage in an inquiry process. Scientific inquiry is another process that provides children with opportunities to develop mathematical concepts and skills in a concrete way. While exploring the beach, a group of children sort, compare, and categorize found objects by their properties, which "reflects children's ability to represent, analyze, and interpret mathematical data" (Gerde, Schachter, & Wasik, 2013, p. 319).

As children investigate their world, they use the same processes that scientists use: observing, classifying, experimenting, predicting, drawing conclusions, and communicating ideas. With the support of student teachers and teachers, children become more systematic and logical in how they use these processes (Gerde et al., 2013). The processes are depicted in Table 11.3. Adapted from the work of Gerde, Schachter, and Wasik (2013), the table features a description of the process as well as the roles of early learning teachers.

Table 11.3 The scientific method.

Step	Action	Children's Experiences	Role of Early Learning Teachers
Step 1	Observing	Children observe the world around them, finding things that intrigue them as they explore and discover. By developing questions about what they see, they become better observers.	Early learning teachers offer descriptions of what is being observed and ask questions to guide and scaffold thinking. New vocabulary can be used. Adequate time is offered for exploration and discovery.
Step 2	Questioning	To continue the scientific inquiry, a question is asked based on the children's interests and what they observed. During the process of generating a question, children learn how to ask scientific questions and to be curious about the world around them.	As children describe their observations, early learning teachers support question development by summarizing and asking questions. Writing out the children's questions help the children to identify new questions that might emerge and that build on previous questions.
Step 3	Predicting and hypothesizing	Children make hypotheses or predictions about the answers to their questions. If they are encouraged to create visual representations of their data, this supports their writing and mathematics skills.	Early learning teachers encourage children to guess what they think might be the answer to their scientific questions. Recording children's hypotheses provides a visual reference. Offering children opportunities to explain their thinking to others reflects the scientific method. Encouraging children to use the words *brainstorm*, *predict*, and *hypothesize* supports vocabulary development.
Step 4	Experimenting and testing	Experimentation or testing occurs when children try to answer their questions. Experimentation is a concrete process that supports concept development. During this stage, children manipulate objects and observe. It is critical that rather than watch a teacher conduct an experiment, children engage in the experience to experiment themselves.	Early learning teachers engage children in describing, finding patterns, comparing, organizing, measuring, and sorting. Invitations to experiment with materials are offered to children. This facilitates children thinking more deeply about their ideas. Early learning teachers draw the children's attention to a chart of their predictions so that they can intentionally test their hypotheses.

continues ▶

▶ *continues*

Step 5	Summarizing and analyzing to form a conclusion	With adult support, children represent data visually by listing, charting, graphing, and sorting all of their findings. This helps children draw scientific conclusions and develop concepts. Children benefit from being invited to provide multiple responses to summarizing questions. Misconceptions that children may have had during the experimentation phase can be re-examined.	During the summary, early learning teachers help children pull together all of their findings from their experimentation. Teachers guide children in reflecting on the predictions they made. Teachers model how to respond to the array of questions. Finally, teachers ask the original guiding question and summarize children's statements verbally and on chart paper.
Step 6	Communicating discoveries	After making discoveries, children share their findings with others. Communicating about their discoveries supports children in the development of scientific concepts. Children will be excited about what they have learned and want to share with others.	Early learning teachers help children develop their communication skills by inviting them to communicate their findings in different ways, such as through verbal discussions or writing and drawing pictures. Early learning teachers communicate children's findings with families to support their engagement.
Step 7	Identifying a new question	The final step of the scientific method is to transfer findings to a new study. Building upon curiosity is important for children because it contributes to them wanting to follow their interests and use their emerging knowledge to experiment, discover, and learn more.	Early learning teachers facilitate step 7 by asking children if they have more questions about what they learned or by following up on observations that children made during the experimental or summarizing steps. Teachers encourage children to identify a new question by making connections between what they have learned and new contexts.

The Role of Early Learning Teachers in Outdoor Math and Science

Early learning teachers are constantly trying to balance their knowledge and beliefs about how young children learn and develop with family expectations and the philosophies of early learning programs. They can feel pulled between preparing children for school and providing rich play environments. If early learning teachers equate math and science with subjects in the school setting that require work in order to learn, they may feel that a structured environment with specific math or science concepts will better prepare children for the formal instruction they will receive in the school system. This may include incorporating more structured methods, such as worksheets for children to complete, into the program. As we have identified throughout this text, worksheets are developmentally inappropriate and do not support a play-based approach to learning. Early learning teachers who use worksheets say that parents expect them. "Perhaps parents expect photocopied worksheets because that is what they recall from their own early schooling experiences" (Hendrick & Weissman, 2011, p. 241). Experiential play is more powerful for allowing children to grasp complicated concepts.

Worksheets designed to provide children with math and science experiences are part of a teacher-led and teacher-directed classroom that involves scripted teaching. The teacher's input is low because such resources are developed by others. The teacher's role becomes photocopying sheets from a book and providing them to the children. The children's input is low, as they are the passive recipients of these worksheets. These worksheets differ from experiential play. Quality early learning programs provide rich documentation of children's learning experiences during play, and displaying the results of the various play experiences and children's discoveries help families to understand the value of learning math and science within a play-based, constructivist approach. Worksheets do not work (Kashin, 2015).

Play is children's work (Paley, 2004). However, play does not mean that "anything goes" in the early learning space. Miller and Almon (2009), in *Crisis in the Kindergarten: Why Children Need to Play in School*, described a healthy kindergarten as one that does not deteriorate into chaos. Nor is it so tightly structured by adults that children are denied the opportunity to learn through their own initiative and exploration. The authors call for a balance of "child-initiated play in the presence of engaged teachers and more focused experiential learning guided by teachers" (Miller & Almon, 2009, p. 12). The key to advancing child-initiated play is to have the active presence of the early learning teacher, combined with intentional teaching through playful learning. Adults in the early learning play space make this happen by developing open, experiential, fun places to explore, discover, and play.

Setting Up an Environment to Support Scientific Inquiry

In the chapter on language and literacy, it was recommended that early learning teachers create a print-rich environment to encourage language and literacy development. An easy way to incorporate science into the early learning environment is to create discovery areas with materials that are rich in scientific possibilities. Designing quality discovery areas requires early learning teachers to carefully select a variety of materials (such as magnifiers, a balance scale, prisms, plants, and unique materials that are new to children) that will introduce children to the wonders of the natural world (Gamble & Cota-Robles, 2015). If the additional natural materials, books, and manipulatives are rotated into discovery spaces, they will continue to be of interest to the children. These can reflect seasonal changes.

The types of materials provided for children will depend on the type of science being explored. As outlined in Figure 11.6, there are five types of science that guide early learning experiences. Each is described below.

Physical science relates to physical knowledge and involves hands-on exploration of materials used to investigate the properties of objects. For example, at the water table, tubing, measuring cups, funnels, turkey basters, and eyedroppers will foster an understanding of volume, weight, gravity, and force. *Life science* involves children observing and formulating questions about the characteristics of things that are living. Caring for a classroom pet or observing birds, squirrels, insects, and worms in the natural habitat will help children develop a deeper understanding of living things. *Earth science* relates to the properties of earth materials such as rocks or shells. *Technology* involves distinguishing between natural and manufactured items. Simple machines like apple peelers, clocks, or egg timers invite hands-on investigations into how machines function. *Social science* focuses on a social perspective and involves discussion and activities about conserving and recycling (Davies et al., 2014). By brainstorming ways to repurpose discarded objects, children develop problem-solving skills, higher-order thinking, and environmental stewardship principles. Information about environmental science that focuses on sustainability (recycling, reusing, and repurposing) is provided in the final chapter of this text.

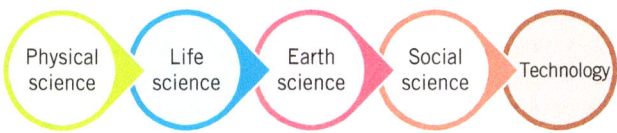

Figure 11.6 Types of sciences in early childhood programs.

Photo 11.8 Exploring water.
Used with Permission of Rosalba Bortolloti

Sand and Water Play

Having opportunities to play at sandpits and water tables provides children with experiences rich in mathematical and scientific learning. Although classic play materials such as sand and water have largely disappeared from children's play spaces, these materials are essential for children's learning (Miller & Almon, 2009). When adults do not recognize the play value inherent in sand and water, they may consider removing them, especially if there are more structured experiences that focus on academic preparation.

Children are drawn to play with sand and water. Sand and water play are messy. Messy play is an essential part of childhood because of the enormous play opportunities and developmental potential. Therefore, early learning teachers are required to embrace it and support children in engaging in such play. Imagine being at a beach. The experience that you are visualizing is probably soothing and relaxing. It is for children as well. Just because an experience is messy does not mean that it does not have enormous play and developmental potential (Hawkins, 2002). Some teachers position the sand and water play tables close to the door of the classroom to help ease children who are experiencing separation anxiety into the program. Children find these experiences soothing when they are stressed. In addition, sand and water play lays the foundation for logical mathematical thinking, scientific reasoning, and cognitive problem solving (Charlesworth, 2015). These sensory experiences are easily incorporated into both indoor and outdoor early learning environments.

Sand and water play allow for scientific inquiry and the opportunity to apply knowledge and skills of mathematical concepts such as measuring, volume, size, shape, and weight. These natural materials provoke children with a sense of wonder while they pour, pound, sift, drain, and pack the water and sand. Ideally, in the early learning environment, sand and water tables are placed side by side, as the exploration and discoveries of the media will expand when combined. Outdoors, children require access to water when playing in the sandbox, as this helps them gain skills in discovering the creation of three-dimensional sculptures, which in turn advance their math, science, and creative attributes. The materials and supplies for sand and water play are carefully chosen. Consideration is also given to safety (i.e., nontoxic, smooth edges), quality and durability (materials must withstand use by multiple children), flexibility (for multiple usage), and play value (what the child can do with it). Students and early learning teachers planning for a sand and water experience have many options for materials and supplies.

The Development of Mathematical Concepts

Young children have a natural desire to explore and understand the world around them. Mathematics is another means by which they acquire information about their environment and begin to understand the world. Well before kindergarten, children have an interest in and the ability to engage in significant mathematical thinking and learning (Clements & Sarama, 2014). According to *Foundations for Numeracy: An Evidence-Based Toolkit for Early Learning Teachers* (Canadian Child Care Federation [CCCF] & Canadian Language and Literacy Research Network, 2010), research has shown that "knowledge of quantity emerges early in life and develops significantly during a child's first three years" (p. 13). Infants can tell the difference between small quantities—for example, between two items as opposed to three. Toddlers typically learn their first number word (usually *two*) at around 24 months of age. By the time children reach 4 years of age, they are able to compare quantities. They become experienced with using math words like *more* or *less*.

Being aware that young children develop math concepts from a very early age is significant to early learning teachers. In recent years, there has been an emphasis on literacy readiness and, in comparison, mathematical readiness has had a minimal focus in home and early learning environments. Research is showing strong evidence that mathematical readiness is also important. For example, Clements and Sarama (2014) suggested that a complete mathematics program may contribute to children's later learning of other subjects, including literacy. "Much of the recent research has reported that mathematics does in fact support the development of literacy" (CCCF & Canadian Language and Literacy Research Network, 2010, p. 13). Recognizing that mathematical concepts develop early in children's lives, early learning teachers have a responsibility to create opportunities that will support them in engaging in play experiences that are diverse and supportive of various mathematical concepts.

The term *numerosity* is used to describe the ability to discriminate arrays of objects based on the quantity of presented items (Coubart, Izard, Spelke, Marie, & Streri, 2014). Research suggests that infants have an "intuitive sense of approximate magnitude (i.e., how much there is) called *ordinality*" (CCCF & Canadian Language and Literacy Research Network, 2010, p. 13). The ability of children to learn the concepts of numerosity and ordinality depends on two important cognitive factors: mental representation of information and the memory of information. At age 2, "children can mentally represent and remember one, two, and sometimes three items." Between the ages of 2 and 3, "children are not only aware of the concept of small numbers," they can "also begin to learn how to solve simple nonverbal calculations involving one and two items." This is basic arithmetic. Older preschool children can solve problems involving three or four items, and by the time they reach 4 years of age, they can begin to understand the more complex arithmetic problem of inverse relation between addition and subtraction. If one item is added and one item is taken away, the answer is still that there are two items ($2 + 1 - 1 = 2$): "adding one and taking away one cancel each other out" (CCCF & Canadian Language and Literacy Research Network, 2010, p. 14).

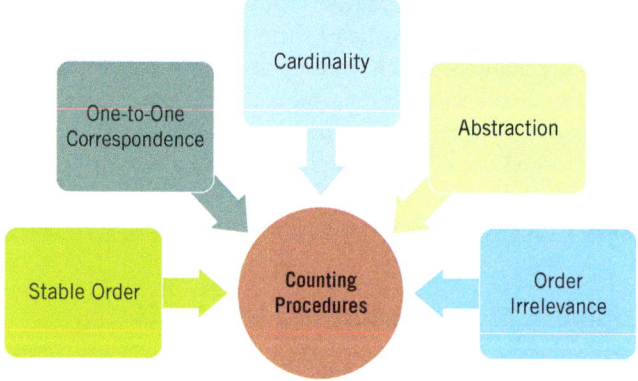

Figure 11.7 Counting procedures.

Counting Procedures

Between the ages of 2 and 3, children begin to use language related to mathematics, such as incorporating number words into their play experiences. "Children appear to know very early that number words all represent different quantities and that the sequence in which they say these number words is important" (CCCF & Canadian Language and Literacy Research Network, 2010, p. 14). There are five implicit principles that are thought to guide preschool children's development of counting procedures, as illustrated in Figure 11.7 and described below:

- **Stable order** refers to the fact that number words are always used in the same order (i.e., counting in the order of "1, 2, 4" is incorrect).
- **One-to-one correspondence** means that one, and only one, number word can be assigned to each counted object in a set (i.e., an item in a set that has been assigned "2" cannot also be assigned "5") (CCCF & Canadian Language and Literacy Research Network, 2010). When each child has a cookie at snack, there is one cookie per child. This is one-to-one correspondence. It is still one-to-one correspondence when each child has two cookies. When children understand that for snack each child will have one or two cookies, they are beginning to understand the concept that one group has the same number of things as another.
- **Cardinality** refers to the act that the value of the last number word used when counting indicates the quantity of items in the set (i.e., counting "1, 2, 3, 4" means that there are four items in the set).
- **Abstraction** means that any set of items can be counted (i.e., a book, two bananas, and three pencils can be counted together as a set of six items).
- **Order irrelevance** means that items can be counted in any order (i.e., counting from right to left, left to right, or in no particular sequence results in the same total number of items) (CCCF & Canadian Language and Literacy Research Network, 2010).

The Difference Between Counting by Rote and Rational Counting

Although children may be able to count to 10 by rote memory, they may have difficulty understanding that they can have two cookies each. Reciting the numbers from 1 to 10 may appear easy for children. When asked to point and count the 10 blocks that are lined up, a child may point to the same block more than once. It takes time and experience for children to develop the one-to-one correspondence concept so that they can move from rote to rational counting (Clements & Sarama, 2014). There is a difference between rote counting and rational counting. Rote counting involves the memorization of numbers. Rational counting tells children "how many there are." For children to count rationally, they need to demonstrate one-to-one correspondence. This is a skill that generally does not occur until the kindergarten years because relating the concept of one-to-one correspondence to rational counting is a complex skill. This process requires children to keep track while reciting a stable order of numerals to their one-to-one counting (Clements & Sarama, 2014). Children require play experiences that embed opportunities for them to develop number sense, which are the way in which numbers and tools of measurement work within a given culture. Toddlers and preschoolers encounter numbers every day. They celebrate birthdays as they blow out three candles on a cake and hold up three fingers to demonstrate their age. They see numbers on appliances, the television, and tablets; by their front door; and on car licence plates. In order to count, children require language. Some of the earliest language experiences involving counting come from nursery rhymes, finger plays, and counting books (Phillipson, Sullivan, & Gervasoni, 2017).

By the end of kindergarten, most children count sets that contain a quantity of items for which they know the number words: if they know the numbers up to 12, they can accurately count a set with 12 items. Not all children develop these essential principles, and some still struggle with them even into the higher grades. "Those who are not proficient counters and who do not know the essential principles by the time they enter Grade 1 may be at risk for difficulties with mathematics" (CCCF & Canadian Language and Literacy Research Network, 2010, p. 14). Researchers have identified counting as a worthwhile focus in early learning programming.

Concrete mathematical experiences are essential to the development of counting skills. Children need to touch and feel the items they are counting. Early learning teachers encourage children to count with their fingers. *Finger gnosis* is the term used to describe counting with fingers. Introducing children to the use of their fingers to count supports them in developing mathematical abilities (Penner-Wilger & Anderson, 2013).

There are many opportunities within early childhood programs to encourage learning mathematical concepts daily, such as counting items to reciting finger plays. These strategies support the development of the most important area of mathematical learning: counting. In addition to counting procedures, early learning teachers emphasize a number of other mathematical concepts during children's play episodes, such as geometry and measurement, pattern, sequence, seriation, comparison, and classification, as described below.

Geometry and Measurement

"Geometry and measurement have been called the second most important area of mathematical learning" (CCCF & Canadian Language and Literacy Research Network, 2010, p. 15). What makes geometry and measurement important is their real-world connections. Geometry is about shapes. During their early years, children benefit from being in environments that are rich with opportunities to explore the shapes in their world (Clements & Sarama, 2014). Each object in the environment has its own shape (Charlesworth, 2015). According to Charlesworth (2015), much of the play and activity of an infant revolves around learning about shapes. As children develop, they continue to learn about shapes when they handle objects. Some objects are easier to grasp than others. Some roll, some do not. Some objects are smooth like a spoon, while others are sharp like a fork (Sperry Smith, 2009). When children are classifying, shape is often a basic attribute that they use for comparison. Children usually enjoy having opportunities to experience shapes in their world. They benefit from having opportunities to experiment in creating representations of shapes either two dimensionally in drawings or three dimensionally from clay, sand, and play dough (Charlesworth, 2015).

Measurement is an often neglected mathematics topic for young children (Clements & Sarama, 2014), even though it is one of the easiest concepts to incorporate into children's play. Measurement involves assigning numbers of units to physical quantities such as height, weight, length, and volume. It also involves no physical quantities such as time and temperature (Knaus, 2015). Measurement helps children describe and compare things, as well as record and keep track of information. These skills support children in being able to capture and make predictions about how things may grow and change (Reys, Lindquist, Lambdin, & Smith, 2014).

Early learning teachers provide children with many real-life tools that spark children's interest in mathematical principles. Such tools can be divided into categories: linear measurement (rulers, tape), weight and mass measurement (scales, thermometers), and those that measure volume or capacity (cups, spoons). Measurement brings math and science principles together, such as when children plant seeds and then measure their growth on a daily basis.

Pattern

As children explore the world around them, they develop other mathematical concepts, including pattern. Mathematics is the science and language of patterns and is basic to all mathematical thinking (Charlesworth, 2015). If infants are cared for in a predictable way, they begin to recognize and anticipate the rhythm or pattern of their care. Toddlers experience patterns with movement and rhythm. For example, early learning teachers share a clapping pattern and encourage children to clap along. Preschoolers are able to predict and anticipate events because they have learned about pattern. A pattern is a regular arrangement of objects, numbers, and shapes (Clements & Sarama, 2014). Certain materials such as blocks, beads, mud puddles, and shapes lend themselves to patterns. See Figure 11.8 for an example of a pattern with shapes and colours. During play experiences, when appropriate, early learning teachers encourage children to identify patterns, to practise repeating a pattern (circle, square, circle, square, circle, square), and to grow patterns. Growing patterns are patterns that change from one value to another in a predictable manner. For example, children may start with a certain number of objects, which represent the first *term* of the pattern. Then more objects are systematically added to the previous term, with the pattern that is established. Children generate growing patterns with beads, blocks, and marbles (Rivera, 2015).

Sequence

Similar to pattern, sequence is a mathematical concept that children internalize early in life. Sequence refers to the organization and order of successive events and experiences. When children recognize sequences, they are developing a sense of order, logic, and reason. Children in early learning programs recognize the sequencing of their day, and they become able to predict what will happen next. Similarly, they observe sequences in nature, such as the melting of snow or the falling of leaves. As children listen to stories, they begin to understand the sequence of events and are able to consider how the story unfolds or what comes next (Sousa, 2014).

Figure 11.8 A pattern of shapes and colours.

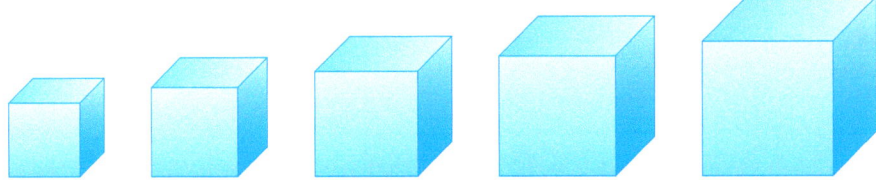

Figure 11.9 How do these blocks represent seriation?

Seriation

Lining up blocks in order from largest to smallest is an example of seriation. In doing so, children exhibit sequencing words, such as *first* and *last*, *beginning* and *end*, and *next to* (Clements & Sarama, 2014). Of the five blocks in Figure 11.9, which one is the smallest and which one comes last? This is an example of a question you can ask children to challenge their seriation skills. Seriation is a mathematics concept that involves organizing or ordering things in a logical way. As children play with different sizes of teddy bear counters, they may put them in order from "baby" to "daddy" bear. As an extension of this type of play, children may be encouraged to tell a story connecting play to math and language. Outdoors, children benefit from having access to materials such as rocks, where they experience moving them from smallest to largest or vice versa. They can tell stories about building roads and paths leading to special places.

Comparison

To be able to pattern, sequence, and seriate, children require skills in being able to compare. When comparing, children discover a relationship between two things or a group of things in connection with a specific attribute. Children may compare by size, quantity, length, age, or other attributes. During play experiences, look for times when you can note that children may be comparing. For example, during block play, when children build a larger garage for a truck that is bigger and a smaller one for one that is shorter, children are comparing. Early learning teachers help children with this skill by modelling basic comparing words, such as *large* and *small*, *big* and *little*, *long* and *short*, *fast* and *slow*, *cold* and *hot*, *near* and *far*, and *thick* and *thin*, to name a few. Can you think of any others (Charlesworth, 2015)?

Classification

In math, as in science, an understanding of constructing logical groups and classifying is essential (Charlesworth, 2015). Classifying is a way of comparing. Classification refers to putting things together and naming the group, such as smooth rocks and rough rocks or rectangular blocks and square blocks. Children naturally engage in sorting activities during play. When adults participate as a play partner, they help children to identify the attributes by which they sorted the materials. This facilitates children in gaining or developing their classification skills. There are many attributes that distinguish items in a collection or the different ways objects can be sorted. These include colour, shape, size, material, pattern, texture, and function (Charlesworth, 2015).

Subitizing

Often associated with mathematical concepts in kindergarten, it is helpful for early learning teachers to understand subitizing as the next level from one-to-one correspondence. "The ability to recognize a small number of briefly presented items without counting

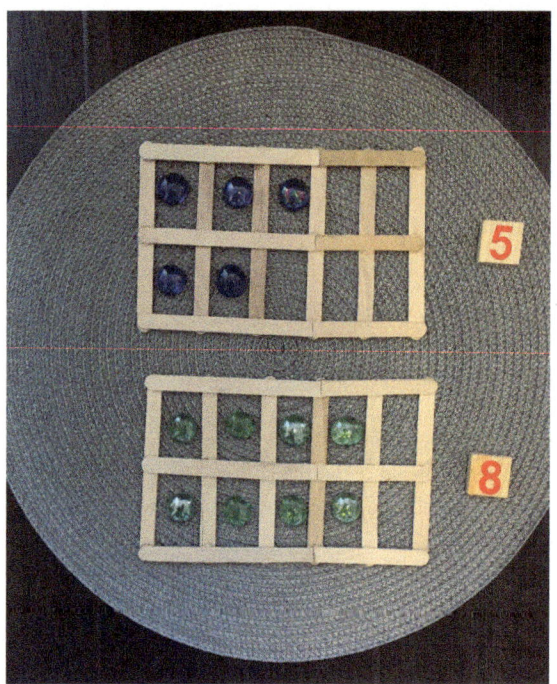

Photo 11.9 Subitizing with glass gems and 10 frames.
Used with Permission of Diane Kashin

items one by one is called subitizing" (McMullen, Hannula-Sormunen, & Lehtinen, 2013, p. 137). Subitizing is instantly seeing how many glass gems are placed in the frame, as depicted in Photo 11.8. Early learning teachers can encourage subitizing with the use of 10 frames purchased or created with materials such as sticks.

THE LANGUAGE OF MATHEMATICS

The language of mathematics is part of the development of verbal communication skills. People all around the world, of all ages, speak math (Rosales, 2015). Can you think of any math words that you could use with young children? How many "math words" (any words that relate to math) can you think of? Write them down.

STOP ... THINK ... DISCUSS ... REFLECT

Discuss your list with a classmate. Who had the longer list? When you compare your lists, you are using math language. Identify the math words you used to compare. How might you incorporate this type of language into a conversation with children? Are there some early learning experience centres where it is easier to incorporate these words than others? If so, which ones? Why? How might you try to incorporate math into experience centres that normally do not focus on math, such as a music and movement centre?

When you were comparing your lists of math words, were words such as *plus*, *minus*, and *equals* used? Would you consider *down*, *between*, and *to the left* as words describing mathematical relationships? There are different types of math words. *Positional* words are those that describe place. The most difficult positional word concepts for young children are left and right. These are also sometimes the most difficult for adults, too! Do you rely on a ring or a watch to help sort out your left hand from your right? Some other examples of positional words include *in*, *out*, *outside*, *apart*, *over*, *under*, *top*, *bottom*, *middle*, and *together*. Other types of math words are *directional* words. As children use a pulley to move an object, they may describe the experience as moving the object "forward." This is an example of a *directional* word. Can you think of others? *Sequence* words are very important, as they help children develop a sense of order. The ability to sequence is a skill needed to solve more complex problems found in number systems. Lining up farm animals gives children a chance to use sequence words such as *first and last*, *beginning and end*, *before and after*, and *next to*. *Shape* words help children to categorize and identify everyday objects. They can use the word *round* to describe a clock. They can also call it a *circle*. Other shape words include *sides*, *corners*, *flat*, *box*, *carton*, *tube*, *triangle*, and so on. The final category of math language words is *number* words, which describe our numbers system. These words help children to compare quantities and to recognize relationships. Examples of number words include *more, less, the same, many, fewer, greater than*, and *less than*. How might you use number words at snack time? What about when children are playing with blocks or are in the dramatic play centre?

A NUMBERS-RICH ENVIRONMENT

To promote literacy, early learning environments have literacy materials distributed throughout; to promote mathematics, so should there be numbers and math materials (Clements & Sarama, 2014). Early learning teachers set the stage for children to develop mathematical concepts by providing sufficient materials that will intrigue children to explore them. The materials and the environment are rich with objects that can be used to explore shape and number concepts during everyday play experiences (Van Hoorn et al., 2011), in both the indoor and the outdoor play spaces. Counting books should be available. Other books, such as *Three Little Pigs*, also reinforce math concepts. Blocks, rocks, sand, water, large boxes, plastic containers, and digging materials should be easily accessible to children during their outdoor play.

Just as labelling the environment with words supports children's language and literacy development, early learning teachers record numbers. Children may find labelling with numbers to be easier than writing words. The number *1* really only involves a short stroke of a marker or crayon. Having math materials available will reinforce children's explorations with concepts. Manipulatives are easily handled concrete objects, such as puzzles, pegboards, and objects that can be used as counters (beads, rocks, buttons). Children use these manipulatives in ways that help them understand or explore mathematical concepts. These materials support children's quest to gain knowledge in sorting, classifying, comparing, and counting. Of course, an early learning environment that supports mathematical concepts will always have a substantial set of unit blocks, as they naturally promote shape and number concepts. For a list of materials and supplies that encourage mathematical experiences and could be added to the indoor and outdoor play spaces, refer to Table 11.4.

Mathematical Invitations and Provocations

All that we do with children should be invitational to support the premise that children learn through play. Play is freely chosen. Early learning teachers set up invitations that, if responded to, become what is known as provocations inspired by the Reggio Emilia approach (Novakowski, 2015). If the invitation is ignored, it becomes an opportunity to reflect on why. Could it be that the children were just not interested? Was the invitation hidden away in a corner? Was it presented during a time when children were busy with

Table 11.4 Materials and supplies for mathematics.

Pattern blocks	Parquetry blocks	Objects for sorting and seriating
Colour cubes	Lacing boards	Beads and string
Linking cubes	Pegboards and pegs	Wooden blocks
Attribute blocks	Games and puzzles for number recognition	Counting number books
Tangrams	Scales	Tabletop building toys
Tools for measurement	Play money	Counters such as poker chips, buttons, checkers, rocks

other experiences? It is here that the invitation provides us with a gift—an opportunity to reflect, improve, and change.

The best way to approach math with young children is to make it a meaningful part of their day (CCCF & Canadian Language and Literacy Research Network, 2010). Creating flexible schedules in early learning environments is an important role of early learning teachers. The flow of the day determines the availability of opportunities to learn through play as well as during routine and transitional times. When mathematical concepts are interwoven into the daily routine, there are many experiences that will involve children using their number concepts. Think about a normal day in the life of a preschool environment. Begin at arrival time. What could you do during this time to incorporate numbers? The process of getting ready for lunch involves mathematical concepts; what do you think they might be?

STOP ... THINK ... DISCUSS ... REFLECT

Write down as many ideas you can come up with for incorporating math concepts into arrival and lunchtime. Consider other times of the day, such as tidying up, snack time, and when families pick up children. How many ideas do you have for involving numbers or other math concepts at these times? Write these down. What about group experiences, or what many teachers describe as "gathering time"? Can you think of ways to involve math? Again, write them down and then compare your list with another student. Compare your answers and reflect on what you have learned about creating a math-rich environment. Is there ever a time that we can oversaturate the environment with math concepts? If so, how? How might our actions affect the child's play both positively and negatively?

OBSERVATION

Any time early learning teachers observe children's play, there are opportunities to see that

> they are naturally attracted to mathematical features in their environment. For example, they spontaneously compare the size of objects, they use number words often, they make attempts at counting, and they pay attention to characteristics of patterns and shapes, including symmetry when they build with towers and blocks. (CCCF & Canadian Language and Literacy Research Network, 2010, p. 6)

To address children's strengths and interests related to mathematics, early learning teachers observe their play so that they may scaffold learning opportunities to extend the types of experiences that connect children's play to mathematics. Take notes as children play with mathematics. How do you know that children are at the level they should be for math learning? There are standards for mathematical learning that can be referred to when observing children's experiences with math; however, we caution that if your jurisdiction has such standards, you should avoid testing children's mathematical abilities. Testing children will take the joy out of learning and is not necessary in preschool.

Science and Math Connections

Science interactions support vocabulary development by exposing children to a variety of new words in meaningful contexts. The scientific method involves practices described using verbs such as *observe, predict, estimate, sort,* and *experiment*. As children engage in these practices, they learn new nouns to label what they are seeing—*roots, pods, stems*—and adjectives to describe attributes—*sticky, pointy, more than, less than* (Gerde et al., 2013).

The Literacy Connection

Discussing objects that are not present or events in the past or future supports the development of abstract reasoning and is related to literacy skills. While engaged in science activity, children make predictions and plan explorations. When they plan what they should do to find out whether seeds need water to sprout, they use language in the future tense. When talking about seeds sprouting, children are required to reason and talk about changes they have not yet experienced.

Children's literature supports providing hands-on opportunities to apply science and mathematical skills. Integrating these areas of exploration into early learning programming creates an interweaving rather than a compartmentalization of math and science concepts. Math and science principles can be learned during play. Creating games from books is a good way to provide math experiences, especially if they are adapted from a children's story. Games with spinners allow for numeral recognition and counting practice. Lotto games let children use their matching skills, practise one-to-one correspondence, and build on early counting skills. More complex games involve circular paths, both short (10 to 20 spaces) and long. Taking these types of games as examples and creating your own game based on a book would be an excellent way to incorporate literature and math. For example, the children's story *The Prince Child* by Maranke Rinck (2004) has vibrant illustrations of animals, each describing the gift the animals are bringing to the prince child, who, the story reveals, ends up being a toad with a crown. A lotto game can be created, and the children inspired by the story will be intrigued to match each animal with the gift being brought to the prince. Using the same book, children can spin a wheel and move a game piece around a circle representing each animal, and they could collect cards representing the gifts.

Math and science can be used to support literacy development and vice versa. The content of children's literature can serve as the basis for conversations between children and adults around concepts. Creating science charts, producing graphs, recording numerical data, and recording findings in journals provide an important connection between math, science, and language and literacy development (Brenneman, Stevenson-Boyd, & Frede, 2009).

The Music and Movement Connection

There are many finger plays, nursery rhymes, and children's songs that use math words. How many monkeys are jumping on the bed? What happened to Humpty Dumpty?

Children love to move their bodies, and it isn't difficult to relate their movements to mathematical language. Imagine children singing "Ring around the Rosie." What movements might the children be making? What math words could you use as an early learning teacher to reinforce the children's understanding?

The Art Connection

Through art, children can experiment with and practise a number of mathematical concepts. Children can print vertical, horizontal, and diagonal lines. They combine lines to form shapes. This is just one example of combining mathematics and art. Can you think of others? What happens when children mix paint colours? When red and yellow are combined, they equal orange. This is an illustration of a math concept. How would you document this for the children? Children can experiment with symmetry when they create nature mandalas. Mandalas are an ancient art form. When using natural materials, there is a connection between art, math, and science.

The Cooking Connection

Cooking with children is an experience that can involve all of the senses: hearing, touching, tasting, smelling, and seeing. Cooking is a hands-on experience. Children who participate in cooking may feel like they are role-playing adult behaviours. Children learn by imitating the adults in their world. Cooking is an excellent way to encourage and reinforce many skills. These include mathematics (measuring, counting, ordering, etc.). Cooking clearly involves science. Children can observe and identify the parts of a raw egg (the shell, the yolk, the white). Depending on the cooking method and recipe chosen, children can see the egg transform to hard-boiled, soft-boiled, scrambled, or fried. Encourage the children to predict changes and then to test the accuracy of their prediction.

Photo 11.10 Nature mandala.

Used with Permission of Diane Kashin

"What will happen when we cook the egg for 10 minutes in boiling water?" Lead the children into an investigation of the origins of the egg. Imagine the possibilities. Cooking also involves language, art, health, safety, and nutrition. Cooking provides opportunities in social and emotional development (taking turns, sharing, trying new experiences) and physical development (small muscle actions such as chopping and stirring, large muscle actions such as kneading and mixing). It is the ultimate learning experience and can produce delicious results. As with all experiences with young children, it is the *process* of cooking that leads to learning, not the finished product.

TERMS THAT INFLUENCE EARLY LEARNING PLAY ENVIRONMENTS

Here, we introduce you to three additional terms that are used when exploring math and science in children's play.

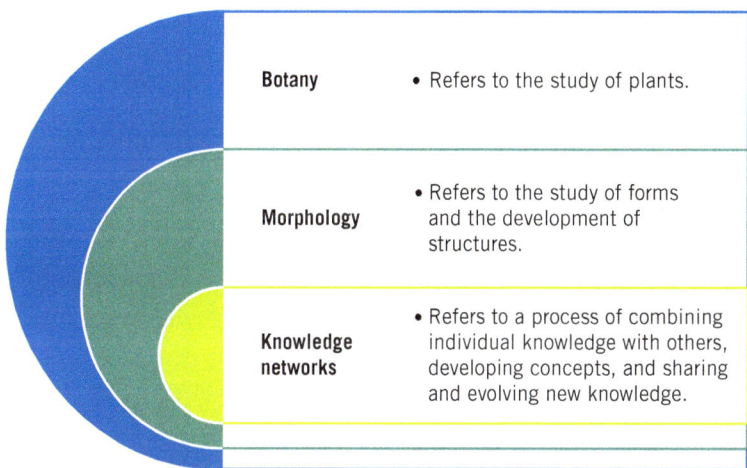

SUMMARY

Chapter Preview

- Mathematical and scientific experiences are significant to children's play and development.
- Math and science experiences during the early years offer children powerful ways of knowing about the world. Being engaged with math and science during the early years provides children with opportunities to formulate the foundational skills required for more formal instruction given in the school system.
- Early learning teachers offer children play environments that support them learning about science, technology, engineering, and math (STEM), as these are identified as twenty-first-century learning skills.
- Early learning teachers recognize the importance of mathematics and science as core areas of play and how play supports children in learning about the various concepts associated with these areas of inquiry.

Theory

- Our understandings of how math and science concepts are presented to young children are based on the theories of Piaget and Vygotsky and learning through play.
- According to Piaget's theory, children acquire knowledge through interaction with their environment and distinguish three types of knowledge: physical, logical-mathematical, and social knowledge.
- Lev Vygotsky promoted a more social context for constructivism— "it is through others that we develop into ourselves" (Vygotsky, 1981, p. 181).
- Higher levels of learning coincide with higher-order thinking skills. Benjamin Bloom (1956) identified six levels of higher-order thinking, from knowledge at the lowest level to evaluation at the highest.

Defining Science, Mathematics, and Scientific Inquiry

- Simply put, science involves processes, content, and concepts, and mathematics is about numbers.
- Scientific inquiry involves the process of questioning, predicting, investigating, analyzing, explaining, and communicating as a way to learn about the world.

The Importance of Science and Mathematics

- David and Francis Hawkins suggested that early learning programs offer children a variety of materials that may be used for exploration and "messing about."

Concept Development in Science and Mathematics

- Concept growth and development begins in infancy.
- Concepts are the building blocks of knowledge. They allow children to organize and categorize information
- As children develop, their thinking related to mathematical and scientific concepts goes through four distinct stages involving representation: concrete, semi-concrete, semi-abstract, and abstract.

Science, Mathematics, and Development

- Mathematical and science concepts begin when life begins.

Learning Science and Math through Play

- Math and science are learned from a variety of experiences, materials, and role models.
- Through playing, exploring, dialogue, collaboration, problem solving, curiosity, reflection, and reasoning, learning about science and math evolves.
- Bruner advocated that for children to gain concept attainment, early learning teachers must support modes of knowledge representation. He identified them as enactive, iconic, and symbolic.

Playing with Science Is to Celebrate Wonder

- Children are natural wonderers.
- Early learning teachers embrace children's sense of curiosity and wonderment by providing stimulating, invigorating, and experiential learning opportunities.

The Scientific Method for Young Children

- Early learning teachers encourage children to engage in an inquiry process.
- Children use a process of observing, classifying, experimenting, predicting, drawing conclusions, and communicating ideas.

Setting Up an Environment to Support Scientific Inquiry

- Worksheets are developmentally inappropriate and do not support a play-based approach to learning math and science.
- Documenting children's work supports children, families, and early learning teachers in understanding the value of learning math and science within a play-based, constructivist approach.
- Early learning teachers strike a balance between child-initiated play with the active presence of the early learning teacher and intentional teaching through playful learning.
- An early learning environment has materials that are rich in science possibilities and that will introduce children to the wonders of the natural world.
- The types of materials depend on the type of science being explored. There are five types identified: physical, life, earth, technology, and social sciences.
- Sand and water play provides children with experiences rich in mathematical and scientific learning.

The Development of Mathematical Concepts

- Mathematics learning begins in infancy. Mathematical experiences and learning during the early years contribute to children's later learning of other subjects, including literacy.
- Between the ages of 2 and 3, children begin to use language related to mathematics, incorporating number words into their play experiences.
- The five implicit principles that are thought to guide preschool-aged children's development of counting procedures are stable order, one-to-one correspondence, abstraction, cardinality, and order irrelevance.
- There is a difference between rote counting and rational counting. Rote counting involves the memorization of numbers. Rational counting tells children "how many there are." For children to count rationally, they need to demonstrate one-to-one correspondence.
- Other mathematical concepts that early learning teachers introduce children to during their play experiences include geometry and measurement, pattern, sequence, seriation, comparison, and classification.

The Language of Mathematics

- Math has its own language. There are different types of math words, including positional, directional, sequence, shape, and number words.

A Numbers-Rich Environment

- Early learning teachers set the stage for children to develop mathematical concepts by providing sufficient, intriguing materials. The environment is rich with objects that support the exploration of concepts such as shape and number during play experiences.

- Early learning teachers label things in the environment with numbers, in addition to labelling with words for literacy.

Observation

- Reflection is an important part of observation. Early learning teachers and students observe the environment and consider where mathematical concepts can be introduced, supported, and reinforced.

Science and Math Connections

- Math and science are naturally connected to other areas, including literacy, art, music, movement, and cooking.

REVIEW QUESTIONS

1. Describe Piaget's three types of knowledge, and give an example of each.
2. According to the theories of Vygotsky, how do children learn best? What implications does this have for math and science?
3. Benjamin Bloom identified six levels of thinking. How does this relate to teaching and learning about math and science?
4. What are the simple definitions of math and science?
5. What is meant by concept development in math and science? Describe some math and science concepts.
6. What are some of the first concepts children encounter as infants and toddlers?
7. Why do you think our sense of wonder dissipates over time and that there is a distinct difference between a child's and an adult's sense of wonder?
8. Describe how the processes that make up the scientific method are interconnected.
9. Why are worksheets inappropriate? How would you explain to parents that there is a better way to support the development of math and science skills in their children?
10. Explain what a child needs to know in order to count rationally, rather than engage in rote counting. What is the difference?
11. What is meant by the language of math? What types of math words are there? Give an example of each.
12. Highlight how an early learning teacher–created game board based on a children's story connects literacy to mathematical concepts.

MAKING CONNECTIONS

Theory to Practice

1. Find a suitable container for classification. You would be looking for something that has equal compartments for sorting. Get a collection of natural items for sorting—small rocks, small shells, acorns, and so on. Practise sorting these by different attributes—colour, texture, shape, and size. Can you think of some cognitively challenging questions that you could ask children

while they are in the process of sorting these items? Once you have practised this experience, present it to some children and record your observations of their processes for classification. Did your questions lead the children to higher-order thinking?

2. Visit your local museum or science centre to get inspired. What did you learn? How can you take your learning and create a developmentally appropriate experience for children? Would you take children on a field trip to a museum or a science centre? Why or why not?

3. Look around your house and find an item that you wonder about. Perhaps you wonder where the item came from or how it works. Perhaps you do not know the history of the item and wonder about who owned it before you. Perhaps you wonder about how it was made. Look at your wonder closely, from all angles. Notice details. Now sketch the wonder with pencil and paper. Are you able to capture the details? Now add colour to your sketch with paints, pencils, pastels, or markers. After that, you can represent the wonder three dimensionally with plasticine or clay. What scientific processes and mathematical concepts were explored while you conducted this experience? Now take your wonder to the children and recreate the experience.

4. Take the time to observe children whenever you can. The next time you are in an early learning environment, walk around the room and take digital images of potential areas where math can happen in meaningful ways. Reflection is an important component of observation, so view the digital images you have taken and choose two different areas or experience centres to practise observing children as they play. Take some notes and more images and reflect on your findings. What could you do to encourage mathematical experiences for children? Remember not to limit your observations to just the indoor environment. Consider the potential for math in the outdoors!

DIGITAL PORTFOLIO ENTRIES

Potential portfolio entries for your digital portfolio could include the following:

- When I think of math and science I wonder about . . .
- As an early learning student, my role in introducing math and science into learning environments with children is . . .
- I wonder if I have sufficient passion and knowledge about math and science to be able to effectively . . .
- I am concerned that my understanding of math or science concepts may . . .

CURIOUS?

Do a library search for children's play and math and science to find out more regarding the latest research on the varying perspectives presented.

CHAPTER 12
Music, Movement, and Play

Rawpixel.com/Shutterstock

> ❝ Music expresses that which cannot be said and on which it is impossible to be silent. ❞
>
> —Victor Hugo (1802–1885)

LEARNING OUTCOMES

After reviewing this chapter, you should be able to:

- Describe reasons why music and movement may not be presented to children in the same way as other programming experiences.

- Outline the historical influence of music and movement, including the contemporary perspectives.

- Explain why music and movement are important for children during their early years.

- Describe how music and movement support the child's psychomotor development, social and emotional development, cognitive development, and aesthetic appreciation.

- Outline the considerations that early learning teachers make when introducing songs and related music and movement experiences to children.

- Describe the roles of early learning teachers in presenting music and movement to children.

Sharing Stories of Practice

When I was first hired at an early learning centre after graduation, I was surprised to observe that children were exposed to music all day long. For the first few days I thought, "Wow, this is neat—I am hearing music from the local radio station—the golden oldie hits." I would sing along to the songs. It gave me a sense of comfort. After a few days, I found myself feeling less comfortable. When we took children on walks, the radio was attached to the buggy. When children were outside, music played through the speakers, and when they were trying to settle down for their nap, the station was still on, but lowered. It was adult music, and it seemed out of place in an environment that was supposed to be devoted to play.

By the end of my second week, I was using much of my energy to deal with the music. I was constantly fighting my feelings of disequilibrium. I began to question if children also needed to use some of their precious energy to block out the music, which I had now determined to be noise. I also wondered if this was healthy for children—were they acquiring a sense of and appreciation for music? Finally, I determined that I needed to speak with my colleagues. My colleagues were interested in my feelings and open to discussing this practice. One colleague indicated that she thought that because so many children now grow up in homes with music and the television playing constantly, this was more of a comfort to the children than a hindrance. Another colleague thought that because, in her opinion, most early learning teachers were not musically inclined, this was a way to expose children to music.

We collectively determined that we would try an experiment. We would reduce the times when the music was on and reduce the volume of the music. We decided to include calming music when the children were settling down to rest and nature-related music when they were outdoors. Over a month-long period, we noticed significant changes in the children. They were calmer and seemed less frenetic outdoors with the natural-themed music. When we played children's music, the children seemed more inclined to move and dance. We also noticed that some children were using the music centre more frequently and talking about musical concepts!

My advice to new teachers—music, like all early learning experiences, is developmentally and inclusively appropriate for all children. When children have access to instruments, they initiate their own experiences, especially when teachers provide the materials, space, and time for music. Music is as important as all of the other experiences. It is incorporated into the environment at appropriate times so that children develop an appreciation for it. Choose how to present music with the same care as blocks, outdoor play, math, or science.

Katie, ECE graduate, 2015

CHAPTER PREVIEW

Many researchers and educational experts have reported the benefits of music and movement to children's whole development (Ehrlin & Gustavsson, 2015; Welch, 2015). Music and movement are important components of the experiences extended to children during their early years. Music play engages children in physical, social, cognitive, kinesthetic, and communicative challenges. The National Association for Music Education (2017), in its early childhood education position statement, identifies that:

- All children have musical potential. Every child has the potential for successful, meaningful interactions with music. The development of this potential, through numerous encounters with a wide variety of music and abundant opportunities to participate regularly in developmentally appropriate music activities, is the right of every young child.

- Children bring their own unique interests and abilities to the music learning environment. Each child will take away that bit of knowledge and skill that he or she is uniquely capable of understanding and developing. Children must be left, as much as possible, in control of their own learning. They should be provided with a rich environment that offers many possible routes for them to explore as they grow in awareness and curiosity about music.
- Very young children are capable of developing critical thinking skills through musical ideas. Children use thinking skills when making musical judgments and choices.
- Children come to early childhood music experiences from diverse backgrounds. Their home languages and cultures are to be valued and seen as attributes that enrich everyone in the learning environment.
- Children should experience exemplary musical sounds, activities, and materials. Their play and learning time is valuable and should not be wasted on experiences with music or activities of trite or questionable quality.
- Children should not be encumbered with the need to meet performance goals. Opportunities should be available for children to develop accurate singing, rhythmic responses to music, and performance skills on instruments. Each child's attainment of a predetermined performance level, however, is neither essential nor appropriate.
- Children's play is their work. Children should have opportunities for individual musical play, such as in a "music corner," as well as for group musical play, such as singing games. Children learn within a playful environment. Play provides a safe place to try on the roles of others, to fantasize, and to explore new ideas. Children's play involves imitation and improvisation.
- Children learn best in pleasant physical and social environments. Music learning contexts will be most effective when they include (1) play, (2) games, (3) conversations, (4) pictorial imagination, (5) stories, (6) shared reflections on life events and family activities, and (7) personal and group involvement in social tasks. Dominant use of drill-type activities and exercises and worksheet tasks will not provide the kind of active, manipulative, and creative musical environment essential to the development of young minds.
- Diverse learning environments are needed to serve the developmental needs of many individual children. Children interact with musical materials in their own way based on their unique experiences and developmental stages. One child may display sophistication and confidence in creating songs in response to dolls. Another child, in the same setting, may move the dolls around without uttering a sound—but this "silent participator" leaves the area content in having shared the music play. The silent participator often is later heard playing in another area softly singing to a different set of dolls—demonstrating a delayed response.
- Children need effective adult models. Parents and teachers who provide music in their child's life are creating the most powerful route to the child's successful involvement in the art (p. 1).

The National Association for Music Education (2017) advocates for children to experience music in play-based environments. Children benefit when music is available as free choice, in small groups, and integrated across the curriculum. Ideally, early learning teachers will ensure that children are exposed to traditional children's songs, folk songs, classical music, and music from a variety of cultures and styles as well as musical instruments.

Music and movement are interconnected. Movement opportunities help children become more aware of their bodies, what their bodies can do, and how they may use their bodies in their space. Music develops auditory discrimination, phonemic awareness acquired from rhyming words, and abstract thinking related to mathematics (Ehrlin & Gustavsson, 2015). Despite the importance of music and movement, there is growing concern among researchers that early learning teachers do not emphasize this part of the program to the extent of other programming areas. This may be due in part to not having sufficient exposure or training in music and movement to fully support this programming area (Ehrlin & Gustavsson, 2015). Ehrlin and Gustavsson (2015) identified that limited importance is placed on early learning teachers developing sufficient knowledge and skills in singing and playing as it relates to music (Ehrlin, 2012; Garvis & Pendergast, 2011; Sundin, 1995). Yet as the relationship of music to academic skills and brain functioning becomes more apparent, there is a need for early learning teachers to increase their understanding and practices of music in early learning programs. It can no longer be viewed as an "add on" or "nice to have" (Ehrlin & Gustavsson, 2015).

Early learning teachers are increasingly being put under pressure to offer children under the age of 5 experiences that support them in academic preparation, rather than to engage them in the broad-spectrum learning that occurs through play (Association of Canadian Deans of Education [ACDE], 2016). For some families, there can be a gap in their knowledge about how music play relates to child development and learning. For example, many families may not know the connection between music and movement, language development, mathematical concepts, and overall brain development (Lindeman, 2016). Early learning teachers play an important role in sharing with families how musical attributes support children's development.

STOP ... THINK ... DISCUSS ... REFLECT

Think about how families instinctively use music to comfort children. What are some of the ways adults use music with children? Why do you think these actions offer children a sense of comfort?

As you explore this chapter, think about the music and movement experiences you have had in your life. Think about the kind of music you are attracted to. What kinds of music make you want to move, dance, or sing? Can you keep the beat by counting? Does singing out loud give you joy? Does it help you relieve stress? Music and movement relate to all developmental domains. How are music and movement related to play? In this chapter, we highlight the relationship of music to movement and how music and movement are integrated into children's play

HISTORICAL INFLUENCES OF MUSIC AND MOVEMENT

The importance of music and movement to play has long been identified as an important feature of childhood. For example, in *The Principles of Psychology*, Herbert Spencer (1896) identified four types of play: physical play, artistic-aesthetic play, games, and mimicry. Artistic-aesthetic play includes music and movement as a key element.

Jean-Jacques Rousseau and Maria Montessori both advocated for children to be given the opportunity to experience music in their lives. Rousseau stressed the importance of adults providing environments that respected children's natural ways of knowing and learning. Music and movement are natural for children and interconnected from a growth and development perspective. Children cannot flourish without access to both. He indicated that adults have a role in singing to children, starting with simple songs. He believed that by exposing children to music and singing, their voices would, over time, become accurate, uniform, and flexible (Isenberg & Jalongo, 2010).

Montessori incorporated sound exploration activities in the children's environment. For example, she developed a set of mushroom-shaped bells so that children could discover various musical concepts. These bells offer children many musical discovery options. Through exploration of the mushroom bells, children can discover sounds, patterning, how to create music, how to vary sounds, and what happens when bells are combined with other musical instruments.

Another leader who has influenced our understanding of the importance of music in the lives of young children is Carl Orff (1895–1982). Using a child-centred approach, he established a school that incorporated movement through gymnastics with music and dance. He believed that children needed the freedom to spontaneously react, create, and produce their own music and rhythmic responses. Orff role modelled and supported children in using their imaginations to explore making music with their voices and simple instruments.

Howard Gardner (1996) has provided a contemporary approach, identifying music as one of the eight types of intelligences. The others are linguistic, logical-mathematical, spatial, bodily-kinestic, interpersonal, intrapersonal, and naturalistic intelligences. Gardner indicated that music appreciation offers heightened perceptual discrimination, body awareness, and a sense of pitch and melody. He suggested that musical intelligence is aligned with linguistic intelligence (Earle, 2013).

As outlined in Table 12.1, according to Gardner's theory, musical intelligence, bodily-kinesthetic intelligence, linguistic intelligence, and spatial intelligence are essential for children's development. Music and movement contribute to enhancing each of the intelligences outlined. They are also interrelated to understanding the concepts of physics and mathematics for *logical-mathematical intelligence* and have connections to *interpersonal intelligence,* since music brings people together, and *intrapersonal intelligence*, since music contributes to the development of the self. Music connects to *naturalistic intelligence*, as it can be a significant way in which children relate to nature.

Table 12.1 Gardner's multiple intelligences related to music and movement.

Music intelligence involves skill in the performance, composition, and appreciation of musical patterns. Music intelligence is having the capacity to recognize and compose musical pitches, tones, and rhythms.

Bodily-kinesthetic intelligence entails the potential of using one's whole body or parts of the body to solve problems. This includes using mental abilities to coordinate movement with music.

Linguistic intelligence involves the skills of words, either spoken or written. It is the ability to read, write, tell stories, and memorize the meaning of words.

Spatial intelligence involves the potential to recognize, adapt, and use the varying types of space, such as wide space and more confined areas.

Contemporary views suggest that children benefit from music based on four elements:

- **Listening:** This requires children to have access to a variety of music, including music from their culture, classical music, and easy listening music based on the interests of the children and at appropriate times.
- **Moving:** This requires children to have time and space to experiment with body movements and rhythm as music is played.
- **Playing:** This requires children to have access to music, instruments, and dramatic play props that will support them in acting out their interpretations of the music.
- **Singing:** This requires children to have an early learning environment that supports them in having exposure to song, opportunities for singing and experimenting with words, and instruments and dramatic play props (Welch, 2015).

Morin (2001) indicated the need for early learning teachers to develop a concept of play and to think about how play relates to the musical learner. She identified that "play, like music, is symbolic, meaningful, active, rule-governed, and episodic" (p. 25). Morin categorized music play as follows:

> *Cooperative music play* recognizes the role of socialization in children's learning and requires children to interact and communicate; *functional music play* encompasses exploring the environmental and musical sounds, sound production techniques, and resources that introduce musical concepts and ideas; *constructive music play* is an extension of exploration and involves creative idea development such as improvisation, composition, instrument-making, or sound recording; *dramatic music play* uses instruments or singing in role playing, make-believe, or story-telling contexts; *kinesthetic music play* involves the movement response to recorded music or instrumental or vocal sounds, with or without objects like streamers or scarves; and *games with rules* include more structured music experiences such as singing, clapping, or dancing games with predetermined actions and/or socially developed rules. (p. 26)

Early learning teachers incorporate play and learning experiences with strategies that promote music and movement through exploration and discovery in the early learning environment.

THE IMPORTANCE OF MUSIC AND MOVEMENT

The early years are critical in terms of children learning how to unscramble the aural images of music and to develop mental representations for organizing the music of the culture (Welch, 2015). This process is similar to the young child engaging in the "language babble" stage necessary for language development.

As outlined in Table 12.2, children develop musically through a predictable sequence to basic music competence. This includes singing in tune and marching to a beat (Guilmartin & Levinowitz, 1996; Yüksel, 2016). Children are born with the potential to learn and develop musical skills and talents, just as they are able to develop art or science skills. Children's interest in music and movement is influenced by their play environments and role models.

Music and movement are important experiences and features of early learning programs. Children flourish in exploring musical options in environments where early learning teachers have thoughtfully planned for this area of the program. Ideally, music and movement are transparent in both the planned portion of the program and in children's spontaneous play. The more opportunities children have to explore music through spontaneous play, the more likely they are to create music and engage in exploration (Lindeman, 2016).

Photo 12.1 Children's interest in music is influenced by their environments.

Used with Permission of Angela Roy

Table 12.2 The sequence of music and movement with young children.

Infants' Developmental Sequence of Music	Infants' Developmental Sequence of Movement
■ Are sensitive to loud and soft sounds. ■ Are soothed by soft, rhythmic, melodious sounds (Isenberg & Jalongo, 2010). ■ The more lively the music, the more active the response—eyes or head turn toward music.	■ Respond to music using the entire body. ■ Infants who are sitting tend to bounce to the music. ■ Infants in an upright position may move from side to side or bounce up or down. ■ Infants turn body toward music, wave hands and feet.
Toddlers' Developmental Sequence of Music	**Toddlers' Developmental Sequence of Movement**
■ May imitate sound. ■ May try to make sound with toys or household objects. ■ Will react positively to music by clapping or bouncing to the music they are familiar with. ■ May hum sounds during play. ■ Are able to discriminate among sounds and songs. ■ Are interested in musical instruments.	■ Respond to music using fine and gross motor skills with various body parts relevant to the music—arms and legs for some, upper torso for others. ■ Respond to the tempo of the music by moving body fast or slow. ■ Dance to music and produce some words with the dance.
Preschoolers' Developmental Sequence of Music	**Preschoolers' Developmental Sequence of Movement**
■ Begin to recognize songs and sing the songs with accuracy. ■ Able to play a simple rhythm instrument such as bells or sticks.	■ Body movements become more coordinated and refined to music. ■ Movements such as heel to toe and tiptoes are evident.

continues ▶

▶ *continues*

■ Able to reproduce rhythm patterns. ■ Begin to recognize the sounds of different musical instruments such as horn, bells, flutes, etc. ■ Able to sing familiar songs from beginning to end, some with basic musical concepts such as high/low, fast/slow, loud/soft. ■ Participate in group singing games and make up parts to songs with rhythm. ■ Participate in listening to music. ■ Begin to experiment with sounds.	■ Action songs completed with varying moves to music. ■ Songs are sung as movements take place. ■ Able to switch from one movement to another with speed and success. ■ Movements become more creative and varied among the children, using the whole body with the music to jump, hop, and walk.
Kindergarten-Age Developmental Sequence of Music	**Kindergarten-Age Developmental Sequence of Movement**
■ Able to illustrate pitch, rhythm, and melody. ■ Able to produce musical concepts of fast/slow, high/low on keyboard. ■ Able to reproduce sounds, tones, and patterns. ■ Able to produce a vocal range of five to six notes (Isenberg & Jalongo, 2010). ■ Able to produce new words for songs.	■ Movements are well coordinated with music. ■ Combine two movements at the same time, such as marching and keeping the beat with instruments.
School-Aged Developmental Sequence of Music	**School-Aged Developmental Sequence of Movement**
■ Able to sing "in tune." ■ Begin to sing simple two-part harmony with role modelling. ■ Able to sing more complicated songs from memory. ■ Able to identify the types of music that are preferred. ■ Able to produce music on musical instruments.	■ Movements match musical characteristics. ■ Movements move from simple to complex with ease. ■ Improvising of movements completed with ease. ■ Complex moves in dances achieved.

Early learning teachers often use the terms *creative movement*, *movement*, and *creative dance* interchangeably. Dance differs from movement. *Dance* is a more formal, structured movement. It integrates the mind and the body (Menzer, 2015). Dance is generally based on a foot pattern and body movement that are used to depict the language of the music, including the verbal message, beat, and tone. *Creative movement* refers to the process of children using their bodies, usually with music, to communicate an idea, a feeling, an image, or a belief. It is a noncompetitive activity. *Movement* refers to physical movement of the body that helps to develop skills such as balance, coordination, body awareness, and self image.

STOP ... THINK ... DISCUSS ... REFLECT

Think about creative movement and movement. How do you envision ensuring that children have exposure to both types of movement in the indoor and outdoor environments? How might they differ, depending on location? What happens if you personally are not comfortable with these concepts?

Music is more than singing; it is a way in which children and adults communicate. Music and movement comprise a way in which culture is transferred from one generation to the next. In many cultures, children are introduced to music and movement through dance and song at a very young age. Often family and community gatherings have a strong focus on music, with very young children joining in with song and movement. The Yamaha philosophy is that "music is a common language that unites people across international boundaries" (Yamaha Corporation, 1994, p. 295). Music, creative movement, and dance are interconnected. They include children singing, rhyming, clapping, chanting, tapping, marching, and doing simple dances.

Many researchers highlight the benefits of music and movement on early brain development. According to Habibi (2012) and Welch (2015), music accelerates brain development in young children, particularly in the areas of the brain responsible for processing sound, language development, speech perception, and reading skills. The International Foundation of Music Research (2017), based at the University of Texas, indicates that there is substantial evidence to suggest that music appreciation begins during pregnancy and continues as nurtured through childhood. It outlined that there is sufficient research to suggest that babies are aware of and respond to various sounds, including music, while in the mother's womb. For example, at birth, a baby may turn in the direction of the voice of the mother. Newborns quickly recognize the mother's voice over other voices. They develop the skills to distinguish and respond to changes in a person's voice or pitch before their first birthday. Through the movement of their arms and legs and their babbling and cooing, they express their response to the voice and pitch changes. Enriching music and movement experiences contribute to many aspects of brain development. As we think about the brain working by electrical currents, when children are engaged in movement, they are supporting the brain in replenishing the oxygen levels needed for functioning. The brain produces a chemical called endorphins. This chemical contributes to the child's energy level. Movement is one of the body's fuels responsible for developing the energy levels.

Albin (2016) identified that children with developmental delays benefit from having a combination of physical therapy and creative dance. The combination requires children to engage in physical and cognitive actions. As well, the activity improves their memory, increases physical fitness, and encourages self-expression.

CURIOUS?

On the Internet, search for *music and brain development* to learn more about the relationship of music to brain development during the early years.

As shown in Figure 12.1, Lindeman (2016) outlined benefits to children when they are exposed to music and movement.

Music and movement experiences are inclusive of all children. All children can become engaged in music and movement at various levels. Children who may have developmental delays or difficulties with attention receive comfort from music. Children on the **autism spectrum**, in particular, may find solace in music. Music supports children in stabilizing moods, increases frustration tolerance, and serves as an emotional outlet. Music provides children with an understanding of social-emotional cues. As children grow, music becomes a way to socially connect with each other (Petruta-Maria, 2015).

autism spectrum Refers to a range of conditions children may have that are characterized by difficulties with social skills, repetitive behaviours, speech, and nonverbal communication. Children may have unique strengths and differences.

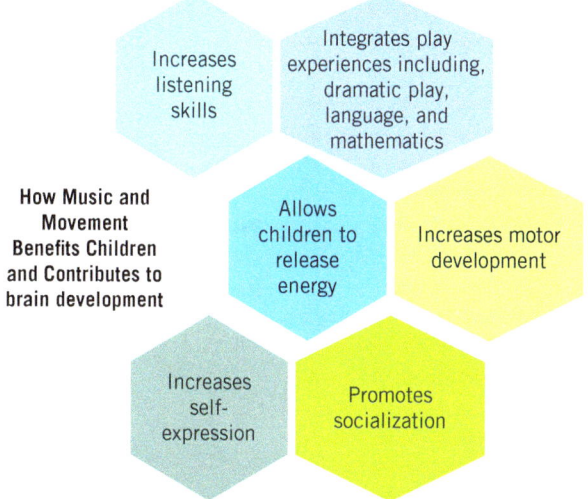

Figure 12.1 How music and movement benefits children.

Early learning teachers think about ways to incorporate music and movement into the play of children. There is a need to provide a variety of musical options to children so that they can develop personal choices. It is important for music from families and cultures to be incorporated into the early learning environment.

Do an Internet search to discover more benefits of music for children with exceptionalities, such as those who may be on the autism spectrum.

Music, Movement, and Child Development

Music and movement contribute to the overall development of the young child, as identified in Figure 12.2. Early learning teachers consistently observe young children to gain a sense of their developmental phase, interests, and capabilities. Examining children's interests and capabilities is of particular importance with music and movement because children may express their musical interests in a variety of ways, such as by listening to music, moving to music, reproducing music, exploring different movements with their bodies, or examining how musical instruments work.

Researchers continue to examine the relationship of music and movement to development. As new research becomes available, the importance of music in the early learning years becomes more evident. For example, recent music neuroscience research indicates that a steady beat affects attention behaviours in humans (Geist, Gesit, & Kuznik, 2012). Geist, Gesit, and Kuznik (2012) indicated that a steady beat is generally processed in the premotor cortex of the brain. This is the same area related to attention. Grahn and Rowe (2013)

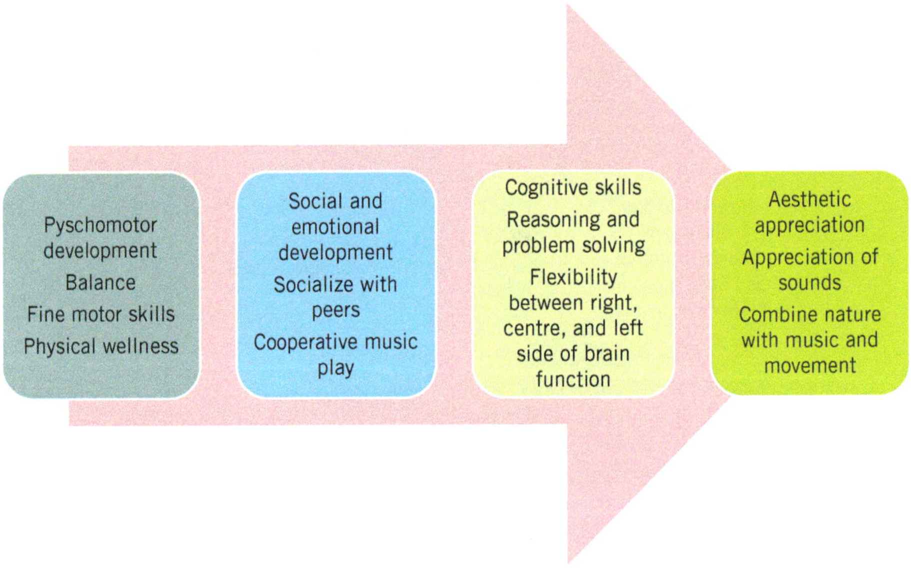

Figure 12.2 Music, movement, and child development.

timing Refers to the ability to feel and express beat.

determined that children's **timing** is fundamental to both movement and music. Beat and timing skills affect children's ability in sport skills, music performance, speech flow, handwriting, and performance of motor tasks (Grahn & Rowe, 2013; Kuhlman & Schweinhart, 2010; Slater, Tierney, & Kraus 2013). Mathematics, reading achievement, self-control, and gross motor skills are influenced by children's skills in beat and timing. Children are more likely to listen when they are engaged in listening to steady beats than when listening to verbal instructions only (Geist et al., 2012). If children do not have experiences and activities that will allow them to develop timing and beat during their early years, this will have a lifelong effect (Goswami, Huss, Mead, Fosker, & Verney, 2013).

cross-lateral movement Refers to laterality, focus, and centring. Laterality is the ability to coordinate the left and right sides of the body. Focus is the ability to coordinate the front and back of the body. Centring refers to coordinating the top and bottom of the body.

There is a relationship between children's **cross-lateral movement** and learning how to read. According to Levinowitz (1998), the development of cross-lateral movement is required for children's eyes to move from one side of the paper to the next—this is a brain function that requires movement from one side of the brain (right side) to the midsection to the other side (left side). Children benefit by being in early learning programs that provide numerous music and movement experiences that require them to use both sides of their brain in movement. Dancing with scarves, crawling like a baby, and walking like a turtle or elephant can achieve this important movement.

Psychomotor Development

Music and movement constitute an important activity that supports children's psychomotor development from as early as 3 months old. For example, when babies are exposed to music, they move their arms and legs in response to the music. Toddlers begin to move their upper torso and their feet to the music. This enhances their ability to develop balance and to lift one foot and then the other. Preschoolers become more efficient in their movements. Music and movement contribute to children expanding their balancing skills and their fine motor skills, such as when they use musical instruments like shakers. School-aged children further expand their psychomotor skills when they combine physical activity in response to music while producing music by singing or performing karaoke.

As discussed throughout this text, children today require as many opportunities for physical activity as possible. Music and movement are easy, natural strategies to use with children to incorporate physical movement into their daily lives. If children do not develop competence in movement during their early years, it may result in a poor body image. Movement skills also affect children's ability or interest in participating in physical sports or other physical activities (Castelli, Glowacki, Barcelona, Calvert, & Hwang, 2015). Through music and movement, children develop the kinesthetic skills of knowing how their body moves within their space. This is required to be successful in sports.

According to Levinowitz (1998), there is a profound connection between rhythm and movement. Levinowitz (1998) suggested that

> The study of rhythm can be thought of as the study of all aspects of flow of music through time. We experience rhythm as the flow of our movement through space. From the developmental perspective, children must experience rhythm in their bodies before they can successfully audiate rhythm in their minds. The early childhood years are crucial for using the body to respond as a musical instrument in many ways to many different kinds of music. Real musical instruments, like tools, can then become simply extensions or amplifications of the body's ability to be musically expressive. (p. 1)

When children experience music and movement activities, those who struggle with movement will become more active, and their motor movement will become more developed (Castelli et al., 2015; Lindeman, 2015). For example, when children perform a motor skill to the beat while singing and moving from one motor movement to the next, such as jumping and hopping, they expand their abilities to engage in more complicated motor movements. Being exposed to psychomotor development opportunities contributes to children being able to move their bodies, use their bodies, and build confidence in their abilities to manoeuvre their bodies as they desire. Psychomotor development is effective when it incorporates listening, moving, playing, and singing (Lindeman, 2015) in various activities.

Photo 12.2 Children express an interest in music from a very young age.
Used with Permission of Gill Robertson

Social and Emotional Development

Music and movement offer children another way to socialize with their peers. For example, when preschool children enjoy music, they will talk to each other about the music they like, identify the songs and games they wish to play, and observe their peers using musical instruments and then share information about them.

When children are involved in music and movement, such as in chase songs or games, the children may call out the names of those who are being chased or provide words of encouragement, such as "run faster . . . quick." These actions support one another; they introduce cooperative play and build self-esteem.

According to Williams (2014), when children from low-income families have been exposed to early learning environments that include music, they have improved emotional regulation (Brown & Sax, 2013) compared to children in non-arts-enriched programs. Music and movement also increase the social and communication skills of children (Williams, Berthelsen, Nicholson, Walker, & Abad, 2012). Music and movement extend beyond the group experience and the music and movement centre. For example, it may become prevalent in the dramatic centre. Music allows children to enact roles different from the usual familiar family-type roles in the dramatic centre (although children will use music to rock the babies in the dramatic centre). When children become connected to music—and with props—the possibilities are endless, such as becoming rock stars in the dramatic centre. Musical instruments may be used in many parts of dramatic play. For example, cowbells are used for police or fire truck sirens. Tambourines are used for doorbells, and clappers are used when playing "Three Billy Goats Gruff."

CURIOUS?

Do an Internet search to learn more about how music may be incorporated into children's dramatic play.

Early learning teachers expand music and movement across the program as a way to support children's social development. For example, children may note that there are various musical instruments in experience centres such as the block area. This becomes a conversational trigger and exploratory opportunity, while also increasing *cooperative music play*. Children communicate with each other to learn more about the musical attributes of items and experiences in the play space.

Many activities that align with improving children's executive functioning skills have a common coordinated movement element—for example, dance, martial arts, and yoga (Williams, 2014). Movement and music activities that have a dance or action component enhance the brain–body neural connections in children. These, in turn, support children's self-regulation skills. Think of the children you may hear saying, "We will sing, and you do the actions" or "Let's play the song and do the actions." For many children, having exposure to music is an important strategy for them to express themselves and to become part of a group. Music and movement experiences that encourage the participation of children help them in gaining competence with peers, in groups, and with cooperative skills. Action songs such as "Head and Shoulders, Knees and Toes" or "The Hokey Pokey" support various aspects of children's social development.

The application of social play categories, as described in Chapter 2, to music and play increases socialization and its function in the music play culture of children. When children have the freedom and respect of adults, they will engage in music play similar to other play. They will develop strategies for managing disputes and solve problems of noise on their own (Williams, 2014).

STOP ... THINK ... DISCUSS ... REFLECT

When you think of music and movement in an early learning program, what do they look like to you? How are they different from the arts and science experiences extended to children? Why are they different? Is music a social or a solitary activity? Why? How do you support children with diverse cultures or strengths in becoming involved in music? Why would you wish to do this as an early learning teacher?

Cognitive Development

Music and movement experiences directly support brain stimulation and development (Bergman-Nutley, Darki, & Klingberg, 2014). The connections that are formed between the cells of the brain, known as synapses, are developed with stimulation. During the early years, it is important for the synapses to be strengthened through appropriate experiences. Children require experiences such as music and movement for optimal development; otherwise there is a risk that this area will not develop to its fullest potential. For example, research suggests that one's singing voice generally develops during the first seven years of life. If children do not have any further exposure to music in their lifetime, the skills they acquired during the early years are generally what they have during adulthood.

Some researchers suggest that music and movement experiences increase children's overall intelligence, as identified by Gardner (discussed earlier in the chapter). Researchers suggest that music and movement contribute to the development of one's attitudes, interest, motivation, and life focus. It also contributes to self-confidence and self-esteem (Bergman-Nutley et al., 2014). As outlined in Figure 12.3, Bruner (1968) suggested from a cognitive psychology perspective that children's abilities in the musical and kinesthetic domains tend to progress through three stages: (1) enactive, (2) iconic, and (3) symbolic. Bruner's enactive stage of development corresponds to Piaget's sensorimotor stage, as described in Chapter 2, whereby children benefit from experiences that focus on simple, repetitive movements with people and objects.

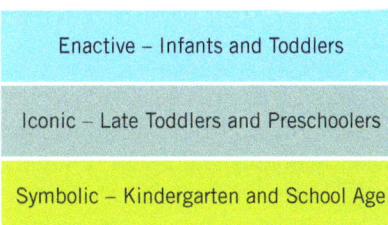

Figure 12.3 Bruner's stages of musical and kinesthetic domains.

During the *enactive stage*, predominantly experienced by infants and toddlers, the physical activity and music are linked (Mang, 2005). For example, adults will combine music and movement in their daily communication with infants and toddlers as they sing "Moving up and down" and as they bounce them on their knees. Toddlers and young preschoolers will share their delight as they sing and engage in action songs such as the "Eensy Weensy Spider" or "Head and Shoulders."

The *iconic stage* of development, experienced primarily by late toddlers and preschoolers, combines real objects with pictorial representations. During this phase, children require experiences that allow them to use their imaginations (Piaget, 1962) and assert their autonomy. Musical games such as "London Bridge Is Falling Down" encourage children to effectively incorporate music and movement as they use their hands and arms stretched out to make a bridge. Children experience the interconnectivity to music, movement, and language when early learning practitioners combine music experiences with action and words.

Children at the *symbolic stage* are usually of kindergarten age and school age. At the beginning of this phase, the children use abstract symbols, including language, to represent ideas. As they progress cognitively, they use advanced abstract processes that may include "words, musical notation, and the movement and gesture of dance" (Isenberg & Jalongo, 2010, p. 157). This is supportive of Piaget's stage of development known as symbolic/dramatic play, where children begin to express fantasy, use props, and take on roles other than being children.

Early learning teachers and student teachers expose children to music in a variety of ways, so that they have the opportunity to develop tonal aspects of rhythm and melody (Lindeman, 2016). For example, when children are able to participate in a song such as "Head and Shoulders," they are practising skills in linking words to actions and sequencing what comes first, second, and third. As children gain more complex musical abilities, such as being able to play an instrument, they require higher-level thinking skills, such as application, synthesis, and evaluation, as identified in Bloom's taxonomy. Music is considered a language. Through music and movement children require and develop cognitive skills similar to those used in mathematics and language and literacy (Bergman-Nutley, Darki & Klingberg, 2014).

Music requires children to utilize both their memory skills and classification skills. For example, when children are exposed to music with instruments, they are required to classify the different sounds and rhythms that they hear. They use their memories to be able to replicate beat patterns. Singing songs adds to children's language acquisition, as it introduces them to vocabulary and rhyme (Bergman-Nutley et al., 2014).

CURIOUS?

Do an Internet search to learn more about how music is thought of as being similar to learning a second language.

Recent studies show that music and movement support cognitive abilities, particularly spatial abilities, higher reasoning and motor skills, and higher achievements in math, language, and science (Flaugnacco et al., 2015). The earlier children are exposed to music, the more opportunity their brains have to respond to the various musical tones. Early learning teachers and student teachers ensure that there are many opportunities for children to sing, improvise, move, and dance across the program.

Photo 12.3 When children are exposed to various types of music and movement from a young age, it becomes part of their lifestyle.

Used with Permission of Angela Roy

AESTHETIC APPRECIATION

Music and movement provide another venue for children to gain aesthetic appreciation. Early learning teachers ensure that the places where children experience music are appealing to them. Children require intrigue within their indoor and outdoor environments (Dietze & Kashin, 2016). This supports and models the importance of aesthetic appreciation.

Early learning teachers and students can pose questions to the children that help them listen to the various sounds, tones, and movement of the music. Offering children music that introduces them to various musical instruments, such as bells, horns, cellos, or drums, increases options for music and movement and exposure to soft and gentle or more vigorous music. Varying the music types is important because this is how children learn to listen to the various attributes of music and to determine how they feel about each type of music (Ehrlin & Gustavsson, 2015). Aesthetic appreciation for music is extended when music and movement are combined. Early learning teachers, student teachers, and children listen to music and move their bodies to the music. This contributes to children using their bodies within the spaces made available for music and movement. Movement and music assist children in devising ways to use their bodies differently in the space provided. For example, early learning teachers offer children experiences that require them to squish their bodies into small spaces or be as big as a giant. Think of a ballerina. Ballerinas develop the ability to listen to the music and have their bodies respond to it. They bring aesthetic appreciation to the eye.

Music and movement are part of our natural surroundings. When music is presented to children in the outdoor environment, the early learning teacher and children compare aspects of the music to the sounds in the natural environment. For example, there may be music that includes the sounds of water or wind or birds. Children compare that music to the sounds present in their environments. This advances their connection to nature and aesthetics. This also assists children in being able to reproduce new sounds with their voices or instruments. The natural environment combines music and movement opportunities with the child's world. Children are encouraged to combine sounds and movement. When they hear and feel the wind, children replicate the sound and the movement of the wind. These types of activities heighten the children's observation skills and their ability to appreciate the beauty of their environment.

Presenting Music and Movement to Children

Early learning teachers and student teachers plan music and movement experiences with children and support spontaneous activities. Music and song can be presented to children throughout the day, both indoors and outdoors, rather than being available at specific times during the day. For example, simple, familiar songs may be used to transition from one experience to another. Although children should not be put in the position of needing to wait for activities or directions, at times this may occur. Music and movement are used at such times to make the waiting experience pleasant. Music brings children together at a group-time experience and is used to bring parents, extended families, and children together.

Presenting music to children may be challenging for some early learning teachers and student teachers, especially for those who feel they cannot sing or are self-conscious about singing in front of their colleagues (Ehrlin & Gustavsson, 2015). As challenging as it may be, quality early learning programs offer children rich music and movement experiences. Early learning teachers benefit from gaining practical knowledge about music and movement and acquiring skills that will support children in developmentally appropriate music and movement programming (National Association for Music Education, 2017).

Photo 12.4 Music offers children a way to engage in self-expression.

Used with Permission of Gill Robertson

Table 12.3 Children's singing progression.

Age	Child Response	Suggested Experiences
3 months	Recognizes pitches sung by mother.	Sing to baby while rocking or providing daily care routines.
3 to 9 months	Babbles a few pitches. Responds to primary caregiver singing.	Sing, move infant's hands and feet, repeat sounds made by infant, introduce nursery rhymes.
9 to 18 months	Produces words; tries to repeat what is heard.	Sing one to two lines of a song.
18 to 24 months	Sings more pitches; starts to make up jingles.	Offer same songs for children to be able to learn and reproduce; encourage children to make up songs.
2 to 3 years	Sings familiar songs; participates in singing games.	Sing songs with children; offer singing games.
3 to 4 years	Sings songs in totality.	Sing songs with varying pitches; offer small-group musical experiences.
4 to 5 years	Sings with more accurate pitch and rhythm; repeats tonal patterns.	Increase number of songs; combine songs with rhymes such as "Miss Mary Mack."

Dietze & Kashin adapted this from Lindeman (2015).

Presenting Songs to Children

Early learning teachers and student teachers support children in experiencing music through songs in a variety of ways, including through group music presentation, professional recordings, and family contributions. Lindeman (2015) identified that children's singing skills are progressive. Table 12.3 illustrates children's singing progression.

In addition to the singing progression, it is important that early learning teachers have an understanding of what is meant by **pitch**, **pitch matching**, and **vocal range**, as these concepts guide teachers in how songs are presented to children (Corrigall & Schellenberg, 2016).

Pitch and rhythmic discrimination are central to children learning music. Rhythmic synchronization, in turn, is essential for the experience of music (Corrigall & Schellenberg, 2016).

Early learning teachers have a role in supporting young children in being exposed to a variety of music and ways to produce music. Often, the latter is done through group singing. One of the most common problems with young children singing in groups is that "some adults do not begin the song on a pitch that is comfortable for the majority of children" (Kim, 2000, p. 153). Rather, early learning teachers use their own comfort singing range. This is generally too low for preschool children (Kim, 2000). Offering children opportunities to use high pitches through echoing and through imitation of natural songs supports them in their pitch matching and vocal range.

Greenberg (1979) classified children's vocalization into five stages, as seen in Table 12.4.

Greenberg identified that it is not until the age of 5 years or later that children generally are able to reach the higher tones with much accuracy. Children are required to be able to control the physical mechanism needed to produce these tones. This takes time and experience.

Barrett (2006) suggested that invented song is a common feature of young children's musical and life experiences. She identified three categories of invented song that early

pitch Refers to the highness or lowness of the musical sound.

pitch matching Refers to matching the musical sounds to the highness or lowness of the song (Kim, 2000).

vocal range Refers to the distance between the highest and the lowest notes the voice can match (McDonald & Simons, 1989).

Table 12.4 Five stages of vocalization.

Stage I	The first vocalization (birth to 3 months)
Stage II	Experimentation and sound imitation (3 to 18 months)
Stage III	Approximation of singing (18 months to 3 years)
Stage IV	Singing accuracy in limited range (3 to 4 years)
Stage V	Singing accuracy with expanded range (after 4 years)

learning teachers should be familiar with. They are identified as imaginative, narrative, and potpourri.

In imaginative song, the child's focus is on the **melodic contour** rather than the **lyric content**. Narrative songs contain varied lyric and melodic content. Nonsense words and phrases are incorporated into the song. Potpourri songs combine elements of songs the children know with original melodic and lyric materials. When children have stimulating environments, invented songs will develop. As they progress in their invented song, they increasingly draw on the musical forms of their culture to make "standard songs" that reflect their life experiences. This activity aligns with language and problem-solving skills (Barrett, 2006).

Young children require songs that are simple, short, and repetitive, with only a few notes. Traditional music such as "Twinkle, Twinkle, Little Star" offers early learning teachers, students, and children with an introduction to music that is familiar and developmentally appropriate. As singing experiences are scaffolded, children between the ages of 4 and 5 years benefit from having many songs with a limited tonal range and catchy tunes or tonal patterns. Children master simple songs when they are repeated several times over several days. Early learning teachers offer the first verse initially. Once the children have mastered that verse, additional verses are added (Corrigall & Schellenberg, 2016).

Children require the music experience to offer them a sense of curiosity and intrigue. Introducing instruments such as autoharp enhances the children's interest in the relationship of singing to the sounds of the instrument. "The advantage of using an autoharp is that children can be invited to strum it in time to the singing, because all one must do to control the note is press down firmly on the correct key" (Hendrick & Weissman, 2007, p. 279). As children become more proficient with a song, building on both music and language, the early learning teacher changes the words—some of which are nonsense words.

Singing songs from various cultures is a positive way to introduce children to the cultures of the children in the early learning environment. If early learning teachers do not have experience with music from different cultures, many child-appropriate recordings are available. It is important that early learning teachers become familiar with the material before introducing it to the children. Early learning teachers and children may use technology to explore all types of music.

THE ROLE OF THE EARLY LEARNING TEACHER IN PROMOTING MUSIC AND MOVEMENT

Throughout this chapter, we have provided examples of ways in which early learning teachers can introduce music and movement to children. We know from the literature that a variety of factors influence how early learning teachers can incorporate music and movement into the early learning environment. These influencers include the level of

---

melodic contour The way in which each sound and silence connects along a curve.

lyric content The composition in verse that is sung to make up a song.

training in music and movement, values and beliefs about the importance of music and movement to the development of the whole child, experience and confidence in presenting music and movement experiences, the physical space, the program, and the resources available.

> ## STOP ... THINK ... DISCUSS ... REFLECT

When you think of children and music and movement, what are the key attributes that you believe an early learning teacher must exhibit? How do early learning teachers introduce music and movement if they themselves are not comfortable with it? How does your philosophy about music and movement fit with the information shared in this chapter?

When we think of the success of music and movement, it requires early learning teachers to explore their values and beliefs about music and movement. Staff attitudes affect the quality of the experiences that are extended to children. Often, when early learning teachers suggest that music and movement are not their strong areas of programming, it is because they do not have sufficient background and experience in these areas. This leads to a general lack of confidence (Castelli et al., 2015; Lindeman, 2015). Initially, early learning teachers may suggest that they do not have a repertoire of music and movement experiences to draw upon; however, music and movement include the performance of nursery rhymes and songs, finger-plays and action songs, alphabet and counting songs, and associated movement activities that emphasize beat and rhythm, which most have experience with from their childhood. As outlined in Box 12.1, there are many ways in which early learning teachers can bring musical experiences to children in early learning environments.

Early learning teachers have many roles and responsibilities in promoting music and movement. One of the most challenging roles for early learning teachers is to observe children's play to ensure that the music and movement experiences remain "focused and evolve as musical play without deteriorating into random tag, rough-and-tumble, or chasing games" (Van Hoorn, Nourot, Scales, & Alward, 2007, p. 287). As identified in Sharing Stories from Practice at the beginning of this chapter, when music and movement are

> ### Box 12.1 Strategies for introducing music into early learning environments.

- Create a centre with musical instruments. Encourage children to explore it, and then play a guessing game of which instrument is making which sound.
- Place a portable keyboard in the play space with photos of musicians.
- Set up the dramatic centre as a musical theatre with a stage, microphones, and instruments.
- Provide tape recorders for children to record various sounds.
- Provide various bells for children to explore.
- Make maracas with children.
- Introduce a rain stick in the science area.
- Fill jars with water, and have children explore the sounds they make.
- Invite families to share their cultural music.

Photo 12.5 Children explore music through experiences such as "The Bear Went over the Mountain."

Used with Permission of Gill Robertson

presented appropriately, they have a very positive influence on children and the feeling tone of the play space. Alternatively, if early learning teachers use music to distract or entertain, it does merely that. The potential of children being sparked to develop a sense of music will not occur.

Early learning teachers examine the types of music and movement experiences introduced to the children and the reasons for exposing the children to them. As in other early learning play opportunities, the early learning teacher devises the music experiences based on the particular needs, interests, learning, and development of the children. For example, when children are playing in the rain, rain songs and props such as umbrellas may be made available. When early learning teachers choose the musical experiences based on their own interests, and without children having a connectedness to it, the activities become teacher directed. Children require opportunities to explore music and the freedom of improvisation with music.

Early learning teachers ensure that children have exposure to singing and singing games, playing instruments, movement to music and moving to music with props, and listening to music. They may also include relaxation activities to music such as yoga.

MUSIC AND MOVEMENT EXPERIENCE CENTRES

Early learning teachers incorporate a variety of strategies that support young children's exposure to music and movement into the daily program. The music and movement experience centre, similar to other experience centres, is designed to have materials that will trigger children's curiosity and allow them the opportunity to explore and create music. Movement evolves from the music. For example, a sound system may be set up with a microphone so that children can hear and play with projecting their voices. There may be recording equipment so that they have the pleasure of singing and then replaying their singing. Musical instruments such as drums, guitars, sticks, keyboards, tambourines, and various shakers are rotated in the experience centre. Children make important discoveries about music when they have opportunities to explore music boxes.

Music, culture, and dramatic play are interconnected. When the music and movement centre has dance costumes available, including scarves, headbands, and ribbons, along with a variety of music, children will create interesting play, dance, and dramatic play options. When children are given such opportunities to incorporate music into various kinds of play, they require flexibility to move the materials to the appropriate play spaces. Children are provided with musical resources such as CDs, and they are given materials and opportunities to make music in their own way.

Music centres are offered to the children both indoors and outdoors. When children have exposure to instruments such as drums outdoors, the sound and the overall experience differ from those in an indoor play experience. The dramatic play with instruments takes on new creative attributes when it is available outdoors. For example, children may develop a music experience in the park, or they may decide to have a wedding in the park. Musical instruments offer innovative experiences for the children.

Musical Instruments

Early learning teachers ensure that a variety of musical instruments are placed within the indoor and outdoor environments. Simple instruments such as keyboards, drums, rhythm sticks, tambourines, shakers, and autoharps offer children the opportunity to explore music, movement, and related concepts such as sound, rhythm, patterning, and creating. Musical instruments are important tools for children to experience as they develop an ear for the various sounds that each instrument makes. Children learn about musical instruments through experimentation. To provide children with this freedom to explore, it is advantageous to think about where children may go to bang on the instruments or increase the sound of the music. This is an essential part of them exploring music.

When Early Learning Teachers Have Limited Skills in Music and Movement

There are many resources available to support and guide early learning teachers in providing music and movement experiences to children. Other ideas include the following:

- **Use a variety of music to encourage children to engage in music and movement.** Expose children to different types of music, such as classical, contemporary, folk, or country. Encourage children to move to the music, and have dialogue with them about how the music makes them feel.
- **Encourage versatility in their movements.** Use a variety of questioning techniques that will encourage children to move their bodies in different ways. For example, have the children move only their legs, their tummies, or their upper torsos.
- **Offer items that the children may move with.** Use broomsticks, umbrellas, and feathers with a variety of music. Make musical instruments such as maracas out of plastic bottles.
- **Sing songs with the children.** Offer children a variety of songs to sing with you. Choose songs that move up or down the scale.
- **Invite children to discover music together.** Have children use musical instruments together to see what they may create.

Table 12.5 Movement words to use with children.

Body Parts	Actions	Space
■ Head	■ Swing	■ Diagonal
■ Face	■ Push	■ Shape
■ Nose	■ Pull	■ Large
■ Back	■ Walk	■ Tiny
■ Ankle	■ Gallop	■ Far
■ Heels	■ Slide	■ Near
■ Toes	■ Leap	■ Beside
■ Bones	■ Rock	■ Under
■ Stomach	■ Stomp	■ Curved
■ Elbows	■ Crawl	■ Round
■ Spine	■ Sway	■ Zigzag
■ Knees	■ Bend, curl, flex	■ In/out

- **Teach children songs with movement.** Teach children the song "Rig-a-Jig-Jig." Discuss with the children which movements are best suited for each verse (Morin, 2001).
- **Incorporate movement vocabulary.** Offer children exposure to daily discussions and activities using movement vocabulary. See Table 12.5.
- **Combine music and movement experiences.** Determine ways to combine music and movement experiences with other experience centres, such as the art, dramatic play, and science areas.

OBSERVATION AND DOCUMENTATION

Early learning teachers learn important information about children through observation and documentation. The observational and documentation tools used are intended to provide the early learning teachers and students with information about:

- The type of music each child enjoys;
- How each child responds to various types of music;
- How music and movement are incorporated into the children's play;
- The types of activities that sparked spontaneous music and movement play;
- The types of musical instruments favoured;
- How the music is a social or solitary play experience.

Many early learning teachers use charts to document this information. Others use video, as it allows the children to share the musical activity with their families. As they continue to acquire information on the relationship of music and movement to development, early learning teachers and children must become inspired to explore it to its fullest. Children require early learning teachers to listen, to observe, and to know who they are so that environments may be prepared to allow for active exploration, creative play, and discovery.

TERMS THAT INFLUENCE EARLY LEARNING PLAY ENVIRONMENTS

We conclude this chapter with three additional terms that support the theory of children's play. These terms are used when examining children's potential learning experiences.

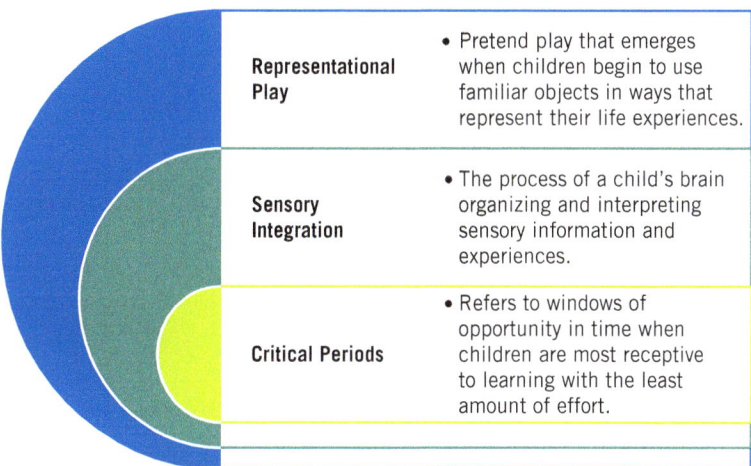

SUMMARY

Chapter Preview

- Music and movement involve children in physical, social, cognitive, kinesthetic, and communicative challenges.
- There is growing concern among researchers that early learning teachers may not be emphasizing this area of programming to the extent they emphasize other programming areas.

Historical Influences of Music and Movement

- The importance of music and movement was first identified by Jean-Jacques Rousseau, followed by Herbert Spencer, Maria Montessori, and Carl Orff.
- From a contemporary perspective, Gardner identifies that music intelligence aligns with linguistic intelligence. Bodily-kinesthetic and spatial intelligence are needed for the movement portion of music and movement.
- Morin indicated the need for early learning teachers to understand the relationship of music and play. Children respond to music when it is associated with play.
- Morin categorizes music play into five categories: cooperative music play, functional music play, constructive music play, dramatic music play, and kinesthetic music play.

The Importance of Music and Movement

- Music and movement are important aspects of a child's whole development.

- Dance, creative movement, and movement are interrelated, but each has distinct characteristics.
- Through music and movement, cultural aspects are transferred from one generation to the next.
- Music and movement are incorporated into a child's play and environment in a variety of ways.

Music, Movement, and Child Development

- Music play supports brain development, psychomotor development, social and emotional development, and cognitive development.
- Bruner identified that children's abilities in the musical and kinesthetic domains progress through three stages: the enactive stage, the iconic stage, and the symbolic stage. These stages are related to Piaget's stages of cognitive development.
- Various studies suggest that children who have had experience with music have high levels of spatial abilities, higher reasoning and motor skills, and higher achievements in math, language, and science.

Aesthetic Appreciation

- Music and movement contribute to children developing aesthetic appreciation for music and their environment.

Presenting Music and Movement to Children

- Music, movement, and song should be presented to children throughout the day in ways that will support children in appreciating music and movement.
- By being aware of the pitch that is used relative to the skills of the children, early learning practitioners can present songs to children.
- Greenberg identified five stages of children's vocalization. He believed that children are at least 5 years old before they are able to reach higher tones with accuracy.
- Barrett indicates that invented song is common among children.

The Value of Music and Movement to Children with Atypical Development

- Music and movement constitute an effective communication strategy for children who have atypical developmental patterns.

The Role of the Early Learning Teacher

- Early learning teachers can provide children with play experiences that include a variety of music and movement opportunities, including singing, singing games, playing instruments, movement to music, and listening to music.
- Early learning teachers ensure that children have opportunities to explore music and movement in areas similar to other play experience centres. Music centres are offered both indoors and outdoors, with a variety of intriguing materials, including musical instruments and related artifacts, rotated in the centres.
- There are a variety of music and movement experiences that early learning teachers may offer children, even if they do not have a background in music.
- Observation and documentation help early learning practitioners to gain information on each child's interest and skill in music and movement.

REVIEW QUESTIONS

1. Describe the importance of music and movement to the lives of young children.
2. How does the historical perspective of music and movement affect our practice today?
3. What does Gardner tell us about music intelligence, bodily-kinesthetic intelligence, and linguistic and spatial intelligence?
4. How do Morin's categories of play inform an early learning practitioner practice?
5. What is the importance of music and movement to child development?
6. How do music and movement affect brain development?
7. What are the key considerations that early learning practitioners must make when introducing songs to young children?
8. What is the value of music and movement to children with atypical development?
9. Describe the diverse roles that early learning teachers have in promoting music and movement in an early learning environment.

MAKING CONNECTIONS

Theory to Practice

1. You are working in an early learning environment where music and movement are secondary to other programming areas such as blocks, science, and art. What strategies would you put in place to advance the knowledge, skills, and opportunities of early learning teachers and children in this area of programming?
2. Visit two early learning environments and do an inventory of the music and movement experiences that are offered to children. What are they? How do they relate to children's interests? What is the role of the early learning practitioner?
3. You have been asked to design and implement a music experience that may pique children's interests. On what basis would you choose the materials? Why? How would you scaffold the materials? Why?
4. A parent comes to you to identify that he would prefer his child learn the alphabet rather than use the drum set outdoors. How would you respond? What steps would you take to support the parent in gaining comfort in knowing how music supports children's development?

DIGITAL PORTFOLIO ENTRIES

Here are possible digital portfolio entries to support your knowledge and experience of the relationship between music and movement and children's play and learning.

- Now, when I think about music and movement and children, I wonder about . . .
- If I were to develop a musical skill to share with children, I think I would . . .
- I see how families and community can support children's music by . . .
- I wonder how children will respond when I bring music outdoors. Will it be different from music indoors?

CHAPTER 13
Bringing Technology into Child's Play: A New Perspective

Rawpixel.com/Shutterstock

> " I have been impressed with the urgency of doing. Knowing is not enough; we must apply. Being willing is not enough; we must do. "
>
> —Leonardo da Vinci (1452–1519)

LEARNING OUTCOMES

After exploring this chapter, you should be able to:

- Explain various perspectives and recommendations about the use of technology with young children, and relate them to the responsibility of early learning teachers.

- Highlight the benefits and concerns, including equitable issues, of using technology with children in their play environments.

- Explain the stages that children experience when beginning to use technology.

- Discuss strategies that early learning teachers use to facilitate play with technology devices, choose software, and observe children while using the technology.

- Discuss principles of professional development and learning for early learning teachers related to technology.

Sharing Stories of Practice

As I think about my beginnings as an early learning teacher and then examine societal changes, I realize it is time to face reality—I am living at a time where there is a cultural and **digital divide**. Today's children are exposed to so much new technology from birth. I know from Statistics Canada that Canadian children rank among the highest in the world in terms of living in households with access to computers; I also know that there are gaps within our society. These gaps are like a digital divide. I know early learning teachers who have adapted to the new technologies of this era and those who have not even become comfortable with email. I have a friend who is very active on social media, and she keeps telling me about new articles she has read or groups she has joined. She told me about a Facebook group called Technology in Inquiry-Based Learning where she learned about coding with preschoolers. She then set up a coding experience with the children she worked with that was play based. I can't imagine what that looked like. I don't even understand what coding means. My friend tells me that children need to learn to code as twenty-first-century learners and that we need to get on board as twenty-first-century teachers. I guess I am still in the twentieth century! I feel like I am in a state of disequilibrium. I am not even sure if technology is appropriate for children. Is it really play based?

Amela, ECE graduate, 2010

CHAPTER PREVIEW

In this chapter, we introduce you to the topic of technology in the lives of young children. Technology is a very broad and complex topic. We explore the controversies, benefits, and challenges of the integration of technology into early learning programs as a tool to support playing and learning. We examine how early learning teachers can use technology to expand play experiences. We look at how technology integration can contribute to the social, physical, language, and cognitive development of children.

Creating child-initiated, responsive play environments is one of the most challenging roles of an early learning teacher. As we think about technology, we need to consider how it fits with play. If technology is being used, how does it support quality and active play experiences?

Children come to early learning environments with varied experiences with technology. Think about households that may have multiple television sets, tablets, surround sound systems, home theatres, smartphones, and computers with wireless Internet capability. Think about your own family; would you characterize it as **high tech** or **low tech**? When even household appliances have "smart" capacities and toys have electronic functions, some families today are considered extremely high tech. Others may not have the resources to afford wireless Internet or have purposely limited the technology in their household. Technology brings into focus differences and inequities in our communities. There are areas of our country and family circumstances that prohibit easy access to high-tech devices and outputs. This in turn influences children's play and learning opportunities at home and in their early learning programs. Children who do not have access to devices or who are not in early learning programs that are incorporating technology in the play experiences will not have the same skills as their peers when

digital divide Refers to the gap between demographics and regions that have access to technology and those that do not or that have restricted access.

high tech Complex technological devices

low tech Devices that are simple, such as a pencil grip to help children to write.

Photo 13.1 Siblings interacting with a tablet.
Used with Permission of Andrea Stirling

digital age A period that began in the 1970s with the widespread use of computers.

information age Another term for the digital age specific to readily available information made possible by omnipresent computers and devices.

they start their formal schooling (Buckingham, 2013). One of the challenges for future early learning teachers is to learn about how to effectively weave technology into early learning programs.

As the early learning teacher who shared her story of practice that begins this chapter indicated, we are in the twenty-first century, which is often referred to as the **digital age** or the **information age** and which has a major focus on science, technology, engineering, arts, and mathematics (STEAM). These changes are influencing teaching and learning in early learning programs. To support children in the early years, early learning teachers help children to engage with technology in playful ways so that they develop particular skills consistent with twenty-first-century teaching and learning. To benefit from digital learning, children need to develop inquiry and critical thinking skills "to select and process useful and reliable information from various sources" (Kong et al., 2014, p. 71). Children will also need to develop communication and collaboration skills, as the digital and information age requires these skills more than ever before (Kong et al., 2014). Figure 13.1 illustrates essential skills for the twenty-first century that now influence early learning programs. Consider how these can be applied to children in ways that support play, incorporate technology, and honour play-based learning perspectives.

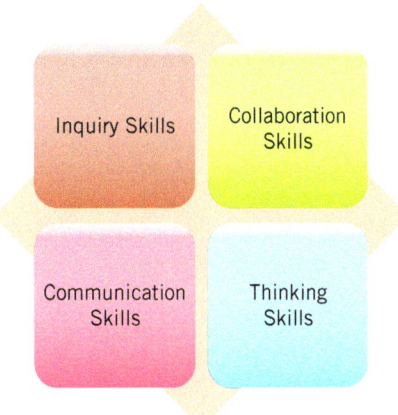

Figure 13.1 Skills for the twenty-first century.

With advances in technology happening at a rapid rate, the world of early learning is also changing. Hrannar (2014) made an extensive list of what could be considered obsolete in present and future education. A few examples are the following:

- Computer rooms that are separated from the learning environment.
- Learning environments without wi-fi (wireless Internet).
- Banning cellphones and tablets from learning enivronments.
- Not using social media such as Facebook and Twitter.
- Traditional libraries that do not have access to devices for editing and creating, such as 3D printers.

Think about the things that Hrannar identified as obsolete, and discuss why they might be considered so. Think about your own educational experience as well as what might be considered passé in early learning and why.

To read Hrannar's (2014) complete list, see http://ingvihrannar.com/14-things-that-are-obsolete-in-21st-century-schools/.

When you think about your own experiences in school, from the early years to the college or university years, how have things changed? What do you think happens to teachers at all levels who do not change with the times? What does it tell you about being a lifelong learner?

DEFINING TECHNOLOGY

Broadly defined, technology is anything invented or created by humans to solve problems. Everything, except what is created by nature, is therefore technology. Technology has a long history, from the invention of fire-starting tools and the wheel to present-day

Photo 13.2 Playing with light.
Used with Permission of Diane Kashin

new technologies that include advancements in computer technology. Current research is emphasizing that technology in early learning programs "supports and increases young children's skills in social, cognitive, language, literacy, writing and mathematics realms" (McManis & Gunnewig, 2012, p. 15). The use of technology in play-based programs is positioned to change the way children engage in play, exploration, and their overall learning experiences (Dietze & Kashin, 2013). Such findings suggest that early learning teachers require the skills to integrate technology into play-based experiences with children that follow sound pedagogical principles. Using technology with children is changing the landscape of play-based early learning environments. From low-tech experiences with light projection to high-tech interactive whiteboards, early learning environments are technical places!

With technology being such a broad topic, in this chapter we focus on devices, such as tablets, computers and cellphones, and on the products or outputs of these devices that are viewed, read, played, or created on these devices (Plowman & McPake, 2013). This definition of technology appears in Figure 13.2. Various devices are featured in

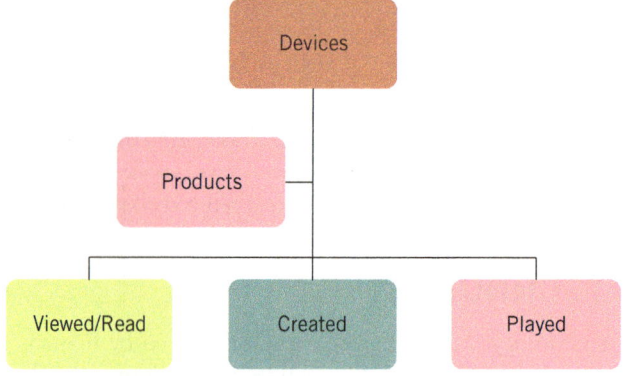

Figure 13.2 Defining technology.

420   Chapter 13   Bringing Technology into Child's Play: A New Perspective

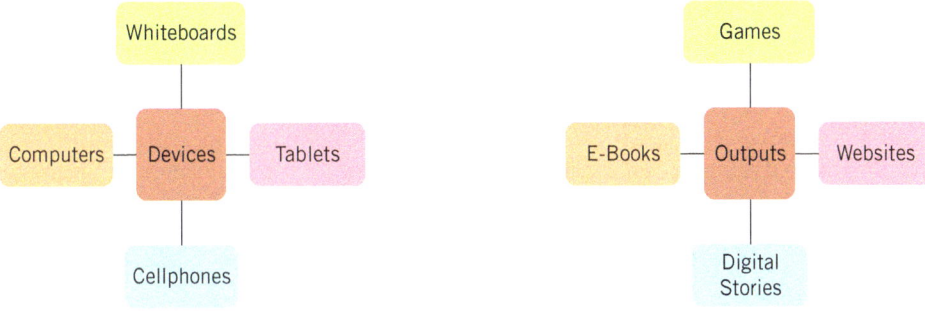

Figure 13.3 Devices.

Figure 13.4 Outputs.

Figures 13.3 and 13.4, along with examples of products or outputs of these devices. This chapter considers a number of technology devices and outputs that can be integrated into early learning programs and their relationship to play and learning, recognizing that it is near impossible to keep up to date with all devices and products, as new ones are being developed every day.

Consider a situation in which a group of children are closely examining a frog that they discovered during an outdoor nature play experience. Their early learning teacher knows that the children are excited and want to spend time with the little creature. However, she is also aware that the children know that the frog will have to be released before they return to the centre. By capturing the experience on video with her cellphone (a device), the early learning teacher has captured the moment, and the children can relive it. Then they can do an Internet search to learn more about the frog, which takes them to a website (an output). As they learn about types of frogs and are able to identify that they had a found a tree frog, the children begin to share their ideas about where the

Photo 13.3 From frog to digital story.
Used with Permission of Diane Kashin

frog went after its release. They decide that they want to create a digital story about a family of tree frogs (an output). Think about this example. How is the sense of inquiry and play-based learning combined with technology in the play experience? Presently and futuristically, what learning opportunities would children miss if technology was not in their environments?

Salonius-Pasternak and Gelfond (2005) suggested that the advancement of technology in children's play, whether it be with computers or toys with motors, is the first qualitatively different form of play to be introduced since before the turn of the twentieth century. We maintain that if the principles of constructivism, experiential learning theories, and the progressive education movement (Dewey, 1938; Vygotsky, 1978) are considered, children will have opportunities to discover, make choices, and experience the impact of their decisions when playing with technology (Dietze & Kashin, 2013).

VARIOUS PERSPECTIVES ABOUT THE USE OF TECHNOLOGY WITH YOUNG CHILDREN

There is a growing controversy about the role that technology should play in the lives of young children in a world where technology is not going away (Wagner & Compton, 2015). Examining the varying perspectives about technology use with young children will help you understand the various positions that you may come to experience in your work with children. Understanding the context of the various perspectives helps you in thinking about your beliefs and philosophy of how play and technology fit in early learning environments.

> **STOP ... THINK ... DISCUSS ... REFLECT**
>
> How do you think technology has changed the way children play today from when you were growing up? Should children be exposed to devices and outputs during their early years? Why or why not? How do we know what is best?

One perspective that some early learning teachers may take is to decide not to provide children with access to devices because of the concern expressed by a number of experts, including educators and psychologists, who have attested that these devices stifle children's learning and creativity (Buckingham, 2013). More than 10 years ago, Elkind (2007) stated that technology should not be a substitute for play experiences and that professionals should be cautious about technology in children's places of play. Does his position remain current today? Others suggest that opportunities for children to learn through play are being reduced because of the amount of time they are spending in front of television or computer screens or using technology-assisted toys (Plowman, McPake, & Stephen, 2010). However, another perspective views technology as a process that can contribute to opportunities to play while learning (Dietze & Kashin, 2013).

Throughout this text, we have maintained that play equals learning. From this perspective, if we consider how technological devices can be incorporated with play, these devices can be educational and support children's development. The National Association for the Education of Young Children (NAEYC) and the Fred Rogers Center for Early Learning

Photo 13.4 Playing with the concepts of coding.
Used with Permission of Andrea Stirling

and Children's Media (2012), in their position statement *Technology and Interactive Media as Tools in Early Childhood Programs Servicing Children from Birth through Age 8*, offer guidance on how young children learn and develop. Their position statement acknowledges the opportunities and challenges of using technology in early learning programs.

Parikh (2012) identified that, despite the challenges, one of the key messages in the joint statement is that "when used intentionally and appropriately, technology is an effective tool to support learning and development" (p. 10). Advocates who use technology with children are clear that certain activities that violate children's active play opportunities, such as electronic worksheets, should be viewed as being inappropriate. Technology is not used as a substitute for active play; it is an enhancement of children's play experiences (Dietze & Kashin, 2013). When used intentionally by early learning teachers, technology can promote effective play extensions, learning, and development (NAEYC & Fred Rogers Center for Early Learning and Children's Media, 2012). For example, consider an early learning teacher who searches YouTube for videotapes of the children's favourite book.

CURIOUS?

What is your favourite children's book? For instance, if you like *Pete the Cat* by Eric Litwin and search YouTube, you would find many related videos. Can you find videos related to your favourite book? How do you think you could use these videos with children?

TECHNOLOGY AND CHILDREN'S CREATIVITY

Creativity, imagination, and problem solving are essential skills needed for critical thinking and innovation. Children's imagination correlates with the learning process. For example, when children engage in imaginary play, they formulate images and ideas that are then transferred to their self-expression, which could influence their communication through storytelling, art, or creative movement.

What is the relationship of technology to children's creativity? Is there a place for children's expression of creativity through technology? Should early learning teachers assume that creativity is limited to art and can be expressed only with paint, paper, markers, and crayons? Why or why not? Consider what might happen after children view a YouTube clip of their favourite storybook. Do you think their curiosity might be triggered about making movies? Might they want to turn another cherished storybook into a movie that they film themselves? What would the role of the early learning teacher be in facilitating children's potential ideas?

If these questions cause tension for early learning teachers because they have considered creativity only in terms of art, in thinking, in practice, and in philosophical orientation **disequilibrium** might occur. Disequilibrium can be described as tension that builds when new information collides with prior knowledge, beliefs, or values. Banaji, Burn, and Buckingham (2010) pointed to research that has identified that technology can promote creativity, but it is important that early learning students and teachers are not using technological devices and outputs for their own sake. Technology is a tool that may be used for promoting or expanding various types of play experiences.

Early learning teachers may oppose the tool and its place in early learning environments because of the correlation to lack of physical literacy and increased levels of obesity (De Jong et al., 2013). There has long been a concern that increased exposure to television, and now the addition of different kinds of screens (computers and tablets), means that children are spending less time engaged in full body play (De Jong et al, 2013). Because of the growth in computer games, there may be a concern that the violent aspects of some of these games may lead to aggressive behaviour (Przybylski, 2014). There is concern that the use of computers and the exposure to television can stifle children's learning and creativity, leading children to become passive consumers (Buckingham, 2013). With child development specialists and experts debating whether television, computers, and videos take time away from children participating in quality play experiences with other children, it is understandable why some teachers may stand in opposition to their use.

Some of the tension and resistance surrounding the use of technology with children may stem from the lack of inclusion of this topic area in early learning training programs

disequilibrium According to Piaget's theory, when children encounter new information, they try to reduce the tension caused by this state of disequilibrium by developing new schemes or adapting old ones (Labouvie-Vief, 2015).

Photos 13.5 and **13.6** Early learning students using technology in class.

Used with Permission of Diane Kashin

(Dietze & Kashin, 2013; McManis & Gunnewig, 2012). The reason for this could be early learning faculty not pursuing professional learning in the area of how technology supports children's play. If faculty have not examined the current perspectives on technology, they may not have included technology in their pedagogy (Dietze & Kashin, 2013), or they may be using technologies that have not typically been designed for the educational purpose for which they are using it (Koehler & Mishra, 2009). This may mean that early learning students complete their studies without having explored ways to incorporate appropriate technology with the principles of interactive and exploratory play. This can result in new graduates either leaving technology out of their practice or using it with children in ways that are not conducive to active play or **developmentally appropriate** (McManis & Gunnewig, 2012).

developmentally appropriate Refers to a practice grounded in research and reflective of child development, often referred to as DAP (developmentally appropriate practice) (Gestwicki, 2013).

STOP ... THINK ... DISCUSS ... REFLECT

Think about your own experiences in high school, college, or university. Has technology been integrated into your learning experiences? Are you encouraged or discouraged to use laptops, cellphones, and tablets in class? What do you think are the benefits of using these devices? What would be some reasons why faculty do not support their use?

According to Plowman and McPake (2013), there is no concrete evidence available to decide one way or the other about computers and digital media, although widespread media coverage has explored the advantages and disadvantages. Plowman and McPake suggested that, in the absence of such evidence, several myths about children's experiences with technology have emerged. We list four here:

1. **Childhood and technology do not mix.** Plowman and McPake (2013) did not find evidence, after a decade of research, that children are being harmed by technology use. In interviews with families, some expressed concern about children becoming addicted to video games and about the health issues around cellphone use, but they did not express concern that children's experiences with technology were having a detrimental effect on behaviour, health, or learning.
2. **Young children are "digital natives."** The term **digital natives** was coined by Prensky (2001) in reference to college students. It is true that today's children have been born into the digital world and therefore are considered natives. However, Plowman and McPake (2013) suggested that, based on their research findings, not all children are comfortable with technology. Depending on their life experiences, some children may find technology overwhelming. Children benefit from the appropriate support from adults when using technology. Digital natives are different from **digital immigrants**, who were not born into the digital age.
3. **Technology hinders social interaction.** Plowman and McPake (2013) suggest that there is a fear that the lure of technology will lead to children's lack of engagement with their families because of the demands of busy working lives. Technology use may be seen as "electronic babysitting" (Plowman & McPake, 2013, p. 29). Plowman and McPake proposed that this is not the case for 3- and 4-year-old children. They found that digital media actually provided a "stimuli for questions about the world and for the development of their own narratives and imaginative responses" (p. 29). With the right support, digital media encourage commmunication and actually support social interaction (Plowman & McPake, 2013).

digital natives and digital immigrants Digital native is a label for the generation of people born into the digital age, whereas digital immigrant refers to those people who learned to use computers at some stage in their lifetime. They were not born into the digital age (Wang, Myers, & Sundaram, 2013).

4. **Technology dominates children's lives.** According to Plowman and McPake (2013), technology does not necessarily dominate children's lives. In their studies, they found that children used some sort of device with a screen every day. Computers were used to visit developmentally appropriate websites and to view video clips or missed television programs with other family members. Children often spoke with relatives via Skype. However, families were not concerned about overuse of technology, even though they were aware of concerns expressed by researchers and experts.

Researchers and experts have expressed concern about the overuse of technology (Voogt & McKenney, 2017). This has contributed to differing viewpoints on the use of technology. However, technology is not going away; it is part of our society. In the upcoming sections, we take the position that there is a need for early learning teachers to incorporate technology into play, when it is developmentally appropriate. We will introduce you to a number of perspectives about the relationship of technology to children's play and learning. This chapter is intended to provoke discussion about how technology, using developmentally appropriate practice, can be adopted effectively in early learning centres beginning with the role of the early learning teacher. In the next section, we discuss the role of the early learning teacher in promoting technology in children's play.

Television was first invented in 1927 and had become part of almost every household by the 1990s (Baughman, 1992). Research has found that some television shows, such as *Sesame Street* and *Blue's Cues*, can promote early academic skills. However, children younger than 30 months cannot learn from television and videos in the same ways as they do from real-life experiences. Conversely, the use of interactive media that allows for children to act and respond may facilitate more learning (Radesky, Schumacher, & Zuckerman, 2015). More research is being conducted every day. While it is the responsibility of early learning teachers to stay current with new findings, we suggest that examining past research on television use is a good opportunity to make connections and reflections.

Photo 13.7 Playing with technology.
Used with Permission of Andrea Stirling

CURIOUS?

Add the words *the impact of television on children* to your search engine, and read an article from the 1980s or 1990s. What learning can be extrapolated from this article to the issue of children and new technologies?

Understanding your role in facilitating play with technology includes assisting children, families, and colleagues to experience technology in a positive light. To be effective, early learning teachers must have a thorough understanding of children's play and how technology can enhance the play experience. Providing support to children, while using technology, requires knowledge about play, technology devices and outputs, and the roles of early learning teachers. Effective observation skills and the ability to pose open-ended questions that will support the children in exploring and problem solving while playing with technology are essential. Helping children to be successful with technology in their play is an important aspect of your role. Although working with technology may be controversial and challenging, many early learning teachers also find it a rewarding area.

STOP ... THINK ... DISCUSS ... REFLECT

What is it about your own use of technology in your personal life that you find rewarding? Is it the opportunity to communicate and interact with others? How might you offer these same opportunities to children? Many years ago, children used to write to pen pals to learn about life in other countries. What technological advances can support this concept, and what would be the benefits or disadvantages compared to having a pen pal?

TECHNOLOGY AND EARLY LEARNING

Technology opens new learning opportunities. Marshall McLuhan (1994) suggested that electronic media would change our way of thinking, similar to when societies were introduced to print media. Digital media are viewed as another form of communication, similar to both oral and print methodologies. A systematic literature review conducted by Hsin, Li, and Tsai (2014) of studies of how technologies influence children's learning found that they had positives effects across developmental domains, particularly in the social domain. Technology enhanced children's interactions with others.

Research on technology and early learning has focused on children as consumers of technology rather than on their role as creators using technology (Hsin, Li, & Tsai, 2014). The problem is that the amount of research has not kept pace with the rapid increase in devices and outputs (Radesky et al., 2015). We will examine the benefits of using technology with young children, to help you understand the importance of it's integration with children's play and learning. We encourage you to keep current with advances in research in this rapidly growing area of early learning.

THE BENEFITS OF USING TECHNOLOGY WITH YOUNG CHILDREN

The decision to incorporate technology into children's play is guided by teachers' beliefs or philosophies about how children learn. Often, we examine our beliefs and assumptions by reviewing positions taken by experts in the field. Since technology began being available in early learning centres, experts have examined its influence on children's play. As illustrated in Table 13.1, some researchers indicate that there are benefits to incorporating it into early learning environments. For example, children can draw shapes and pictures on the screen, and they can receive immediate feedback when using letter recognition software. Early learning teachers and student teachers benefit from examining the literature as a way to help determine their philosophical position on technology and play. Table 13.1 serves as a way for you to reflect on your own philosophy.

When using technology with children, early learning teachers examine it on the same merits as other forms of play. The core question to be asked is: How does technology contribute to children's quality play experiences? For example, if children are interested in music and you are able to find software that is rich in sound, music, action, and voice, then is technology is appropriate to use with children? If children are interested in outdoor climbing opportunities, is it appropriate to substitute outdoor play for activities using the computer or other technology devices?

Having technology in the early learning environment is a strategy that may be used to promote exploratory learning in a collaborative setting. Children communicate with others and use technology tools to write information, talk with peers, listen, and read

Table 13.1 The benefits of technology.

T	Technology devices and outputs are intrinsically motivating for young children and contribute to cognitive and social development (Tomporowski, McCullick, & Pesce, 2015).
E	Enhancement of self-concept and improvement of attitudes about learning can occur with technology use (Potvin & Hasni, 2014).
C	Children demonstrate increased levels of spoken communication and cooperation during computer use (Rost & Candlin, 2014).
H	Hours spent with technology can offer children opportunities to share leadership roles (Aubrey & Dahl, 2014).
N	New interactive technologies allow children to develop their curiosity, problem solving, and independent thinking skills. These are powerful for brain development (Sousa, 2016).
O	Opportunities for using technology as a tool are enhanced when early learning teachers use it to support observations and documentation (Blackwell, Lauricella, & Wartella, 2014).
L	Lives of children with exceptionalities can be enhanced. They improve their self-esteem, mobility, communication, and sense of control (Crowley, Holzman, Santiago, & Vanyi, 2016).
O	Opportunities to use technology are considered important to twenty-first-century learning. Children benefit when invited to experience robotics, coding, and tinkering with technology (Crowley, Holzman, Santiago, & Vanyi, 2016).
G	Game playing online supports children's growing interests and emerging digital literacy (Holloway, Green, & Livingstone, 2013). Game playing supports children's literacy, play, and learning (Kankaanranta, Koivula, Laakso, & Mustola, 2017).
Y	Young children who have exposure to educational software that is close to real-world experiences have an opportunity to learn about aspects of life that they would not otherwise learn about (Buckingham, 2013).

Photo 13.8 Computers in the classroom.
Used with Permission of Diane Kashin

either pictorial icons or written words. As you will note later in the chapter, computers and tablets may be tools that positively contribute to advancing children's literacy skills and support children with varying strengths and exceptionalities (Buckingham, 2013).

Constructivists who support computers in early learning centres remind us that preschool children learn through the experience gained from the use of **concrete objects**. For example, Bredekamp and Copple (1997) compared children manipulating figures on the screen to Cuisenaire rods. They suggested that if children learn to use the computer in developmentally appropriate ways, there are ample opportunities for children to manipulate objects and gain similar learning to that gained with traditional objects. The computer requires children to think in new and different ways from the thinking that occurs with concrete play materials. Children require software that provides them with activities and situations that make demands on them to explore in groups and engage in autonomous learning and that takes into account the sociocultural context of the learning experience (Buckingham, 2013).

concrete objects Objects that can be touched and manipulated by children in their play and that often reinforce a particular concept.

THE ROLE OF INFORMATION AND COMMUNICATION TECHNOLOGIES

New technologies are changing traditional views of teaching and learning in the early years. Beschorner and Hutchison (2013) suggested that, in the twenty-first century, a more inclusive definition of literacy is necessary to include multimedia and computer-based print. This wider definition is needed because young children frequently see family members using the Internet and often use interactive media for a variety of purposes themselves. New literacies, skills, strategies, and dispositions are required when reading

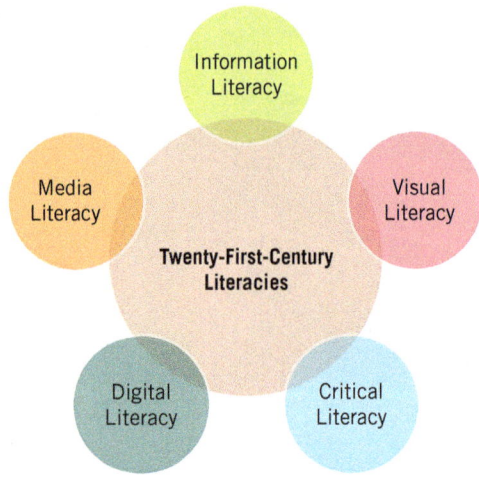

Figure 13.5 Literacies for the twenty-first century.

and writing on the Internet. Traditional literacy involves reading, writing, speaking, and listening. Now, as outlined in Figure 13.5, advances in technology have contributed to new literacies for the twenty-first century (Tompkins, Campbell, Green, & Smith, 2014). Each of these literacies will be explored as it relates to early learning programs.

How can these literacies can be supported during the early years? Consider information literacy, which is the ability to locate, evaluate, and use information. What information would be useful to young children? Can they build a proficiency for locating information on the Internet, and is this an opportunity to support early learners in being able to evaluate the usefulness and appropriateness of information? What about visual literacy? There are many applications that allow children to practise producing visual messages. Being able to visually represent is an indicator of cognitive development (Ontario Ministry of Education, 2014). Opportunities for visual literacy are multiple in the twenty-first century (Tompkins et al., 2014).

Children require critical thinking skills in order to become critically literate. "An essential aim of early childhood education is to promote effective thinking in young children (Costello, 2013, p. 1). Critical literacy is defined as the ability to question, challenge, and evaluate (Leu, Everett-Cacopardo, Zawilinski, McVerry, & O'Byrne, 2014). Consider how early learning teachers can support this type of literacy in a developmentally appropriate way. Digital literacy is the ability to use digital technology and communication tools. Media literacy is the ability to question, analyze, and create media (Buckingham, 2013). For example, Nikky, Fariba, and Emily are using a tablet to shoot a movie about the small world they created, which they call "water world." After they view the movie, they recognize that some of what they filmed is blurry. Their early learning teacher, Adam, helps them use an editing tool; once they are satisfied with their finished product, they decide they want to send it to their families. Adam takes out his laptop, and the children compose the content of an email message. Adam helps each child send the email to his or her family. This is twenty-first-century teaching and learning!

As outlined in Figure 13.6, early learning teachers benefit from developing and maintaining the technology skills needed for devices and programs that are consistent with current practices used in families and within society. Without current and relevant practices, it is a challenge to support and facilitate twenty-first-century skills with children.

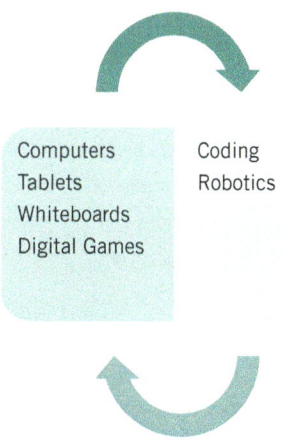

Figure 13.6 Technology devices and programs that support early learning programs.

Computers

Computers have a much longer history in early learning programs than newer devices such as tablets and whiteboards. More than 25 years ago, Clements and Nastasi (1993) identified that, in the early 1980s, already 25 percent of early learning programs had computers. They cited research from the 1980s that suggested that children approach computers with competence and comfort, and appear to enjoy exploring this "new medium" (p. 190). Computer use has continued to grow, and computers are now integrated into the learning environment.

Haugland and Wright (1997) identified stages and corresponding activities that children typically go through when computers are used. These stages and corresponding activities remain relevant today. The stages are discovery, involvement, self-confidence, and creativity. Table 13.2 provides the stages and an overview of some behaviours that an early learning teacher may observe in children. These stages are similar for children's use tablets and cellphones.

Early learning teachers can use a combination of developmentally appropriate practice guidelines as well as the characteristics and strengths and capabilities of children that blend their active play with computers and related technology. For example, Gage, a 3-year-old, loves to sing. Initially, the early learning teacher assisted him in going to YouTube to find karaoke videos. Three months later, using the icons on the computer, Gage goes to the site independently. He has progressed through the first three phases of using the computer in his active play experiences.

Tablets

Tablets function in much the same way as computers but are more accessible in terms of space and cost. When technology is integrated into early learning environments in meaningful ways, it can transform literacy development (Hutchison & Reinking, 2011). According to Beschorner and Hutchison (2013), tablets have not been extensively studied as a literacy-teaching tool in early learning programs, but there is evidence that older children have benefited from their inclusion in the classroom. The touchable interface feature of tablets makes the tool especially suitable for young children. Tablets can be

Table 13.2 Stages of computer use.

	Stage	Activity
I.	Discovery	Child observes interesting images and sounds.
		Adult models the use of the mouse.
		Child begins to use the mouse.
		Adult provides physical and verbal support.
		Child begins to explore software.
		Child may observe how peers use software.
		Child examines specific features of the program.
II.	Involvement	Child uses the mouse and the keyboard.
		Child manipulates the software.
		Child follows pictorial directions.
		Child participates in social interaction with others, including turn-taking.
		Child begins to remember how to use the software.
III.	Self-confidence	Child begins to use the computer on own.
		Child is able to find icons for programs.
		Child provides guidance to others.
		Child is willing to explore new software with confidence.
		Child talks about what he or she is doing with the computer.
		Child moves between one site and another or between programs.
IV.	Creativity	Child uses the computer in a variety of ways.
		Child combines personal expression with creativity.
		Child tries new ways to create materials.

used to read, write, and communicate, which supports the development of new literacies and promotes children's independence and confidence (Neumann & Neumann, 2014).

Newmann and Neumann (2014) purported that evidence suggests that tablets have the potential to enhance specific emergent literacy skills such as alphabet knowledge, print concepts, and emergent writing. However, they have cautioned that the optimal use of tablets for early literacy is dependent on the type of scaffolding used by the adult and the availability and quality of applications. As research continues to evolve, tablets are simultaneously appearing more frequently in early learning environments. Early learning teachers benefit from using their understanding of child development, learning, and play to recognize the most appropriate ways to incorporate them into their programs.

STOP ... THINK ... DISCUSS ... REFLECT

How do you read books? Do you read them on a tablet? Do you think tablets will replace children's exposure to real books? Do you think this is a problem? What is the difference between reading e-books and reading traditional books? How might families that promote paperless environments respond to early learning programs that continue to use paper books?

Photo 13.9 Learning with tablets.

Used with Permission of Maria Luberto

Paciga and Quest (2017) recommended five tips for reading e-books with young children.

1. Sit in close proximity to co-engage in e-reading experiences.
2. Place the tablet on a stable surface to stabilize the device.
3. Read e-books multiple times.
4. Help children to learn to wait their turn in order to interact with the interactives and clickables.
5. Consider the child's developmental level and the child as an individual, including his or her particular interests, when choosing e-books.

Do an Internet search for readings one books versus print books for young children. What have you discovered?

Interactive Whiteboards

Interactive whiteboards are also becoming a feature of many early learning environments. These connect to computers and tablets and are often placed on a wall where children can sit in a group to view and interact with the content. Plowman (2016) discussed the use of interactive whiteboards as still tending to be associated with instruction rather than play. The whiteboards generally support a directive pedagogy that is not congruent with early learning practice.

A study conducted by Bourbour, Vigmo, and Samuelsson (2015) on interactive whiteboards provided examples of imaginative uses that illustrated children's interests as a point of departure. Their examples indicate that whiteboards can help children engage in problem-solving activities and provide multisensory experiences. The use of whiteboards in a way that supports play depends on the experience, philosophy, and training of early learning teachers. It also depends on the teacher's understanding of play (Voogt & McKenney, 2017). As with many forms of new technology, there is not ample research to make an informed decision about incorporating interactive whiteboards in early learning environments.

Digital Games

According to Plowman (2016), the use of digital games tends to create a divide among educators. The research on digital gaming in education often focuses on older children. Advocates of game playing suggest that it promotes collaboration and problem solving and that it is intrinsically motivating to children. Nolan and McBride (2014) question whether digital games fit the concepts of play and suggest that more research is needed.

Kankaanranta, Koivula, Laakso, and Mustola (2017) determined that digital games can be beneficial because they motivate children. Children are attracted to the imaginary worlds of digital games and the opportunities to share their experiences with peers. The use of digital games requires early learning teachers to apply a critical lens to their use so that they support children's play in meaningful ways.

> ### STOP ... THINK ... DISCUSS ... REFLECT
>
> What do you think about the use of digital games in early learning? When children "play" with these games, are they really playing? Would you advocate for their use, or would you suggest that there are issues related to integrating digital games in the learning environment.

Coding

Coding is the language of the digital age that is necessary to program a computer. There are now countless products for teachers and parents that focus on helping children to develop computing skills (Portelance, Strawhacker, & Bers, 2016). Does coding have a place in early childhood education? At what age can children learn to code in a way that supports the development of computing skills and is still considered play?

At the beginning of the chapter, Amela discussed the importance of introducing a coding experience to children. What does that mean, and how do early learning teachers include coding in early learning programs? In Box 13.1, Deanna Pecaski McLennan, an early learning teacher in Ontario, describes how she has incorporated coding into children's experiences and makes suggestions on how coding can be used in early learning programs.

> **Box 13.1   Coding with kindergarteners.**

In our emergent kindergarten classroom, we use children's interests to guide our programming. Over the course of a week, I noticed that the children had been exploring maps: they were creating and using them in their pirate dramatic play, referring to printed maps as they rode the tricycles outside and directing one another using student-created maps to the "hidden treasure" in our classroom. I was familiar with the coding that older children were doing and eager to implement it in a meaningful way in our classroom. I knew that the children's interests in maps was the spark I needed. During whole-group time, I introduced the term *coding* to children. I explained that coding was the language that computers use in order to perform a specific task and that we can also give directions to one another using the same type of language. I presented the children with a simple grid that I made using masking tape on a clear sensory bin lid and various props (a gold coin, mini plastic spider and bats, a mini figure).

Wanting to expand the children's interest in treasures, I placed the gold coin on one end of the grid and the mini figure on the other. I asked children to look at the grid and consider the different ways the figure could travel to the gold. We agreed on four basic commands—"go right," "go left," "go up," and "go down"—and then, following the children's directions, I moved the figure until it successfully reached the gold. The children were enthusiastic about this new game, and we continued to explore many variations of it over the next several days. After the children had some practice manipulating the props and giving directions, I introduced obstacles into the grid. I added a number of random plastic spiders and bats and encouraged the children to move the figure around these in order to successfully reach the gold. Once the children had tried a few ways and mastered this, I provided them with coding cards that had symbols to represent the directions. This supported children in planning out and "writing" the many different paths the figures might travel.

I noticed that the children continued to create their own coding stories and games using additional props from around our room during subsequent play times. Over time, we tried many activities in order to improve and extend their coding interest and skill, including:

- Creating grids using stickie notes and encouraging the children to code in order to discover sticker "treasures" hidden underneath
- Integrating coding outdoors by creating masking tape or chalk grids on the pavement, motivating the children to use props and stories from outdoors in their explorations
- Using printed photos of our neighbourhood landmarks and inviting children to code the path they take to travel from home to school
- Retelling favourite stories on the coding grid using props (e.g., helping the Gingerbread Man escape the many animals who want to eat him)
- Adding number and arrow dice to the grid and encouraging the children to create their own coding games
- Incorporating our knowledge of coding directions into creative movement outdoors and in the gym
- Applying our knowledge and practising coding using mini robots (e.g., Code and Go Robot Mouse)
- Introducing more formal coding activities using technology (e.g., Scratch, Scratch Jr.)

It has been exciting to witness the children's growth in incorporating coding in more sophisticated ways in their play. I have noticed many benefits, including substantial math and literacy abilities emerging from these explorations, and I feel that by including coding in our classroom, children are embracing activities that are preparing them for life in a digital future and instilling in them twenty-first-century competencies. To learn more about coding in our classroom, visit www.mrsmclennan.blogspot.ca or connect with me @McLennan1977.

Source: Used with permission of Deanna Pecaski McLennan

Robotics

Research is being conducted about including **robotics** in early learning environments. Robotics offer children opportunities to design and create their own robots using technology. The growth of robotics is a sign of the maker movement, the popularity of tinkering, and the recent attention to STEM (science, technology, engineering, mathematics) learning.

robotics A branch of technology concerned with the design and use of robots.

While research on robotics has focused on later schooling, there is evidence to suggest that "teaching these subjects during foundational early childhood years can be an engaging and rewarding experience for young learners" (Bers, Flannery, Kazakoff, & Sullivan, 2014, p. 145). Early learning teachers assess the developmental appropriateness of robotics based on standards and best practices (NAEYC & Fred Rogers Center for Early Learning and Children's Media, 2012). For example, in an early learning environment, Maria placed a number of plumber pipes, connections, a sketch pad, a tablet with an interesting configuration that used the plumber pipes, and a note to the children, asking how they might create such a configuration. Such experiences promote the types of thinking that children require for robotics projects: logic, planning and linear thinking, prototyping, problem solving, and following ideas. Now, think about how this could be expanded to include other STEM concepts.

The research suggests that children as young as 4 years old can build and program simple robotics projects. Developmentally, the building of robotics supports fine motor skills, collaboration, and teamwork. From a learning perspective, robotics support experimenting with concepts of engineering, while playing in a creative way (Bers et al., 2014).

TECHNOLOGY AND PLAY

Mildred Parten's (1932) classic work on children's stages of social play provides further insight into how technology supports quality play experiences (Freeman & Somerindyke, 2001). As described in Chapter 2, play is categorized into six categories: unoccupied, onlooker, solitary, parallel, associate, and cooperative. Parten's categories, combined with

Photo 13.10 Taking a "selfie."

Used with Permission of Ben Bortolotti

Vygotsky's constructivist, social-cultural perspective—including the positive influences of peer learning and the zone of proximal development—reinforce that technology equipment such as computers provides a venue to promote collaborative learning during the preschool years. There is merit in examining the relationship between Parten's play and Vygotsky's perspective on how children learn in relation to the use of technology in early learning programs.

During play, children are active participants in manipulating devices and outputs while they explore concepts, perform activities, and develop problem-solving and decision-making abilities. To illustrate how play and technology can be integrated into early learning programs, we share the story of Jamill and Liam. They use the resources made available to them to explore, create, experiment, and discover new opportunities in their play.

Jamill and Liam, both 4 years of age, have different play interests and styles. For example, Jamill plays computer games in the creative area, where she uses paints, clay, and other mixed media materials to create fascinating work. Liam frequently uses the block, construction, and climbing areas. Anita, the early learning teacher, brought a variety of new materials to the block centre: planks, cylinders, large cedar cubes, measuring sticks, and cars. She also placed a tablet in the area.

As the children explored the area, it appeared as though they were intrigued to find the tablet set up in the block area. Anita had loaded a number of unique block structures on the screen for the children to examine. As Jamill scrolled through the images, Liam became interested in an image that had amazing ramps. The children engaged in rich discussion about what they saw and how they could begin a construction project.

The two children began a construction project. They used the planks to develop ramps; they incorporated the cylinders and large cedar cubes into the structure. They sought out other materials, such as ropes, funnels, and containers, and incorporated them into the structure.

Jamill and Liam referred to the images on the tablet screen periodically, especially when they seemed to be at a standstill with ideas. Jamill, at various stages, with the help of Anita, took photos and then transferred them to the tablet. Each time a new image was taken, the children told Anita about the structure. They verbalized what they had done and how they were going to add to the structure.

Over the next several days, the children brought additional materials from home to add to the structure. They returned to the electronic file to examine the initial photos of the structure, as well as the documentation that was taken throughout the construction. The children had conversations about the structure and why it had been built in the specific manner it was. As more children and adults became interested in the structure, they incorporated new ideas into it. They had other children provide suggestions, and parents provided input. One father who was working on road construction brought photos of the three highway ramps that he was involved with constructing. This sparked the children to add a garage area with graters and cranes near the structure.

The children used email to send photos of the structure to their parents. Anita and the children continued to add new resources, including a couple of transformers.

Although the project began from the interests of Jamill and Liam, over the next few weeks, it became a project that received input from other children and their families. A number of children experimented with new configurations, new uses for the structure, and ways of adding new features. They took pictures, shared them with families, and received immediate feedback from adults and children about their structure. Families made comments at the beginning of the day, through email during the day, and again at the end of the day. The children continued to extend and make modifications to the structure. They used the Internet to search for more ideas.

Throughout the project, many design principles were examined, ideas were tried, research was completed, new language was learned, and rich child-to-child and adult–child communication occurred. This project brought play and technology together. The use of the Internet for research and taking the digital photos, combined with transferring them to family emails, contributed to the children extending their play. The questions posed and suggestions made by adults and other children about how to further enhance the structure expanded the depth of the project. Families and early learning teachers collectively supported the children's interests and learning.

This example illustrates how technology can enhance a play episode. Children extended their play over several days and created opportunities for adults to become part of their play and their learning community.

> ### STOP ... THINK ... DISCUSS ... REFLECT
>
> How did technology support Jamill and Liam in their play? What was the role of the early learning teacher in combining technology with play? Were the children negatively affected by using technology? If so, how and why? If not, why not?

TECHNOLOGY AND CHILDREN'S DEVELOPMENT

Advocates of technology integration indicate that it positively influences children's development. If presented appropriately, technology supports the social, emotional, cognitive, and physical development of children between infancy and 6 years of age (Chaudron, 2015). For example, technology may enhance children's verbal and written language skills and increase their social-emotional development. If used appropriately, it also enhances children's self-esteem. Inappropriate use of technology includes replacing human interaction to create a solo experience (Chaudron, 2015). Figure 13.7 features an overview of the developmental aspects of technology use.

Figure 13.7 Technology and development.

Source (left to right): Used with Permission of Andrea Stirling, Used with Permission of Ben Bortolotti, Used with Permission of Diane Kashin, Used with Permission of Diane Kashin, and Used with Permission of Andrea Stirling.

Table 13.3 Categories of social play with devices.

Type of Social Interaction	Characteristics
Active Navigator	Children have experience or expertise with the device.
	Children appear to be child experts at using the device.
	Children have access to devices at home.
	Children provide support to other children.
Vicarious Navigator/Super-Onlooker	Children observe and watch from the sidelines.
	Children show individual interest in the program operation.
	Children do not claim control over the device.
	Children do not share their knowledge with others.
	Children do not exhibit leadership skills.
Spectator	Children observe and show an interest and sense of curiosity in technology.
	Children may not actively engage in the use of devices.

Freeman and Somerindyke (2001) outlined three categories of children's social play that occur with computers. Chaudron (2015) added to research on how children use technology. Combining Freeman and Somerindyke's work with Chaudron's perspectives provides early learning teachers with insight into technology and children's learning. Even with the emergence of new technologies such as tablets, Freeman and Somerindyke's categories remain relevant. They are active navigators, vicarious navigators/super-onlookers, and spectators. Table 13.3 provides an overview of the type of social interaction and common characteristics that children may exhibit at each phase.

Freeman and Somerindyke (2001) indicated that active navigators can be classified into three categories:

- *Consolidated navigators* use computers independently and explore how to solve problems.
- *Mouse navigators* are able to manoeuvre the mouse to reflect items on screen and to meet their needs.
- *Program navigators* use the program with proficiency.

Each of these phases contributes to the level of socialization that children engage in. For example, because of their comfort with technology, active navigators are more likely to share their knowledge and help other children than are children who are super-onlookers or spectators. As children become more comfortable with their technology tools and capabilities, they are more likely to connect with other children.

Technology can serve as a catalyst for social interaction and conversations related to what the children are exploring. Chaudron (2015) indicated that children socialize significantly in early learning environments where computers and technological devices are available. They learn to negotiate to take turns. They support one another by helping each other to use the software, such as deciding what icons to click. As well, they celebrate when they have completed a task or created something of interest. This is known as a **shared problem space**.

shared problem space A way to organize the technology resources available to children that supports their curiosity or area of exploration. The early learning teacher facilitates discussions that help the children explore answers to their questions and incorporate their findings into new learning.

Think about this example: Johnston, the early learning teacher, provided four children with a digital camera to use and showed them which button to push for video. When the video was played back to them, they were fascinated by the conversations they captured. This led them to want to do more recording. They determined that they would be thoughtful about what they said, so they created a script, used props, and then recorded it. They played the recording again and again. Then Johnston transferred the viewing of the video from the camera to the interactive whiteboard.

STOP ... THINK ... DISCUSS ... REFLECT

Think about other ways the early learning teacher and children could use the recording. How might it be shared with families? How could the experience be extended?

Children take different initiatives with technology than in other areas of play. This contributes to increasing one's self-concept and self-esteem. For example, when children, with the support of early learning teachers, explore the software, share ideas, ask their peers for assistance, and observe how peers use technological devices and outputs, they gain knowledge and skills that lead to self-confidence. These actions contribute to social and emotional development attributes and personal self-esteem (Chaudron, 2015).

CURIOUS?

Do an Internet search to gain different perspectives on how experts approach the topic of technology and children's development.

Software applications that require children to use a variety of thinking and problem-solving skills increase the likelihood that they will work with a peer. For example, software such as *Facemaker* has children make faces. In observing Mahamad and Parker, the more faces they made, the more they giggled and the more they shared with one another how they were going to add to their drawing. Parker asked Mahamad how he got the thick, green squiggle line on the drawing. As they created new ideas, more children walked over to the area to observe what they were doing and to join in the activity. This illustrates the socialization and communication skills consistent with preschool development. Unique learning and proficiency emerge and evolve as children use technology effectively.

Examine the story of Jamill and Liam presented earlier in the chapter. Note how the initial project began with two children and then expanded to include more children and adults. Think about how Jamill and Liam had discussions with other children and adults. Examine how the children asked Anita for help and how, at times, children helped each other. These actions support the foundation of socialization skills. It is interesting to note that children appear to seek help from one another and seem to prefer help from peers over help from the teacher.

During the early years, children require software that promotes written and expressive thoughts and has visual representation (Chaudron, 2015). For example, software that encourages the young child to use symbols or discover and invent with symbols increases both language development and creativity (Isenberg & Jalongo, 2014).

When children "create" their personalized stories, their sense of curiosity, inquiry, and problem solving is further developed. For example, when children use pictorial icons, words, colour menus, and unique characters, their language and thinking skills are stimulated because they are using more than one or two dimensions in their learning. By recording their stories on a tablet or computer, using a combination of words and pictorial representation, children experience how words and pictures are used to tell a story. They also see how print carries a message. Children appear to edit their stories and verbalize what they are doing when they move or create objects on the screen.

Technology Supports Inclusivity

There are many examples that illustrate how technology opens up new avenues for children with language impairments. There are software applications that can be used to acoustically alter speech sounds so that children are more likely to distinguish them. Children who have language impairments are able to hear the rapidly changing sound elements and sequences of normal speech over and over. As children master skills, the activities become progressively more advanced. This enables them to continually increase their rate of speech processing, which in turn leads to normal speech perception (Denning & Moody, 2013; Ennis-Cole & Smith, 2011).

Children who are on the autism spectrum may also benefit from using digital devices to support their language development. For example, Stokes (2017) identified that various modes of technology support children with autism by contributing to a number of skills, including:

- Overall understanding of their environment;
- Expressive communication skills;
- Social interaction skills;
- Attention skills and motivation skills;
- Overall independent daily functioning skills.

Many children who are autistic are visual learners; they think in pictures. A combination of verbal instructions and visual cues, such as facial expressions and hand gestures, helps them to understand language acquisition. Software applications that provide virtual peers help children produce more "contingent" sentences than when they were paired with real-life children (Denning & Moody, 2013; Ennis-Cole & Smith, 2011).

As with other aspects of the early learning program, early learning teachers examine the strengths, interests, and potential materials and resources that support children in expanding their play and learning opportunities. For children who express an interest in technology, early learning teachers research the types of technology resources that would support active play and extend the play so that children engage in more complicated and complex play.

Is There a Digital Divide?

The use of technology can reveal issues of inequity among children and families and early learning programs. For example, children from diverse ethnic backgrounds, children living in inner cities or rural communities, children with disabilities, and children whose first language is not English are disadvantaged in terms of accessibility to technology and adult role models (Willis, Weiser, & Kirkwood, 2014). These inequities may disadvantage children in both their general cognitive skills and their ability to function in our digital society (Willis et al., 2014). This requires early learning teachers to ensure that they think about who is using the technology, how they are using it, and if they are using it.

The declining cost of technology contributes to early learning programs being able to offer children experiences with technology in their play that allow them to explore and learn about their world in different ways. For many families, the early learning program is where their children will be exposed to technology. This includes children being exposed to technological terms and the use of various programs.

Early learning teachers understand that by offering children opportunities to engage with technology, children are being given options for understanding various life experiences through action, verbal, pictorial, and written experiences. These skills complement the twenty-first-century skills discussed earlier in the chapter.

The attitudes of adults either promote or hinder children's access to technology. Early learning teachers benefit from reflecting on their attitudes on and behaviours toward the use of computers and related technology with young children. This reflective process may help to identify how some situations have the potential to lead to inequity among the children and may help to examine processes and procedures that could reduce or create barriers that may have the potential to lead to inequitable issues. Early learning teachers benefit from seeking information from families on the level of access to technology in the home environment. Such insight helps to guide how to enhance the use of technology in the early learning setting. Children who do not have access to or have limited access to technology require exposure to digital devices that encourage exploration of how technology can support their play.

Technology can support families as a means of increased communication. Connecting to families and sharing children's experiences during the day are improved with the use of technology. Technology tools can help early learning teachers to strengthen connections with families. Early learning teachers have a responsibility to share knowledge of child development and learning. Technological tools offer efficient and accessible ways to exchange information and resources with families. Families, in turn, "can use technology to question, seek advice, share information about their child, and feel more engaged in the program and their child's experiences there" (NAEYC & Fred Rogers Center for Early Learning and Children's Media, 2012, p. 7). Early learning students and teachers learn that technology tools can be used in many beneficial ways and should be able to use these ethically in practice. For example, having a smartphone with you during the day should not mean that it is used for excessively for personal use. It should also never be used to share images of children without family consent.

THE ROLE OF THE EARLY LEARNING TEACHER

Above all, according to the joint position statement on technology, the use of technology tools and interactive media should not harm children (NAEYC & Fred Rogers Center for Early Learning and Children's Media, 2012). As outlined in Figure 13.8, early learning teachers have diverse roles in promoting technology.

Early learning teachers consider the overall health and welfare of children. "Access to technology tools and interactive media should not exclude, diminish, or interfere with children's healthy communication, social interactions, play, and other developmentally appropriate activities with peers, family members, and teachers" (NAEYC & Fred Rogers Center for Early Learning and Children's Media, 2012, p. 5). Early learning teachers ensure that children are not exposed to violent or highly sexualized images or anything else that can be damaging. It is the role of early learning teachers to protect children

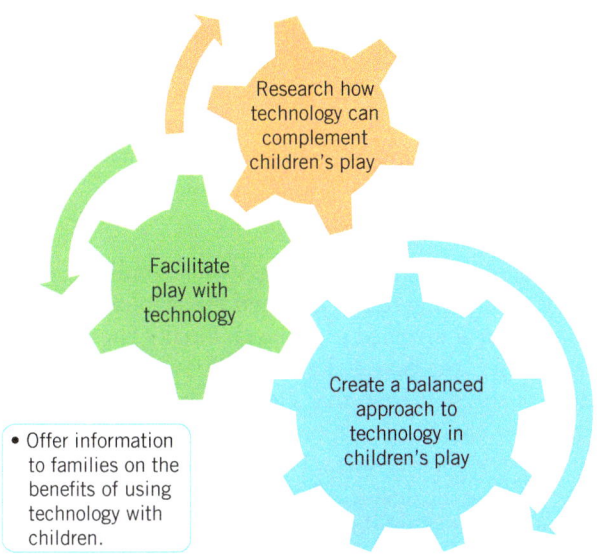

Figure 13.8 The role of early learning teachers in promoting technology.

and to keep abreast of emerging issues with technology use, such as exposure to electromagnetic fields and radiation from cellphones (NAEYC & Fred Rogers Center for Early Learning and Children's Media, 2012).

The role of the early learning teacher is to seek a balanced approach. Technology does not replace other experiences in early learning programs. Developmentally appropriate teaching practices always guide the selection of any classroom materials, including technology and interactive media. "Technology and media should not replace activities such as creative play, real-life exploration, physical activity, outdoor experiences, conversation, and social interactions that are important for children's development" (NAEYC & Fred Rogers Center for Early Learning and Children's Media, 2012, p. 5). Is there any age that is too young for exposure to technology?

In 2015, the American Academy of Pediatrics reversed an earlier recommendation that children under 2 years should not have exposure to screen time. Now they recognize that there are benefits to such things as video chatting for infants and toddlers. Imagine how wonderful it would be for a 14-month-old child to communicate with grandparents living in another country. Technology has benefits and can support learning, thinking, collaboration, communication, and creativity. Consistent with a balanced approach are limits at any age.

In your recent memory, can you recall a cellphone or tablet being used to occupy young children? Just as in the past when televisions were used to keep children busy, mobile devices are now being used to occupy or distract children. The role of early learning teachers is to offer families a wider perspective on the implications of using devices as a **behavioural regulation tool**. Early learning teachers help families recognize that, although these devices help in the short term, their use can be detrimental in the long term, as children need to develop internal mechanisms of self-regulation (Radesky et al., 2015).

Facilitating Children's Play with Technology

Early learning teachers are responsible for supervising and facilitating play at a number of experience centres, both indoors and outdoors. Generally, teachers become involved with using technology in children's play when children ask for help or if there is a need for intervention. Early learning teachers observe how children engage in play and introduce

behavioural regulation tool
Refers to an item or activity used with children to control their impulses and to have them behave in appropriate ways.

technology if they are able to identify how it may expand or deepen children's play. Plowman and Stephen (2005) suggested that there are three broad categories of adult involvement in computer play. We have adapted these categories to reflect technology-related devices in general terms. Plowman and Stephen identified them as reactive supervision, guided interaction, and a hybrid approach. An overview of each follows.

Reactive Supervision

Reactive supervision is described as keeping a check on the children using the technology tool. This may include monitoring turn-taking and the amount of time children use the devices. Teachers may become involved with the children if there is a request for help or if a child requires a turn with the device. This supervision does not provide teachers with a clear understanding of the skill level that children exhibit with a technology device. Teachers may not see how children incorporate active play experiences with technology (Plowman & Stephen, 2005), or vice versa. However, excessive monitoring and interacting to correct children's use of the device may prevent children from developing the confidence to explore the use of the technology tool or to take risks and try new ideas.

Guided Interaction

This category refers to the child–adult interaction that occurs as the technology is being used. For example, early learning teachers may work with a group of children to explain how to use a particular piece of software, they may pose questions that lead children to explore alternative strategies, or they may illustrate how a particular tool is used. Effective guided interaction is one of the most powerful strategies that early learning teachers use with children. To be effective, it requires small groups of children and time.

Hybrid

This model combines reactive supervision with guided interaction. Early learning teachers engage in observations to determine the competency levels, the needs of the children, and the required resources relative to play interests that are being expressed or executed. This guides the approach that the early learning teachers use with the children and the types of technology devices presented.

Choosing Applications

There is an abundance of computer software available on the market. Early learning teachers examine the software to determine how it meets the needs, learning, and interests of an individual child and groups of children. For example, they look at its unique features, such as how the children will learn through exploration, imagination, creative problem solving, and self-guided instruction. They ensure that it reflects and builds on what children know. They examine it to determine how many senses children will use and the potential versatility it brings to the play experience. They examine it relative to how the software will expand concrete play experiences across the early learning programs.

Choosing software that promotes discovery enhances learning. Children work best with software that is *open-ended* because it provides them with opportunities to discover, make choices, and experience the impact of their decisions. *Open-ended software* refers to applications that encourage children to explore, discover, wonder, make choices, problem solve, collaborate, and view the results of their choices. Children make real choices rather than choosing from a menu with options. Children flourish at integrating technology

Table 13.4 Questions to consider when choosing software or applications for young children.

- Does the software or application require purchasing?
- How will the purchase of this software or application support the early learning play philosophy?
- How does the software support the child's interests and developmental phase?
- How does the software support the child's background and experiences and what the child already knows?
- How much physical manipulation is required for the child to use the software or application?
- How does the use of the application connect with the child's learning?
- How does the software encourage exploration, imagination, and wonderment?
- How many senses, such as sound, music, and voice, are used?
- How will the application support cooperation and child interaction?
- How does the software support open-ended discovery?
- How easy is it to understand the instructions?
- How does the software support children completing concrete tasks?
- How will the software adjust to the level of difficulty required?
- Does the software provide children with positive verbal and visual cues?
- Does the software support a child working alone or in a group?

with play when they have projects to engage in rather than merely "free explore" time (Plowman & McPake, 2013). Discovery-type software motivates children to actively search for diverse ways to solve tasks. This differs from drill-and-practice software that leads children to gains in certain rote skills.

Early learning teachers examine the developmental levels and interests of the children for whom the application is intended. For example, how does the software reflect how children think? The opening menu of software for 3-year-olds would be pictorial, whereas the opening menu for 5-year-olds may require some word recognition. Likewise, what are the choice of characters and the level of action? This will influence how the children use the software. The intended purpose of the software is examined. For example, is the software intended to support language development? Is the purpose to provide children with opportunities to create pictures or stories? A number of guidelines can be followed when choosing software. Table 13.4 provides potential questions to guide the selection of software.

Observing Children

Early learning teachers have the unique advantage of acquiring information about children's interests and levels of developmental milestones as they interact with technology. It provides teachers with a window into children's thinking processes (Chaudron, 2015). Observing children using technology provides insight into their strengths that may not be observed in other play episodes. For example, Marley, at the age of 4, does not show any interest in books and has limited contact with the other children. However, while using a tablet, she recognizes words, documents words to support her art, and communicates with other children. Her level of socialization and literacy skills is much more pronounced with the use of technology than at other experience centres.

The early learning teacher can devise a set of questions that are asked of the children. The questions are directed at what children are doing at that moment. Examples of questions to consider include:

- What is the reason you are doing this?
- Why do you use this function?
- What does this mean?
- How will this take you to . . . ?

The questions chosen avoid steering the child to specific activities. Questions such as Could you show me this? or What would happen if? or Have you tried this? will reduce your ability to assess the child's knowledge of and ability to use the software. Contextual inquiry observations give us an opportunity to view how children use the software and how to support them in using added functionality of the software or application.

Early learning teachers can use software or applications as well as devices to support the documentation process. Devices such as tablets or smartphones can be used "to take photos, record video and audio, and make notes, then integrate them into daily blogs and online portfolios that parents can access" (Parnell & Bartlett, 2012, p. 51). This is considered digital documentation. There are numerous applications available to support the use of this type of documentation, some of which require purchasing and others of which are available without charge. Early learning teachers engage in ongoing professional learning and development in order to make decisions about incorporating digital documentation in their practice.

Professional Learning and Development

Early learning teachers play a key role in the integration of technology into child's play. One of the biggest challenges or roadblocks to integrating technology into early learning environments is training.

Teachers who participate in continuous learning and development on the use of technology and how it may benefit children appear to be more successful in integrating technology into early learning programs (NAEYC & Fred Rogers Center for Early Learning and Children's Media, 2012). When teachers know the software and the technology, there is an enhanced level of interaction among teachers and children.

Early learning teachers new to integrating technology into the early learning program benefit from having role models to whom they can turn for knowledge about computers, as well as for emotional support and reassurance (NAEYC & Fred Rogers Center for Early Learning and Children's Media, 2012).

The following practices support early learning teachers in integrating technology into programs for young children.

Linking Technology with Children's Interests

Time: Early learning teachers require time to explore technology and acquire the skills necessary to effectively infuse technology into early learning environments. There is merit to allowing early learning teachers to explore the software and applications without distractions.

Training structure: Early learning teachers require a variety of teaching and learning opportunities and strategies related to how technology supports children's play.

Collaborative development: Just as young children learn best in a collaborative environment, early learning teachers also benefit from this type of setting. Because early learning teachers' skills and interests may vary, a nonthreatening environment in which the technology can be explored leads to enriching the children's technology opportunities. Role modelling can be part of this process, as this allows teachers with less experience to observe and then gradually build their confidence.

Linking technology with children's interests and program philosophy: How technology is used in the early learning program should support the program's philosophy. This helps to guide how technology is integrated into children's play (NAEYC & Fred Rogers Center for Early Learning and Children's Media, 2012). The technology available in the early learning program is relevant to the program philosophy and intended learning outcomes for the children. This provides a meaningful context for learning about technology and transferring this knowledge to the early learning environment.

TERMS THAT INFLUENCE EARLY LEARNING PLAY ENVIRONMENTS

We conclude this chapter with three additional terms that relate to children and early learning teachers' experiences with technology.

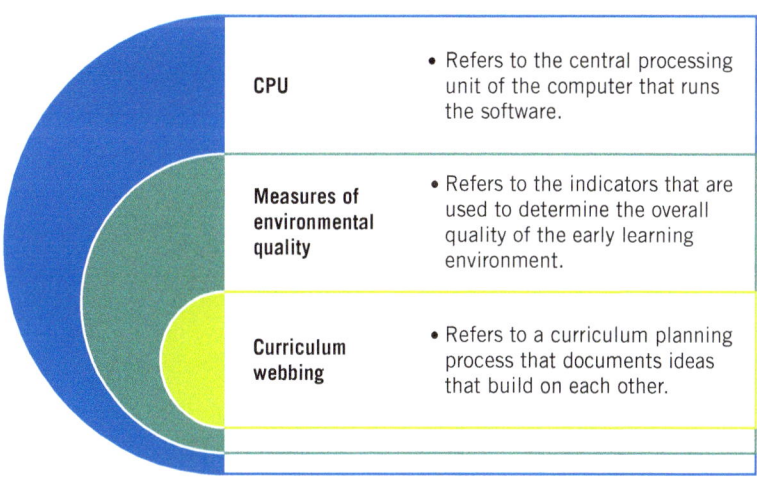

SUMMARY

Chapter Preview

- The role of technology in the lives of children requires an examination of the benefits, controversies, challenges, and perspectives as it relates to play.
- The essential skills for the twenty-first century, including the ability to use technology, now influence early learning programs.

Defining Technology

- Technology is any device that increases or assists children's ability to play, explore, discover new learning, and extend their potential.

Various Perspectives about the Use of Technology with Young Children

- Many early learning teachers oppose the use of technology with children because of their fear that it erodes play and will lead to health issues such as childhood obesity and aggressive behaviour.
- The NAEYC's position statement outlines that early learning teachers have the responsibility to assess, evaluate, and develop strategies for implementing technology, while providing each child with equitable access to technology.

Technology and Children's Creativity

- Technology supports children's creativity, imagination, and problem solving, all which are skills needed for critical thinking and innovation.

Technology and Early Learning

- Technology is part of children's lives.

The Benefits of Using Technology with Young Children

- Various technologies are motivational for some children. If used appropriately, technology will enhance children's play and their self-concept.
- Children share leadership roles and initiate interactions when using technology.

Role of Information and Communication Technologies

- Advances in technology have contributed to new literacies, including information literacy, visual literacy, critical literacy, digital literacy, and media literacy.
- Technologies in early learning programs include the use of computers, tablets, digital games, interactive whiteboards, coding, and robotics.

Technology and Play

- Technology, if introduced at the right time in the play environment, can enhance the play episode.

Technology and Child Development

- Technology contributes to the cognitive, social, emotional, language, and physical development of children.
- Technology can cause inequitable issues among children, families, and genders.
- Children with disabilities may benefit from access to technology.

Technology Supports Inclusivity

- Technology offers children with various disabilities support that contributes to their socialization, play, interests, and learning.

Is there a Digital Divide

- Early learning teachers and student teachers understand that children from diverse ethnic backgrounds, children living in inner cities or rural communities, children with disabilities, and children whose first language is not English may be disadvantaged due to accessibility to technology and adult role models.
- Early learning teachers examine how technology may be used to support children and families in communication about the program and children and their play.

The Role of the Early Learning Teacher

- Early learning teachers and student teachers gain skills in facilitating play with technology, take a balanced approach to technology in play, and promote technology in play when it is appropriate to the play.

Facilitating Children's Play with Technology

- Early learning teachers participate in a variety of ways with children using technology. Reactive supervision, guided interaction, and a hybrid approach provide different types of guidance to children. Observations of children's use of technology and their play interests guide early learning teachers in their facilitating practice.
- Choosing software and applications is challenging. Children require open-ended software that supports their interests, skills, and capabilities. There are key questions that can guide teachers in determining the needs and types of software to support children's use of computers.

Professional Learning and Development

- Early learning teachers require training and development in technology. This requires time, training structure, collaborative development, and having a clear philosophy about technology and children's play.

REVIEW QUESTIONS

1. Discuss the debates about using technology with children in early learning programs.
2. Discuss six benefits of using technology with children.
3. Describe how Parten's stages of social play relate to children's social behaviours when using computers.
4. Highlight how technology supports cognitive, physical, social, and emotional development.
5. Describe how technology supports inclusivity.
6. Describe the roles and responsibilities of early learning teachers in integrating technology into early learning centres.

MAKING CONNECTIONS

Theory to Practice

1. Interview an early learning teacher to gain information on how technology is used in the early learning centre. How is it used to enhance the play experiences of children? Is it used by more than one child at a time? How do children use the technology? What is the value of having technology in an early learning centre? What are the challenges?
2. View six websites that offer software or applications for infants, toddlers, preschoolers, and school-aged children. Examine the software using the questions outlined in the chapter. What are your findings? Are you able to effectively evaluate software online? If not, how do early learning teachers ensure that the software they are purchasing is suitable for their children?
3. Visit an early learning centre that uses technology. Examine the software and applications that are available to the children. How, as an early learning student, do you prepare yourself to know about software and applications so that you may support children?
4. You are required to develop an interactive newsletter for families that links children's play with the use of technology. What key messages would you incorporate onto the poster board? Why?

DIGITAL PORTFOLIO ENTRIES

Potential portfolio entries for your digital portfolio could include:

- When I think of technology and children's play, I wonder about. . .
- As an early learning student, what is my role in introducing technology into learning environments with children?
- I wonder if I have sufficient technology skills to be able to effectively.
- I am concerned about children's play and technology because. . .

CURIOUS?

Do a library search for *children's play and technology* to find out more about the latest research on the varying perspectives presented in this chapter.

CHAPTER 14
Taking Play to the Next Level

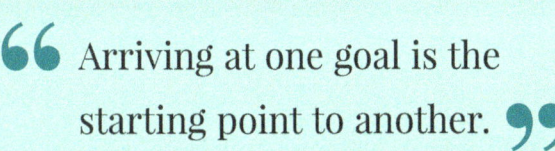

Rawpixel.com/Shutterstock

> " Arriving at one goal is the starting point to another. "
>
> —John Dewey (1859–1952)

LEARNING OUTCOMES

After exploring this chapter you should be able to:

- Outline terminology issues and relate them to the role of early learning teachers.
- Describe what reconceptualizing and postmodern perspectives mean.
- Explain how early learning teachers' practices support the contents of the Truth and Reconciliation report.
- Examine values, beliefs, and images within the early learning and play environment.
- Explain how advocacy for children's rights, determinants of health, family engagement, and action research influence early learning teachers philosophies and practices.
- Describe the relationship of sustainability to early learning and play.

Sharing Stories of Practice from the Authors

Throughout this text, you have had an opportunity to read stories from a diverse set of early learning teachers. We hope that you have been able to hear the voices of these dedicated professionals and are able to relate to their stories. As the authors of the text, we will be using this final chapter to explore contemporary issues of play that may influence and scaffold your learning to the next level as you continue to think critically about, and reflect on, current thinking and theories about children's play and learning.

Taking into consideration all of the chapters you have read in this text, you may now feel inspired to consider your own treatise on play—to contemplate your play mission or your vision for play for children. You may see this as a time to engage in and practise reflection, while you consider your values and beliefs. You may consider doing this in collaboration with others. You may think about how to incorporate your ideas and new vision into your current and future practice as an early learning professional. In each chapter, we have attempted to share the voices of many early learning teachers with you. We have tried to present stories, research, and information as objectively as possible. You may have detected our voice throughout. Yes, we have a vision for play and hope that you have seen ways in which we shared it with you throughout the text and in this final chapter.

Beverlie's Story

The first phase of my career involved working with children in family settings. I learned from Anne and Jane and Brett and Kelly the importance of their freedom to play. They were happiest when they were playing in dress-up clothes or in the garden making mud pies. They expressed a sense of wonderment when they observed butterflies or bees on the flowers. It was the simple environment in which we played, talked, laughed, and explored where we made connections, expanded ideas, and embraced their sense of wonderment.

The next phase of my career led me to explore the importance of school-aged children having a place to play after school. There, in public schools, we organized play experiences that allowed children to "play." I did not support children doing homework; rather, I wanted them to run and jump and hop and skip. I wanted them to have a venue where they could engage in solitary or group play. My mantra was that children learn best through play.

I learned throughout my career that there are trends, there are new thoughts, and there are preferred processes that researchers and educators insist are best for the children. My values and beliefs are strong—children need play, and they benefit from having early learning teachers in their environments that pay attention to them, their play ideas, and their play episodes. Children benefit from being in environments that offer them a sense of wonder, exploration, experience, curiosity, and success both indoors and outdoors. I believe that early learning teachers benefit from continuously examining the new research and determining what it means in their practice. I am an advocate of teachers "stretching themselves" by trying new ideas and experimenting with perspectives and practices that move them beyond their comfort zone. Embracing the feelings of disequilibrium is healthy and is necessary for professional development and practices to evolve. Early learning teachers have a key role in advancing new knowledge that we gain from observing children and supporting them in their play. My vision continues—please open the doors and let the children play!

Diane's Story

When I began to practise as an early learning teacher, I dismissed the theory that I had become acquainted with in my college courses. When creating play and learning experiences for the children, I followed a theme approach. At first, I was challenged and happy to be teaching young children, but gradually I began to question this approach of program planning based on overriding, week-long themes. I knew that there was something more to teaching, learning, and facilitating play opportunities with children. At the time, I was experiencing cognitive dissonance. Festinger (1962) first presented the theory of cognitive dissonance, which is premised on the idea that when there is inconsistency between two cognitions, a psychological state of dissonance will develop. These two cognitions, or understandings, clash until an individual seeks to resolve the dissonance through choice or action (Delaney, 2015). At first, I made the choice to block out new understandings about children's authentic play experiences, but as I kept seeing that children were often not interested in the themes I presented, I choose to take action.

I began to recognize that when children deviated their play from the theme activities, their connections and engagements with peers increased, their language changed, and their overall depth of play was much more intense than when exploring theme-related activities. I could see learning taking place. I began to look for children's authentic interests that emerged during their play. Interestingly, it was during play, when the children themselves were faced with cognitive dissonance, that I could see real meaning in their experiences.

As I reduced my rigid theme-based program planning, I noted that the children began to develop more abstract thought, and my own development coincided with theirs. I started to ask questions and reconsider choices. I was seeking alternatives and deliberating. I can now see the correlation with my own development. As I examined my practice, engaged in self-reflection, participated in a community of practice, and examined new research on early childhood pedagogy, I sought out and continue to seek new perspectives from others. These perspectives sometimes result in cognitive dissonance, but I embrace these cognitive knots as part of the learning process and my own development. It is my hope that early learning teachers will seek new meaning in their practice and continue to be critically reflective to avoid habituation. Embracing disequilibrium leads to new meaning. Finding the deeper meaning in children's play will lead to possibilities that could never be imagined if old habits, such as planning around themes, continue. It is my vision that early learning teachers will seek the new, embrace dissonance, and continually reflect on their values and beliefs to become active advocates for play-based learning for children. Make your voice heard; the children are depending on you.

CHAPTER PREVIEW

Loris Malaguzzi (1998) suggested that children have a right to a new, restored image that elevates their position to one of collaborator, communicator, and co-constructer with the adults in their lives. For early learning teachers, the same parallel exists vis-à-vis their relationship to other educators. Early learning teachers benefit from engaging in creating an image that elevates their position to one of collaborator, communicator, and co-constructer with educators from all levels across the spectrum and with children. For many years, early childhood education has been recognized as a distinct sector from teachers in the school system. With that distinction come varying qualifications from program to program or region to region (Phillips, Austin, & Whitebook, 2016). Access to professional development varies from region to region, and quality is inconsistent. Compensation for the profession is relatively low, resulting in employee turnover (Hall-Kenyon, Bullough, MacKay, & Marshall, 2014). All of these factors are connected to early learning teachers suffering from an image that impedes their feeling of self-worth, which can lead to insecurity and stress. It can also result in a desire to engage in practices that will lead to continuous growth and development to overcome negative images (Phillips et al., 2016).

As outlined by Phillips, Austin, and Whitebook (2016), "Quality early childhood education lies squarely in the interactions that transpire between teachers and children" (p. 139). This reinforces the importance of creating images for both children and early learning teachers that should ascend in tandem. As the rivers are crossed and the paths are retraced, it is time to reconceptualize how we view and position early childhood education, including the roles and responsibilities of early learning teachers (Weyer, 2016).

Photo 14.1 Sliding down the hill.
Used with Permission of Diane Kashin

We are committed to the belief that children learn best through play; therefore, collectively we have a responsibility as early learning students, teachers, colleagues, and interdisciplinary educators to bridge the gap and gain an understanding of the importance of play to children's development and lifelong learning. Advocating for play supports an image of the early learning teacher as having a strong voice with beliefs that are entrenched in research, theory, and practice.

TERMINOLOGY CHALLENGES AND DEBATES

You may have noticed throughout the chapters in this text that we have referred to those working in early childhood education as early learning teachers. There is great debate regarding the terminology in our profession. For example, in 2016, the Lawson Foundation and their partners, the Canadian Outdoor Play Working Group, developed an outdoor play glossary of terms. Their goal was to clarify terms associated with outdoor play and to "build a shared understanding of language used in dialogue on outdoor play across Canada" (Lawson Foundation, 2017, p. 1). In the same way, there are many interchangeable terms within the early childhood sector. For instance, early childhood educators, early childhood teachers, early years teachers, child-care providers, and child-care practitioners are common terms. To add to the confusion, kindergarten teachers working in the school system may also view themselves as early learning teachers. Increasingly, in some provinces, teams of early learning teachers with different designations work together and refer to themselves as early learning educators. In this edition, we have used the term *early learning teacher* because it appears to be an inclusive term that represents current contexts.

We believe that it is important to focus on play, exploration, wonderment, and discovery in the early years. Empirical research and policies guide us in positioning both the indoor and the outdoor environments as essential places for children's play. How the environments are designed, the materials within the environments, and the adult–children interactions within the play spaces influence the depth, breadth, and discoveries that children will experience. We view play as the cornerstone for children's learning. We hope that the use of the terms *early learning teacher* and *early learning programs* demonstrates our desire to be inclusive. It by no means represents the final word on issues of terminology. As you read further, you will be introduced to other terms and concepts to consider.

PROGRAMMING AND CURRICULUM

You may have noticed that in this text we use of the term *programming* more often than *curriculum*. These terms are often used interchangeably, especially now that the majority of provinces across Canada have established curriculum frameworks intended to guide early childhood education programming (Dietze & Kashin, 2016). One of the cautions we ask you to consider is the connotation associated with the term **curriculum**. The term *curriculum* is generally associated with an approach that is used to plan and execute programs in elementary school classrooms (Dietze, 2006). In a more traditional sense, curriculum is the plan of intended learning outcomes and the related activities that will be carried out by the teaching staff in order to help children acquire predefined developmental or subject skills (Gestwicki, 2013). However, contemporary views, such as those held by educators from Reggio Emilia, view curriculum in a broader sense, as process related and co-constructive (Biermeier, 2015).

Since the term *curriculum* has its origin in the educational sector and it primarily targets cognitive learning (Dietze, 2006), we have emphasized the word *program* for its broader focus. The term *program* offers an alternative that we feel is associated with

curriculum Refers to the materials, content, and teaching strategies that learners will use and interact with for the purpose of achieving defined outcomes.

Photo 14.2 Expressing identity with open-ended materials.
Used with Permission of Diane Kashin

learning in a play-based environment. Rather than deliver a prepared curriculum, early learning teachers engage in co-constructing and delivering a program based on children's interests, ideas, previous learning, and strengths. Offering children play options rather than a prescribed curriculum results in the evolution of a dynamic environment that challenges both children and teachers to scaffold and expand on their ideas and learning. A process-related program is by its very nature co-constructed with teachers, children, and families contributing to the ideas, environment, and reflective processes.

Emergent Programming

The preprimary schools in Reggio Emilia, Italy, have influenced this approach to programming known as emergent programming. The term **emergent curriculum** is used to refer to an approach that emerges from the interests of the learner and is co-constructed with the teacher (Jones, 2012). However, the process of emergent curriculum assumes a higher level of effectiveness when it goes beyond interests to focus on children's thinking (Dietze & Kashin, 2016). *Emergent* and *curriculum* might be contradictory terms in some situations. We ask you to consider emergent programming as that which involves leading children to new levels of exploring, wonderment, thinking, tinkering, and scaffolding across the zone of proximal development within a social context. Taking this perspective to the next level, early learning teachers are encouraged to expand the types of play, places, and duration of play opportunities that occur in the outdoors. When considering both the indoor and the outdoor environments and having discussions about how and why emergent programming evolves, a more holistic approach to programing occurs. Integrating this theory into practice, the role of the teacher becomes one that is accountable for facilitating an environment that is rich in play, exploration, and learning. By demonstrating how play supports learning and making it visible and accessible, early learning teachers respect and encourage co-construction in practice. The process has transformative possibilities. We describe emergent programming as a pedagogy of infinite empowering play and learning possibilities for children, teachers, families, and communities.

As outlined in Figure 14.1, a cycle for emergent programming begins with a play experience and embeds a process of observation, documentation, and reflection among children, teachers, and families. Teachers engage in an observation process that includes various types of documentation, listening, and connecting children's current play with previous play. With written observations and digital imagery, the play experiences and learning can be documented and related to children's previous play. New types of play and learning may be identified through discussions and reflections with peers, children, and families. By

> **emergent curriculum** Refers to what emerges from the play of children and their teachers. It is based on children's interests and is co-constructed by the children, the teachers, and the environment (Jones, 2012).

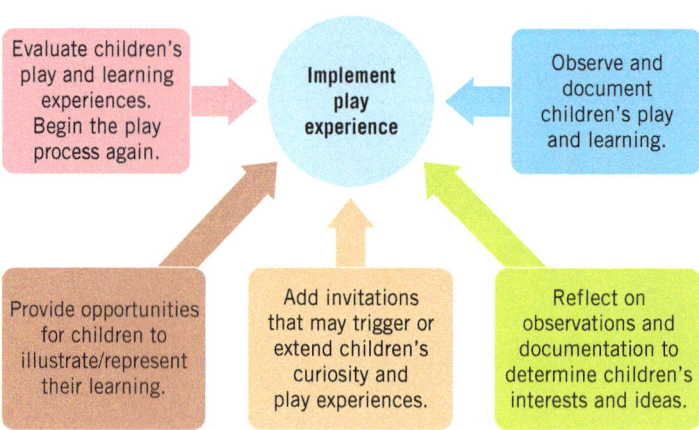

Figure 14.1 Emergent programming cycle.

examining the various types of data collected and documented, teachers use their findings to guide the choice of materials to be placed in the environments and the time and space provided. Children's learning is made visible when they are given opportunities to represent and re-represent their learning either two or three dimensionally and in many languages. When children's play and learning is made visible, documented, and shared for others to review and interpret, collaboration and co-construction occurs. When the analysis of the documentation leads to new play experiences, the documentation becomes pedagogical. With multiple perspectives informing practice, the process can begin again. Recognizing that some children are nonverbal, including infants and toddlers, early learning teachers assume the role of researcher and interpreter of children's play and learning to provide for materials, space, and time to enhance children's experiences.

Communities of Practice

Early learning teachers who engage in emergent programming with children and each other take on the role of teacher as researcher (Biermeier, 2015). This practice, which requires searching for meaning within children's play experiences, is enhanced when it is not an isolated endeavour. Communities of practice align with the view of the teacher as researcher, which connects with the practice of reflection. Reflection is more than "just informal thinking or talking with others about your work; it is an essential part of your teaching practice" (Curtis, Lebo, Cividanes, & Carter, 2013, p. 4). Communities of practice support collaborative efforts among early learning teachers to negotiate knowledge, improve teaching, and seek solutions to issues and problems (Ampartzaki, Kypriotaki, Voreadou, Dardioti, & Stathi, 2013). Wenger, McDermott, and Snyder (2002) put forth the idea of professionals coming together with distinctive identities that are purposely set up to deepen knowledge and improve practice. Establishing communities of practice that support play as a vehicle of learning will take your practice to the next level.

Photo 14.3 Reflecting on documentation in a community of practice.

Used with Permission of Diane Kashin

Table 14.1 Communities of practice that guide individual perspectives.

Know Yourself	What captures your attention when you study the photos?
	What surprises you?
Consider What Engages Your Heart and Mind	What details in the photos show children's competencies and potential?
See the Child's Point of View	What do the children seem drawn to and excited about? What might the children be thinking about or trying to accomplish?
Examine the Environment: Physical, Social, Cognitive, and Emotional	How does the organization of the space and materials influence children's play?
	What is it about the space or materials that kept the children engaged?

Communities of practice can occur in person, or the group can use a variety of technologies. When like-minded individuals who share a common purpose come together, reflection and collaboration will support continuous professional learning. If the purpose is to study play, thinking and sharing your views about how children learn through play is a way to begin. Studying photos and asking thinking lens questions, as featured in Table 14.1, adapted from Curtis and colleagues (2013), will help to frame your discussions.

In communities of practice, early learning teachers may consider perspectives that will take their thinking and practice to higher levels. To do this requires embracing opportunities to learn about new research, concepts, and ideas and to consider how these will inform practice. In the following section, we introduce you to topical issues that are currently influencing or have the potential to influence early learning policies and practices.

Postmodernism

The movement identified as postmodernism has been influencing perspectives and practices since the late twentieth century (Ogunyemi, 2015). Rajshree (2012) and Ogunyemi (2015) identified that from a theory and practice perspective, postmodernism is most visible in early learning programs. Ogunyemi (2015) suggested that early learning programs such as Montessori, Reggio Emilia, High Scope, and Te Whariki are frequently used as "models across the globe [and] are closely linked with postmodernism" (p. 2494). There are many perspectives on the meaning of postmodernism. For example, Mühlpachr (2006) identified that it "stands for more or less developed theories of the current conditions of modernization processes and particularly the outcomes of these processes" (p. 61). Meanwhile, Penn (2005) suggested that "Postmodernists consider that there are many different kinds of voices, many kinds of styles, and take care not to value or privilege one set of values over another" (p. 28). Early learning teachers benefit from considering the tenets of postmodernism and what it means to them and, subsequently, to their practice.

Ogunyemi (2015) cited DeLushmutt and Braund (1996) as suggesting that constructivism is the underlying theory of postmodernism in early childhood education and that knowledge, ideas, and language are invented or constructed when of interest or needed by individuals and groups. Similarly, Ryan and Grieshaber (2005) identified that a postmodern perspective in early learning is based on the assumption that teaching enacts power relations, making multiple voices necessary to prevent privilege (Ryan & Grieshaber, 2005).

Early learning teachers who embrace postmodern perspectives create environments whereby the lived experiences of families and children are acknowledged. Core questions that lead the teacher to explore new ways of thinking and knowing are encouraged.

Exploring new theories and ideas is embraced. In essence, thinking and questioning theories, ideas, and things that differ from current practice lead us to think "outside the box," and this is celebrated, as it advances practice. To advance practice, changes may be required. Change can be uncomfortable, and some teachers may resist change. When one embarks on a journey to be an early learning teacher, it is important to accept cognitive dissonance as part of professional growth.

Add the phrase *postmodernism in early childhood education* to your search engine. What new information about this perspective did you gain? How does this information transfer to your practice? Why?

THE TRUTH AND RECONCILIATION COMMISSION OF CANADA: A CALL TO ACTION

As outlined by the Childcare Resource and Research Unit (2017), "Early childhood education and care (ECEC) is a critical policy issue for Canada's Indigenous people" (p. 1). Over the past several years, educators, researchers, and policy developers have been strong advocates of working toward establishing a sustainable Indigenous early childhood education system reflective of culturally and locally appropriate values and beliefs of Indigenous communities. The importance of ensuring that **Indigenous families** and communities have access to early learning programs that are culturally relevant was reinforced on June 3, 2015, when the Truth and Reconciliation Commission of Canada (TRC, 2015) report was released. Among the 94 recommendations was one specific to early childhood education: "a recommendation in the substantial education calls upon federal, provincial, territorial, and Indigenous governments to develop culturally appropriate programs for Indigenous families" (p. 1). The report identified that by establishing culturally appropriate programs with Indigenous families and communities, such action could contribute to addressing the legacy of the residential schools and, as importantly, support reconciliation (First Nations Information Governance Centre, 2017).

As we have outlined throughout this text, the early years set the foundation for children's language, culture, and connections to their families and communities. These perspectives are reinforced throughout the TRC document. As well, according to the First Nations Information Governance Centre (2017), 86 percent of families and guardians surveyed identified that parents and communities are the main source of children's cultural education. This reinforces the importance of partnerships among early learning teachers, programs, and families.

Indigenous families Also known as First Peoples or Aboriginal peoples, those who identify as being the original inhabitants of a given region.

Add the words *truth and reconciliation in Canadian early childhood education programs* to your search engine to gain further information on how the TRC report can guide early childhood programs.

As we think about early learning teachers taking the next step in their practice, it is beneficial to examine the recommendations brought forth in the TRC document. Ideally, there will be discourse and engagement among various communities of practice members as a way to understand, interpret, and bring meaning both theoretically and practically in terms of what reconciliation means in relation to early learning programs. To begin to understand the scope of reconciliation, early learning teachers are encouraged to work toward gaining insight into understanding the history of the residential schools, what is meant by Indigenous presence and place, the value of families and communities both on and off reserves, and how pedagogy and oral languages support learning and transference of culture.

Taylor (2017) identified that early learning teachers' benefit from understanding what culturally appropriate curricula mean from an Indigenous perspective. She suggested that "we begin by endeavour[ing] to gain an understanding of an Aboriginal view of child-rearing" (p. 49). As identified by Muir and Bohr (2014), the Indigenous view of children may be different from non-Indigenous views of children and child-rearing. Muir and Bohr indicated, "Aboriginal children are openly recognized and respected as persons and are thus encouraged to make their own decisions about how they wish to explore their environment" (p. 70). Children who are given the freedom to make their own decisions are increasingly engaging in democracy and community engagement. Understanding these views help early learning teachers to examine their current practices and philosophies in relation to these types of perspectives. Ideally, early learning teachers will invest the time to learn more about how varying cultures within early learning programs can enhance the quality of programming for children and the professional practice among teachers.

STOP ... THINK ... DISCUSS ... REFLECT

When you think about your role in examining the TRC report, how can you go about fully understanding its context? How do you envision this will influence your practice? Why? How might understanding the content of the TRC report strengthen your practice and next steps?

INTERCULTURAL COMMUNICATION COMPETENCE

Across Canada, early learning teachers will experience early learning programs that bring together families from various cultural and religious backgrounds. As outlined by Jandt (2016), **intercultural communication competence** is an essential skill needed to communicate effectively with people of diverse cultures. This competence is of particular importance to early learning teachers because their role modelling with children and families influences children's sense of belonging within the play environment.

intercultural communication competence Jandt (2016) defined this as "the ability to communicate effectively and appropriately with people of other cultures" (p. 53).

Jandt (2016), building on the work of Chen (1990), identified four skill areas that are necessary to become a competent intercultural communicator. As outlined in Figure 14.2, these skill areas have been adapted to reflect how they relate to the roles and responsibilities of competent early learning teachers.

Early learning teachers who are developing in their practice combine intercultural competence with ethics. This means that early learning teachers develop the values, attitudes, and skills required to address families with differing cultural backgrounds with the same respect that they wish to experience. As well, they encourage families of diverse cultures to share their ideas and experiences with the teachers and children in the early

Personality Strength	Communication Skills
Early learning teachers know themselves and exhibit positive attitudes. Friendly and flexible approaches to all children and families are exhibited.	Early learning teachers have the ability to select the appropriate behaviours in diverse contexts and situations that support children and families in gaining a sense of comfort in the environment.
Cultural Awareness	**Psychological Adjustment**
Early learning teachers acknowledge and respect cultural differences. They exhibit an understanding of how cultures vary and have effective skills with interaction management across cultures.	Early learning teachers develop skills to adapt to and support families in new environments. They understand and support families experiencing culture shock, stress, or discomfort due to new situations.

Figure 14.2 Intercultural communication competence.

learning centre. This supports all children and adults in the environment to develop an undersanding of similarities and differences and to value and celebrate the similarities and differences that contribute to new play experiences and learning in the environment.

Early learning teachers who explore, research, and embrace new perspectives beyond their own contexts can see the bigger picture. Diversity in thinking helps early learning teachers to consider multiple points of view and perspectives regarding the possibilities of expanding options and programming for children and appreciating children's play and learning.

STOP ... THINK ... DISCUSS ... REFLECT

Think about moving to a new country where you do not know the language, do not have access to your usual food, and do not have access to your family. How might that experience change your perspective on intercultural communication competence? Why? What kinds of supports would you find helpful?

VOICE AND EMPOWERMENT

For early learning teachers, whether working directly with children and families or peers, voice and empowerment are necessary strategies for continuous improvement. According to Holcomb-McCoy and Bryan (2010), empowerment is a process of

> increasing personal, interpersonal, or political power so that individuals, families and communities can take action to improve their situations . . . that fosters power (i.e., the capacity to implement) in disenfranchised and powerless groups of people—for use in their own lives, in their communities, and in their society. (p. 262)

Empowerment is related to key professional practices of early learning teachers such as **self-efficacy** and **resilience** (Kim & Bryan, 2017). For example, self-efficacy, from the perspective of early learning teachers, refers to the belief that they have in their capabilities to accomplish a specific task, goal, or change in practice (Ball, 2014). Confidence

self-efficacy As put forth initially by psychologist Albert Bandura (1977), refers to the belief in one's ability to succeed in specific situations or to accomplish tasks.

resilience Refers to one's capacity to bounce back from difficult situations.

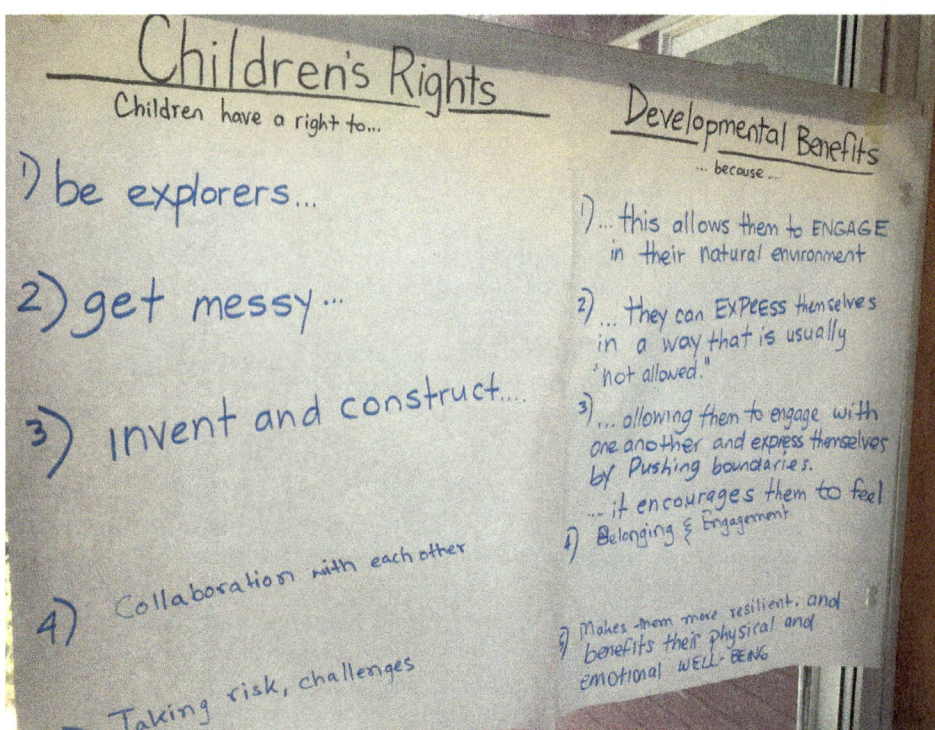

Photo 14.4 Examining outdoor play.

Used with Permission of Diane Kashin

and competence are foundational to empowerment. Resilience refers to an early learning teacher's capacity to overcome adverse circumstances and risk factors. Resilience converges with empowerment, as the two concepts are interrelated to internal power and the ability to take action to make change (Brodsky & Cattaneo, 2013). Empowerment is evident when early learning teachers take action to pursue change. In Photo 14.4, early learning teachers are reflecting on the importance of outdoor play from a developmental and rights perspective in order to make authentic changes to their practice to increase children's opportunities to play outside.

According to Kim and Bryan (2017), empowerment is measured at two levels: the personal and the community levels. They outlined that personal empowerment refers to "individuals' perceived abilities, capacities, skills, and mastery to make their voices heard and influence others to improve their life's situation" (p. 169). Community empowerment is focused on the process of social or political action that individuals or groups engage in to achieve goals that influence communities, institutions, practices, or policies (Kim & Bryan, 2017).

For early learning teachers, empowerment is associated with finding one's voice. We ask that you find your voice as an early learning teacher. *Voice* is "what people mean when they speak of the core of the self" (Gilligan, 1993, p. xvi). Voice can be seen as a metaphor of development extending well beyond the expression of a point of view. "Voice is a powerful psychological instrument and channel, connecting inner and outer worlds" (Gilligan, 1993, p. xvi). To have a voice is also relational; it depends on listening and being heard. Voice also reflects the empowerment possible when the voice is heard. For example, if you believe that children require more time and quality experiences outdoors because of the research you have conducted on its benefits to children, it is essential that you ensure that your voice is heard. Theory is foundational to practice and to supporting early learning teachers in finding their voice.

Early learning teachers have an important role in society to advocate for children and families. Collectively, early learning teachers who are empowered to have their voices heard can address barriers to programs, policies, and perspectives by continuously engaging in developing competence and self-confidence in practice.

CRITICAL PEDAGOGY

Early learning teachers and students who embrace **critical pedagogy** are concerned with the idea of a just society in which people have control of their lives (Aliakbari & Faraji, 2011). Proponents of critical theory and pedagogy "believe that these goals are satisfied only through emancipating oppressed people which empowers them and enables them to transform their life conditions" (Aliakbari & Faraji, 2011, p. 77). Critical pedagogy provides a conceptual tool with which to critique social, political, and equity issues within children's environments (Kilderry, 2004).

> **critical pedagogy** A philosophy of education focused on challenging the dominant discourse or status quo to seek social justice.

When early learning teachers are purposeful in their roles and practice, including providing children with multiple opportunities to experience play, a program evolves through a collaborative process of teaching and learning. Children, families, and early learning teachers collectively have a voice in ideas, explorations, and discoveries. However, early learning teachers who accept a prescribed program or curriculum that contradicts present research and practice are without a voice. Critical pedagogy challenges any form of domination or oppression. Who is heard and who is allowed to speak changes the power structure within the environment and ultimately the play experiences that children engage in. Play experiences influence the children's ability to have a sense of wonder, exploration, discovery, and reflection. When early learning teachers, families, and children share in the play and learning process with voices heard and heeded, a shift in power occurs. Socially shared visions, mediated learning, and joint activities that are systematic lead to change and achieving a shared long-term vision. These are essential in advancing early learning programs. When early learning teachers set priorities, advance partnerships, and embrace new alliances, "reshaping the discourse and vision" (Weyer, 2016, p. 19) occurs. This leads to improved opportunities, practices, and discoveries on many levels.

RECONCEPTUALIZATION IN EARLY LEARNING

Reconceptualization refers to the act or process of rethinking how a new concept may evolve and become current practice. Reconceptualization involves critically examining the assumptions and knowledge base that have traditionally guided the field of early childhood education with the goal of reframing values, beliefs, and practices to reflect new or revised research (Kessler, 2014). Reconceptualizing in early learning supports the belief that dominant discourses should be challenged. In early learning literature, that has included challenges to the conceptualization of quality (Dahlberg, Moss, & Pence, 1999), developmentally appropriate practice (Kessler & Swadener, 1992), and many other areas that are considered "best practice," as reconceptualists challenge the idea that there is one single universal truth (Dahlberg & Moss, 2005). The reconceptualization movement in early learning aligns with postmodernist ideals of seeking multiple perspectives to inform practice.

In the spirit of looking at the world in new and creative ways to broaden your perspectives, we ask you to critically think about what you have read and reflected on throughout this text. For early learning teachers, this means engaging other views and exploring a world of profound diversity. Process, engagement, dialogue, and co-construction take precedence over routines and prescribed practices. Rather than doing what has always been done, early learning teachers can look beyond prescribed and habituated practices to embrace new thinking appropriate for the twenty-first century.

Integrating Twenty-First-Century Skills in Early Learning

As outlined in Chapter 11, understanding the skills and experiences that children need in the twenty-first century, including those that focus on science, technology, engineering, and math (STEM), is an example of early learning teachers, researchers, and policymakers thinking critically about current and future societal and educational issues. Thinking critically is important for everyone: children and adults alike. The research on STEM reminds early learning teachers of the importance of creating play-based environments that model and teach **critical thinking** skills. Are you a critical thinker? What does it take to be a critical thinker? Writer Bell hooks (2010) articulated, "One need not be either an intellectual or an academic to engage in critical thinking." Any time that "we ponder the question of who, what, when, where, how, and why," we are on the path of critical thought (p. 187). This leads us to new places of thinking, learning, and practice.

As identified by Beers (2016), the key to integrating twenty-first-century skills into early learning environments is for children to be surrounded with early learning teachers who are committed to ensuring that there are opportunities for children to make connections among peers and with materials, apply their past learning with new ideas, and participate in exploration and discovery. Organizing the environment, thinking critically about how experiences are authentic, and using information differently advance children's abilities to use information and concepts in new ways. The early learning teacher is the role model and guide.

> **critical thinking** Thinking that is purposeful, reasoned, and goal directed, involving solving problems, formulating inferences, calculating likelihoods, and making decisions.

Values and Beliefs

More than 20 years ago, Balaban (1995) identified that "Critical to truly seeing and understanding the children we teach is the courage to reflect about ourselves. Facing our biases openly, recognizing the limits imposed by our embeddedness in our own culture and experience, acknowledging the values and beliefs we cherish, and accepting the influence of emotions on our actions are extraordinary challenges" (p. 49). How do values and beliefs influence your practice both positively and negatively?

Values and beliefs about play require reflection if there is a lack of alignment. Stating that you believe in play is not enough if your values are not evident in practice. For example, if you spend most of your time during the day not focusing on the children who are independently playing but rather on the children who are having difficulty managing within the environment, reflection is required. If you spend most of your time in the environment attending to other pressing needs, such as housekeeping or program planning, at the expense of facilitating children's play, it is time to stop and think. How do your values coincide with your beliefs?

STOP ... THINK ... DISCUSS ... REFLECT

What do you value about children's play? What do you make visible about your values and beliefs about children's play? Why? What might you wish to advance in your practice?

One of the most important professional development experiences an early learning teacher engages in is examining the values that influence practice. Values influence everything, whether they have been intentionally identified or not. Clarifying and aligning values and beliefs supports how you provide for play and facilitate children in their play experiences (Curtis et al., 2013). Considering images and views of children, their families and teachers also support the place of play in the learning environment. If you believe that children have the right to play, there should be evidence of this in practice.

The Image of the Child

Do you believe that children have rights as well as needs? What is your image of the child? What is your image of the early learning teacher? The central notion for the philosophy of Reggio Emilia resides in the concept of images. By critically thinking about images, early learning teachers can begin to view the children and the roles of teachers from different perspectives. The image of the child is where teaching should begin (Malaguzzi, 1993). When children, teachers, and families are viewed as capable, competent, and rich in potential, the learning environment will support children's play and development (Ontario Ministry of Education, 2014). The image of the child as having a right to play is empowering (Dietze & Kashin, 2016).

Sobel and Larimore (2016) identified that children being viewed as powerless, passive receptacles into which knowledge or skills are poured is no longer aligned with current research. As outlined by Shanker (2016), children flourish in environments where they have the opportunities to develop executive functioning and self-regulation skills that include caring, fairness, and justice skills. Such skills contribute to children engaging in and modelling empathic and reflective skills that contribute to creating an environment that supports the foundations and conditions for learning: belonging, well-being, engagement, and expression (Ontario Ministry of Education, 2014). In the twenty-first century, it is time for early learning teachers to embrace practices that align with current research and perspectives. As outlined in Figure 14.3, early learning teachers of the twenty-first century benefit from adapting professional practices that include the desire and practices to embrace reflections, questions, and change.

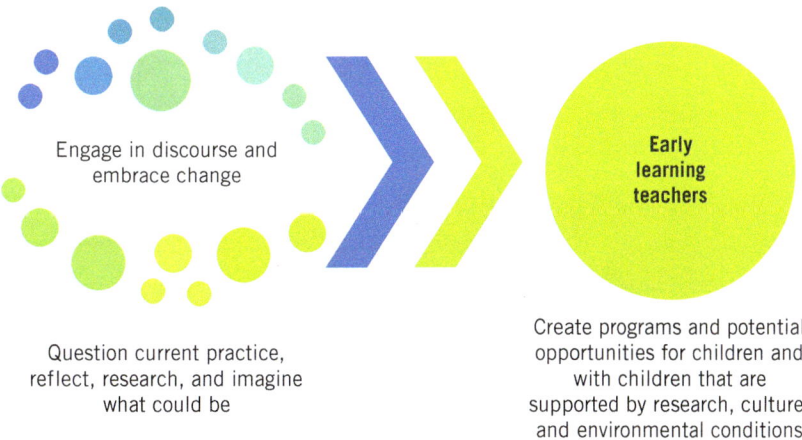

Figure 14.3 Professional practices for early learning teachers in the twenty-first century.

Malaguzzi (1998) stressed the importance of early learning teachers being open to change and the reconstruction of themselves. Kim (2014) identified that the examination and reflection process that can occur when creating or revisiting various types of documentation is an ideal time for early learning teachers to reflect on their practice and imagine how they could expand their practice to further support children. Using reflection practice; questioning one's values, beliefs, and practices; and being open to change are valued and encouraged as core principles within professional practice (Phillips et al., 2016). These professional practices align with an image of the teacher as a researcher who is engaged in action research (Dietze & Kashin, 2016; MacNaughton, Rolfe, & Siraji-Blatchford, 2010). Combining research with practice is essential in exhibiting professional practice. MacNaughton, Rolfe, and Siraji-Blatchford (2010) identified that "research is best conceptualized simply as a tool that helps us answer important questions about early childhood" (p. 3). Malaguzzi (1998) suggested that education without research is "education without interest" (p. 73). Continual internal dialogues and discussions with others provide ongoing discourse, training, new knowledge creation, and theoretical enrichment. Early learning teachers make their research practices visible, such as when preparing documentation of their work with children (Fu, 2002; Kim, 2014). Internal dialogues and discussions with others may lead to rethinking practice, which in turn contributes to shifting practices that are inconsistent with play-based learning.

As the image of the early learning teacher evolves, developing a teacher-researcher perspective is a core step in moving the profession forward. Early learning teachers who develop their teacher-research skills gain in-depth skills of analyzing practice, which are necessary in leading change based on evidence-based practice (Dietze & Kashin, 2016). Kellett (2011) identified that children should be active participants in the research process. Research "with" rather than research "on" children is advocated so that children's voices are being heard, respected, and incorporated into any research agenda (Dietze & Kashin, 2016). In nurturing, respectful environments, children have the skills and abilities

Photo 14.5 Exploring and playing outside.

Used with Permission of Michelle Thornhill

to identify areas of research that they wish to engage in and why such areas are important. Adults benefit from ensuring that children and families are partners in research.

Critically Rethinking Practice

There has been a movement for more than 25 years by scholars in early childhood education and related fields to challenge notions and status quo in practice (Cannella, 2010). Early childhood leaders require early learning teachers to engage in deconstructing taken-for-granted assumptions and practices and reconceptualize their thought processes and practices (Duncan, Eaton, & Te One, 2013). Early learning teachers, children, and families being in environments that stress and make multivocal and multiconceptual narratives visible when imaging what could be and in practice increases distributions of respect and power (Cannella, 2010).

There are many ways in which early learning teachers develop new practices and shift their thinking about what had been previously accepted in their practice. For example, think about those early learning teachers who still practise the ritual of using a calendar with 3-year-olds without fully examining its contribution to supporting children's learning. As identified by Wardle (2007), "According to Piaget, preoperational children cannot possibly do the calendar activity in a meaningful way" (p. 2). How might shifting thinking about these practices change the experiences for and with children? Think about the following example highlighted by Duncan, Eaton, and Te One (2013). They engaged in dialogue that led to a critical change in thinking process. Their early learning team chose to explore the "what-ifs" of changing their gaze of thinking about centre-based, child-centred practice to focusing on what learning in early childhood education would look like if the emphasis was on early childhood education being embedded in the community. They discovered, through this process, their desire to shift their perspectives of "seeing the child as a 'child in the setting', to seeing the child 'within and across' settings" (p. 199). Engaging in these types of explorations takes early learning teachers to new places of discovery and practice. We challenge early learning teachers to think about and reflect on where our practices come from and why we maintain practices without exploring new possibilities. Early learning teachers are encouraged to question practices and bring forth new ways of programming that reflect evidence-based practices.

Whether early learning teachers are open to rethinking some practices depends on their disposition toward change. Sometimes, such changes require early learning teachers to examine the workplace environment, including the program philosophy, team approach to working with children, and values that colleagues have about children and families. When values and philosophies do not align, early learning teachers may need to prepare to leave the security of the environment to join new colleagues who emulate a shared philosophical orientation (Phillips et al., 2016).

PROFESSIONAL DISPOSITIONS

In the process of research in practice, early learning teachers can demonstrate a predisposition to critical thinking. **Professional dispositions** are the tendencies and processes early learning teachers use to think and act in certain ways that are valued by the field (Swim & Merz, 2016). Professional dispositions become a way in which early learning teachers exhibit their professional practice through the strategies used to examine the why, how, and what one does in one's practice (Swim & Merz, 2016). They have been referred to as habits of mind. Critical thinking is one of many dispositions associated with professional practice. Knowledge can be acquired without having the disposition to use

professional dispositions
Includes attitudes, values, and beliefs demonstrated through both verbal and nonverbal behaviours as early learning teachers interact with children, families, colleagues, and communities (National Council for Accreditation of Teacher Education, 2007).

Table 14.2 Two examples of professional dispositions and indicators.

Disposition	Description	Professional Practice Indicators
Collaboration	The ability to work together with others.	■ Cooperates with others. ■ Makes contributions to the group effort. ■ Shares information, resources, and materials with others. ■ Assists or mentors others. ■ Supports group decision making. ■ Makes relevant contributions to discussions.
Reflection	The ability to review, analyze, evaluate, and reflect on your experiences.	■ Accepts and incorporates suggestions. ■ Identifies own biases and prejudices. ■ Demonstrates self-analysis. ■ Uses reflective tools such as documentation in practice. ■ Uses reflective practices to set goals. ■ Recognizes situations that call for creative problem solving and collaboration.

it. Early learning teachers and students may have the skills required to be critical thinkers but not necessarily be in the habit of using this skill to the fullest. In turn, they may have knowledge about the importance of play but not the disposition to create and support a play-based learning environment for children (Phillips et al., 2016).

If you were to create an inventory of the professional dispositions that you think early learning teachers benefit from believing in and practising, what would be on your list? In Table 14.2, two examples are included along with associated behavioural indicators. If an early learning teacher were demonstrating one of these dispositions, the list of indicators outlines the corresponding professional practices that would ideally be seen or displayed.

STOP ... THINK ... DISCUSS ... REFLECT

What other dispositions do you think early learning teachers and students may wish to cultivate in their work with children? Aside from the dispositions identified, what do you believe is important to add? Think about this and then add to the two examples in Table 14.2. Identify the disposition, describe it, and then make a list of indicators that you believe would be essential professional practices to be exhibited. When you have completed this, compare your list with that of a peer or colleague. As a collaborative exercise, create a chart of all of the dispositions identified by the group. Why is it important to examine this at this phase of your learning? How does it affect the work you do with cooperating teachers? Why?

reflective practice As defined by Schön, thoughtfully considering one's own experiences in applying knowledge to practice while being coached by professionals in the discipline (Schön, 1996).

Reflective Practice

To deepen their understanding of their beliefs, values, and philosophy, early learning teachers use **reflective practice** (Lemon & Garvis, 2014). In Table 14.2, one of the dispositions listed refers to reflective practice. In 1987, Donald Schön introduced the concept of reflective practice as a critical process in refining one's artistry or craft in a specific discipline. Schön recommended reflective practice as a way to recognize consonance between individual practices and those of successful practitioners. Reflective practice is aligned with critical thinking and dispositions and is viewed by researchers as a vital professional practice (Miller, Cable, & Devereux, 2005). Through reflective practice, early learning teachers are encouraged to think beyond current practice and begin to notice practice and to ask questions such as "What could this be, why and how could this occur, and what might we do next time?" (Arthur, Beecher, Death, Dockett, & Farmer, 2012).

Research on teaching has shown that effective and quality practice is linked to inquiry, **evidence-based practice**, reflection, and continuous professional growth. Mason (2002) introduced the idea of early learning teachers engaging in a process of "noticing" in relation to their practice. Mason indicated that all aspects of working with children depend on how what is noticed about children, environments, and relationships is used in reflection and action. Throughout the process of noticing, and through the framing of self, "reflection becomes a necessary mechanism for the enhancement of professional learning and therefore engenders much more active and demanding prospects for practice" (Loughran, 2006, p. 52). Reflective practice offers insight into many aspects of children's play, their interests, their strengths, and opportunities for new curiosity triggers.

Strategies and tools for reflective practice may include portfolio development, action research, journal writing, and mentoring relationships (Lemon & Garvis, 2014). The ability of early learning teachers to reflect on their own practice provides them with feedback that nurtures their self-esteem and professional growth (Dietze & Kashin, 2014). The greatest challenge to accepting an inquiry paradigm is transforming the image that early learning teachers have of themselves. If we see ourselves as already knowing, we are rigid rather than dynamic thinkers. Rigid thinkers are unlikely to see themselves as learners whose primary task is to grow, develop, and engage in action research in their practice. Children benefit from teachers who are committed to continuously examining research and engaging in new ways of thinking and knowing. This leads to empowering children's opportunities for curiosity to be triggered and acted upon. Conversely, without new ways of knowing and engaging in current practices, children are destined to have static and rather boring learning experiences, which in turn reduce their opportunities to have rich play experiences to embrace (Biermeier, 2015; Dietze & Kashin, 2017).

If we ponder the question of who, what, when, where, how, and why, as suggested by hooks (2010) in relation to reflective practice, we can practice reflection. In Figure 14.4, you will see a cognitive organizer, which will help you to critically think about reflective practice.

evidence-based practice A process of making decisions based on current high-quality research in the professional literature, professional judgments based on situations and evaluation of the situation, and philosophy and children and family context.

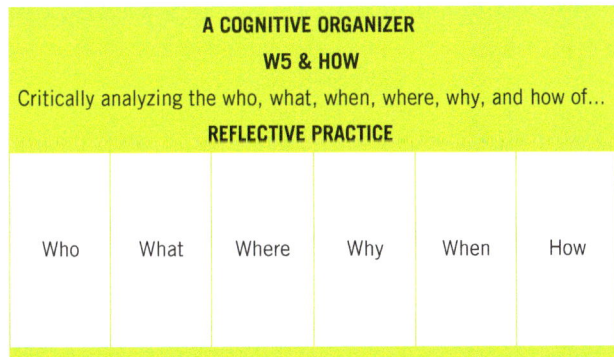

Figure 14.4 A cognitive organizer for reflective practice.

Cognitive organizers can be used to break down many different topics related to early learning. Another useful tool is the schematic concept map. This can be used with children as a way to program and as a tool for reflective practice (Birbili, 2006). Early learning teachers who take the time to engage in reflective practice can begin to see the impact it has on children and make connections about how their approaches influence on the rights of children.

Children's Rights

As identified in Chapter 1, in 1989, the Convention on the Rights of the Child (CRC) became the first legally binding international convention to affirm human rights for all children. World leaders recognized then that children needed a special convention because those under 18 years of age often need more care and protection than adults. The leaders wanted to ensure that the world recognized that children have human rights too. The CRC stressed that the focus on human rights must include civil, cultural, economic, political and social rights. It has achieved near-universal acceptance.

The provisions and principles of the CRC guide the mission of UNICEF (United Nations International Children's Emergency Fund) as an international advocate for the protection of children's rights. The CRC outlines the basic human rights that children everywhere have. They are the right to:

- Survival;
- Develop to the fullest;
- Protection from harmful influences, abuse, and exploitation;
- Participate fully in family, cultural, and social life.

The four core principles are nondiscrimination; devotion to the best interests of the child; the right to life, survival, and development; and respect for the views of the child.

In the Reggio Emilia world view, children have rights rather than simply needs. They have a right to be collaborators and a communicators. Ideally, adults support and encourage children in possessing and exhibiting their strength, competence, and potential. This informs a view of children as protagonists, occupying a primary role in their learning. Children as protagonists have the right to be collaborators within a community of learners (Biermeier, 2015; Cadwell, 2003; Gandini, 2004).

To view children as protagonists of their own experiences of learning is to view them as having rights. Children have the right to express their understanding of the world through many languages. Malaguzzi reinforced the importance of children having the right to environments that are flexible and responsive to the needs and interests of children (Gandini, 2012). Children have the right to be in early learning environments that support them in constructing their knowledge through play and that build upon current and previous interests, knowledge, and experiences (Biermeier, 2015). Children's right to play and learning requires early learning teachers to understand that the construction of children's learning is most meaningful to children when they are given the opportunities to experiment, explore, and absorb the aspects of new information that make sense to them, rather than teachers assuming that they know what children should learn and when they should learn particular concepts (Hamre et al., 2012).

The consideration of rights has propelled a world view for early learning programs. How does the consideration of children's rights influence your view? Is your pedagogical orientation to children's play affected by the concept of children's rights? Rights rather than needs can scaffold thinking about play to the next level of practice.

Becoming an Advocate of Play

Recognizing that play has such positive attributes for and with children, it is distressing that there are conflicting attitudes and practices toward play in early learning environments. In our society, there are many who are increasingly focused on academic skills such as pre-literacy and elementary arithmetic manipulations in early childhood programs (Association of Canadian Deans of Education [ACDE], 2013). If you believe that children's play and play-based learning need to be the driving philosophy for early learning environments, then becoming an advocate of play is an essential step in your professional practice.

Advocacy is usually defined as the act of advocating for a cause. Oliver and Klugman (2004) suggested that if you want to advocate for play-based learning for young children, the first step is to clarify your own philosophy about how children learn best and most naturally. Advocacy begins with your own beliefs, values, and knowledge. Expanding your knowledge involves reviewing current research on the role of play in the lives of young children. Documenting what you know about the link between play and learning is an essential aspect to your practice. Acting collectively will lead to transformation. In Photo 14.6, a group of early learning teachers have come together to reflect on outdoor play and have created a gallery of advocacy statements.

Action Research

Kurt Lewin first identified action research in the early 1900s for the business community. Today, action research is based on the process of thinking, doing, reflecting, and evaluating (Tobin, 2006). When undertaken by early learning teachers, action research involves looking at one's own practice or a situation involving children's development,

Photo 14.6 Advocacy statements.

Used with Permission of Diane Kashin

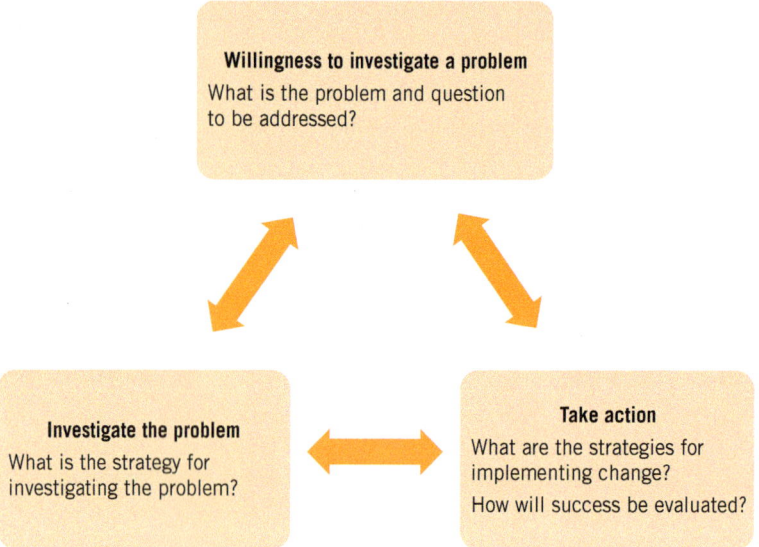

Figure 14.5 Steps in action research.

behaviour, areas of interest, social interactions, learning difficulties, family involvement, or learning environments and then reflecting on it and seeking support and feedback from colleagues. It is an approach to professional development in which early learning teachers systematically reflect on their work and make changes to their practice (Tobin, 2006).

As outlined in Figure 14.5, action research involves three basic steps (Smith, Willms, & Johnson, 1997). The first step is a willingness to investigate a problem that requires investigation. Although we do not support the calendar ritual, we use it to illustrate how action research may evolve within early learning programs. Think of children who have difficulty sitting still for the morning circle focusing on the calendar. The second step involves investigating the problem or situation, including the collection of data related to the problem. Here, an early learning teacher's role might be to record instances of children's inattention to the daily rituals of the calendar. The final step is to take action. In this case, it would involve abandoning this daily rote exercise. The early learning teacher who engaged in action research would return to the first step and begin the cycle again. Action research "is a way for educators to step back, think, and develop a more in-depth understanding of their goals. In essence, it is a process that supports educators in reconstructing or creating new knowledge while strengthening their beliefs and practices" (Dietze et al., 2014, p. 3). When early learning teachers have support to incorporate action research into their practice, the process allows opportunities for changes to practice that ultimately support children in their play (Dietze et al., 2014).

Health Determinants

The World Health Organization (WHO) is an authority for health within the United Nations. The determinants of health are grouped into seven broad categories: socio-economic environment, physical environments, early childhood development, personal health practices, individual capacity and coping skills, biology and genetic endowment, and health services. The fact that early childhood development is considered a

Table 14.3 World Health Organization's 10 facts about early childhood development as determinants of health.

FACT ONE	Brain and biological development depends on the quality of stimulation in the infant's environment, whether it be at the family level or elsewhere. Early child development is a lifelong determinant of health, well-being, and learning skills.
FACT TWO	Addressing early childhood development means creating the conditions for children from prenatal to 8 years to thrive equally in their physical, social, emotional, language, and cognitive development.
FACT THREE	Safe, cohesive, child-centred neighbourhoods, communities, and villages matter for early child development.
FACT FOUR	In order to improve the state of early child development, global communities need to continuously improve the conditions for families to nurture their children by addressing economic security, flexible work, information and support, health, and quality child-care needs.
FACT FIVE	Barriers of access to programs and services that have been demonstrated effective in supporting early childhood development need to be removed.
FACT SIX	Children require stimulating, supportive, and nurturing care when their parents are not available. High-quality child care and early childhood education can improve children's chances for success in later life.
FACT SEVEN	Early child development is a cornerstone of human development and should be central to how we judge the success of societies. Measuring the state of early child development with a comparable approach throughout the world will provide a way for societies to judge their success.
FACT EIGHT	Success in the area of early child development requires a partnership, not only among international, national, and local agencies but also with the world's families.
FACT NINE	Many in the international development community agree that child survival and child development are not in conflict, but program financing in the international development community has not yet reflected this understanding.
FACT TEN	Among all the social determinants of health, early childhood development is the easiest for societies' economic leaders to understand. Improvement means not only better health but also a more productive labour force, reduced criminal justice costs, and reductions in other strains on the social safety net. National and international fiscal and monetary institutions need to recognize that spending on early child development is an investment and incorporate it into policy accordingly.

determinant of health is significant. WHO has identified 10 facts about early child development as a social determinant of health, as outlined in Table 14.3. These facts reinforce why early learning teachers consistently draw upon research to inform their practice and why they advocate on behalf of children.

Healthy Living and Sustainability

The growing trend toward adopting environmental sustainability principles in early learning programs is part of a broader sustainability movement. To be sustainable in an early learning setting is a practice that is visible on a daily basis with children and colleagues (MacDonald, 2015). MacDonald (2015) identified the importance of children, their families, and early learning teachers creating societies that value sustainability in both sustainable thinking and practices.

Photos 14.7 and 14.8
Sustainable materials for children.

Used with Permission of Diane Kashin

Think of some commonplace materials that children may use in their play, or consider some of the consumable materials that are purchased for children's art experiences. Is there a way to reduce consumables and increase natural and synesthetic materials? For example, think about the content in Chapter 6 on loose parts. How might loose parts, rather than commercially bought materials, become prominent in the early learning program? How might children and early learning teachers connect with recycling centres to access materials? How might families support and embrace environmental sustainability practices within the early learning program? Decisions made about sustainable practices are reinforced by decisions made about play materials and play spaces. For example, a dramatic play area could have purchased pots, utensils, and synthetic pretend food. On the other hand, it could collect cooking equipment from a second-hand shop and natural materials such as leaves or seedpods for pretend food. Involving children and families as active participants and leaders in sustainable practices has transformative possibilities that can lead to true engagement in role modelling environmental stewardship.

CURIOUS?

Use a search engine of your choice to look up *environmental stewardship in early learning programs* to gain more information on how early learning teachers may support children in being stewards of the environment.

Children's play, including sustainability practices, correlates with children's creative thinking and problem solving and with children using materials in unique and innovative ways.

FAMILY RIGHTS AND FAMILY ENGAGEMENT

Early learning teachers ensure that children and families are the core of the program. Families, when encouraged, can contribute great richness in experiences, resources, and perspectives to the early learning program. Including the input of others is essential in a reflective practice, and families have a right to be included. There are many ways to encourage families to have a strong connection to the early learning program. The use of pedagogical documentation is one way to encourage and promote having the voices of families, children, and teachers heard (Kim, 2014). Family involvement differs from family engagement.

As identified by the U.S. Department of Health and Human Services (2016) and the U.S. Department of Education (2016), family engagement refers to the systematic process that early learning teachers and families use in contributing to planning, implementing, and evaluating programming and promoting children's experiences, learning, and wellness. The depth of the partnership may vary for each family, depending on culture, preference, availability, and sense of empowerment. Early learning teachers develop dispositions that value the family's strengths, culture, and aspirations for their children.

Simply put, parent involvement is often more of a "doing to," whereas engagement is a "doing with" (Ferlazzo, 2012). You might recall a time when members of your family attended an event at your school. Most likely it was the school that set the agenda for the evening. This is considered family involvement, where the focus is placed "on what the parents can do to help the school realize its intentioned outcomes for children, or on what the parents' hopes, dreams or intentions for their children may be or on what the school can do to help parents realize their personal or family agendas" (Pushor, 2007, p. 3). With engagement, early learning teachers enter into a community of practice where, collectively, families and early learning teachers create a shared vision to support children and their world.

FINAL THOUGHTS

In this final chapter, we hope that you have envisioned the possibilities for this shared world, particularly as they connect to play. We end the chapter with information about an organization devoted to the transformative power of play. Right to Play is a leading international humanitarian and development organization devoted to using the power of play to build essential skills in children around the world. This organization is about taking action as a collective. Right to Play creates a safe place for children to learn and fosters the hope that is essential for children to envision and realize a better future. Figure 14.6 illustrates the

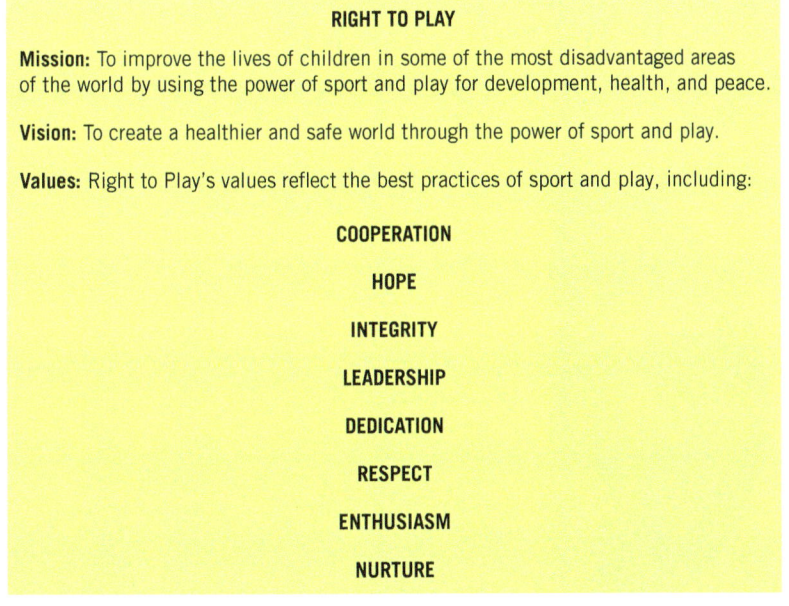

Figure 14.6 Right to Play.

Photo 14.9 All children have a right to play.
Used with Permission of Bora Kim

organization's mission, vision, and values. Consider these in relation to your own developing vision for play. Can you imagine the world being a better place if all children had the right to play?

Froebel (1887) so long ago clearly identified that children learn and develop through play. He advocated for early learning programming to be play focused and for children to have diversity in their play experiences. Children have the right to play. The play environments that we expose children to during their early years become a blueprint for their health, wellness, development, and lifetime dispositions and achievements. Let the children play.

TERMS THAT INFLUENCE EARLY LEARNING PLAY ENVIRONMENTS

We conclude this chapter with three additional terms that support the theory of children's play. These terms are used when advocating for children's play.

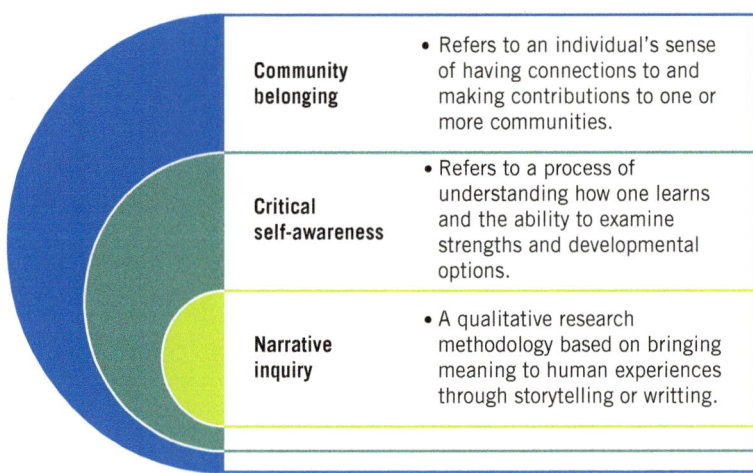

Community belonging	• Refers to an individual's sense of having connections to and making contributions to one or more communities.
Critical self-awareness	• Refers to a process of understanding how one learns and the ability to examine strengths and developmental options.
Narrative inquiry	• A qualitative research methodology based on bringing meaning to human experiences through storytelling or writting.

SUMMARY

Chapter Preview

- Early learning teachers and children benefit from reframing their images of being competent and capable individuals.

Terminology Challenges and Debates

- Many interchangeable terms are used in the early learning field, including the terminology used to identify adults who work with children. Terminology challenges have historical roots and can reflect different perspectives of children and early learning teachers.

Programming and Curriculum

- These two terms can be used interchangeably, even though they have different meanings. *Curriculum* is the approach to education that is employed in public school classrooms. We use the word *program* for its broader focus. Curriculum has been associated with the traditional prescribed methodologies and intended learning outcomes to be achieved. Programs are co-constructed among families, teachers, and children.

Emergent Programming

- Emergent curriculum refers to an approach that emerges from the interests of children. When it goes beyond interests to focus on children's thinking, it assumes a transformational position.
- Emergent programming involves a process of observation, documentation, and reflection among children, teachers, and families.

Communities of Practice

- Communities of practice support collaborative efforts among early learning teachers to negotiate knowledge, improve teaching, and seek solutions to issues and problems. Communities of practice deepen knowledge and improve practice.

Postmodernism

- A postmodern perspective in early learning is based on the assumption that teaching enacts power relations, making multiple voices necessary to prevent privilege. It evolved from the modern romantic view.

The Truth and Reconciliation Commission of Canada

- The importance of ensuring that Indigenous families and communities have access to early childhood programs that are culturally relevant was reinforced on June 3, 2015, when the Truth and Reconciliation Commission of Canada (TRC) report was released.

- Early learning teachers benefit from understanding the content of the TRC report and its relationship to understanding culture and inclusive practice.

Intercultural Communication Competence

- Intercultural communication competence is an essential skill used to communicate effectively with families from various cultural and religious backgrounds.
- There is a relationship between intercultural competence and ethics.

Voice and Empowerment

- Voice is what people mean when they speak of the core of the self. Voice can be seen as a metaphor of development.
- When teachers, families, and children share in the learning process with voices heard and heeded, a shift in power occurs.

Critical Pedagogy

- Critical pedagogy refers to the idea of a just society in which people have control of their lives.
- Critical pedagogy challenges any form of domination or oppression.

Reconceptualization in Early Learning

- Reconceptualization involves critically examining the assumptions and knowledge base that have traditionally guided early learning with the goal of reframing it. It is one facet of postmodern thought. A key element of postmodernism is openness to the presence of many voices and views.

Integrating Twenty-First-Century Skills in Early Learning

- Early learning teachers understand the skills and experiences that children need in the twenty-first century, including those that focus on science, technology, engineering, and math (STEM).

Values and Beliefs

- Early learning teachers are encouraged to face biases openly and acknowledge how values and beliefs can positively or negatively influence their practice and children's experiences within the early learning environment.

The Image of the Child

- The central notion for the philosophy of Reggio Emilia resides in the concept of images. By critically thinking about images, early learning teachers begin to view children and the role of teachers from different perspectives.
- Both children and early learning teachers are strong, committed, intellectual builders of theories.

Critically Rethinking Practice

- There are many ways in which new practices develop and shift thinking about current practices.
- Early learning teachers are encouraged to question practices and bring forth new ways of programming that reflect evidence-based practices.

Professional Dispositions

- Professional dispositions include attitudes, values, and beliefs demonstrated, both verbally and nonverbally, when interacting with children, families, colleagues, and communities.

Reflective Practice

- Reflective practice involves thoughtfully considering one's own experiences in applying knowledge to practice. Research on effective teaching has shown that effective practice is linked to inquiry, reflection, and continuous professional growth.
- Tools for reflective practice can include portfolio development, pedagogical documentation, action research, journal writing, and mentoring relationships.

Children's Rights

- In 1989, the Convention on the Rights of the Child affirmed the full range of human rights for all children, including civil, cultural, economic, political, and social rights. It has achieved near-universal acceptance.
- The four core principles are nondiscrimination; devotion to the best interests of the child; the right to life, survival, and development; and respect for the views of the child.

Becoming an Advocate of Play

- Early learning teachers who believe that children's play and play-based learning is a core philosophy for early learning are encouraged to become advocates of play.
- Advocacy is usually defined as the act of advocating for a cause. The first step to becoming an advocate of play is for early learning teachers to clarify their philosophy about how children learn best and most naturally.

Action Research

- Action research is one of the best strategies to encourage empowerment. Action research is an approach in which early learning teachers systematically reflect on their work and make changes in their practice.
- The three basic steps to action research are (1) a willingness to investigate a problem that needs to be investigated, (2) an investigation of the problem and the collection of data related to the problem, and (3) taking action.
- Action research has been referred to as the opportunity to change.

Health Determinants

- The determinants of health can be grouped into seven broad categories: socioeconomic environment, physical environments, early childhood development, personal health practices, individual capacity and coping skills, biology and genetic endowment, and health services.
- The World Health Organization (WHO) has identified 10 facts about early child development as a social determinant of health that early learning teachers support in their practice.

Healthy Living and Sustainability

- Sustainability is not a "lifestyle choice" but a way of life that becomes part of daily practice in early learning environments.
- Decisions made about play materials and play spaces are two examples of how to reflect on sustainability issues.

Family Rights and Family Engagement

- Family engagement is distinct from family involvement. With engagement, early learning teachers enter into a community to create with families a shared world.
- Play has transformational possibilities for this shared world. All children have the right to play.

REVIEW QUESTIONS

1. How does terminology influence the early learning profession?
2. Describe the cycle of emergent programming.
3. Explain what is meant by a postmodern perspective, and relate this paradigm to the reconceptualization movement in early learning.
4. Demonstrate critical thinking by applying the concept of image to a cognitive organizer—who, what, where, why, when, and how.
5. Describe the role of early learning teachers in promoting sustainability, health determinants, and family engagement.

MAKING CONNECTIONS

Theory to Practice

1. Write your own treatise on play, which can become your play mission for the work you do with children.
2. Identify five short-term and five long-term professional goals that you can identify for your further growth and development.
3. Identify and implement an action research project.
4. Develop a policy for sustainability that could be applied to an early learning setting.

DIGITAL PORTFOLIO ENTRIES

Potential portfolio entries for your digital portfolio could include the following:

- When I think of my role as an advocate for children's play, I wonder about. . .
- As an early learning teacher, I view my role in action research as. . .
- Finding my voice will require me to. . .
- I wonder how terminology influences beliefs, values, and ideas because. . .

CURIOUS?

Do a library search on being a child's advocate for play. What are the varying roles that early learning teachers must be prepared to practise? Why?

References

Acar, H. (2013). Landscape design for children and their environments in urban context. In M. Özyavuz (Ed.), *Advances in landscape architecture* (pp. 291–324). Rijeka, Croatia: InTech.

Acar, H. (2014). Learning environments for children in outdoor spaces. *Social and Behavioral Sciences, 141*(25), 846–853.

Active Healthy Kids Canada. (2007). *Older but not wiser: Canada's future at risk. Canada's report card on physical activity for children & youth—2007*. Toronto, ON: Author. Retrieved from http://dvqdas9jty7g6.cloudfront.net/archivedreportcards/full-english-report-card-2007.pdf

Adamson, L. B., Bakeman, R., Deckner, D. F., & Nelson, P. B. (2012). Rating parent–child interactions: Joint engagement, communication dynamics, and shared topics in autism, down syndrome, and typical development. *Journal of Autism and Developmental Disorders, 42*(12), 2622–2635.

Adamson, P. (2013). *Child well-being in rich countries*. Florence, Italy: Innocenti Research Centre. Retrieved from https://www.unicef-irc.org/publications/683

Ahlskog-Björkman, E., & Björklund, C. (2016). Communicative tools and modes in thematic preschool work. *Early Child Development and Care, 186*(8), 1243-1258.

Ahn, J., & Filipenko, M. (2007). Narrative, imaginary play, art, and self: Intersecting worlds. *Early Childhood Education Journal, 34*(4), 279–289.

Albin, C. M. (2016). The benefit of movement: Dance/movement therapy and Down syndrome. *Journal of Dance Education, 16*(2), 58–61.

Alcock, S. (2000). *Documentation: Pedagogical or pathological?* Kelburn, New Zealand: Institute for Early Childhood Studies, Victoria University of Wellington.

Al-Dhamit, Y., & Kreishan, L. (2013). Gifted students' intrinsic and extrinsic motivations and parental influence on their motivation: From the self-determination theory perspective. *Journal of Research in Special Education Needs, 15*(1), 1–11.

Alfonso, S. (2017). Implementing the project approach in an inclusive classroom: A teacher's first attempt with project-based learning. *Young Children, 72*(1).

Aliakbari, M., & Faraji, E. (2011). Basic principles of critical pedagogy. *International Proceedings of Economics Development and Research, 17*, 78–85.

American Psychological Association. (2017). *Resilience guide for parents & teachers*. Retrieved from http://www.apa.org/helpcenter/resilience.aspx

Ampartzaki, M., Kypriotaki, M., Voreadou, C., Dardioti, A., & Stathi, I. (2013). Communities of practice and participatory action research: The formation of a synergy for the development of museum programmes for early childhood. *Educational Action Research, 21*(1), 4–27.

Anderson, K., & Ball, J. (2011). Foundations: First Nations and Métis families. In D. Long & O. Dickason (Eds.), *Visions of the heart: Canadian Aboriginal issues* (pp. 55–89). Toronto, ON: Oxford University Press.

Änggård, E. (2011). Children's gendered and non-gendered play in natural spaces. *Children Youth and Environments, 21*(2), 5–33.

Arthur, L., Beecher, B., Death, E., Dockett, S., & Farmer, S. (2012). *Programming & planning in early childhood settings*. South Melbourne, Australia: Cengage Learning Australia.

Asaridou, S. S., Demir-Lira, Ö. E., Goldin-Meadow, S., & Small, S. L. (2016). The pace of vocabulary growth during preschool predicts cortical structure at school age. *Neuropsychologia, 98*, 13–23.

Association of Canadian Deans of Education (ACDE). (2013). *ACDE's accord on early learning and early childhood education*. Retrieved from https://www.trentu.ca/education/sites/trentu.ca.education/files/ACDE%20Accord%20on%20Early%20Learning.pdf

Association of Canadian Deans of Education (ACDE). (2016). *Early learning and early childhood education: An accord by the Association of Canadian Deans of Education*. Retrieved from http://www.csse-scee.ca/docs/acde/ACDE_Accord_on_Early_Learning.pdf

Atherton, F., & Nutbrown, C. (2016). Schematic pedagogy: Supporting one child's learning at home and in a group. *International Journal of Early Years Education, 24*(1), 63–79.

Athey, C. (2007). *Extending thought in young children: A parent–teacher partnership*. London, UK: Sage Publications. (Original work published 1991.)

Aubrey, C., & Dahl, S. (2014). The confidence and competence in information and communication technologies of practitioners, parents and young children in the Early Years Foundation Stage. *Early years, 34*(1), 94-108.

Aubrey, C., Ghent, K., & Kanira, E. (2012). Enhancing thinking skills in early childhood. *International Journal of Early Years Education, 20*(4), 332–348.

Australian Early Development Census. (2014). *Brain development in children*. Retrieved from https://www.aedc.gov.au/resources/detail/brain-development-in-children

Azhari, N. F. N., Qamaruzaman, N., Bajunid, A. F. I., & Hassan, A. (2015). The quality of physical environment in workplace childcare centers. *Procedia-Social and Behavioral Sciences, 202*, 15–23.

Bai, S., Repetti, R., & Sperling, J. (2016). Children's expressions of positive emotion are sustained by smiling, touching, and playing with parents and siblings: A naturalistic observational study of family life. *Developmental Psychology, 52*(1), 88–101.

Bailey-White, S., & Stewart, R. A. (2016). Improving access to books for young school-age children one library at a time. *PNLA Quarterly, 80*(3).

Balaban, N. (1995). Seeing the child, knowing the person. In W. Ayers (Ed.), *To become a teacher: Making a difference in children's lives*. New York, NY: Teachers College Press.

Ball, J. (2014). *Hearing all children's voices: The potential of mother-tongue based multilingual education to promote educational equity.* Global Summit on Childhood, Association for Childhood Education International, Vancouver, Canada, April 14–16.

Banaji, S., Burn, A., & Buckingham, D. (2010). *The rhetorics of creativity: A literature review.* Newcastle, UK: Creativity, Culture and Education.

Bandura, A. (1977). Self-efficacy: Toward a unifying theory of behavioral change. *Psychological Review, 84*(2), 191.

Banning, W., & Sullivan, G. (2011). *Lens on outdoor learning.* St. Paul, MN: Redleaf Press.

Barnes, H. (2008). The value of superhero play. *Putting Children First, 27,* 18–21.

Barnes, R. (2015). *Teaching art to young children.* New York, NY: Routledge.

Barnett, L., & Owens, M. (2015). Does play have to be playful? *The Handbook of the Study of Play, 2,* 453.

Barrett, M. S. (2006). Inventing songs, inventing worlds: The "genesis" of creative thought and activity in young children's lives. *International Journal of Early Years Education, 14*(3), 201–220.

Barton, E. E. (2015). Teaching generalized pretend play and related behaviours to young children with disabilities. *Exceptional Children, 81,* 489–506.

Bateman, A. (2013). Responding to children's answers: Questions embedded in the social context of early childhood education. *Early Years, 33*(3), 275–288.

Bates, E. (2014). *The emergence of symbols: Cognition and communication in infancy.* Cambridge, MA: Academic Press.

Battiste, M., & Henderson, J. Y. (2009). *Protecting indigenous knowledge and heritage: A global challenge.* Saskatoon, SK: Purich Publishing.

Baughman, J. L. (1992). *The republic of mass culture: Journalism, filmmaking, and broadcasting in America since 1941.* Baltimore, MD: Johns Hopkins University Press.

Beers, S. Z. (2016). *Teaching 21st century skills: An ASCD action tool.* Alexandria, VA: ASCD Publishing.

Beets, M. W., Weaver, R. G., Moore, J. B., Turner-McGrievy, G., Pate, R. R., Webster, C., & Beighle, A. (2014). From policy to practice: Strategies to meet physical activity standards in YMCA afterschool programs. *American Journal of Preventive Medicine, 46*(3), 281–288.

Belknap, E., & Hazler, R. (2014). Empty playgrounds and anxious children. *Journal of Creativity in Mental Health, 9*(2), 210–231.

Beloglovsky, M., & Daly, L. (2015). *Early learning theories made visible.* St. Paul, MN: Redleaf Press.

Bentley, D. F. (2013). *Everyday artists: Inquiry and creativity in the early childhood classroom.* New York, NY: Teachers College Press.

Berg, S. (2015). Children's activity levels in different playground environments: An observational study in four Canadian preschools. *Early Childhood Education Journal, 43*(4), 281–287.

Bergen, D. (2002). The role of pretend play in children's cognitive development. *Early Childhood Research & Practice, 4*(1), n1.

Bergen, D. (2009). Play as the learning medium for future scientists, mathematicians, and engineers. *American Journal of Play, 1*(4), 413–428.

Bergman-Nutley, S., Darki, F., & Klingberg, T. (2014). Music practice is associated with development of working memory during childhood and adolescence. *Frontiers in Human Neuroscience, 7,* 926.

Berk, L. E. (2013). *Child development.* Toronto, ON: Pearson Education.

Berk, L. E., & Meyers, A. B. (2013). The role of make-believe play in the development of executive function: Status of research and future directions. *American Journal of Play, 6*(1), 98.

Berris, R., & Miller, E. (2011). How design of the physical environment impacts early learning: Educators and parents perspectives. *Australasian Journal of Early Childhood, 36*(4).

Bers, M. U., Flannery, L., Kazakoff, E. R., & Sullivan, A. (2014). Computational thinking and tinkering: Exploration of an early childhood robotics curriculum. *Computers & Education, 72,* 145–157.

Beschorner, B., & Hutchison, A. (2013). iPads as a literacy teaching tool in early childhood. *Online Submission, 1*(1), 16–24.

Bhroin, M. N. (2007). A slice of life: The interrelationships among art, play and the "real" life of the young child. *International Journal of Education and the Arts, 8*(16), 1–24.

Biermeier, M. A. (2015). Inspired by Reggio Emilia: Emergent curriculum in relationship-driven learning environments. *YC Young Children, 70*(5), 72.

Bilton, H. (2002). *Outdoor play in the early years management and innovation* (2nd ed.). London, UK: David Fulton Publishers.

Bilton, H. (2014). *Playing outside: Activities, ideas and inspiration for the early years.* London, UK: Routledge.

Birbili, M. (2006). Mapping knowledge: Concept maps in early childhood education. *Early Childhood Research and Practice, 8*(2).

Bjorklund, D. F., & Causey, K. B. (2017). *Children's thinking: Cognitive development and individual differences.* Thousand Oaks, CA: Sage Publications.

Blackwell, C. K., Lauricella, A. R., & Wartella, E. (2014). Factors influencing digital technology use in early childhood education. *Computers & Education, 77,* 82–90.

Blair, C. (2009). Self-regulation and school readiness. *The International Child and Youth Care Network.* Retrieved from http://www.cyc-net.org/cyc-online/cyconline-oct2009-blair.html

Bloom, B. S. (1956). *Taxonomy of educational objectives.* New York, NY: Longmans, Green.

Bodrova, E. (2008). Make-believe play versus academic skills: A Vygotskian approach to today's dilemma of early childhood education. *European Early Childhood Education Research Journal, 16*(3), 357–369.

Bodrova, E., Germeroth, C., & Leong, D. J. (2013). Play and self-regulation: Lessons from Vygotsky. *American Journal of Play, 6*(1), 111.

Bodrova, E. & Leong, D. (1996). *Tools of the mind: The Vygotskian approach to early childhood education.* Upper Saddle River, NJ: Merrill-Prentice Hall.

Bodrova, E., & Leong, D. J. (2007). *Tools of the mind.* Columbus, OH: Pearson.

Bodrova, E., & Leong, D. J. (2009). Tools of the mind: A Vygotskian-based early childhood curriculum. *Early Childhood Services: An Interdisciplinary Journal of Effectiveness, 3*(3), 245–262.

Bodrova, E., & Leong, D. J. (2012). Assessing and scaffolding: Make-believe play. *YC Young Children, 67*(1), 28.

Bodrova, E., & Leong, D. J. (2015). Vygotskian and post-Vygotskian views on children's play. *American Journal of Play, 7*(3), 371.

Boss, P. (2001). *Family stress management: A contextual approach* (2nd ed.). Thousand Oaks, CA: Sage Publications.

Bourbour, M., Vigmo, S., & Samuelsson, I. P. (2015). Integration of interactive whiteboard in Swedish preschool practices. *Early Child Development and Care, 185*(1), 100–120.

Brady, E. (2009). Environmental aesthetics. *Encyclopedia of Environmental Ethics and Philosophy, 1,* 313–321.

Bredekamp, S., & Copple, C. (1997). *Developmentally appropriate practice in early childhood education* (rev. ed.). Washington, DC: National Association for the Education of Young Children.

Brenneman, K., Stevenson-Boyd, J., & Frede, E. C. (2009). Math and science in preschool: Policies and practice. *Preschool Policy Brief, 19.*

Brodsky, A. E., & Cattaneo, L. B. (2013). A transconceptual model of empowerment and resilience: Divergence, convergence and interactions in kindred community concepts. *American Journal of Community Psychology, 52*(3–4), 333–346.

Bronfenbrenner, U. (1979). Contexts of child rearing: Problems and prospects. *American Psychologist, 34*(10), 844.

Brosterman, N. (1997). *Inventing kindergarten.* New York, NY: Henry N. Abrams.

Broström, S. (2015). Science in early childhood education. *Journal of Education and Human Development, 4*(2), 1.

Brown, E. (1975). Developmental characteristics of clay figures made by children from age three through the age of eleven. *Studies in Art Education, 16*(3), 45–53.

Brown, E. (1984). Developmental characteristics of clay figures made by children: 1970–1981. *Studies in Art Education, 26*(1), 56–60

Brown, E. D., & Sax, K. L. (2013). Arts enrichment and preschool emotions for low-income children at risk. *Early Childhood Research Quarterly, 28*(2), 337–346.

Bruce, T. (2012). *Learning through play: For babies, toddlers, and young children* (2nd ed.). London, UK: Hodder Education.

Bruner, J. (1957). Discussion. In J. S. Bruner, E. Brunswik, & L. Festinger (Eds.), *Contemporary approaches to cognition* (pp. 151–156). Cambridge, MA: Harvard University Press.

Bruner, J. (1966). *Toward a theory of instruction.* Cambridge, MA: Harvard University Press.

Bruner, J. (1968). *Toward a theory of instruction.* New York, NY: W. W. Norton.

Bruner J. (1972). The nature and uses of immaturity. *American Psychologist, 27,* 687–706.

Bruner, J. S. (1961). The act of discovery. *Harvard Educational Review, 31,* 21–32.

Bruner, J. S. (1976). Early rule structure: The case of peekaboo. In R. Harre (Ed.), *Life sentences.* London, UK: Wiley.

Bruner, J. S., Sylva, K., & Genova, P. (1976). The role of play in the problem solving of children 3–5 years old. In J. S. Bruner, A. Jolly, & K. Sylva (Eds.), *Play: Its role in development and evolution.* New York, NY: Basic Books.

Buckingham, D. (2013). *Media education: Literacy, learning and contemporary culture.* Hoboken, NJ: John Wiley & Sons.

Buis, T. (2014). *Perspectives of preschool educators on early childhood education's impact and role on school readiness and the social-emotional development of children* (Doctoral dissertation). California State University, Sacramento, CA.

Cadwell, L. B. (1997). *Bringing Reggio Emilia home: An innovative approach to early childhood education.* New York, NY: Teachers College Press.

Cadwell, L. B. (2003). *Bringing learning to life: The Reggio approach to early childhood education.* New York, NY: Teachers College Press.

Callaghan, K. (2013). The environment is a teacher. In Ontario Ministry of Education, *Think, feel, act: Lessons from research about young children* (pp. 11–15). Toronto, ON: Ontario Ministry of Education.

Campbell, S., Torr, J., & Cologan, K. (2014). Pre-packaging preschool literacy: What drives early childhood teachers to use commercially produced phonics programs in prior to school settings. *Contemporary Issues in Early Childhood, 15*(1), 40–53.

Canadian Association for Young Children. (2016). *Position statement on play.* Retrieved from http://www.cayc.ca/sites/default/files/attachments/CAYC%20Position%20Paper%20on%20Play.pdf

Canadian Child Care Federation (CCCF) & Canadian Language and Literacy Research Network. (2010). *Foundations for numeracy: An evidence-based toolkit for early learning practitioners.* Retrieved from http://eyeonkids.ca/docs/files/foundations_for_numeracy.pdf

Canadian Diabetics Association. (2016). https://www.diabetes.ca/about-diabetes

Canadian Heritage. (2007). https://www.tbs-sct.gc.ca/rpp/2006-2007/pch/pch01-eng.asp

Canadian Institute of Child Health. (2008). http://www.cich.ca/index_eng.html

Canadian Standards Association. (2014). CAN/CSA-Z614-07. Retrieved from http://shop.csa.ca/en/canada/injury-prevention/cancsa-z614-14/invt/27019532014

Cannella, G. (2010). Reconceptualizing movements: Foundations for the critical rethinking of childhood policy. *International Critical Childhood Policy Studies, 3*(1), 1–6.

Canning, N. (2010). The influence of the outdoor environment: Den-making in three different contexts. *European Early Childhood Education Research Journal, 18*(4), 555–566.

Carlson, A. (2002). *Aesthetics and the environment: The appreciation of nature, art and architecture.* New York, NY: Psychology Press.

Carroll, C. (2013). *The effects of parental literacy involvement and child reading interest on the development of emergent literacy skills* (Doctoral dissertation). The University of Wisconsin–Milwaukee, Milwaukee, WI.

Carsley, S., Liang, L. Y., Chen, Y., Parkin, P., Maguire, J., & Birken, C. S. (2017). The impact of daycare attendance on outdoor free play in young children. *Journal of Public Health (Oxford), 39*(1), 145–152.

Cartwright, G. P., & Cartwright, C. A. (1974). *Developing observation skills*. New York, NY: McGraw-Hill.

Casey, B. M., Pezaris, E. E., & Bassi, J. (2012). Adolescent boys' and girls' block constructions differ in structural balance: A block-building characteristic related to math achievement. *Learning and Individual Differences, 22*(1), 25–36.

Casey, T. (2011). Outdoor play for everyone: Meeting the needs of individuals. In J. White (Ed.), *Outdoor provision in the early years*. London, UK: Sage Publications, Ltd.

Castelli, D. M., Glowacki, E., Barcelona, J. M., Calvert, H. G., & Hwang, J. (2015). Active education: Growing evidence on physical activity and academic performance. *Active Living Research*, 1–5.

Cecil, N. L. (2017). *Striking a balance: A comprehensive approach to early literacy*. Abingdon, UK: Taylor & Francis.

Center on the Developing Child at Harvard University. (2016). http://developingchild.harvard.edu/

Cevher-Kalburan, N., & Ivrendi, A. (2016). Risky play and parenting styles. *Journal of Child and Family Studies, 25*(2), 355–366.

Chaillé, C. (2008). *Constructivism across the curriculum in early childhood classrooms: Big ideas as inspiration*. Boston, MA: Allyn & Bacon/Pearson Education.

Chambers, B., Cheung, A. C., & Slavin, R. E. (2016). Literacy and language outcomes of comprehensive and developmental-constructivist approaches to early childhood education: A systematic review. *Educational Research Review, 18*, 88–111.

Chapman, L. H. (1978). *Approaches to art in education*. Boston, MA: Houghton Mifflin Harcourt.

Charlesworth, R. (2015). *Math and science for young children*. Boston, MA: Cengage Learning.

Chaudron, S. (2015). *Young children (0–8) and digital technology: A qualitative exploratory study across seven countries (EUR–Scientific and Technical Research Reports)*. Luxembourg: Publications Office of the EU.

Chaudry, A., & Wimer, C. (2016). Poverty is not just an indicator: The relationship between income, poverty, and child well-being. *Academic Pediatrics, 16*(3), S23–S29.

Chen, G. M. (1990). Intercultural communication competence: Some perspectives of research. *Howard Journal of Communications, 2*(3), 243–261.

Cherry, K. (2016). Extrinsic vs. intrinsic motivation: What's the difference? Retrieved from http://psychology.about.com/od/motivation/f/difference-between-extrinsic-and-intrinsic-motivation.htm

Chiao, J. Y., Li, S. C., & Seligman, R. (2016). *The Oxford handbook of cultural neuroscience*. Oxford, UK: Oxford University Press.

Chiarotto, L. (2011). *Natural curiosity: Building children's understanding of the world through environmental inquiry: A resource for teachers*. Toronto, ON: Laboratory School at the Dr. Eric Jackman Institute of Child Study, Ontario Institute for Studies in Education, University of Toronto.

Childcare Resource and Research Unit. (2017). Retrieved from http://www.childcarecanada.org

Christakis, E. (2016). *The importance of being little: What preschoolers really need from grownups*. New York, NY: Penguin Random House.

Christenson, L. A., & James, J. (2015). Building bridges to understanding in a preschool classroom: A morning in the block center. *YC Young Children, 70*(1), 26.

Christian, K. M. (2012). *The construct of playfulness: Relationships with adaptive behaviors, humor, and early play ability*. Cleveland, OH: Case Western Reserve University.

Christie, J. F., & Wardle, F. (1992). How much time is needed for play? *Young Children, 47*(3), 28–33.

Chudacoff, H. P. (2007). *Children at play: An American history*. New York, NY: NYU Press.

City of Vancouver. (2016). Retrieved from http://vancouver.ca/news-calendar/our-city.aspx

Clements, D. H., & Nastasi, B. K. (1993). Electronic media and early childhood education. In B. Spodek (Ed.), *Handbook of research on the education of young children* (pp. 251–275). New York, NY: Macmillan.

Clements, D. H., & Sarama, J. (2014). *Learning and teaching early math: The learning trajectories approach*. New York, NY: Routledge.

Cloward Drown, K. K., & Christensen, K. M. (2014). Dramatic play affordances of natural and manufactured outdoor settings for preschool-aged children. *Children Youth and Environments, 24*(2), 53–77.

Cohen, L., & Uhry, J. (2007). Young children's discourse strategies during block play: A Bakhtinian approach. *Journal of Research in Childhood Education, 21*(3), 302–315.

Common Sense Media. (2013). *Zero to eight: Children's media use in America 2013*. Retrieved from https://www.commonsensemedia.org/research/zero-to-eight-childrens-media-use-in-america-2013

Conner, J., Kelly-Vance, L., Ryalls, B., & Friehe, M. (2014). A play and language intervention for two-year-old children: Implications for improving play skills and language. *Journal of Research in Childhood Education, 28*(2), 221–237.

Connors, M. (2016). Creating cultures of learning: A theoretical model of early care and education policy. *Early Childhood Research Quarterly, 36*(2), 32–45.

Copley, J. V. (2010). *The young child and mathematics* (2nd ed.). Washington, DC: NAEYC; Reston, VA: National Council of Teachers of Mathematics.

Corbett, B. (1979). *A garden of children*. Grand Rapids, MI: Froebel Foundation.

Cornett, C. E., & Smithrim, K. (2001). *The arts as meaning makers*. Toronto, ON: Pearson Education.

Corrigall, L., & Schellenberg, E. G. (2016). Music cognition in childhood. In G. McPherson (Ed.), *The child as musician* (2nd ed.). New York, NY: Oxford University Press.

Costello, P. J. (2013). *Thinking skills and early childhood education.* New York, NY: Routledge.

Coubart, A., Izard, V., Spelke, E. S., Marie, J., & Streri, A. (2014). Dissociation between small and large numerosities in newborn infants. *Developmental Science, 17*(1), 11–22.

Counsell, S., Escalada, L., Geiken, R., Sander, M., Uhlenberg, J., Van Meeteren, B., . . . Zan, B. (2015). *STEM learning with young children: Inquiry teaching with ramps and pathways.* New York, NY: Teachers College Press.

Cremin, T., Glauert, E., Craft, A., Compton, A., & Stylianidou, F. (2015). Creative little scientists: Exploring pedagogical synergies between inquiry-based and creative approaches in early years science. *Education 3–13, 43*(4), 404–419.

Crowley, K., Holzman, P., Santiago, F., & Vanyi, J. (2016). Guideline #1: When implementing technology for young children, a child's safety is the primary goal. In *Technology and Young Children.* Retrieved from http://www.patriciaholzman.com/uploads/5/7/2/2/.../_technology_and_the_young_child.pdf

Cuffaro, H. K. (1995). *Experimenting with the world: John Dewey and the early childhood classroom.* New York, NY: Teachers College Press.

Curtis, D., & Carter, M. (2007). *Learning together with young children: A curriculum framework for reflective teachers.* St. Paul, MN: Redleaf Press.

Curtis, D., Lebo, D., Cividanes, W. C., & Carter, M. (2013). *Reflecting in communities of practice: A workbook for early childhood educators.* St. Paul, MN: Redleaf Press.

Dahlberg, G., & Moss, P. (2005). *Ethics and politics in early childhood education.* London, UK: Routledge-Falmer.

Dahlberg, G., Moss, P., & Pence, A. R. (1999). *Beyond quality in early childhood education and care: Postmodern perspectives.* Abingdon, UK: Psychology Press, Taylor & Francis Group.

Damon, W. (1984). Peer education: The untapped potential. *Journal of Applied Developmental Psychology, 5*(4), 331–343.

Daniels, E., & Gamper, C (2011). The yin and yang of Montessori and Waldorf in early childhood education. *Commongroundmag,* 62–63. Retrieved from http://learningcompanion.files.wordpress.com/2010/12/commonground-decjan-nlcarticle_page_4.jpg

Davidson, J. I. (1996). *Emergent literacy and dramatic play in early education.* Belmont, CA: Wadsworth Publishing.

Davies, D., Howe, A., Collier, C., Digby, R., Earle, S., & McMahon, K. (2014). *Teaching science and technology in the early years (3–7).* London, UK: Routledge.

De Jong, E., Visscher, T. L. S., HiraSing, R. A., Heymans, M. W., Seidell, J. C., & Renders, C. M. (2013). Association between TV viewing, computer use and overweight, determinants and competing activities of screen time in 4- to 13-year-old children. *International Journal of Obesity, 37*(1), 47–53.

Delaney, K. (2015). Dissonance for understanding: Exploring a new theoretical lens for understanding teacher identity formation in borderlands of practice. *Contemporary Issues in Early Childhood, 16*(4), 274–389.

DeLashmutt, G., & Braund, R. (1996). Postmodernism and you: Education. URL: http://www.crossrds.org/doteduc.htm.

Denning, C. B., & Moody, A. K. (2013). Supporting students with autism spectrum disorders in inclusive settings: Rethinking instruction and design. *Electronic Journal for Inclusive Education, 3*(1), 6.

Derr, V., & Kellert, S. R. (2013). Making children's environments "R.E.D.": Restorative environmental design and its relationship to sustainable design. In E. Pavlides & J. Wells (Eds.), *Proceedings of the 44th annual conference of the Environmental Design Research Association.* Providence, RI.

De-Souza, D., & Radell, J. (2011). Superheroes: An opportunity for prosocial play. *YC Young Children, 66*(4), 26.

Dewey, J. (1903). Democracy in education. *The Elementary School Teacher, 4*(4), 193–204.

Dewey, J. (1934). *Art as experience.* New York, NY: Minton, Balch & Company.

Dewey, J. (1938). *Experience and education.* New York, NY: Touchstone.

Dewey, J. (1944). *Democracy and education: An introduction to philosophy of education.* London, UK: Macmillan. (Original work published 1916.)

Dewey, J. (1999). *The child and the curriculum, and the school and society.* Chicago, IL: The University of Chicago Press. (Original work published 1956.)

Dietze, B. (2006). *Foundations of early childhood education: Learning environments and childcare in Canada.* Toronto, ON: Prentice Hall.

Dietze, B. (2013). How accessible and usable are our neighbourhood playgrounds for children who have mobility restrictions or use mobility devices? *Canadian Children, 38*(2), 14–20.

Dietze, B. (2016). *Loose parts and tinkering = Learning.* Retrieved from http://www.cccf-fcsge.ca/2017/07/25/a-blog-the-importance-of-increasing-childrens-outdoor-play-opportuniites

Dietze, B., & Kashin, D. (2012). *Playing and learning in early childhood education.* Toronto, ON: Pearson.

Dietze, B., & Kashin, D. (2013). Shifting views: Exploring the potential for technology integration in early childhood education programs. *Canadian Journal of Learning and Technology, 39*(4), 1–13.

Dietze, B., & Kashin, D. (2014). The value of narrative inquiry as a provocation to learn, develop and conceptualize professional learning in early childhood education. *Early Childhood Education, 42*(1).

Dietze, B., & Kashin, D. (2016). *Empowering pedagogy for early childhood education.* Toronto, ON: Pearson.

Dietze, B., & Kashin, D. (2017). *Outdoor play training.* Retrieved from http://www.outdoorplaytraining.com

Dietze, B. & Kim, B. (2014). An assessment tool in support of creating children's outdoor play environments with a sense of wonder. (Unpublished).

Dietze, B., Penner, A., Ashley, S., Gillis, K., Moses, H., & Goodine, B. (2014). Listening to faculty: Developing a research strategy in early childhood education. *Transformative Dialogues: Teaching & Learning Journal, 7*(1).

Donley, S. (1987). *Drawing development in children.* Retrieved from http://www.learningdesign.com/Portfolio/DrawDev/kiddrawing.html

Dowling, M. (2014). *Young children's personal, social and emotional development*. Thousand Oaks, CA: Sage Publications.

Drew, W. F., & Nell, M. L. (2015). Children discovery workshop: How everyone can grow through constructive play. *Teaching Young Children, 8*(2), 22–24. Retrieved from http://flscaeyc.org/wp-content/uploads/2015/02/TYCv8n2ChildrensDiscoveryWorkshop.pdf

Driscoll, A. S., & Nagel, N. (2005). *Early childhood education, birth–8: The world of children, families, and educators*. Boston, MA: Allyn & Bacon.

Dueck, C. (2016). Pathway to stewardship. (Draft). Retrieved from http://campkawartha.ca/pdf/Pathway-to-Stewardship.pdf

Duhn, I. (2012). Making "place" for ecological sustainability in early childhood education. *Environmental Education Research, 18*(1), 19–29.

Duncan, J., Eaton, S., & Te One, S. (2013). The golden thread: Rethinking learning outcomes in early childhood education. *New Zealand Journal of Teachers' Work, 10*(2), 196–208.

Durham, S. (2015). Blocks: "Standard" equipment for today's primary classrooms. *YC Young Children, 70*(1), 52.

Earle, K. (2013). *Meeting the needs of your most able pupils in art*. London, UK: Routledge.

Eckhoff, A. (2008). The importance of art viewing experiences in early childhood visual arts: The exploration of a master art teacher's strategies for meaningful early arts experiences. *Early Childhood Education Journal, 35*(5), 463–472.

Edwards, C., & Gandini, L. (2015). Teacher research in Reggio Emilia: Essence of a dynamic, evolving role. *Voices of Practitioners*, Winter, 89–103.

Edwards, C. P., Gandini, L., & Forman, G. E. (1998). Educational and caring spaces. In C. P. Edwards, L. Gandini, & G. E. Forman. (Eds.), *The hundred languages of children: The Reggio Emilia approach—Advanced reflections* (pp. 161–178). New York, NY: Ablex Publishing.

Ehrlin, A. (2012). *Learning from each other: An ethnographic study of music in preschool in a multilingual environment* (Doctoral dissertation). Örebro University, Örebro, Sweden.

Ehrlin, A., & Gustavsson, H. O. (2015). The importance of music in preschool education. *Australian Journal of Teacher Education, 40*(7), 32–42.

Eisner, E. W. (1976). *The arts: Human development and education*. Richmond, CA: McCutchan Publishers.

Elkind, D. (2004). The problem with constructivism. *The Educational Forum, 68*(4), 306–312.

Elkind, D. (2007). *The power of play: Learning what comes naturally*. Cambridge, MA: Da Capo Press.

Elkind, D. (2015). *Giants in the nursery: A biographical history of developmentally appropriate practice*. St. Paul, MN: Redleaf Press.

Ellis, J. J. (1973). *Why people play*. Upper Saddle River, NJ: Prentice-Hall.

Ellis, N. C. (2015). Cognitive and social aspects of learning from usage. In T. Cadierno & S. Eskildsen (Eds.), *Usage-based perspectives on second language learning* (pp. 49–73). Berlin, Germany: DeGruyter Mouton.

Englebright Fox, J., & Schirrmacher, R. (2014). *Art and creative development for young children*. Boston, MA: Cengage Learning.

Ennis-Cole, D., & Smith, D. (2011). Assistive technology and autism: Expanding the technology leadership role of the school librarian. *School Libraries Worldwide, 17*(2), 86.

Epstein, A. S. (2009). *Me, you, us: Social-emotional learning in preschool*. Ypsilanti, MI: HighScope Press.

Epstein, A. S. (2014). *The intentional teacher: Choosing the best strategies for young children's learning* (rev. ed.). Washington, DC: National Association for the Education of Young Children.

Ergler, C. R., Kearns, R., & Witten, K. (2016). Exploring children's seasonal play to promote active lifestyles in Auckland, New Zealand. *Health & Place, 41*, 67–77.

Erikson, E. H. (1963). *Childhood and society* (2nd ed.). New York, NY: W. W. Norton.

Ernst, J. (2014a). Early childhood educators' preferences and perceptions regarding outdoor settings as learning environments. *International Journal of Early Childhood Environmental Education, 2*(1), 97–125.

Ernst, J. (2014b). Early childhood educators' use of natural outdoor settings as learning environments: An exploratory study of beliefs, practices, and barriers. *Environmental Education Research, 20*(6), 735–752.

Evans, G. W., & Wachs, T. D. (2010). *Chaos and its influence on children's development*. Washington, DC: American Psychological Association.

Ewing, R., Callow, J., & Rushton, K. (2016). *Language and literacy development in early childhood*. Cambridge, UK: Cambridge University Press.

Fawcett, M., & Watson, D. (2016). *Learning through child observation*. Philadelphia, PA: Jessica Kingsley Publishers.

Feeney, S., Moravcik, E., & Nolte, S. (2013). *Who Am I in the Lives of Children? An Introduction to Early Childhood Education*. Upper Saddle River, NJ: Pearson.

Fehr, K., & Russ, S. (2016). Pretend play and creativity in preschool-aged children: Associations and brief intervention. *Psychology of Aesthetics, Creativity, and the Arts, 10*(3), 296–308, doi:10.1037/aca0000054

Ferlazzo, L. (2012). *The differences between parent involvement and parent engagement*. Retrieved from http://earlylearningwa.org/

Fernald, A., & Weisleder, A. (2015). Twenty years after "meaningful differences," it's time to reframe the "deficit" debate about the importance of children's early language experience. *Human Development, 58*(1), 1–4.

Festinger, L. (1962). *A theory of cognitive dissonance* (Vol. 2). Stanford, CA: Stanford University Press.

First Nations Information Governance Centre. (2017). http://fnigc.ca/

Fisch, K., & McLeod, S. (2012). *Did you know 2.0*. (Video file). Retrieved from http://www.youtube.com/watch?v=FNjuDf_3DKoorld?

Flannigan, C. (2015). *The influence of loose parts on preschool children's play behaviours*. (Unpublished master's dissertation). Mount Saint Vincent University, Halifax, NS.

Flaugnacco, E., Lopez, L., Terribili, C., Montico, M., Zoia, S., & Schön, D. (2015). Music training increases phonological awareness and reading skills in developmental dyslexia: A randomized control trial. *PLoS One, 10*(9).

Fleet, A., Patterson, C., & Robertson, J. (2012). *Conversations: Behind early childhood pedagogical documentation.* Jamberoo, Australia: Pademelon Press.

Flesch, R. (1955). *Why Johnnie can't read: And what you can do about it.* New York, NY: HarperCollins.

Florez, I. (2011). Developing young children's self-regulation through everyday experiences. *Young Children, 66*(4), 46–51.

Follari, L. (2014). *Valuing diversity in early childhood education.* Upper Saddle River, NJ: Pearson Education, Inc.

Follari, L. (2015). *Foundations and best practices in early childhood education: History, theories, and approaches to learning.* Upper Saddle River, NJ: Pearson Higher Education.

Forman, G. (2005). The project approach in Reggio Emilia. In V. C. Fosnot (Ed.), *Constructivism* (2nd ed., pp. 212–221). New York, NY: Teachers College Press.

Fraser, B. J. (2012). Classroom learning environments: Retrospect, context and prospect. In B. J. Fraser, K. Tobin, & C. J. McRobbie (Eds.), *Second international handbook of science education* (pp. 1191–1239). Haarlem, Netherlands: Springer.

Fraser, S. (2012). *Authentic childhood.* Toronto, ON: Nelson Education.

Fraser, S., & Gestwicki, C. (2002). *Authentic childhood: Exploring Reggio Emilia in the classroom.* Boston, MA: Cengage Learning.

Freeman, N. K., & Somerindyke, J. (2001). Social play at the computer: Preschoolers scaffold and support peers' computer competence. *Information Technology in Childhood Education, 203,* 13.

Friedberg, M. P., & Berkeley, E. P. (1970). *Play and interplay: A manifesto for new design in urban recreational environment.* Basingstoke, UK: Macmillan Publishers.

Friendly, M., & Prabhu, N. (2010). Can early childhood education and care help keep Canada's promise of respect for diversity? *Occasional Paper, 23.*

Froebel, F. (1887). *The education of man.* London, UK: D. Appleton and Company.

Fromberg, D. P. (2002). *Play and meaning in early childhood education.* Boston, MA: Allyn & Bacon.

Frost, J. L. (1992). *Play and playscapes.* Clifton Park, NY: Delmar.

Frost, J. L. (2012). The changing culture of play. *International Journal of Play, 1*(2), 117–130.

Frost, J. L., Wortham, S. C., & Reifel, R. S. (2001). *Play and child development.* Upper Saddle River, NJ: Merrill-Prentice Hall.

Frost, J. L., Wortham, S., & Reifel, S. (2008). *Play and child development* (3rd ed). Upper Saddle River, NJ: Merrill-Prentice Hall.

Frost, J. L., Wortham, S. C., & Reifel, R. S. (2012). *Play and child development.* Upper Saddle River, NJ: Pearson.

Fu, V. R. (2002). The challenge to reinvent the Reggio Emilia approach: A pedagogy of hope and possibilities. In V. Fu, A. Stremmel, & L. Hill (Eds.), *Teaching and learning: Collaborative exploration of the Reggio Emilia approach.* Upper Saddle River, NJ: Merrill-Prentice Hall.

Gadzikowski, A. (2013). *Challenging exceptionally bright children in early childhood classrooms.* St. Paul, MN: Redleaf Press.

Galda, L., & Pellegrini, A. D. (2015). Dramatic play and dramatic activity: Literate language and narrative understanding. In J. Flood, S. B. Heath, & D. Lapp (Eds.), *Handbook of research on teaching literacy through the communicative and visual arts: Volume II, A project of the International Reading Association* (p. 455). New York, NY: Routledge.

Gallahue, D. L. (1993). Motor development and movement skill acquisition in early childhood education. In O. N. Saracho & B. Spodek (Eds.), *Handbook of research on the education of young children* (pp. 24–41). New York, NY: Routledge.

Gamble, W. C., & Cota-Robles, S. (2015). *Guiding curiosity: Nurturing young scientists.* Retrieved from https://store.bookbaby.com/book/guiding-curiosity-nurturing-young-scientists

Gandini, L. (1994). Not just anywhere: Making child care centers into "particular places." *Child Care Information Exchange, 48.*

Gandini, L. (1998). Educational and caring spaces. In C. Edward, L. Gandini, & G. Forman (Eds.), *The hundred languages of children: The Reggio Emilia approach—Advanced reflections.* Westport, CT: Greenwood Publishing Group.

Gandini, L. (Ed.). (2004). *In the spirit of the studio: Learning from the atelier of Reggio Emilia.* New York, NY: Teachers College Press.

Gandini, L. (Ed.). (2005). *In the spirit of the studio: Learning from the atelier of Reggio Emilia.* New York, NY: Teachers College Press.

Gandini, L. (2012). *History of the experiences of the Reggio Emilia municipal infant-toddler centres and preschools.* Retrieved from http://learningmaterialswork.com/

Gardner, H. (1993). *Multiple intelligences.* New York, NY: Basic Books.

Gardner, H. (1996). Probing more deeply into the theory of multiple intelligences. *NaSSP Bulletin, 80*(583), 1–7.

Garvis, S., & Pendergast, D. (2011). An investigation of early childhood teacher self-efficacy beliefs in the teaching of arts education. *International Journal of Education & the Arts, 12*(9), 1–15.

Geist, K., Geist, E. A., & Kuznik, K. (2012). The patterns of music: Young children learning mathematics through beat, rhythm, and melody. *YC Young Children, 67*(1), 74.

Genishi, C., & Dyson, A. H. (2014). Play as the Precursor for Literacy Development. In E. Brooker (Ed.), *The SAGE handbook of play and learning in early childhood* (p. 228). Thousand Oaks, CA: SAGE Publications.

Genishi, C., & Dyson, A. H. (2015). *Children, language, and literacy: Diverse learners in diverse times.* New York, NY: Teachers College Press.

Georgeson, J., & Campbell-Barr, V. (2015). Attitudes and the early years workforce. *Early Years, 35*(4), 321–332.

Gerde, H. K., Schachter, R. E., & Wasik, B. A. (2013). Using the scientific method to guide learning: An integrated approach to early childhood curriculum. *Early Childhood Education Journal, 41*(5), 315–323.

Gesell, A. (1940). *The first five years of life: A guide to the study of the preschool child, from the Yale Clinic of Child Development.* New York, NY: Harper & Brothers.

Gestwicki, C. (2013). *Developmentally appropriate practice: Curriculum and development in early education.* Boston, MA: Cengage Learning.

Gibson, S. A., & Moss, B. (2016). *Every young child a reader: Using Marie Clay's key concepts for classroom instruction.* New York, NY: Teachers College Press.

Gilligan, C. (1993). *In a different voice: Psychological theory and women's development.* Cambridge, MA: Harvard University Press.

Given, L. M., Cantrell Winkler, D., Willson, R., Davidson, C., Danby, S., & Thorpe, K. (2016). Parents as coresearchers at home: Using an observational method to document young children's use of technology. *International Journal of Qualitative Methods, 15*(1).

Glasser, W. (1998). *Choice theory: A new psychology of personal freedom.* New York, NY: HarperCollins.

Gleave, J., & Cole-Hamilton, I. (2012). *A literature review on the effects of a lack of play on children's lives.* London, UK: Play England.

Golbeck, S. L. (2005). Building foundations for spatial literacy in early childhood. *YC Young Children, 60*(6), 72.

Goldstein, J. (2012). *Play in children's development, health and well-being.* Brussels, Belgium: Toy Industries of Europe.

Göncü, A., Mistry, J., & Mosier, C. (2000). Preschoolers' classroom activities and interactions with peers and teachers. *Early Education and Development, 24*(3), 321–329.

Göncü, A., Thermer, U., Jain, J., & Johnson, D. B. (1999). Children's play as cultural activity. In A. Göncü (Ed.), *Children's engagement in the world: Sociocultural perspectives* (pp. 148–170). New York, NY: Cambridge University Press.

Goodenough, F. (1956). *Exceptional children.* New York, NY: Appleton-Century Crofts.

Gopnick, A., Meltzoff, A. N., & Kuhl, P. K. (2001). *Scientist in the crib: Minds, brains, and how children learn.* New York, NY: HarperPerennial.

Goswami, U., Huss, M., Mead, N., Fosker, T., & Verney, J. P. (2013). Perception of patterns of musical beat distribution in phonological developmental dyslexia: Significant longitudinal relations with word reading and reading comprehension. *Cerebral Cortex, 49*(5), 1363–1376.

Gotay, C. C., Katzmarzyk, P. T., Janssen, I., Dawson, M. Y., Aminoltejari, K., & Bartley, N. L. (2013). Updating the Canadian obesity maps: An epidemic in progress. *Canadian Journal of Public Health, 104*(1), e64–e68.

Gowrie South Australia. (2015). *Sense of agency.* Retrieved from http://www.gowriesa.org.au/sites/default/files/rs-sense-agency.pdf

Grahn, J. A., & Rowe, J. B. (2013). Finding and feeling the musical beat: Striatal dissociations between detection and prediction of regularity. *Cerebral Cortex, 23*, 913–921.

Greenberg, M. (1979). *Your children need music: A guide for parents and teachers of young children.* Englewood Cliffs, NJ: Prentice Hall.

Greenman, J. (1988). *Caring spaces, learning places: Children's environments that work.* Redmond, WA: Exchange Press, Inc.

Greenman, J. (2005). Places for childhood in the 21st century: A conceptual framework. *Beyond the Journal: Young Children on the Web,* May.

Greenfield, P. M. (2016). Social Change, Cultural Evolution, and Human Development. *Current Opinion in Psychology, 8,* 84-92.

Grella, M. A. (2015). *Nurturing the aesthetic: Learning to care for the environment in a Waldorf School* (Unpublished dissertation). Antioch University, Yellow Springs, OH.

Grieshaber, S., & Hatch, J. A. (2003). Child observation and pedagogical documentation as effects of globalisation. *Journal of Curriculum Theorizing, 19*(1), 89–102.

Groves, N. J., Kesby, J. P., Eyles, D. W., McGrath, J. J., Mackay-Sim, A., & Burne, T. H. (2013). Adult vitamin D deficiency leads to behavioural and brain neurochemical alterations in C57BL/6J and BALB/c mice. *Behavioural Brain Research, 241,* 120–131.

Guerrero, M. D., Hoffmann, M. D., & Munroe-Chandler, K. (2016). Children's active play imagery and its association with personal and social skills and self-confidence. *Journal of Imagery Research in Sport and Physical Activity, 11*(1), 47–57.

Guilmartin, K. K., & Levinowitz, L. M. (1996). *Music and your child: A guide for parents and caregivers.* Princeton, NJ: Center for Music and Young Children.

Guyton, G. (2011). Using toys to support infant-toddler learning and development. *YC Young Children, 66*(5), 50.

Habibi, A. (2012). *Music training speeds up brain development in children.* Retrieved from http://theconversation.com/music-training-speeds-up-brain-development-in-children-61491

Halliday, M.A.K. (1975). *Learning how to mean: Explorations in the development of language.* London: Edward Arnold.

Hall-Kenyon, K. M., Bullough, R. V., MacKay, K. L., & Marshall, E. E. (2014). Preschool teacher well-being: A review of the literature. *Early Childhood Education Journal, 42*(3), 153–162.

Hamre, B. K., Pianta, R. C., Burchinal, M., Field, S., LoCasale-Crouch, J., Downer, J. T., & Scott-Little, C. (2012). A course on effective teacher-child interactions: Effects on teacher beliefs, knowledge, and observed practice. *American Educational Research Journal, 19*(1), 88 123.

Hanline, M. F. (1999). Developing a preschool play-based curriculum. *International Journal of Disability, Development and Education, 46*(3), 289–305.

Hansel, R. R. (2015). Bringing blocks back to the kindergarten classroom. *YC Young Children, 70*(1), 44.

Harmon, D. B. (1951). *The coordinated classroom.* Grand Rapids, MI: American Seating Co.

Harper, S. (2004). Schemas in areas of play. *Playcentre Journal, 121,* 8–9.

Haskins, C. (2012). Order, organization, and beauty in the classroom: A prerequisite, not an option. *Montessori Life: A Publication of the American Montessori Society*, 24(2), 34–39.

Hathaway, W. E. (1995). Effects of school lighting on physical development and school performance. *The Journal of Educational Research*, 88(4), 228–242.

Haugland, S. W., & Wright, J. L. (1997). *Young children and technology.* New York, NY: Allyn & Bacon.

Havighurst, R. J. (1952). *Developmental tasks and education.* New York, NY: Longsmans, Green.

Hawkins, D. (1974). Messing about in science. In D. Hawkins (Ed.), *The informed vision: Essays on learning and human nature.* New York, NY: Agathon Press.

Hawkins, D. (1983). Nature closely observed. Daedalus, 65-89.

Hawkins, D. (2000). *The roots of literacy.* Boulder, CO: University Press of Colorado.

Hawkins, D. (2002). *The informed vision: Essays on learning and human nature.* New York, NY: Algora Publishing

Hendrick, J., & Weissman, P. (2007). *Total learning: Developmental curriculum for the young child.* Upper Saddle River, NJ: Merrill-Prentice Hall.

Hendrick, J., & Weissman, P. (2011). *Total learning: Developmental curriculum for the young child* (8th ed.). London, UK: Pearson Higher Education

Hendrick, J., & Wiseman, P. (2006). *The whole child* (8th ed.). Upper Saddle River, NJ: Pearson.

Henniger, M. (2002). *Teaching young children: An introduction* (2nd ed.). Upper Saddle River, NJ: Pearson Education.

Heppell, G. (2013). Risk assessment not risk-aversion. *Belonging Early Years Journal*, 2(1), 14–17.

Hermon, A., & Prentice, R. (2003). Positively different: Art and design in special education. *International Journal of Art & Design Education*, 22(3), 268–280.

Herrington, S., & Pickett, W. (2015). *Canadian position statement on active outdoor play.* Retrieved from http://stage.participaction.com/sites/default/files/downloads/Participaction-PositionStatement-ActiveOutdoorPlay.pdf

Hinkley, T., Carson, V., & Hesketh, K. D. (2015). Physical environments, policies and practices for physical activity and screen-based sedentary behaviour among preschoolers within child care centres in Melbourne, Australia and Kingston, Canada. *Child: Care, Health and Development*, 41(1), 132–138.

Hirsch, E. (1996). *The block book.* Washington, DC: National Association for the Education of Young Children.

Hirsh-Pasek, K., & Golinkoff, R. M. (2009). The great balancing act: Optimizing core curricula through playful pedagogy. In E. Zigler, S. Barnett, & W. Gilliam (Eds.), *The pre-K debates: Current controversies & issues.* Baltimore, MD: Paul H. Brookes Publishing Co.

Hobson, J., Hobson, R., Cheung, Y., & Calo, S. (2015). Symbolizing as interpersonally grounded shifts in meaning: Social play in children with and without autism. *Journal of Autism Development Disorder*, 45, 42–52.

Hoel, D. G., Berwick, M., de Gruijl, F. R., & Holick, M. F. (2016). The risks and benefits of sun exposure 2016. *Dermato-Endocrinology*, 8(1).

Holcomb-McCoy, C., & Bryan, J. (2010). Advocacy and empowerment in parent consultation: Implications for theory and practice. *Journal of Counseling and Development: JCD*, 88(3), 259.

Holloway, D., Green, L., & Livingstone, S. (2013). *Zero to eight: Young children and their internet use.* Retrieved from http://eprints.lse.ac.uk/52630/1/Zero_to_eight.pdf

hooks, B. (2010). *Teaching critical thinking: Practical wisdom.* New York, NY: Routledge.

Hoorn, J., Nourot, P., Scales, B., & Alward, K. (2011). *Play at the center of the curriculum.* Upper Saddle River, NJ: Pearson.

Houen, S., Danby, S., Farrell, A., & Thorpe, K. (2016). Creating spaces for children's agency: "I wonder. . .": Formulations in teacher–child interactions. *International Journal of Early Childhood*, 48(3), 259–276.

Houser, N. E., Roach, L., Stone, M. R., Turner, J., & Kirk, S. F. (2016). Let the children play: Scoping review on the implementation and use of loose parts for promoting physical activity participation. *AIMS Public Health*, 3(4), 781–799.

Howard, E. (2015). Authentic assessment explained. *Lethbridge College Learning Connections.* Retrieved from http://www.lc2.ca/item/239-authentic-assessment-explained

Hrannar, I. (2014). *14 things that are obsolete in 21st century schools.* Retrieved from http://ingvihrannar.com/14-things-that-are-obsolete-in-21st-century-schools/

Hsin, C. T., Li, M. C., & Tsai, C. C. (2014). The influence of young children's use of technology on their learning: A. *Educational Technology & Society*, 17(4), 85–99.

Hunt, T., & Renfro, N. (1982). *Puppetry in early childhood education.* New York, NY: Renfro Studios.

Hunter-Doniger, T. (2016). Snapdragons and math: Using creativity to inspire, motivate, and engage. *YC Young Children*, 71(3), 30.

Hutchison, A., & Reinking, D. (2011). Teachers' perceptions of integrating information and communication technologies into literacy instruction: A national survey in the United States. *Reading Research Quarterly*, 46(4), 312–333.

Hyson, M., & Tomlinson, H. B. (2014). *The early years matter: Education, care, and the well-being of children, birth to 8.* New York, NY: Teachers College Press.

Indigenous and Northern Affairs. (2016). *Indigenous peoples and communities.* Retrieved from http://www.aadnc-aandc.gc.ca/eng/1100100013785/1304467449155

International Foundation of Music Research. (2017). https://www.nammfoundation.org/

International Play Association Canada (IPA). (2014). *Declaration on the importance of play.* Retrieved from http://ipaworld.org/ipa-declaration-on-the-importance-of-play/

Isbell, R., & Raines, S. C. (2012). *Creativity and the arts with young children.* Boston, MA: Cengage Learning.

Isenberg, J. P., & Jalongo, M. R. (2001). *Creative expression and play in early childhood* (3rd ed.). Upper Saddle River, NJ: Merrill-Prentice Hall.

Isenberg, J. P., & Jalongo, M. R. (2010). *Creative thinking and arts-based learning: Preschool through fourth grade.* Upper Saddle River, NJ: Merrill.

Isenberg, J. P., & Jalongo, M. R. (2013). *Creative thinking and arts-based learning: Preschool through fourth grade* (6th ed.). Upper Saddle River, NJ: Pearson Education.

Isenberg, J. P., & Jalongo, M. R. (2014). *Why is play important? Social and emotional development, physical development, creative development.* Upper Saddle River, NJ: Pearson Allyn Bacon Prentice Hall.

Isenberg, J. P., & Jalongo, M. R. (2015). *Creative thinking and arts-based learning: Preschool through fourth grade* (7th ed.). Upper Saddle River, NJ: Pearson Education.

Ishai, A., Ungerleider, L. G., Martin, A., Schouten, J. L., & Haxby, J. V. (1999). Distributed representation of objects in the human ventral visual pathway. *Proceedings of the National Academy of Sciences, 96*(16), 9379–9384.

Jacobi-Vessels, J. L. (2013). Discovering nature: The benefits of teaching outside of the classroom. *Dimensions of Early Childhood, 41*(3), 4–10.

Jacovina, M. E., McNamara, D. S., & Allen, L. K. (2015). *Higher order thinking in comprehension.* New York, NY: Taylor and Francis, Inc.

Jalongo, M. R. (1999). On behalf of children "How we respond to the artistry of children: Ten barriers to overcome." *Early Childhood Education Journal, 26*(4), 205–208.

Jalongo, M. R. (2000). *Early childhood language arts: Meeting diverse literacy needs through collaboration with families and professionals.* Boston, MA: Allyn and Bacon.

Jandt, F. (2016). *An introduction to intercultural communication: Identities in a global community* (8th ed.). Thousand Oaks, CA: Sage Publications Inc.

Jenkins, E. (1986). How original is it? The models on which children base their writing. *Educational Review, 38,* 151–160.

Jennings, H., & Carlisle, R. (2013). Spaces for active play: Developing child-inspired play space for older children. *Australasian Parks and Leisure, 16*(3), 8.

Jensen, E. (1999). *Teaching with the brain in mind.* Alexandria, VA: Association for Supervision and Curriculum Development.

Johnson, J. E., Christie, J. F., & Wardle, F. (2005). *Play, development, and early education.* Toronto, ON: Pearson.

Johnson, J. E., Christie, J. F., Yawkey, T. D., & Wardle, F. P. (1987). *Play and early childhood development.* Glenview, IL: Scott, Foresman & Co.

Johnson, K., Caskey, M., Rand, K., Tucker, R., & Vohr, B. (2014). Gender differences in adult-infant communication in the first months of life. *Pediatrics, 134*(6), e1603–e1610.

Jones, E. (2012). The emergence of emergent curriculum. *YC Young Children, 67*(2), 66.

Jones, E., & Nimmo, J. (1994). *Emergent curriculum.* Washington, DC: National Association for the Education of Young Children.

Jones, E., & Reynolds, G. (2011). *The play's the thing: Teachers' roles in children's play.* New York, NY: Teachers College Press.

Jones, E., & Reynolds, G. (2015). *The play's the thing: Teachers' roles in children's play.* New York, NY: Teachers College Press.

Joyce, R. (2012). *Outdoor learning: Past and present.* New York, NY: McGraw Hill Open University Press.

Kable, J. (2013). Let the children play. *Rattler (Sydney), 108,* 19–22. Retrieved from https://search.informit.com.au/documentSummary;dn=845473626390039;res=IELAPA

Kamal, M., Bener, A., & Ehlayel, M. S. (2014). Is high prevalence of vitamin D deficiency a correlate for attention deficit hyperactivity disorder? *ADHD Attention Deficit and Hyperactivity Disorders, 6*(2), 73–78.

Kamii, C. (2016). Can adults teach number concepts to young children? *Beginnings Professional Development Workshop,* 59–62.

Kamii, C., Miyakawa, Y., & Kato, Y. (2004). The development of logico-mathematical knowledge in a block-building activity at ages 1–4. *Journal of Research in Childhood Education, 19*(1), 44–57.

Kankaanranta, M., Koivula, M., Laakso, M. L., & Mustola, M. (2017). Digital games in early childhood: Broadening definitions of learning, literacy, and play. In M. Ma & A. Oikonomou (Eds.), *Serious Games and Edutainment Applications* (pp. 349–367). Cham, Switzerland: Springer International Publishing.

Karpov, Y. V. (2014). *Vygotsky for educators.* Cambridge, MA: Cambridge University Press.

Kashin, D. (2009). *Reaching the top of the mountain: The impact of emergent curriculum on the practice and self-image of early childhood educators.* Saarbrücken, Germany: Lambert Academic Publishing.

Kashin, D. (2015). Worksheets don't work: Try Reggio-inspired mathematics. Retrieved: https://tecribresearch.wordpress.com/2015/08/23/worksheets-dont-work-try-reggio-inspired-mathematics/

Katerina, M. (2012). *Natural light in learning environments* (Unpublished master's thesis). University of Nicosia, Cyprus.

Katz, L. G., & Chard, S. C. (2012). *Engaging children's minds: The project approach* (2nd ed.). New York, NY: Ablex Publishing Corporation.

Kellett, M. (2011). Empowering children and young people as researchers: Overcoming barriers and building capacity. *Child Indicators Research, 4*(2), 205–219.

Kellogg, E. (2010) *David Hawkins and the pond study.* Bloomington, IN: Xlibris Corporation

Kellogg, R. (1979). *Children's drawings/children's mind.* New York, NY: Avon Publishing.

Kemple, K. M., Oh, J., Kenney, E., & Smith-Bonahue, T. (2016). The power of outdoor play and play in natural environments. *Childhood Education, 92*(6), 446–454.

Kessler, S., & Swadener, B. (1992). Introduction: Reconceptualizing curriculum. In *Reconceptualizing the early childhood curriculum: Beginning the dialogue.* New York, NY: Teachers College Press.

Kessler, S. A. (2014). Reconceptualizing the early childhood curriculum: An unaddressed topic. In M. N. Bloch, B. B. Swadener, & G. S. Cannella, (Eds.), *Reconceptualizing early childhood care and education, a reader: Critical questions, new imaginaries, and social activism* (pp. 33–45). New York, NY: Peter Lang.

Kilderry, A. (2004). Critical pedagogy: A useful framework for thinking about early childhood curriculum. *Australian Journal of Early Childhood, 29*(4), 33–38.

Kim, B. (2014). *"Sometimes I like to see what I'm doing": Children's voices in outdoor play pedagogical documentation* (Doctoral dissertation). Mount Saint Vincent University, Halifax, NS.

Kim, J. (2000). Children's pitch matching, vocal range, and developmentally appropriate practice. *Journal of Research in Childhood Education, 14*(2).

Kim, J., & Bryan, J. (2017). A first step to a conceptual framework of parent empowerment: Exploring relationships between parent empowerment and academic performance in a national sample. *Journal of Counseling & Development, 95*(2), 168–179.

Klatte, M., Bergström, K., & Lachmann, T. (2013). Does noise affect learning? A short review on noise effects on cognitive performance in children. *Frontiers in Psychology, 4*, 578.

Knaus, M. (2015). *Maths is all around you*. Sydney, Australia: Bloomsbury Publishing.

Koehler, M. J., & Mishra, P. (2009). What is technological pedagogical content knowledge. *Contemporary Issues in Technology and Teacher Education, 9*(1), 60–70.

Kohut, T. (2015, November 24). Nearly 1 in 5 Canadian children living in poverty: Report. *Global News Report*. Retrieved from http://globalnews.ca/news/2360311/nearly-1-in-5-canadian-children-living-in-poverty-report/

Kong, S. C., Chan, T.-W., Griffin, P., Hoppe, U., Huang, R., Kinshuk, D. R., . . . Yu, S. (2014). E-learning in school education in the coming 10 years for developing 21st century skills: Critical research issues and policy implications. *Educational Technology & Society, 17*(1), 70–78.

Koralek, D. (2015). Introduction to special issue: Social studies: From a sense of self to a sense of the world. *Young Children, 70*(3), 6–8.

Kostelnik, M., Gregory, K., Soderman, A., & Whiren, A. (2011). *Guiding Children's Social Development and Learning*. Cengage Learning.

Kostelnik, M., Whiren, A., Soderman, A., Rupiper, M., & Gregory, K. (2016). *Guiding children's social development and learning* (8th ed.). Boston, MA: Cengage Learning.

Kovačević, M. (2016). *The analysis of pretend play in American (pre-)school children, and its portrayal in movies* (Doctoral dissertation). Josip Juraj Strossmayer University of Osijek, Osijek, Croatia.

Krathwohl, D. (2002). A revision of Bloom's taxonomy: An overview. *Theory in Practice, 41*(4), 212–218.

Krishnamurti, J. (2000) Educating the educator. *Parabola, 25*(3), 85–89.

Kritchevsky, S., Prescott, E., & Walling, L. (1969). *Planning environments for young children: Physical space*. Madison, WI: National Association for the Education of Young Children.

Kritchevsky, S., Prescott, E., & Walling, L. (1977). *Planning environments for young children: Physical space*. Washington, DC: National Association for the Education of Young Children.

Kucer, S. B. (2014). *Dimensions of literacy: A conceptual base for teaching reading and writing in school settings*. Routledge.

Kuh, L. P. (Ed). (2014). *Thinking critically about environments for young children: Bridging theory and practice*. New York, NY: Teachers College Press.

Kuhlman, K., & Schweinhart, L. J. (2010). *Timing in child development*. Ypsilanti, MI: HighScope Educational Research Foundation. Retrieved from https://www.interactivemetronome.com/IMW/IMPublic/Research/High%20Scope%20Research.pdf

Labouvie-Vief, G. (2015). *Integrating emotions and cognition throughout the lifespan*. New York, NY: Springer.

Land, N., & Danis, I. (2016). Movement/ing provocations in early childhood education. *Journal of Childhood Studies, 41*(3), 26–37.

Lane, D. (2014). *The story of the sand pile (1886)*. Nature Explore Program. Retrieved from https://natureexplore.org/the-story-of-the-sand-pile-1886/

La Paro, K. M., & Gloeckler, L. (2016). The context of child care for toddlers: The "experience expectable environment." *Early Childhood Education Journal, 44*(2), 147–153.

Lawson Foundation. (2017). *Outdoor play strategy*. Retrieved from http://lawson.ca/wp-content/uploads/OutdoorPlayInfoGraphic.pdf

Lee, C. B., Koh, N. K., Cai, X. L., & Quek, C. L. (2012). Children's use of meta-cognition in solving everyday problems: Children's monetary decision making. *Australian Journal of Education, 56*(1), 22–39.

Lee, J., Collins, D. A., & Winkelman, L. (2015). Connecting 2-D and 3-D: Drafting blueprints, building, and playing with blocks. *YC Young Children, 70*(1), 32.

Lee, M. (2015). Power shift: Play and agency in early childhood. *Childhood & Philosophy, 11*(22).

Lees, R. B., & Chomsky, N. (1957). Syntactic structures. *Language, 33*(3 Part 1), 375–408.

Lehmann-Haupt, C. (2002). David Hawkins, 88, historian for Manhattan Project in 1940's. *New York Times*, March 4. Retrieved from http://www.nytimes.com/2002/03/04/us/david-hawkins-88-historian-for-manhattan-projectin-1940-s.html

Lemon, N., & Garvis, S. (2014). Encouraging reflective practice with future early childhood teachers to support the national standards: An Australian case study. *Australasian Journal of Early Childhood, 39*(4), 89.

Leu, D. J., Everett-Cacopardo, H., Zawilinski, L., McVerry, G., & O'Byrne, W. I. (2007). New literacies of online reading comprehension. *The Encyclopedia of Applied Linguistics*. doi:10.1002/9781405198431.wbeal0865

Levin, D. E. (2015). Technology play concerns. In D. P. Fromberg & D. Bergen (Eds.), *Play from Birth to Twelve: Contexts, Perspectives, and Meanings* (2nd ed., p. 225). New York, NY: Routledge.

Levinowitz, L. M. (1998). The importance of music in early childhood. *General Music Today, 12*(1).

Li, J., Hestenes, L. L., & Wang, Y. C. (2016). Links between preschool children's social skills and observed pretend play in outdoor childcare environments. *Early Childhood Education Journal, 44*(1), 61–68.

Li, L., Quinones, G., & Ridgway, A. (2016). Noisy neighbours: A construction of collective knowledge in toddlers' shared play space. *Australasian Journal of Early Childhood, 41*(4), 64.

Liberman, J. (1990). *Light: Medicine of the future: How we can use it to heal ourselves now*. Rochester, VT: Inner Traditions/Bear & Co.

Lifter, K., Mason, E. J., & Barton, E. E. (2011). Children's play: Where we have been and where we could go. *Journal of Early Intervention, 33*(4), 281–297.

Lightman, E., Mitchell, A., & Wilson, B. (2008). *Poverty is making us sick: A comprehensive survey of health and income in Canada*. Toronto, ON: The Wellesley Institute.

Lindeman, C. (2015). *Musical children: Engaging children in musical experiences*. New York, NY: Routledge.

Lindeman, C. (2016). *Musical classroom: Backgrounds, models, and skills for elementary teaching*. New York, NY: Routledge.

Lindeman, K. W. (2013). Response to intervention and early childhood best practices: Working hand in hand so all children can learn. *YC Young Children, 68*(2), 16.

Lindeman, K. W., & Anderson, E. M. (2015). Using blocks to develop 21st century skills. *YC Young Children, 70*(1), 36.

Loughran, J. (2006). A response to "Reflecting on the self." *Reflective Practice, 7*(1), 43–53.

Lowenfeld, V. (1947). *Creative and mental growth: A textbook on art education*. New York, NY: Macmillan Co.

Lowenfeld, V. (1978). *Creative and mental growth*. New York, NY: Macmillan

Lowenfeld, V., & Brittain, W. L. (1982). *Creative and mental growth* (7th ed.). New York, NY: Macmillan.

Lowenfeld, V., & Brittain, W. L. (1987). *Creative and mental growth* (8th ed.). Toronto, ON: Pearson.

Luckenbill, J., & Schallock, L. (2015). Designing and using a developmentally appropriate block area for infants and toddlers. *YC Young Children, 70*(1), 8.

Ludlow, S. (2012). Maximising the potential of the "third teacher": Indoor developmental play environments: 3–8 yrs. *TEACH Journal of Christian Education, 3*(1), 6.

MacDonald, M. (2015). Early childhood education and sustainability: A living curriculum. *Childhood Education, 91*(5), 332–341.

MacNaughton, G., Rolfe, S. A., & Siraj-Blatchford, I. (2010). *Doing early childhood research: International perspectives on theory and practice* (2nd ed.). Crows Nest, Australia: Allen & Unwin.

Magar, E. C., Phillips, L. H., & Hosie, J. A. (2008). Self-regulation and risk-taking. *Personality and Individual Differences, 45*(2), 153–159.

Malaguzzi, L. (1991). La integración de la diversidad: Contexto social en que se produce. *Infancia: Educar de 0 a 6 años*, (6), 4–8.

Malaguzzi, L. (1993). For an education based on relationships. *Young Children, 49*(1), 9–12.

Malaguzzi, L. (1994). Your image of the child: Where teaching begins. *Child Care Information Exchange*, 52.

Malaguzzi, L. (1998). History, ideas, and basic philosophy: An interview with Lella Gandini. In C. Edwards, L. Gandini, & G. Forman (Eds.), *The hundred languages of children: The Reggio Emilia approach to early childhood education* (2nd ed., 49–97). Greenwich, CT: Ablex Publishing Corporation.

Malaguzzi, L. (2001). *Early childhood education in Reggio Emilia*. Barcelona, Spain: Rosa Sensat.

Malone, T. W., & Lepper, M. R. (1987). Making learning fun: A taxonomy of intrinsic motivations for learning. *Aptitude, Learning, and Instruction, 3*, 223–253.

Mang, E. (2005). The referent of children's early songs. *Music Education Research, 7*(1), 3–20.

Mann, L., Power, D., & MacLellan, V. (2013). Development of menu planning resources for child care centres: A collaborative approach. *Canadian Children, 38*(2).

Mardell, B., LeeKeenan, D., Given, H., Robinson, D., Merino, B., & Lin-Constant, Y. (2009). The zooms: An experiment in using documentation to promote schoolwide teacher research. *Voices of Practitioners, 11*, 1–15.

Mardell, B., Wilson, D., Ryan, J., Ertel, K., Krechevsky, M., & Baker, M. (2016). *Towards a pedagogy of play*. Retrieved from http://pz.harvard.edu/sites/default/files/Towards%20a%20Pedagogy%20of%20Play.pdf

Markussen-Brown, J., Juhl, C. B., Piasta, S. B., Bleses, D., Højen, A., & Justice, L. M. (2017). The effects of language- and literacy-focused professional development on early educators and children: A best-evidence meta-analysis. *Early Childhood Research Quarterly, 38*, 97–115.

Martinez, S. L., & Stager, G. S. (2014). The maker movement: A learning revolution. *Learning & Leading with Technology, 41*(7), 12–17.

Maslow, A. H. (1987). *Motivation and personality* (3rd ed.). New York, NY: Harper & Row.

Mason, J. (1982). *The environment of play*. New York, NY: Leisure Press.

Mason, J. (2002). *Researching your own practice: The discipline of noticing*. London, UK: Routledge.

Massing, C., Kirova, A., & Hennig, K. (2016). The role of first language facilitators in redefining parent involvement: Newcomer families' funds of knowledge in an intercultural preschool program. *Journal of Childhood Studies, 38*(2), 4–13.

Matteoni, M. E. (2013). *The benefits of sociodramatic play: A resource book for early childhood educators and parents* (Unpublished master's thesis). California State University, Sacramento, CA.

Maxim, G. W. (1993). *The very young child: Guiding children from infancy through the early years*. New York, NY: Macmillan Publishing.

Maxwell, L. E., Mitchell, M. R., & Evans, G. W. (2008). Effects of play equipment and loose parts on preschool children's outdoor play behavior: An observational study and design intervention. *Children Youth and Environments, 18*(2), 36–63.

Mayer, C., & Trezek, B. J. (2015). *Early literacy development in deaf children*. Oxford, UK: Oxford University Press.

Mayfield, M. (2001). *Early childhood education and care in Canada: Contexts, dimensions and issues.* Toronto, ON: Prentice-Hall.

McClintic, S. (2014). Loose parts: Adding quality to the outdoor environment. *Texas Child Care Quarterly, 38*(3). Retrieved from http://www.childcarequarterly.com/pdf/winter14_parts.pdf

McCloskey, G. (2016). *Improving executive functions.* Eau Claire, WI: PESI, Inc.

McDonald, D. T., & Simons, G. M. (1989). *Musical growth and development: Birth through six.* New York, NY: Schirmer Books.

McLean, K., Jones, M., & Schaper, C. (2015). Children's literature as an invitation to science inquiry in early childhood education. *Australasian Journal of Early Childhood, 40*(4), 49.

McLuhan, M. (1994). *Understanding media: The extensions of man.* Cambridge, MA: MIT Press.

McManis, L. D., & Gunnewig, S. B. (2012). Finding the education in educational technology with early learners. *YC Young Children, 67*(3), 14.

McMullen, J. A., Hannula-Sormunen, M. M., & Lehtinen, E. (2013). Young children's recognition of quantitative relations in mathematically unspecified settings. *The Journal of Mathematical Behavior, 32*(3), 450–460.

McNeal, J. U. (1992). *Kids as customers: A handbook of marketing to children.* Lanham, MD: Lexington Books.

McVicker, C. J. (2007). Comic strips as a text structure for learning to read. *The Reading Teacher, 61*(1), 85–88.

Menzer, M. (2015). *The arts in early childhood: Social and emotional benefits of arts participation: A literature review and gap-analysis (2000–2015).* Washington, DC: National Endowment for the Arts.

Miller, E., & Almon, J. (2009). *Crisis in the kindergarten: Why children need to play in school.* New York, NY: Alliance for Childhood.

Miller, J. (1993). *The holistic curriculum.* Toronto, ON: OISE Press.

Miller, L., Cable, C. & Devereux, J. (2005). *Developing early years practice.* London, UK: Routledge.

Mincemoyer, C. C. (2013). Loose parts: What does this mean? *Penn State Extension: Better Kid Care.* Retrieved from http://extension.psu.edu/youth/betterkidcare/earlycare/our-resources/tip-pages/tips/loose-parts-what-does-this-mean

Mincemoyer, C. C. (2016). Authentic assessment—What's it all about? *Penn State Extension: Better Kid Care.* Retrieved from https://bkc.vmhost.psu.edu/documents/HO_Authentic Assessment.pdf

Monighan-Nourot, P., Scales, B., Van Hoorn, J., & Almy, M. (1987). *Looking at children's play: A bridge between theory and practice.* New York, NY: Teachers College Press.

Montessori, M. (1949). *The absorbent mind* (Vol. 1). Wheaton, IL: The Theosophical Publishing House.

Moomaw, S. (2013). *Teaching STEM in the early years: Activities for integrating science, technology, engineering, and mathematics.* St. Paul, MN: Redleaf Press.

Moore, R. (2006). Playgrounds: A 150-year-old model. In H. Frumkin, R. Geller, & I. L. Rubin (Eds.), *Safe and healthy school environments.* Cambridge, MA: Oxford University Press.

Moore, R. C. (1990). *Childhood's domain: Play and place in child development.* London, UK: MIG Communications.

Morin, A. (2016). *Understanding executive functioning issues.* Retrieved from https://www.understood.org/en/learning-attention-issues/child-learning-disabilities/executive-functioning

Morin, F. (2001). Cultivating music play: The need for changed practice. *General Music Today, 14*(2), 24–29.

Moritz Rudasill, K., Rimm-Kaufman, S. E., Justice, L. M., & Pence, K. (2006). *Temperament and language skills as predictors of teacher-child relationship quality in preschool.* Early Education and Development, 17(2), 271-291.

Morrison, M. (2010). Are kids seeing more fast food ads? *Ad Age,* November 8.

Moyles, J. (2014). *The excellence of play.* London, UK: McGraw-Hill Education.

Mühlpachr, P. (2006). Social determinants of education in the postmodern society. In *Selected educational problems: The past-the present-the future.* Krakow, Poland: Oficyna Wydawnicza Impuls.

Muir, N. M., & Bohr, Y. (2014). Contemporary practice of traditional Aboriginal child rearing: A review. *First Peoples Child & Family Review, 9*(1), 66–79.

Munroe, E., & MacLellan-Mansell, A. (2013). Outdoor play experiences for young First Nation children in Nova Scotia: Examining the barriers and considering some solutions. *Canadian Children, 38*(2).

Murphy, L. (2014). *Do preschool teachers value block play?* Paper presented at the Annual Conference of the Association for the Study of Play (TASP), Rochester, NY.

Nairn, A., & Fine, C. (2008). Who's messing with my mind? The implications of dual-process models for the ethics of advertising to children. *International Journal of Advertising, 27*(3), 447–470.

Nath, S., & Szücs, D. (2014). Construction play and cognitive skills associated with the development of mathematical abilities in 7-year-old children. *Learning and Instruction, 32*, 73–80.

National Aboriginal Health Organization (NAHO). (2012). http://www.naho.ca/

National Association for Music Education. (2017). https://nafme.org/

National Association for the Education of Young Children (NAEYC) & Fred Rogers Center for Early Learning and Children's Media. (2012). *Technology and interactive media as tools in early childhood programs serving children from birth through age 8: Joint position statement of the National Association for the Education of Young Children and the Fred Rogers Center for Early Learning and Children's Media at Saint Vincent College, approved January 2012.* Retrieved from http://www.naeyc.org/files/naeyc/file/positions/PS_technology_WEB2.pdf

National Childcare Accreditation Council (NCAC). (2007). A national quality framework for early childhood education and care. Retrieved from http://www.bing.com/search?q=National+Childcare+Accreditation+Council+(2007)&go=&filt=all&qs=n&sk=&first=11&FORI

National Council for Accreditation of Teacher Education. (2007). *Performance-based accreditation standards*. Washington, DC: Author.

Natural Curiosity. (2011). *Building children's understanding of the world through environmental inquiry: A resource for teachers*. Retrieved from http://www.naturalcuriosity.ca/pdf/NaturalCuriosityManual.pdf

Neill, P. (2013). Open-ended materials belong outside too! *High Scope, 27*(2), 1–8. Retrieved from http://www.highscope.org/file/NewsandInformation/Extensions/ExtVol27No2_lowrez.pdf

Nell, M. L., Drew, W. F., & Bush, D. E. (2013). *From play to practice: Connecting teachers' play to children's learning*. Washington, DC: National Association for the Education of Young Children.

Ness, D., & Farenga, S. J. (2016). Blocks, bricks, and planks: Relationships between affordance and visuo-spatial constructive play objects. *American Journal of Play, 8*(2), 201.

Neumann, M. M., & Neumann, D. L. (2014). Touch screen tablets and emergent literacy. *Early Childhood Education Journal, 42*(4), 231.

New, R. S. (1998). Theory and praxis in Reggio Emilia: They know what they are. In C. P. Edwards, L. Gandini, & G. E. Forman (Eds.), *The hundred languages of children: The Reggio Emilia approach—advanced reflections* (p. 261). Westport, CT: Greenwood Publishing Group.

Newcombe, N. S., Levine, S. C., & Mix, K. S. (2015). Thinking about quantity: The intertwined development of spatial and numerical cognition. *Cognitive Science, 6*(6), 491–505.

Newman, L. S. (1990). Intentional and unintentional memory in young children: Remembering vs. playing. *Journal of Experimental Child Psychology, 50*, 243–258.

Nicholson, S. (1971). How not to cheat children: The theory of loose parts. *Landscape Architecture, 62*(1), 30–34.

Nicolopoulou, A. (2010). The alarming disappearance of play from early childhood education. *Human Development, 53*(1), 1–4.

Nicolson, S., & Shipstead, S. G. (2002). *Through the looking glass: Observations in the early childhood classroom*. Upper Saddle River, NJ: Prentice Hall.

Niranjanan, J. (2016). *Enhancing preschool ELL's early literacy skills through socio-dramatic play*. Retrieved from http://hdl.handle.net/1828/7127

Nolan, J., & McBride, M. (2014). Beyond gamification: Reconceptualizing game-based learning in early childhood environments. *Information, Communication & Society, 17*(5), 594–608.

Nordic Council of Ministers. (2014). *Biophilia: Creativity as an educational and scientific tool*. Retrieved from https://www.mfa.is/media/nordurlandaskrifstofa/NordBio-faktaark-Biophilia.pdf

Nordlund, C. (2013). Waldorf education: Breathing creativity. *Art Education, 66*(2), 13–19.

Novakowski, J. (2015). *Reggio-inspired mathematics: Richmond School District #38*. La Vergne, TN: Lightning Source Inc.

Obesity Action Coalition. (2016). *What is childhood obesity?* Retrieved from http://www.obesityaction.org/understanding-obesity-in-children/what-is-childhood-obesity

Ogunyemi, F. T. (2015). Promoting constructivist early childhood education in a post-modernist era: Challenges for Nigeria. *International Journal for Cross-disciplinary Subjects in Education, 5*(2), 2494–2503.

Oliver, S. J., & Klugman, E. (2004). Speaking out for play-based learning: Becoming an effective advocate for play in the early childhood classroom. *Child Care Information Exchange, 155*, 22–25.

Oncu, E. C. (2015). Preschoolers' usage of unstructured materials as play materials divergently. *Education Journal, 4*(1), 9–14. Retrieved from http://www.sciencepublishinggroup.com/journal/paperinfo.aspx?journalid=196&doi=10.11648/j.edu.20150401.13

Ontario Ministry of Education. (2013). *Ontario's early years policy framework*. Toronto, ON: Author. Retrieved from http://www.edu.gov.on.ca/childcare/OntarioEarlyYears.pdf

Ontario Ministry of Education. (2014). *How does learning happen? Ontario's pedagogy for the early years*. Toronto, ON: Queen's Printer.

Ontario Ministry of Education. (2016). *The kindergarten program 2016*. Retrieved from https://www.ontario.ca/document/kindergarten-program-2016

Oostermeijer, M., Boonen, A. J., & Jolles, J. (2014). The relation between children's constructive play activities, spatial ability, and mathematical word problem-solving performance: A mediation analysis in sixth-grade students. *Frontiers in Psychology, 5*.

Oppermann, E., Anders, Y., & Hachfeld, A. (2016). The influence of preschool teachers' content knowledge and mathematical ability beliefs on their sensitivity to mathematics in children's play. *Teaching and Teacher Education, 58*, 174–184.

Opree, S. J., Buijzen, M., van Reijmersdal, E. A., & Valkenburg, P. M. (2014). Children's advertising exposure, advertised product desire, and materialism: A longitudinal study. *Communication Research, 41*(5), 717–735.

Ostroff, W. (2012). *Understanding how young children learn: Bringing the science of child development to the classroom*. Retrieved from https://www.amazon.ca/Understanding-How-Young-Children-Learn-ebook/dp/B00916USOM#reader_B00916USOM

Ott, J. N. (1976). Influence of fluorescent lights on hyperactivity and learning disabilities. *Journal of Learning Disabilities, 9*(7), 417–422.

Otten, J. J., Hirsch, T., & Lim, C. (2017). Factors influencing the food purchases of early care and education providers. *Journal of the Academy of Nutrition and Dietetics, 117*(5), 725–734.

Oudeyer, P., & Kaplan, F. (2007). The progress-drive hypothesis: An interpretation of early imitation. In K. Dautenhahn & C. Nehaniv (Eds.), *Models and mechanisms of imitation and social learning: Behavioural, social and communication dimensions* (pp. 361–377). Cambridge, UK: Cambridge University Press.

Paciga, K. A., & Quest, M. (2017). It's hard to wait: Effortful control and story understanding in adult-supported e-book reading across the early years. *Journal of Literacy and Technology, 18*(1).

Pacini-Ketchabaw, V., & Nxumalo, F. (2015). Unruly raccoons and troubled educators: Nature/culture divides in a childcare centre. *Environmental Humanities, 7*(1), 151–168.

Paley, V. (2001). *In Mrs. Tully's room.* Cambridge, MA: Harvard University Press.

Paley, V. G. (1981). *Wally's stories: Conversations in the kindergarten.* Cambridge, MA: Harvard University Press.

Paley, V. G. (1986). On listening to what the children say. *Harvard Educational Review, 56*(2), 122–132.

Paley, V. G. (1990). *The boy who would be a helicopter: The uses of storytelling in the classroom.* Cambridge, MA: Harvard University Press.

Paley, V. G. (2004). *A child's work: The importance of fantasy play.* Chicago, IL: University of Chicago Press.

Parachute. (2017). http://www.parachutecanada.org/

Parikh, M. (2012). Technology and young children: New tools and strategies for teachers and learners. *Young Children, 67*(3), 10–13.

Parnell, W. A., & Bartlett, J. (2012). iDocument: How smartphones and tablets are changing documentation in preschool and primary classrooms. *Young Children, 67*(3), 50–57.

Parten, M. B. (1932). Social participation among pre-school children. *The Journal of Abnormal and Social Psychology, 27*(3), 243.

ParticipACTION. (2015). *The biggest risk is keepings kids indoors: The 2015 ParticipACTION report card on physical activity for children and youth.* Toronto, ON: Author.

Pascal, C. E. (2009). *With our best future in mind: Implementing early learning in Ontario: Report to the premier by the special advisor on early learning.* Toronto, ON: Government of Ontario.

Payler, J., Georgeson, J., & Wong, S. (2016). Young children shaping interprofessional practice in early years settings: Towards a conceptual framework for understanding experiences and participation. *Learning, Culture and Social Interaction, 8,* 12–24.

Pear Cohen, E., & Gainer, R. (1984). *Art: Another language for learning.* New York, NY: Schoken Books.

Pearce, A., Kirk, C., Cummins, S., Collins, M., Elliman, D., Connolly, A. M., & Law, C. (2009). Gaining children's perspectives: A multiple method approach to explore environmental influences on healthy eating and physical activity. *Health and Place, 15*(2), 614–621.

Peirson, L., Fitzpatrick-Lewis, D., Morrison, K., Ciliska, D., Kenny, M., Usman, M., & Raina, P. (2015). Prevention of overweight and obesity in children and youth: A systematic review and meta-analysis. *CMAJ Open, 3*(1), e23–e33.

Pence, A., & Pacini-Ketchabaw, V. (2008). Discourses on quality care: The "investigating quality" project and the Canadian experience. *Contemporary Issues in Early Childhood, 9*(3), 241–255.

Penn, H. (2005). *Unequal childhoods: Young children's lives in poor countries.* London, UK: Routledge.

Penner-Wilger, M., & Anderson, M. L. (2013). The relation between finger gnosis and mathematical ability: Why redeployment of neural circuits best explains the finding. *Frontiers in Psychology, 4.*

Perry, B. D. (2004). *Maltreatment and the developing child: How early childhood experience shapes child and culture.* Inaugural lecture at the Margaret McCain Lecture Series. Retrieved from http://www.hopereinstherapy.com/pdfs/perry.pdf

Perry, R. (1997). *Teaching practice: A guide for early childhood students.* London, UK: Routledge.

Petersen, L., & Levine, S. (2014). Early block play predicts conceptual understanding of geometry and mathematical equivalence in elementary school. *SILC Showcase,* September. http://bit.ly/1nwuS4Q

Petruta-Maria, C. (2015). The role of art and music therapy techniques in the educational system of children with special problems. *Procedia-Social and Behavioral Sciences, 187,* 277–282.

Phillips, D., Austin, L. J., & Whitebook, M. (2016). The early care and education workforce. *The Future of Children, 26*(2), 139–158.

Phillipson, S., Sullivan, P., & Gervasoni, A. (2017). Engaging families as the first mathematics educators of children. In *Engaging Families as Children's First Mathematics Educators* (pp. 3–14). Singapre: Springer Singapore.

Physical & Health Education Canada (PHE). (2013). http://www.phecanada.ca/

Piaget, J. (1928). *Judgment and reasoning in the child.* London, UK: Routledge & Kegan Paul. (Original work published 1923.)

Piaget, J. (1952). *The origins of intelligence in children.* New York, NY: International Universities Press.

Piaget, J. (1962). *Play, dreams and imitation in childhood.* New York, NY: W. W. Norton.

Piaget, J. (1970). *Science of education and the psychology of the child.* (D. Coltman, Trans.). New York, NY: Viking.

Piaget, J. (1974). *Understanding causality.* New York, NY: W. W. Norton. (Original work published 1971.)

Piasta, S. B., Pelatti, C. Y., & Miller, H. L. (2014). Mathematics and science learning opportunities in preschool classrooms. *Early Education and Development, 25*(4), 445–468.

Plowman, L. (2016). Learning technology at home and preschool. In N. J. Rushby & D. W. Surry (Eds.), *The Wiley handbook of learning technology* (pp. 96–112). Hoboken, NJ: Wiley Blackwell.

Plowman, L., & McPake, J. (2013). Seven myths about young children and technology. *Childhood Education, 89*(1), 27–33.

Plowman, L., McPake, J., & Stephen, C. (2010). The technologisation of childhood? Young children and technology in the home. *Children & Society, 24*(1), 63–74.

Plowman, L., & Stephen, C. (2005). Children, play, and computers in pre-school education. *British Journal of Educational Technology, 36*(2), 145–157.

Plympton, P., Conway, S., & Epstein, K. (2000, June). Daylighting in schools: Improving student performance and

health at a price schools can afford. Paper presented at the American Solar Energy Society Conference, Madison, WI.
Poest, C. A., Williams, J. R., Witt, D. D., & Attwood, M. E. (1990). Challenge me to move: Large muscle development in young children. *Young Children, 45*, 4–10.
Poole, H. G. (2016). Rainstorm activities for early childhood music lessons inspired by teachable moments. *General Music Today, 30*(1), 11–15.
Portelance, D. J., Strawhacker, A. L., & Bers, M. U. (2016). Constructing the ScratchJr programming language in the early childhood classroom. *International Journal of Technology and Design Education, 26*(4), 489–504.
Potvin, P., & Hasni, A. (2014). Interest, motivation and attitude towards science and technology at K–12 levels: A systematic review of 12 years of educational research. *Studies in Science education, 50*(1), 85–129.
Prairie, A. P. (2013). Supporting sociodramatic play in ways that enhance academic learning. *YC Young Children, 68*(2), 62.
Prellwitz, M., & Skar, L. (2007). Usability of playgrounds for children with different abilities. *Occupational Therapy International, 14*(3), 144–155.
Prensky, M. (2001). Digital natives, digital immigrants: Part 1. *On the Horizon, 9*(5), 1–6.
Pressley, M., & Allington, R. L. (2014). *Reading instruction that works: The case for balanced teaching*. New York, NY: Guilford Press.
Provenzo, E. F., & Brett, A. (1983). *The complete block book*. Syracuse, NY: Syracuse University Press.
Przybylski, A. K. (2014). Electronic gaming and psychosocial adjustment. *Pediatrics, 134*(3), e716–e722.
Public Health Agency of Canada. (2016). http://www.phac-aspc.gc.ca/index-eng.php
Pushor, D. (2007). Welcoming parents: Educators as guest hosts on school landscapes. *Education Canada, 47*(4), 6–11.
Pye, K. (2013). *Childcare practitioners' perceptions of risk taking in early learning programs* (Unpublished honors thesis). Mount Saint Vincent University, Halifax, NS.
Qu, L., Shen, P., Chee, Y. Y., & Chen, L. (2015). Teachers' theory-of-mind coaching and children's executive function predict the training effect of sociodramatic play on children's theory of mind. *Social Development, 24*(4), 716–733.
Radesky, J. S., Schumacher, J., & Zuckerman, B. (2015). Mobile and interactive media use by young children: The good, the bad, and the unknown. *Pediatrics, 135*(1), 1–3.
Rafal, C. T. (1996). From co-construction to takeovers: Science talk in a group of four girls. *The Journal of the Learning Sciences, 5*(3), 279–293.
Rajshree. (2012). Themes of postmodern education. *International Journal of Scientific and Research Publications, 2*(12).
Ramani, G. B., Zippert, E., Schweitzer, S., & Pan, S. (2014). Preschool children's joint block building during a guided play activity. *Journal of Applied Developmental Psychology, 35*(4), 326–336.
Ramasubbu, S. (2014). *A close look at the online spending behaviour of children*. Retrieved from http://www.huffingtonpost.com/suren-ramasubbu/a-close-look-at-the-online-spendiong-behaviour-of-children_b_6036106.html
Raphael, D. (2014). Social determinants of children's health in Canada: Analysis and implications. *International Journal of Child, Youth and Family Studies, 5*(2), 220–239.
Reicher, D. (2000). Nature's design rules: Leading the way toward energy-efficient schools. *Learning by Design*. Retrieved from http://www.asbj.com/ibd/2000/00inprint/00reicher.html
Reifel, S., & Greenfield, P. M. (1982). Structural development in a symbolic medium: The representational use of block constructions. In G. E. Forman (Ed.), *Action and thought: From sensorimotor schemes to symbolic operations* (pp. 203–233). Cambridge, MA: Academic Press.
Reys, R. E., Lindquist, M., Lambdin, D. V., & Smith, N. L. (2014). *Helping children learn mathematics*. Hoboken, NJ: John Wiley & Sons.
Richards, J. C., & Rodgers, T. S. (2014). *Approaches and methods in language teaching*. Cambridge, MA: Cambridge University Press.
Ridgers, N. D., Knowles, Z. R., & Sayers, J. (2012). Encouraging play in the natural environment: A child-focused case study of Forest School. *Children's Geographies 10*(1), 49–65.
Rinaldi, C. (1998). Projected curriculum constructed through documentation—Progettazione. In C. P. Edwards, L. Gandini, & G. E. Forman (Eds.), *The hundred languages of children: The Reggio Emilia approach—Advanced reflections* (pp. 113–125). New York, NY: Ablex Publishing.
Rinaldi, C. (2006). Documentation and research. In *In Dialogue with Reggio Emilia: Listening, researching and learning* (pp. 97–101). New York, NY: Routledge.
Rinck, M. (2004). *The prince child*. Smyrna, TN: Lemniscaat USA.
Rivera, F. (2015). The distributed nature of pattern generalization. *PNA, 9*(3), 165–191.
Robertson, N. (2016). The complexity of preschool children's dramatic play behavior and play styles in Australia: A mixed methods study. *Asia-Pacific Journal of Research in Early Childhood Education, 10*(2), 71–92.
Rogers, A., & Russo, S. (2003). Blocks: A commonly encountered play activity in the early years, or a key to facilitating skills in science, math and technology. *Investigating, 19*(1), 17–21.
Romero, M. S., García, E. A., & Jiménez, G. A. (2015). *Children, spaces and identity*. Oxford, UK: Casemate Publishers.
Roopnarine, J. L., & Davidson, K. L. (2015). Parent-child play across cultures. *The Handbook of the Study of Play, 2*, 85.
Rosales, A. (2015). *Mathematizing: An emergent math curriculum approach for young children*. St. Paul, MN: Redleaf Press.
Rosenblum, S., Waissman, P., & Diamond, G. W. (2017). Identifying play characteristics of pre-school children with developmental coordination disorder via parental questionnaires. *Human Movement Science, 53*, 5–15.
Roskos, K. A., Christie, J. F., & Richgeis, D. J. (2003). The essentials of early literacy instruction. *Young Children, 58*(2), 53–60.
Ross, M. (2000). *Sandbox scientist: Real science activities for little kids*. Chicago, IL: Chicago Review Press

Rost, M., & Candlin, C. N. (2014). *Listening in language learning*. New York, NY: Routledge.

Rubin, K. H., Fein, G. G., & Vandenberg, B. (1983). Play. *Handbook of Child Psychology, 4*, 693–774.

Rubin, L. (2013). *To look closely: Science and literacy in the natural world*. Portland, ME: Stenhouse Publishers.

Russ, S. W., & Wallace, C. E. (2013). Pretend play and creative processes. *American Journal of Play, 6*(1), 136.

Russell, B. M. (2015). Supporting play and executive function: It's how children learn. *Texas Child Care Quarterly, 29*(3). Retrieved from http://www.childcarequarterly.com/pdf/winter15_play.pdf

Ryan, S., & Grieshaber, S. J. (Eds.). (2005). Practical transformations and transformational practices: Globalization, postmodernism, and early childhood education. *Advances in Early Education and Day Care, 14*.

Ryan, K., Woytovech, C. J., Bruya, L., Woytovech, A., Shumate, B., Malkusak, A., & Sievers, J. A. (2012). Loose parts: The collaboration process for a school playground. *Journal of Kinesiology & Wellness, 1*.

Salonius-Pasternak, D. E., & Gelfond, H. S. (2005). The next level of research on electronic play: Potential benefits and contextual influences for children and adolescents. *Human Technology: An Interdisciplinary Journal on Humans in ICT Environments*. Jyväskylä, Finland: University of Jyväskylä, Agora Center.

Sandseter, E. (2016, June 14). *Risky play? Adventurous play? Challenging play?* Retrieved from https://ellenbeatehansensandseter.com/

Sandseter, E., & Kennair, L. (2011). Children's risky play from an evolutionary perspective: The anti-phobic effects of thrilling experiences. *Evolutionary Psychology, 9*(2), 257–284.

Sandseter, E. B. H. (2007). Risky play among four- and five-year-old children in preschool. *Vision into practice: Making equality a reality in the lives of young children* (pp. 248–256).

Sandseter, E. B. H., & Sando, O. J. (2016). "We don't allow children to climb trees": How a focus on safety affects Norwegian children's play in early-childhood education and care settings. *American Journal of Play, 8*(2), 178.

Santer, J., & Griffiths, C. (2007). *Free play in early childhood: A literature review*. London, UK: National Children's Bureau.

Santrock, J. (2010). *Adolescence* (13th ed.). New York, NY: McGraw-Hill.

Santrock, J. (2015). *A topical approach to lifespan development*. Columbus, OH: McGraw-Hill Higher Education.

Sarlo, C. A. (2013). *Poverty: Where do we draw the line?* Fraser Institute. Retrieved from https://ssrn.com/abstract=2354442

Sawyer, R. K. (1997). *Pretend play as improvisation: Conversation in the preschool classroom*. Mahwah, NJ: Lawrence Erlbaum Associates.

Scarlett, W., & New, R. (2007). Play. In R. New & M. Cochran (Eds.), *Early childhood education: An international encyclopedia* (Vol. 3, pp. 626–633). Westport, CT: Praeger.

Schön, D. A. (1996). *Educating the reflective practitioner: Toward a new design for teaching and learning in the professions*. San Francisco, CA: Jossey-Bass.

Schwarz, T., & Luckenbill, J. (2012). Let's get messy! Exploring sensory and art activities with infants and toddlers. *YC Young Children, 67*(4), 26.

Scott, E. (2008). *Your child and stress: Causes of stress in your child's environment*. Retrieved from http://stress.about.com/od/studentstress/a/school_anxiety_4Htm

Seagoe, M. V. (1970). An instrument for the analysis of children's play as an index of degree of socialization. *Journal of School Psychology, 8*(2), 139–144.

Shanahan, T. (2016). Relationships between reading and writing development. In C. A. MacArthur, S. Graham, & J. Fitzgerald (Eds.), *Handbook of writing research*. New York, NY: Guilford Publications.

Shanker, S. (2016). *Self-reg: How to help your child (and you) break the stress cycle and successfully engage with life*. New York, NY: Penguin Random House.

Sharifnia, E., Vidiksis, R., Orr, J., Dominguez, X., Goldstein, M., & Kamdar, D. (2015). Developing preschool scientists: Identifying best practices for using tablets to support early science teaching and learning. In *Society for Information Technology & Teacher Education International Conference* (pp. 1745–1750). Waynesville, NC: Association for the Advancement of Computing in Education (AACE).

Siegel, D. J. (2016). *Mind: A journey to the heart of being human*. New York, NY: W. W. Norton & Company, Inc.

Sim, S. S., Berthelsen, D., Walker, S., Nicholson, J. M., & Fielding-Barnsley, R. (2014). A shared reading intervention with parents to enhance young children's early literacy skills. *Early Child Development and Care, 184*(11), 1531–1549.

Siraj, I., & Asani, R. (2015). The role of sustained shared thinking, play and metacognition in young children's learning. In S. Robson & S. Flannery Quinn (Eds), *International Handbook of Young Children's Thinking and Understanding* (pp. 403–415). London, UK: Routledge.

Siraj-Blatchford, I. (2009). Conceptualising progression in the pedagogy of play and sustained shared thinking in early childhood education: A Vygotskian perspective. *Education and Child Psychology, 26*(2), 77–89.

Skebo, C. M., Lewis, B. A., Freebairn, L. A., Tag, J., Ciesla, A. A., & Stein, C. M. (2013). Reading skills of students with speech sound disorders at three stages of literacy development. *Language, Speech, and Hearing Services in Schools, 44*(4), 360–373.

Skinner, B. F. (1957). *Verbal behavior*. Englewood Cliffs, NJ: Prentice-Hall.

Slater J., Tierney A., & Kraus N. (2013). At-risk elementary school children with one year of classroom music instruction are better at keeping a beat. *PLoS ONE, 8*(10). Retrieved from https://www.ncbi.nlm.nih.gov/pmc/articles/PMC3795075/

Smilansky, S. (1968). *The effects of sociodramatic play on disadvantaged preschool children*. New York, NY: Wiley and Sons, Inc.

Smilansky, S., & Shefatya, L. (1990). *Facilitating play: A medium for promoting cognitive, socio-emotional, and academic development in young children*. MD: Psychosocial & Educational Publications.

Smirnova, E. O., & Riabkova, I. A. (2016). Psychological features of the narrative-based play of preschoolers today. *Journal of Russian & East European Psychology, 53*(2), 40–55.

Smith, P. K., Cowie, H., & Blades, M. (2015). *Understanding children's development*. Chichester, UK: John Wiley & Sons.

Smith, S., Willms, D. G., & Johnson, N. A. (1997). *Nurtured by knowledge: Learning to do participatory action research*. Ottawa, ON: IDRC.

Sobel, D. (2014). Learning to walk between the raindrops: The value of nature preschools and forest kindergartens. *Children Youth and Environments, 24*(2), 228–238.

Sobel, D., & Larimore, R. (2016). *Nature cements the new learning: A case study of expanding a nature-based early childhood program from preschool into the K–5 curriculum in public schools in Midland, Michigan*. Keene, NH: Antioch University New England.

Solly, K. S. (2015). *Risk, challenge and adventure in the early years: A practical guide to exploring and extending learning outdoors*. New York, NY: Routledge.

Sousa, D. A. (2014). *How the brain learns to read* (2nd ed.). Thousand Oaks, CA: Corwin Press.

Sousa, D. A. (2016). *How the special needs brain learns*. Thousand Oaks, CA: Corwin Press.

Spencer, H. (1896). *The principles of psychology (Los principios de la sicología)*. New York, NY: Appleton and Co.

Sperry Smith, S. (2009). *Early childhood mathematics* (2nd ed.). Boston, MA: Allyn & Bacon/Pearson.

Šramová, B. (2014). Media literacy and marketing consumerism focused on children. *Social Behavioral Sciences, 141*, 1025–1030.

Stadler, M. A., & Ward, G. C. (2005). Supporting the narrative development of young children. *Early Childhood Education Journal, 33*(2), 73–80.

Staempfli, M. (2009). Reintroducing adventure into children's outdoor play environments. *Environment and Behaviour, 41*(2), 268–280.

Stankovic, D., Tanic, M., Kostic, A., Vrecic, S., Kekovic, A., Cekic, N., . . . Vrecic, S. (2015). Resurgence of indoor environment of preschool building. *Procedia Engineering, 117*, 737–750.

Statistics Canada. (2013). *CANSIM 202-0802: Persons in low income families*. Retrieved from http://www12.statcan.gc.ca/census-recensement/2013/dp-pd/index-eng.cfm

Statistics Canada. (2016). http://www12.statcan.gc.ca/census-recensement/2016/dp-pd/index-eng.cfm

Statistics Canada. (2017). http://www.statcan.gc.ca/eng/start.

Stokes, S. (2017). Just relax? Understanding the self-regulation needs and strategies for success for students with autism spectrum disorder. *Closing the Gap*. Retrieved from https://www.closingthegap.com/article/just-relax-understanding-self-regulation-needs-strategies-success-students-autism-spectrum-disorder/

Stokrocki, M. (1988). The development of children through clay modeling, *School Arts, 57*(9), 34–35.

Storli, R., & Sandseter, E. B. H. (2015). Preschool teachers' perceptions of children's rough-and-tumble play (R&T) in indoor and outdoor environments. *Early Child Development and Care, 185*(11–12), 1995–2009.

Strong-Wilson, T., & Ellis, J. (2007). Children and place: Reggio Emilia's environment as third teacher. *Theory into Practice, 46*(1), 40–47.

Sundin, B. (1995). *Children's musical development*. Stockholm, Sweden: Liber.

Sutterby, J. A., Frost, J. A., & Frost, B. (2006). *Play behavior on a playground designed for upper elementary children*. Unpublished industry report.

Sutton, M. J. (2011). In the hand and mind: The intersection of loose parts and imagination in evocative settings for young children. *Children Youth and Environments, 21*(2), 408–424.

Sutton-Smith, B. (1997). *The ambiguity of play*. Cambridge, MA: Harvard University Press.

Swim, T. J., & Merz, A. H. (2016). Professional dispositions of early childhood educators. In D. Couchenour & J. K. Chrisman (Eds.), *The Sage encyclopedia of contemporary early childhood education*. Thousand Oaks, CA: Sage Publications Inc.

Szabó, M. K. (2014). EPA-0996–Sensory-perceptual experiences and object play in autism spectrum disorder. *European Psychiatry, 29*, 1.

Szekely, I. (2015). *Playground innovations and art teaching*. Art Education 37–42. Retrieved from http://www.tandfonline.com/doi/pdf/10.1080/00043125.2015.11519304

Tannock, M. T. (2008). Rough and tumble play: An investigation of the perceptions of educators and young children. *Early Childhood Education Journal, 35*(4), 357–361.

Taylor, B. (2017). Toward reconciliation: What do calls to action mean for early childhood education? *Journal of Childhood Studies, 42*(1), 48–53.

Tepylo, D. H., Moss, J., & Stephenson, C. (2015). A developmental look at a rigorous block play program. *YC Young Children, 70*(1), 18.

Thaichon, P. (2017). Consumer socialization process: The role of age in children's online shopping behavior. *Journal of Retailing and Consumer Services, 34*, 38–47.

Tippett, C. D., & Milford, T. M. (2017). Findings from a pre-kindergarten classroom: Making the case for STEM in early childhood education. *International Journal of Science and Mathematics Education, 1*(15), 67–86.

Tobin, K. G. (2006). *Doing educational research* (Vol. 1). Rotterdam, Netherlands: Sense Publishers.

Tokarz, B. (2008). Block play: It's not just for boys anymore. *Exchange Press, 181*, 68.

Tolley, K. (2014). *The science education of American girls: A historical perspective*. New York, NY: Routledge.

Tompkins, G., Campbell, R., Green, D., & Smith, C. (2014). *Literacy for the 21st century*. Melbourne, Australia: Pearson Australia.

Tomporowski, P., McCullick, B., & Pesce, C. (2015). *Enhancing children's cognition with physical activity games*. Champaign, IL: Human Kinetics.

Topal, C. W., & Gandini, L. (1999). *Beautiful stuff! Learning with found materials*. Oakland, CA: University of California Press.

Tough, J. (2012). *The development of meaning: A study of children's use of language* (Vol. 118). New York, NY: Routledge.

Tough, P. (2009). Can the right kinds of play teach self-control? The school issue: Preschool. *New York Times*, September 27. Retrieved from http://www.skatekidsonline.com/parents_teachers/Vygotsky_Can_the_Right_Play_Help_Updated.pdf

Tovey, H. (2007). *Playing outdoors: Spaces and places, risk and challenge*. Maidenhead, UK: Open University Press.

Tremblay, M. S., Gray, C., Babcock, S., Barnes, J., Bradstreet, C. C., Carr, D., . . . & Herrington, S. (2015). Position statement on active outdoor play. *International Journal of Environmental Research and Public Health*, 12(6), 6475–6505.

Trister-Dodge, D., Colker, L., & Heroman, C. (2014). *The creative curriculum for preschoolers*. Washington, DC: Teaching Strategies.

Truth and Reconciliation Commission of Canada (TRC). (2015). *Truth and Reconciliation Commission of Canada: Calls to action*. Retrieved from: http://www.trc.ca/websites/trcinstitution/File/2015/Findings/Calls_to_Action_English2.pdf

Turbert, D. (2014). *Sunglasses: Protection from UV eye damage*. Retrieved from https://www.aao.org/eye-health/glasses-contacts/sunglasses-3

Twain, M. (1876). *The adventures of Tom Sawyer*. Leipzig, Germany: Leipzig, Bernhard, Tauchnitz.

Ullrich, H. (2014). *Rudolf Steiner*. London, UK: Bloomsbury Publishing.

Upitis, R. (2005). Architecture, complexity science, and schooling in the early years. Hawaii International Conference on Arts and Humanities. Unpublished manuscript.

U.S. Department of Education. (2016). https://www.ed.gov/

U.S. Department of Health and Human Services. (2016). https://www.hhs.gov/

Van Hoorn, J., Nourot, P., Scales, B., & Alward, K. (2011). *Play at the center of the curriculum* (5th ed.). New York, NY: Prentice-Hall.

Van Hoorn, J., Nourot, P. M., Scales, B., & Alward, K. R. (2007). *Play at the center of the curriculum* (4th ed.). Upper Saddle River, NJ: Pearson Merrill/Prentice Hall.

Vasta, R., Miller, S. A., & Ellis, S. (2004). *Child psychology* (4th ed.). Hoboken, NJ: Wiley.

Vecchi, V. (2010). *Art and creativity in Reggio Emilia: Exploring the role and potential of ateliers in early childhood education*. New York, NY: Routledge.

Verdine, B. N., Golinkoff, R. M., Hirsh-Pasek, K., Newcombe, N. S., Filipowicz, A. T., & Chang, A. (2014). Deconstructing building blocks: Preschoolers' spatial assembly performance relates to early mathematical skills. *Child Development*, 85(3), 1062–1076.

Voogt, J., & McKenney, S. (2017). TPACK in teacher education: Are we preparing teachers to use technology for early literacy? *Technology, Pedagogy and Education*, 26(1), 69–83.

Vygotsky, L. (1978). Interaction between learning and development. In M. Gauvain & M. Cole (Eds.), *Readings on the development of children* (pp. 34–40). New York, NY: Scientific American Books.

Vygotsky, L. S. (1967). Play and its role in the mental development of the child. *Soviet Psychology*, 5, 6–18.

Vygotsky, L. S. (1976). Play and its role in the mental development of the child. In J. Bruner, A. Jolly, & K. Sylva (Eds.), *Play: Its role in development and evolution*. New York, NY: Penguin.

Vygotsky, L. S. (1978). *Mind in society: The development of higher psychological processes*. Cambridge, MA: Harvard University Press.

Vygotsky, L. S. (1980). *Mind in society: The development of higher psychological processes*. Cambridge, MA: Harvard University Press.

Vygotsky, L.S. (1981). The development of higher forms of attention in childhood. In J.V. Vertsch (Ed.), The conept of activity in Soviet psyhology (pp. 189-240). Armonk, NY:Sharpe.

Vygotsky, L. S. (2004). Imagination and creativity in childhood. *Journal of Russian & East European Psychology*, 42(1), 7–97.

Wagner, T., & Compton, R. A. (2015). *Creating innovators: The making of young people who will change the world*. New York, NY: Simon and Schuster.

Waite, S., Wickett, K., & Huggins, V. (2014). Risky outdoor play: Embracing uncertainty in pursuit of learning. In T. Maynard & J. Waters (Eds.), *Outdoor play in the early years* (pp. 71–85). Maidenhead, UK: Open University Press.

Waite-Stupiansky, S. (1997). *Building understanding together: A constructivist approach to early childhood education*. Boston, MA: Cengage Learning.

Wang, Q. E., Myers, M. D., & Sundaram, D. (2013). Digital natives and digital immigrants. *Business & Information Systems Engineering*, 5(6), 409–419.

Ward, S., Blanger, M., Donovan, D., Vatanparast, H., Muhajarine, N., Engler-Stringer, R., . . . Carrier, N. (2017). Association between childcare educators' practices and preschoolers' physical activity and dietary intake: A cross-sectional analysis. *BMJ Open*, 7, e013657.

Wardle, F. (2007). Rethinking early childhood practices. In K. M. Paciorek (Ed.), *Annual editions: Early childhood education 08/09* (29th ed., p. 104). New York, NY: McGraw-Hill Companies, Inc.

Wasserman, L. H., & Zambo, D. (2013). *Early childhood and neuroscience: Links to development and learning*. New York, NY: Springer.

Weber, E. (1984). *Ideas influencing early childhood education: A theoretical analysis*. New York, NY: Teachers College Press.

Wee, B. S. C., & Anthamatten, P. (2014). Using photography to visualize children's culture of play: A socio-spatial perspective. *Geographical Review*, 104(1), 87–100.

Weisberg, D. S., Hirsh-Pasek, K., & Golinkoff, R. M. (2013). Guided play: Where curricular goals meet a playful pedagogy. *Mind, Brain, and Education*, 7(2), 104–112.

Weitzman, E., & Greenberg, J. (2002). *Learning language and loving it*. Toronto, ON: The Hanen Centre.

Welch, G. F. (2015). Singing and vocal development. In G. McPherson (Ed.), *The child as musician: A handbook of musical development* (2nd ed.). New York, NY: Oxford University Press.

Wellhousen, K. (2002). *Outdoor play, every day: Innovative play concepts for early childhood*. Boston, MA: Cengage Learning.

Wenger, E., McDermott, R. A., & Snyder, W. (2002). *Cultivating communities of practice: A guide to managing knowledge*. Cambridge, MA: Harvard Business Press.

Werner, C. D., Linting, M., Vermeer, H. J., & Van IJzendoorn, M. H. (2015). Noise in center-based child care: Associations with quality of care and child emotional wellbeing. *Journal of Environmental Psychology, 42*, 190–201.

Wessel, L. A. (2017). Shifting gears: Engaging nurse practitioners in prescribing time outdoors. *The Journal for Nurse Practitioners, 13*(1), 89–96.

Weyer, M. (2016). 3 things lawmakers can do now for our youngest learners. *State Legislature Magazine*, December. Retrieved from http://www.ncsl.org/bookstore/state-legislatures-magazine/3-things-lawmakers-can-do-now-for-our-youngest-learners.aspx

Whitebread, D., Basilio, M., Kuvalja, M., & Verma, M. (2012). *The importance of play*. Brussels, Belgium: Toy Industries of Europe (TIE).

Whitehurst, G. J., & Lonigan, C. J. (1998). Child development and emergent literacy. *Child Development, 69*(3), 848–872.

Wien, C. A. (2011). Learning to document in Reggio-inspired education. *Early Childhood Research & Practice, 13*(2), n2.

Wilkinson, R. (2015). *Risky play in Icelandic preschools* (Unpublished master's thesis). University of Akureyri, Sólborg, Iceland.

Williams, K. E. (2014). Contemporary cultures of service delivery to families: Implications for music therapy. *The Australian Journal of Music Therapy, 25*, 148–173.

Williams, K. E., Berthelsen, J. M., Nicholson, S., Walker, S., & Abad, V. (2012). The effectiveness of a short-term group music therapy intervention for parents who have a child with a disability. *Journal of Music Therapy, 49*, 23–44.

Willis, J., Weiser, B., & Kirkwood, D. (2014). Bridging the gap: Meeting the needs of early childhood students by integrating technology and environmental education. *International Journal of Early Childhood Environmental Education, 2*(1), 140–155.

Willows, N. D., Hanley, A. J. G., & Delormier, T. (2012). A socioecological framework to understand weight-related issues in Aboriginal children in Canada. *Applied Physiology, Nutrition, and Metabolism, 37*, 1–13.

Wilson, R. A. (2010). Aesthetics and a sense of wonder. *Exchange: The Early Childhood Leader's Magazine*, May–June, 24–26.

Wolfgang, C. H., Stannard, L. L., & Jones, I. (2001). Block play performance among preschoolers as a predictor of later school achievement in mathematics. *Journal of Research in Childhood Education, 15*(2), 173–180.

Wolfgang, C. H., & Wolfgang, M. E. (1992). *School for young children: Developmentally appropriate practice*. Boston, MA: Allyn & Bacon

Wood, D., Bruner, J. S., & Ross, G. (1976). The role of tutoring in problem solving. *Journal of Child Psychology and Psychiatry, 17*(2), 89–100.

Woolfolk, A. (1987). *Educational psychology*. Englewood Cliffs, NJ: Prentice Hall.

Woolley, H., & Lowe, A. (2013). Exploring the relationship between design approach and play value of outdoor play spaces. *Landscape Research, 38*(1), 53–74.

World Health Organization (WHO). (2012). *Population-based approaches to childhood obesity prevention*. Retrieved from http://apps.who.int/iris/bitstream/10665/80149/1/9789241504782_eng.pdf

World Health Organization (WHO). (2016). *World health statistics 2016: Monitoring health for the SDGs sustainable development goals*. Geneva, Switzerland: Author.

World Health Organization. (2017). 10 facts about early child development as a social determinant of health. Retrieved from http://www.who.int/maternal_child_adolescent/topics/child/development/10facts/en

Worth, J. (1990). Developing problem-solving abilities and attitudes. In J. Payne (Ed.), *Mathematics for you the young child* (pp. 39–61). Reston, VA: National Council of Teachers of Mathematics.

Worth, K. (2010). Science in early childhood classrooms: Content and process. *Early Childhood Research & Practice, 12*(2), 1–7.

Wright, F. L. (1957). *A testament*. New York, NY: Harper & Rowe.

Wright, S. (2012). Flipping Bloom's Taxonomy. Retrieved: http://plpnetwork.com/2012/05/15/flipping-blooms-taxonomy/

Yamaha Corporation. (1994). *Creating music for tomorrow: Young musicians speak*. (Videotape). Orange County, CA: Yamaha Corporation of America.

Yavuz, L. C. (2016). The effects of loose parts and nature-based play on creativity in the Montessori early childhood (3–6 year old) classroom. *Masters of Arts in Education Action Research Papers, 141*. Retrieved from http://sophia.stkate.edu/maed/141

Yüksel, D. (2016). *Using songs in teaching English to very young learners* (Master's thesis). Eastern Mediterranean University (EMU)–Doğu Akdeniz Üniversitesi (DAÜ), Cyprus.

Yule, C. U. (2014). *The statistical study of literary vocabulary*. Cambridge, MA: Cambridge University Press.

Zamani, Z. (2012). The comparison of cognitive play affordances within natural and manufactured preschool settings. *Proceedings of the 44th annual conference of the Environmental Design Research Association*. Seattle, WA.

Zurek, A., Torquati, J., & Acar, I. (2014). Scaffolding as a tool for environmental education in early childhood. *International Journal of Early Childhood Environmental Education, 2*(1), 27–57.

Index

Note: Page numbers followed by *f*, *t*, and *b* represent figures, tables, and boxes respectively.

A

Aboriginal children, obesity in, 12–14
   socioecological framework, 13–14, 13*f*
Absolute poverty, 23
Abstraction, 376
Acar, H., 15
Access, 149
Accessibility, 70
Accommodation, 197
Accord on Early Learning and Early Childhood Education, 33
Action research, 471–472, 472*f*
Active engagement, 49–50
Active navigators, categories of, 439
Active places, 178
Active play, 138–144, 314. *See also* Outdoor play
   art, 139
   blocks, 139
   constructive play experience centres, 138
   discovery and science, 139
   early learning teachers
      attitudes and abilities, 141–142
      facilitation roles, 142–144
      roles of, 141*f*
   games with rules, 141
   program schedules, 142
   sociodramatic, 140–141
   woodworking, 139
Active play zone, 131
Adaptability, 199
Adaptation, 66
Adult play, 60
Adults, in children's play
   modeling and exhibiting positive attitudes, 68
   observation and documentation, 69
   participation of, 69–70
   preparing appropriate environments, 69
   promoting play
      in and with nature, 69
      and opportunities for expansive discoveries, 69
The Adventures of Tom Sawyer (Twain), 5
Adventurous play, 125–129. *See also* Risk-taking/risky play
   definition of, 126*f*
   reasons why being essential, 129*f*
Advocacy, 471
Aesthetic appreciation
   music and movement
      experiences with children, 406
   songs presentation, 407–408
      imaginative, 408
      narrative, 408
      potpourri, 408

Aesthetic experience, 223
Aesthetics, 247
Affinity play zones, 131–132
Affinity spaces, 213
Agency, 10, 367
Alphabetic principle, 348
Alphabetic principle, 334
Amanita virosa mushroom, 148
American Academy of Pediatrics, 443
Analyzing play spaces, 134–137, 136*t*
Anthamatten, P., 18
Art
   child development and, 225–231
      cognitive, 227–229
      emotional, 229–231
      physical, 227
      social, 229
   defining, 220–221, 221*f*
   early learning teachers and, 242–247
   open-ended art materials. *See* Open-ended art materials
   outdoor play and, 139
   overview, 218–220
   visual arts in early childhood programs, 221–225
   visual language experiences, principles of, 231–232
Art and child development
Articles, of UN Convention on the Rights of the Child, 9–10
Articulation, 105
Artwork, stages of, 232–235
   clay development, 234–235
   drawing, 233–234
Assessments
   authentic, 92–93
   risk assessment document, 128*t*
   risk–benefit, 128
Assimilation, 197
Association of Canadian Deans of Education, 33, 118
Associative play, 64
Authentic assessment, 92–93
   defined, 93
   traditional observation *vs*., 93, 93*t*
Autism spectrum, 398
Autonomy, 10
Availability, 199

B

Balance, 179
Barnett, L., 6
Barton, E. E., 5
Battiste, M., 18
Behaviour, play spaces affecting, 181–182, 181*t*
Behavioural regulation tool, 443

Behaviourist theory, 322
Bentley, D. F., 220
Big ideas, 82
Biophilia, 123
Block play
   accessories for, 263, 263*f*
   affective domain, 267
   and arts, 271–272
   and cognitive development, 267
   and creativity, 271–272
   defined, 253
   early learning play environments, terms influencing, 282
   early learning teachers' role in. *See* Early learning teachers' role
   and engineering, 270–271
   and gender, 272
   historical perspective, 254
      late-nineteenth-century block systems, 255
      twentieth century, 255–257
   inclusive practice, 272
   and language development, 268, 269*f*
   as learning opportunities for children, 263–272, 266*t*
   and math, 269
   physical skills, 267–268
   and science, 270–271
   stages, 257–259, 258*t*, 259*t*
   types of, 260–262
Blocks, outdoor play and, 139
Bloom, Benjamin, 358
Bloom's taxonomy, 358–359, 358*f*, 359*f*
Bodily-kinesthetic intelligence, 394*t*
Body mass index (BMI), 11–12
Body play, 56
Botany, 385
Boy Who Would Be a Helicopter (Paley), 304
Brain development, 25–28
Brief notes, 99*t*
Bristle blocks, 261
Brittain, W. L., 221
Bronfenbrenner, Urie, 40–43
Brown, E., 232, 234
Bruner, Jerome, 31*t*, 44, 51, 369, 403
Bruner's theoretical construct, 66
Buckley, Helen, 52
Built environment, 14

C

Canadian Association for Young Children (CAYC)
   position statements, 16, 32–33
Canadian Health Measures Survey (CHMS), 12
Canadian Institute of Child Health, 26
Canadian Outdoor Play Working Group, 454

Canadian Position Statement on Active Outdoor Play (Herrington & Pickett), 125
Canadian Standards Association (CSA)
 Children's Playspaces and Equipment Standards, 148
 for equipment, facilities, and surfaces, 147t–148t
 playground safety standards, 115–116, 116t
Cardboard bricks, 262
Cardinality, 376
Caring places, 166–167
Challenging play, 125–129. *See also* Risk-taking/risky play
 definition of, 126f
 reasons why being essential, 129f
Child development and art, 225–231
 cognitive, 227–229
 emotional, 229–231
 physical, 227
 social, 229
Child development and outdoor play, 14–16, 15f, 117–118
 appreciation for, 123–124
 challenging, adventurous, and risky play, 125–129
  definitions of, 126f
  reasons why being essential, 129f
  risk assessment document, 128t
 cognitive development, 119–120
 emotional development, 120–121
 natural light exposure, 122–123, 122f
 physical development and movement, 121–122, 121f
 physiological and psychological development, 16
 play spaces, planning, 129–132
  active zone, 131
  affinity play zones, 131–132
  consideration of, 130f
  experiential play zones, 131
  nature zone, 131
  physical movement zone, 131
  quiet learning and, 131–132
 skills gained, 118f
 social development, 120
 vitamin D, 16
Child-guided discovery, 144
Child-initiated exploration, 143
Children
 behaviour affected by play spaces, 181–182, 181t
 brain development, 25–28, 27f
 conversational roles, 331
 cross-lateral movement, 400
 culture, 18–20, 21t
 development, technology and, 438–442, 438f, 439t
 learning through play, 78–80
 obesity, 11–14
 participation in emerging literacy, 335
 singing progression, 407t
 types of discoveries made through watching, listening, and discussing play with, 102–105
Children's competence, 199
Children's play. *See also* Play
 construction, 157
 discovering and making meaning of, 101, 102t
 duration of, 156
 places of, 158–163. *See also* Play spaces
 sensorimotor, 156
 societal concerns and, 10–25
 symbolic, 156
 types of, 155
Children's Playspaces and Equipment Standards (CSA), 148
Children's rights, 470
A Child's Work (Paley), 337
Child with His or Her Own Agenda, 331
Chomsky, Noam, 322
Christiansen, Ole, 256
Christie, J. F., 4
Chronosystem, 41–43
Circadian rhythms, 16
Circulation patterns, 179
Classical theories, 28, 29t
 practice theory, 65
 recapitulation theory, 65
 recreation/relaxation theory, 65
 surplus energy theory, 65
 themes, 30
Clay, Marie, 333–334
Clay development, 234–235
 dawning realism, 235
 pre-schematic, 234
 schematic, 234
 scribbling, 234
Closed questions, 342
Co-construction, 79
Co-construction of knowledge, 97
Coding, 434, 435b
Cognitive development
 art and, 227–229
 music and movement, 403–404, 403f
 outdoor play and, 119–120
Cognitive-developmental theory, 66
 Bruner's theoretical construct, 66
 Piaget's theory, 66
 Sutton-Smith's theory, 66
Cognitive organizer, for reflective practice, 469f
Co-inquirer, 79
Co-investigator, 79
Cole-Hamilton, I., 5
Colonization, 13
Comenius, John Amos, 29t
Common Sense Media, 17
Communication strategies, 332
Communities of practice, 457–458, 458t
Community attributes, 172–174
Community belonging, 476
Community culture for language and literacy, 343–344
 art centre, 346–347
 blocks, 347
 dramatic play centre, 345
 math and science, 347
 music and movement, 347
 observations, 344–345
 outdoor play, 347
 shared group reading with children, 346
 writing and book centres, 345–346
Community empowerment, 462
Complexity, analyzing play spaces, 136
Complex unit, 136
Computers, 431
 usage, stages of, 432t
Concrete objects, 429
Conflict resolution, 308, 308b
Connection, 198
Consolidated navigators, 439
Constructionist theory, 43
Construction play, 157
Constructive music play, 395
Constructive play, 206
 areas, 138
 stage, 63
Consumerism, 22–23
Contemporary theories, 28, 30–31, 31t
Contextual influences, 348
Convention on the Rights of the Child (CRC), 470
Cooperative-competitive play, 64
Cooperative music play, 395, 402
Cooperative play, 64, 282
Co-playing, 70
Core schema, 198
Cornett, C. E., 220
Counting procedures, 376, 376f
CPU (central processing unit), 447
Creative confidence, 314
Creative movement, 397
Creative play, 207
Creativity
 with art experiences, strategies for encouraging, 238–239
 intelligent materials and, 194
Critical pedagogy, 463
Critical periods, 413
Critical self-awareness, 476
Critical thinking, 464
Critical thinking skills, 111
Cross-lateral movement, 400
Cuffaro, H. K., 194
Cultural artifacts, 80
Cultural attributes, 172–174
Cultural identity, 14
Cultural norms, 20
Culture, 18–20, 21t, 338–339
Curriculum, 455. *See also* Programming/curriculum
 defined, 81
 emergent, 81
 thinking, 80
Curriculum webbing, 447

Index 503

D

Dance, 397
Dawning realism
  clay development, 235
  drawing, 234
Declaration on the Importance of Play (IPA), 8
Decontextualized language, 337, **342**
Delormier, T., 13
Design considerations, for play spaces, 177–179, 178f
  active places, 178
  balance, 179
  circulation patterns, 179
  flex zones, 179
  green space, 177–178
  large-group places, 178–179
  quiet places, 178
  small-group places, 178
  spatial partitioning, 179
Developmentally appropriate, 425
Dewey, John, 29t, 194, 222
Didactic materials, 282
Dietze, B., 16, 18, 93, 112–113, 130, 175, 186, 195, 198, 202
Digital age, 418
Digital divide, 417, 441–442
Digital games, 434
Digital immigrant, 425
Digital native, 425
Directional words, 381
Discovery, outdoor play and, 139
Disequilibrium, 424
Dispositions, 338
Divergent thinking, 192
Documentation. *See* Pedagogical documentation
Dramatic play, 205, 286–287
  adult's participation in, 299–301
  characteristics of, 291–292
  criteria of, 292, 292f
  defined, 289–290
  developmental stages, 292–294, 293t
  early learning environment, 311–314
    guns/war play/superheroes, 312–314
    terms influencing, 314
  examination, questions to support, 302t
  experiences for children in, 295
  formal/scripted, 294
  importance of, 295–298
  informal, 294
  multiple intelligences and, 288, 288f
  music, 395
  observation and documentation, 301
  planning and facilitating, 302–304
  provocations for, 309
  scope of, 289f
  setting up for, 309–310
  story drama, 306–309
    teacher theatre, 307
    Tools of the Mind classroom, 307–309
  story/interpretive drama, 294
  themed areas, 300–301

  theoretical foundation, 287–290, 287f
  time, 310
  types of
    pantomime, 305
    puppets, 306
    story play, 304–305
Drawing stages
  gang, 234
  pre-schematic, 233–234
  schematic, 234
  scribbling, 233
Drew, Walter, 256
Duplo® Blocks, 261

E

Early Learning and Early Childhood Education, 49–50
Early learning teachers' role, 272–282, 273f
  in art experiences, 242–247
  as cheerleader, 341
  children's behaviour, observation/documentation of, 277–280
    anecdotal records, 278–279
    checklists/rubrics, 279, 279t
    conversational notes, 279
    digital documentation, 280
    example of, 278t
  and dialogue with children, 281–282, 281b
  as director, 341
  in dramatic play, 299–301, 300t
  as entertainer, 341
  environmental factors and, 274–275
  as helper, 341
  in inquiry-based environments, 81f
  in language and literacy development, 341–343
  limited skills in music and movement, 411–412
  in music and movement promotion, 408–410, 409b
  observational and documentation tools used by, 412
  in organizing block play space, 276, 277t
  in outdoor math and science, 372–373
  in outdoor play
    attitudes and abilities, 141–142
    developing appreciation for, 123–124, 124f
    facilitation roles, 142–144
    roles of, 141f
  philosophical perspective, determination of, 273–274
  in play, 68–69
  questions helping selection of materials, 195
  reflection and development, 282
  as responsive partner, 341
  role modelling, 280–281
  as social director, 303
  as stage manager, 303
  in technology usage, 442–443, 443f

  choosing applications, 444–445, 445b
  facilitating play, 443–444
  observing children, 445–446
  professional learning and development, 446
  as timekeeper, 341
  as too-quiet teacher, 341
Earth science, 373
E-books, tips for reading, 433
Ecological theory, 40, 43–44
Edgeworth, Richard Lovell, 254
Educators of Reggio Emilia, 158
Electronic devices, 17–18
Emergent curriculum, 81
Emergent curriculum, 456–457, 456f
Emergent literacy, 325
Emergent programming, 105
Emilia, Reggio, 470
Emotional development
  art and, 229–231
  outdoor play and, 120–121
Empowerment, 461–463
  community, 462
  defined, 461
  personal, 462
  resilience, 461–462
  self-efficacy, 461
Enactive stage, cognitive development, 404
Enclosure, 198
English language learners (ELLs), 339
Enveloping, 198
Environment, as third teacher, 157–158
  considerations while designing, 158f
Environmental aesthetics, 168–170
Environmental/ecological systems, 40f
  chronosystem, 41–43
  exosystem, 41
  macrosystem, 41
  mesosystem, 41
  microsystem, 40
Environmental order perspectives and practices, 175t
Environmental quality, measures of, 447
Ephemeral art, 241
Epistemology, 213
Erikson, Erik, 30t, 287
Evidence-based practice, 469
Executive function, 297
Executive functioning skills, 43
Exosystem, 41
Experiential play zones, 131
Expressive language, 325

F

Family literacy, 340
Family rights and engagement, 474–475
Fantasy play, 338
Fawcett, M., 77
Fibonacci, Leonard, 368
Fibonacci sequence, 368

Fight-or-flight response, 172
Flannigan, C., 195
Flexibility, 199
Flexible schedules and order, 174–175, 175*t*
Flex zones, 179
Floor blocks, 260, 261
Fluid materials, 157
Foam blocks, 261
Formal/scripted drama, 294
Form of objects, 182
Fred Rogers Center for Early Learning and Children's Media, 422–423
Free play, 6, 111
Freud, Sigmund, 297
Froebel, Friedrich Wilhelm, 6, 28, 29*t*, 76, 113, 114, 124, 187, 218, 222–223, 254–255
Frost, J. L., 114
Functional music play, 395
Functional/sensorimotor play, 60, 62

G

Gainer, R., 220
Games with rules, 63, 141
Gang stage, of clay development, 234
Gardner, Howard, 31*t*, 394, 403
Genova, P., 51
Gleave, J., 5
Göncü, A., 20
Gotay, C. C., 11
Grammar, 328–329
Graphemes, 334
Green space, 177–178
Grieshaber, S., 76
Guerrero, M. D., 5
Guided interaction, 444
Guided play, 70

H

Hall, G. Stanley, 76, 113
Hanen Centre OWL strategy, 331–335
 language skills and play, 331–332
Hanley, A. J. G., 13
Hatch, J. A., 76
Hawkins, David, 203, 362–363
Hawkins, Frances, 363
Hazards, 126–127. *See also* Risk-taking/risky play
 levels of, 127*t*
Health determinants, 472–473
 WHO facts about, 473*f*
Healthy living and sustainability, 473–474
Healthy risk-taking play, 41
Henderson, J. Y., 18
Hermon, A., 243
Higher-order thinking, 289
High tech, 417
Historical factors, 14
Hoffmann, M. D., 5
Hollow blocks, 262
How Does Learning Happen? (Ontario Ministry of Education), 43, 158

I

Iconic stage, cognitive development, 404
Imagination, 335
Imaginative play, 57
Imaginative song, 408
Imitation, 335
Imitative role play, 292
Inclusivity, technology and, 441
Indigenous families, 459
Individual, 14
Infant, play spaces for, 132
Informal dramatic play, 294
Information age, 418
Information and communication technologies
 coding, 434, 435*b*
 computers, 431, 432*t*
 digital games, 434
 interactive whiteboards, 434
 robotics, 435–436
 tablets, 431–433
In Mrs. Tully's Room (Paley), 305, 337
Inner speech, 325
Inquiry-based learning, 81, 81*f*
Intelligent materials, 194–195
Intentional imaginative play, 59
Interaction, 335
Interactionist theory, 322–323
Interactive whiteboards, 434
Intercultural communication competence, 460–461, 461*f*
International Foundation of Music Research, 398
International Play Association (IPA), 7
 Declaration on the Importance of Play, 8
Interpersonal intelligence, 394
Interpersonal relationships, 14
Interpretation, 89–90
Interpretive drama, 294
Intrapersonal intelligence, 394
Intrinsic motivation, 44–49, 48*t*
Intrinsic play, 55–56
Investigative triggers, 105
Isaacs, Susan, 86
Isenberg, J. P., 62, 66

J

Jalongo, M. R., 62, 66, 246
Jenkins, E., 236
Johnson, J. E., 4

K

Kashin, D., 16, 93, 112–113, 130, 175, 186, 195, 198, 202
Kinesthetic music play, 395
Knowledge
 modes of representation, 369, 369*t*
 networks, 385
 types of, 357, 357*f*
Kostelnik, M., 229
Krishnamurti, J., 246

L

Landscape art, 241
Language
 community culture for, 343–344
 decontextualized, 337, 342
 development. *See* Language development
 expressive, 325
 learning methods, 320, 323–325, 324*f*
 of mathematics, 380–381
  materials and supplies, 381, 382*t*
 play and, 325–327
 pragmatics, 329–330
 receptive, 325
 theoretical frameworks of, 322–323, 322*f*
Language acquisition device (LAD), 322
Language development
 characteristics of, 327–330
 defined, 324
 grammar, 328–329
 play and, 325–327, 332–333
  communication skills, 332
  verbal interaction, 333
 pragmatics, 329–330
 stages of, 330–331, 330*t*
 variations in, 338–340
  culture, 338–339
  English language learners, 339
  family, 339–340
  motivation, 338
 vocabulary, 329
Language of the materials, 194
Large-group places, 178–179
Larimore, R., 38
Late-nineteenth-century block systems, 255
Lawson Foundation, 149, 454
Learning, play and
 active engagement, 49–50
 intrinsic motivation, 44–49, 48*t*
 play as process rather than product, 50–52
Learning journals, 99*t*
LEGO, 256
Levinowitz, L. M., 401
Lewin, Kurt, 471
Life science, 373
Life scripts, 314
Lifter, K., 5
Linguistic intelligence, 394*t*
Listening behaviour, 335
Listening to children
 observation and, 96, 102–105
 responsive play space environment, 165–166
Literacy, 325
 child participation, 335
 community culture for, 343–344
 development
  characteristics of, 333–334
  stages of, 334, 335*f*
  variations in, 338–340

Literacy (*continued*)
  emergent, 325
  environment, setting up, 347–348
  family, 340
  play and language, 325–327
  skills, and play, 335
Literate behaviours, 326–327
The Little Boy (Buckley), 52–53
Locke, John, 29*t*, 254
Logical-mathematical intelligence, 394
Logical-mathematical knowledge, 357, 357*f*
Loose parts
  benefits of, 202*f*
  children's play
    and development with, 195–197, 196*t*
    and learning evolving with, 205–207
    and schemas with, 197–198
  choosing, for early learning environments, 198–200
    considerations for, 199, 199*f*
    outdoors and indoors, 200
  classification of, 190–192, 192*f*
  conceptual understanding of, 187–188
  defined, 115, 186, 188
  early learning teachers and, 209–210, 210*f*
  fixed equipment *vs.*, 201–202, 201*t*
  learning options offered by, 186
  outdoor play, 137–138
  strategies for enhancing use of, 210–212
  theory of, 193–194
  thinking and, 190, 192
  tinkering with, 202–203, 204*t*
  types of, 200*t*
  values of, 192*f*
Low tech, 417
Lowenfeld, V., 221, 232, 234
Lyric content, 408

M

MacLellan, V., 11
Macrosymbolic play, 156
Macrosystem, 41
Make-believe play, 292
Make-Believe Play Practice, 307
Maker movement, 202. *See also* Tinkering
Malaguzzi, Loris, 30*t*, 194, 223, 453
Mann, L., 11
Mardell, B., 78
Martinez, S. L., 202
Maslow, Abraham, 30*t*, 48
Mason, E. J., 5
Master players, 291
Math and science, 355–356
  concept development in, 364–365
  defined, 361–362
  and development, 365–367
  importance of, 362–364
  learning through play, 367–369, 367*f*
  outdoor, role of early learning teachers in, 372–373

  playing, and children's wondering, 369–371
  theoretical foundation, 357–360
    Bloom's taxonomy, 358–359, 358*f*, 359*f*
    knowledge, types of, 357, 357*f*
Mathematical concepts, development of, 375–380
  classification, 379
  comparison, 379
  counting procedures, 376, 376*f*
  geometry and measurement, 377–378
  pattern, 378, 378*f*
  rote counting *vs.* rational counting, 376–377
  sequence, 378
  seriation, 379
  subitizing, 379–380
McNeal, J. U., 22–23
Melodic contour, 408
Mesosystem, 41
Messing about, 362–364, 363*f*, 363*t*
Messy play, 374
Metacognition, 98
Metacommunication, **332**
Microsymbolic play, 156
Microsystem, 40
Modern theories, 28, 29*t*–30*t*, 65–67
  cognitive-developmental theory, 66
  neurobiological theory, 66–67
  psychoanalytic theory, 66
  themes, 30
Moments of science, 371
Montessori, Maria, 5, 29*t*, 187, 254, 255–256, 394
More knowledgeable other (MKO), 77–78
Morin, F., 49, 395
Morphology, 329, 385
Motivation, 338
Motor illiteracy, 121
Motor skills, 40, 56
  art and, 227
  outdoor play and, 121–122, 121*f*
Motoring movement play, 57
Mouse navigators, 439
Movement, 397. *See also* Music and movement
Movement skills. *See* Motor skills
Movement vocabulary, 412, 412*t*
Multimedia, 247
Multiple intelligence, 288, 288*t*
  related to Music and movement, 394, 394*t*
Munroe-Chandler, K., 5
Music and movement
  aesthetic appreciation. *See* Aesthetic appreciation
  autism spectrum, 398
  experience centres, 410–412
    musical instruments, 411
  historical influences of, 393–395
  importance of, 395, 397–399, 399*f*

  child development, 399–400, 400*f*
  cognitive development, 403–404, 403*f*
  psychomotor development, 400–401
  social and emotional development, 402–403
  multiple intelligences related to, 394, 394*t*
  overview, 391–393
  promoting, early learning teachers' role in, 408–410, 409*b*
  sequence with young children, 396–397*t*
Music intelligence, 394*t*
Musical instruments, 411

N

NAEYC. *See* National Association for the Education of Young Children (NAEYC)
Narrative inquiry, 476
Narrative modes of thinking, 66
Narrative songs, 408
Narratives/storytelling, 337–338
National Aboriginal Health Organization (NAHO), 13, 14
National Association for Music Education, 392
National Association for the Education of Young Children (NAEYC), 422
National Childcare Accreditation Council (NCAC), 26
Nativist theory, 322
Natural environment, 149
Naturalistic intelligence, 394
Natural light
  outdoor play and exposure to, 122–123, 122*f*
  as responsive play space environment, 171, 171*f*
Natural loose parts, 190, 191, 192*f*
Natural play space, 124
Natural textures, 182
Nature zone, 131
navigators, categories of, 439
Neill, P., 205
Nesting blocks, 255
Neurobiological theory, 66–67
Nicholson, Simon, 187–188, 193
Noise pollution, 172
Nordlund, C., 223
Novelty preference, 321
Numbers-rich environment, 381–382
Numerosity, 375

O

Obesity, children and, 11–14
  in Aboriginal children, 12–14
    socioecological framework, 13–14, 13*f*
  facts about, 11*t*
Obesity Action Coalition, 11

Observation, 382–383
  concept, 84
  considerations, 85f
  history, 76
  outdoor play, 145–146, 146t
  in past, 76, 77
  pedagogical documentation vs., 91–92, 91f
  play and learning, 80–82
  purpose, 84–85
  questions to be supporting, 85, 86
  science and math connections
    art, 384
    cooking, 384–385
    literacy, 382
    music and movement, 383–384
  skills required for, 84
  types of discoveries, 102–105
  ways of acquiring information, 94–98
    determining metacognition, 98
    developing purposeful observations, 95
    examining children's play patterns and actions, 96
    examining co-construction of knowledge, 96–97
    examining expression of meaning and representation, 97
    examining information from varying perspectives, 95
    involving children and adults, 95
    listening to children, 96
    organizing tools, 95
    recognizing biases and perceptions, 95–96
    reviewing documented observations, 96
One-to-one correspondence, 376
Onlooker play, 64
Open-ended art materials, 239–242
  chalk, 240
  clay, 240
  collage materials, 240
  crayons, 240
  paint, 240
  paper, 240
  sand, 240
  ways to display, 241f
Open-ended questions, 282, 342–343
Open-ended software, 444–445
Operant conditioning, 322
Oppen, Karl, 257
Oral language, 325
Ordered time, 174
Order irrelevance, 376
Ordinality, 375
Orff, Carl, 394
Organisation for Economic Co-operation and Development (OECD), 23
Orientation, 198
Outdoor play, 14–17, 15f, 347. See also Active play
  appreciation for, 123–124
  child development. See Child development and outdoor play
  cognitive development, 119–120
  complexities of, 112–113, 112f
  early learning teachers in
    attitudes and abilities, 141–142
    developing appreciation for, 123–124, 124f
    facilitation roles, 142–144
    roles of, 141f
  emotional development, 120–121
  historical perspective on, 113–117
  materials for, 137–138. See also Loose parts
  and natural light, exposure to, 122–123, 122f
  observation and documentation of, 145–146, 146t
    CSA standard for environment, 147t–148t
    environment examination, 146–148
  physical development and movement, 121–122, 121f
  reasons to observe children during, 101
  skills gained from, 118f
  social development, 120
  spaces, 129–132
    active zone, 131
    affinity play zones, 131–132
    analyzing, 134–137, 136t
    consideration of, 130f
    examining use of, 134
    experiential play zones, 131
    infant, 132
    nature zone, 131
    physical movement zone, 131
    preschool children, 133
    quiet learning and, 131–132
    school-aged children, 133–134
    toddler space, 132–133
  for today and tomorrow, 117
Owens, M., 6
OWL (observing, waiting, and listening) strategy. See Hanen Centre OWL strategy

P

Paley, Vivian, 304–305, 337–338
Pantomime, 305
Parachute, 115
Parallel play, 64, 70
Parquetry blocks, 261
Parten, Mildred
  classifications of social play, 63–64
ParticipACTION, 16
Passive Child, 331
Pearce, A., 18
Pear Cohen, E., 220
Pedagogical documentation, 76, 77, 86–89
  as cyclical process, 89
  observation vs., 91–92, 91f
  outdoor play, 145–146, 146t
  strategies, 88f, 99–101, 99t
  tools of, 88
Pedagogy, 31
Peer play with rules, 59
Persistence in role play, 292
Personal empowerment, 462
Pestalozzi, Johann Heinrich, 29t, 77
Phonics approach, 323–324
Photographs, 99t
Physical development
  art and, 227
  outdoor play and, 121–122, 121f
Physical knowledge, 357, 357f
Physical literacy, 121
Physical movement zone, 131
Physical science, 373
Piaget, Jean, 5, 6, 86, 196, 197, 287–288, 345, 357, 403, 404
  on body play, 56
  cognitive-developmental theory, 66, 119, 187, 197, 229
  perspectives on play, 30t
  stages of play development, 60, 62–63, 62f
    functional/sensorimotor play, 60, 62
    games with rules, 63
    symbolic/dramatic play, 62–63
Picture and alphabet blocks, 261
Pitch, 407
Pitch matching, 407
Play
  brain development and, 25–28, 26f
  characteristics of, 54–56
    active, 54
    child initiated and focused, 54
    episodic, 56
    intrinsic, 55–56
    process oriented, 55
    rule governed, 56
    symbolic and transformational, 55
  consumerism, 22–23
  culture and, 18–20, 21t
  defined, 4–8
  electronic devices and, 17–18
  origin of, 4–8
  overview, 2–4
  poverty, 23–25
  process, 56–60
  societal concerns and, 10–25
  stages and types, 60–65, 61t
  theories and theorists, 28–31, 65–67
  tinkering in, 202–203, 204t
  work vs., 5
Play environment, 8
Play spaces
  behaviour affected by, 181–182, 181t
  cultural and community attributes, 172–174
  designations, 180f
  design considerations, 177–179, 178f
    active places, 178

Play spaces (*continued*)
  balance, 179
  circulation patterns, 179
  flex zones, 179
  green space, 177–178
  large-group places, 178–179
  quiet places, 178
  small-group places, 178
  spatial partitioning, 179
effective, characteristics of, 176–180
for exploration and freedom to play, 173–174
flexible schedules and order, 174–175, 175t
outdoor play, 129–132
  active zone, 131
  affinity play zones, 131–132
  analyzing, 134–137, 136t
  consideration of, 130f
  examining use of, 134
  experiential play zones, 131
  infant, 132
  nature zone, 131
  physical movement zone, 131
  preschool children, 133
  quiet learning and, 131–132
  school-aged children, 133–134
  toddler space, 132–133
perspectives on, 177t
physical play space, 176
traditional, considerations for, 179–180
responsive environments, 163–172
  caring place, 166–167
  characteristics of, 163f
  environmental aesthetics, 168–170
  feeling tone, 164–165, 164f–165f
  listening to children, 165–166
  natural light, 171, 171f
  provocations, 167
  stress-free, 171–172
space, 176–177
Play tutoring, 70
Play unit, 136
Poor diet, 172
Portfolio, 99t
Positional words, 380–381
Positioning, 198
Position Statement on Active Outdoor Play, 32–33
Postmodernism, 458–459
Potential units, 136
Potpourri song, 408
Poverty, 23–25
Power, 10
Power, D., 11
Practice theory, 65
Pragmatics of language, 329–330
Pratt, Caroline, 254, 256
Prentice, R., 243
Pre-schematic stage

clay development, 234
drawing, 233–234
Preschool children
  modes of reader response for, 335
Preschool children, play spaces for, 133
Prestructured play, 6
The Principles of Psychology (Spencer), 393
Process
  defined, 50
  of play, 56–60
  product *vs.*, 50–52
Process-based art, 225
Product
  defined, 50
  play as process *vs.*, 50–52
Professional dispositions, 467–468
  action research, 471–472, 472f
  advocacy, 471
  children's rights, 470
  examples of, 468t
  health determinants, 472–473
    WHO facts about, 473f
  healthy living and sustainability, 473–474
  reflective practice, 468–470
    cognitive organizer for, 469f
Program navigators, 439
Program schedules for outdoor play, 142
Programming/curriculum, 455
  communities of practice, 457–458, 458t
  emergent, 456–457, 456f
  postmodernism, 458–459
Projectile movement, 182
Prop boxes, 309, 309b
PRoPELS acronym, 293
Provocation, 309
Provocations, 31
  defined, 167
  forms of, 167
  in indoor and outdoor environments, 167
Psychoanalytic theory, 66
  repetition, 66
  role switching, 66
Psychomotor development, music and movement, 400–401
Public Health Agency of Canada, 10, 24
Public parks, 117
Puppets, 306

Q

Questions
  closed, 342
  open-ended, 342–343
  thought-provoking, 343
Quiet learning and, 131–132
Quiet places, 178

R

Radial schema, 198
Rational counting, rote counting *vs.*, 376–377

Reactive supervision, 444
Reading Recovery Program, 334
Recapitulation theory, 65
Receptive language, 325
Reconceptualization, in early learning, 463–464
  rethinking practice, 467
  twenty-first-century skills in, 464
  values and beliefs, 464–465
    image concept of, 465–467
Recreation/relaxation theory, 65
Reflective practice, 90–91, **468**–470
  cognitive organizer for, 469f
  core questions, 90–91
Reggio Emilia, 6, 77
  educators of, 81, 86, 158, 218
  environment as the third teacher, 157–158, 158f
  pedagogical documentation, 86, 87
  visual arts in early childhood programs, 223–225
Reggio-inspired programs, 157
Relative poverty, 23
Reluctant Child, 331
Repetition, 66
Representational play, 413
Resilience, 43, 461–462
Responsive play space environments, 163–172
  caring place, 166–167
  characteristics of, 163f
  design considerations, 177–179, 178f
  environmental aesthetics, 168–170
  feeling tone, 164–165, 164f–165f
  listening to children, 165–166
  natural light, 171, 171f
  provocations, 167
  stress-free, 171–172
Rhythm, study of, 401
Riabkova, I. A., 6, 7
Richter Building Block systems, 255
Right to Play, 475, 475f
Risk assessment document, 128t
Risk–benefit assessments, 128
Risk management, 127
Risk reframing, 149
Risk-taking/risky play, 125–129
  definition of, 126f
  reasons why being essential, 129f
  risk assessment document, 128t
Robotics, 435–436
Role switching, 66
Rotation, 198
Rote counting *vs.* rational counting, 376–377
Rousseau, Jean-Jacques, 394
Rule governed play, 56

S

Safe risk, 127, 128
Sand and water play, 374–375
Sand play, 113

Vitamin D, 16
Vocabulary, 329
Vocalization, stages of, 407, 408t
Vocal range, 407
Voice, and empowerment, 461–463
Vygotsky, Lev, 30t, 36, 288, 290–291, 298, 322–323, 325–326, 338, 345, 357, 369

W

Waldorf approach, 223
Wardle, F., 4
Watson, D., 77
Wee, B. S. C., 18
Weikart, David, 30t
Whole language approach, 323
Willows, N. D., 13
Wondering, children, playing and, 369–371
Woodworking, 139
Work *vs.* play, 5
World Health Organization (WHO)
  on health determinants, 472–473, 473f
Written language, 345

Y

Yamaha Corporation philosophy, 398
Young children, scientific method for, 371–372t, 371–380
  early learning teachers' role, 372–373

Z

Zone of proximal development (ZPD), **78**, **264**, 323

Scaffolding, 127, **323,** 334, 369
Schemas, 197–198
Schematic stage
　clay development, 234
　drawing, 234
School-age children
　modes of reader for, 335
School-aged children, play spaces for, 133–134
Science. *See* Math and science
Science, outdoor play and, 139
Scientific inquiry, 361
　setting up environment to, 373–375
Scott, E., 4
Scribbling
　clay development, 234
　drawing, 233, 233*t*
Scripted drama, 294
Self-efficacy, 14, **461**
Self-regulation, 43
Self-regulation skills, 121
Semantics, 329
Sensorimotor play, 60, 62, 156
Sensory integration, 413
Sequence, defined, 378
Sequence words, 381
Seriation, 379
Shanker, S., 46
Shared problem space, 439
Sign language, 348
Simple play unit, 136
Skinner, B. F., 322
Small-group places, 178
Small world play, 213
Smilansky, Sarah, 120
　contributions to stages of play, 63
Smirnova, E. O., 6, 7
Smithrim, K., 220
Sobel, D., 38
Socialable Child, 331
Social and emotional development, music and movement, 402–403
Social-conventional knowledge, 357, 357*f*
Social development
　art and, 229
　outdoor play and, 120
Social director, early learning teacher as, 303
Social isolation, 70
Social play, 206–207
　Parten's classifications of, 63–64
　Seagoe's contributions to, 64–65
Social science, 373
Society, 14
Sociocultural environments, 14
Sociocultural theory, 288
Sociodramatic play, 140–141, 297
　variations in, 298–299
Solitary play, 64
Spatial intelligence, 394*t*
Spatial partitioning, 179

Spatial reasoning, 264
Spencer, Herbert, 393
Šramová, B., 22
Stable order, 376
Stage manager, early learning teacher as, 303
Stager, G. S., 202
Steiner, Rudolph, 29*t*
STEM, 356
Stokrocki, M., 232, 234
Story acting, 305
Story/interpretive drama, 294
Story play, 304–305
Storytelling. *See* Narratives/storytelling
Stress-free environment, 171–172
Structured materials, 157
Subitizing, 379–380
Super complex unit, 136
Surplus energy theory, 65
Sustainability, 199
Sutton, M. J., 188
Sutton-Smith's theory, 66
Sylva, K., 51
Symbolic/dramatic play, 62–63
Symbolic play, 156
Symbolic stage, cognitive development, 404
Syntax, 329
Synthetic loose parts, 190, 191, 192*f*

T

Table blocks, 260
Tablets, 431–433
Teachable moments, 274, 355
Teacher theatre, 307
Technology, in child's play, 373, 417–419, 436–438
　benefits of, 428–429, 428*t*
　and children's development, 438–442, 438*f*
　and creativity, 424–427
　defined, 419–422, 420*f*
　devices, products/outputs of, 420–421, 421*f*
　and early learning, 427
　and inclusivity, 441
　information and communication. *See* Information and communication technologies
　myths about, 425–426
　and young children, 422–423
Terminology challenges/debates, 454
Themed dramatic play areas, 300–301
Theoretical frameworks, of language, 31, 322–323, 322*f*
　behaviourist theory, 322
　interactionist theory, 322–323
　nativist theory, 322
Theories and theorists, 28–31
　classical, 28, 29*t*
　　practice theory, 65
　　recapitulation theory, 65
　　recreation/relaxation theory, 65

　　surplus energy theory, 65
　　themes, 30
　contemporary, 28, 30–31, 31*t*
　modern, 28, 29*t*–30*t*, 65–67
　　cognitive-developmental theory, 66
　　neurobiological theory, 66–67
　　psychoanalytic theory, 66
　　themes, 30
Theory of mind (ToM), 289, 289*f*
Thinking curriculum, 80
Thinking lens, 193
Thinking out loud, 227
Thought-provoking question, 343
Timing, 400
Tinkering. *See also* Loose parts
　defined, 111, **202**
　in play environments, 202–203, 204*t*
Toddlers, play spaces for, 132–133
ToM. *See* Theory of mind (ToM)
Tools of the Mind classroom, 307–309
Toward a Healthy Future: Second Report on the Health of Canadians, 25
Trajectory, 198
Transcript, of play episode, 291*b*
Transient art, 226
Transporting, 198
TRC. *See* Truth and Reconciliation Commission of Canada (TRC)
Tree blocks, 261
Truth and Reconciliation Commission of Canada (TRC), 459–460
Twain, Mark, 5
Twentieth century, block play in, 255–257
Twenty-first-century skills, for teaching and learning, 418, 419*f*

U

UN Convention on the Rights of the Child, 9–10
UNICEF (United Nations International Children's Emergency Fund), 470
Unit blocks, 261
Unoccupied behaviour, 64

V

Values and beliefs, 464–465
　image concept of, 465–467
Verbal communication, 292
Verbal make-believe, 292
Video recordings, 99*t*
Visual arts in early childhood programs, 221–225
　Dewey's approach, 222
　Froebel's approach, 222–223
　project-based approach, 224
　Reggio Emilia approach, 223–225
　Waldorf approach, 223
Visual language
　defined, 231
　developing, through art, 231–232
Visual-spatial construction play objects, 253

Index　**509**